The Kennedy Imprisonment

A Meditation on Power

The Kennedy Imprisonment

A Meditation on Power

GARRY WILLS

Little, Brown and Company
Boston   New York   Toronto   London

FIRST BACK BAY EDITION

Acknowledgments for material quoted in this book
appear on page 304

LIBRARY OF CONGRESS CATALOGING IN PUBLICATION DATA

Wills, Garry.
   The Kennedy imprisonment.
    1. Kennedy family.   2. Power (Social sciences)
   1. Title.
E843.W54   973.922′092′2   81-18649
ISBN 0-316-94371-1 (pb)   AACR2

MV-NY
Published simultaneously in Canada
by Little, Brown & Company (Canada) Limited

PRINTED IN THE UNITED STATES OF AMERICA

To the Other Garry Willses

Garry S. (1884–1956)
Garry L. (1961–)

Contents

PART FOUR: CHARISMA

PART FIVE: POWER

There lurks about the fancies of many men and women an imaginary conception of an ideal statesman, resembling the character of which Alcibiades has been the recognized type for centuries. There is a sort of intellectual luxury in the idea which fascinates the human mind. We like to fancy a young man in the first vigour of body and in the first vigour of mind, who is full of bounding enjoyment, who excels all rivals at masculine feasts, who gains the love of women by a magic attraction, but who is also a powerful statesman, who regulates great events, who settles great measures, who guides a great nation. We seem to outstep the moenia mundi, *the recognized limits of human nature, when we conceive a man in the pride of youth to have dominion of the pursuits of age, to rule both the light things of women and the grave things of men. Human imagination so much loves to surpass human power, that we shall never be able to extirpate the conception.*

— WALTER BAGEHOT, of Bolingbroke

Introduction

THOUGH REVIEWERS have treated several of my books as biographies, I have never written a biography. What interests me about political figures is what the electoral response to them reveals about our culture. My first exercise in this vein was *Nixon Agonistes* (1970), in which I tried to observe — in the words of the preface — how "what is best and weakest in America goes out to reciprocating strengths and deficiencies in Richard Nixon." I was not so much writing about Nixon's life as about the American "reaction, over the years, to Nixon's career, campaign, and presidency."

The title of my book on Ronald Reagan (1987) was explicit. The subject was *Reagan's America*. I devoted much of that book to American religiosity, to the fascination with Hollywood and celebrity, to the sports imagery Reagan always used about life and politics.

My book on the Kennedy phenomenon was cast in the same mold. It was more about public fascination with the Kennedys — stronger, perhaps, in 1981 than now — than about any one Kennedy's biography. That is why it was subtitled *A Meditation on Power*. When I finished the book, I was already working on lectures and classes that became *Cincinnatus: George Washington and the Enlightenment* (1984). I thought of the two as companion studies, one looking at the way Washington used power, the other looking at the way power used the Kennedys. The point of both books is stated in the epilogue to this one: "There is something twistable in the hand about power — something tricky and unpredictable, 'amphisbaenic,' backward-striking."

No one more deeply understood that truth than Washington. He knew that power is often the enemy of its wielder, and can be tamed only by a willingness to sacrifice it. Washington had an internal gyroscope that told him when to resist the intoxications of office — and the authority that accrued to him was, as a result, unromantic but stable. The contrast with Richard Neustadt's view of power, adopted by the Kennedys, is constantly implied in *Cincinnatus*.

> Washington realized that power is a tree that grows by a constant prudent trimming. . . . This apparent paradox — that power grows by cutting it back — is far removed from the hydraulic view of power that fills so much of modern political writing, the view that power is drained away by so many vents and leaks that one should acquire the largest *amount* of it at every opportunity. Why, if you are carrying something in a sieve, pour out spoonfuls on your own?

Of course, it is not much of a criticism to say that modern politicians are not as great as George Washington. Who is? But what mattered to me, at the time, was the communication of ideas about power back and forth between Washington and his public. The symbols used by and about Washington subtly conveyed his sense of republican duty and restraint. Most of *Cincinnatus* is a study of those symbols, and of what they tell us about the ideals of the young American nation.

By contrast, it is more a judgment on our time than on any or all of the Kennedys that so much of their impact was registered in the tabloids, or in tabloid terms even among intellectuals. One of the most interesting cultural phenomena of recent decades was the eagerness of the clerisy to embrace the shallowest symbols of Kennedy potency — Arthur Schlesinger gloating over Marilyn Monroe comes to mind. William Manchester's biographical early book, *Portrait of a President* (1961), was, for my study of presidential symbols, more useful than Manchester's later mine of information, *The Death of a President*. Manchester was the Parson Weems of the Kennedy cult; and the significant difference between the two authors was not in the sophistication of the later man but in the qualities he meant to glorify. Manchester admired Mrs. Kennedy, for instance, because her superior culture made Presidents Truman and Eisenhower "both look like Hottentots" (political correctness had not arrived in 1961), and she "is, in her *comme il faut* way, just as U [upper class] as her husband." It is a different moral world (as well as intellectual one) that Weems's Washington inhabits. The cherry tree story is a symbolic one (derived from the Scottish writer James Beattie), but what it celebrates — truth telling — is far removed from being *comme il faut*. And Weems tells many *true* stories that celebrate basic virtues — e.g., Washington's willingness to sacrifice his whole plantation rather than give comfort to a foraging British enemy. The status of Washington as a charismatic leader in Max Weber's sense — a "graced" nation-founder — forms a startling contrast with the trivialization of the term "charisma" in Kennedy's circle. When we read how the Kennedys were celebrated, we learn things about ourselves, the celebrants, that we might prefer to forget. That is why I ended this book with a contrast drawn between Kennedy and Martin Luther King. The admiration for King was coded to express quite different ideals of power, assertion, and success.

The tarnishing of the Kennedy patina was in its early stage when I wrote *The Kennedy Imprisonment*. There has been a good deal of indiscriminate beating up on all things Kennedy in the fifteen-year interval. I would adopt a different tone, to take that into account, if I were writing it now. The conspiratorial views of Kennedy involvement in the death of Marilyn Monroe were just beginning to surface — and they seemed to me as flimsy then as they do now. But other damaging facts have also appeared. Nigel Hamilton has found Kennedy's "appeasement" editorial in the Harvard *Crimson,* which he rightly says might have denied Kennedy the presidency — or even his election as Senator — if it had been known earlier. Doris Kearns Goodwin learned things about Joseph Kennedy that make him even more sinister than I suspected, though perhaps more pathetic — how he ordered his own daughter's lobotomy without telling his wife; how he secreted caches of cortisone — hard to get, at the time, by others who needed it — so that his son's illness could be treated, wherever he traveled, without fear of exposure by doctors out of the old man's control. Of all the Kennedy books written since I did mine,

I found Goodwin's *The Fitzgeralds and the Kennedys* the most useful and informative.

The most dated part of my book lies in the details of the Cuban missile crisis. Documents released since then show, among other things, that Robert Kennedy was not as pacific throughout as he claimed to be in his own account of the matter. I have not tried to update the chapter, since the main points I made are still the basic ones, in my opinion — that Kennedy irresponsibly put humiliating the Russians on a par with removing the missiles, that he lied to the American public about events leading up to the crisis (especially the assassination attempts aimed at Castro), and that placation of American hysteria (what Eugene Rostow called a sense of psychic crowding) took precedence over descriptions of the actual threat. The new material confirms what was known when I wrote about the secret trade-off of our missiles in Turkey for Khrushchev's withdrawal of the missiles from Cuba. Some claim that this proves Kennedy showed restraint. But his concession was secret; Russian capitulation was humiliatingly public, accepted to meet our ultimatum — Kennedy wanted not just the removal but a demeaning of his foe. Only the restraint of Khrushchev led to a happy conclusion. America had to *seem* virtuous and all-powerful, the John Wayne of nations. This is pleasant for psyches dependent on such self-puffery. It could also, in a nuclear world, have been suicidal.

Some critics said, at the time of my book's publication, that it had too much about sex. The first 17 percent or so of its pages are devoted to sex and gender issues. The amusing thing is that critics who deplored this went on to spend about 90 percent of their reviews on the subject. It may have been a mistake to start with sex — many people do not read books through. But I put it first as the *least* of the five subjects I arranged in ascending order of importance. The aim of the book was to show how themes of power discernible in interpersonal relationships — not only with transient lovers but with wives, workers, and fellow conspirators in silence — show up in the public arena as well, and affect attitudes toward party and national power. A great deal more is known about Kennedy's sexual affairs than when I wrote, and about its relation to his presidency — for instance that he realized he should end what he called his "poon days" after entering the White House, but that he could not.[1] But I would not spend more time on the matter now. The book as I conceived it is a matter of five concentric rings. A pebble dropped in the first and narrowest one causes the other four circles to ripple out, covering wider and wider areas of concern. The pebble dropped is the concept of power as macho "conquest," of getting one's way, visibly and triumphally, with Khrushchev as well as with sycophants (whom I call, here, Honorary Kennedys). It is the spirit that made John Kennedy tell an ally to do in an old Honorary Kennedy, Arthur Krock, when he was no longer sufficiently useful: "Bust it off in old Arthur. . . . Tuck it to Arty."[2]

Some Kennedy retaliation was attempted after this book was published. Eunice Kennedy Shriver, as a member of the board of trustees for Holy Cross College, had voted with her fellows to give me an honorary degree from that institution. When the book appeared before commencement, she lobbied the college's president to rescind the degree, threatening not to attend commencement if he went ahead with the offer (a threat she stuck to when the degree was given anyway). She lost that time; but if she had won, would she really have? That is the kind of meditation on power I hope the book can still provoke.

G.W.
May 1994

1. See *Washington Post*, p. B1, May 29, 1987.
2. Ben Bradlee, *Conversations with Kennedy* (New York: W. W. Norton, 1975), pp. 141, 161.

The Kennedy Imprisonment

A Meditation on Power

Prologue

Brothers

Then spake the King: "My house hath been my doom"

— TENNYSON, *The Passing of Arthur*

HAMPTON, NEW HAMPSHIRE, February 22, 1980: This night seems made to vindicate Frank Capra's version of democracy. Hollywood snow falls rhythmically in large wet flakes, late for the ski trade but doubly welcome after delay. The American hockey team has just, unexpectedly, beat the Russians. On the press bus, the Eastern Establishment, in the form of the New York *Times* reporter, is cheering, *"That'*ll teach the commie bastards." And, to top it all, an American prince is riding by night to visit the homes of his people; riding on a creaky bus. "Senator Kennedy likes to travel with the press," his aides are explaining, at this very moment, to hostesses along the arranged route. The Secret Service wants to keep Kennedy in its sleek car: every time he gets on the bus, they have to take out reporters' bags, search them for bombs, and seal the doors of the luggage compartment. It's a dangerous thing to be an American prince.

But Edward Kennedy has much to prove, now that there is nothing for him to win. Despite a head cold and his bad back, he remounts this spavined Rosinante and rides it to another doorway. He knows what is ahead — squeezing through small homes packed with people, feigning delight at nibbles on homemade cake, at a ritual slurp of freshly brewed coffee. At one home, after taking something for his dry throat, he assures the housewife: "That's good water."

This is an exercise the Kennedys perfected. Veterans of other campaigns, of other brothers, took it as one of the laws they had written: a Kennedy in the front room of anyone's house means the wife's vote is certain, and the wife will work on the husband. But the woman's vote is a different matter in 1980, and so is the Kennedy technique. Tonight's series of "coffees" is clearly marked on the schedule CLOSED TO THE PRESS. These homes are so jammed that Kennedy will not have room to shrug out of and into his coat — it gets left on the bus. But the pencil press nags at Tom Southwick, the press secretary increasingly insecure (he will soon resign), till he lets us in. The TV crews are just as happy to watch, on their equipment, replays from the Olympic hockey game — which gives Kennedy his opening remark of the evening, repeated from house to house: "I bring you *good* news" (shaking his left hand at "good" as if to get water out of his watch), "the American hockey team beat the Russian team, and *they* were a significant underdog too" (left forefinger points up in a long scooping motion on "they"). It is the epitome of false cheer. Instead of warming the crowd up, he disorients it. What has gone wrong?

These New England houses in a heavily Catholic state should be Kennedy territory. In one of them I study the kitchen calendar, from Our Lady of the Miraculous Medal Parish. Questions are so many "fat balls," served up for Kennedy to knock out of the park — health care, veterans' rights, shipyards. He barely bothers to swing. Phrases out of the past are lifted up, but no longer placed in an architectonic whole, in a Kennedy rhetoric of liberalism overarching local bread-and-butter issues. A woman asks, "What do you think is the future of the UN?" He gives the fending-off answer used to placate right-wing foes of the organization, though she is clearly its friend: the do-gooder agencies *do* do some good — WHO and UNICEF, UNESCO and the FAO. The woman, impatient, asks if the UN can grow toward a world government. "I'm interested in that," Kennedy says, in his uninterested way. But we must also make the world "safe for diversity" (his brother's line from the American University speech, so out of context here as to seem a deliberate caricature). Before leaving the house, I ask the UN questioner if his answers satisfied her. She shrugs: "I guess he can't say more than that in this campaign." By now, she is admitting, Kennedy must bear his liberalism with a shamefaced doggedness, advertising its and his own doom. He actually *ducks* fat balls.

Going from the bright night back into the bus is like entering a rusty muffler. Sniffles blend with cigarette smoke, and with the question endlessly posed here: Why is he, how *can* he be, so bad? He has lost all sense of scale. In little rooms he is too loud, in large halls too mumbly. He seems to be talking to audiences somewhere else — mainly in the past. When a Kennedy cannot do a "coffee" right, things are truly upside down. This very week I saw Howard Baker make hostesses glow in their own homes, complimenting them, giving their coffee cake heartfelt munches. Kennedy cannot even *eat* right — one of the American politician's basic skills.

That is a special problem these days, since everywhere Kennedy goes he is cutting birthday cake. All his years in politics he has reminded people, come February, that he shares a birthday with George Washington. Now, even that reference gets out of hand. Speaking in Newmarket, he shouts: "George Washington was a southern Senator, and *he* was followed in the presidency by a man from Massachusetts." No politician is above making up a little history when it serves, inventing a Senate past for Washington; but Kennedy has done it to equate President Carter with George Washington — not the surest way of diminishing an opponent. Reporters long ago gave up counting Kennedy's malapropisms. Hide and seek is only fun if the quarry will at least pretend to hide. One cannot expose a clumsiness that is proclaimed. "Oliver Wendell Holmes, who was Chief Justice of the United States," Kennedy tells the students at West High School.

So dazed is he and stumbling, now, that some who do not witness the spectacle day by day think the press is picking on him. That was probably true, three months earlier; but since then regard for him has been increasing in the press bus, along with pity. This campaign is out of synch with perception of it — a set of multiple time-lags. When he seemed to be gaining, he was losing; now, in loss, he is subtly growing. At one of the coffees, an angry voice shouts: "Did you anticipate that the press would turn on you as it has?" Kennedy smiles: "We've got a few in the room, so we better look out." The slight laugh makes him provoke a bigger one: "Want me to point 'em *out*, so you can go *get* 'em?" Kennedy, once the darling of the press, is reduced to the ploys of George Wallace, the reporters' bogeyman.

As Kennedy began his campaign in November, flying the huge chartered jet, trailing a presidential entourage, the press resented his arrogance, the assumption that to run was to win, that he would prevail by sheer drift, inheritance, and Carter's default. *Then* his mistakes mattered, his apparent lack of purpose. Then critics were harsh, swift to say this man in the imperial panoply had, intellectually, no clothes on, that "there is no there there." But now a there is beginning to appear, and the press is quick to throw clothes over his nakedness — all too late. The change began a month ago when President Carter beat Kennedy two-to-one in the Iowa caucus votes. Some on Kennedy's own team were counseling withdrawal. They saw the defeats stretch out before him, all through a spring and summer; and so did he. He would, in time, lose twenty-four of the thirty-four primaries, twenty of twenty-five state caucuses. But instead of dropping out, he drew himself together and gave the speech that should have opened the race, the Georgetown speech — wage and price controls, gas rationing, an international commission to study Iran's grievances in the hostage affair; strong stuff, defiant of campaign evasions, an abrupt end to hedging and a declaration of purpose worth all future effort. If he was going down anyway, better to go down for principle, for the embattled liberalism other Senators, running scared, would no longer champion.

Some people thought Kennedy was doing himself, not liberalism, the big favor, drawing it down with him to dignify his fall. Battered as the liberal program might be, it was not so clearly doomed as Kennedy's race. But Kennedy, it turned out, could not be accused of opportunism; which takes, at the least, some clarity of purpose. His mind drifted away again from specifics of his Georgetown speech. Gas rationing disappeared from his rhetoric. The economy was neglected for weeks at a time, though he had declared it the central issue. Scheduling and staff matters were neglected. After his severe effort at focus, Kennedy lapsed back into the daze that numbed others in his campaign. He would rouse himself to eloquence at one stop, and ramble at the next. His attention span seemed to stretch for minutes, not for days (or even hours).

What won grudging respect was his will to go on, the lack of complaint as old allies fell away; the absolute refusal to criticize his critics, to indulge even fleeting bitterness. There was only one thing Kennedy could prove now, that he was not a spoiled kid — the thing on which everything else had depended, back when no one realized that. He campaigned like a dethroned king doing penance. It was painful to watch, even for reporters who had gloated at earlier setbacks.

Ghoulish journalists have for a long time called assignment to Kennedy "the death watch." If there is another Dallas, the networks want to be there. But this is another kind of death watch — not standing by on the chance of assassination, but witnessing the certain dissipation of a vast complex of hopes, the end of the entire Kennedy time in our national life. Rose Kennedy, on the eve of her ninetieth birthday, tells New Hampshire's old folks to vote for her ninth child, and the emotion she calls up is nostalgic regret, not campaign enthusiasm. The emotionally wounded wife and three traumatized children are produced by the candidate like scars, not ornaments. "Come up, Patrick," Kennedy gestures at a morning rally, and the twelve-year-old, so clearly resentful, stands just off the platform edge and refuses. Joan Kennedy, rising to speak, breathless and inducing breathlessness in all who watch, moves as carefully as a wire walker on the first trip over Niagara. Will she fall?

How did it all come apart so fast? Only last summer, Kennedy led Carter two-to-one in the polls. The President was seeking him out for debate, giving up the incumbent's advantage, fearful of the even greater advantage of being a Kennedy. But that, too, had been a lagging perception, one out of synch with events. Edward Kennedy had inherited various simulacra of power, not its reality; he both was and was not "a Kennedy" as his brothers had defined that political entity. And both being and not being like them hurt. His life has become, over the years, a broken chain of tangled memories, full of gaps and overlaps. He lives out of sequence with himself, the youngest child and oldest son alive; the kid brother who must father all his brothers' kids. Nearing fifty, he lives cramped inside the diminutive "Teddy."

At age twenty-nine, Edward Kennedy was Assistant District Attorney for the County of Suffolk, preparing his first Senate race. At the same age, his oldest brother had died in war.

At age forty-three, Edward Kennedy had been a Senator from Massachusetts for thirteen years — the senior Senator for eleven years. He was considered by many (including Jimmy Carter, out of office in Georgia), the strongest contender for the Democratic nomination coming up a year later. At age forty-three his elder brother Robert had been killed while campaigning.

At forty-six, Edward Kennedy ignited the Democratic "mini-convention" in Memphis and seemed to all observers his party's favorite. At the same age, his brother the President was shot in Dallas.

Of his four dead siblings, two died in their twenties, two in their forties. He had become his father's father when he reached the age of thirty: the financier who drove his brothers toward office had a crippling stroke just before Edward won a Senate seat. Later, it was Edward who had to pierce his father's shell of incomprehension with news that the President was dead. It was Edward who buried the father one year after Robert was shot. It was Edward who stood by in smock and face mask to assist at the cesarean birth of Robert's last child after Robert's death, blood from the incision spraying his mask. Day by day, he mixes death and life.

Both press and public were astounded at the way Kennedy bore up under defeat after defeat, Tuesday after Tuesday, in the 1980 campaign. But he has long been initiated into loss. When he was twelve, his brother and his brother-in-law were killed in war. When he was sixteen his sister died in a plane crash. When he was thirty-one, his brother was shot. When he was thirty-two, his aide, and the pilot of a chartered plane, died in the crash that broke Edward Kennedy's back. When he was thirty-six another brother was shot. After that last blow, maudlin in the woozy early hours in Alaska, he kept repeating to reporters, "They're going to shoot my ass off the way they shot Bobby's." He rarely showed fear, however; seemed, indeed, too jaunty to some — with the effort that heaves several lives' weight into the air again. After Robert was killed, he told his aide Dun Gifford: "I can't let go. We have a job to do. If I let go, Ethel will let go, and my mother will let go, and all my sisters."

Because of Kennedy's determination, there is a wounded youthfulness about him that deceives. He will be the kid brother till he dies. Because they died too young, he will be young in a grotesque way when he is old. The proper sequences have been irrevocably mixed. He is allowed neither youth nor age, neither death nor fully living. John, campaigning, had Robert and Edward to work for him. Robert had Edward to advise and be his surrogate. Edward has no one but ghosts at his side, and they count more against than for him, eclipse him with bright images from the past. Where they were praised too fulsomely, he is bound to be judged too harshly. He inherits the illusions of his brothers' followers with the accumulated venoms of their foes; and both tend to disinherit him.

Once brother drew on brother for fresh strength; now brother drains brother, all the dead inhibiting the one that has lived on. Edward has managed to outlast three brothers without ever catching up to one of them. Just as he seems to overtake them, their glory either recedes from him, or fades in the public's eyes. It was pretty evanescent stuff to begin with, the glory; but one can hardly look to him for that perception. To show ingratitude toward the ghosts would just make them harder to shake off. Meanwhile, he inherits all their children, while his own partly slip away from him, victims of his own victimhood, and of his wife's.

There has been too much dying for the Kennedys, which makes the whole nation, not just traveling reporters, mount a kind of death watch over Edward Kennedy. An editor of *Harper's* took offense at the family gift for disaster: "Given the intensity of his family's will to death . . . ," he wrote in 1980. Will to death, indeed. Were Lee Harvey Oswald, and Sirhan Sirhan, Kennedy wish-fulfillments? This almost demented charge shows how deep the Kennedy fascination has entered into the national psyche, and how odd the manifestations of it can become. He only partly died with each brother, and some resent that. What right has he to live?

> *Guthrum the good is fallen,*
> *Are you too good to fall?*

If Kennedys have a will to death, then Edward's life proclaims his lack of willpower. His very courage to go on, his lack of self-pity, are used against him.

James MacGregor Burns called Edward Kennedy "late-born," a description echoed constantly in other people's writings. But, even more important, Kennedy was early stranded, deprived of his own sources of strength and support, forced into the arena by a father and brothers who are not around to help him with the fight. Burton Hersh quotes a friend of the Senator: "When Ted wants to consult with someone he trusts completely he gets in a room alone, and locks the door, and talks to himself." He communes with ghosts. Years ago, one of John Kennedy's mistresses told her son: "The old man would push Joe, Joe would push Jack, Jack would push Bobby, Bobby would push Teddy, and Teddy would fall on his ass." It need not have worked that way, if one or more of the first four men had lived longer. But they did not. Having pushed the younger brother for a while, they could not hold him up or steady him under trial, as each had been steadied, earlier, by the others.

At the end of a campaign day in New Hampshire, I had dinner with reporter Jim Dickenson of the Washington *Star,* and his wife, Molly. How does Kennedy go on, we wondered. Jim said: "If this is the American dream, you can have it. Wealth, looks, family, office, power — he has what his daddy wanted for him, and look where it's got him. Who on earth would want to be Kennedy now?" The center for so long of prying envy, he had become an object of pity for those who watched him up close, what there was to watch. Constantly on display, Kennedy is forever hidden, known only to a few — and those few sometimes wonder if they know him. Does he know himself? Has he a self to know, apart from the vanished older icons of Kennedy self-possession?

We went back to the Wayfarer Inn in Manchester, and met California Governor Jerry Brown wandering with a lone aide down the hall.

"Where you been?" Brown asked me.

"Following Kennedy."

"How's he doing?"

"It seems bleak."

"Yes?" There was no show of glee at this report about a rival candidate. "Well ... it's hard, I guess, to handle decline." He said it meditatively, knowing his own campaign was gliding down, and knowing that we knew. Jim later remarked, "We just heard Jerry Brown's concession speech."

Molly, a Brown admirer, said, "Yes, but it was more than that. You could tell what was happening to Kennedy affected him." This was more than an unsuccessful campaign. I had thought to pursue the matter with Brown, but just then Theodore White bustled up to lecture Brown on the Roman Empire.

It was more than a campaign ending. Kennedy was being forced, every day, to demonstrate that he was not as good as his brothers. His every effort at recommending himself worked to condemn him. He could not make the counterclaim, that his *brothers* were not as good as his brothers, that Camelot had been a fabric of political unreality. In this campaign, Kennedy was like the last climber in a human chain going up a mountainside, tied to the prowess of the four men above him. But then, in rapid succession, all four men fell, and the very strength that had been drawing him upward now hung a dead weight below him. Each time he stirred to go higher, he just slipped back. The "Kennedy legacy" had become a very literal burden, made his life a constant labor with death.

I

SEX

Sexuality must not be described as a stubborn drive, by nature alien and of necessity disobedient to a power which ex-
hausts itself trying to subdue it and often fails to control it
entirely. It appears rather as an especially dense transfer
point for relations of power: between men and women,
young people and old people, parents and offspring, teachers
and students, priests and laity, an administration and a population.

— MICHEL FOUCAULT

1

The Father

Like the other young men of his circle he thought chastity a dangerous state, and he seems early to have taken practical steps to avoid incurring the risks attendant on it.
— DAVID CECIL, *Young Melbourne*

THE TERM "imprisonment" came to mind as I watched Edward Kennedy shake hands with well-wishers at Boston's Pier Four — another stop in his marathon 1980 birthday party. In this ritual of giving himself, every gesture outward was inhibited, visibly checked. He moves, of course, in the stiff constraints of his back brace — at outdoor events, reporters wondered whether it was just the brace or if he wore a bulletproof vest. But there is more to his stiffness with people than medical complaint. That is most obvious when women approach him. With men, he can sometimes do the locker-room punch on the arm, clumsily hug an "old boy." But he subtly tenses when women come near, and puts his hand far out for primmest shaking. He has been burned too often by tabloid pictures of him merely walking near a pretty blonde. A kiss on the cheek may be quite continental, but that is a luxury denied him, now, in public. He lives within an invisible cage of his own forging, sealed in by his own actions outward, by the reputation of his former prowess. The ladies' man can barely shake a lady's hand, so crippled is he by his past.

An air of barely suppressed sexual exuberance was always part of Kennedy campaigns. The day after the Pier Four party, I went with

Steve Neal of the Chicago *Tribune* to look at films of those old
campaigns in the Kennedy Library. Even Bobby had been grabbed
at by young women as if he were a rock star. The Charles Guggen-
heim documentary on his life has a touching moment when a girl
reaches out to pat his hair, almost reverently, in the turmoil of
shouts and handshakes. Of course, the "jumpers" of the 1960 campaign have entered legend. Murray Kempton wrote, of John Kennedy's motorcade:

> John F. Kennedy treated southern Ohio yesterday as Don Giovanni
> used to treat Seville. His progress, as ever, was an epic in the history
> of the sexual instinct of the American female. Outside Dayton, a
> woman of advanced years but intact instinct sat with her dog.
> Kennedy passed; she waved; he waved back; in that moment of truth
> she clasped her dog and kissed his wet muzzle. Jack Kennedy is
> starting to enjoy these moments, and he is starting to enjoy them as
> a man of taste. He turns back now and goes on waving; the lingering
> hand gestures and the eye follows; its object is always a quietly
> pretty girl and the hand says that, if he did not have miles to go and
> promises to keep, he would like to walk with her where the mad
> river meets the still water.

For the youngest — in some ways the sexiest — Kennedy to run
a sexless campaign in 1980 was a sharp but not a strange reversal.
There is a kind of inevitability to it. I have said that Edward forged
his own bars around him; but that is only partly true. Family tradition helped put them there. A very important and conscious part
of the male Kennedy mystique is a pride in womanizing. Only Robert broke free of this — he had other demons. But, with that exception, what Montaigne wrote of some aristocratic families in his
day was literally true of the Kennedys: "We know how some lament
being consecrated to celibacy before the age of choice; but I have seen
some truly lament their being consecrated to licentiousness before the
age of choice. The parent's vice can be the cause. . . ." The Kennedy
boys were expected by their father to undertake a competitive discipline of lust; and he let them know that he was still in the competition himself. Here is the testimony of Mary Pitcairn, who dated
John Kennedy, but later married Senator Kenneth Keating:

Mr. Kennedy always called up the girls Jack was taking out and asked them to dinner. He came down and took me to the Carleton Hotel — then the fanciest dining room in Washington. He was very charming. He wanted to know his children's friends. He was *very* curious about my personal life. He really wanted to know. He asked a lot of personal questions — *extraordinarily* personal questions. And then — I'll *never* forget this — he told me a lot about Gloria Swanson, how wonderful she was and how he kept in touch with her. When he brought me home, he called her up from my apartment. She was at the Plaza Hotel in New York. He said, "I'm going to call her up and make a date for tomorrow night," or something. Which he did.

Gloria Swanson has described the way Joseph Kennedy flaunted her presence on a ship to Europe, even though Rose Kennedy was traveling with them. According to Mary Pitcairn, he was similarly uninhibited in the home he shared with Rose:

> He did something that I heard he did to everyone. After dinner he would take you home and kiss you goodnight as though he were a young so-and-so. One night I was visiting Eunice at the Cape and he came into my bedroom to kiss me goodnight! I was in my nightgown, ready for bed. Eunice was in her bedroom. We had an adjoining bath. The doors were open. He said, "I've come to say goodnight," and kissed me. Really kissed me. It was so silly. I remember thinking, "How embarrassing for Eunice!" . . . I think all this confused Jack. He was a sensitive man and I think it confused him. What kind of object is a woman? To be treated as his father treated them? And his father's behavior that way was blatant. There was always a young, blond beautiful secretary around.

I have been quoting from *The Search for JFK* by Joan and L. Clay Blair, Jr. (1976). The Blairs tried to interview all of John Kennedy's early friends, male and female. The attributes most frequently mentioned in this mass of interviews are John Kennedy's intelligence, his womanizing (often connected with his father's), his bad back and bad stomach, and his habit of expecting others to pay for things because he never carried cash.

The father's "skirt chasing" was notorious. He not only pursued his own sons' "dates," but the dates of those sons' friends. Edward

McLaughlin, John's Navy friend, was engaged to Elizabeth Drake, whom he later married. Mrs. McLaughlin remembers how Kennedy's father took her to dinner:

> He asked me how much I thought Eddie would make when he started working. I said I didn't know but that he hoped to be a lawyer. Mr. Kennedy said he paid his butler more than Ed would ever make. He said I was wasting my time with Ed. I was a nice-looking girl and I could do better than that. I couldn't even eat I was so nervous. And I began to see the handwriting on the wall. I got out of there as fast as I could. I didn't think I'd ever hear from him again, but I did. He called again. And I — foolish me — went again, twice more I think. It was a challenge in a way. I thought I could handle this guy. Nothing was going to happen. But each time he got tougher to fend off. The third time, I really had a rough time getting out of his apartment. I literally ran out. And then I'd see him down at the Cape and he'd be perfectly charming. I've had other girls tell me almost identical stories. He was just that kind of guy.

When the young Charlotte McDonnell went to visit Kathleen Kennedy at her father's Waldorf Towers suite, Kennedy pretended to Will Hays, the movie censor, that she was his "girl in the bedroom":

> I was about sixteen at the time and pretty shook up. I could not imagine *my* father walking in to the room and saying, "Hey, would you believe it? Will Hays thought I had a girl in the bedroom." When you're sixteen years old and you've been born and bred in the convent and you've got a very strict father who never deviated from any line, morally or ethically — it did shake me up. But Kick and Jack didn't seem to care. I think maybe they were so used to it. . . . They just didn't seem to have the same, for lack of a better word, moral values. Although that is not really the proper word. Respect for women.

When the Blairs asked, "Was that also true of Jack?" she answered, "Yes."

Far from covering up his affairs, Joseph Kennedy tried to claim more of them than there were — even when it might hurt his business ventures (shocking Will Hays was not the best way to get motion pictures approved). He obviously thought this was part of his charm; and three of his four boys must have agreed, since they tried to emulate his "conquests."

I have seen it written and heard it said that Joseph — or John or Edward — Kennedy showed an Irish Catholic approach to women, idolizing the wife at home, but recognizing the human frailty caused by original sin, hoping for forgiveness in the confessional. But, as we shall see, the father rarely stressed his own Irish background; and the family line, picked up in a number of the Blairs' interviews, was that the father had an "English" attitude toward women — which meant, they thought, a continental or sophisticated air. Joseph Kennedy was so little Irish that he wanted to ape the English, and his children became intense anglophiles. In calling his attitude "English," they were putting what they considered the best light on it.

Irish Catholics in America have been, if anything, puritanical about sex, and Kennedy wanted people to know he had escaped that particular form of ethnic narrowness; that he was a man of the world, making his own rules, getting what he wanted, ready to indulge without guilt the one sensual pleasure that interested him. His bad stomach forbade drinking, smoking, or fancy foods; he was too restless to enjoy leisure; the arts were nonexistent to him. That left women, where he tried to exhibit a connoisseur's taste and a conquistador's prowess. Here he not only indulged himself; the family indulged him too. The sons seemed to take a borrowed pride in their father's "manliness," and imitated it. Even the daughters put the best face on his philandering. Some of those who told the Blairs that the father's attitude was "English" picked up that designation from Kathleen Kennedy, who became the Marchioness of Hartington. Before her marriage to the Marquis, Kathleen wrote her brother Jack in the Navy: "I can't really understand why I like Englishmen so much, as they treat one in quite an offhand manner and aren't really as nice to their women as Americans, but I suppose it's just that sort of treatment that women really like. That's your technique isn't it?"

Montaigne said that some aristocrats not only claim a license themselves but arrange a similar freedom for their sons: "It is the fashion in our country to put sons in the best homes where, as pages, they may be trained to noble manners. And it is called a discourtesy for anyone to refuse a gentleman his wishes." But if Joseph Kennedy thought sexual freedom an aristocratic trait, he was giving aristocracy a new definition from the jazz age. After his rejection by the brahmins of Boston, he oriented his world around New York and Hollywood, around the sports and journalism and cinema stars of the roaring twenties. A starlet would have disgraced the better Boston families; but Kennedy displayed his actresses as so many decorations, as signs that he was looking to new centers of power and of popular acclaim. The Boston gentry were exclusive. He would be expansive, open and racy. He was steering his family down the course that made them staples of the tabloids. As he told Gloria Swanson: "The Cabots and the Lodges wouldn't be caught dead at the pictures, or let their children go. And that's why their servants know more about what's going on in the world than they do. The working class gets smarter every day, thanks to radio and pictures. It's the snooty Back Bay bankers who are missing the boat."

The father's fascination with starlets, sports heroes, and worldly journalists was passed on to his sons. Even Robert Kennedy, the most reflective of them, the nonwomanizer, had the family interest in entertainers and athletes — in Rafer Johnson and Andy Williams and Marilyn Monroe. He would ultimately alert his brother against Frank Sinatra's circle — but only after their sister Patricia had married into that circle.

The journalist to whom Joseph Kennedy was closest, over the years, was Arthur Krock of the New York *Times,* a voice of the American journalistic establishment, politically very conservative, but "liberal" in his moral views. The two cemented their joint purposes with a male camaraderie of conquest — exactly the relationship John Kennedy would later have with *Newsweek*'s Ben Bradlee. Krock inadvertently occasioned John Kennedy's first serious trouble over sex. The New York *Times*man tried to find journalistic jobs for his beautiful protégées; Frank Waldrop, editor of the Washington *Times-Herald* in 1941, remembers that when Krock called him and said, "I've got another one for you," Waldrop answered, "What are you, our staff procurer?" The "one" Krock had got was Inga Arvad, a European beauty contest winner who had Nazi connections. Arvad later told her son, "Krock was a skirt-chaser." Women were passed around in the Krock–Kennedy circles; but so was news of them — the FBI soon had tape recordings of Arvad in bed with a naval intelligence officer, John Kennedy. That ended the future President's intelligence days in Washington, and almost ended his military service altogether. Only his father's intervention with James Forrestal, then Undersecretary of the Navy, kept John Kennedy in uniform after this, his first assignment. He later omitted this first tour of duty from his Navy biography.

It seems clear in retrospect that John Kennedy was not jeopardizing his country when he persisted in seeing Inga Arvad (even after his dismissal from intelligence work because of her); but he was certainly jeopardizing his career — which was his father's only concern. Inga Arvad's son remembers: "She thought old Joe was awfully hard — a really mean man. He could be very charming when she and Jack were with him but if she left the room he'd come down on Jack about her and if Jack left the room, he'd try to hop in the sack with her. He did that one weekend at the Cape, she said. She thought it was a totally amoral situation, that there was something incestuous about the whole family."

Krock had earlier helped initiate the Kennedy boys into intrigues, even when the father was giving them a rare warning. Joseph Jr. had struck up a shipboard romance with a movie actress, and was too open about it. His father wanted this son to be President; so he imposed a curfew on Joe, and on John who shared a cabin with him. But once the father had checked the boys in for the night, they escaped out a sealed servant door. In his *Memoirs,* Krock pretends he deduced this from the boys' presence at later carousals; but in the oral history at the Kennedy Library, where he speaks more frankly, he admits he opened the door for them. Despite that cruise's specific injunction, the father radiated a "boys will be boys" ethic around his sons. As Montaigne says, aristocratic pretensions can train one to licentiousness.

Joseph Kennedy's new breed of boys being boys made a questionable aristocracy. Norman Mailer did not quite get the point when he described the situation. In his famous 1960 essay for *Esquire,* "Superman Comes to the Supermarket," Mailer rejoiced that America's "beggars of glamor" were to be given a new kind of political heroism: "America's politics would now be also America's favorite movie. . . . America believed in athletes, rum-runners, aviators; even lovers, by the time Valentino died." Now it would believe in Kennedys, who — thanks to the father — had a bit of rum-running dash and Valentino glitter to them.

In 1938, Ambassador Kennedy watched the King and Queen of England arrive at Ascot for the Gold Cup races. His wife wrote of that day: "When Joe first saw the royal procession, he commented, 'Well, if that's just not just like Hollywood.' " Kennedy's career in the movies was comparatively short; but it was not a mere incident in his life. He was dazzled by Hollywood, and loved to use its glitter on others. As a movie producer, he had early copies of films to show his family and visitors — something he managed to do long after he had left the business. Even when entertaining the royal couple in London, he showed them early releases of American films. At Hyannis Port there was a movie every night during the summer, which awed the children's visiting friends.

Only John seems to have inherited his father's *consuming* interest in the movies, in the myths and gossip of Hollywood. As President he even called the set where *Advise and Consent* was being filmed, to learn when he could get an early print. He watched films constantly in the White House. And he was as interested in the actors' private lives as in their screen performances. The adoring Kenneth O'Donnell admits: "His fondness for Frank Sinatra, which perplexed a lot of people, was simply based on the fact that Sinatra told him a lot of inside gossip about celebrities and their romances in Hollywood." Not only was Sinatra the President's private Rona Barrett — he was also one of the President's favorite topics of conversation. Judith Campbell (later Mrs. Exner), who had been recommended to Kennedy because "she looks like Elizabeth Taylor" (in 1960, the subject of most movie gossip), says Kennedy's conversations in the White House returned again and again to Frank Sinatra's affairs.

> Oh, but he loved gossip. He adored it. That was something he was always asking me about on the telephone and in person. He would say, "Who's Frank seeing now?" or "I heard Frank is seeing so-and-so and isn't she married?"

He thought Frank's temperament was a riot. He was amused at the havoc Frank could cause and at the way people around him would cower in fear.

Almost immediately Jack started pumping me for gossip, most of it directed at Frank. What was Frank doing? Was it true that he was seeing Janet Leigh? We went through the same routine.

Mrs. Exner does not seem to realize that her own glamour for Kennedy came largely from the fact that she had been Sinatra's mistress.

Every time we talked on the phone, and I am referring to before and after our meeting at the Plaza, he invariably would ask, "Have you seen Frank lately?" I would answer, "No," or "Yes, I saw him on the set," or "He called last night and I wasn't home," or whatever was the circumstance at the moment. Jack would say, "Ohhh, you still want to see Frank?" I would say, "We're just friends, Jack." Then he'd say, "Okay, okay," in almost a little boy's "See if I care" voice. Then the very next day, "See Frank? Where did you go last night? I called and you weren't home."

Kennedy pursued "stars" (Sonja Henie and Gene Tierney) the way his father had. And since his father had taken Gloria Swanson and other mistresses to Hyannis Port, daring any in the family to object, John Kennedy met his women in the White House. The Hyannis Port competition for women, which made that compound partly a fraternity house, was repeated in the executive mansion. Mrs. Exner was a prize up for grabs, not only between brothers but among Kennedy "gofers" as well:

He asked about Frank again, and although I felt that his interest in Frank was genuine, I found it a little annoying that I always seemed to remind him of Frank. Then as we walked into the [White House] dining room, he said, "Have you heard from Teddy?"
    That stopped me. "You mean your brother?"
    "Yes. Has Teddy called you?"
    "Of course not," I said. "You should know that."
    "Well, I just wondered."
    Jack never forgot what Teddy had tried in Las Vegas. Several times when we were in bed he said, "Boy, if Teddy only knew, he'd

be eating his heart out." I think he got a big kick out of the fact that
he had succeeded where Teddy had failed.

When Mrs. Exner ferried Kenneth O'Donnell to the secret apartment
kept by Kennedy during the Los Angeles convention, O'Donnell
made a grab at her, and was astonished when she resisted. Everyone
joined the game, with no preliminary niceties. Part of the father's
aggressive charm, passed on to the sons and their imitators, was a
merry effrontery, a freshness and candor of rapacity, what Montaigne
calls his own "impertinently genital" approach. Burton Hersh has
described the family manner, as exemplified by Edward Kennedy:
"College girls who went out with him reported back that he made his
expectations clear early and with great undisguised feeling, and took
it more as a curiosity than an affront if his straightforward-enough
offer was not instantly accepted." Even a custodian of the Kennedy
legends, James MacGregor Burns, was astounded at the openness of
the youngest Kennedy's "series of brief flirtations and longer, more
intense involvements," and quotes a friend of his in Congress: "I have
told him ten times, 'Ted, you're acting like a fool. Everybody knows
you wherever you go. . . . Jack could smuggle girls up the back way
of the Carlyle Hotel. But you're not nearly as discreet as you should
be.' He looks down with a faint smile and says: 'Yeah, I guess you're
right.' But he never listens."

The family game of "chasing" is part of the self that was built up
by all three imitators of their magnetic father. Passing women
around, and boasting of it, to other men and other women, was a
Kennedy achievement:

> As soon as I was introduced to Angie [Dickinson], she let out a
> shriek: "You're Judy Campbell?" I told her I was and she said,
> "John has told me so much about you!" All I could say was, "Oh,
> really?" At first I thought she meant Rosselli [a Giancana associate],
> but then I realized that she meant John Kennedy. She kept saying,
> "Oh, I'm so glad to see you. I've heard so much about you."

Kennedy's curiosity and candor about his own and other people's sex
lives may indicate why his favorite book was Cecil's *Young Melbourne,* a gossipy and superficial look at "lives of the aristocrats" in
Regency England. Betty Spalding was astonished at Kennedy's in-

trusive questions, as Mary Pitcairn had been by Joseph Kennedy's: "He would say personal things to me. I mean, ask me personal questions about women and marriage — and later he talked to me about his sex life with Jackie."

Ben Bradlee also describes Kennedy's appetite for gossip about the sex life of others: "The four of us got on the subject of a guest at the birthday party last night (who shall here be nameless), who had told Jackie and Tony that he had not slept with his wife for the last sixteen years. This kind of dirt the president of the United States can listen to all day long." It is clear from Bradlee's book what conversation Kennedy enjoyed: "Tonight's last minute miscellany included: Why none of us had women friends with large bosoms." And: "Before we left we reminisced about the night of the West Virginia primary, the dirty movie we had seen, whose plot the president seemed to recall remarkably well, given his preoccupations that night." Kennedy could not even wait for a child to grow up before speculating about its sex life. Complimenting the Bradlees on their infant son, he said: "My God, he's a good looking child. Those eyes. He's going to do a helluva business." That must be what his own father said of the infant Kennedy.

When not gossiping about sex, Kennedy liked to fantasize about it with the help of movies. Even Ben Bradlee was surprised at the President's taste:

> The movie was James Bond, and Kennedy seemed to enjoy the cool and the sex and the brutality.

> The president was determined to see a movie, even though Jackie said the choices were strictly limited. Jackie read off the list of what was available, and the president selected the one we had all unanimously voted against, a brutal sadistic little Western called *Lonely Are the Brave*. Kennedy watched, lying down on a bed placed in the front row, his head propped up on pillows.

Obviously only one vote counted in that room. Those without a taste for low movies must have found the famous Kennedy charm wearing thin come nightfall: "We dined alone with the president last night. Jackie did not appear. We saw a dreadful movie about some Englishmen in a German prison camp."

Joseph Kennedy, a man of strong will and low tastes, passed on both traits to his son. He aspired upward to the White House and downward to tabloid heaven. John Kennedy reached both places; and though the tabloids cruelly exploited his widow in later years, the son had been groomed for the one place just as surely as he was for the other. It is difficult to become an American prince.

2

The President

IN 1960, as a graduate student in New Haven, I was discussing
Mailer's *Esquire* article with another graduate student, a woman.
What, I asked her, would happen if Kennedy's womanizing became
even better known? (The reputation was already there, winked at
several times by Mailer in his piece.) "That will help him," she replied. Why? "It will show he knows how to get what he wants."
The liberal world was so bored with avuncular "Ike" that it welcomed a President who had the nerve to wear a rake's rather dingy
halo. It is easy to forget that the Sinatra "rat pack" was considered a
liberal phenomenon in the late fifties. After all, it admitted one black
performer to its carousings.

The graduate student in New Haven, afire for liberal causes, was
also excited by John Kennedy's sexual image, which was not "irrelevant" for her — as it later became for those trying to hide Kennedy's
affairs. It was, precisely, a basis of *political* appeal. Power was one,
over women or over Khrushchev. As Kathleen had written to her
brother in the South Pacific, "It's just that sort of treatment that
women really like." Women could trust a man who "treats 'em
rough" to be tough in other contexts too.

I thought of that graduate student when I went to work for a
magazine where a female writer was described to me as "a Kennedy-

style celebrity-fucker." She too admired New Frontiersmen for their macho. But by the time Sammy Davis, Jr. was embracing Nixon and Frank Sinatra was subsidizing Agnew, that woman had become a feminist — and a critic of Edward Kennedy. Mailer was right to see things poised for a massive swing of mood in 1960; but he could not see how wide the mood would ultimately veer from his own (and the Kennedy) view of male heroism. The sexual revolution launched with a glorification of aggression would lead, finally, to profound criticism of it.

But all that was far ahead when John Kennedy became the first movie-star President. It is hard to remember that the "sexual revolutionaries" of the 1950s — male *and* female — had been brought up on the cult of Hemingway, of dominating men, hunters, bull-fighters, risk-takers. This was the Hemingway called on in the first sentence of Kennedy's *Profiles in Courage*. Mailer voiced the creed of that time during and after the 1960 campaign:

> The film studios threw up their searchlights as the frontier was fi-
> nally sealed, and the romantic possibilities of the old conquest of
> land turned into a vertical myth, trapped within the skull, of a new
> kind of heroic life, each choosing his own archetype of a neo-renais-
> sance man, be it Barrymore, Cagney, Flynn, Bogart, Brando or Sin-
> atra, but it was almost as if there were no peace unless one could
> fight well, kill well (if always with honor), love well and love
> many, be cool, be daring, be dashing, be wild, be wily, be resource-
> ful, be a brave gun.

Naturally, there was no occasion to talk of female heroism. Woman's role was to be one of the "many" getting "well loved." They were to revolve (replaceably) about the hero, like the freshets of nubile bodies circling Sean Connery in James Bond movies, the favorite entertainment of Mailer's "Superman" in the White House.

It may seem pointless to notice that John Kennedy had extra-marital affairs. Politicians are not famous for fidelity. The male politician's ego reaches out to manipulate others, to dominate; and with women that domination often takes a crude sexual form. Lyndon Johnson, for instance, tried to put his brand on everyone around him, and was colorfully direct about the nature of the branding iron used on women. But John Kennedy's womanizing was different in both scale and intensity. It led him to take political and personal risks, from the time of Inga Arvad to that of Sam Giancana's lover, Judith Campbell; risks even his father and brothers thought foolhardy. It would in time enmesh most of his entourage in a complex set of lies and cover-ups. And it seems never to have abated. Few politicians — much less Presidents — would candidly inform a Prime Minister of England that they get headaches if they go for long without a woman.

When Kennedy said that to Harold Macmillan, he was assuming his sister Kathleen's view of the *English* attitude toward sex — an attitude celebrated in Kennedy's favorite book, Cecil's life of Melbourne: " 'I was afraid I was going to have the gout the other day,' writes Lord Carlisle to a friend. 'I believe I live too chaste: it is not a common fault with me.' It was not a common fault with any of them. In fact, an unmarried man was thought unpleasantly queer if he did not keep under his protection some sprightly full-bosomed Kitty Clive or Mrs. Bellamy, whose embraces he repaid with a house in Montpelier Square, a box at the opera and a smart cabriolet in which to drive her down to Brighthelmstone for a week's amorous relaxation."

The sheer pace of Kennedy's sex life, its serial and simultaneous variety, awed his friends and competitors. Rip Horton, a Choate friend who was with the teenage John Kennedy at his sexual initiation in a bordello, remembers what Congressman Kennedy's bachelor pad was like in the fifties:

> I went to his house in Georgetown for dinner. A lovely looking blonde from West Palm Beach joined us to go to a movie. After the movie we went back to the house, and I remember Jack saying something like, "Well, I want to shake this one. She has ideas." Shortly thereafter, another girl walked in. Ted Reardon was there, so he went home and I went to bed figuring this was the girl for the night. The next morning, a completely different girl came wandering down for breakfast. They were a dime a dozen.

They were, in fact, so interchangeable he had trouble keeping them straight, according to Charlotte McDonnell: "I got a letter from Jack from the South Pacific. When I opened it up, I saw it wasn't meant for me. He had written two letters and got the envelopes mixed up. The salutation was 'Dearest ———.' She must have been some starlet." Anthony Gallucio, a friend of Joseph Jr., who worked in John Kennedy's campaign, told the Blairs:

> The male side of the family were all like that. They came by it naturally — from the father, who chased anything in skirts. Girls would come around and Jack would get all excited. He was like a kid. He really liked girls. But it was just physical and social activity for him. He'd just keep moving. Italians get emotionally involved. But Kennedy never got emotionally involved. He'd sleep with a girl, and then he'd have Billy [Sutton] take her to the airport the next day.

Senator George Smathers of Florida, known as a ladies' man himself, was Kennedy's closest social friend on the Hill during their early Washington days. He says: "Jack liked girls. He liked girls very much. He came by it naturally. His daddy liked girls. He was a chaser."

But according to the English tennis star Katherine Stammers, who dated Kennedy just after the war, Kennedy did not so much "like" girls as use them, at a fast turnover rate: "He really didn't give a damn. He liked to have them around and he liked to enjoy himself, but he was quite unreliable. He did as he pleased. I think he was probably spoiled by women. I think he could snap his fingers and they'd come running."

We have seen that his father tried to discourage a woman from marrying one of John Kennedy's friends. The Blairs found that the son, too, tried to discourage others from getting married. And the wives of those already married resented his attempt to keep their husbands still "on the chase." The wife of a Navy friend, James Reed, complained:

> Jack would frequently ask Jim to parties — but not me! It was a male prowling thing and Jack couldn't understand why Jim couldn't leave me behind and prowl with him. Maybe this is acceptable in the "upper class" [her husband, too, called Kennedy's attitude an aristocratic "English attitude"]. I think Jack felt this was being manly. But, it seemed to me, he had a contempt for women, possibly because of his father's attitude toward women.

Friend after friend traces the speed of female turnover to a total lack of emotional involvement. Leonard Nikoloric, another Navy pal, said: "Girls were almost an obsession with him. We liked them too, but we didn't make a career of it the way he did." The journalist John White, who dated Kathleen Kennedy, told Herbert Parmet: "He was completely driven to dominate them. Once he got them, he lost interest and moved on to the next." It is the classic Don Juan attitude: by putting them on the list, you cross them out of existence. Conquest erases the conquered. In Montaigne's words: "As soon as we can make them ours, we are no longer theirs." The cancellation could take place so fast that a woman might well wonder if she was still *there*. Judith Campbell contrasts the active lovemaking of Frank Sinatra with Kennedy's supine passivity:

> I understood about the position he had to assume in lovemaking when his back was troubling him, but slowly he began excluding all other positions, until finally our lovemaking was reduced to this one position. It is impossible for me to pinpoint when I first realized it, because it was such a gradual process, but slowly I began to feel that he expected me to come into bed and just perform. There would be a moment of stillness when I came into bed and it was almost like he expected me to roll over and put my arms around him and make love to him. . . . I was there to service him.

Inga Arvad's son heard the same complaint from her: "If he wanted to make love, you'd make love — now. They'd have fifteen minutes to get to a party and she'd say she didn't want to. He'd look at his watch and say we've got ten minutes, let's go. There was a certain amount of insensitiveness, an awful lot of self-centeredness." He had this terrible itch that needed constant scratching, and the attention was on the itch, not on the replaceable scratchers. As Lord Rochester wrote of a profligate duchess:

> *She'll still drudge on in tasteless vice*
> *As if she sinn'd for exercise.*

The crowded, compulsive schedule of Kennedy's sex life went beyond that of most politicians, beyond even that of his father or brothers, though it was grounded in the father's code. Charles Spalding, one of Kennedy's closest friends, said:

> He was always interested in seeing whether he had it or didn't have it. Can I do it or can't I do it? To me, that always accounted for a lot of the numbers, if you will. And the other thing I think is having a very, very strong father. All kids, I suppose, want to be better than their fathers. That's part of the game. Mr. Kennedy was a very strong and also a very worldly fellow.

Besides the competition with other males, and especially his father, there was a testing of himself, his potency. Did he "have it" for girl after girl? Could he maintain the numbers? To understand this discipline of lust, it is useful to turn again to Montaigne, that shrewd observer of sexual behavior, who says the ill or aging sometimes must rely on the tickle of lust to reanimate them. This was especially true of the chronically ailing Kennedy, who had the physical assertiveness of the partly crippled.

It is becoming more obvious as time passes, and the sequestration of medical records is pierced, that Robert Kennedy was not exaggerating when he said his brother passed half his days on earth in terrible pain. He was sickly from birth, with allergies, an unstable back, and other unspecified illnesses that shuttled him in and out of hospitals all through his youth, and that were followed by the carefully hidden Addison's disease of his later years. With a truly staggering willpower Kennedy refused to acquiesce in his own debilities; not only rose again and again after collapsing, but took on further challenges. He seems to have needed danger and risk and adventure, physical or moral, to keep an edge on his life. If he took to his bed, it would not be to die. He courted danger — driving fast (he turned a car over on himself and Torbert Macdonald in Europe, and crashed into a dock with his PT boat in the Pacific). He went out for sports that were clearly beyond his physical capacity — spurred on, as always, by his father, who wrote him at Harvard: "Good luck to you on the swimming and as to football, remember to be as good as the spirit is." He volunteered for PT boat service, though a boat that size, repeatedly slamming the water, would rattle his back viciously. He had a cult of courage that helps explain his interest in football players, war heroes, and astronauts.

Some thought Kennedy would not endorse Franklin Roosevelt, Jr.'s slurs, in the 1960 campaign, at Hubert Humphrey's "draft dodging"; but Kennedy advised journalists to look up his opponents' war records. Referring to Nelson Rockefeller's diplomatic service in Latin America during World War II, he asked *Newsweek*'s Ben Bradlee, "Where was old Nels when you and I were dodging bullets in the Solomon Islands?" Kenneth O'Donnell says that President Kennedy stopped mocking Douglas MacArthur after reading his World War I citation for bravery on the battlefield. Military service and manhood went together in his mind, and he was quick to accuse an opponent of shirking. During his youngest brother's Senate race against Eddie McCormack, he asked Bradlee, "When are you going to send one of your ace reporters to look into Eddie's record?" Bradlee asked what that meant, and Kennedy said McCormack had resigned from the Navy, the day he graduated from Annapolis, on flimsy medical excuses. "Dave Powers had all the information and he'll give it to you."

I think it is only fair to assume that Kennedy's constant self-testing, the lashing of his body back to a sense of its powers, contributed to his continual, almost heroic sexual performance — a way of cackling at the gods of bodily debility who plagued him, "I'm not dead yet." This performance would be especially important in the macho world he admired, the Hemingway-Mailer-Sinatra world, because he was denied two items in its trinity of manliness, broads and booze and brawls. Among his many ailments, Kennedy had inherited his father's weak stomach, which precluded drinking — which, de facto, eliminates most occasions for brawling.

Kennedy senior, who had or thought he had ulcers most of his life, drank no alcohol and ate bland food. His way of taking a young girl out to lunch was to show up in her hotel room, invite himself in, and send two eggs down to be soft-boiled not more than three minutes — according to Charlotte McConnell he carried the fresh eggs in his pockets, and wrote his instructions on their shells. His second son, too, did not drink or eat rich foods. The Blairs quote many people wondering at his huge appetite for ice cream, though he disconcerted hostesses by picking without interest at the meals they served him. Abstention from drinking is very noticeable when you spend long hours in nightclubs, as John and his father did — in fact, it takes an almost inexplicable taste for such places to stay in them while not drinking. During long nights in the Solomon Islands, where there was little to do but drink, Kennedy gave away his liquor coupons. But even a teetotaler can keep his macho credentials in order if he doubles the order on broads to compensate for nonperformance at the booze.

Kennedy's ailments no doubt gave him license with some women, beginning with those of his family. Even the puritanical Eunice, aware of the courage of his daily life, remained as loyal to the President as did the puritanical Robert. They realized how many pleasures were denied him. Cripples are often very strong in that part of them that is not directly incapacitated. Those closest to Kennedy understood his need to demonstrate virility to himself and others.

But, if anything, this understanding at the personal level raises in more pointed fashion the political implications of large-scale satyriasis. Risk-taking may be the right therapy for an individual; but the commander of a PT squadron should know ahead of time if one of his officers administers self-therapy by crashing expensive boats into valuable docks.

In the same way, a woman a day might help keep the doctor away; but an omnivorous approach to women can compromise the presidential policy as well as reputation. Kennedy had more reason than most people to know this — he was certain, from an early age, that the FBI had at least one set of tapes taken while he made love to a woman suspected of espionage. His father had told him to fear J. Edgar Hoover's use of such tapes. And his grandfather Fitzgerald had been driven from a political campaign by threats to reveal his relationship with a "Toodles" Ryan. Yet, incredibly, John Kennedy continued to make compromising assignations in the White House itself. When he inherited Judith Campbell from Frank Sinatra, he was making love to another woman who might be under investigation — and, as it turned out, was. Overlapping her affair with the candidate, and then with the President, she was intimate with Sam Giancana, who was (a) more or less permanently under investigation for suspected criminal activities, and (b) being approached by the CIA to help assassinate Castro. On several grounds the President's love life was bound to end up in another FBI folder.

Why would a man take such risks? The answer seems obvious: *be-*

cause they were risks. (Montaigne: "Both the act and depictions of it should have a whiff of the criminal about them.") According to Campbell, he tried to arrange even more compromising meetings than their White House trysts, including a threesome arrangement in a hotel room. Like his father inviting Gloria Swanson to travel openly with him on the steamer to France, Kennedy asked Campbell to fly on Air Force One. As she comments on this incident: "I think he just loved intrigue." Setting up risky meetings could take more of his energy than did completion of the tryst. As John Buchan's hero, Richard Hannay, says in *The Thirty-nine Steps,* "It was risks after all that he was chiefly greedy about."

The love of risk, the taste for compromising intrigues and hair-breadth escapes, may lead to an "interesting" life; but it can lead, as well, to international trouble if indulged in the White House. Kennedy admired risk-takers, not only on the football field or the field of battle, but in everyday life. People around him were constantly challenged to display their macho. Those who advised against the Bay of Pigs invasion, Harris Wofford has revealed, were mocked by the President for "grabbing their nuts" in fear. On the other hand, told that his appointment of Robert Kennedy as Attorney General would cause a storm of protest, he turned to his brother and said, "Let's grab our balls and go." Ballsiness was a category as important to him as to Hemingway or Mailer, and he must have been delighted when Joseph Alsop began referring to him at Washington dinner parties as "a Stevenson with balls." The adventurous services appealed to Kennedy, while President as well as in his Navy years — the PT raiders, the Green Berets (whose romantic symbol he invented), the CIA's "special action" teams, the counterinsurgents who promised to perform for him like real-life James Bonds (and who did some of their jungle exercises to an admiring audience at Hyannis Port). Kennedy was intrigued by the U-2 pilot Gary Francis Powers, considering him weird but brave. Later, he admired the legendary counterinsurgent Edward Lansdale.

Admiration for the courage that takes risks can have odd policy consequences, as we shall see. But this very love of dash and freedom had conspicuous exceptions on the "new frontier." The Kennedy administration, brashly taking on bureaucrats, was timorous if not obsequious with the oldest bureaucrat in town, J. Edgar Hoover.

When Robert Kennedy needed information on the layout of the University of Alabama, during the integration struggle there, he did not ask the FBI field office to check facts, but caused a terrible flap by asking the Pentagon to make air photos of the campus. While Justice Department marshals risked their lives at black demonstrations in the South, FBI agents stood on the sidelines taking notes. The series of unworthy southern choices for the federal bench was caused, in part, by superficial FBI reports on the candidates.

These derelictions continued, as Victor Navasky notes in his book on the Kennedy Justice Department; yet J. Edgar Hoover was mysteriously immune to the Kennedy feistiness. Not only did Robert allow Hoover's noncooperation; the Attorney General himself cooperated with requests from Hoover — like that for a phone tap on Martin Luther King. Granted, Hoover was a sacred cow; but the Kennedys showed a passivity toward him out of keeping with their activism in other areas, an activism that positively courted risk. Arthur Schlesinger remembers the priorities of postelection euphoria:

> On Wednesday night after the election he relaxed at dinner with several friends. The group fell into an animated discussion of what the President-elect should do first. One guest suggested that he fire J. Edgar Hoover of the Federal Bureau of Investigation, another that he fire Allen W. Dulles of the Central Intelligence Agency. Kennedy, listening with apparent interest, egged his friends on. When they opened their papers the next morning, they were therefore a little irritated to read a Kennedy announcement that Hoover and Dulles were staying in their jobs.

No explanation was given. Dulles would have to go after the Bay of Pigs. But Hoover kept doing outrageous things, and remained. The President would take on U.S. Steel and Nikita Khrushchev, but not Mr. Hoover. The Attorney General would cut corners to "get Hoffa," but he breathed no wish to get, or even check, his own subordinate at the Justice Department. To guarantee protection for civil rights demonstrators, he formed new kinds of legal posses, but he let FBI agents stand on the sidelines useless and unrebuked. As Navasky wrote: "It was ironic that the FBI — the only intelligence agency directly under the Attorney General's jurisdiction — was the only agency which he did not feel free to bully, pressure, harass, and pull rank on." There was no "ballsiness" in either Kennedy's attitude toward Hoover.

The strange passivity of Robert, this most energetic man, is noticeable in one other area, the investigation of his brother's death. He not only showed a lack of curiosity about the killer (or killers); he took steps to quash rumors of conspiracy — gave exclusive post-assassination interview rights to William Manchester, who opposed any conspiracy talk; sequestered the autopsy report; supported the Warren Commission without even reading its report. Harris Wofford argues persuasively that Robert feared the uncovering of CIA plots to kill Castro, since these involved Sam Giancana, who involved Judith Campbell, who would involve the dead President. As Navasky says: "Any list of RFK priorities would have to begin with his brother's reputation." If that is the case, then the Kennedy servility toward Hoover is explained. From the time of Inga Arvad, Hoover had knowledge that could have ruined the Kennedy reputation and career. Hoover was willing to use that kind of information on targets like Dr. King and Philip Berrigan; but the information was more potent *unused* where men in power were concerned. The mere threat of its use kept such men "in line."

In fact, one of John Kennedy's motives in appointing Robert to the Justice Department was no doubt to have his most trusted agent "handle" Hoover. That appointment was risky at the public level; Kennedy courted charges of nepotism, and Robert was young for the job. But it was a *caution* taken at the private level — no other man was Kennedy's intimate as Robert was, privy to the family secrets, certain to do anything to keep them secret, speaking for the family in sessions with Hoover. Another person, given the choice of ruining Dr. King's reputation or John Kennedy's, might hesitate. But not John Kennedy's brother.

To many people's surprise, Robert Kennedy earned a reputation as his brother's "best appointment." His record at Justice was mixed, as Navasky has argued, but it included many achievements. There may, indeed, have been a compensatory ardor in Kennedy's work for civil rights. He had to assemble his own team and use his own devices, since he had denied himself any opposition to Hoover's wiretapping, to his obstruction in the integration cases, to his slipshod screening of federal judges. There is an air, in the later Robert Kennedy, of doing penance — not, I think, for his own earlier "ruthlessness," as it is fashionable to say; but for his own later sense of helplessness against a man who brazenly frustrated the government's support of civil rights. Robert had been appointed by his brother to contain the threat of Hoover — which made him acquiesce in Hoover's campaign to destroy King. That was a terrible burden to sustain; and it makes a mockery of any talk that John Kennedy's sexual affairs were irrelevant to his politics. His brother's earlier freedoms put Robert Kennedy in a moral prison.

3
Sisters and Wives

And the old man — having his mistresses there at the house for
lunch and supper. I couldn't understand it! It was unheard of!

— BETTY SPALDING, visitor at Hyannis Port

IN 1970, my wife and I were at Eunice and Sargent Shriver's house
in Rockville, Maryland, for a dinner welcoming Patricia Lawford
back from Europe. It was the first time we had seen Joan Kennedy,
who was a natural beauty with little makeup on, still looking much
younger than her years. Edward Kennedy came late from the Senate
floor; we were already seated. But from the moment he arrived there
was a hum of invisible wires strung across the room, from Kennedy
to Kennedy, alive with continual semiprivate communication. Eunice, no matter what the conversation in her vicinity, heard and
laughed at each of Edward's jokes at another table, and vice versa.

When their nurse took the Kennedy children swimming at Tag-
gert's Pier, back in the thirties, they all wore the same color bathing
hats, so they could be distinguished from the other children — you
knew at once if it was a *Kennedy* in trouble, or if one had not been
rounded up for the trip home. Ever since they have been wearing invisible caps that signal to each other on a radio frequency no one else
can use.

Driving home, I asked my wife if she had noticed this phenomenon, and its corollary — she had. The corollary was that Joan Kennedy barely said a word at table, or was addressed, after her husband
arrived. She wears no invisible cap; she sends no signals. There are

honorary Kennedys and real Kennedys, as Sargent Shriver has had occasion to learn. But Joan Bennett Kennedy suffered a double disadvantage at the family table — she is not only not a Kennedy, but not a man. My wife and I were not surprised, a few years later, when reports of Joan Kennedy's drinking became public.

One has to be tough to marry into so close a family, to fight for attention, for one's own space to turn around in. Inga Arvad's son claimed there was something almost incestuous in the closeness of Kennedys to Kennedys; and, in her innocent way, Rose Kennedy bears out that insight: "Joe thought the children would never be married because they all enjoyed going out together so much. They were stimulated by each other's interests and plans, problems and ambitions." Ethel Skakel could become a Super-Kennedy, taking all their competitive games (even the breeding one) to new extremes. Jacqueline Bouvier could make her bargain, mark off her space, and let the family flow, a little bit awed, around her quiet pose. But Joan Bennett was shoved, half a century after the mold had been broken, into Rose Kennedy's role; and not even Rose's own daughters can live that way anymore.

Gloria Swanson, having agreed to Rose's humiliation on a steamer trip to Europe, ingenuously wonders how the wife could put up with such boorishness:

> Virginia [Swanson's friend] grasped the curious situation in which she was taking part the first day on the ship, but whether Mrs. Kennedy did or not I couldn't tell. Only a few years older than me, Rose Kennedy was sweet and motherly in every respect. Most of the time she and her female relative treated Virginia and me like a pair of debutantes it was their bounden duty to chaperon. . . . If she suspected me of having relations not quite proper with her husband, or resented me for it, she never once gave any indication of it. In fact, at those times during the voyage when Joe Kennedy behaved in an alarmingly possessive or oversolicitous fashion toward me, Rose joined right in and supported him. In the salon after dinner one evening, he openly and without apology talked and joked confidentially with me and left the other three women to converse among themselves; but when a man at the next table turned his chair around to look at me, Joe became white as chalk, leaped to his

feet and loudly ordered the other man to mind his own business
and stop staring at me. Before I could think of how to conceal my
mortification, I heard Rose emphatically agreeing with Joe's action,
saying she didn't understand how I stood being on constant public
display, unable to travel two steps without my husband or somebody else to protect me. She thought it was shocking. Was she a
fool, I asked myself as I listened with disbelief, or a saint? Or just a
better actress than I was?

Of course Rose knew. And of course she had to pretend she did not.
That kind of acting came naturally to women of her generation and
faith and social position. The men in the family, and even her daughters, were not embarrassed by the mother's plight, but proud of her
submissiveness to it. If courage is ballsiness, that is by definition not
a quality for women. Their nobility is in patience, in long-suffering,
in just those things that would disgrace a man. This attitude is displayed by Tito Gobbi, the great baritone, in his 1979 autobiography.
Boasting of his mother's uncomplaining virtue, he wrote:

> My good-looking father had been playing the Don Giovanni and
> my grandfather — who had a patriarchal tendency to summon the
> family together when advice or reproof was called for — did so
> then. I think he principally wished to assure my mother of his sup-
> port, but before he could say anything *she* addressed *him,* together
> with the rest of the assembled family. "Thank you very much for
> your concern for me," she said, "and I hope what I am going to say
> will not lessen your affection for me. But one thing I must ask you
> to understand. I am proud of my husband and will not have any-
> thing said against him." In point of fact I suppose it might be said
> that my wise mama was the winner in the end. For the last twenty
> years of her life my father never left her side and he adored her to
> the end.

The woman should wait for her wandering husband to come home,
and then take care of him in his old age. Meanwhile, she must never
complain, never let on that she knows what everyone around her
knows. Not only will Joseph Kennedy take Gloria Swanson into his
home, Rose Kennedy will talk of that in her own book as an honor
done to their abode:

Gloria Swanson was our house guest for a couple of days in Bronxville and brought along her small daughter, who was about the age
of our Pat, who was about ten. They got along well together, and
Pat took her down to show her the Bronxville public school and
meet her classmates and perhaps show off a little, as she did by introducing her as "Gloria Swanson's daughter." Nobody believed
her. They all just grinned, thinking it was a joke. After all, Gloria
Swanson was, to them, practically a supernatural being, so she
wouldn't be in Bronxville.

But Rose knew why she was in Bronxville. As she knew why she was
on the boat to France.

When Joseph Kennedy was in Hollywood, during his many long
absences, Rose took it as her duty not to disturb his work:

> It may seem unusual, but I did not think it was vital for my hus-
> band to be on hand for the birth of the babies . . . I knew he worked
> hard for us. . . . In the same spirit and for the same reason, as the
> years went on and our children grew and went through the inevita-
> ble period of childhood accidents and diseases (though the latter
> were more frightening then than now), I saw no point in mention-
> ing these to Joe if he was away and telephoned me for the family
> news. There was little or nothing he could do to help the situation
> at a distance, so why worry him? How could he do his own work
> well if his thoughts were preoccupied with concern for a beloved
> child? I remember once, for instance, when he was in California and
> telephoned me within a matter of minutes after I arrived home
> from a car accident that had put a good-sized gash in my forehead. I
> was feeling shaky. In fact, when the call came I was lying on my
> bed pulling myself together and drinking coffee. But I spoke natu-
> rally, gave him news of the children and told him what a fine day it
> was: a perfect day for golf. Then I drove to the hospital where the
> doctor took five stitches in my forehead.

When Rose was at the Court of St. James's, Eunice heard of her
mother's appendectomy from the newspapers — she had not wanted
to worry the children. When Rose saw her son John at Mass on the
morning of his inauguration, she avoided him — she did not want
to embarrass the President-Elect with her makeshift snow garb. A
woman's virtue is not to embarrass the men of the family, obstruct

their careers, dim their accomplishments. In fact, she must not only excuse her husband's lack of attention to her, but make her forgiveness so manifest that no one else will have trouble forgiving him. Arthur Krock told the Blairs that Rose's attitude made it unnecessary for any outsider to feel sorry about Joseph Kennedy's wanderings: "It was the way of the world as far as I knew it and the way of *his* world. I was not concerned about what happened to him in that respect. It never bothered me at all because Rose acted as if they didn't exist, and that was her business, not mine."

There can, as singer Gobbi says, be a noble pride in such refusal to complain. Once, when Rose almost broke into tears after the death of her second son, she pulled herself together again and told her companion, "No one will ever feel sorry for me." But that was something beyond her control. Others did feel sorry. Mary Pitcairn Keating, who visited Hyannis Port while dating John Kennedy, says:

> Of course, she never saw things or acknowledged things she didn't want to, which was great. I had the feeling that the children just totally ignored her. Daddy was it. I mean, I was the one who went out and picked her up when she was coming down to Washington for dinner. When the children went to Europe, Mr. Kennedy would come down to the boat with a couple of his Catholic legmen, but Mrs. Kennedy never did. At the Cape, Mrs. Kennedy was always by herself. You know that little house she had by the beach? She'd take her robe and her book down there. When she went to play golf, she'd go by herself. She did everything by herself. I never saw her walking with one of the children on the beach. . . . She was sort of a non-person.

Rose said she put up her separate little cottage at Hyannis Port to get away from the noise of a large family. It became a cell, not of loneliness but of study and prayer. Rose Kennedy belonged to the last generation of Catholic women who could combine, in some measure, the two vocations held up to them by the nuns — marriage and the convent. Rose traveled, prayed, and read much of her life in a chosen solitude. My own Irish grandmother, who was also called Rose and raised a large family, came to live with my parents after her husband died; and she turned her room, complete with prie-dieu and statues, into a chapel for her spiritual reading and rosaries. This double life was easier for Rose Kennedy, since she had nursemaids to bring up the children till they were old enough for boarding school. As she herself writes, "I did little diaper changing." Her file card, to keep track of the children's health records, became famous when she went to England. But that was surely a minimal labor for one with nine children to keep track of. There is no questioning her deep affection for her children, her duties gladly performed. But she was soon shut out of the active philandering life of her sons; and though she traveled some with Eunice, even the girls preferred the company of their father and the games of their brothers.

"Joe and I had agreed that the responsibility for education of the boys was primarily his, and that of the girls, primarily mine." Which meant that the boys went to secular schools, which would promote their careers in the world, while the girls were sent to convent schools. There was a division of labor. Boys play, girls pray. But the Kennedy girls wanted to play, too — and did it as strenuously as the boys. Women visitors at Hyannis Port found themselves forced into games where the Kennedy boys and Kennedy girls were equally ferocious. Kate Thom, wife of a Navy friend of John's, told the Blairs:

> I remember Eunice was in a sailing race and didn't have a crew. I'd never been in a boat in my life and I was made her crew. They were in everything to win, not just to participate. I remember how cruel I thought she was because she kept barking orders at me and if I did something wrong she'd scream. But she knew what she was doing and what she had to to win. And we won the race. . . . And I was pregnant at the time.

There is a famous story of Joseph Jr. throwing Edward out of his boat, during a race, for clumsy handling of a jib. Mrs. Thom may not know how close she came to going overboard herself. Mary Pitcairn Keating says, in the Blairs' interviews: "I was a bridesmaid in Eunice's wedding. She was highly nervous, highly geared, and worshipped Jack. I always thought she should have been a boy."

Another woman who visited the Kennedy home with Mrs. Thom remembers: "We were organized from the moment we arrived. The Kennedys organized everybody. I hated playing tennis, so Eunice invited me to play golf. The next day we played touch football, which was hideous. But we *had* to play and it was relentless." Later, Jac-

queline Kennedy's independence was marked by her successful refusal to play "dumb football." But in her engagement days, as one
can see from photographs in the Kennedy Library, even she was
dragged into the family softball game.

What rebellion the girls expressed was not in defense of their
mother, but in efforts to join their father's world, the world of male
play and politics. They were expected to work only in wartime; they
could not run for office themselves. Their task was to marry and raise
children. But the oldest marriageable sister did not take up the pious
role of Rose — she would marry a non-Catholic, an anti-Irish
Englishman, part of that world Joseph Kennedy aspired to. It was
Kathleen, who thought of womanizing as an English trait, who
married the Marquis of Hartington.

The next sister, Patricia, joined her father's world in a different
way, marrying not only an Englishman but a movie star who ran
with Sinatra's crowd. Eunice, the strongest of the sisters, helped her
brothers campaign but married a man who was given part control of
the family business; Jean did the same. These sons-in-law did work
the father thought of as below his own boys, but still above the girls.
The in-laws would help service the careers of Kennedy after Kennedy. They had married all of them. Torbert Macdonald, John's
friend from Harvard football days, fell in love with Kathleen; but he
realized he was too independent to become what he called "a corporate son-in-law," and broke off the attachment.

The exceptional Kennedy in-laws married the brothers who were
murdered. Ethel Skakel had several advantages in her own right. She
came from a large and competitive Catholic family, and she was the
strong one, the Eunice, of her sisters. But, more important, she married the brother who was not a "chaser," the one male in whom the
mother's piety took root. If the rule of the father was that boys play
while girls pray, pious Robert was to that extent womanish. He did
not challenge his father's rakish habits; but neither did he try to
emulate them. He was left out of his brother's carousings, and felt
excluded from the friendships John formed at Choate and in the
Navy. John often called his brother a puritan. A visitor to Hyannis
Port during the war told the Blairs: "Bobby came home from Harvard. He was a scrawny little guy in a white sailor suit. He was very
upset that we were sneaking booze in the kitchen. He was afraid his

father might catch us and he knew his father's wrath. But Kathleen handled him. She told him to get lost." On another occasion he came in while John was entertaining friends, and was ignored; going up the stairs he asked plaintively, "Aren't you glad to see me?" He was left out of the fraternity house side of Hyannis Port. Herbert Parmet claims that "Not until after Jack's death did Bobby Kennedy shed his jealousy over his brother's closeness to Torby [Torbert Macdonald]."

Unlike his brothers — Joseph Jr. was unmarried when he died at twenty-nine, and John did not marry until he was thirty-six — Robert settled down early. He was married by the age of twenty-five, and started raising his large family, to which he was devoted. Around children, Robert was almost maternal — not the strict disciplinarian his father had been, the man whose wrath he feared when grown-up children "sneaked" Scotch to Navy friends. The "boiler room girls," who became famous after Chappaquiddick, said he indulged his children when they came into his Senate office, sat on the laps of secretaries and pretended to type. Esther Newberg recalled, in her oral history for the Kennedy Library:

> Christopher said to Matthew, when he was sitting on my lap eating a mouthful of crackers and the Senator was in his doorway, "Show the lady how you learned to whistle." And he turned around all over a brand new suit and he showed me how he learned to whistle. Crackers everywhere! It was just a mess! The Senator thought it was amusing. I wanted to slap the kid in the face, but it really was kind of cute.

But if Robert was "feminine" in his piety and maternal instinct toward those he loved, he was the fiercest Kennedy competitor, the one who played touch football with a grim determination worthy of war, all bony elbows and fierce beaked face. The first time he met James Hoffa, Robert said he thought him "not so tough" — and challenged him to a push-up contest. Robert's ruthlessness became a family joke — and, like most such jokes, would have lacked point if it lacked a basis in fact. When Robert visited Edward after the plane crash that almost killed the youngest brother, the patient opened his eyes and smiled groggily, "Is it true you're ruthless?"

Robert's piety just made his fighting spirit more awesome — he

not only wanted to win but to destroy evil, whether that was embodied in the Communists he helped Joseph McCarthy hunt for a
while or in Hoffa's corrupt teamsters. John did not ask Robert to organize his campaigns out of mere family loyalty. He knew that Robert would be demanding on subordinates, up to and past the point
of abrasiveness. Friends of Robert regretted, when he ran for office
himself, that he had no "Bobby" of his own to "kick ass" in the
lower echelons of aides. It was this harsh and ruthless side of Robert
that gave poignancy to his later concern for the poor, and made his
brother take seriously his plea for restraint in the Cuban missile
crisis.

Joseph Kennedy might not have recognized himself in the puritan
Robert but for the latter's almost kamikaze physical daring and cult
of athletic prowess. He would prove he was a true Kennedy down to
his final days — climbing mountains, shooting rapids. If he was a
more cautious skier and driver than his brothers, it was because he
calculated risks with a more economical insistence on what is needed
to *win*. In remorseless determination to reach his goal, the puritan
resembled his predator father more than did any other son (or
daughter). And he married a scrapper of his own sort. Ben Bradlee
wonders at Ethel's will to win:

> Another time Kennedy and I were playing at Hyannis Port with
> Ethel and she was about seven months pregnant. I had not played
> golf for a couple of years, as I remember, and I had never played
> that course. The stakes were again ten cents a hole. Once I asked
> Ethel what club she thought I should use, because I was unfamiliar
> with the course and unsure of my own judgment. She suggested a
> five iron, and I clocked it pretty good, only to see it go sailing way
> over the green. I turned around to the sound of gales of laughter
> from Ethel and the president. She wanted to win so badly she had
> purposely suggested too much club.

Jacqueline Bouvier was tough in a different way. John Kennedy
did not marry her until the bachelor state began to pose a threat to
his career. Even as late as 1980, Governor Brown of California found
that an unmarried presidential candidate is suspected either of homosexuality or of promiscuity — he was damned if he traveled with
Linda Ronstadt, and damned if he didn't. It seems unlikely that

John Kennedy would have been accused of homosexuality. But his large and growing number of heterosexual affairs might prove damaging to any effort at the White House. It was during the 1952 race for the Senate that speculation about Kennedy's marrying came to a head. The *Saturday Evening Post* ran an article calling him "just about the most eligible bachelor in the United States, and the least justifiable one." Kennedy obviously took those last five words in several senses; after delaying the announcement long enough to let the article have its impact, he told the world he was marrying Jacqueline Bouvier, twelve years his junior, an ideal political choice. She was a Catholic by upbringing, but with a worldly background as well. She had not gone to convent schools, but to Vassar. Her father, whom she deeply admired, was a famous rake, "Black Jack" Bouvier. Like Kathleen Kennedy, she married a man who resembled her father in his attitude toward women. When Senator Jack met Black Jack, she recalled: "They were very much alike. We three had dinner before we were engaged, and they talked about politics and sports and girls — what all red-blooded men like to talk about." Like Rose Kennedy, but for very different reasons, she would not criticize her husband's affairs with other women. It was part of the world she knew, where fame and money and glamour cost something.

The political calculus of John's wedding was so obvious that even Professor Burns, in his early biography, wrote: "At least one good friend doubts that Kennedy would be married today if he had lost his Senate battle." And Burton Hersh calls that remark "as sybilline and penetrating as any ever made concerning the oncoming President." But if he had struck a good bargain with his marriage, so had she. Her later arrangement with Onassis showed what was transferable from the Kennedy contract — power, money, fame. No other coin was current in both realms. She too, even the ethereal Jacqueline, was more than half in love with Hollywood. And if Onassis was a womanizer, one might expect better taste in one who chased Maria Callas than in Judith Campbell's lover — though one hesitates at the report of whale-testicle coverings for the bar stools on Onassis's yacht. Jacqueline Kennedy did not enter tabloid heaven when it came time to marry Onassis — that had been done earlier; she merely achieved its empyrean.

Joan Bennett Kennedy was not in the league of these tough

ladies. Like Ethel, she was a Manhattanville student, with the
Madames of the Sacred Heart, when she met a law student named
Kennedy. But her Kennedy was not the monogamous Robert. It
was Edward, the nicest of the Kennedy playboys, but playboy still,
at least for some crucial years of their marriage. She tried to play
touch football like Ethel. As if to prove her worth, the new Kennedy
bride told journalists: "Ted taught me to play tennis and golf, to
waterski and be a much better skier than I was."

But, try as she would, she was on the outmost rim of the concentered Kennedy family. The nucleus was the father. Around him
circled the sons, near to the point of disappearing, at times, into
this center of family gravity. Outside that tight ring came the
women Kennedys, wife and daughters. Outside that, the male in-
laws, Sargent Shriver running the Merchandise Mart, Stephen Smith
financing campaigns out of the patriarchal stock. Outside that ring,
the female in-laws — but even here Joan was not an equal to the
other two; she came in a distant third, farthest from the family's
animating center — till she spun out, alone, into darkness.

The caution with which she bore her barely mended pride, during
the 1980 campaign, impressed many viewers. But it was miraculous that any mending had occurred. She had been, over the years,
systematically broken down and almost discarded in a world of men
who shy superstitiously from losers and of women who go with their
men no matter what. Myra McPherson, in her book on political
wives, interviewed a frequent visitor in Hyannis Port, who told her:
"They all really got on Joan, to the point where I felt sorry for her.
I remember one day we were all going sailing, and everyone had on
old blue jeans and Joan came down in a leopard skin bathing suit.
Ethel said, 'Really, Joan, did you expect the photographer?' Everyone snickered, Joan was helpless, unable to quip back with some
smart crack. That's what you had to do."

The results of this long attritive living with the Kennedys came to
frighten Edward Kennedy at last. And no wonder. Burton Hersh's
book contains this searing passage: "A longstanding journalistic
friend of the Kennedy family remembers stopping at Kennedy's
house in Hyannis Port a couple of summers ago to talk and have a
drink. As he was leaving, Kennedy suggested that the visitor hadn't
had a chance yet to say hello to Joan, and led him around to the back

of the house; Joan lay crumpled up, passed out in the back seat of
one of the Kennedy cars. 'She was a rag mop,' the friend observes.
'I've seen drunks often enough, but what I was looking at there was
the result of a two- or three-day bender. I think Kennedy just
wanted me to see what he was up against. If something got printed,
he was prepared for that." In a man's world of winners one must be
tough enough to go on, even when the losers can't.

4

The Prisoner of Sex

By a kind of compensation the source of his power was the cause
also of his downfall.

— WALTER BAGEHOT, of Bolingbroke

THE NIGHT AFTER that Pier Four rally where I first noticed how
checked are all Edward Kennedy's public gestures out toward
women, there was a little "birthday party" for staff and press in the
motel we stayed at. Joan Kennedy was just ahead of me in the buffet
line, and I tried to kid her gently about adding a year to her husband's age in a speech earlier that day. She knitted her brow in an
effort to understand, but said nothing. Her husband saw her talking
to me and hastened over. "Come join us, Joansy." She was swept to a
small protective table with familiar aides around her.

Kennedy's task during the campaign was to produce Joan and
protect her at the same time, and these were antithetical aims. Her
absence would be an indictment of him as a family man. Yet her
presence was an absence even more startling — she was so clearly
disoriented by the glare; misread her short, carefully prepared
speeches; wore an orange mask of makeup which cracked, on occasion, and let the tears seep through.

Kennedy's "Joan problem" was not simply that he had to protect
her while producing her, hide and expose simultaneously. The real
problem was that he *could* not protect her. Often as he thanked her,
guided her, deferred to her, he touched her as cautiously as he did
the women who gushed up to him for handshakes. There was a

troubled space between them; each reached across it only rarely, tentatively. During the St. Patrick's Day parade in Chicago, when security problems were anticipated, she skittered at noises and clutched for him, but he was marching defiantly forward and did not notice. The few times they tried to kiss in public were tense moments for them both. It is hard to put together sundered intimacies with half a nation watching.

So the imprisonment was complete. Not only could he not reach out in public, even innocently, to women supporters. He could not reach out to his own wife with any confidence of finding her. Once he may have neglected her. Now, try though he would, he could barely locate her.

The philanderer's compiling of lists means crossing women off, erasing them. The philanderer's punishment is the inability to call back the one woman he may want once she has been erased. The very word "conquests," used of seduction, poses the problem in a military metaphor. It is one thing to conquer a people, quite another to rule it, to win it over. The power to conquer is often a delusion, even at the national level; and almost always at the personal level. Power to destroy hurts the destroyer if there is not a concomitant power to restore. The child, angry at not getting the station he wants on a radio, has the power to smash it; but this is not useful power, the power to make it speak again. It is easy to smash the intricate circuitry of a marriage; but what if one should want to make the other partner speak again some day? Edward Kennedy was trying, all thumbs, to put back the most costly and complicated inner workings of a delicate speaking apparatus, a marriage, in front of the voters of New Hampshire. And he was failing.

The failure was not his alone. The entire Kennedy family was too much for Joan (or for most people) to cope with. Nor was Edward the worst husband she might have found in that family. It puzzled me all through the 1980 campaign to hear people say they would vote again for one of the older brothers, but not for Edward; he lacked character. His character flaws, such as an outsider can judge, seemed to me neither as deep nor as crippling as those displayed by other Kennedys, beginning with the father. Then why was the judgment on Edward's shortcomings so harsh?

One reason may be that he seems to have got caught more than a reasonably prudent man should. If the others symbolically "got away with murder," getting away with it took managerial discipline that might be relevant to presidential performance. William Buckley even wrote that what disqualified Edward Kennedy, in the light of Chappaquiddick, was his poor head for cover-ups. It was not important that he was, in Buckley's words, "drunk and horny" that night (questionable assertions), but that he could not tidy up the mess more deftly.

The friend of Richard Nixon and Spiro Agnew may place cover-up skills higher on the list of presidential qualities than others would, but this youngest son *does* seem to have been caught a good deal — repeatedly caught speeding, caught cheating in college, caught doing God-knows-what at Chappaquiddick. Some amateur psychiatrists put this down to a death wish in the last brother left alive, claim that he may subconsciously desire the comparative immunity that has come to his brothers after death. That kind of speculation is amusing to the speculator but of little use to anyone else. The trouble with it is that Kennedy started getting caught — at Harvard, at the University of Virginia — long before there was any "legacy of death" for the Kennedys.

One reason for this brother's public indiscretions may simply be the fact that he is the first Kennedy male in three generations to break the family taboo on drinking. His grandfather kept a tavern, but did not touch his own wares. His father did not drink himself, and strictly rationed the family's predinner drink to one, even for visitors. Joseph Jr., John, and Robert drank rarely, and very little on the rare occasions. By all accounts, none was seen drunk, in private or in public; which means that when they took risks, they were calculated risks, not the improvisations of befuddlement. Some of Edward's getting caught may be the result of lowered defenses. When he sped away from police in Charlottesville, then hid in the back seat after parking his car, he may have been avoiding the suspicion of driving while intoxicated. He was hiding the evidence — himself. The "Jock" sessions at which a whole group schemed up a solution to Kennedy's Spanish problem sounds well lubricated. If Kennedy had determined in any cold-headed way to cheat, he would hardly have invited in so many witnesses to the decision. And at Chappaquiddick there was just enough drinking to make the impulse to hide that fact affect the complex of decisions and, mainly, nondecisions that undid Kennedy.

It may seem no defense to say a man gets himself into trouble by appearing intoxicated in public. But there is a sense in which this gives Joan somewhat less to complain of than Jacqueline had. For Edward, handsome and besieged by beautiful admirers, to slip on occasion out of weakness should be more acceptable to a wife than the calculated regimen of John Kennedy, the daily dose of sex taken, as it were, for muscle tone. One can say, by the standards of cover-up artistry, that John Kennedy showed political skill in marrying a woman who would not object to this regimen (not terminally, at least); but there is a coldbloodedness to this that seems less admirable in a person, no matter how useful it may be to a leader.

As for other charges against Edward's character, I cannot (since I am a teacher) condone cheating on exams. But I do not regard that act as dishonorable as lying about one's authorship of a book in order to keep the Pulitzer Prize. And if we are to measure public virtue by public service, as the founders of this nation did, Edward Kennedy has served his constituency and the nation in the Senate long after it became clear that such service involved risking his life. He has bent the Kennedy ego to cooperative work among his peers. He has shown legislative concern for refugees, the aged, the ill, by doing the drudgery of his Senate homework. He does not try to take the glamour and leave hard work to others. He labors at being a good Senator — the only Kennedy who has ever done that. This Kennedy has not misused the power of his office as Robert did, wiretapping Martin Luther King. He has not risked the national dignity as John did, taking a "gangster's moll" into White House bedrooms.

Ah, but this Kennedy was involved in a woman's death on Chappaquiddick Island. Much as there is to criticize in Kennedy's behavior that night — and the thing most to be criticized is that we still know so little of that behavior — the narrowly sexual charges leveled at Kennedy seem, in this case, a bum rap. It is the irony of Don Juan's life to get caught on a night when he is not prowling for women. There were many knowing winks about the idea of six married men getting six single "girls" together in an isolated spot — as if Edward Kennedy needed this elaborate arrangement to find female companionship. The irony is completed when we learn that, though Kennedy has a hard time showing respect for women, he *did* respect the six assembled at Chappaquiddick. For that we have the best pre-Chappaquiddick evidence, that of the women themselves.

One of the most touching transcripts in the Kennedy Library's oral history project comes from Esther Newberg and Rosemary Keough, and was made on May 22, 1969, a year after Robert Kennedy's murder, not long before their own attendance at the Chappaquiddick party. They were asked to speak about Robert Kennedy's last campaign, for which they ran the nerve center of information called "the boiler room." They admit they had trouble impressing old political types with the importance of clearing all information through them; but they said that one exception to this was the candidate's younger brother, who *did* look to them for information, on a professional basis. Esther Newberg said: "He really knew that even if we didn't have it written down in books, we had it in our heads. He didn't look down on us, as you might expect, as a group of pool secretaries for instance. I think he respected what some of us knew."

Much that has been written about Chappaquiddick either asserts or implies that the party was based on a *lack* of respect, was an "office party" in the stereotypical sense. Yet Kennedy's respect was shown not only during the campaign, but afterward, well before Chappaquiddick. In the summer of 1968, after the murder of Robert Kennedy, Joseph Gargan arranged the *first* party for the boiler room girls at Cape Cod. This was to thank them for their work in Robert's ill-fated campaign. Edward and Joan Kennedy threw a cocktail party for them. The women were put up at various Kennedy homes — Mary Jo Kopechne stayed with the Shrivers. The Chappaquiddick party was to be a repetition of that innocent first gathering. Since it was to be held at the Edgartown races, there were no Kennedy homes to put them in — the women stayed at a motel. The Hyannis Port compound could not be used to entertain them, so Gargan rented a cottage. Kennedy's attitude toward this party, as to the first one, was dutiful; he was discharging a debt for his brother, not arranging an orgy. I delay discussion of his later conduct for a later page, since my topic here is sex. Chappaquiddick is discussed in a haze of innuendo, typified by a 1980 bumper sticker in New Hampshire: "Ted Kennedy drives women to the drink." Yet sex was the least important aspect of the Chappaquiddick tragedy.

It may seem Kennedy has such a genius for getting caught that he is caught even when there is nothing to catch him out in. Well, not quite. But he does receive a kind and intensity of criticism he has not earned all by himself. His father and brother were more single-minded philanderers than he, but their activity was kept away from the mass of the electorate. Now that their record is better known, Edward alone survives to take the brunt of moral dismay these revelations caused in naive admirers. A nun who taught my daughter in parochial school kept a picture of President Kennedy in her classroom and spoke of him as a saint. It is fairly certain she will not look at Edward Kennedy through the same haze of hagiography. Even those who claim that their opinion of the dead President has not been altered are ready to look with sharper eyes of suspicion on his brother — and would have done so at the President if they had known then what they do now.

But a deeper cultural reason for Edward Kennedy's difficulties comes from the vitality of modern feminism. John Kennedy was the beneficiary of a first sexual revolution, the one proclaimed in Norman Mailer's gushy welcome to Superman at the Supermarket. But Mailer and Hugh Hefner — and Edward Kennedy — are the victims of a counterrevolution, one that says woman's highest destiny is *not* to become another notch on some hero's gun. Joan Kennedy, a victim in so many ways, is the beneficiary of this counterrevolution; she says the liberation movement helped get her out on her own, continue her education and her music, without looking to her husband's family for applause that never came. And if she is to be the beneficiary, her husband must be the victim. The graduate student of my era, who rejoiced in John Kennedy's sexual reputation, has been replaced by "sisters" on campus, twenty years later, who think of such "chauvinism" as a political issue, just as the earlier liberal had — but one, now, that works against the Kennedys, not for them.

This criticism of Kennedy macho was first mounted in a massive and rather clumsy way by Nancy Gager Clinch, in her book *The Kennedy Neurosis* (1973), which had all the faults of "psychobiography" at its worst. But by the time Edward actually ran for President, the criticism had become more refined. Suzannah Lessard's article "Kennedy's Woman Problem, Women's Kennedy Problem" was rejected by *The New Republic,* which had commissioned it; but the piece ran (to an audience made more attentive by the rejection), in *The Washington Monthly,* and some at *The New Republic* felt embarrassed by the rejection. Lessard admitted: "In the Bible Belt, it would take courage to say that philandering is of no importance. But in New York the danger lies in saying that it matters." Yet she found Kennedy's pattern of "semi-covert, just barely personal and ultimately discardable encounters" degrading to women and revelatory of the Kennedy attitude toward power.

Kennedy's voting record on "women's issues" like the Equal Rights Amendment and abortion has been praised by the National Organization for Women. But people notice that he has few women in high positions on his staff, and those few are not among the most intimate or powerful. Here his imprisonment takes on its exquisite, its cruel thoroughness. Just when it is important for him to show a greater trust in and reliance on women, his reputation makes him hold them off in public. He cannot win. Some ask him to take women into his political apparatus; but a suspicious public whispers about any women who get near him. He suffered for trying to honor Robert's boiler room workers. Even innocent meetings have been given tabloid treatment. Burnt so often, how can he work intimately with a woman, keep her late at the office, thank her fondly for good work done?

The moralizers at the end of *Don Giovanni* lay it on rather thick for most of us; but it is true, in quite specific ways, that licentiousness throws chains around itself. Earlier Kennedys were more subtly bound — the father's mistreatment of his wife was more obvious than the callousness he formed around himself. But Edward inherits the handiwork of his elders as well as the links he has added on his own, and by now he is so heavily chained he can hardly move naturally in the presence of women.

It may seem unfair for the inheritor of all that libidinous imperialism to live in the postcolonial era of sexual reations. The power over women that was promised him, almost as his birthright, has turned on him, has tripped him up. Power has a way of doing that.

II

FAMILY

You will hear everlastingly, in all discussions about newspapers, companies, aristocracies, or party politics, this argument that the rich man cannot be bribed. The fact is, of course, that the rich man is bribed; he has been bribed already. That is why he is a rich man.

— GILBERT CHESTERTON

5

Semi-Irish

We have again been cheated of the prospect of a Catholic President.

— MURRAY KEMPTON, 1961

IT IS THE OLD STORY: for "one of your own" to get elected, he must go out of his way to prove he is not *just* one of your own. The first Catholic President had to be secular to the point (as we used to say in Catholic schools) of supererogation. And John Kennedy had the right credentials. Theodore Sorensen vouched for the fact that "he cared not a whit for theology." Jacqueline Kennedy told Arthur Krock: "I think it is unfair for Jack to be opposed because he is a Catholic. After all, he's such a poor Catholic. Now if it were Bobby: he never misses mass and prays all the time." Herbert Parmet quotes a close friend's judgment that Kennedy had "no sense of piety as an internal characteristic." As Charles Kinsella puts it in Edwin O'Connor's novel: "I got the Catholic vote because everybody knows I am one. I got the non-Catholic vote because the others don't think I'm a very good one. Or, as they'd put it, I'm not 'typical.' "

But one must quote O'Connor with care. The Kennedy legend makes much of the Boston Irish background on both sides of John Kennedy's family. It sees him growing up in a world of bowler-hatted Boston pols with outlandish nicknames like Knocko and Onions, where Honey Fitz is always singing "Sweet Adeline." But Murray Kempton saw through it all during the 1960 campaign:

"There is a myth that Boston is his home. It is only the place where he went to college. He is a Cambridge man and he looks at Boston as Harvard looks at Boston, in some middle distance between amusement and disgust." Kennedy's parents moved from Brookline to New York in 1926, when he was nine years old, and he grew up there, went to school there, before going to prep school in Connecticut. True, he spent summer vacations at Hyannis Port, just as he spent winter vacations in Palm Beach — but that did not make him a resident of Massachusetts or of Florida. When he decided to run for Congress in 1946, he had not lived in Boston for twenty years; he had to take out rooms at the Bellevue Hotel to be his official residence.

Later, people would remember the cry of "carpetbagger" raised against Robert Kennedy when he ran for the Senate in New York. But the charge had first been leveled at John Kennedy, and with better reason. Robert had been only one year old when his family moved to New York. That state was his home for all his young life. And, just to make the border-crossing story more complex, Edward was actually born in New York, though he would follow John's example — and claim his old residential apartment — in running for the Senate from Massachusetts.

The loyal Kenneth O'Donnell admits that "Jack Kennedy himself was a stranger in Boston, having lived as a youth in New York and at Hyannis Port on Cape Cod." But he suppresses the accusation that hurt most: Kennedy was called the Miami candidate, a Floridian like his father. In 1946, Kennedy senior had to hire local politicians to instruct his son in the state's ways. David Powers remembered with wonder that "It took Jack three months before he found out that Mother Galvin wasn't a woman" but a pol known for bounty in dispensing favors. So much for the Edwin O'Connor view of Kennedy as a kind of Ivy Shamrock sprung from Honey Fitz, Purple Shamrock with class.

Though Joseph Kennedy was the first in the family to get out of Boston, his father had taken care to make that departure possible. The state legislator's son was educated at Boston Latin School and Harvard, where he could learn to talk like the brahmins. During the war John Kennedy got mad at a Navy friend's surprise over his father's diction — he did not have the "lower class" Boston accent.

The son was angry that anyone would *expect* his father to "talk mick."

The grandfather of the future President, Patrick Joseph Kennedy, had a certain contempt for the Irish weaknesses he ministered to as a bartender. He did not drink himself — asked to celebrate some occasion with a toast, he would fill a shot glass with beer. He was a man anxious to forget his own origins. Elected to the state legislature, he could put "liquor dealer" as his occupation — he did not tend bar anymore. Later, with sensitivities further honed, he would identify himself only as "trader." His son, in turn, got out of the liquor business just before John Kennedy's campaign for the House of Representatives.

Though Joseph Kennedy would later be embarrassed by his florid father-in-law, John (Honey Fitz) Fitzgerald, it should be remembered that Fitzgerald too went to Boston Latin and was enrolled at the Harvard Medical School when his father died and he had to go to work. As soon as he rose in the world, John Fitzgerald affected brahmin ways, playing polo, hobnobbing with Sir Thomas Lipton, fox hunting. Later, when Edward Kennedy thought of riding with a polo team, his father told him Kennedys were not polo society. He was referring to John Fitzgerald's unsuccessful attempts to become assimilated on horseback.

But if John Fitzgerald was only semidetached from his own father's "shanty" background, he sprang his daughter almost entirely free. She was schooled not only at Manhattanville, the "best" school for Catholic ladies, but abroad with German aristocrats. She was a catch for the young bank president, who first suffered the condescension of Honey Fitz, and then spent years repaying it a thousandfold.

With this beautiful wife at his side, Joseph Kennedy did everything he could to be accepted by the "real" Boston. Not content to vacation with the wealthy Irish at Nantasket, he went to the WASP playground at Cohasset — where the country club blackballed him. Years later he recalled every such rebuff; and, according to Ben Bradlee, so did his son. Even the tranquil and pious Rose Kennedy once asked a Harvard student from one of the brahmin families, "When are the nice people of Boston going to accept us?" As late as 1957, the New York *Times* could quote her husband's protest at being called an Irishman: "I was born in America. My children were born here. What the hell do I have to do to be called an American?" After his graduation from Harvard, where he was not accepted into the best clubs, Joseph Kennedy kept trying to ingratiate himself at class reunions, furnishing the beer and entertainment; but when he was booed at the twenty-fifth one, he attended no others. Richard Whalen wrote: "In years to come, for a number of reasons he found sufficient, Kennedy adopted an attitude toward Harvard that friends and classmates sadly described as hatred." The family sensitivity was passed down. To paraphrase Jacqueline Kennedy, it was unfair for the Kennedys to be treated as Irish, they were such poor Irishmen; they tried so hard to be anything but.

Convinced at last that he would always be just another Irishman in Boston, Kennedy decided in 1926 to "purge his trousers cuff of the Boston Irish" (in Kempton's words) by moving to fashionable New York addresses: Riverdale, Westchester, Bronxville. When he did not get the cabinet position he aspired to under Roosevelt (Secretary of the Treasury), the only honorific that appealed to him was Ambassador to the Court of St. James's, the diplomatic post even brahmins look up to. There was no Irish hatred of the English among Kennedys. Just the opposite. Most of the heroes (and some of the in-laws) of the Kennedys were English.

Though he realized that his son would have to learn the Irish wards in Boston, he carefully put him in hands other than Honey Fitz's, and he approved when his chosen mentor blew up at the ex-Mayor for entering the campaign headquarters. Joe Kane shouted, "Get that son of a bitch out of here," and John Kennedy did not defend his grandfather. He was learning, like his father, to use the Irish connection only when necessary.

If anything, John Kennedy went further than his father in dissociating himself from Irish ways. His famous reluctance to wear hats was put down to vanity — he must not have thought they became him. But doing interviews for their book, the Blairs soon learned that an Irish politician's hat was his trademark in Boston — just as Al Smith's had been in New York: "Talk of hats — style, size, and so on — cropped up all through our political interviews." Edward Gallagher, one of those deputed by John's father to instruct him in Boston politicking, bought the candidate a hat and tried to make him wear it. John refused. He had not come to join the Irish pols, and certainly not to look like them. He just wanted their votes.

Six of Joseph Kennedy's children married — not one to an Irish spouse. They had not been brought up to respect their own. In fact, only four of the six married fellow Catholics. Nor were "vocations" ever a serious prospect for any Kennedy in this large family. The mother's was not the strongest voice in domestic matters. The parish priest was no figure of importance. There was no hint of jansenist views on sex. In all these ways, the Catholic families of Edwin O'Connor's stories — or Elizabeth Cullinan's — have little to do with the secular and rootless environment of the Kennedy family. Joseph Kennedy took his family with him to various parts of America and the world, trying to win acceptance on his own terms in several societies — New York, Florida, Hollywood, London — where he could "make a splash" without fully belonging. Phil Kinsella, speaking for the family O'Connor partly modeled on the Kennedys, could say of the novel's fictionalized Boston, "This has always been our base." Joseph Kennedy's children could not say that. They had a floating base. Their base was the father.

Joseph Kennedy's loyal inner circle of business subordinates was all Irish; but they were flunkies. They did the work for which Kennedy felt his sons would be too good — only sons-in-law were expected to perform the chores of his lifelong henchmen, the personal attendants Gloria Swanson called his "Four Horsemen." In the words of Richard Whalen: "Throughout his career, it was Kennedy's standard operating procedure to move from job to job behind a protective cordon of cronies." Dragonflying from this venture to that, he needed a mobile team of men he could trust entirely, who had no other interest than his own shifting concerns, whose base was his person as fully as the children's base was paternal.

The father's rootlessness is reflected in his business attitude. When President Roosevelt put him in charge of the Securities and Exchange Commission, he was called a traitor to the business community he came from. But he was never part of any "community." He operated in a series of raids — saw opportunity, struck fast, and moved on. Banking, movies, liquor, land — he was in and out of these ventures, cutting his losses, always moving. He did not stay long enough to get entangled in the stable concerns of business, cer-

tainly not in any business responsibility to the circumambient community. He was a predator on other businessmen, not their partner.
He looked down on them, just as he did on the Boston Irish. If he
was forced to be one of them, he would make sure that his sons were
not. He must earn enough from other capitalists to keep his family
clean of any further contact. When President Kennedy, in the midst
of the steel dispute, said his father "always told me that businessmen
are sons-of-bitches," he was not joking; it was the literal truth. Even
for associates of higher standing than businessmen, there was little
real respect. Through the years Kennedy cultivated and, when necessary, flattered Arthur Krock. But Krock told the Blairs, "I've often
reflected since those days that he probably never liked me at all, but
found me useful and thought he might be able to make use of me."
All others were to be used; but not the family. That was what the
others were being used *for*.

Joseph Kennedy scrambled up with a desperate ambition. His
constant emphasis on self-improvement was the other side, the escape side, of his self-contempt. If he was not always rising, he would
be just a Boston Irishman, just another businessman — a crass mick.
As he told Arthur Krock, "For the Kennedys it is the shit house or
the castle — nothing in between." The castle was what he hoped to
arrive at; the shit house was where he had been. He had no credentials but his latest achievement — no community to lean back on, no
base but the one he forged for himself every day, the clearing he
made for his family in a hostile environment. The endless catechiz-
ing of his children on the need to win, the competitive edge he
sharpened in each of them, reflected his own inner urgencies. If he
did not keep winning, there was nothing to support him. The drag-
onfly, with nothing to light on, would just fall straight down forever.

Gloria Swanson gives a convincing picture of the threat failure
presented to Kennedy. The film Kennedy had tailored for her, *Queen
Kelly,* was unshowable; he stood to lose over a million dollars and —
worse — to appear ludicrous, to hear the boos that drove him from
the Harvard class reunion echoing all around the nation.

An hour later he charged into the living room of the bungalow,
alone, cursing Von Stroheim and Le Baron and Glazer. Stopping

abruptly, he slumped into a deep chair. He turned away from me, struggling to control himself. He held his head in his hands, and little, high-pitched sounds escaped from his rigid body, like those of a wounded animal whimpering in a trap. He finally found his voice. It was quiet, controlled. "I've never had a failure in my life," were his first words. Then he rose, ashen, and went into another searing rage at the people who had let this happen. . . . Bravo, I wanted to say. If you're forty years old and you've never had a failure, you've been deprived. Failure is a part of life, too.

But failure could not be part of Kennedy's life. One failure was enough to send him all the way back to the shit house, to prove he was nothing but a shanty mick. Kennedys don't lose. If they do, they are not Kennedys, as Joseph defined them, with their own code and their own excellence, hovering without props in the air by sheer energy of levitating ambition. If (God forbid) they should fail, they would simply be Honey Fitz's in-laws.

When Joseph Kennedy's own ambitions for the presidency were frustrated, he turned to his surrogates, his sons. They would become a tiny and enclosed aristocracy of talent, with a material base entirely provided by him. They need not scramble, or be predators. They would live on the heights to which he lifted them. It was an astonishing act of will, to create a kind of space platform out of his own career, one from which the children could fly out to their own achievements and come back for refueling. As this one or that one took on a new challenge, the children were informed by the custodian of their patrimony that "You have just made a political donation" to the new flight.

The wonder is not simply that the whole thing could be held together by the fierce drive of one man's will, but that, under the blowtorch of that willpower, none of the children rebelled. Of course, the sons would edge away from some of the old man's prejudices, his anti-Semitism, his attitude toward blacks. But it is nonsense to say they differed from him deeply in politics. He had no ideology but achievement, and that became theirs. I spoke earlier of the way Kennedys have of talking mainly with other Kennedys, of forming a circle that others are only partly let into. That is the circuit forged by the old man's desires, the communications system of the little society made to hover in air by his sheer energy. That circuitry animates them all, and to drop out of it would be death for them.

The semi-Irishness of the Kennedys can be gauged by a comparison that was often raised *because* the Kennedys were Irish. Another large Irish family, cosmopolitan, talented, tight-knit, has been likened to them over the years — sometimes in mirror-image formulae, such as: the Kennedys are the Buckleys of the Left, or the Buckleys are the Kennedys of the Right. Granted, neither side of this comparison seems to have relished the conjunction. When Robert Kennedy refused to go on William Buckley's TV show *Firing Line* and a reporter asked why, Buckley ferociously answered: "Why does the meat shun the grinder?"

Both sides rightly sense the comparison is ill-grounded just because it relies on the Irish Catholic connection. But there are real similarities, precisely in terms of this rejection. They resemble each other negatively, by their strenuous push *off from* the stereotypes people keep trying to use in order to link them. The suggested first comparison not only misses the point, but reverses it: the two families are similar only to the extent that they have ceased, deliberately, to be Irish in the accepted sense.

William Frank Buckley (1881–1958) deserves his own Richard Whalen — who would, no doubt, get as little cooperation from the Buckleys as the Kennedys gave to Whalen. The son of a Texas sheriff, young Will Buckley was a frontier scrambler who anticipated some of Lyndon Johnson's experiences. Born on the Brazos River, he grew up in San Antonio, where an educated Basque priest made him yearn for a more cultured world. He taught school to Mexican Americans, and worked his way through the University of Texas, where he became a campus leader, editor of the school paper. After finishing law school, he became an oil speculator — as natural an entry into the financial world, for a Texan, as was Joseph Kennedy's apprenticeship to banking in Boston.

Like the Kennedy patriarch, Buckley was a loner, launching individual raids on targets of opportunity, defying the big oil companies. Kennedy, however, diversified, jumped from one successful enterprise to others of entirely different sorts. Buckley, after hitting oil in Mexico, kept free-lancing on the same lines all his life. Thus the

Buckleys ended up land rich and oil poor, with too many options on sites with too little oil. The father's "big killings" came at longer and longer intervals and almost ceased with his retirement. When James Buckley was dragged, kicking and screaming, to the revelation of his income during the 1980 Senate race in Connecticut, people were surprised at how little it was. But Buckley had never reached the financial stratosphere Joseph Kennedy moved in.

For one thing, the Buckley father seemed less driven. Given financial competence, he broadened his interests. He admired good prose, and exacted it from his children with the sort of dedication that made Joseph Kennedy try to plaster a Harvard football letter on each of his sons' chests. Here, at least, Buckley was more successful. Only two of the Kennedys — Robert and Edward — won their H. Every Buckley child, so far as I know, writes well — though no Kennedy, without a ghost, found it easy to commit English prose. The elder Buckley, who once taught Spanish, kept Spanish servants and insisted that his children speak both that language and French. He had them all tutored in music. (Joseph Kennedy liked to play classical records as background to conversations, which made Arthur Schlesinger claim that he had a taste for the stuff — it seems to others to belie that fact. Kennedy did not want to go to concerts, just to have classical muzak to soothe him — and, on one recorded occasion, to irritate others.)

The Kennedys liked to work and play as a team — on boats, footballing over the lawn (more ardent than deft), or in politics. The Buckleys are individualists in practice as well as theory. They take their sports and politics in comparative isolation from each other — John Buckley hunting, Priscilla golfing, James bird-watching, William skiing.

While less single-mindedly attached to each other, the Buckleys are also less thoroughly detached from their origins — some have even married Irish spouses. Religion gets more than lip service from most Buckley children. Their father not only stuck to one line of business, but was ideologically single-tracked as well. Both patriarchs were America-Firsters who opposed entry into World War II, though their sons were quick to enlist in that struggle. Both were anti-Communists in the Cold War period — indeed, both were friends of Joseph McCarthy. But Joseph Kennedy was flexible in his politics in order to be undeviating in support of his sons' political ambitions. John Kennedy told Dorothy Schiff, "My father would be for me if I were running as head of the Communist Party." No Buckley son felt he could make that boast.

Despite these and other differences, there are remarkable similarities between the two clans — some, of course, just accidental. There is no deep significance to the fact that James Buckley succeeded in time to the Senate seat Robert Kennedy had held, or that both ran as "carpetbaggers." The size of the families is not a matter for surprise, given the religious upbringing of both mothers. Rose Kennedy began her family of nine children before Aloise Buckley (a New Orleans belle) began hers of ten — the oldest Kennedy son was born in 1915, the oldest Buckley in 1920. During the twenties, the two women were more or less continuously pregnant (William Jr. was born in 1925, the same year as Robert Kennedy). The last Kennedy child (Edward) was born in 1932, the last Buckley (Carol) in 1940.

More profound similarities lie in the relation of the children to their parents. The mother was, in both cases, pretty, cultured, and retiring; clearly not the major force in the family. Kenneth O'Donnell, stressing the importance of the women's vote in Boston, said: "In an Irish home, the mother's word is law." If that is the case, then neither the Buckley nor the Kennedy home was Irish. One daughter of Aloise Buckley told me that her first memories of her mother's room — where she retired as Rose Kennedy did to her "hut" on the beach — were of holy water and perfume.

In both families the father was dominant, though he traveled much away from home. Both men combined the discipline of an executive driving his underlings with a paternal affection that showed best in memos. Each man was rootless, restless, going where the action took him, living in a variety of homes simultaneously — south in winter, north in summer, Europe often. The children were tutored and sent to secular schools that would advance their careers — eventually Yale became for the Buckleys what Harvard was for Kennedys. To some degree the Buckleys freed their daughters from convent backgrounds — while Kennedy girls were at Manhattanville, the Buckleys were at Smith. But neither father liked to see his daughters aim at anything but homemaking.

Though Buckley's cultural aspirations were deeper than Kennedy's, they were no less anglophile, in defiance of Irish memories. John Kennedy grew up admiring Lords Tweedsmuir and Cecil, at an age when William Buckley's hero was Albert Jay Nock, who modeled his *Freeman* on the English *Spectator,* the better to mock American vulgarity. As Joseph Kennedy exchanged his "low Boston" accent for brahmin, the Buckleys acquired a "mid-Atlantic" mode of speech partly modeled, in William Jr.'s case, on the Oxford diction of Willmoore Kendall. It is no wonder this same Buckley told an interviewer: "I simply wasn't aware that we were somewhere along the line taxonomized as Irish Catholics until somebody told me, and that was fifteen years after I graduated from college." That was not a thing his own family would have impressed on him.

Buckleys, no more than Kennedys, rebelled against their strong father. The children gradually rid themselves of their parents' anti-Semitism and prejudice against blacks, but this was seen as a forgivable generation lag in the admired rulers of the clans. There were no open breaks. Buckley, having less financial power, had to welcome his sons into the family business — something unthinkable for Kennedy. But even Buckley seems to have been happier at the thought that some of his boys would become writers or scholars than that they would keep poking at the largely dry holes he left them. Buckleys, though less fused in a single system than the Kennedys, do have special antennae for each other, making it hard sometimes for in-laws fully to belong.

The main difference between the families is that the Kennedy father pushed farther out, aspired higher, and fueled more ambitious flights than did the Buckley father. This means the Buckleys are only semi-semi-Irish, when compared with the Kennedys' full semi-Irishness (the condition of John's rise to the presidency). But if that differentiates them, the thing that makes them similar is the fact that each man *did* push off from his point of origin, to create a private world for his children, a rootless aristocracy of merit. Though no one is entirely free of ancestral influence, these men's families do not exemplify their ethnic heritage so much as the American *escape* from origins toward opportunity.

6
Semi-English

Irish-Americans, particularly those who live in the Boston area,
are almost to a man staunchly anti-British.

— DAVID NUNNERLY, *President Kennedy and Britain*

WHEN JOHN KENNEDY WENT to Washington for his work in naval
intelligence (and his trysts with Inga Arvad), he met John White, a
journalist who was dating his sister Kathleen. White, who thought
Kennedy a shallow playboy, was surprised by one sign of depth: "He
said his favorite book was *Seven Pillars of Wisdom* by T. E. Lawrence.
That was extraordinary taste. Genuine taste."

Perhaps. In 1941 Kennedy was enthusiastic about John Buchan's
memoir, *Pilgrim's Way,* in which Buchan praised his friend
"Lawrence of Arabia" and said, "I could have followed Lawrence
over the edge of the world." Lawrence lived the kind of adventure
story Buchan wrote — he served, in fact, as model for "Sandy" in
Greenmantle. Lawrence could write, in *Seven Pillars:* "Blood was always on our hands; we were licensed to it." James Bond's agent
number, remember, is his license to kill. Lawrence presented his
qualifications as a translator of Homer this way: "I have hunted wild
boars and watched wild lions, sailed the Aegean (and sailed ships),
bent bows, lived with pastoral peoples, woven textiles, built boats
and killed many men." It is the code of Norman Mailer's neo-Re-
naissance man: "kill well (if always with honor), love well and love
many, be cool, be daring, be dashing, be wild, be wily, be resourceful, be a brave gun."

It did not hurt that Buchan was made Lord Tweedsmuir for his services to the British government. Kathleen Kennedy married an English lord, which was not possible for John Kennedy; but the two books he always referred to as his favorites were by British lords — *Pilgrim's Way* by Tweedsmuir, and *The Young Melbourne* by Lord David Cecil. Both books came out within a year of his own *Why England Slept,* at a time when Kennedy was a defender of England's imperialist politicians. Both books gave him a wildly romantic view of aristocrats. From Cecil's *Melbourne* he seems to have derived his impression that English aristocrats have naked women emerge from silver dishes at their banquets (the moral *Time* magazine drew from the book). The Melbourne described by Cecil, a doting descendant, was all the things Kennedy wanted to be — secular, combining the bookish and the active life, supported by a family that defied outsiders. The Arthur Schlesinger line on Kennedys as "slow maturers" was laid down by Cecil: "He was the sort of character that, in any circumstances, does not come of age till middle life. His nature was composed of such diverse elements that it took a long time to fuse them into a stable whole."

The family loyalty of the Kennedys is presented by Cecil as a Melbourne trait. Melbourne House must have seemed to Kennedy a remarkable anticipation of Hyannis Port:

Children brought up in gay and patrician surroundings seldom react against them with the violence common in more circumscribed lives. If their tastes differ from those of the people round them, they have the leisure and money to follow them up in some degree; and anyway, their ordinary mode of living is too agreeable for them to conceive any strong aversion to it. Further, the Milbanke half of William's nature was perfectly suited by his home. He loved the parties and the sport and the gossip; he felt at home in the great world. Nor was his other side starved at Melbourne House. He had all the books he liked, he could listen enthralled to the clever men cleverly disputing, while his native tenderness bloomed in the steady sunshine of the family affection. His brothers and sisters were as fond of him as of one another. And, in the half-laughing, unsentimental way approved by Lamb standards, they showed their feelings. He returned them. His brothers were always his closest men friends, his favourite boon companions. What could be better fun than acting with George, arguing with Frederick, racing with Peniston? He was equally attached to his sisters, especially "that little devil, Emily."

The Melbourne set described in such a dreamy glow is the fulfillment of Joseph Kennedy's dream for his own children, aristocratically free of the need to climb, to do business, to court others: "Born in the centre of its most entertaining circle, he found himself, without any effort on his part, elected to its best clubs, invited to its most brilliant parties. And he had the talents to make the most of his advantages." Some resemblances were almost eerie — Melbourne, for instance, had a retarded son he cared for with great affection. Other resemblances John Kennedy could arrange — both Melbourne's wife and one of his lovers were named Caroline.

Cecil was sentimental in describing Melbourne as an eighteenth-century man whose circle and class kept wit alive into Queen Victoria's time. But John Kennedy must have felt that Cecil was a contemporary reporter on the English ruling class when he took six months off from Harvard studies to be a "courier" for his father in London. David Nunnerly, in *President Kennedy and Britain* (1972), describes the undergraduate's initiation into English country life:

> Englishmen of his own generation, like David Ormsby-Gore and "Billy" Hartington, he found altogether more sophisticated and confident than his American contemporaries. They were hardly the angry young men of the 1930s: in fact politics was for them rather light-hearted, certainly no obsession, though this very idea of politics invigorating rather than dominating society much appealed to Kennedy. But the other aspects of the British way of life equally appealed to him. He immensely enjoyed his leisured week-ends in the country homes of the great aristocratic families. At first through his father's position, he found himself regularly invited for weekends at the Chatsworths and Lismores, respectively the English and Irish ancestral homes of the Devonshires, with whom he later strengthened his ties through his sister Kathleen's marriage to the Marquis of Hartington. The presence of other house guests, many of whom were public figures, like the Edens and the Randolph Churchills, was in a sense history come alive for him. It had, as Arthur Schlesinger put it, "a careless elegance he had not previously encountered." The new perspective on life to which he was exposed

was of special importance since it was acquired in his formative and impressionable years, during which period he might otherwise have been content to have remained a shy and somewhat introverted personality. Instead, and as one of his intimate friends later recalled, somewhat to his own surprise, "He found his British friends very agreeable and he got on very well with them; and gradually what I would call the anti-British elements he grew out of and by the end you couldn't have found a more British person."

Nunnerly properly stresses the confidence of the class Kennedy was meeting. The Harvard undergraduate naively extended that trait to every single Englishman in his first published book, *Why England Slept:* "No discussion of Britain's psychology would be complete unless some mention were made of the natural feeling of confidence, even of superiority, that every Englishman feels." It was a heady vision to take back with him into classrooms where even Boston brahmins looked provincial now.

John Buchan, in *Pilgrim's Way,* takes a view of English aristocrats at least as rosy as Lord Cecil's. Here, for instance, is his Lord Asquith: "The Prime Minister, Mr. Asquith, had in his character every traditional virtue — dignity, honour, courage, and a fine selflessness." If Lytton Strachey was less dazzled by Asquith, his view would not alter Kennedy's admiration for these aristocrats:

> Who would guess from this book [of Asquith's] which has just come out (*Occasional Addresses*) with its high-minded orotundities and cultivated respectabilities, that the writer of it would take a lady's hand, as she sat behind him on the sofa, and make her feel his erected instrument under his trousers? (this I had very directly from Brett, to whose sister it happened at Garsington, and who told me as much of it as her maiden modesty allowed — egged on by Ottoline — and all of it to Carrington).

But Buchan, an imperialist admirer of Cecil Rhodes who served as a colonial official in several countries, had more to tell Kennedy about aristocratic *politics*. He presents himself as a defender of democracy "properly understood," but says this must not amount to a denigration of the "great men" England needs to survive. He thought the people of England had gone soft, and hoped his adventure tales would brace them for new risks. His ideal was T. E. Lawrence, worshipped as a superman on the James Bond scale:

> Physically he looked slight, but, as boxers say, he stripped well, and he was as strong as many people twice his size, while he had a bodily toughness and endurance far beyond anything I have ever met. In 1920 his whole being was in grave disequilibrium. You cannot in any case be nine times wounded, four times in an air crash, have many bouts of fever and dysentery, and finally at the age of twenty-nine take Damascus at the head of an Arab army, without living pretty near the edge of your strength.

For Kennedy, who lived at the edge of his slight strength — defying illness, risking dangerous sports, driving recklessly — Buchan's "crush" on his hero proved contagious, as we learn from John White. Kennedy's statistics-laden senior paper, published as *Why England Slept,* should be read in conjunction with Buchan's memoir. The latter supplies the romantic ideology partly covered over by the scholastic pose of the former. Both books appeared in the same year (1940), and their attitudes came from the same class, one that Ambassador Kennedy was cultivating as he supplied his son with evaluations of the British leaders, journals, and problems.

Since Joseph Kennedy opposed America's entry into England's war, and was harshly criticized by the British after Roosevelt recalled him, there has been a tendency to treat him as just another "isolationist" like Senator Borah or Colonel McCormick. But Kennedy considered Borah a pacificist, and his son's book castigates him for trying to disarm America. No Kennedy shared McCormick's anglophobia. In fact, Joseph Kennedy dearly loved a lord, and did not throw his strong will — the only one that mattered — against his daughter's decision to marry one. Rose Kennedy remembers how her husband glowed with pride in their suite at Windsor Castle: "Well, Rose, this is a helluva long way from East Boston, isn't it?" Arrived in England, Kennedy quickly joined the fashionable Cliveden Set, and imbibed its antiwar position. Franklin Roosevelt was soon wondering to Henry Morgenthau: "Who would have thought that the English could take into camp a red-headed Irishman?" To James Farley he said: "Joe has been taken in by the British government people and the royal family." The wonder of it, according to Heywood Broun, was that this American cultivating lords and ladies came from an Irish background "where the kids are taught to twist the lion's tail even before they learn to roll their hoops."

The distinctive mark of Joseph Kennedy's "isolationism" was its paradoxical nourishment from *foreign* sources. This circumstance set Kennedy at some distance from other Americans who opposed the war. Since British "appeasers" claimed their policy was meant to buy time for rearming, Kennedy was not opposed to war preparation as such, like Borah. Nor was he optimistic about America's avoiding "entanglement." He wanted the country armed to the teeth, for any emergency. It was England's failure to do this that trapped her in a position where rapid mobilization could only be accomplished by adopting totalitarian disciplines herself. This was the background of Kennedy's disastrous later press conference in Boston — the one that ended all his presidential hopes when he said that "democracy is finished in England."

Because Kennedy's views fit imperfectly with those of other American isolationists, his son's book *Why England Slept* — which reflects those views — has regularly been misread. It is customary for authors to tell us the book departed from the elder Kennedy's position. Arthur Schlesinger makes an even stranger claim: *"Why England Slept* was a singularly dispassionate statement to be flung into America's most passionate foreign policy debate of the century — so dispassionate, indeed, that it was impossible to conclude from the text whether the author was an interventionist or isolationist."

No one who reads the book's original foreword can think it rose above foreign policy debates. Henry Luce cut all but a few paragraphs of that foreword in the book's 1961 reprint, the version familiar to most readers now. But in 1940, a campaign year, *Why England Slept* was recommended between its own covers as an attack on Roosevelt for not alerting the public to impending war dangers. Luce, of course, was backing Wendell Willkie's candidacy in 1940, as was Arthur Krock, who gave the book what little style it possesses. In arranging for these two sponsors, Joseph Kennedy was easing away from what he thought would be the disaster of Roosevelt's policies — he hoped to inherit the Democratic party for himself if Roosevelt fell. He was playing for big stakes at this period, but without Roosevelt's cold nerve. Having set up a confrontation with his leader, Kennedy shied off at the last minute. By that time, his son's book was out.

In the 1940 foreword, Luce argued that Roosevelt was unrealistic in his dismissal of the war threat. He denied that this was just a campaign ploy: "Surely Mr. Roosevelt couldn't just be playing politics if he really thought we might be in for a war." Luce had to admit that Willkie, too, had presented himself to the Republicans as a peace candidate. But this was understandable in the first stage of an outsider's campaign. "Since his opponents (in both parties) have had eight years to play politics, Mr. Willkie may reasonably be given eight days." But this newcomer was not frozen in the antiwar stance Luce attributed to Roosevelt: "Very soon Mr. Willkie must meet the psychological test which Mr. Kennedy has so ably staged. Perhaps he will have met it magnificently before this book is off the press."

The "test" proposed by the book was this: How can a modern democracy be brought to arm itself in peacetime sufficiently to deter war, or to win it, without having to adopt totalitarian ways? England failed that test, according to Kennedy, for two reasons, one structural, one specific to the thirties. The structural problem arises from the very nature of democracy, which caters to people's present wants instead of addressing future threats. The more transitory problem was England's pacifism of the thirties, fed on unrealistic hopes raised by the League of Nations. America, necessarily, suffers from the first problem; but it might still bring itself to arm, because it had not been fatally infected with the League's pacifism.

Throughout his book, Kennedy accepts and repeats Stanley Baldwin's assertion that "a democracy is always two years behind the dictator." Absolute rulers can plan ahead, free of the necessity of coaxing votes from the populace: "A democracy will merely try to counter-balance the menaces that are actually staring it in the face." Thus the effort to rearm England had to be abandoned in the crucial year, 1935, because of the General Election: "For election year is the time when the public rules — it is then that the politicians acknowledge its superiority. Then, as at no other time, do they try to strike on the policy most acceptable to the mass of voters." Dictators manage the news to alarm their subjects into activity, while a free press lulls the citizenry: "A democracy's free press gives the speeches of the totalitarian leaders, who state their case in such a 'reasonable' manner that it is hard always to see them as a menace." Even Hitler had a plausible case to make in such a press: "As Hitler pointed out with some truth, in his cleverly worded letter to Daladier in August, 1939, shortly before the outbreak of the war, much of what he had done in Europe rectified wrongs that had been done at Versailles, and which should have been righted long before."

Beyond this continuing problem of a democracy, England of the 1930s had gone soft under the preaching of idealists (the John Buchan view). "Numerous political federations and councils throughout the country opposed it [rearmament] also. Groups, like the League of Nations, protested that it was a desertion of collective security; and others, like the National Peace Council, the National League of Young Liberals, the National Council of Evangelical Free Churches, were equally outspoken in their opposition. In any discussion of groups opposed to rearmament, no list would be complete without including the completely pacifist wing of the Labour Party led by men like George Lansbury and Dick Shepherd. Though the number of people who supported their advocacy of complete and final abolition of all weapons of warfare was limited, yet their indirect influence was considerable."

England, in short, had an enemy within, for which young Kennedy was supplying a kind of Attorney General's List. The country's spirit had been sapped by dangerous books: "The whole spirit of the country was pacifistic — probably more strongly than it had ever been. Numerous books against war like *Cry Havoc!* by Beverly Nichols were widely circulated and avidly read. In an article on *Illusions of Pacifists,* the writer began, 'Disarmament and peace are among the most discussed topics of the day.'" Kennedy repeatedly denounces "the strength of the pacifist movement and the general feeling against disarmament," "the strongly peaceful attitude of the people."

The structural and the incidental problems, combined, posed the dilemma for British statesmen (who were wise enough to see the danger): how to flatter the people's pacific instincts enough to get elected, yet defy them enough to rearm? The resolution of this problem depended on buying time. Since that was the goal, it became for Kennedy the justification of the appeasers:

> In his [1936] acceptance address, Chamberlain announced the policy that was to become known as "appeasement." Appeasement to us now has a bad sound — it connotes Munich and backing down. In a vague way we blame it for much of Europe's present trouble, but there was more to it than that when Chamberlain announced it back in 1937. It was a double-barreled policy; he would "continue our program of the re-establishment of our defence forces, combined with a substantial effort to remove the causes which are delaying the return of confidence in Europe." That Chamberlain's policy was not merely an unsuccessful effort "to remove the causes delaying the return of confidence" is not popularly realized. It is the other part of his program, "continuing our program of the re-establishment of our defence forces," with which we are chiefly concerned.
>
> The policy of appeasement, while it was partly based on a sincere belief that a permanent basis could be built for peace, was also formulated on the realization that Britain's defence program, due to its tardiness in getting started, would not come to harvest until 1939.
>
> Taking all these factors into consideration, the Munich Pact appears in a different light from that of a doddering old man being completely "taken in." It shows that appeasement did have some realism; it was the inevitable result of conditions that permitted no other decision.

But time ran out on the men trying to overcome the mass's dangerous reluctance to face danger, and Baldwin became a scapegoat while Chamberlain became a figure of sad comedy.

The Cliveden Set had taught Joseph Kennedy that the British public was at fault for the country's weakness — especially the labor unions:

> The question has come up again and again, as the great increase in production has been made by the recent great sacrifices of labor in England — why wasn't this done more than a year ago? Why didn't the Chamberlain Government organize labor in this way? Why

weren't strikes outlawed months before, as was done on June 6?
Why wasn't labor conscripted and the country organzied at the end
of 1938 and through 1939? This has all been done by Mr. Bevin, the
new Minister for Labor under the Churchill Government. But Mr.
Bevin was the great leader of the Trade Unions in England before
the war. What was his and Mr. Greenwood's attitude at that time
about this problem?

So strong was John Kennedy's defense of the ruling class in his
earlier draft that even his father told him to tone it down. The book
should not look like a whitewash. So there is a perfunctory "blame
all around" conclusion, which — like the book's rambling structure — encourages people to call it evenhanded where it is just confused. The only real criticism of the rulers in the body of the book is
directed at Baldwin's "great mistake" in telling the truth about the
1935 election — admitting that he played down the need to rearm
during the election period, to gain time for developing his plans:

> The speech Baldwin delivered was one of the gravest political
> "boners" that any politician ever made. His "appalling frankness"
> has resulted in his being blamed for the entire condition of Britain's
> armaments. Although a master politician, he made the most ele-
> mentary mistakes in phrasing, and from this time on he became the
> political scapegoat for Britain's failure to rearm. Much of what
> Baldwin said was true, but the manner in which he worded the
> truth made it appear that he had put his party's interest above the
> national interest, and that was fatal.

It is hard to see, in retrospect, how reviewers took seriously a book
that presented Baldwin's speech as the appeasers' one great mistake.
The whole book is a hodgepodge of disconnected and ill-grounded
assertions: "There is no lobby for armaments as there is for relief or
for agriculture." The basic argument was hard to follow, since the
volume was first planned as a chronological treatment of military
production, year by year. For this Ambassador Kennedy supplied
masses of ill-related statistics and charts, shoved into the different
time slots. The argument was made, as it were, in the interstices of
this less ambitious account — and it derives less from a reasoned
chain of thought than from the father's odd blend of prejudices,

fears, and ambitions. The book, like the Ambassador, is anglophile-isolationist and warhawk-appeasing. Even in its amended version it struck Luce as too charitable to the appeasers: "On the very difficult subject of Munich, I agree with Mr. Kennedy to the extent that he rebuts the cheap-and-easy vilification of Mr. Chamberlain by many American writers. I do so even though, on balance, I cast my own jury-vote against Mr. Chamberlain."

Why England Slept was a passable undergraduate paper that never quite became a book. The disparate things stuffed into it have obscured its principal argument; its only unity comes from a cluster of attitudes John Kennedy had drawn from his reading, his experience of England, and his dependence on his father for information and point of view. That is why the book should be read in relation to his contemporary enthusiasms for Lords Cecil and Tweedsmuir. The "English attitude" toward politics was, for young Kennedy, the English attitude toward sex. He admired adventurer-aristocrats, who could save the people by guiding them, sometimes without their knowledge. The book's only importance is its way of striking these notes. They would sound for a long time in Kennedy's political career.

It is said that Kennedy's early friendship for Joseph McCarthy derived simply from his father's ties to the man, or from the Irish Catholic constituency of Massachusetts. But the heated attack on pacifist books, authors, and organizations in *Why England Slept* shows that Kennedy thought subversive ideas could undermine people's will to resist. It might be necessary, in such circumstances, to limit civil rights — the right to strike, the "misleading" tendency of a free press. A country exposed to peril by an enemy within may have to submit to a period of voluntary totalitarianism:

> The nation had failed to realize that if it hoped to compete successfully with a dictatorship on an equal plane, it would have to renounce temporarily its democratic privileges. All of its energies would have to be molded in one direction, just as all the energies of Germany had been molded since 1933. It meant voluntary totalitarianism because, after all, the essence of a totalitarian state is that the national purpose will not permit group interest to interfere with its fulfillment.

This is the earliest formulation of "Ask not what your country can do for you, but what you can do for your country."

Sometimes enlightened leaders must hide from their subjects the reasons for their acts (avoiding Baldwin's mistaken candor with the electorate), or even the acts themselves. The world of aristocratic rakes like Melbourne has an underside, the dark area where T. E. Lawrence moves, and Richard Hannay, and James Bond, all the Green Berets and gentlemen spies of the CIA. Presiding over this potentially dangerous world is the honor of the aristocrats, their code of national service. When it came time for Kennedy to praise his forebears in the United States Senate, he sought men with Melbourne's sense of personal honor, which precludes a servile deference to constituents. All eight of his heroes are praised for defying the electorate, sometimes quixotically:

> It may take courage to battle one's President, one's party or the overwhelming sentiment of one's nation; but these do not compare, it seems to me, to the courage required of the Senator defying the angry power of the very constituents who control his future. It is for this reason that I have not included in this work the stories of this nation's most famous "insurgents" — John Randolph, Thaddeus Stevens, Robert LaFollette, and all the rest — men of courage and integrity, but men whose battles were fought with the knowledge that they enjoyed the support of the voters back home.

Kennedy's father tried to instill in each of his children a sense of their own worth. It was a miniature aristocracy he created, hovering above the Irish-American scene. Those clustered on that space platform did not so much have roots as sources — and the principal source was an imagined English aristocracy of public service.

7

Honorary Kennedys

I would have the courtier devote all his thought and strength of
spirit to loving and almost adoring the prince he serves above all
else, devoting his every desire and habit and manner to pleasing
him.

— CASTIGLIONE

VICTOR NAVASKY ATTRIBUTES much of Robert Kennedy's success
in the Justice Department to the talented circle of men he calls
"honorary Kennedys." Though Kennedys are attuned mainly to
Kennedys, their superheated mutual admiration sets up a magnetic
field energizing others in their vicinity. Without being fully admitted to the family (even by marriage), friends and allies rotate loyally
and lend their skills. Navasky studied the resources this system made
available to Attorney General Kennedy. Not only could he recruit
from his own cluster of friends and past associates, but from those of
his father and brothers. People who would not have served at second
or third level posts, just for a minor title, were happy to serve a
Kennedy. And their performance was spirited, not only from a sense
of obligation or office, but from reinforcing motives of pride and
ambition — to make a *Kennedy* recognize their ability.

The use of honorary Kennedys was not restricted to formal ap-
pointments at the Justice Department. When the Attorney General
took it as a family obligation to free those captured at the Bay of
Pigs invasion, powerful friends organized a private ransom fund.
Cardinal Cushing, for instance, pledged the first million dollars. In
Navasky's words: "He called upon a Kennedy potpourri, a public-

private mix of family, friends, ad hoc committees, free-lance lawyers, sympathizers, bankers and power brokers within, without and throughout the government, the network, the charismatic authority structure, the honorary Kennedys."

When, as Senator from New York, Kennedy decided to do something about slum conditions in Bedford-Stuyvesant, he set up the same kind of task force. McGeorge Bundy was now at the Ford Foundation, Burke Marshall at IBM, Douglas Dillon back at his firm — the voices of wealth and influence. Civil rights workers from Robert's Justice Department — including the admired John Doar — dropped other work and took up Robert's project. Money and talent were instantly available for the Senator's personal poverty program.

When, sudden and late, Kennedy decided to run for President in 1968, he could compensate for prior delay by turning to this instantly mobilizable network. Jack Newfield describes his first move: "So the phone calls began to go out, and dozens of men agreed to abandon their families, and their jobs with law firms, newspapers, and universities, and go to Indiana, or Oregon, or California, to work for the Restoration."

Joseph Kennedy had organized the first generation of honorary Kennedys, which included Arthur Krock, William Douglas, and James Landis. The fast-moving businessman knew how to use the talents of such adjuncts, but he had neither the leisure nor the reputation to acquire them on the scale that his sons later did. To have courtiers, you must maintain a court — something he made possible for his family rather than himself. For every Krock he collected, his sons would have dozens of bright journalists in tow. At different times, the honorary Kennedys included Philip Graham, Ben Bradlee, Joseph Alsop, Bill Lawrence, Roland Evans, Sander Vanocur, Hugh Sidey, Hayes Gorey, Henry Brandon, Theodore White, Charles Bartlett, Anthony Lewis, Art Buchwald, Pete Hamill, Jack Newfield, Jeff Greenfield, John Bartlow Martin, and — ironically — Roger Mudd. For every Dean Landis of Harvard Law, the sons would have courtier-professors bowing in with book after book. Arthur Schlesinger abandoned his major work on the New Deal to write — endlessly — for and about the Kennedys. He and James MacGregor Burns alternate volumes on the Kennedys, creating one-man libraries.

Service for one brother became a claim on the next, building up ring on ring of variously influential allies. Loyalty was expected of them, understandably. If the real Kennedys set family above all else, those who share in the Kennedy magic without owning it by birth should, clearly, take up their share of service to the clan. Navasky describes the reaction when Nicholas Katzenbach, Robert's friend and successor as Attorney General, "disloyally" refused to issue a statement exonerating Kennedy from all complicity in FBI buggings.

> Katzenbach rationalized his resolution of the conflict between loyalty to law and loyalty to friend by arguing — to himself and to RFK — that there was no conflict, that by leaving out the requested language he was acting in Robert Kennedy's best interest as well as the Justice Department's. Nevertheless, he had violated one of the unspoken tenets of the Kennedy code — that when there is a disagreement between a hard-core Kennedy and an honorary Kennedy such as Katzenbach, the former prevails, even when a non-Kennedy like Johnson happens to be President — and the relationship was never quite the same thereafter. The story is important less for what it shows about Katzenbach's decision than for what it suggests about Kennedy's assumption in dealing with other members of the extended Kennedy family: that where the formal requirements of the legal system and the informal requirements of politics or personal obligation conflict, the code of the Kennedys should prevail, or at least be given great weight.

In the 1968 campaign, Robert told Jack Newfield how McNamara had observed the Kennedy-first rule: "Bob McNamara twice turned down the Vice Presidency just because he felt I should get it." The standards varied as one went up or down the social scale of Kennedy attendants. A *gran rifiuto* was expected of Robert McNamara. For Paul ("Red") Fay, an aborted checkers game would show proper respect for John Kennedy's supremacy: "I was winning the first game when I noticed a warning look in his eyes. He coughed suddenly, sending the checkers onto the floor or helter-skelter across the checkerboard. 'One of those unfortunate incidents of life, Redhead,' he said with a touch of a smile. 'We'll never really know if the

Under Secretary was going to strategically outmaneuver the Commander-in-Chief.' "

The natural order of things was several times enforced on Sargent Shriver, as Harris Wofford describes in his book *Of Kennedys and Kings*. Shriver's interest in running for governor of Illinois had to be sacrificed in 1960 to the presidential race of John Kennedy — lest he distract people with another Catholic who was part of the senior Kennedy's business world. When Lyndon Johnson thought of offering the vice-presidency to Shriver, and Bill Moyers said that Robert would not object, Kenneth O'Donnell blurted, "The hell he wouldn't." Then, when Humphrey considered Shriver for the same post, Edward Kennedy vetoed the idea. When Shriver did accept appointments from President Johnson — to the poverty program, and as Ambassador to France — this caused hard feelings in the family, reaching their climax in the 1968 race. Wofford writes: "It was the first time when family loyalty broke down, to the disservice of both Shriver and Kennedy — and Johnson — each of whose effectiveness would have been greater if they could all have worked together."

But Shriver remained an in-law, so no final break occurred. With those less bound to the family, retaliation for disloyalty could be savage. Arthur Krock, who had spent decades serving the career of Joseph Kennedy, was bitterly opposed to the civil rights movement of the sixties. He refused to endorse John Kennedy because of the 1960 platform statement on civil rights. Kennedy, once in office, arranged for attacks on Krock to run in *Newsweek,* and was disappointed that they were so mild. "Tuck it to Krock," he told Ben Bradlee. "Bust it off in old Arthur. He can't take it, and when you go after him he folds."

Bradlee, meanwhile, was serving Krock's old functions, clearing things he wrote about Kennedy with Kennedy himself, informing the President when *Newsweek* planned to publish anything critical of the administration. But Fletcher Knebel quoted in print a Bradlee remark about Kennedy's sensitivity to criticism, and the punishment that followed confirmed the accusation: for three months Bradlee was banned from Kennedy festivities, and from other social gatherings where the President's influence extended. In front of Bradlee himself, Kennedy told the British Ambassador not to invite *News-*

week's man to an embassy party. Only after he had been fully chastened was he readmitted to court — never to make the same mistake of risking candor while Kennedy lived.

Loyalty, which won honorary Kennedys their reflected glory, also exacted a price. Kennedy's bright staff at Justice worked hard, cut corners, got things done. But the cost was a certain suspension of judgment before Kennedy priorities. Family pride was forfeit to the task of "getting Hoffa," and the loyalists supported this effort, even when it meant prosecuting on a dubious charge, with no issue at stake, by a major commitment of resources to the hunt. Navasky says of Hoffa's Nashville indictment, "Never in history had the government devoted so much money, manpower and top level brainpower to a misdemeanor case." The charge, which would have brought a maximum penalty of one year, was conflict of interest in a truck-leasing firm Hoffa openly set up. This was not a crime that cried to heaven; it was just an opportunity to get Hoffa, and the honorary Kennedys — with one honorable exception — dutifully went along (though they would not, in fact, win a conviction):

> Within the Department, Byron White, Nicholas Katzenbach, Burke Marshall (who flew down in the middle of the trial with Howard Willens, First Assistant in the Criminal Division), former labor law professor Archibald Cox and Ramsey Clark were among those consulted on the case, and with the exception of Clark — whose experience as a private attorney with the trucking industry convinced him that the evidence was insufficient to show a significant departure from the practices of the trucking industry — they all felt a legitimate case might be made.

Honorary membership in the family could entail dangers. And why not? Being a real Kennedy is even more dangerous. Dean James Landis, loyal to the Kennedys for many years, was one of those people who suffer a mental block in dealing with the IRS. For some years, he had deposited his income tax payments in a special account rather than with the government. When this came to light, he paid taxes, interest, and penalty; there was no evidence of attempt to defraud; with anyone else, the case would have been dropped. But that might open the Kennedys to a charge of favoritism, so the Justice

Department was compensatorily rigorous. Navasky concludes his analysis of the case:

> The code of the Kennedys was profoundly entangled with James Landis's fate. His tax delinquency was discovered because he was on the Kennedy White House staff. It was brought to old Joe's attention because the district Director of the IRS shared the nation's image of the clannish, behind-the-scenes way the Kennedys do business. The case proceeded through channels partly because the Kennedys had officially disqualified themselves, partly because it was *not* part of the Kennedy way of doing business for Robert to tell his old University of Virginia tax professor, Mortimer Caplin, to get him off the hook at the expense of the integrity of the tax code, partly because Kennedy loyalists didn't want the Kennedy Administration vulnerable to charges of fix. Landis pleaded guilty so as not to embarrass the Kennedys, despite evidence that a not-guilty plea might have been sustained. He was sentenced to confinement, seldom the case in failure-to-file convictions, undoubtedly in part as a tribute to his importance as a member of the Kennedy family.

To circle in tight family orbits, ringed about with powerful satellites, is to create a field of influence very gratifying — until the satellites, reversing nature, begin to tug at the center of their own system, pulling it in contrary directions. This happened to Robert when the number of real Kennedys diminished, and the honorary family members were all concentered on him. Other galaxies collapsed inward, around his, after his father's stroke, his brother's death. Edward, the youngest Kennedy, was more Robert's satellite, at this stage, than a center in his own right. The subordinates, neatly sorted out before, now collided; clogged the air around Robert, inhibiting his motions with their friendly crowding; deafened him with advice.

This problem became acute when Robert Kennedy tried to free himself of the Vietnam war his brother helped initiate. Robert had named three of his children after powerful men in his brother's administration — Averell Harriman, Douglas Dillon, and Maxwell Taylor. It was a way of binding the system together; the honorary Kennedys around the older brother were honored in their turn by the younger brother. But in the period leading up to the 1968 campaign, these three "wise men" were supporting the war they helped President Kennedy launch. The natural order of things is for honorary Kennedys to move toward the oldest living heir; but one test of President Kennedy's growing influence had been his ability to attract ever more powerful men toward him, men who — even while serving Kennedy — had positions and reputations of their own at stake. Besides, the Kennedy heir had himself supported the Johnson escalations when they first occurred — along with stellar members of the Kennedy team like Robert McNamara, the Bundy brothers, the Rostow brothers. These people all felt they were being true to a Kennedy legacy. *Robert* had departed from the course his brother set.

Even some of those closest to Robert — including his younger brother — joined those who had been close to John Kennedy (e.g., Schlesinger, Sorensen, Salinger) in urging Robert not to run against Lyndon Johnson in 1968. Other members of the Kennedy team were dropping out of the Johnson White House — but, like McNamara, they went quietly, not risking outright confrontation with an incumbent Democratic President. And when Robert Kennedy began to critize the war, his comments were cautious, muted, contrite ("there is blame enough for everyone"), and invariably joined with some expression of good will toward President Johnson. This meant that the "old guard" was still welcome at Robert's home, Hickory Hill, where their voices were raised in the rivalry of friendly advisers, all with claims on Robert through his brother or his father. They were part of the dead man's legacy, the Kennedy promise. Many resented Kennedy's apparent willingness to squander the family's future hopes in a quixotic race against Johnson. They thought of *him* as disloyal to his name.

In this period, Robert showed signs of wanting to break out of his own protective cordon of family powers. He sought new and younger advisers — creating, inevitably, more honorary Kennedys who would clash with the older ones. Generations of such family retainers now clamored for his ear. The "first generation" were veterans of the Adlai Stevenson campaigns who had switched to Kennedy. They claimed to uphold the authentic liberal tradition — Arthur Schlesinger, for instance, and Kenneth Galbraith. Schlesinger began with doubts that Robert should take on Johnson, then shifted as the candidate's own desires became clearer. Galbraith thought he should run from the start; and, when he didn't, joined Eugene McCarthy's campaign. This member of the old guard outran Robert's own hotheaded young staffers.

The second generation was made up of those who had run his brother's campaigns. They, too, were divided — Kenneth O'Donnell, for instance, wanted to take on Johnson. But the weightiest members of that team thought this would be foolish — and theirs were the arguments Robert himself had used when advising his brother. Don't make gestures; go in to win; forget liberal sentiment; count the votes. The vote counters could not come up with the right numbers, so they told him not to run.

Another generation was made up of those recruited into President Kennedy's cabinet and staff. The "big guns" here were all supporters of Johnson and the war. They spoke, for the public, as Kennedy men. They made the war Kennedy's war — how dare Robert attack it?

The fourth generation of honorary Kennedys came from Robert's associates in the Justice Department — men like Burke Marshall, John Seigenthaler, Edwin Guthman. They, too, initially opposed a 1968 campaign.

Last came Kennedy's Senate staffers, the press secretary Frank Mankiewicz and the two "kids" who served as administrative assistants, speechwriter Adam Walinsky and legislation-drafter Peter Edelman. These people were free of echoes and memories from President Kennedy's time, and vividly alert to the distress of college students over the war. Often Robert's heart slipped off from his head's calculations to share the sentiments of these "kids." And, while the older Kennedy guard of journalists upheld the Vietnam war — Joseph Alsop outstanding in this group — Kennedy cultivated a new circle of adversary journalists: Jack Newfield, Jeff Greenfield, Pete Hamill, Jimmy Breslin, David Halberstam. When Robert died, these writers would be his elegists — as Theodore White and Hugh Sidey had been for his assassinated brother.

Naturally, the young staffers and newsmen were resented by older servants of family glory — not simply because they were Johnnys-come-lately, but because they were reckless with the family's future hopes. They seemed to think in terms of a demonstration rather than a restoration. Guardians of the legacy were rightly upset when the young firebrands dragged Robert Kennedy off to consult with Tom Hayden, or with street gang leaders. If Kennedy was willing to take communion with Cesar Chavez today, to recommend sending blood to the Viet Cong, what might he do tomorrow? Take communion with a pacifist like Dorothy Day? Become Eldridge Cleaver's friend? Go — as his Justice Department colleague, Ramsey Clark, finally did — to Hanoi? Or, like Clark, defend the Berrigan brothers? Where would it all end?

At least part of Robert Kennedy — and that the oldest part, the successful campaign manager — shared these reservations about his new cohorts. Kennedys do not run campaigns as a form of moral gesture. They run to win; and know what that takes; and do what is necessary. The young guard around Kennedy had an open contempt for "old politicians" like Mayor Daley. But longstanding associates of the Kennedys knew what Daley had done for them in the past and could do in the future — and Robert knew that best of all. Shortly before his death, he told Jimmy Breslin, "Daley is the ball game." But if that was so, what was he doing in a different ball park entirely, palling around with Cesar Chavez?

The truth is that Robert Kennedy agreed to run, not out of total agreement with his "kids," but in the belief that he could beat Eugene McCarthy first and then win back the old machine types he would need. That is why Robert ran a "law and order" campaign, and refused to debate McCarthy in Indiana and Oregon, though all his younger aides felt he was honor-bound to do so. The strains of the coalition Kennedy was trying to put together showed over and over in Oregon. And then, when he agreed to debate in California, Robert was willing to win in his old ruthless way — he played on white fears of blacks moving into lily-white Orange County, a ploy even Schlesinger called "demagogic."

In Oregon the honorary Kennedys were fighting for custody of "their" man. Those who felt he had to debate McCarthy went to his suite hoping to make him reverse his decision. Kennedy, standing there in his shorts, blew up. Jules Witcover describes the scene:

> Kennedy ordered the room cleared except for a few of the old professionals. He called one of them into the bedroom. "They're press-

ing in on me," Kennedy told him. And then, looking at the old pro, he added: "Don't tell me you're buying these guys." It was a political crunch, and time for political decision making. "I don't know what they're doing here," Kennedy said of his young speechwriters. "I didn't even want them out here." Outside in the corridor, Walinsky, Greenfield and others were milling around, talking loudly. Kennedy, still dressed only in his shorts, went to the door, opened it and stalked out. "I thought we decided that," he told them angrily. "Why are you standing around here making noise? If you want to do something, go out and ring doorbells." And then, turning to Adam [Walinsky] and Jeff [Greenfield] he barked: "Besides, I don't see why my speechwriters aren't writing speeches instead of playing the guitar all the time." And he stormed back inside. This last was a slow burn erupting. Sometimes during the campaign, Walinsky and Greenfield would get aboard the campaign plane and start playing and singing folk songs while others, including the candidate, tried to work. Now the group in the corridor broke up, and Kennedy dressed for the rally. Adam and Jeff came to [Fred] Dutton's room later, properly chastised, announcing they were returning to Washington to write their speeches. Dutton laughed it off, and told them to do the same. That was the end of it — but there was no debate in Oregon.

Kennedy's young followers were acutely embarrassed by the way their candidate deferred to McCarthy when he could not avoid him. The man who made such a cult of courage, the man who had challenged Jimmy Hoffa to do push-ups, actually turned and ran when his path crossed McCarthy's in Oregon. The two men, without knowing it, were touring the same park outside Portland. Jeremy Larner, on McCarthy's staff, saw the rival press bus and sent three of his aides to block Kennedy's car while Larner brought McCarthy to it. Larner's candidate would only saunter toward the car, so Larner ran ahead to hold it:

My charge carried me right up to Kennedy, who was sitting on top of the back seat with his brown and white spaniel next to him, just like in the photographs. Kennedy shrank a little, as if I were going to grab him. He was smaller than I thought, and his eyes were a brilliant blue. Every second I could hold him talking would bring McCarthy that much closer into camera range.

"Senator McCarthy is coming," I grinned. "Why don't you stick around and talk with him?" I was standing over him and he was looking at me with a look of exquisite hurt. Did we think he was running from fear?

"Isn't that too bad!" he said. He turned to his driver and the driver floored it, the kids jumped for their lives. So Kennedy rolled down the hill without looking back, and I stood with the *Life* photographer shouting "Coward! Chicken!" — for truly he was running away. It turned out that we had held him just long enough for the TV crews to get McCarthy coming and Kennedy speeding off. That night all Oregon saw our backs, and heard the shouts of Coward. Followed by McCarthy capturing the Kennedy press bus and shaking hands with Kennedy's abandoned press.

After Kennedy's death, Larner felt contrite about taunting him; but even Kennedy's people were a bit sickened at the thought that their man was following the old politics — not risking his greater name in debate — even at the cost of running out on the young. There was no way to please all the honorary Kennedys; and their division had left the aggressive Robert Kennedy inwardly divided and uncharacteristically wavering.

Those closest to him at that point sensed that his resort to old political ways violated something that had come to birth in Kennedy out of his brother's death. Now he talked wistfully of leaving politics, of becoming a social worker. His feats of brave mountain-climbing and rapids-shooting were nonpolitical ways of recapturing the headlong spirit with which he once campaigned. He ruefully admired the young McCarthyites with nothing to lose, working for their cause with never a compromise. That was how he had fought when he knew no cause higher than his brother's election. But he could not fight for himself that way. When friends regretted that "Bobby" did not have his own Bobby to do his dirty work for him, they were confessing, indirectly, that "Bobby" no longer existed. It was a deeply changed man who was running for office now. Depth had come to him, and with it indecision — the very thing he despised in Adlai Stevenson while working on his 1956 campaign staff.

No one can tell how the 1968 election might have gone if Kennedy had lived. But David Halberstam rightly observes: "Because he had come in late, McCarthy had picked up Kennedy's natural base and as a result Kennedy was forced to appeal to blue-collar people, which contradicted his appeal to blacks and liberals." And Lawrence O'Brien, who had seen more of all the candidates' camps than any other man that year, was overheard on Robert's funeral train: "Couldn't they see? Couldn't they see? He didn't have a chance." Kennedy had given himself an assignment he probably could not live up to — itself a sign of his change from the win-at-all-costs days. He intended to woo Johnson democrats, and Humphrey, through Richard Daley, after polishing off the McCarthy threat. But that would give him hostages in too many camps. The South, with enmities toward him nurtured from civil rights days, thought him a traitor for advocating that blood be sent to the Viet Cong. His "kids" would deny him that superpatriot bloc so necessary to a Democratic candidate. And would his kids themselves stay with him when he went, hat in hand, back to Johnson, to the man they greeted with the shout, "Hey, hey, LBJ, how many kids did you kill today?" Would Johnson receive him? Would Daley?

Robert's hopes from Daley can be gauged by the way he went through a farce of reconciliation for Daley's sake, just at the time when he was deciding to run against Johnson. When Daley made the suggestion, Kennedy had to go along. He had a lingering respect for the man, who had some of his father's gifts and abrasive strength. In fact, the young Robert Kennedy once seemed destined to become a kind of Richard Daley, a tough political manager. Certainly, when he looked back at his earlier career, Kennedy did not find there a Tom Hayden or Jimmy Breslin. Breslin and Hayden and Hamill, like Michael Harrington, were Catholics who broke away from the Daleys and Cushings and Spellmans — from the people young Bobby had revered.

Mayor Daley went to Mass every morning; he never missed his Easter duty — and never forgot an enemy. Kennedy had been that kind of pious gut-fighter. Like Daley, he was not personally corrupt; but he could deal with corruption to achieve some "greater good." The memory of that fact no doubt galled Robert Kennedy in 1968 — the memory of campaign tricks in West Virginia, the nastier memories of plots against Castro. He had shed much of that older self — but he had to confront it again if he meant to deal with Richard Daley.

Daley's intrusion could not have come at a worse time. McCarthy, while losing the popular vote in New Hampshire, had won twenty of its twenty-four delegates. Kennedy had decided to run, and knew he would be called a spoiler after McCarthy had risked the first challenge to the President. Kennedy informed Mayor Daley of his decision — and Daley asked him, first, to explore the idea of an outside commission to review Vietnam policy. It was a project doomed from the outset — President Johnson was not going to let Robert Kennedy set up a panel to criticize him; and Kennedy did not want to work for such a commission while his chance to campaign slipped by. Yet Daley's influence was so great in the party that all sides had to go through the motions of desiring a review panel just because "Hizzoner" did. Johnson asked Sorensen for a list of names, to be delivered to McNamara's replacement at the Department of Defense, Clark Clifford. Robert Kennedy went to the meeting with Clifford. Unwilling to serve on the review board, he had to *say* he would consent, if asked. That gave Johnson his chance to say Robert wanted to use the panel against him. The episode exacerbated conflict with the President, whose response in turn fueled anger in Kennedy's supporters. The honorary Kennedy from days past, Richard Daley, was tripping up new arrivals at that status.

Accounts differ on the timing of Kennedy's decision to run — before New Hampshire, or after; *well* before New Hampshire, or *just* before. Kennedy was sending different signals to different parts of his own support system; agreeing now with one group, now with another; seeing too many sides of the matter to set a simple course. He caused conflicting impressions in others because he was in conflict with himself. That was clear down to the eve of his announcement, when the kick-off speech had been composed and the team of consultants had gone off to whatever empty beds they could find about his house. Even at this point, Robert had dispatched his brother to see Eugene McCarthy, campaigning in Wisconsin, with a proposal out of character for Kennedys in general and for Robert in particular: the two men would be friendly rivals, raising the war issue but not confronting each other in the same primaries. In short, "Let's fight, but not really." Kennedy wanted to take the war issue away from McCarthy without upsetting McCarthy's troops too much — a proposal fully as unworkable as Daley's, and one McCarthy rightly dismissed. Robert was entering the campaign and not entering it at the same time — which accurately reflected his mood on the sleepless night before he announced.

Arthur Schlesinger, having gone to bed at one-thirty, was awakened by a whisper, "Ted! Ted!" It was Edward Kennedy trying to find Sorensen with the unsurprising news that McCarthy had said no. He did not want to wake his brother, who must be fresh for the morning press conference; but Robert was already awake, and he soon wandered into Schlesinger's room, looking morose: "Well, I have to say something in three hours." Schlesinger, who wanted no bitter or final division between Kennedy and McCarthy's followers, said, "Why not come out for McCarthy? Every McCarthy delegate will be a potential Kennedy delegate. He can't possibly win, so you will be certain inheritor of his support." Kennedy gave him a stony stare and said, "Kennedys don't act that way." Kennedys *didn't* act that way. But they didn't back halfway into fights, either. When Schlesinger went down to breakfast and asked Sorensen where the candidate was, he said, "He is upstairs looking for someone else to wake up in the hope of finding someone who agrees with him." Schlesinger continues:

> Ted Kennedy raised his arms in the air: "I just can't believe it. It is too incredible. I just can't believe that we are sitting around the table discussing anything as incredible as this." Vanden Heuvel and I proposed that, as an interim measure, he come out for McCarthy. My impression was that both Teds thought this might be preferable to his declaring for himself. Then Robert entered the room, still in his pajamas. He had heard the last part of our talk. He said, "Look, fellows, I can't do that. I can't come out for McCarthy. Let's not talk about that any more. I'm going ahead, and there is no point in talking about anything else." With that he left. I proposed taking one more look at the situation. There must be some other course besides endorsing McCarthy or running himself. Teddy said, "No. He's made up his mind. If we discuss it any longer, it will shake his confidence and put him on the defensive. He has to be at his best at this damned press conference. So we can't talk about it any more."

The real and honorary Kennedys, who basked in the light of power and moved so confidently, were broken and divided among themselves, serving a divided man, finally abandoning advice in favor of therapy. The Kennedy pride was engaged, but had to be forsworn — Robert would have to fight Johnson while deferring to him. The family glamour had been eclipsed by McCarthy, who claimed the young constituency Robert thought belonged to his brother by right. The support Robert had *assumed,* McCarthy had gone out and *earned;* and now McCarthy could neither be wooed nor fought outright.

Every move Robert made was opposed by one cluster of Kennedy friends. He had to get away from them; yet he could not. He wandered the house asking, listening, for what no one could say. He talked with everyone, with too many, because he could not talk it through by himself. Yet that was the one thing necessary. It was like being back in his father's house, going with questions at night where certain answers would be given — all the sprawl of family and friends united by the fierce will that made everything cohere on the inside, defiant of anything outside. Robert was struggling to lift up the whole complex of Kennedy loyalties and personal ties, make it hover above difficulty, bright as his father had made it shine for a while. But the sheer accumulation weighed him down. He was a captive of his own courtiers, of those who were urging him on and those who were dragging him back, of the different worlds littered about him, of the dead man's teams and the dead man's shadow, of a legacy divided beyond reassembling.

8

Ghosts

It's narrowed down to Bobby and me. So far he's run with the
ghost of his brother. Now we're going to make him run against it.
It's purely Greek: he either has to kill him or be killed by him.
We'll make him run against Jack.... And I'm Jack.

— EUGENE MCCARTHY, 1968

IF ROBERT KENNEDY COULD SEE an older self in Mayor Daley, he
faced in Eugene McCarthy a kind of antiself. For years McCarthy had
been considered the "other Catholic" Senator of presidential stature;
and when McCarthy looked at John Kennedy he clearly thought
there was only one *real* Catholic in the running. During the 1960
convention McCarthy tugged at liberal heartstrings with his tribute
to Adlai Stevenson. But the Kennedys knew he was talking with
Lyndon Johnson about a spot on the Texan's ticket if Kennedy
could be stopped. They took all the praise of Stevenson as an attack
on John Kennedy, on the fake liberal. McCarthy was a natural for a
Johnson ticket, just as Johnson was for Kennedy's — to balance a
northern Catholic with a Southerner.

Unlike John Kennedy, McCarthy took his religion seriously; had
even spent time in a Benedictine monastery. But in other ways Robert could see much of his brother's appeal in this lazy Senator who
moved easily with intellectuals. McCarthy's poems had not won a
Pulitzer Prize; but at least he had written them himself. He had a
buttoned and unrumpled self-possession, a wit that could flick out
and wound, a handsome poise, an equilibrium maintained by mockery. If anything, he made more of personal style than the Kennedys

could — unlike them, he was not afraid to show his contempt for political hacks.

McCarthy is an interesting study in the pride of people trained to embrace humility. He had given up most of the means of satisfying his ambition without giving up the ambition itself. By 1968 he had arrived at a desire for power whose purity was guaranteed by his unwillingness to take any practical steps toward power. He *should* be President because he would not *try* very hard to be. The American people were being tested. If he was not elected, they had failed, not he. All through the 1968 campaign he sought to legitimate a principled indifference as the true prophetic stance. "Don't get excited," he kept telling his enthusiastic young followers. Excitement is undignified. It musses one's hair.

While his young recruits worked day and night for him, he quietly disdained their zealotry. I watched him, that summer, come out of a meeting of Michigan delegates in East Lansing to answer waiting newsmen's questions. "Do you think you won any votes in there?" Well, McCarthy said, these meetings with delegates are mainly a waste of time — a comment that became a self-fulfilling prophecy when the delegates read it the next day in their newspapers.

McCarthy had been stung once by his own ambition, when Lyndon Johnson renewed in 1964 the talk, from 1960, about becoming his Vice-President. Merely continuing that negotiation meant that McCarthy had to undercut his own senior colleague from Minnesota, Hubert Humphrey. But McCarthy crawled partway toward Johnson before being rejected. The humiliation mattered less than his own guilt at yielding to the base scramble for advancement. He would not yield again. So far from bowing to the voters in 1968, he barely bothered, on many occasions, to notice them. He closeted himself with Robert Lowell and made fun of the demeaning aspects of running for office. Refusing to stoop for the crown, he showed his contempt for all those who did — and principally for Robert Kennedy. If the world would not give him the presidency, over the clowns who were running for it, then the world owed him something just for his refusal to join the clowns.

He is still trying to collect what the world owes him — as my wife and I found out later, after a National Book Award presentation: he and a young woman he was escorting saw us sitting with some friends at a restaurant, sat down uninvited, ate an expensive meal, and, after the brandy, left us with the check. It did not come as a surprise, in 1976, when he repeated the campaign act he had disdained in 1968 (when he had a chance) — all, a friend of his assured me, to keep his lecture fees high enough to support him.

As a liberal "Commonweal Catholic" of the forties and fifties, Eugene McCarthy did not share some Irish Catholics' fondness for the other Senator McCarthy. And he still felt, in 1968, that Robert Kennedy was just Joe McCarthy's ex-goon — a cut above Roy Cohn perhaps, but not even up to his older brother's pretensions. Even after Robert was murdered, McCarthy would not utter the minimum words of praise that would unite the two peace campaigns. Robert's team, rebuffed, went to the convention with a new leader, George McGovern, dividing the dissenters' energies. Then, to top it all, McCarthy seemed intent on repairing his treachery to Humphrey in 1964 by refusing to attack the Vice-President for the President's Indochina war.

Yet, despite all his personal flaws and the pettiness of his attitude toward Kennedys, McCarthy was immune to attack from Robert Kennedy. He had done what Robert wished, too late, he had undertaken. He had challenged his party's incumbent, even before Tet; and many thought he deserved the fruits of that challenge. When McCarthy first announced, Robert knew his own young staffers felt disappointed in their boss and envied their rival. Some wore McCarthy buttons on the inside of their lapels. Old Kennedy hands, leaderless after their appeals to Robert, joined McCarthy's effort — Kenneth Galbraith would stay on even after Robert joined the race, after Richard Goodwin went back to his first loyalty. Robert spent the last months of his life lamenting that McCarthy had the "A kids," the ones who went first with the courageous man, the kind who had looked up to his brother. Robert had to run with the "B kids."

Having disappointed his followers by inaction, Robert infuriated many when he did act, coming in as a "spoiler" after McCarthy's New Hampshire upset. Murray Kempton, who had learned to respect Kennedy's concern for the poor, manifested after he won his Senate seat, reacted bitterly to the late entry into competition with

McCarthy. In a telegram to Edward Kennedy, turning down an invitation to his book party, he said: "Sorry I can't join you. Your brother's announcement makes it clear that St. Patrick did not drive all the snakes from Ireland." Kennedy could not feed this resentment by overt attacks on McCarthy. He had to defer to him, praise him, hope for his followers somewhere down the road. That was the odd story of 1968 for this old gut-fighter — he could not attack Daley, nor McCarthy, nor Johnson himself. He had to run against men while bowing to them constantly and asking their pardon. One side of the Kennedy legacy now belonged to the hawks around Johnson, who invoked the late President's pledge to fight all over the globe. It was hard enough for Kennedy to see Johnson usurping his brother's tough rhetoric with the help of President Kennedy's most warlike cabinet members. But when Robert turned to the other side of his brother's legacy — the side that inspired youth — he found an even more dangerous, because more charming, usurper in place, mocking him with a smile and saying, "I'm Jack."

John Kennedy, without any trace of radicalism himself, ignited the hopes of young people in the early sixties. The authorized aspect of this was the Peace Corps. An unplanned — and undesired — result of it led to sit-ins and the march on Washington, the Free Speech movement, the Port Huron Statement. John Kennedy would never, like Robert, consort with Tom Hayden; but he helped, like an inadvertent Dr. Frankenstein, bring Hayden into being. Now Eugene McCarthy had captivated and partially tamed the Kennedy monster, made the shaggier types cut their hair and go "clean for Gene," brought civility back to the protest movement. He had not only inherited the Kennedy youth following, but seemed to have elevated it. Thus, when Robert Kennedy appeared late on the scene, McCarthy could say to his speechwriter Jeremy Larner, "We'll make him run against Jack." Arthur Schlesinger finds this statement meaningless, mere verbal posturing. But the meaning is not hard to find. McCarthy, the man who should (in his own eyes) have been the first Catholic President, now stood where the next Kennedy should have, blocking the mere physical heir with a higher spiritual claim. "So far he's run with the ghost of his brother. Now we're going to make him run against it." Lyndon Johnson feared Kennedy because he was the heir; McCarthy felt that Robert was no heir at all, and had no claim. For Robert Kennedy to attack McCarthy would be to attack the A kids who belonged by right to John Kennedy. It would be attacking his brother.

Kennedy shunned debate with McCarthy in Indiana and Oregon, not simply from the "old politics" rule that the better known does not share platforms with the lesser known. He feared confrontation because, on too many points, he had no good case to make against McCarthy — none that could not have been made against his brother. "He either has to kill him or be killed by him."

McCarthy seemed to have a malignant gift for doing what would diminish Kennedy. He moved ostentatiously free of the constraints that were hobbling his rival. Kennedy attacked the war; but McCarthy pointed out that his opponent would not criticize those who had escalated the war — McNamara and other Kennedy appointees. John Kennedy's first official appointment had reconfirmed J. Edgar Hoover in office; so McCarthy campaigned in 1968 on a pledge to fire Hoover — something Robert Kennedy could not promise. Most important of all, McCarthy attacked President Johnson — the way he spoke of "my" helicopters and "my" fighting men and "my" war. McCarthy indeed had reason to resent the man who had humiliated him in 1964; but his attacks were mild next to those of his followers who asked Johnson, chanting, for his daily "kill count" of Americans. McCarthy only looked daring next to Kennedy, who was strangely tongue-tied about the President.

This restraint puzzled Kennedy's followers. The explanation given was that Kennedy should not trigger Johnson's paranoia. As he told Jack Newfield: "I don't want to drive Johnson into doing something really crazy. I don't want to hurt the doves in the Senate who are up for re-election." Now we know that, with Johnson as with Hoover, Kennedy's hands were tied. He feared what Johnson might release about his brother, going all the way back to the Inga Arvad tapes. In 1967 Johnson started dropping hints to the press that he knew about the Kennedy plots against Castro. He even told Leo Janos of *Time* that the Kennedys "had been operating a damned Murder Incorporated in the Caribbean." Robert could not be certain how much else Johnson had learned from Hoover or the CIA. He had to assume Judith Campbell's simultaneous affair with John Kennedy and Sam Giancana was known to the President from files in either agency.

His own service as Attorney General had not endeared him to Hoover. He did not want to provoke either man into campaign leaks or revelations.

Robert's Johnson problem had been both typified and exacerbated by the Manchester affair in 1966. After the President's assassination, Robert and Jacqueline Kennedy had many reasons for controlling the family image. They wanted a dignified treatment of the national tragedy. They did not want to be pestered by a thousand writers seeking interviews. The high-handedness of some Kennedy aides in dealing with Dallas authorities would need soft-pedaling. The autopsy follow-up could be embarrassing on the matter of Addison's disease. And the search for other assassins could lead in the direction of Cuba, of CIA attempts to use the Mafia against Castro.

To all these motives must be added the problem of future relations with President Johnson. In the aftermath of the assassination, Kennedy friends and aides expressed a hatred of Texas and Texans that focused, understandably if unfairly, on Lyndon Johnson. And, as usual, the resentment of the honorary Kennedys outran that of the real ones. The emotion at the center of things was exaggerated by outsiders, who compensated for their distance from the original fire. On the flight back from Dallas, there were ugly little outbursts, anguished rude comments — some of which Johnson had heard about, some he had not. It was important to control the reporting of these events — and, if possible, to delay any reporting of them. The Kennedy team had to work with Johnson, for a while at least — to appear patriotic (and to be patriotic), to avoid charges of pettiness and desertion when the nation was in crisis. Besides, Robert Kennedy felt Johnson was an aberration, an intruder, whose harmful effect could be controlled if he were forced to accept Robert as his running mate in 1964. As long as that option remained, he told his people to express their loyalty to the new President. Frank reporting of those people's real feelings had to be prevented.

The best way to delay and mute reports on the mood in and after Dallas was to find a sufficiently pliant writer, to exact submissiveness to censorship from him, and to prevent him from publishing for almost five years (till after the 1968 election). The Kennedys were especially worried by the prospect that Jim Bishop would do one of his "day" books — *The Day the President Was Shot.* Bishop liked drama and conflict; and the "us against them" mood of the Kennedy aides would lend itself well to his skills. He must be prevented from interviewing the more outspoken members of the Kennedy entourage.

A cooperative author was ready to hand, respectable enough, but with a record of accommodation to the Kennedys. In 1961, William Manchester sent Pierre Salinger a request for interviews with the President, to be turned into articles and then a book: "I should be eager to have you review the facts in the completed articles." When Manchester finished typing his *Portrait of a President,* the publisher sent proofs to Salinger for review — but not a word had to be changed in a White House very touchy about its image.

To Manchester's credit, it must be said that his adoration was sincere. He had been smitten by the glamour of the Kennedys, and his 1961 book records this case of puppy love:

> Dwight Eisenhower, the painter, declared that he wasn't too certain what was art, but he knew what he liked, and Harry Truman, the pianist, said of something he didn't like that if it was art, he was a Hottentot. Jacqueline Kennedy, the connoisseur, makes both look like Hottentots, if not outright clods. She has a rare visual eye. . . . Cultivated families admire elegance, and John Kennedy sets great store by good form. His circle doesn't include men who wear clocks on their socks, or call Shakespeare the Bard, or say budgetwise.

Manchester was thoroughly dazzled after interviewing the President: "It is an encyclopedic performance, and any writer who has condescended to climbers on the political ladder (while he himself has remained in journalism, which is more of a trampoline) is likely to feel a bit contrite." The President is "frank as St. Augustine," a writer with imperfect spelling "like Fitzgerald," who has "more than ideas in common with" William James, and shared traits with "Caesar and Napoleon" — "and, for that matter, with Tacitus." Jacqueline Kennedy's poetry appears in fragments "like Emily Dickinson's."

Both the President and his wife liked this performance — a proof that they would accept incense from the tinniest thurible. Caroline Kennedy was praised for showing her "membership in the Quality," and Jacqueline because "she has moved from the trivial to the aesthetic, and is, in her *comme il faut* way, just as U as her husband."

Finally, "her fastidiousness has been endorsed by Russell Lynes" — a man, it must be presumed, without clocks on his socks.

There could be no problem in manipulating such a man. Indeed, when Salinger mentioned the assassination book early in 1964, Manchester anticipated demands on him by a preemptive surrender. He wrote to Robert Kennedy: "I agree that it is important that Mrs. Kennedy and you should review the manuscript. If you had not suggested this, I would have. I also agree that no film should ever be made from the book. That would be unthinkable." To manage all aspects of the book's production, Robert demanded that Manchester be released from an option clause with his own publisher and issue the book from Harper & Row, where Evan Thomas would be its editor. Thomas had worked with John Seigenthaler on Robert's *The Enemy Within.* Harper & Row, whose president, Cass Canfield, was related to Jacqueline Kennedy by marriage, had published several books by and about John Kennedy. Members of the firm were themselves honorary Kennedys. Further, most of the American book royalties would have to go to the John F. Kennedy Library. Manchester was, in the Kennedys' eyes, being hired for a task, not contracting for a book whose reward would be his because the resources marshaled for it were his from the outset. He signed an agreement which stated that "the final text shall not be published unless and until approved" by Robert and Jacqueline Kennedy.

It would seem that Robert Kennedy had covered every contingency, binding his author down to an official account of his brother's death. But each effort he made at a totality of control became self-defeating. Kennedy wanted to maintain good relations with President Johnson, and the book became a sore point between them just as the 1968 campaign was taking shape. He wanted to keep the book out of electoral politics — it was not to appear until the end of November in 1968, after the votes were in — but it came out, to sounds of controversy, in 1967. He wanted a dignified account, and was drawn into a sordid squabble. He wanted to protect the President's widow, and the book affair caused the first dip in her popularity polls since the assassination. He wanted a compliant author, yet Manchester's very devotion made him protect his literary "eternal flame" to President Kennedy's memory.

Manchester, to his delight, felt promoted to the position of honorary Kennedy by the 1964 commission. He was allowed access to the
family and to family retainers; was invited to social affairs with them;
compared notes on "their" Kennedy books over lunches with
Arthur Schlesinger. This access led to emotional identification and
excess. When he turned in his manuscript, Evan Thomas had the
grace to be embarrassed for the Kennedys (who had not been embarrassed by Manchester's first effort). The editor wrote to Kennedy's designated censors (Justice Department associates John Seigenthaler and Edwin Guthman) that the book turned John
Kennedy into "the child of Arthur and Guinevere." Jacqueline
Kennedy appears "born of elves in a fairy glade and dressed in such
magic cloth of gold (chosen by Prince Jack) that the Texans in their
polka dot dresses and bow ties are seen as newly arrived scum —
plucked from the dung heap by magical Jack."

That last point was the crucial one. Thomas, while praising the
work as potentially "a great book," wrote the Kennedys that it was
"gratuitously and tastelessly insulting to Johnson," just what they
wanted to avoid. On other matters Manchester had been very oblig-
ing. He understood that Robert did not welcome conspiratorial spec-
ulations about the murder, and he suggested the book's publication
be moved up to counter them:

> I'm convinced that our appearance early next year [1967] will elim-
> inate most of the problems created by irresponsible books about the
> tragedy. For example, Epstein's *Inquest,* a really poisonous book,
> needn't trouble us any longer. With the help of Dr. Burkley and
> Howard Willens I think I've knocked out what, at first reading, ap-
> pears to be the one strong point in Epstein's version.

But on the subject of Lyndon Johnson, Manchester had absorbed all
the grievances, real or imagined, of the honorary Kennedys he interviewed. Even in the earlier book, it should be remembered, his tribute to Kennedy involved a contrast with the "Hottentots" Eisenhower and Truman. In his first draft of the 1967 book, Johnson
became a type of the murderous obtuseness that struck down the
graceful ruler. While admitting he had gone to excess, Manchester
clung to his hatred and wrote Mrs. Kennedy: "Though I tried des-

perately to suppress my bias against a certain eminent statesman who
always reminds me of somebody in a Grade D movie on the late
show, the prejudice showed through."

When various Kennedy deputies started picking at his manuscript, Manchester felt they were inexplicably whittling at the dead
President, with whom he now identified his work and himself.
When Robert Kennedy joined the attack, Manchester seemed to go
to pieces. Evan Thomas felt the situation was getting out of control
and urged Robert Kennedy to send the emotional author a telegram — which was later used to show Robert had approved the
manuscript. Even after Manchester had altered many references to
Johnson, and dropped things that Mrs. Kennedy said would embarrass her (like the search in a mirror for wrinkles on the day her husband was shot), various honorary Kennedys weighed in with contradictory criticisms of the book. Their loyalties were separately
engaged. Arthur Schlesinger, writing his own semiauthorized book,
wanted to defend its historical claims by muting any charge that
Kennedys censor their authors. Richard Goodwin had first inserted
himself into the process with a few minor suggestions, implying
they were all that was needed; but then Mrs. Kennedy made him her
agent, and he took a much harsher line on what must be altered.

The Kennedys were not used to having their courtiers rebel —
and certainly not in the name of a higher loyalty to Kennedyism.
The serialization of the book had been arranged in America and foreign countries — an aspect of publication that had no royalties ear-
marked for the Kennedy Library; so Robert accused Manchester of
trying to profit from his brother's death. It was a charge as unwise as
it was unfair. It convinced Manchester that Robert just did not see
the issues involved. He told others, "This is not the brother of the
man I knew." Manchester would have to defend the President alone,
if necessary. At last he understood how the ruthless "Bobby" had set
out to get Jimmy Hoffa. The old stories of federal agents knocking
on newsmen's doors at night seemed confirmed when Kennedy
showed up at the hotel room where Manchester was hiding under an
assumed name and pounded on the door, demanding that he open
it. (He didn't.) The Kennedy who had shed some of his reputation
as a McCarthyite now seemed a book-burner, vindictive in the treatment of his own chosen author. Sorensen concludes: "The poi-

sonous fallout from this controversy did more than anything else to affix the image of ruthlessness on Bob Kennedy."

Most shocking to Manchester was the way his fairy princess showed her claws. She told others she had "hired" Manchester and could fire him. She threatened him with court action, and said he had no chance against her at the peak of her postassassination popularity: "Anyone who is against me will look like a rat unless I run off with Eddie Fisher" (as Elizabeth Taylor had). *Esquire* ran on its cover a composite photo of Mrs. Kennedy carrying Fisher off on a sled. Mrs. Kennedy told her assistant that she had "the right to destroy the entire transcript" of her interviews with Manchester. She summoned Michael Cowles of *Look* magazine to Hyannis Port and told him to kill the serialization of the book. When he refused, she said, "If it's money, I'll pay you a million." When he said it was not money, she pointedly remarked, "You're sitting in the chair my late husband sat in."

The Kennedy courtiers rallied to her. Arthur Schlesinger told William Attwood of *Look,* "There will never be another Kennedy byline or my byline in *Look.*" The Kennedy lawyers descended to the kind of pettiness they had exhibited against Hoffa. Mrs. Kennedy's lawyers told Manchester he could not give credit to any Kennedy people in the acknowledgments to his book — or, for that matter, to anyone else. "Not even my wife?" Manchester asked. "Not even your wife." The mobilization of high-powered lawyers and advisers — Goodwin, Sorensen, Burke Marshall — drew further attention to the conflict. The very passages marked for criticism came out isolated, harsher than in context. Rumor exaggerated the hostility to Johnson, till the book, even before publication, was known as an anti-Johnson tract. John Connally attacked it as such. Everything the Kennedys did by this time just hurt them more. The crisis management team proclaimed the importance of the crisis. It was called a literary Cuban missile affair, since so many of the same minds were at work on it. The overreaction forced Evan Thomas to defend his writer against his former patrons, causing a split with his friend Seigenthaler. As John Corry wrote, in his account of the affair, "It is a fact that a good many people who got involved in the fight on both sides had inscribed pictures of President Kennedy in their homes and offices. . . . Ultimately, the battle of the book involved only old friends and neighbors, which was inevitable since only old friends and neighbors were ever invited to participate."

This was entirely a squabble between and among honorary Kennedys — a thing that was once considered unthinkable. There were too many cadres of loyalists, with loyalties variously engaged. The Kennedys had relied on the emotions they could arouse; but emotions are often unstable. Charisma dazzles, and flashbulbs woo the lightning bolt. The whole charged circle of electric fascinations was shorting out. The honorary Kennedys, once a source of power, were becoming liabilities. There were too many of them now, and too few real Kennedys. In attempting a totality of control over the image of his brother's death, Robert Kennedy made sure that if anything went wrong, everything would. And it did.

9

The Prisoner of Family

The danger of betraying our weakness to our servants, and the impossibility of concealing it from them, may be justly considered as one motive to a regular and irreproachable life. For no condition is more hateful or despicable, than his who has put himself in the power of his servants.

— SAMUEL JOHNSON, *Rambler* No. 69

FAMILY SERVANTS BECAME honorary Kennedys of a lower sort — John Kennedy inherited his older brother's black valet from Harvard days, and acquired another black valet from Arthur Krock when he entered Congress. ("This big fat colored boy," as Krock put it in his oral history, accompanied Kennedy to the White House.) But strangers brought onto the White House staff had to be disciplined by more than loyalty: they were all required to sign a pledge not to write or give interviews about their period of service with the family. At the time this pledge became known, it was taken as evidence of the Kennedys' superior taste. There would be no undignified dog-walker's account of "John John" in cute moments. Now we know the odd living arrangements of John Kennedy had to be concealed. One way or another, hundreds of people were bound to silence around the private life of the President.

The Kennedys later thought they had bound William Manchester with a double tie, of loyalty and of legal obligation. They did not realize that the two are at odds. Loyalty truly binds only if freely given. To add the note of legality is to absolve, in some measure, from free tribute. Not that Manchester ever thought he was disloyal.

But outsiders blamed him less, the more the Kennedys relied on legal technicalities.

There is a middle echelon of Kennedy retainers that plays an important role in family history. William Douglas and James Landis were honorary Kennedys in the family patriarch's eyes. But his "Four Horsemen" — the business operatives who accompanied him — were glorified "gofers." They had a variety of roles, most of them subservient. The Blairs write: "When the Ambassador took a girl out on the town, he brought along bachelor Joe Timilty. If they were seen, the assumption was supposed to be that the girl was with Timilty." Timilty was a man whose silence did not have to be bought.

Wealthy people acquire a penumbra of errand-running "friends." They are a luxury that soon becomes a necessity. What if a wealthy young man wants to sail, and his serious contemporaries are at work, are following their own projects? It is good to have a school chum who stands by on more or less instant call to crew for him; to take the boat back when the young heir must fly to his next appointment; to supervise the boat boy's shopping for the next sail. If Jacqueline Kennedy needed an escort to the theater, it was nice to have a safe and reliable one she could call on. For years, Truman Capote served this function for New York ladies, observing the code of the attendant — not to gossip to outsiders. (Gossip within the women's own circle is one of the services he was expected to provide.) The fury of the escorted women was so intense, when he broke the code, because the code was so uniformly assumed. One reason for having elegant gofers is to keep outsiders away — just as Manchester was commissioned to keep other authors away. People with a clamorous public need buffers to protect them from paparazzi, autograph-hunters, people who might sit down at one's table or join one's walk. Designated escorts fend off competitors for the escort role. Anyone who took Mrs. Kennedy out had the undoubted virtue, in her eyes, of not being Gore Vidal.

To some extent the Secret Service performed the role of gofer for the Kennedys in office. But a Secret Service agent cannot play golf or raise a jib or join a bridge hand, and at the same time keep his eyes out for potential assassins. So, John Kennedy made his old Navy friend "Red" Fay an Undersecretary of the Navy. This brought him to Washington where he could play golf, tell jokes, and sing "Hooray for Hollywood." Ben Bradlee could not understand the endless appetite of the Kennedys for this latter distraction. But Fay had other services to perform — Kennedy made him the escort for Angie Dickinson on his inauguration night. Fay endlessly obliged, and obligingly ran a picture of himself hooraying Hollywood in his book on the Kennedy years.

Fay was regularly addressed as "Grand Old Lovable" by Kennedy, who understood instinctively how one asserts ownership over another by renaming him. Thomas Broderick told the Blairs: "Jack was always giving people nicknames. He called me Tommie or the Thin Man." To serve its purpose, the name had to be made up by Kennedy himself. Thus men normally called "Jim" by their family and friends became "Jamie" to John Kennedy. "Ben" Bradlee became "Benjy." Inga Arvad was both claimed as a lover and trivialized as one when Kennedy addressed her, invariably, as "Inga-Binga." Kennedy was a Steerforth in the way he could attract people by putting them in their place, expressing superiority and affection in a single name. Steerforth, remember, makes David Copperfield proud that the school hero is familiar enough with him to call him "Daisy." Only shrewd Miss Dartle sees how the name flatters and unmans at the same time:

> "But really, Mr. Copperfield," she asked, "is it a Nickname? And why does he give it you? Is it — eh? — because he thinks you young and innocent? I am so stupid in these things."
>
> I colored in replying that I believed it was.
>
> "Oh!" said Miss Dartle. "Now I am glad to know it. He thinks you young and innocent; and so you are his friend? Well, that's quite delightful!"

Theodore Sorensen (known as "Ted") noticed that Robert Kennedy bristled at "Bobby," yet the President kept using that name. After the assassination, a note from Robert let Sorensen know where the diminutive belonged. It began "Teddy old pal" and ended "Bob."

If the gofers of the rich are a convenience to them — someone to run into town for supplies during a party — they also demand some care and servicing. Loyalty can be presumed, but only if it is prudently re-recruited at sufficiently close intervals. Besides, real affection is normally engaged on both sides. Perhaps the gofers who most entered the Kennedy affections were Ann and Joseph Gargan, the cousins who lost their own parents in childhood. The Kennedy family nursed pious Ann through a period when she seemed to have multiple sclerosis, and she repaid their tenderness a thousandfold when she became the Ambassador's indefatigable nurse after his stroke.

Joseph Gargan went to law school, but subjected his own career to that of Edward Kennedy, with whom he grew up, an almost-brother to the youngest brother, male company to the "stranded" last Kennedy son. Gargan was always ready to clean up after a race, put the sails away — only partly a Kennedy, but a Super-Kennedy because of that. The Ambassador sent Gargan to fetch his car, and forgave him when he hit a tree with it. The father was as forgiving to him as to any of his sons — but only because he expected less of him. *Time* magazine wrote, after Chappaquiddick: "Gargan is used by [Edward] Kennedy largely as companion for carrying out miscellaneous chores — making reservations, ordering food, emptying glasses and drawing baths."

The extra thing Gargan could supply in the pell-mell world of Kennedy competition was thoughtfulness for less privileged gofers. The reminder of a birthday, the joke that deflects a quarrel, the inclusion of a forgotten retainer — it was he who smoothed the social life for his admired patrons.

> [I] was amply recompensed by seeing an exact and punctilious practice of the arts of a courtier, in all the stratagems of endearment, the gradations of respect, and variations of courtesy. I remarked with what justice of distribution he divided his talk to a wide circle; with what address he offered to every man an occasion of indulging some favourite topick, or displaying some particular attainment; the judgement with which he regulated his enquiries after the absent; and the care with which he shewed all the companions of his early years how strongly they were infixed in his memory, by the mention of past incidents, and the recital of puerile kindnesses, dangers, and frolicks. (Johnson, *Rambler* No. 147)

Gargan, who shared Edward Kennedy's "puerile kindnesses, dangers, and frolicks," had also worked in the campaign of Robert Kennedy, where part of his social duty to fellow gofers led him to joke with the "boiler room girls." With his customary thoughtfulness, he did not let them go unremembered. He arranged the first party for them at Hyannis Port; and, the next summer, invited them to the Edgartown regatta. Performing such services not only benefited "the girls," but gratified him. Part of his claim to favored position was his ability to produce a Kennedy at parties where that is the ultimate distinction. And part of Kennedy's debt to this loyalest of gofers was to allow himself to be, periodically, produced.

The last Kennedy has to service all the inherited gofers as well as his own — and all the honorary Kennedys, veterans of 1960 and 1968, who suggest new campaigns, send speeches, line up supporters. These may come in handy some day — though the 1980 race proved that many old speechwriters took more time than they were worth. They all feel they have the one essential bit of advice the candidate must hear. In 1980 Edward Kennedy sought surcease from the buzz of them all by turning off his advice-receiver almost entirely. He is not good at hurting the feelings of those who have some old bond with the family. The tendered services are never entirely refusable, once he has heard them. And the demands made can become quite bizarre — one stalwart from the past even asked that Kennedy inform his own child that its mother had died. ("He is so used to dealing with sorrow.") There are endless weddings, funerals, graduations the family heir must go to, to express the family's gratitude.

That was the meaning of Chappaquiddick. Kennedy was trammeled up in other people's lives because they had suffered at his brother's death. He had to brace himself for endless reminiscings about Robert's campaign — the only thing that bound "the girls," through Gargan and his peers, to "the Senator." Popular gossip made of Chappaquiddick a kind of tawdry orgy. Actually, like many "celebrations" Kennedy is compelled to attend, it was part of his extended death watch or permanent floating Irish wake. Friends have to be sorted out according to which brother they accompanied to meet his killer.

Though Gargan could produce the Senator to awe the "girls," that did not mean he could attract any other people of consequence to this very minor entertainment. The others were friends of Gargan, fellow gofers — the Kennedy chauffeur, John Crimmins; Ray LaRosa, who also drove for Kennedy when called on; Charles Tretter, who had done advance work for the Kennedys; and Paul Markham, whom Burton Hersh calls "Joey Gargan's Gargan." Markham and Gargan went to Georgetown Prep together. Through Gargan, Markham received the Kennedy patronage that helped him become United States Attorney for the state of Massachusetts. Markham had fetched the Kennedy boat to Edgartown, where he was supposed to serve on its crew; but he banged his leg sailing there, and could not race after all. Furthermore, the Shiretown Inn was so crowded he had to give up his room to Kennedy, to stay with Crimmins and the others at the rented house on Chappaquiddick. One who rises by virtue of friendship with a gofer remains a gofer even when he holds the highest federal prosecutor's post in the state. Chappaquiddick was a roll call of the well-paid errand-runners, to honor the errand-dispatchers from campaigns past.

Crimmins, who had brought the Kennedy car over to Martha's Vineyard on the ferry, met Kennedy at the little island airport, early in the afternoon, and drove him to the hotel in Edgartown, where Kennedy dropped his luggage (and turned Markham out of a room). The men then crossed to Chappaquiddick for a swim at the beach just over Dyke Bridge. (Less than twelve hours later the same car would go off this bridge.) Then Kennedy went back to Edgartown and the regatta heat, a competitive chore when (as then) his back was hurting from fatigue and travel — the *Victura* came in ninth.

Kennedy had a postrace drink with fellow skippers and dressed for the cottage cookout; for the twilight milling of sun-dazed people at a resort town, for the maudlin laughter at campaign tales told over again, a listing of glad things remembered across an abyss of sadness. Someone always has his or her "Hooray for Hollywood" at such a gathering, and Kennedy must summon up his brothers' laughter out of the past. It was an important time for the boiler room workers, whose lives (they thought) would never again be as meaningful as when they worked for Robert Kennedy — unless they should get the opportunity, some time, to campaign for the Kennedy whose attention now flattered them. They stayed on and on — past the de-

parture time of the last ferry. Kennedy, of course, claims that he and
Mary Jo Kopechne dashed for the ferry and turned by accident onto
the dirt road leading to Dyke Bridge. But his story is so unsup-
ported, contradictory, or improbable in various of its parts, that we
cannot know for sure what happened during that time for which he
is the only witness.

Perhaps he does not know what happened. Fatigue, drink, panic
were at work on him. Did he black out? He could have left the car
before Miss Kopechne crossed the bridge, and pieced events together
later (Jack Olsen's thesis). Any number of things could have happened — including the presence of another passenger in the car.
Even the testimony of those left at the party is suspect. Robert Sherrill, in *The Last Kennedy,* has shown how jumbled is their account of
comings and goings and mutual time-checks — though the
synchronized support for Senator Kennedy's testimony about when
he left (11:15) emerges with suspicious clarity from this chaos. The
later silence kept by all involved does not inspire confidence. After
every other scandal of this period, journalistic enterprise and check-
books have led to interviews, books, movie or TV presentations
based on at least one of the witness's accounts. There have been none
out of Chappaquiddick. The loyalty of Robert's workers carried over
to Edward's troubles. In the first week after the accident, Esther
Newberg was deputed to give the partygoers' account of the night in
two interviews. But that experience taught the Kennedy team to
impose a total silence: she admitted in both interviews that she did
not remember when the Senator and Ms. Kopechne left the cottage;
her watch was "not working properly" — though she would later
testify to the Grand Jury that she marked the time by looking at her
watch. Apart from these canceled experiments in minimal candor,
the coordinated testimony before the Grand Jury remains the participants' first and last public account.

Three men at the party (Gargan, Markham, and Tretter) were
lawyers, and they invoked a client relationship with Kennedy to justify their silence. But there is little doubt that they would be loyal to
Kennedy with their silence, even if they were not attorneys. What
else are loyalists for? In fact, this episode resembles the Manchester
affair as a tale of the way honorary Kennedys flock to rescue one of
the family in his troubles.

If Chappaquiddick resembles the Manchester controversy in one respect, it began with a fainter but more poignant echo from another night of crisis for the family. After the interval in which something happened that led to Ms. Kopechne's death, Kennedy reappeared, but only dimly, at the rented cottage where the party's aimless milling continued after midnight. Standing by the other car the party was using, Kennedy called out softly to the one man outside the doorway, Ray LaRosa: "Ray, get me Joe." Kennedy sat inside the car waiting for Gargan — and, when he arrived, asked him to get Markham. Why had he not asked for both in the first place? Was Gargan too drunk, fuddled, or panicky at the sight of Kennedy alone? Was a cooler head needed? All we know is that the first loyalist, ever since boyhood, was turned to first — and that Gargan soon brought "Joey Gargan's Gargan" out to the car. The three went off, they say, to dive over and over into Poucha Pond trying to rescue the woman in the car.

Little over a year before this, Kennedy had awakened another loyalist with a whisper through the night — Arthur Schlesinger, sleeping at Hickory Hill where the family was locked in debate over the political future of Robert Kennedy. Then Edward went on to wake Sorensen. He had been probing around the edges of a slumbrous house to report back Eugene McCarthy's refusal to cooperate in the 1968 primaries. He came to the cottage at Chappaquiddick with more disastrous news; but very early the people he called began to consider his own future of primaries and campaigns, and how this night would affect them. The spookiest point of resemblance is that Mary Jo Kopechne had been present, hardly noticed, at Hickory Hill the night of Robert Kennedy's decision to run. She stayed late to type up Sorensen's and Schlesinger's declaration of Robert's candidacy.

Gargan and Markham, both lawyers, did not call for professional help — divers are available at a resort for rescue work, if that was their goal. Nor did they inform authorities that an accident, perhaps a crime, had occurred. They say they left the scene of the accident, drove Kennedy to the crossing for Edgartown, watched him dive into the channel and swim off into the night, then returned to the cottage and — at Kennedy's request — told the women nothing. The next morning they managed to show up at Kennedy's hotel room without being seen by the ferry operator. If all this happened as they say, the two men enter the pantheon of all official friends. And if it didn't happen that way, they ascend even higher for saying that it did. These gofers would go for a human body without complaining, though Markham thereby lost any hope for higher public office.

Kennedy could rely on such loyalty absolutely. That is why he considered for many hours whether to report the accident at all. Though we do not know for sure what happened on Chappaquiddick, there is outside testimony to his actions back at Edgartown; and, in conjunction, those actions plainly indicate that until 9:30 on the morning after the accident, Kennedy either did not know for sure about Ms. Kopechne's death, or pretended not to know. He was confident that, whatever story he told, his two confidants would support him.

Kennedy's secret return to his hotel (either by swimming, as he says, or in a borrowed boat) would allow him to claim he had left Chappaquiddick before the accident occurred, without any inconveniencing testimony from the ferry operator. Back at the inn, Kennedy was either awakened by a noisy party, or pretended to be, and let the innkeeper see him at 2:55 A.M. By 7:30 he was outside the inn, where he met the winner of the previous day's regatta heat, and accompanied him to the hotel's second-story porch where the two talked casually about upcoming races (with no indication on Kennedy's part that he would not be participating in that day's heat).

At 8:00 Gargan and Markham arrived, and went into Kennedy's room. When Charles Tretter, who had trailed Gargan and Markham back to the main island, saw the three men in heated conversation through a window, he began to enter but was waved off angrily by Kennedy. At 8:30 Kennedy went to the inn's desk, ordered the New York and Boston papers, and borrowed a dime for the public phone (Kennedys never have money on them). Gargan says he urged Kennedy to return to Chappaquiddick, where he could find a safely private telephone for the series of messages he had begun to send, calling in other loyalists to salvage the situation. The three men had reached the other side by 9:00, and Kennedy was still at the pay phone near the landing when the ferry returned to fetch the recently discovered body of Ms. Kopechne. Asked if he had heard of the acci-

dent, Kennedy said yes, and took the ferry to Edgartown, where
Gargan was dispatched to the women's motel. While Gargan finally
(and sketchily) told the women what had happened to their friend,
Kennedy told the police there had been an accident.

Gargan and Markham, to defend their failure to inform the police
earlier, claim that Kennedy assured them, before swimming off the
night before, that he would report as soon as he arrived on the other
shore. But the two men went back to the cottage, said nothing to
the others there, and slept till dawn. They did not warn the others
that police were about to descend on them with disorienting news,
because — obviously — they expected no report to trigger that result. In the morning, they hurried the women back to their hotel
without telling them a word. Only when Kennedy was actually
walking toward the police station did Gargan let them know about
the accident. Until then, all options were being maintained — including the option of denial that Kennedy had been involved at all.

One of the early theories about Chappaquiddick was invented by
Jack Anderson, who supposed that Gargan was scheduled to take the
blame. Whether this was seriously considered, the theory naturally
arose, since those who know Gargan have little doubt that he would
take the fall if asked. Such loyalty is touching, and a little scary. It
gives its recipient a kind of parachute for bailing out of sticky situations. But it also tempts that recipient to take risks, on the assumption that he can always walk away untroubled. Kennedy later accused himself of inexcusable delay in reporting the death; but he
could only entertain thoughts of delay because he knew the loyalists
around him would not challenge him or his story, whatever that
turned out to be. Once again, the sources of strength debilitated. He
leaned too long on their passivity. They had nothing to offer but ob-
sequiousness, when he needed stringency and hard talk.

Even in his panic, Kennedy knew that he needed sharper advice
than Gargan could give him — or than he could give himself. One
of the first phone calls he made was to Burke Marshall. Marshall had
been one of Robert's shrewdest and toughest assistants in the Justice
Department. Before Robert's death, Marshall was considered the
leading contender for the Attorney General post in a second Kennedy administration. Burton Hersh says Marshall was known to the
family as a "defuser of blockbusters." So Edward Kennedy, with

three lawyers on the scene, was going for a super-lawyer — itself a signal of the danger he was in. In Hersh's words, "Importing Burke Marshall to deal with a motor vehicle code violation was tantamount to whipping frosting with the great screw propeller of the Queen Elizabeth." There was a precedent for this. John Corry says that the Manchester struggle looked serious only when Burke Marshall appeared to represent the Kennedys. Everyone knew, then, that "bigger guns had taken over."

Kennedy was busy at the telephone. He had to seek out his brother-in-law Stephen Smith, who was on vacation in Europe. Once the campaign manager was alerted, the campaigners would troop in — the old team attracted toward Hyannis Port, in the next several days, as by some magnetizing of their PT tie pins. Robert McNamara showed up, and Sorensen, and Goodwin, offering help and advice. Others had already been dispatched on cleanup chores — William vanden Heuvel to tell the Kopechnes what little he knew of their daughter's death, Dun Gifford to take away the body, an act which, as it turned out, made an immediate autopsy impossible. Gargan held the hands of other gofers. Sorensen wrote the TV defense Kennedy would make after his Grand Jury testimony. Eight lawyers were representing Kennedy by that time. Loyalists were everywhere, putting the best face they could on what had happened.

If Gargan and Markham passed the ultimate test for gofers on that muddled night, the bigger names in the Kennedy entourage performed an equivalent service in the next few weeks. It seems that Kennedy told few of them (if any) much more than he told the rest of us. They submitted to the test of silence, and rallied nonetheless. Men with their own careers, they used their reputations to cover Kennedy's shame. These were not people who could be bought or intimidated. If they helped cover up what happened, they did it out of a primal sense of loyalty, out of the honor code of honorary Kennedys.

Once again newspapers compared this convening of heavyweight talent to the time of the missile crisis. Missiles in Cuba, Manchester writing a book, Robert deciding to run, a girl dead by accident — public and private events mingle around the Kennedy reputation; perspective alters according to the engagement of the family in events that would otherwise be minor, however sad in themselves.

Each crisis is major if a Kennedy is involved; and the missile team gathers. The frightening thing is not that courtiers should assemble to help Edward Kennedy after a car accident. The frightening thing is that making Kennedys look good was no doubt an important motive for these courtiers during the missile crisis itself.

And, sure enough, the men of power and influence repaired whatever was reparable after this disaster. They soothed the Kopechnes, wooed officials, won special treatment. No autopsy was performed. No one else present has ever talked. The only charge brought against Kennedy was for leaving the scene of an accident. He bargained a plea of guilty in return for the minimum sentence, suspended. He lost his driver's license for a year. At the Grand Jury hearing, he was treated respectfully; other witnesses did not have to explain difficulties in their testimony. Despite all the damage Chappaquiddick did to Kennedy, he was reelected to the Senate, welcomed back by his colleagues, and remained a contender for the presidency. He has successfully "stonewalled" attempts to discover more about that mysterious night. William Buckley criticized the way Chappaquiddick was handled; but Sherrill considers it a masterpiece among cover-ups, one in which Kennedy was given the benefit of every legal doubt while cooperating as little as possible with the investigation.

For the first nine hours or so after he drove the woman to her death he said nothing about the accident because, he explained later, he was out of his mind. Then for the next week he stayed in seclusion and avoided the press because, he said, he was recovering from the physical ordeal of the accident (he did break out of his hiding to attend the Kopechne funeral, but he said that was not an "appropriate" time to talk but promised to talk when the time did become "appropriate"). Not long thereafter his attorneys became engaged in a fight to block the inquest from being open, and while that was pending Kennedy excused himself from talking by saying his lawyers wouldn't let him while his case was in litigation. As soon as the inquest was launched, Kennedy had a perfectly fine reason for keeping quiet because the cooperative Judge Boyle ordered all inquest witnesses not to talk about what they had testified. That order held until the inquest transcript was released, which brings us back to the present moment when Kennedy was saying, "The facts of this incident are now fully public, and eventual judgment and understanding rests where it belongs. For myself, I plan no further statement."

Ironically, Kennedy's very success in evading the full scrutiny and pressure of the law disqualifies him for the presidency. A man for whom other men of power and fame are already willing to stretch and bend the law, to whom they will lend the support of their reputations, should not be further raised above the law by holding the nation's highest office. Sherrill quotes, for its irony, Kennedy's later attack on President Nixon's attempted cover-up of Watergate: "If this country stands for anything, it stands for the principle that no man is above the law." No man should be given special treatment. Yet the crush of affectionate loyalists works always for such special treatment of a Kennedy.

The loyalty perdured, though some were angry at Kennedy for damaging the family prospects they all share. Sorensen, after penning Kennedy's TV defense, crossed out references to his brilliant future in a book he was completing on the Kennedy legacy. By being weak, by having to rely on them, he disillusioned his own defenders, who remained loyal to him even as they lost respect for him. Yet reliance on them had led him into this trap. Reliance on the honorary Kennedys can, after a while, sap the strength of real Kennedys. With so many "Kennedys" around, serving him and being serviced by him, he ceased to be fully one himself. In all the bumbling rush to save his reputation, the man disappeared; and people who would do anything to save the family name were, by that very willingness, tainting the name.

III

IMAGE

If you had said to a man in the Stone Age, "Ugg says Ugg makes the best stone hatchets," he would have perceived a lack of detachment and disinterestedness about the testimonial. If you had said to a mediaeval peasant, "Robert the Bowyer proclaims, with three blasts of a horn, that he makes good bows," the peasant would have said, "Well, of course he does," and thought about something more important. It is only among people whose minds have been weakened by a sort of mesmerism that so transparent a trick as that of advertisement could ever have been tried at all.

— GILBERT CHESTERTON

10

Creating the Kennedys

Promise, large promise, is the soul of an advertisement.

— SAMUEL JOHNSON, *Idler* No. 40

ONE OF JOHN KENNEDY'S BOYHOOD FRIENDS told the Blairs that he had never heard of a "PR man" till he met his schoolmate's father. Joseph Kennedy used professional public relations people; but he was his own best manager of reputations. He early learned the techniques for getting attention. In this he resembled the Hollywood "moguls" who could shape American taste though their own sense of taste was deficient. Still, what the moguls did for "starlets," Kennedy would do for his offspring.

He took great pains to have the Kennedys portrayed in public as, invariably, winners. One of the first difficulties he had to face in this project was the existence of one Kennedy who clearly seemed a loser. When his daughter Rosemary proved slow at learning, Kennedy urged her to try harder — that, after all, was how he made his sickly son John play football. As with his other children, he was tenderly compelling, but compelling. He expected results. But he got none. By the time Gloria Swanson, a believer in health foods, suggested that Rosemary try *them,* Kennedy blew up at her; told her not to tempt him with false hopes. He had faced the fact that Rosemary was a permanent loser, retarded from birth; the best doctors could do nothing for her. One of the "Four Horsemen" around Kennedy warned Ms. Swanson that the subject was too sensitive, she should not bring it up again.

But if all the Kennedys could not be winners, they could be made to appear winners. Rosemary's deficiencies were disguised as long as possible — she was even presented at the English court with the rest of the Ambassador's family. And when she went to a home for the retarded, that fact was denied for decades. At first it was said she had entered a convent to teach. When James MacGregor Burns was given access to the family for his first biography, he relayed the family line that Rosemary had a vocation to "help care for mentally retarded children." Joseph Dinneen and Joe McCarthy repeated that story in early biographies. Even when it became clear that Rosemary was not doing any teaching, her father could not confess that she was retarded from birth. He told the press that she had suffered a childhood attack of spinal meningitis. When the Kennedy Foundation was set up, and money was given Archbishop Cushing to establish a home for the retarded, the Archbishop heeded Kennedy's wishes and said the donation was for care of "poor children." Later, when the truth about Rosemary came out, the generosity of the Kennedys helped improve mental care for the handicapped. Eunice Shriver, especially, became identified with the Special Olympics. But for decades Joseph Kennedy succeeded in hiding what he obviously considered a family disgrace.

The impulse to hide weakness led to the sequestration of John Kennedy's medical records. The Blairs, in their search for doctors who had treated the young Kennedy, found it hard to document the precise time and place of various treatments. His bad back had been with him from childhood, but he told John Hersey that it originated in the strain of rescuing his comrades after his boat was sunk. (Those comrades do not remember his mentioning any back injury at the time.) The habit of covering up his multiple health problems culminated in the series of lies about his Addison's disease. When Lyndon Johnson revealed the existence of this problem in the 1960 campaign (thereby incurring Robert Kennedy's fieriest anger), the Kennedy camp issued outright denials. Its spokesmen later rationalized this by saying he did not have Addison's disease because the public wrongly thought the disease invariably fatal: so it would give a false impression to use the term, even though it was the correct one. But they not only did not use the term. They expressly denied it was applicable in any sense, and portrayed Johnson as a candidate willing to invent any lie convenient to his purposes. (The family sealing of the President's autopsy report would later fuel conspiracy theories inimical to Johnson.)

When Edward Kennedy was caught cheating at Harvard, his father took steps to cover that up, too—and he offered employment to the young man who had taken the exam for his son. But the patriarch's skill was more often used for enhancing the family's good points than in suppressing the truth about defects. The selling of his sons began with their Harvard careers, where he urged them on to athletic distinction. He had, from their boyhood days, introduced them to influential people who would sponsor them (later he had Justice William Douglas take Robert to Russia with him). He wanted his sons to study with famous professors — and sent Joseph, the eldest, to the London School of Economics, where Harold Laski not only instructed the boy but let him travel with him. Arthur Krock developed the family line on Laski, one that has been endlessly repeated — that the patriarch disliked Laski's Marxism but wanted his sons exposed to all views. Actually, Kennedy was a celebrity hunter; he was more interested in what a man could do for his boys than in what the man thought. Felix Frankfurter had described Laski as "the greatest teacher in the world." To be thought that by a Frankfurter was to possess power, and Kennedy meant to send his sons where the power was.

The point, in other words, was not to study with Laski, but to *have* studied with him. So, in his *Who's Who* biography, John Kennedy claimed for years that he was a "Student of London Sch. Economics, 1935–36." Actually, his health made him withdraw before he could attend any classes. Unlike his brother, he never studied under Laski, though the family worked hard to develop the impression he had — James Landis, Dean of Harvard Law School, even claimed that Kennedy got his ideas for *Why England Slept* from Laski.

The first major effort at selling John Kennedy was the Ambassador's treatment of his senior paper, which he turned into a bestselling book. Just as studying with Laski mattered less than being known for having studied with him, writing a book mattered less than being known for having written one: "You would be surprised how a book that really makes the grade with high-class people stands

you in good stead for years to come. I remember that in the report
you are asked to make after twenty-five years to the Committee at
Harvard, one of the questions is 'What books have you written?' and
there is no doubt you will have done yourself a great deal of good."

When his son's book appeared, the Ambassador sent a copy to the
Royal Family, another to Churchill. Given Henry Luce's opening
plug for Wendell Willkie, Kennedy was tactful enough not to send
it to Roosevelt. But he did send a copy to Harold Laski, which was a
mistake. Laski, with whom John Kennedy is supposed to have studied, and from whom James Landis claimed he took this very book's
ideas, wrote to the doting father:

> The easy thing for me to do would be to repeat the eulogies that
> Krock and Harry Luce have showered on your boy's work. In fact, I
> choose the more difficult way of regretting deeply that you let him
> publish it. For while it is the book of a lad with brains, it is very
> immature, it has no structure, and dwells almost wholly on the sur-
> face of things. In a good university, half a hundred seniors do books
> like this as part of their normal work in their final year. But they
> don't publish them for the good reason that their importance lies
> solely in what they get out of doing them and not out of what they
> have to say. I don't honestly think any publisher would have looked
> at that book of Jack's if he had not been your son, and if you had
> not been ambassador.

Kennedy no doubt agreed that the book was published because of
his position. After all, that is why he wanted such a position — to
help his boys. And he was less interested in what his son had got out
of the academic exercise than in what he could get out of it as a political exercise — which, it turned out, was a great deal.

It should be remembered that Laski was reading the completed
book, after Arthur Krock's ministrations to its style and the Ambassador's additions to its content. The Blairs show in parallel passages
how literally Kennedy copied extracts from his father's letters
directly into the final text. The senior paper on which the book is
based was even more ragged in structure and style. Carl Friedrich,
the famous political scientist who judged it, explained why the paper
should not get a *magna cum laude:* "Fundamental premise never analyzed — much too long, wordy, repetitious. Bibliography . . . spotty.

Many typographical errors. English diction repetitive. Cum laude plus."

It was unpromising material. But Joseph Kennedy was a great promoter. He had Krock rewrite the manuscript, retitle it, find it an agent. He supplied charts, statistics, and arguments himself. He arranged for Luce to introduce it, in a campaign year, by describing it as relevant to the election. Kennedy paid to send out 250 free copies, over twice the publisher's norm in those days. Thus, blessed by the New York *Times* (in the person of Krock), and the *Time-Life* organization (in Luce), the book sold 80,000 copies in America, enough to put it briefly on the best-seller list in the summer of 1940. An English edition sold well too. Beginning with a school paper that "half a hundred seniors do" every year, the elder Kennedy had created a Promising Young Thinker in the public mind. Much of the Kennedy legend would turn on his future treatment as a scholar, an historian, a writer. When the Ambassador arranged for his son to travel to useful places with press credentials, Krock celebrated him as a brilliant young journalist. Krock even claimed that Kennedy, as a journalistic stringer in England, predicted the surprise 1946 defeat of Winston Churchill, though the Blairs uncovered clip files and letters to disprove that claim. John Kennedy the writer was almost entirely the creation of Joseph Kennedy the promoter. It is significant that, when the father wanted a ghost for his own 1940 book, *Why I'm For Roosevelt,* he did not turn to "the writer" in the family, but to that writer's writer, Arthur Krock.

The next step in the selling of John Kennedy was the celebration of his wartime heroism. The heroism was real. Kennedy saved the life of Patrick McMahon. He undertook the most dangerous assignments in looking for rescuers. His physical courage can never be questioned. If anything, he took unnecessary risks. But to this basis of heroism John Kennedy added a number of legendary embellishments. He released to biographers a preliminary and inaccurate draft of the citation for his Navy and Marine Corps Medal. This citation says his boat was rammed "while attempting a torpedo attack on a Japanese destroyer" and that he "personally rescued three men." The later citation corrected the errors. The attempted torpedo attack becomes a simple "collision" there, and he is said to have "contributed to the saving of several lives." The changes were not incidental.

Kennedy had put his own men in for the Silver Star, a combat medal, and had been put in for one himself. This application was downgraded to the life-saving award given all three officers of the PT boat. (Enlisted man John Maguire assisted in the rescue too, but got no medal.)

Kennedy repeatedly tried to establish that he was on the attack when his boat was sunk. In the account he gave to John Hersey, who first wrote up his adventure for *The New Yorker,* he claimed that "Kennedy saw a shape and spun the wheel to turn for an attack." Later, when the Ambassador arranged for *Reader's Digest* to run a condensation of the *New Yorker* piece (reprints of which became campaign handouts over the years), John took special care that the phrase "turn for an attack" was retained while other sections were cut.

In fact, interviews with others on the boat make it clear that there was no attempted attack. The destroyer loomed over the idling PT boat before anyone knew it was near. This was a sore point for the crew, and even more so for its skipper. After all, two men died in the collision — was Kennedy as negligent in the Solomon Islands as his brother would be at Poucha Pond? It was fear of that charge that made Kennedy falsify the story of his boat's ramming. The event is mysterious in itself. How did a light plywood boat made for speed and maneuverability manage to get itself cut in two by a more ponderous destroyer? It had not happened before. It did not happen again. It was a mystery to Kennedy himself. Just after his rescue, a friend named William Liebenow asked, joking, "How in the world could a Jap destroyer run you down?" Kennedy replied, "Lieb, I actually do not know."

It is not clear from the accounts laboriously gathered by the Blairs whether Kennedy had shut off one or more of his boat's three motors, was idling them, or stalled them, or what watch conditions let an expected boat bear down on 109 without warning. Kennedy would cryptically tell Robert Donovan, after the Bay of Pigs invasion, "That whole story [of PT 109] was more fucked up than Cuba." And Barney Ross, of the PT crew, was astonished when the *New Yorker* account came out, showing an alert crew consciously on the attack — a story that makes the collision even harder to explain. Ross told the Blairs: "Our reaction to the 109 thing had always been that we were kind of ashamed of our performance. . . . I had always thought it was a disaster, but he [Hersey] made it sound pretty heroic, like Dunkirk."

There was nothing in the handling of PT 109 to be very proud of. Its assignment was to intercept destroyers running men and supplies through a strait; or, if they missed at the first passage, to hit the ships as they returned north before dawn. The 109 was part of a four-boat detachment whose leader spotted the Japanese and went for them, expecting the others to follow. Kennedy, for some reason, was out of touch, and did not make that initial attack. He waited for the second chance, two hours later, and was caught off guard. His boat fired none of its torpedos and spotted no enemy ship till the *Amagiri* sliced it in two.

It may be said in extenuation of Kennedy that PT boats in general were poorly equipped with navigation and radio equipment. Their record was dismal — the plywood hulls, the topheavy and unreliable torpedos, made them floating explosions waiting to happen. PT boats were romanticized in war propaganda after one took Mac-Arthur off the Philippines. Recruiting had taken place among Ivy Leaguers and the rich — those who had sailed their own boats — and the individualism of the skippers, together with the unpredictability of the boats' performance, made some Navy officers consider them a menace to the American cause.

If, in 1944, John Hersey had tried to find out how a PT boat could be run down by a destroyer, military censorship would have blocked his effort. Inflation of heroic deeds was encouraged by the whole war atmosphere. It is typical of the "gentleman songsters" aspect of the PT command that Kennedy first told Hersey of his exploit after dining at the Stork Club and going to the theater. Hersey had married an old girl friend of Kennedy's, and the two met at social affairs before and during the war. This was one more confirmation of the Ambassador's belief that knowing the right people would pay off, down the road, in unforeseen ways. "Doing the town" while on leave, Kennedy ran across just the right celebrator of his legend.

If the Navy encouraged exaggeration of its heroes' exploits, it nonetheless downgraded the medal Kennedy was recommended for, and rewrote the citation, and delayed the bestowal for nine months — which suggests to the Blairs that there were some mis-

givings about the accident 109 was engaged in. Kennedy did not get
his medal until his father's friend, James Forrestal, became Secretary
of the Navy. From the time of the Inga Arvad affair, Joseph Kennedy had been closely engaged in the Navy's treatment of his sons.
Through his lobbying, the U.S.S. *Joseph P. Kennedy, Jr.* was commissioned and cadet Robert Kennedy was assigned to serve on it. The
promoter who had opposed entry into the war, and who lost a son to
it, was nevertheless determined to get some mileage out of it for his
other sons' careers.

So the legend was born. On his desk in the Oval Office, Kennedy
kept the cocoanut shell he carved as a message to potential rescuers.
In the legend, this did the trick. In fact, an Australian spotter had
already arranged for the rescue before the cocoanut was received.
From his first race for Congress through his entry into the White
House, Kennedy used his shipmates as campaign speakers. The PT
109 tie clip became a status symbol on the New Frontier. Edward
Kennedy created a sensation by giving them away in Africa. Not
since Theodore Roosevelt charged up San Juan Hill with two journalists at his side had a military episode been so expertly merchan-
dized for its political value. In the White House, Kennedy oversaw
all aspects of the movie made about his adventure, approving the
script and director, choosing the star, Cliff Robertson. (His first
choice, Warren Beatty, turned the President down.)

In time, John Kennedy surpassed his father in skill at creating the
right image for himself. Though a lackluster student at Harvard,
Kennedy left school with material for a book that made him seem a
promising young intellectual. He managed his congressional career
the same way. While not distinguishing himself for legislation or
leadership among his peers, he gave a key speech (on Algeria) and
published a key book (on courage) that attracted public notice. *Profiles in Courage* was a "twofer," not only a prize-winning performance
in itself, but a reminder to readers and reviewers that the war veteran
knew something about courage, about the Hemingway quality of
"grace under pressure" mentioned in the book's first sentence.

John Kennedy is rightly called the author of *Profiles in Courage,* as
he is the author of his own inaugural address. He authorized
each — was the only one who could deliver it; directed the writing;
delivered nothing he did not accept; had final right to delete any-

thing or add anything. His authority could not be overruled. It was all done in his name. But Theodore Sorensen, not the author in any of the senses used above, wrote the inaugural address. And Sorensen, along with Jules Davids and others, wrote *Profiles in Courage.*

The book was put together much like a major speech. Scholars and politicians were canvassed for suggestions. Subjects were chosen to give political balance to the book — three Senators from the South, three from the Midwest, and two Republicans were included lest the Democratic Senator from Massachusetts be accused of making courage a New England or a party monopoly. Yet the Senator from Massachusetts meant to connect himself with a noble tradition — so two Senators from Massachusetts were included in this study of eight Senate heroes. The network of honorary Kennedys was pressed into service. Dean Landis wrote a memorandum that remarkably defines the book's theme. Professors Schlesinger and Commager were asked for suggestions and read drafts. Allan Nevins wrote the introduction. Jacqueline Kennedy brought her history teacher at Georgetown — Jules Davids — into the process. Arthur Krock made suggestions to Sorensen, who was *this* book's Arthur Krock.

This kind of political production is normal, not only for an officeholder's speeches but for his books. The two categories tend, in fact, to merge when a politician is "writing." Books just collect or expand on his speeches, written by various aides. There is no deception in this, because there is no pretense that the man signing his name did all or even most of the writing. But things were complicated in Kennedy's case by the fact that Arthur Krock was lobbying to win the book a *writer's* prize, the Pulitzer.

If the Ambassador was right, if it helps to have written a well-received book, it helps immeasurably more to have received a Pulitzer Prize for having written a book. John Kennedy wanted that award, and was willing to make claims of authorship that went well beyond the political authorization involved in delivering a speech. Indeed, he made claims, and insisted on them repeatedly, that are not sustainable. When it was suggested that Kennedy had not written his own book, he showed anger and threatened suits; his father asked the FBI to investigate his accusers. The Senator displayed notes in his own hand, and dictabelt tapes of his own voice.

But those notes and tapes are now in the Kennedy Library, and

Herbert Parmet's investigation of them destroys Kennedy's claim to have written the book. The notes pertain mainly to one subject — John Quincy Adams, the Massachusetts favorite among Kennedy's chosen heroes; and even these are not drafts of a continuous text. The tapes are a jumble of quotes from secondary sources (many of them passages read straight from Margaret Coit's life of John Calhoun). There is no draft, at any stage, for the book, or for any substantial part of it. The notes show he was keeping up with the progress of the work; but Kennedy was ill, traveling, or campaigning most of the time when the book is supposed to have been composed, and Sorensen was working on it full time — sometimes for twelve hours a day — over a period of six months. Parmet leaves no doubt who did most of the work, and especially who supplied "the drama and flow that made for readability." From his first work on his senior paper at Harvard, Kennedy was never able to sustain a long passage of prose — he assembled that paper in a mad flurry of work with a team of hired secretaries to whom he dictated, pointing out passages for copying, working more as compiler than prose artist.

Sorensen follows the code of the political speechwriter in maintaining that his principal was the author of whatever he signed. Within the constraints of his craft, speaking its code as it were, Sorensen told the truth. But Jules Davids, who wrote lengthy first sketches of four chapters, told Parmet that he and Sorensen did most of the research and drafting of the book. Kennedy loyalists supported the Senator's specific claim to having written the book, though James MacGregor Burns admitted in his oral history report at the Kennedy Library: "I think Sorensen, or whoever was helping him, gave him more help on the book than you or I could get if we were doing one." The rules for Kennedys are different, that's all.

One of the books *Profiles* shoved aside for the 1957 Pulitzer was Burns's own *Roosevelt: The Lion and the Fox,* which was the second choice of the biography panel (consisting of Julian Boyd and Bernard Mayo). The first choice of the judges was Alpheus Mason's *Harlan Fiske Stone: Pillar of the Law.* Three other books were also recommended: Irving Brant's *James Madison: The President, 1809–1812,* Samuel Flagg Bemis's *John Quincy Adams and the Union,* and William N. Chambers's *Old Bullion Benton.* It would have been ridiculous to place Kennedy's work in the company of these biographies, and the two historians did not. But the Pulitzer Advisory Board has the power — and the bad habit — of overruling its own judges' recommendations, and that happened in 1957, when Arthur Krock "worked like hell" (in his own words) to get the prize for Kennedy.

The board, naturally, denied improper influence — which reduced it to the puerile explanation that the Milwaukee *Journal*'s president, J. D. Ferguson, swayed twelve grown men with the news that his twelve-year-old grandson enjoyed *Profiles in Courage*. Herbert Parmet, the best student of this whole episode, is skeptical of the board's rather humiliating explanation of its own act:

> Keeping his hands off would have been out of character for the Ambassador. Allowing the Pulitzer prize to be decided by chance would have been especially unique for a man who placed so much importance on having his son gain literary respectability en route to power, and Hohenberg [historian of the Pulitzer nominations] has admitted to Krock's visibility in the situation. Furthermore, the *Times* correspondent had been "instrumental" in deciding "several" other Pulitzer prizes. His credentials as a lobbyist within that journalism fraternity were first-rate.

Because of his book, Kennedy was chosen to chair a special Senate committee for choosing the five outstanding Senators in America's history. This committee announced its winners just one day before Kennedy won the Pulitzer. Of the five Senators chosen to be honored, three were included in Kennedy's eight "profiles," and the press treated those by referring to Kennedy's text. The book's appearance, his service on the committee, and winning the Pulitzer made up a kind of triple play for Kennedy in the spring of 1957, just as his presidential hopes were surfacing.

In 1981, shortly after a reporter for the Washington *Post* received a Pulitzer Prize, it was discovered that her account was false. In order to advance her journalistic career, she had made up a sensational story. She had to resign in disgrace, and the paper apologized for inadvertently misleading the prize committee. The Pulitzer Prize is given for reporting and writing. The book award is given and accepted on the assumption that the writer's skill is at issue, not the patron's office. In taking the prize, Kennedy falsified the facts of the book's production; and he spent all his remaining years covering up that falsification. He lied to the nation, and conscripted various honorary Kennedys in perpetuating his image as a prize-winning author and historian. This aided his career in many ways. For instance, when he wanted the Republican Robert McNamara, who had just taken over the Ford Company, to come to Washington as his Secretary of Defense, McNamara — who had read and been impressed by *Profiles in Courage* — asked him directly if he had really written it. Kennedy solemnly assured him that he had.

So, a woman tried to advance her career, and is ruined. A student tries to pass Spanish, has a friend take his exam for him, and is kicked out of Harvard. But a Senator claims that he wrote what he did not, and goes blithely on to the presidency. This would pose an ethical problem for a man who did not separate his "image" so clearly from any concern for truth. Putting the best face on one's performance is a fundamental political skill; and it was for Joseph and John Kennedy an imperative of family life. Creating the Kennedy "image" was a basic drive for both men. Sometimes this meant exaggerating what was, admittedly, a heroic episode. Sometimes it meant asserting a nonexistent role as writer. It seems unlikely that either man could distinguish between the two exercises in self-promotion.

The woman reporter who lost her Pulitzer had given herself false credentials when applying for the Washington *Post* job — she claimed to be a Vassar graduate. John Kennedy gave himself false credentials in his *Who's Who* entry — a nonexistent year of study at the London School of Economics. He gave biographers false credentials for his war medal. It was not enough to save one man, at the risk of his own life. He had to save three. The incremental touches of glamour were always sought. The unflattering notes were censored. The collision became an attack. The flattering *New Yorker* article became a Kennedy panegyric when tailored for *Reader's Digest* — and that in turn became a campaign document (and, later on, a movie). Reality was all a matter of arranging appearances for the electorate.

The senior Kennedy had forged a separate world for his children. It hovered above ordinary life. It created reality, as Hollywood renamed starlets and gave them more interesting biographies. Glamour was something other people yearned for; the Kennedys could supply it. An appetite was satisfied on both sides. War propaganda did for heroes what Hollywood promotion did for stars. The super-human does not just happen. It must be contrived. For a time, that master contriver of images, Joseph Kennedy, would see his family outshine any star in the fan magazines, any heroic astronaut on the cover of *Life,* any popular professor on the Harvard campus. In this world, you were whatever you could make people think you were. In that sense, John Kennedy was the writer of *Profiles in Courage.*

11

Style

Summoning artists to participate
in the august occasions of the state
Seems something artists ought to celebrate.

— ROBERT FROST, 1961 Inauguration

WASHINGTON POSITIVELY FIZZED in 1961. Kennedy had assembled a cabinet of all the talents. Brilliant people circulated, telling each other how brilliant they were. As Arthur Schlesinger remembers it:

> Washington seemed engaged in a collective effort to make itself brighter, gayer, more intellectual, more resolute. It was a golden interlude. . . . One's life seemed almost to pass in review as one encountered Harvard classmates, wartime associates, faces seen after the war in ADA conventions, workers in Stevenson campaigns, academic colleagues, all united in a surge of hope and possibility.

Both Schlesinger and Sorensen proudly count up the Rhodes Scholars riding the New Frontier.

These "eggheads" boasted of their worldliness. Harvard professors, moving south, shed weight and wives, changed eyeglasses for contact lenses, worked hard and played hard. Schlesinger delights in the fact that Kenneth Galbraith not only wrote economic tomes but satiric essays in *Esquire* (Schlesinger was writing movie reviews for *Show* while serving in the White House). In describing Richard Goodwin as "the archetypal New Frontiersman," Schlesinger includes among his credentials "dining with Jean Seberg." Sorensen gives the President's friendship with Frank Sinatra as proof of his "range." The crush of intellectuals around Marilyn Monroe, at the President's birthday party, became a favorite memory. Schlesinger included it in his book on Robert:

> Adlai Stevenson wrote a friend about his "perilous encounters" that evening with Marilyn, "dressed in what she calls 'skin and beads.' I didn't see the beads! My encounters, however, were only after breaking through the strong defenses established by Robert Kennedy, who was dodging around her like a moth around the flame." We were all moths around the flame that night. I wrote: "I do not think I have seen anyone so beautiful; I was enchanted by her manner and her wit, at once so masked, so ingenuous and so penetrating. But one felt a terrible unreality about her — as if talking to someone under water. Bobby and I engaged in mock competition for her; she was most agreeable to him and pleasant to me — but then she receded into her own glittering mist."

Other women were more accessible than Marilyn — Myra McPherson interviewed one such "Kennedy girl" for her book *The Power Lovers*. She remembered: "Kennedy set the example. Anyone in his following had to have his doxy." As Graham Greene wrote of Rochester: "He had such an art in gilding his failures that it was hard not to love his faults. . . ."

Harvard's urge toward Washington was so intense that it carried the professors halfway to Hollywood. At the Kennedy Library, the symbol of White House culture is the legendary night Pablo Casals played in the East Room. But Kennedy himself showed more interest in the planning and performances of his own birthday salutes — the first in Madison Square Garden, the second in Washington's National Guard Armory. Richard Adler, who wrote the musicals *Pajama Game* and *Damn Yankees,* was "master of revels" at these parties. For the first one, Adler brought in Marilyn Monroe to croon happy birthday for the President. And he topped himself the next year:

> I directed operations from the balcony through phones to the lighting and sound men, the conductor in the pit and the stage manager backstage. Everybody was in the Armory, waiting. And when the President made his entrance and began to walk to the

Presidential box, I pinned him with a spot and cued six trumpets
for "Ruffles and Flourishes." You know: "Tum-ta-ta, tum-ta-ta,
tum-ta-ta." I tell you, it was terrific! A Roman emperor entering the
Colosseum wouldn't have been more dramatic! Such a roar went up
from the crowd. And right away we went into "Hail to the Chief."
It was fantastic! Then we give the press boys one and a half minutes
for pictures, they like it, and also it adds to the excitement. Meanwhile we are lowering the lights, and I have a drum roll going, and
as each group of lights goes out and the drums get louder and
louder until finally they are *very* loud, and then the orchestra breaks
into the National Anthem, very loud, and at that point I have two
flags up high above the stage, and there are fans behind them, and
the flags are picked up by spots and they billow out and I had a
great singer, John Reardon, to sing the National Anthem, which is
usually dull in a show. Well, I want to say that the minute the National Anthem started and those flags lit up, the crowd was on its
feet, applauding (did you ever see that before?), and after Reardon
finished singing he took a bow, which nobody has ever done before,
and they gave him a wonderful reception. . . . We never had a President like this.

Mr. Adler knew how to please his patron: "This was the President's
party, not one of those culture-vulture programs." It was a giddy
time. Remembering an early White House party for the Radziwills,
Schlesinger writes in *A Thousand Days:* "Never had girls seemed so
pretty, tunes so melodious, an evening so blithe and unconstrained."

Even international fashions seemed to resonate to the anglophile
and "swinging" tastes of Kennedy. Mary Quant's London became
the center of "the action," and Americans itched outward to Petula
Clark's "rhythms of the gentle bossa nova." Schlesinger raved in
Show about Julie Christie, Peter Sellers, and (of course) the Beatles:
"They are the timeless essences of the adolescent effort to deal with
the absurdities of an adult world." *Real* culture was not safe, not dull
and respectable like Eisenhower's early-to-bed shows. It was frisky,
and risqué.

Yet elegant, too: "In an Executive Mansion where Fred Waring
once flourished, one now finds Isaac Stern, Pablo Casals, and the
Stratford Players," Schlesinger assured us. Mrs. Kennedy — whose

next husband would decorate in whale testicles — became the very embodiment of Culture. For the best and the brightest, attracted to her husband, she personified all that was most beautiful. She defied the rule that political wives must wear American clothes and drink American wines. But that, too, separated her husband's White House from the Fred Waring days. Schlesinger approved:

> The things people had once held against her — the unconventional beauty, the un-American elegance, a taste for French clothes and French food — were suddenly no longer liabilities but assets. She represented all at once not a negation of her country but a possible fulfillment of it, a dream of civilization and beauty, a suggestion that America was not to be trapped forever in the bourgeois ideal.

So glittering did the Kennedy style appear that some accused the President of being all style, no substance. Schlesinger answered that such style was itself a political act of substantial import: "His 'coolness' was itself a new frontier. It meant freedom from the stereotyped response of the past. . . . His personality was the most potent instrument he had to awaken a national desire for something new and better." When one man's personality is an administration's most potent tool, then efficient use of resources dictates a cult of that personality. A shrewd administrator must, to achieve his policy goals, maximize the impact of the leader's charm — must, that is, join in the contriving of images to celebrate the prince. Honorary Kennedys had always tended the family image. Now an entire administration would be recruited to that task.

Sorensen's book tells us how carefully Kennedy crafted his symbols. When his back troubles forced him to use crutches, these signs of weakness were abandoned whenever he moved into an area of the White House where he could be seen. On the other hand, his rocking chair was an acceptable sign of relaxation. Even the chair had its carefully chosen "image," making it "a nationally recognized symbol of the traditional values, reflective patience, and practical informality prevailing in the White House." Hugh Sidey called Kennedy's chair "a symbol of him and his administration," with "the full status of F.D.R.'s cigarette holder."

The chair stood for relaxation, not weakness. The President declared the need for "vigah," and sent his "frontiersmen" off on fifty-mile hikes. He cut back on his own golfing, and avoided photographers when he did indulge the sport — he did not want to be compared with grandfatherly Eisenhower at this retirement sport. The putting green on the White House lawn, Ike's spike marks on the Oval Office floor, became objects of ridicule. Yet, away from cameras, Kennedy drove golf balls toward the Washington Monument, and bet "Red" Fay he could not send a drive over the Ellipse fence.

Many of Kennedy's initial moves were planned to provide dramatic contrast with his predecessor's style. No more Fred Waring. No more "Hottentot" taste in the arts. Sorensen's book reveals that the inaugural address was expressly framed to dramatize this difference:

> Few will forget the striking contrast presented by the outgoing and incoming Presidents. One was the likable, dedicated product of the rural Midwest and the Military Academy. The other was the urbane product of the urban East. Both had spent their entire adult careers in the service of their country, yet they were vastly different, not only in age, religion and political philosophy, but in their views of politics as a profession and the Presidency as power. Every eye watched them take their places, the oldest man ever to serve in the office of the Presidency and the youngest man ever elected to it. . . . Their contrast lent added meaning to the phrase: "Let the word go forth from this time and place, to friend and foe alike, that the torch has been passed to a new generation of Americans. . . ."

Sorensen's book breaks off the quote there. But his text, read on that day, continued: "born in this century. . . ." Eisenhower was born in 1890.

Kennedy's task, according to his followers, was to combat the national enervation caused by Eisenhower. If the country had to get "moving again," it was because Eisenhower had brought it to such a total standstill. In this view, presidential style not only establishes an agenda for politics but determines the tone of national life. The image projected by the President becomes the country's self-image, sets the expectations to which it lives up or down. This was the reading of history that made style equal substance; and the Kennedy transition seemed to confirm the reading. If Kennedy could suddenly energize the press, the academy, and the arts, it was because

Eisenhower had previously narcotized them. Only the vigor projected by a President can animate the citizenry.

The canonical first statement of this thesis was Mailer's *Esquire* article on Kennedy as a true hero come to rescue us from Eisenhower
"the anti-hero, the regulator." Arthur Schlesinger quotes that article
with approval in his history of the Kennedy administration. Mailer
had grasped the essential point, according to Schlesinger — that
Kennedy's style was changing the very national identity, freeing the
country from its past (boring) self: "There can be no doubt that
Kennedy's magic was not alone that of wealth and youth and good
looks, or even of all these things joined to intelligence and will. It
was, more than this, the hope that he could redeem American politics by releasing American life from its various bondages to orthodoxy." For Mailer, Kennedy was ending the era of the small town.
Like Sorensen, he saw the contrast with Eisenhower in terms of a
new urbanity:

> The need of the city is to accelerate growth; the pride of the small
> town is to retard it. But since America has been passing through a
> period of enormous expansion since the war, the double-four years
> of Dwight Eisenhower could not retard the expansion, it could
> only denude it of color, character, and the development of novelty.
> The small-town mind is rooted — it is rooted in the small town —
> and when it attempts to direct history the results are disastrously
> colorless because the instrument of world power which is used by
> the small-town mind is the committee. Committees do not create,
> they merely proliferate, and the incredible dullness wreaked upon
> the American landscape in Eisenhower's eight years has been the tri-
> umph of the corporation.

Electing Kennedy would be an adventure, an existential act, re-
minding us that "violence was locked with creativity, and adventure
was the secret of love." We would at last shake off the Eisenhower
spell, the deadening "benevolence without leadership" that had
made the nation sluggish — its architecture empty, its manners sexless, its goals tame: "The life of politics and the life of myth had di-
verged too far, and the energies of the people one knew everywhere
had slowed down."

The cultural revolution Mailer anticipated was, in fact, accomplished, according to President Kennedy's biographers. Yet what was this declaration of the new freedom but an abject profession of servility to the one man — whatever man — sitting in the White House? The apparent compliment to the life of the mind was in fact a profound insult. Those who could only act free with a Kennedy to inspire them confessed that they had been cowed by the mere presence of Eisenhower in the Oval Office.

What, after all, in Ike's avuncular image automatically turned off thought? On the night he was elected, did his stealthy minions, some guardian angels of boredom, slip into newspaper rooms and faculty offices, to stuff invisible pillows in the typewriters? Did they proscribe the reading of philosophy? If so, how was the proscription enforced? Did a painter wake up, late one November morning in 1952, and decide he must pack his brushes away for at least four years? Conversely, did Kennedy's election make a philosopher wake up, look at his morning paper, and say, "At last I can start thinking again?"

Put this way, it seems an absurd claim. Yet that is what Schlesinger and others believed. The appearance of Pablo Casals in the White House became for them a signal that America had adopted art as a national purpose, even as part of the Cold War: "I would hope that we will not leave it to the Soviet Union to uncover the Van Cliburns of the future," Schlesinger wrote. Poor dumb Eisenhower — he not only lost Cuba; he lost Cliburn. He created the pianist gap.

What was the political meaning of Casals (rather than Waring) in the White House? It provided John Kennedy his first opportunity to hear the cellist — and late education is better than none; though there is no evidence that the evening made Kennedy give up his show tunes for Bach. Did Casals need the boost? Hardly. Some of the Harvard faculty types coming to Washington had, no doubt, listened to Casals before; those who had not were as little likely as Kennedy himself to become addicted after this one exposure. Did the "unwashed" make a run for Casals records? If they did, the fad can hardly have lasted very long. Those who listen to Casals because the President endured one night of him will soon, I would bet, backslide in Fred Waring's direction.

What was the result of that fabled night, then? The ones who got most benefit were those who had listened to Casals all along. He did not play better, after that, or Bach sound better; but these listeners felt better — felt bigger. They had been endorsed. Listening to Bach received a presidential seal of approval. The obverse of this is that these people felt smaller under Eisenhower. Their Bach did not have that extra ingredient which can make all the difference — the President was not noticing the listeners as they listened.

This view of things gives to the President a stunning power — to bestow or withhold pleasure in Bach. But he can do this only if those craving for presidential approval have debilitated themselves — have given a ridiculous importance to their own pose as Listeners. David Halberstam argues that "the best and the brightest" were self-corrupting in their confidence — in their assurance that rational gifts and expertise and toughness can set the world straight. But there was a deep sense of social and cultural inferiority under the tough outer whir of analysis and blur of activity. These best and the brightest felt intimidated by the suspicion that Americans consider art and culture "sissy stuff." Yet here was a war-hero President saying it was all right to listen to Bach, to like art and French wines. The embarrassing gush of gratitude for this largesse infects Schlesinger's and Sorensen's books as much as Manchester's. The gratitude is expressed with varying degrees of sophistication, but it is essentially the same in all three men.

Blessed with the approval of this macho President, the cultural monitors would prove that he was not mistaken, that they were not sissies, by taking on Kennedy's own worldly and fast-living air. They would wink at his secret parties in the White House and think that the proper underside of aristocratic graces. The results of this in policy were a "frontier" love of guerrilla boldness, a contempt for dithering Adlai Stevenson and courtly Dean Rusk and moralizing Chester Bowles. Style meant that the President — and those who now dressed like him and spoke like him — did not want to be bored. They talked in wisecracks; wrote witty verse at cabinet meetings; used the code of a superior set. According to Harris Wofford, this style forbade the raising of some questions, the expression of "square" inhibitions, of "preachy" concerns. Chester Bowles was resented for having been right about the Bay of Pigs; but he was exiled from the State Department, not because he was right, but because he was dull. It was every man's duty, around Kennedy, to sound brilliant.

The pursuit of style as if it were substance leaches vitality from the style itself. The Kennedy rhetoric sounds flashy now; raises snickers. This is not simply a matter of passing time and changing fashions. Dr. King's sermons retain their power to move us — but of course they were overtly preachy, moral and old-fashioned. Arthur Schlesinger hailed a cultural revolution, and gave up his monumental work on the Roosevelt years to suppress a report on the Bay of Pigs project at the *New Republic,* to mislead Adlai Stevenson during the missile crisis, to browbeat William Attwood at *Look,* and (in the words of Murray Kempton) "to fall upon William Manchester in the alleys of the American Historical Association." Kennedy did not liberate the intellectuals who praised him; he subverted them. He played to all that was weakest and worst in them. It became apparent that they did not simply want a President who praised them for listening to Bach; they wanted a President who would listen to them, and they were willing to say whatever "played" with him. National purpose would compensate for private failure, would fill with public rhetoric the empty places in them where poetry should have been breeding. Men rose up from the ruins of their family to redeem their country; or preached the comity of nations because they could not abide the members of their own university department.

Benefactors of mankind may start tending to the world, at least in part, to get out of the house. But artists and academicians, writers and the privileged jounalists seem to feel a special responsibility for what goes on in Washington, a personal guilt when things go badly. They are prominent among those who make the threat that they will leave the country if so-and-so gets elected. This threat is not very terrifying, since its auditors would think it a blessing if fulfilled. And I do not personally know any intellectual who has missed a meal, or been put significantly off his feed, by the victory of an unpalatable candidate. But they undoubtedly think they should feel sad, and that the untoward election has blunted their creativity if not their appetite. One catches in faculty gossip about politicians the note of housewives wrapped up in soap operas — the note of a substitute vitality, shared artificial crises that alleviate the speaker's own problems. They may not agree on the merits of a "minimester," but they all hated Nixon. More important, they all agreed to love Prince Charming. We mainly spread havoc under Presidents we love. Camelot was the opium of the intellectuals.

Later, under the dreaded Nixon, celebrators of the New Frontier began to express misgivings about the Imperial Presidency. Schlesinger himself then traced the growth of presidential power, admitting faults in his heroes, Jackson and Roosevelt and Kennedy. But Kennedy's short time in office was not just an acceleration of prior trends. It added something new — not so much the Imperial Presidency as the Appearances Presidency. The man's very looks thrilled people like Mailer: "If the nation voted to improve its face, what an impetus might be given to the arts, to the practices, to the lives and to the imagination of the American." Kennedy was able to take the short cuts he did, command support for rash acts, because he controlled the images that controlled the professional critics of our society. They had been recruited beforehand on minor points of style. He was not Eisenhower — and that was sufficient achievement for the "eggheads" who had been mocking Eisenhower for years. Kennedy was a Steerforth who flattered and tamed the schoolboys by standing up to their master. He was their surrogate, their dream-self, what all the old second lieutenants from World War II wished they had become. Through him they escaped their humdrum lives at the typewriter, on the newspaper, in the classroom. From OSS to MLA is a rude descent.

None of this just happened, of course. Kennedy was a shrewd manipulator of his own appearance and impact. He crafted his non-Eisenhower persona expertly. He monitored reviews of it. He censored undesired impressions. He thought always in terms of public relations, and of managing the press. It was soon discovered that he kept the New York *Times* and *New Republic* from reporting the preparations of a Cuban invasion. But the way he intertwined policy and image-making was not fully revealed until 1974, when a note in Kennedy's hand was found in the Kennedy Library. Written just before the invasion, it says, "Is there a plan to brief and brainwash key press within 12 hours or so?" Those who should be brainwashed are then listed: the New York *Times,* Walter Lippmann, Marquis Childs, and Joseph Alsop. After the invasion, Kennedy sent Maxwell Taylor to brief and brainwash *Time-Life* editors on the disaster. The

President sent a covering letter to Henry Luce asking that the meeting be kept secret. The President said he must "emphasize the need for keeping the fact that this discussion has even taken place completely in the bosom of your official family." He claimed to be giving the editors more information than Congress had received, and that favor should be repaid.

Kennedy was admired by liberals for his nonsentimental realism. He always said ADA types made him uncomfortable. He was "beyond ideology." This calculating approach thrilled the ideologues themselves. Schlesinger said it best: his coolness *was* a new frontier. But few intellectuals saw the contempt mixed with his coolness when it came to manipulating them. When Kennedy suggested that Walter Lippmann be offered an ambassadorship, Schlesinger replied that he might do the administration more good as a columnist. Kennedy worked always to turn journalists into unofficial spokesmen for his administration, and he succeeded with a great many of them. They were there to help him arrange reality, to make style become substance, to define power as the contriving of appearances.

But Kennedy could not have shaped his dazzling facade of style unless he had a genuine feel for many of its components. He liked the kind of glamour he was now in a position to dispense. The largely imaginary English society he had read about was his to "recreate," given all the resources of the White House. The very thinness of his grasp upon Regency England helped him enact a simulacrum of it, without regard for recalcitrant historical particulars. His imagined England was a world of playboy-statesmen, and America's more purchasable intellectuals wanted nothing better. They lined up to celebrate the second coming of a secondhand Lord Melbourne.

12

The Prisoner of Image

Arm, arm, my name!
— SHAKESPEARE, *Richard II*

ROGER MUDD WAS A REGULAR GUEST at Kennedy house parties. Robert Kennedy filmed a relaxed interview with Mudd in the 1968 campaign. It seeemed inevitable that Mudd would interview Edward Kennedy if he ran for President. But Kennedy tried to put it off. All through the summer of 1979, he had been feeding speculation while dodging questions on his future. He hoped to keep the matter buttoned up until October 20, when he had to appear with President Carter at the dedication of the Kennedy Library. But Tom Southwick, his young press secretary, thought it best to get the (presumably sympathetic) session with Mudd out of the way before a heavy schedule of actual campaigning began. On September 29, Mudd was in Hyannis Port to tape what Kennedy thought would be a genial discussion of the nation's plight. Still not an announced candidate, Kennedy planned to repeat his offered-in-sadness strictures on President Carter's competence.

But Mudd, like many reporters who had been close to the Kennedys, had to prove he was not their minion. Edward must submit to the scrutiny his elders evaded. The very charm of John Kennedy, the intensity of Robert, worked against Edward. Their success at contriving appearances now put journalists on guard, made them adopt a compensatory harshness. Defenders of Richard Nixon rightly complained that their man received a ferocious coverage from which Kennedys had largely been exempt. After Watergate, it was a point of pride for journalists to exhibit omnidirectional skepticism.

And so, as Burton Hersh says, "Mudd set Kennedy up." He bore in with personal questions. What was the state of his marriage? Why did he need so many advisers to help him tell the story of Chappaquiddick? What of reports linking him with other women? How does he differ from his brothers? Why did he say he looked at a clock in the car, after fetching Gargan, when there was no clock in the car? Mudd even took on a dramatic role to ask one question in the most offensive manner: "What happens, Senator, if some heckler stands up at a rally, a Kennedy rally, and says, you know, in the loud voice, red-faced, he's angry at you, and he says, 'Kennedy, you know you were drinking, you lied, and you covered up.' What — what are you going to tell him in a situation like that?"

Kennedy was clearly disconcerted at being heckled in his own home by a man he thought his friend. With the cameras turning, he stumbled backward, verbally off-balance and finding no firm ground beneath him. Even when Mudd returned to questions Kennedy had been expecting, he was disoriented, still, and inarticulate:

> MUDD: What would you do different from Carter?
> KENNEDY: Well, in which particular areas?
> MUDD: Well, just take the — the question of — of leadership.
> KENNEDY: Well, it's a — on — on what — on — you know, you have to come to grips with the — the different issues that we're — we're facing. I mean, we can — we have to deal with each of the various questions that we're — we're talking about, whether it's in the questions of the economy, whether it's in — in the areas of energy.

Mudd's editing and later commentary were deftly hostile: they made Kennedy look even more dithery, as his weak answers were distributed throughout the hour show. In his added remarks Mudd said Kennedy's marriage existed "only on selected occasions," and called the Senator a "captive of his bushy-tailed staff." Mudd used shots of the Chappaquiddick scene to back up this judgment: "It is now obvious that Kennedy and his advisers plan to volunteer nothing more on Chappaquiddick, or make any attempt to clear away the lingering contradictions."

All the images of the past were there — the compound at Hyannis Port, scenes of the family clustering around its matriarch, a Kennedy on the hustings, shots of the crowd — but here they were arranged as in a nightmare-reversal of the old iconography of Kennedy brains and bravery. The brothers had lived by expert contriving of appearances; but their survivor was being dismantled, aspect by aspect, in terms of the old impressions. Kennedys were by definition bright and glib — but this one stammered incoherently. Kennedys were tough and took the initiative — but this one collapsed under questioning. Kennedys used TV to create desired impressions — but this one was being destroyed by TV, before our eyes.

Not quite before our eyes, though. CBS, defying Kennedy's wishes, ran the documentary three days before he announced his campaign; but did it on the same night that a rival network ran the movie *Jaws*. The audience for Mudd's show was small; but even that became a disadvantage for Kennedy. Various journalists had received a transcript of the show, and leaked it ahead of schedule, most of them to ridicule it in print. It would have been better for people to see Kennedy than to read the excerpts treated, later, with derision by those who had been friendly to the Kennedys, people like Jimmy Breslin and Mary McGrory. Rambling sentences, spoken, get tied together by inflections, by the tonal trajectory of a thought. Even John Kennedy's expert performance at press conferences left behind a printed record of incomplete, interrupted, circumlocutious answers. For that matter, Mudd was less than word-perfect in *his* performance. One question read in its entirety: "You were not aware — did not — you did not figure that the — that the main road . . ." Asked what, precisely, he wanted to know about Chappaquiddick, Mudd had at first no specific question to offer, then fumbled his way into one: "When you came back to the cottage, after your car had left the bridge, and you got Mr. Markham and Mr. Gargan to go with you, you noticed that the time was approximately 2:15 — 2:20, 12:15 . . ." These things are less noticeable as conversation weaves them into inflected continuities; but Kennedy did not get the benefit of that fact as his more garbled answers were reprinted and made fun of in column after column.

Kennedy not only looked bad in his own right; he was made to look even worse by contrast with exaggerated memories of his brothers' wit and verbal presence of mind. And he was clearly not in charge of the *way* he was portrayed. President Kennedy managed to appear where and how he liked on television. He used the medium; it did not use him. He once rebuked his brother Robert for bringing in a camera crew without preparing him; sent Kenneth O'Donnell to view the film; decided it was not flattering; and had the network kill it. The Kennedy skill at charming or coercing reporters had developed early — John Kennedy had a reference to his father's anti-Semitism taken out of the Dinneen biography. At the Justice Department, Robert Kennedy's agents investigated Victor Lasky for publishing an unfavorable book about his brother. Jacqueline Kennedy was as concerned with the proper control of journalists as any of the family she married into. When the White House staff was sworn to secrecy about its years of service, Maude Shaw had been overlooked. Perhaps, as a British nanny, she was considered discreet by type; or, as a noncitizen, less easily bound to silence. When she published an adoring memoir of her time in the White House, Mrs. Kennedy deeply resented it — perhaps for revealing that she, Maude, had been the first to tell Caroline about her father's death. Mrs. Kennedy asked that this detail be removed from Manchester's book — which shows that she was not merely concerned with accuracy, but with making sure that she was seen in the best light. Mrs. Kennedy was also bitter about "Red" Fay's harmless and playful memoir, perhaps because he mentioned the gossip about rifts in the Kennedy marriage:

> A marriage between a beautiful, enamored young lady and a worldly public figure in his mid-thirties is not as simple a matter as the union of a teen-age boy with the girl next door. . . . There is no question that the demands of public life placed an unusual strain on the marriage of these two bright, attractive young people. Gossip mongers wanted to interpret the slightest deviation from what "newly married Town Square U.S.A." would do as a telltale sign of unrest. . . . With Jack's candidacy for the Democratic nomination now widely recognized, there were persistent idle rumors that Jack and Jacqueline were suffering marital differences.

It was not enough to deny such rumors; one had to pretend they did not exist, erase them from the record entirely.

Edward Kennedy was always the least manipulative of the Kennedy brothers, the most candid and outgoing, the one little given to posing or appearances. When Senator John Kennedy underwent back surgery, he used this moment of apparent weakness to project an image of strength — he was writing a book flat on his back, turning adversity into opportunity. When Senator Edward Kennedy had back surgery following his plane crash, he asked the family's academic courtiers to give him a seminar on political and economic matters. He was not the teacher, but still a pupil. The tame professors came, and performed; but the contrast with Sorensen's use of such men during John's illness was striking.

Eventually, of course, Edward had to come out with his own campaign books; but he simply went through the motions. His brothers planned books to support their political careers in multiple ways. John's theme of courage prompted most reviewers to remind their audience of the author's war record; his concentration on the Senate made him a candidate for the next profile in courage. Robert's *The Enemy Within* gave a "law and order" justification to the author's reputed ruthlessness — people want cops to be tough. That newspapers noticed these books helped their authors. But it has been largely a blessing for Edward that few can remember his books.

In 1968, just after Robert published a collection of speeches to help his campaign (*To Seek a Newer World*), Edward came out with his own collection, *Decisions for a Decade*. It was foolish to publish similar volumes so close together, since the younger brother had to be careful not to outshine the older. Beyond that, however, he succeeded in embarrassing them both by demonstrating that they used the same speechwriters (or writers who cribbed from each other). Peter Lucas, in *The Reporter,* listed eight interchangeable passages from the two books.

Here, for instance, is Robert: "One Latin American President told me succinctly: 'If you want a government that says always "yes, yes, yes," you will soon have to deal with a government that says "no, no, no." ' "

And Edward: "As a Latin American president once said to an American official: 'If you demand a government which says "yes, yes, yes," you may finally get one that says "no, no, no." ' "

Or Robert on local government: "To meet the problem, Jefferson urged the division of the nation, within each state and community, into what he called 'republics of the wards.' "

And Edward: "What we need, in a favorite phrase of Thomas Jefferson, is to 'divide the counties into wards,' creating small units of government." And so on.

The younger brother's lackluster performance may have been expected while older brothers were still around to shine, to get first crack at the best writers, at their brightest phrases. But even after the death of both brothers, on the eve of his own first run for President, Edward issued a book more damaging than helpful to him. *Our Day and Generation* (1979) is a collection of rhetorical snippets from Kennedy speeches interspersed with "family of man" pictures, visual and verbal clichés juxtaposed within wide margins as if to emphasize the poverty of thought.

Naturally, the tame professors paid homage. But this time they gave the game away. Henry Steele Commager took blame for assembling the book, and pretended in the introduction to derive "a consistent philosophy" from the tags and campaign sentences he calls "observations and admonitions." Then, to complete the humiliation of attendants, Archibald MacLeish contributed a foreword that claims more can be learned from these Kennedy "papers" than from "professional pollsters or propagandists."

Trying to use the Kennedy image, Edward has constantly been undone by it. Tricks that worked twice all seem to fail on the third try. Dramatic touches from the older brothers' repertoire become mere bathos when Edward invokes them.

Roger Mudd, in his TV interview, made a sardonic reference to Kennedy's Chappaquiddick speech, forcing the Senator to renounce one of its weepier claims:

> MUDD: Senator, when you gave your television — televised speech after Chappaquiddick, you mentioned thinking that there was some awful curse that was hanging over the Kennedy family. Do you still think that?
>
> KENNEDY: Well, I don't — I don't think so any more. I mean, there were a sudden series of circumstances which happened in fairly rapid sequence at that time, which I think probably helped me to reach that — that observation. In the period of the last ten years, I — I think life has been — been much more probably nor-

mal in — by general standards, and it's been — been able to reach a
sense of — of perspective of life on it, which I — I wouldn't say
that that viewpoint is — is mine any — any longer.

This last of the glamorous Kennedys, pleading to be treated as "normal," has traveled far from the memories of Camelot.

The worst blow came when commentators like John Chancellor
compared the Chappaquiddick talk to Nixon's Checkers speech.
That had always been a symbol, for Kennedy admirers, of the contrast between their man and the Republican he defeated. Nixon had
"no class," as John Kennedy put it; no taste, no sense of style. He
crawled and whined his way back onto the ticket with Eisenhower in
1952, making an emotional appeal to the public to let him run despite rumors about a "slush fund." He invoked his dog. Now it was
a Kennedy's turn to plead that constituents would keep him in the
Senate. He invoked his curse. *Life* magazine treated Kennedy as a
bumbling contriver of appearances, one who not only did not contrive what he wanted, but was caught trying to: "He was simply
hustling heartstrings, using words, cashing in on the family credibility." John Chancellor said that Nixon at least had the excuse of a
presidential campaign's pressures — an excuse Kennedy lacked. It is
the ultimate betrayal of Kennedy appearances to come off second
best to Richard Nixon. Theodore Sorensen, the verbal cosmetician,
labored hard on the hopeless assignment Edward gave him. But
everything he did just made things worse. Quoting himself, Sorensen had Edward recite the closing paragraph of *Profiles in Courage.*
Life observed: "There was also some decidedly awkward talk of morality and courage, including an eloquent passage from his brother's
book, which Teddy recited as though oblivious to the way the
meaning rebuked him."

Each time he evokes his brothers, he seems to dwindle beside the
shadowy evocations. Yet he must go on evoking them. He is a prisoner of his brothers' charm, which he must trade in even as he seems
to cheapen it. It was regard for the family name, and a sense of the
family power, that made him seek Kennedys first, not the police, at
Chappaquiddick. And it was that very delay that made him, and the
family, look so bad. And having relied on the image while trying to
preserve it, he had to keep using it to rescue him from the trap it had

led him into. All the ghosts had to be summoned now. Only if people were bowing to the ghosts could he hope to slip by the constable. He was using the Kennedy name, but using it up. The Kennedy loyalists came and served, but they looked ridiculous doing it — like the professors who bowed to his speechwriters' platitudes. Other people gave in, one more time, to the Kennedy influence; but grumbled as they did so. The whole point of being a Kennedy was, in the father's scheme of things, to look good. But now being a Kennedy meant looking bad, and making others look bad, even as the Kennedy name won a series of dim little victories over minor officials. At least seven people had to be distracted by what remained of the Kennedy dazzle:

1. Edgartown Police Chief Dominick Arena, watching the recovery of Ms. Kopechne's body, was told that Senator Kennedy wanted him back at the police station. Arena did not have Kennedy brought to him, to the radio car which was the sole communications center of his police force. He left the car with the divers, crossed on the ferry, and heard Kennedy's admission of involvement. He asked for a statement, and left the Senator alone with Gargan to confect it. Gargan took down the minimal statement. Arena then typed it; Kennedy was not even asked to sign it. Arena demanded no expansion on the statement, and therefore did not learn about others on the island — which meant that the partygoers slipped away, to be asked no official questions for six months. Then Arena let the body be removed without an autopsy. He did not cite Kennedy for leaving the scene of an accident until pressured by journalists' questioning. He felt obliged to be cooperative, even to the point of personal risk, when dealing with a Kennedy. "I've been so cooperative that they're going to put me on the stand and make a jackass of me."

2. Dr. Donald Mills, the substitute medical examiner, did not give the body an external observation. He did not turn it over. He pulled down Ms. Kopechne's slacks only far enough to feel her "tummy" (his word). He sent the body to the mortuary expecting an autopsy, but was flustered into signing a release when a man came to him speaking for Senator Kennedy. "I was almost pushed to the point of irrationality and blackout as I did my best to answer the barrage of questions." The doctor's reward for being impressed by "the Kennedy man" (as he called Dun Gifford) was, he later said, to

live with accusations that he had been bought by Kennedy money. The power of the Kennedys is precisely that they do not need to buy deference.

3. Dukes County Special Prosecutor Walter Steele led reporters away from any gossip about the party, and carpentered the minor charge which Kennedy plea-bargained with Steele's support.

4. District Attorney Edmund Dinis kept the case away from the Grand Jury as long as possible. Dinis asked for a Pennsylvania court to exhume the body for an autopsy, but had too little information to support his request. Three months after the accident, he had not talked to any of the partygoers.

5. Judge Bernard C. Bronminski, who presided over the exhumation hearing in Pennsylvania, was facing reelection in a heavily Catholic district, and delayed his finding until after the election. Then he decided against exhumation, since fuller medical evidence might lead to "speculation" — as if slimmer evidence *reduced* ill-grounded speculation.

6. Judge Wilfred Paquet brought in a priest to pray for the Grand Jury when he addressed it, and counseled inaction.

7. Judge James Boyle put on the strangest performance. He (a) presided at the leaving-of-the-scene hearing, and volunteered that Kennedy had been punished enough, a statement that should have disqualified him from (b) presiding over the later inquest on Ms. Kopechne's death where (c) he blocked, directed, or took over the questioning process, defending Kennedy before (d) accusing Kennedy of perjury, after which, as he later admitted, (e) he was required by law to issue an arrest warrant, though (f) he didn't. Judge Boyle is the best example of the way men of independent standing react to the aura of power around a Kennedy, even while they resent or belittle that aura. It is Edward Kennedy's fate to be treated in terms of an image he is felt not to have earned. The image by which he is judged may have been false or hollow from the outset; but that does not help him. If for no other purpose, it remains valid for one — to tie his actions to stylistic claims he can neither fully embody nor entirely relinquish.

IV

CHARISMA

What a strange Nemesis lurks in the felicities of men! In thy mouth it shall be sweet as honey, in thy belly it shall be bitter as gall! Some weakly organized individual, we will say at the age of five-and-twenty, whose main or whole talent rests on some prurient susceptivity, and nothing under it but shallowness and vacuum, is clutched hold of by the general imagination, is whirled aloft to the giddy height; and taught to believe the divine-seeming message that he is a great man: such individual seems the luckiest of men: and, alas, is he not the unluckiest?

— THOMAS CARLYLE

13

Counterinsurgency at Home

Eisenhower embodied half the needs of the nation, the needs of the timid, the petrified, the sanctimonious, and the sluggish. What was even worse, he did not divide the nation as a hero might (with a dramatic dialogue as the result); he merely excluded one part of the nation from the other. The result was an alienation of the best minds and the bravest impulses from the faltering history which was made. America's need in those years was to take an existential turn, to walk into the nightmare, to face into that terrible logic of history which demanded that the country and its people must become more extraordinary and more adventurous, or else perish.

    — NORMAN MAILER, "Superman Comes to the Supermarket"

PRESIDENT EISENHOWER'S CRIME, in Norman Mailer's eyes, was a government by committee. Committees are not creative. They stifle originality, impose conformity. Eisenhower had let problems go untended in order to preserve the country's (and his own) tranquillity. An "existential" leadership would dare to go "outside channels," to confront the unexpected with a resourceful poise of improvisation.

Schlesinger and Sorensen, official historians, portray their leader as just the "existential" hero Mailer pined for. His first job was to dismantle the protective procedures Eisenhower had woven around the presidency. Kennedy wanted to be exposed, not shielded — out on the battlements, scanning all horizons, not seated in his chamber sifting documents. His ideal was the Franklin Roosevelt celebrated by Schlesinger and Burns and Neustadt. Richard Neustadt's 1960 book, *Presidential Power,* became the "hot" item of the transition. In it, Roosevelt and Eisenhower were contrasted — Roosevelt as a man free from procedural entanglements, Eisenhower as the slave of them:

> Where Roosevelt let his channels and advisers become orderly he acted out of character. With Eisenhower, seemingly, the case is quite the opposite. Apparently he had a sense of power and a source of confidence as unlike Roosevelt's as were the two men's methods. For Eisenhower the promotion of disorder was distinctly out of character. When he could not work through a set procedure, or when channels failed him, or when his associates quarreled openly, he grew either disheartened or enraged. . . . Eisenhower has been a sort of Roosevelt in reverse.

Which meant that Kennedy, to imitate Roosevelt, had to become a sort of Eisenhower in reverse.

Neustadt, who had been appointed during the 1960 campaign to prepare for the transition, turned in his first report to the candidate on his airplane:

> After a time, Archibald Cox, who was aboard, said that the Senator was ready to see him but cautioned against conversation; "he's saving his voice for Chicago." Neustadt, going back to Kennedy, handed him a bundle of memoranda and said, "You don't have to say anything — here are the memoranda — don't bother with them till after the election." One memorandum listed priority actions from election to Thanksgiving. Another dealt with cabinet posts. Another was called "Staffing the President-Elect"; sensing Kennedy's affinities, Neustadt added to this appendixes discussing Roosevelt's approach to White House staffing and to the Bureau of the Budget. Half an hour later Kennedy bounded out of his compartment in search of Neustadt. Finding him, he said, "That Roosevelt stuff is fascinating." Neustadt said, "You're not supposed to read it now." Kennedy repeated, "It's fascinating."

At his first session with Kennedy after the election, Neustadt gave him a copy of *Presidential Power* and recommended that he read chapters three and seven. Schlesinger continues: "Kennedy, almost as if surprised at the limited assignment, said, 'I will read the whole book.' When he did, he found an abundance of evidence and analysis to support his predilections toward a fluid presidency."

There would be no Sherman Adams in Kennedy's White House. The President would direct his own operation. All bottlenecks to fluidity had to be broken up. The National Security Council, for one. Under Eisenhower, this was a coordinator of information coming to the President. Kennedy meant for it to be his own arm reaching out — through, over, or around the government — to get things done. Schlesinger applauded the birth of what became the Vietnam-planning organ of government:

> Mac [Bundy] was presently engaged in dismantling the elaborate national security apparatus built up by the Eisenhower administration. . . . Richard Neustadt had taken great pleasure during the interregnum in introducing Bundy to the Eisenhower White House as the equivalent of five officers on the Eisenhower staff. Bundy promptly slaughtered committees right and left and collapsed what was left of the inherited apparatus into a compact and flexible National Security Council staff. With Walt Rostow as his deputy and Bromley Smith, a remarkable civil servant, as the NSC's secretary, he was shaping a supple instrument to meet the new President's distinctive needs.

A pattern was being set, by which the President's special teams actively took on an adversary role toward the rest of the executive branch.

Kennedy's appointments reflected his sense of priorities. Dean Rusk, a southern gentleman acclimated to Eastern Establishment ways as head of the Rockefeller Foundation, would be custodian of the State Department's traditional duties toward other countries. But McGeorge Bundy would supply the ideas on foreign policy, from his office in the White House. Schlesinger felt that Washington could pose no difficulty too great for a man who had been king of the hill in Cambridge: "Bundy possessed dazzling clarity and speed of mind — Kennedy told friends that, next to David Ormsby Gore, Bundy was the brightest man he had ever known — as well as great distinction of manner and unlimited self-confidence. I had seen him learn how to dominate the faculty of Harvard University, a throng of intelligent and temperamental men; after that training, one could hardly doubt his capacity to deal with Washington bureaucrats." It is an interesting psychological point — and typical of the time — that Schlesinger considers the enemy to be dealt with, not as hostile foreign powers, but as the bureaucracy.

Dean Rusk soon became the butt of jokes emanating from Bundy's circle of bright men at the White House. David Halberstam describes Rusk's patience during this ordeal: "He resisted the impulse to react to stories being told about him, but at times the anger and irritation would flash through. 'It isn't worth being Secretary of State,' he once told Dick Goodwin, 'if you have a Carl Kaysen at the White House.' Substitute for the name Kaysen the name Bundy." Rusk, it was said with condescension, actually liked to attend meetings. It was a point of pride at the White House not to hold meetings. Sorensen boasts: "Not one staff meeting was ever held, with or without the President." The few meetings the President had to call were shams: "He never altered his view that any meeting larger than necessary was less flexible, less secret and less hard-hitting. . . . No decisions of importance were made at Kennedy's Cabinet meetings and few subjects of importance, particularly in foreign affairs, were ever seriously discussed. The Cabinet as a body was convened largely as a symbol, to be informed, not consulted."

Kennedy's men felt they had broken the logjam caused by Eisenhower's committee approach to government. Sorensen describes his leader's attitude this way:

> He ignored Eisenhower's farewell recommendation to create a First Secretary of the Government to oversee all foreign affairs agencies. He abandoned the practice of the Cabinet's and the National Security Council's making group decisions like corporate boards of directors. He abolished the practice of White House staff meetings and weekly Cabinet meetings. He abolished the pyramid structure of the White House staff, the Assistant President–Sherman-Adams-type job, the Staff Secretary, the Cabinet Secretary, the NSC Planning Board and the Operations Coordinating Board, which imposed, in his view, needless paperwork and machinery between the President and his responsible officers. He abolished several dozen interdepartmental committees which specialized in group recommendations on outmoded problems. He paid little attention to organization charts and chains of command which diluted and distributed his authority. He was not interested in unanimous

committee recommendations which stifled alternatives to find the lowest common denominator of compromise.

The Kennedy teams lived on the move, calling signals to each other in the thick of the action — as Sorensen put it, like basketball players developing plays while the game moved on; not, like Eisenhower's people, withdrawing into football huddles after every play. In his 1963 book on Kennedy, Hugh Sidey celebrated the escape from Eisenhower: "John Kennedy, it is clear, recaptured all the power and more which Dwight Eisenhower ladled out to his Cabinet officers. In fact, Kennedy in the first weeks nearly put the Cabinet on the shelf as far as being a force in policy matters, and he rarely bothered to dust it off. His government became a government by function, not by organizational chart."

If Kennedy thought the State Department was not his to be used, but an alien thing to be tamed, he was bound to feel the same way about the Defense Department. It, after all, bore much of the blame for letting a missile gap develop. Eisenhower had won election with a promise that he would go to Korea. Kennedy had promised, in effect, that he would go to the Pentagon — and he did so in the person of Robert McNamara. A product of the Harvard Business School, McNamara had been part of a team that planned the expansion of the Air Force during World War II, a team (known as the Whiz Kids) that went intact to the Ford Motor Company after the war. McNamara had just become the president of Ford (the first one not to bear the family name) when Kennedy called him to Washington. This intellectual-as-manager would assert civilian control over a Pentagon in love with the giant implements of massive retaliation. And, having done that, he would be called on for advice in every area of government. Sorensen describes the man's extraordinary impact on the President:

> The Secretary of Defense, Robert McNamara, was clearly the star and the strong man among the newcomers in the Kennedy team. His own staff and subordinates ranked with Bob Kennedy's and Douglas Dillon's as the best in Washington and possibly in history. . . . In eleven years with Kennedy I never saw him develop admiration and personal regard for another man as quickly as he did with Robert McNamara, enabling the McNamaras to be excepted

from the general Kennedy rule of keeping official and social friendships separate.

Kennedy's successor in the presidency would be equally impressed by
McNamara's brains and discipline. For years, intelligent men re-
mained convinced that the Vietnam war could be won, because
McNamara told them so, and McNamara always delivered.

A President who treated his own executive branch as something
to be raided, prodded, or ignored was bound to deal with Congress
as an adversary. Kennedy's own lackluster performance as a Representative and Senator derived in large part from his sense that real
power lay with the executive branch (if only a non-Eisenhower
would come along to energize it). Congress was, in his mind, the
epitome of government by committee. Its principal power was to
obstruct, to "deadlock" the system (as James MacGregor Burns argued in an influential book of the period). A strong President was
needed to use all his power against the recalcitrant legislative branch.

The President early decided to take on the committee system at its
strongest node, that obstacle to all legislation, "Judge" Howard
Smith's House Rules Committee. Kennedy packed the committee,
with Speaker Sam Rayburn's help, but this was a pyrrhic victory.
Schlesinger admits: "It was a close and bitter business, and the memory of the fight laid a restraining hand on the administration's
priorities for some time to come." This assertion of power had
drained power away — something that did not fit the Neustadt conception of power; but the lesson was lost on Kennedy.

Instead, Kennedy concluded that, if outright confrontation failed,
then circumvention of the process must be relied on — executive
orders instead of legislation, extensions of authority for the team
players, isolation of the less responsive parts of government. Let the
uncooperative agencies atrophy, while a few vigorous men took on
more and more general tasks. Sorensen describes the process: "It was
largely through the President's confidence in McNamara's competence that the Department of Defense began to play a far greater role
in areas in which other agencies were concerned: civil rights, defense,
space, intelligence, paramilitary operations, foreign aid and foreign
policy in general." A small band of likeminded men, in conferences
that were "flexible, secret, and hard-hitting," might save the sluggish

democracy despite itself. This "happy band of brothers" came straight from the pages of John Buchan. Kennedy's fascination with counterinsurgency in other countries is well known. More important is the extent to which he viewed his own administration as a raid of mobile "outsiders" on the settled government of America. He had assembled a hit-and-run team to cut through enemy resistance, go outside channels, forgo meetings, subvert committees, dismantle structures. Democracies need such strong (and often secret) leadership by an enlightened few pitted against the many dullards of the bureaucracy.

Kennedy had been encouraged by his father to despise professional diplomats. As Ambassador, Joseph Kennedy mocked the "striped-pants set," and carved his way to a controversial independence in England — hoping to save his country from war, to shock those at home with the hard facts of England's demise. The tough realism of that posture, the cutting through "crap," came naturally to the man who was a loner in the business world, carrying out a series of raids, at odds with his fellow entrepreneurs' corporate routines. Both father and son believed in inspired amateurs, in the gentlemen saviors of their country.

As President, Kennedy conveyed his lack of respect for the State Department in many ways, once calling it "a bowl of jelly." Schlesinger, by 1978, had come to see some flaws in this contemptuous attitude:

> The Kennedys had a romantic view of the possibilities of diplomacy. They wanted to replace protocol-minded, striped-pants officials by reform-minded missionaries of democracy who mixed with the people, spoke the native dialects, ate the food, and involved themselves in local struggles against ignorance and want. This view had its most genial expression in the Peace Corps, its most corrupt in the mystique of counterinsurgency. The gospel of activism became the New Frontier's challenge to the cautious, painstaking, spectatorial methods of the old diplomacy.

Abroad, counterinsurgency meant that a regime like Diem's could not fight off insurgents alone; it was too mired in the past, too crippled by old compromises with the colonial power. But a team without such ties, a fresh force with clean hands, could purge and reform the administration while propping it up. It could fend off insurgents *and* alter the Vietnamese establishment. The assignment at home was not very different. In order to get the country "moving again," make it clean and tough enough to confront the Russians, crisis teams would have to save the bureaucracy from itself, take over its duties, force it to join the successful operation of the outsiders. Henry Fairlie rightly called this a vision of "guerrilla government."

That ideal gives its real meaning to a term that became popular in and around the Kennedy presidency. James David Barber claims that *charisma* was "a much pawed-over concept Kennedy brought back to clarity." But that was hardly the case. Kennedy's admirers stretched and cheapened the sociological term adopted, half a century earlier, by Max Weber. Yet there was an unnoticed justice in the application of this word to the New Frontier. Weber distinguished three kinds of authority — traditional, relying on the inertia of sacred custom; legal, based on contractual ties; and charismatic, based on the special gifts of a single ruler. Charismatic leadership is transitory — the "grace" is attached to one person, who must constantly revalidate it in action ("existentially," according to the sixties jargon). It serves, amid the collapse of order or old ways, to bind together a new effort — the embodiment of a cause in George Washington or Mao Zedong. The founders of states, or of religious orders (a favorite Weber illustration), have to exert *personal* authority, since they have no preexisting majesty of office or sanction of law to draw upon.

In Kennedy's case, personalized leadership consciously distanced itself from the "traditional" father-king role of Eisenhower and the "legal" order of bureaucratic committees. Power came from Kennedy's person, according to Schlesinger, which had to be displayed, deployed, brought to bear. His "cool" was his program, style and vigor his credentials. Kennedy's term in office was later studied as just one more stage in the development of an Imperial Presidency. But his own followers saw it as a radical break with the institutional passivity of the post-Roosevelt presidency. They were returning to the last President who had been charismatic in Weber's sense. Franklin Roosevelt, given special powers to deal with the crisis of the Depression, broke free of tradition, defied the two-term rule, took on himself the sacred mantle of war leader, and made policy by sheer personal fiat. Aspiring to a Rooseveltian presidency, Kennedy hoped, without benefit of depression or war, to assume emergency powers and assert a ruling charisma. Thus point after point in Reinhard Bendix's analysis of Weber's concept has its application to the New Frontier (a term which was itself intended to cut the new administration free of settled ways). In *Max Weber: An Intellectual Portrait*, Bendix articulates the different aspects of charismatic authority.

1. Charismatic leadership is "the product of crisis and enthusiasm"; it has an "emergency character." The pressure of danger makes followers look to the single hero who is fearless and can save them. Accounts by New Frontiersmen make it sound as if the Kennedy presidency was just one crisis-meeting after another. Some of these crises were undoubtedly posed by circumstances beyond the team's control. But there was a tendency to court new crises (e.g., the U.S. Steel confrontation) or sharpen them once they occurred (e.g., the imposition of a deadline for removing the Cuban missiles). Kennedy tried to instill a sense of crisis during his campaign by exaggerating the slim (and, it turned out, erroneous) evidence of a "missile gap" that put America in imminent danger of destruction.

Sorensen's account of the administration is gleefully crisis-oriented. He admiringly counts sixteen of them in Kennedy's first eight months as President. The atmosphere is perfectly caught by Halberstam: Kennedy bequeathed to Johnson "crisis-mentality men, men who delighted in the great international crisis because it centered the action right there in the White House — the meetings, the decisions, the tensions, the power, *they* were movers and activists, and this was what they had come to Washington for, to meet these challenges." Kennedy had come to office sounding the alarm over a missile-gap crisis — as he had sounded the alarm in 1940 over England's airplane-gap crisis at the beginning of World War II. (A. J. P. Taylor has demonstrated that the first gap was no more real than the later one.) In his inaugural address he asked the nation to welcome "the role of defending freedom at its maximum hour of danger." In his first State of the Union address he said: "Before my term has ended we shall have to test again whether a nation organized and governed such as ours can endure. The outcome is by no means certain." To convey a sense of crisis over Cuba, he risked alerting Castro to the Bay of Pigs invasion by saying, in a TV interview just before the landing: "If we don't move now, Mr. Castro may become a much greater danger than he is now." He tried to "jolt the democracy" (as his 1940 book recommended) by calling up the spectre of a civil-defense gap. Sorensen admits that Kennedy was just trying to lend urgency to the Berlin crisis: "The President's aim was to bestir a still slumbering public; and he succeeded beyond his own expectations and desire." Debate over who would be saved in the bomb shelters became hysterical, with talk of shooting neighbors who tried to crowd in. "The confusion and panic were aggravated by the Kennedy administration's lack of a comprehensive shelter program, a clear-cut shelter policy or even an authoritative voice placing the whole program in perspective." Kennedy meant to frighten people a little so they would flock toward him. Since the charismatic leader's special powers grow from special dangers, the two feed on each other. For some crises to be overcome, they must first be created.

2. "The charismatic leader is always a radical who challenges established practice by going to 'the root of the matter.' He dominates men by virtue of qualities inaccessible to others and incompatible with the rules of thought and action that govern everyday life." Many people have noticed the way Kennedy, without being radical himself, seemed to inspire a wave of radical action, from the freedom rides to the Free Speech movement. He sent out young people in the Peace Corps to be missionaries for American values; but many seemed to catch the values of the countries they went to. This was not his intent; but the very act of sending them out was radicalizing — it was adventurous, and it reflected the contemptuous attitude Kennedy's people had for older means of diplomatic suasion and propaganda. Insofar as the charismatic leader asserts an entirely personal authority, he *delegitimates* the traditional and legal authorities. Attempting to prop up the Saigon regime, Kennedy's Vietnamese ambassadors and advisers actually called its slim claims further into question. And the same was true, in less degree, of the bureaus and agencies at home. While deferring to the FBI himself, Robert Kennedy made clear to others that it could not be relied on in the protection of civil rights workers. While expressing formal regard for "Secretary Rusk" (never, even in private, was it "Dean"), the President made clear his slight regard for the State Department.

By relying on a few "generalists" Kennedy signaled the lack of authority in most branches of his own administration.

Charismatic authority is constructive only when it builds order from chaos. When it tries to supersede continuing forms of authority, it destabilizes despite itself. The more insistent became Kennedy's personal call to follow him, the less compelling was any order that did not issue directly from him. The nontransferability of such personal authority was evident in the refusal of many Kennedy followers to treat President Johnson as fully legitimate. Johnson's authority came from procedures and legal precedent, not from the personal charisma of his predecessor.

3. Charismatic leadership works through "a loose organizational structure." Criticism of Eisenhower's "structures" was endlessly repeated among Kennedy's followers. When authority flows from a *person,* that authority cannot be delegated. The magic touch must be bestowed by the ruler himself. He must go out among the people, lead the action. Everything must be referred to him, decided by him, must bear his mark, embody his style. He must be in constant touch with everything that goes on. As Hugh Sidey wrote of Kennedy: "He wanted all the lines to lead to the White House, he wanted to be the single nerve center." And when he cannot act personally, he must do so through a personal emissary created ad hoc, not through official, impersonal machinery.

4. Thus, though the organizational structure of charismatic leadership is loose, it calls up "disciples, chosen for their qualifications, who constitute a charismatic artistocracy within the wider group of followers." The power of these aristocrats does not come from their office but from their proximity to the person of the ruler. Members of his family are especially valued carriers of the charisma. The creation of "honorary Kennedys" was thus an instrument of rule, not only in the Justice Department but in the White House itself. In order to speak for the "graced" ruler one must, in some measure, *be* the ruler, be merged in his auriole. Sorensen rejoiced in being thought of as Kennedy's alter ego or second self, and many other people tried to win that distinction.

5. In economic as in other ways, charismatic leadership does not rest on settled modes, but prefers "risky financial transactions. . . . Such economic activities are worlds apart from the methodical man-

agement of a large-scale corporation, in which success depends upon professional competence and an everyday steadiness in the conduct of affairs that is incompatible with the indispensability of any individual and the sporadic character of very risky transactions." Though the nation's economy was less porous to Kennedy's guerrilla raids than was the bureaucracy, his model for political action was the jolly piratical creed of his predator father. When the Cubans captured at the Bay of Pigs needed ransom money, the Attorney General went outside governmental channels, used family charisma for remedial action. He did the same thing, as Senator, in setting up his own social program for Bedford Stuyvesant. These "raids" for political action and advantage were privately financed — like the Kennedy campaign itself, for which the elder Kennedy bought his son his very own airplane, the *Caroline*. And once in office, that son's foreign moves took on "the sporadic character of very risky transactions."

When John Kennedy reached the White House, his father retired gracefully into the background. Schlesinger and others saw in this a demonstration that all fears of his father's influence were groundless. But the father did not have to speak or be present to have an effect on the President. Joseph Kennedy had labored to create a separate world for his family, an aristocracy floating free of lesser ties, where image and power would be controllable, resources instantly mobilizable for the family's advantage. John Kennedy, by his personalization of the authority of the President, simply drew up the United States government — or as much of it as could be lifted — into that encapsulated world of charmed Kennedy power, of charisma.

14

Enjoy! Enjoy!

[Theodore White observes] his rule that there is something improper about disliking a politician.

— MURRAY KEMPTON

THE PRESIDENCY OF DWIGHT EISENHOWER was such an ordeal for
American liberals because they had been excited by the prospect of
having Adlai Stevenson in office. Stevenson first promised intellectuals the sense of belonging that they came to experience, at last,
with Kennedy. In fact, it was a profound mystery to most intellectuals that the American people had been able to reject their hero in
1952. This so disillusioned Murray Kempton that he swore never to
vote again in a presidential election. The idea that the "best man"
could win in that forum was dashed forever in the anguish of Adlai's
loss. John Kenneth Galbraith writes of that election: "It would be
hard for the young to understand not only our surprise but our
shock at the outcome . . . we learned that the natural order had come
to an end."

Richard Neustadt felt the shock, and noticed the even greater
scandal — that some *intellectuals* supported Eisenhower:

> The striking thing about our national elections in the Fifties was
> not Eisenhower's personal popularity; it was the genuine approval
> of his candidacy by informed Americans whom [sic] one might
> have supposed would know better. . . . To place him in the White
> House without losing him as hero seems both reasonable and pru-
> dent on the part of average citizens, no matter what their general

view of politics or Presidents. The same thing can be said of the
Republican professionals who managed Eisenhower's nomination
in 1952; their action appears reasonable and prudent in *their* terms.
They twice had tried a leading politician [Dewey] as their candidate; this time they wanted most of all to win. But when it comes
to journalists, and government officials, and business leaders, and
professors, who joined in the parade or urged it on, one deals with a
phenomenon decidedly less reasonable. . . . When one finds attitudes of this sort in the circle of articulate observers one wonders at
the meaning for American society.

For such people, the choice of Eisenhower over Stevenson was an affront to reason sufficient to shake one's faith in democracy. If the
people could be so manifestly wrong, maybe they were incapable of
self-government after all. McCarthyism had been scary enough — for
a while the Senator from Wisconsin had commanded majority support in the polls. But the passing sway of a demagogue could be
weathered. Eisenhower posed a more serious problem. He was not a
demagogue, in the Neustadt view of things; just a dope. But dopes,
if they last in government, may be even more serious threats to democratic values than impassioned fanatics who quickly burn themselves out. Dopes not only have personal durability; under their prolonged sway the nation can lapse into narcolepsy, let all its problems
breed in the darkness, storing up trouble.

For John Kennedy, who had taken his view of democracy from
John Buchan, the choice of Eisenhower was no mystery. He knew,
and had written in *Why England Slept,* that democracies like to take
the easy way, to avoid looking at problems until it is too late. That is
why they need strong leaders, willing to administer timely jolts to
the people as a form of therapy. But this did not fit well with an
older American liberalism, which feared power and trusted the people — the liberalism for which Adlai Stevenson spoke when he asked
that the "cup" of power pass him by. Friends of Kennedy laughed at
the mere idea of his asking to be spared the cup of power.

What Neustadt's book signified was the willingness of American
liberals to confess that the older liberalism could not cope, it must
be jettisoned. There should be an "end of ideology" in the name of
"existential" leaders — Schlesinger instanced Hemingway and
Camus — for whom "authenticity" in action was the test, a sense of

one's own will to deal with life. Neustadt's Roosevelt was seen
through such postwar filters of existential leadership. He was a manipulative man, a tough pragmatist experimenting, one who did not
go by the rules but imposed his will. There would be no more talk of
fearing power. The brave man must take up power as a joyful encounter with reality. The failure to do that was, in fact, Eisenhower's
greatest flaw:

> Eisenhower also lacked Roosevelt's enjoyment. At least until his
> seventh year the politics of power in the Presidency never was his
> sport; not recreation for him; certainly not fun. . . . What kept expe-
> rience from sharpening his sense of power and his taste for it? . . .
> He wanted to be arbiter, not master. His love was not for power but
> for duty.

The mood of the time can be seen in the fact that the very terms
Neustadt uses to criticize Eisenhower would once have been terms
of praise. And that fact becomes more interesting when we realize
that every criticism directed at Eisenhower could be doubled upon
Adlai Stevenson. Stevenson was even *less* the jolly warrior, the master
manipulator, the seizer and user of power. Truman had called him a
"Hamlet." The Kennedy people learned to despise him for wanting
things he would not openly work to win. They mistreated him and
he came back for more. In moving from Stevenson to Kennedy, liberals had not — as Eleanor Roosevelt feared — given up their principles; they had finally seen the solution to the Eisenhower problem.
They had gone back to the true sense of power exemplified by Mrs.
Roosevelt's husband.

Neustadt's was just the first in a series of books that told Presidents they must, above all else, love power and seek it with un-
bounded gusto. The theme of them all was "Enjoy! Enjoy!" Neustadt led off:

> Roosevelt's methods were the product of his insights, his incentive
> and his confidence. No President in this century has had a sharper
> sense of personal power, a sense of what it is and where it comes
> from; none has had more hunger for it, few have had more use for
> it, and only one or two could match his faith in his own compe-
> tence to use it. Perception and desire and self-confidence, combined,

produced their own reward. No modern President has been more nearly master in the White House. Roosevelt had a love affair with power in that place. It was an early romance and it lasted all his life. . . . For Roosevelt, this was fun.

From now on, having fun in the White House would be a presidential task. It was his duty not to be merely dutiful. Lack of enjoyment was of itself a disqualification for office. Vigor can emanate only from the President's own appetite for the life of power: "The more determinedly a President seeks power, the more he will be likely to bring vigor to his clerkship. As he does so he contributes to the energy of government." A long literature of common sense had taught men to suspect power and the men who thirst for it. Now that literature would be turned on its head. The man who is suspect is the one who shows any suspicion over power and its uses. The old view had been discredited in the deadening Eisenhower days: "His virtue was supposed to be that he was above politics, and disenchantment with him rarely seems a disenchantment with this odd criterion. Instead it is all Eisenhower's fault that he is not what temperament and training never equipped him to be."

Theodore White, in his first *Making of the President* volume, took up the theme of power as a beneficial intoxicant:

[Theodore and Franklin Roosevelt] not only understood the *use* of power; they knew the *enjoyment* of power, too. And that is the important thing. Whether a man is burned by power or enjoys power, whether he is trapped by responsibility or made free by it; whether he is moved by other people and outer forces or moves them — this is the essence of leadership. John F. Kennedy had known much of the quality of leadership in American life long before he became President in 1960 — the legends, delights, songs, deals and reach of power.

Needless to say, the official Kennedy literature is drearily joyful in repeating how much fun Kennedy had being President. Schlesinger sang along: "Not since Franklin Roosevelt had there been a President who so plainly delighted in innovation and leadership." Sorensen too: "John F. Kennedy was a happy president. . . . He liked the job, he thrived on its pressures.

Since it was a President's duty to seek all the power he could get, and our duty to choose men with this appetite, it was clearly our duty to relinquish the power — to be as glad that he seized it as he was in the act of seizure. He ennobled us by instilling awe for his office. Sorensen put this creation of awe among the great human achievements of all time:

> One of John Kennedy's most important contributions to the human spirit was his concept of the office of the Presidency. His philosophy of government was keyed to power, not as a matter of personal ambition but of national obligation; the primacy of the White House within the Executive Branch and of the Executive Branch within the Federal Government, the leadership of the Federal Government within the United States and of the United States within the community of nations.

The founders of this nation would have been surprised to hear that executive supremacy is a noble cause; and other nations might wonder at the elevation of American power over all other countries as a contribution to the human spirit. But I suppose we are lucky Sorensen did not make his pyramid of power — America over all, the executive over America, the President over the executive — culminate in the title he celebrated while writing Kennedy's campaign speeches: the Commander-in-Chief. During the Watergate days, Alexander Haig was mocked for telling William Ruckelshaus, in the Special Prosecutor's office, that his Commander-in-Chief had given him an order. The President is the Commander-in-Chief of the Armed Forces, not of the citizenry at large. But in his 1960 campaign Kennedy assured us that the American people yearn for leadership: "They want to know what is needed — they want to be led by the Commander-in-Chief." And the President was not only the Commander-in-Chief of all American people but of the whole free world — he must be "a man capable of acting as the Commander-in-Chief of the grand alliance." Hugh Sidey significantly called his chapter on counterinsurgent warfare in other people's countries "Commander in Chief." Needless to say, the Constitution did not set up military titles for foreigners to obey. But Kennedy-Sorensen was convinced that all the world's free people yearned for a leader who enjoyed the widest powers he could lay claim to. Thus was "the human spirit" itself vindicated.

The new awe for the presidential role rubbed off on the President's very working space:

> The whole White House crackled with excitement under John Kennedy, but the soundproof oval office, the very center and stimulant of all the action, symbolized his own peace of mind. The tall French windows opened onto the completely renovated flower garden of which he was inordinately proud. Even on gloomy days the light pouring in through those windows on the blue rug and freshly painted cream-colored walls bathed his ash splint rocking chair and two beige couches, brought in for more friendly talks, in a quiet glow.

Breathless description of that office became a set piece in post-Kennedy hymns to the presidency. In his later book, *The Kennedy Legacy,* Sorensen said that the Nixon people first began to use capital letters for the Oval Office. He forgot Theodore White's 1961 book:

> But the exercise of the President's power must be framed by reason, by the analysis of reality as it can only be seen from the President's desk — and by leading other men to see this reality as he alone perceives it. A hush, an entirely personal hush, surrounds this kind of power, and the hush is deepest in the Oval Office of the West Wing of the White House, where the President, however many his advisers, must sit alone. The Oval Office, thirty-five feet long by twenty-eight feet, four inches wide, is almost too peaceful and luminous a place to echo to the ominous concerns that weigh upon the man who occupies it. Its great French windows, eleven and a half feet high, flood it with light, so that even on somber days it is never dark. From the south windows the President can, in leafless winter, see through the trees all the way to the Washington Monument and beyond; he can, by craning, see west to the Memorial where Lincoln broods. The three windows on the east open out on the lawn, on the rose garden and the brilliance of flowers in spring and summer; when he chooses the President can enter or leave the Oval Office by one of these east windows, which opens as a door, going to or from his private dwelling place in the heart of the White House. The tones of the room are as perfect as its proportions. The

gray green expanse of carpeting, into which is woven the Great Seal
of the United States, is keyed to the same pastel tonality as the
cream-beige walls and the beige drapery. The room changes somewhat from President to President, as it has changed from Eisenhower to Kennedy. Where in Eisenhower's time the room possessed an uncluttered, almost overpowering openness as one
approached the seven-foot, four-inch dark walnut desk at which Eisenhower (as all other Presidents since 1902) sat, it has been softened now with two new curving cream-white sofas before the fire-
place that invite the visitor to a respectful closeness with the
President.

There is more — much more — of the description; pages more. It
culminates at the principal cult object within the shrine, the Presidential Telephone: "The telephone is silent — it rings with few or
no incoming messages, it quivers, generally, only as he exerts his will
through it."

Hugh Sidey, in his 1963 book on John Kennedy, called the last
chapter "The Oval Office":

> There was an awesome presence in that Oval Chamber which was
> then quiet, cool, sunlit — the very heart of this nation's meaning,
> the very core of freedom, thirty-five feet long by twenty-eight feet,
> four inches wide. To an outsider the feeling of awe is always
> there — any man who walks into that office senses it. I wondered if
> the President ever got used to it, and then I decided that he never
> does either.

Earlier Sidey had described it as "the biggest office in the world," and
in his book on President Ford he would call it "the epicenter of
power." But the prize for bedazzlement by the room goes to John
Hersey, in the book he wrote about his old Yale football coach,
Gerald Ford:

> This room was an egg of light. I had seen that each person who
> came into it was lit up in two senses: bathed in brightness and a bit
> high. I had clearly seen each face, to the very pores, in a flood of
> indirect candlepower that rained down from a pure-white ceiling
> onto the curving off-white walls and pale-yellow rug and bright

furnishings in shades of gold, green, and salmon. But there were also dazzling parabolas of power here; authority seemed to be diffused as an aspect of the artificial light in the room, and each person who came into this heady glow seemed to be rendered ever so slightly tipsy in it and by it — people familiar with the room far less so, of course, than first-time visitors, some of whom visibly goggled and staggered and held on tight as they made their appeals; but even the old hands, even the President's closest friends, and even the President himself, sitting in a bundle of light behind the desk of the chief, seemed to me to take on a barely perceptible extra shine in the ambiguous radiant energy that filled the room.

Hersey takes us on tour, as others have, but spares us the dimensions-down-to-inches. He likes the furniture, especially a grandfather clock whose "forceful ticking inexorably marked the moments of history — and of nonhistory — in this room of light." The office itself was now a superhuman dwelling place, as Theodore White made embarrassingly clear in his genuflections at the shrine: "For the laws of Congress cannot define, nor can custom anticipate, the unknown — and this is where the great Presidents must live, *observant of the law yet beyond the law, Chief Executive and High Priest of American life at once.*" (Italics added)

Charisma, in the Weberian sense, is not transferable — even to members of the "graced" leader's own family. But later Presidents would be measured by the expectations Kennedy raised. He did not so much elevate the office as cripple those who held it after him. His legend has haunted them; his light has cast them in shadow. For the cult of power launched by Neustadt continued into the seventies. The "in" book on the presidency during that decade was James David Barber's *Presidential Character* (1972); and no work better illustrates how the fads of an academician's graduate school days remain his dogmas in later life. His first scholarly work is the outgrowth of those fads, and he is inclined to defend that work against later evidence. Barber tests presidential character entirely by Neustadt's norms, and especially by the capacity to *enjoy* the exercise of power. The subchapter on Roosevelt's character is titled, "Franklin's Growth to Joy in Work." We are told that his upbringing gave him the self-confidence that led to a "hunger for results." This makes for contrast with Eisenhower and Coolidge, who are "guardians of the proper system," working through channels. Barber's Eisenhower fails, like Neustadt's, by the dutiful rather than joyful exercise of power: "Why then did Eisenhower bother to become President? Why did he answer those phone calls on the golf links [those symbolic golf links]? Because he thought he ought to. He was a sucker for duty, and he always had been. Dutiful sentiments which would sound false coming from most political leaders ring true from Eisenhower." The Coolidge-Eisenhower type is not result-oriented: "Its political weakness is its inability to produce, though it may contribute by preventing." Nonetheless the nation's "unfinished business" accumulates under this type. So: "Eventually some leader ready, to shove as well as to stand fast, someone who enjoys the great game of politics, will have to pick up the pieces."

Another leftover of the sixties was Arthur Schlesinger's claim that John Kennedy was a late developer, but one who showed great capacity for growth through experience, making him an "existential" leader who learned by doing. All these notes are struck in the Barber sections on Kennedy. The Roosevelt-Kennedy type has a "sense of the self as developing, demonstrated externally in evidence of openness, experiment, flexibility, and growth." Though Kennedy did not develop during his congressional years, his response to the Bay of Pigs and the missile crisis showed that he was capable of growth in office. "Along the way he discovered what he believed." He demonstrated "the capacity to incorporate experience." Thus "the inner confidence he had acquired as a youth freed him to grow as President, through one crisis after another, to a grasp of the full potentialities of the office." Naturally, those potentialities involved a sense of enjoyment in power, one radiated to others: "Jack left people feeling they could do better and enjoy it. . . . He found Earth an exciting place to live, and said so. His emphasis on arousing democracy to action is obvious from 'Ask not. . . .' "

Barber's addition to the Neustadt-Schlesinger cult of enjoyed power was the set of four categories he set up for "typing" modern Presidents. This was meant to be a predictive tool, though Barber's later use of it for that purpose has been wrong when not hedged. Jimmy Carter read the Barber book on the way to the presidency, and felt he could be the type implicitly praised throughout, the "active-positive" Roosevelt-Kennedy type; and Barber gave cautious support to that expectation. Jody Powell, Carter's press secretary, dutifully reported that the President enjoyed his time in the White House.

Barber does not say where he picked up his four categories. One would think his scientific claims called for methodological explicitness. But he just posits the types by fiat. True, one of the "baselines," as he calls it, was almost a given at the time he wrote:

> The second baseline is positive-negative effect toward one's activity — that is, how he feels about what he does. Relatively speaking, does he seem to experience his political life as happy or sad, enjoyable or discouraging, positive or negative in its main effect. The feeling I am after here is not grim satisfaction in a job well done, not some philosophical conclusion. The idea is this: is he someone who, on the surfaces we can see, gives forth the feeling that he has fun in political life?

At this point, presumably by some mixing of his file cards, Barber attributes to Henry Stimson the quote I gave above on page 178 from Theodore White, on the enjoyment of power as the test of a leader. Aside from that mixup, Barber's "baseline" is pure Neustadtism.

Barber might have graded all Presidents along this single line, as a continuum; in fact, he ends up doing that. But he has methodological aspirations that require the creation of separate boxes, so this baseline must be intersected at right angles with another, the "active-passive" one that grades a man on his energy or lack of it, depending on his "stance toward environment." It might seem that the two things run parallel rather than at right angles. After all, the enjoyment of power and the exercise of it are naturally concomitant; and one who dislikes it will not be active in using it. But the actual cases Barber discusses suggest that he is distinguishing self-image from reciprocal expectations of others. That is made clear in the psychobiographical episodes Barber uses — which, in turn, reveal that another sixties fad has been taken over for pseudo-scientific exploitation. Positive or negative attitude toward oneself, positive-negative attitude toward one's environment — what are they but the two basic attitudes, yielding four "life positions," of Transactional Analysis as that was popularized in Eric Berne's *Games People Play*

(1964) and Thomas Harris's *I'm OK — You're OK* (1967). Though Barber pretends not to be judgmental in ranking his four types, he clearly sees them in the order of preference set by Berne and Harris. The person who "feels good about himself and others" is the adult. The other types are deficient.

Harris's "I'm Not OK — You're OK" is the child's world, of low self-esteem and high regard for others. In Barber that becomes the active-negative presidency of Richard Nixon or Lyndon Johnson, where there is active striving to win approval, but the very striving tends to defeat its object: "Active-negative types pour energy into the political system, but it is an energy distorted from within."

Harris's "I'm Not OK — You're Not OK" is the adolescent's disillusioned state, tending toward withdrawal if not autism. This becomes Barber's passive-negative (or Coolidge-Eisenhower) type, which "does little in politics and enjoys it less" because of "low self-esteem based on a sense of uselessness." Presidents of this type tend "to withdraw, to escape from the conflict and uncertainty of politics by emphasizing vague principles (especially prohibitions) and procedural arrangements" — all those damn Eisenhower *committees.*

Harris's "I'm OK — You're Not OK" is the rebellious adolescent stage tending toward crime. Whom could Barber put here? Not Richard Nixon, who committed crimes in office — he has already been slotted as a childish "active-negative." Actually, no Presidents really fit this slot, so Barber pulls a fast one on us, tacitly redefining his norms rather than spoil the quadripartite symmetry of his scheme. He puts Taft and Harding in this category because they had "low self-esteem (on grounds of being unlovable, unattractive)." That should make them *negative* types, not positive — but he introduces a second note to keep them from slipping over to keep company with Eisenhower and Coolidge. He says they have a "superficial optimism" that somehow survives the low self-image. In other words, they have high expectation of others — which should, by parallel with the other types, put them in the active as well as the positive category! They are being forced into the mold, to keep the mold intact.

Harris's "I'm OK — You're OK" is the healthy adult world in which people joyfully take up "the wager of action." That obviously is Barber's ideal — the Roosevelt-Kennedy "active-positive" presidency combining "high self-esteem and relative success in relating to the environment." The whole rickety structure was put together to give a quasi-systematic justification for the Neustadt presidency: "The man shows an orientation toward productiveness as a value and ability to use his styles flexibly, adaptively, suiting the dance to the music. He sees himself as developing over time toward relatively well defined personal goals — growing toward his image of himself as he might yet be."

What is consistent in Barber's analysis comes from the Neustadt continuum. What is inconsistent comes from the Berne-Harris categories. Even Neustadt, in a later edition of his *Presidential Power*, finds it useless to consider Johnson and Nixon along with Wilson and Hoover as exemplars of a single type: "I admire but am doubtful of a scheme that crowds these four into a single square." He would doubt more, probably, if he reflected that Barber also put John Adams in that square. The differences are so much more important than the similarities that the grid becomes distortive, even if one assumes that Barber has "correctly" assigned people by his own norms. Yet even that assumption is dubious. Barber has clearly read the biographical evidence with a bias toward "typing" people. Intimates of Dwight Eisenhower would be amused to learn he had a low self-esteem; yet that is what is called for, if he is to fit Barber's purposes, so that is what he acquires. The man condemned for being dutiful is given the duty of fitting in. He might comfort himself with the fact that he shares room in this low category with that other President who lacked self-esteem, George Washington.

All this might be dismissed as games academics play, except for the fact that Barber's book was taken fully as seriously as Neustadt's — testimony to an intellectual need for the glorification of Kennedy (and power) at the expense of both Eisenhower *and Stevenson*. What Stevenson lacked was the "balls" (in Joseph Alsop's words) to shake the nation out of Eisenhower's lethargic grip. It was not enough for Neustadt's liberals to be liberal. They had to be liberals in love with power. To suspect power was to doubt oneself; and self-doubt reduced a man to Adlai helplessness.

Barber's book is just one vivid example of the way the Kennedy appetite for power was used to grade all subsequent Presidents, none of whom has earned the "A" rating of active-positive. A contributing reason for their failure may be the very establishment of such a grading system.

15
Delegitimation

The White House is small, but if you're not at the center it seems enormous. You get the feeling that there are all sorts of meetings going on without you, all sorts of people clustered in small groups, whispering, always whispering.

— LBJ TO DORIS KEARNS

"CAMELOT" ENDED in November of 1963. But its effects were just beginning to be felt. The Kennedys have been a presence in the White House ever since, bedeviling later occupants. Charisma, the uniquely *personal* power, delegitimates *institutions*. Rule by dazzlement cannot be succeeded by mere constitutional procedure. Reinhard Bendix states the problem: "Such a transformation from charismatic leadership to traditional domination occurs most frequently when the problem of succession must be solved. In a strict sense that problem is insoluble, for charisma is an inimitable quality that some higher power is believed to have bestowed upon one person. Consequently a successor cannot be chosen at all. Instead, the followers wait in the hope that another leader will appear who will manifest his own charismatic qualification."

No sooner was President Kennedy dead than his followers began to think and speak of a restoration. Lyndon Johnson was at best an interlude, at worst a usurper — intrusive, in any case; out of the proper order of things. The loonier Left tried to involve Johnson in the assassination itself. Others more vaguely blamed Texas for the President's death, and made the Texan successor guilty by association. For some, Johnson had murdered, if nothing else, a style. For

William Manchester, it was an abomination to have a vulgarian inside that magic egg of blinding whiteness, John Kennedy's Oval Office.

Awareness of these criticisms dulled the political instincts of Lyndon Johnson. A man as large as Paul Bunyan in the Senate had been pre-shrunk in a White House where Kennedy aides snickered at him. And even when he came to power, he could take no revenge upon them. In fact, he had to woo them, ask for their help, try to maintain a continuity of authority. And the more he tried to do this, the less could he be his own uninhibited self. His salty style had to be toned down. He tried to assume an alien dignity that came across, on TV, as acute discomfort. His insecurities were exposed by this situation, as by no other. George Ball rightly observed of him, ringed by Kennedy's Rhodes Scholars, that Johnson did not suffer from the lack of a good education but from his sense of lacking a good education.

The true wound inflicted on Johnson was not that the Kennedys considered him a usurper but that they came, in time, to make him feel like one himself. The Kennedys, he complained, would never let him rule in his own right. The more he deferred to them, the more they made his White House theirs, even before he had left it. This odd personal struggle between two shadow-presidents reached its climax in 1966 when Robert Kennedy returned from a Paris meeting with peace negotiators. A garbled leak had the Senator from New York carrying on negotiations for the United States. When Kennedy visited Johnson, he was attacked for releasing such a story. "I think the leak came from someone in your State Department," Robert told the President. "It's not my State Department," Johnson thundered at him. "It's *your* State Department."

Johnson was President in name only, or President only for taking blame. All the credit for his own initiatives in civil rights or the poverty program seemed to go to the Kennedys. He was President only over things that went wrong. No wonder he confided to Doris Kearns:

> It would have been hard on me to watch Bobby march to "Hail to the Chief," but I almost wish he had become President so the country could finally see a flesh-and-blood Kennedy grappling with the

daily work of the Presidency and all the inevitable disappointments, instead of their storybook image of great heroes who, because they were dead, could make anything anyone wanted happen.

From the very moment he took office, Robert Kennedy became an obsession to him. Eric Goldman said he spent more time and energy on "the Bobby threat" than on any other matter in those early days. He relived those days for Kearns:

> Every day as I opened the papers or turned on the television, there was something about Bobby Kennedy; there was some person or group talking about what a great Vice President he'd make. Somehow it just didn't seem fair. I'd given three years of loyal service to Jack Kennedy. During all that time I'd willingly stayed in the background; I knew that it was *his* Presidency, not mine. If I disagreed with him, I did it in private, not in public. And then Kennedy was killed and I became the custodian of his will, I became the President. But none of this seemed to register with Bobby Kennedy, who acted like he was the custodian of the Kennedy dream, some kind of rightful heir to the throne. It just didn't seem fair. I'd waited for my turn. Bobby should've waited for his. But he and the Kennedy people wanted it now.

Even the Kennedy people who worked energetically for Johnson remained suspect; and if they began to express any doubts about policy, that was taken as a defection to the Kennedy government in exile. Robert McNamara prosecuted the war in Vietnam more vigorously than anyone in Johnson's administration. But when he began to sense the futility of his own efforts, he could not make a case for withdrawal to Johnson. The President saw this as a Kennedy plot. The Kennedys had got him into this war; now they would tell him to get out; and he would look the fool either way:

> McNamara's problem was that he began to feel a division in his loyalties. He had always loved and admired the Kennedys; he was more their cup of tea, but he also admired and respected the Presidency. Then, when he came to work for me, I believed he developed a deep affection for me as well, not so deep as the one he held for the Kennedys but deep enough, combined with his feelings about

the office itself, to keep him completely loyal for three long years. Then he got surrounded by Paul Warnke, Adam Yarmolinsky, and Alain Enthoven; they excited him with their brilliance, all the same cup of tea, all came to the same conclusion after old man Galbraith. Then the Kennedys began pushing him harder and harder. Every day Bobby would call up McNamara, telling him that the war was terrible and immoral and that he had to leave.

The same course of suspicion darkened Johnson's relations with McGeorge Bundy, and George Ball, and Bill Moyers. His circle of power shrank, by voluntary withdrawal or suspicious expulsion. He became a man exposed, at odds with his own government, sensing enmity everywhere.

The impact of "Camelot" on what followed was profound; but I think it has often been misunderstood, or inadequately stated, because of the trivialization of the word "charisma" during the sixties. It is said that Johnson's problem was his lack of charisma as mere glamour, mere sophisticated ease of manner; that John Kennedy had created an appetite for such points of style and Johnson could not satisfy that yearning; that the New Frontier had inflated expectations of the presidential office in a way that enabled Johnson to launch ambitious programs without having the flair to bring them off. But if we take charisma in its sociological sense, of a *personal* rule pitted against traditional and legal procedures, Johnson was forced to take up a charismatic role. He could not rest in the office he held on such tenuous terms, in a government establishment he felt disloyal to him. He tried to use his Senate skills and a few cronies to conduct his own kind of "guerrilla government," defiant of Georgetown, the press, the bureaucracy. He reverted to Texas hyperbole and a personal war waged from his ranch as much as from the White House — "Son," as he told a military aide gesturing toward his presidential helicopter at an Army camp, "they are all my helicopters." *His* war, waged almost as much against its critics at home — even those in his own government — as against the far-off shadowy enemy. The real impact of Kennedy on his successors was not so much an inflation of the office they succeeded to, but the doomed way they imitated his attempt to rule *against* the government. Inheriting a delegitimated set of procedures, they were compelled to go outside the procedures too — further delegitimating the very office they held.

This was most apparent in the administration of Richard Nixon. Narrowly defeated by Kennedy in 1960, Nixon was mesmerized by Kennedys. Even during that first race, Nixon's attacks on Kennedy seemed half-envious, never contemptuous. Murray Kempton observed at the time: "Mr. Nixon is cursed by the illusion that he is playing dirty with his betters." Like Johnson, Nixon felt compelled to mimic where he could not scorn — the Nixon inaugural address was slavishly imitative of Kennedy's more successful one. Yet he also felt an urgency to defile what he aspired to. As soon as he was in the White House, Nixon acquired a team of "gumshoes" to smear his foes. Their first assignment, during Nixon's first summer in office, was Chappaquiddick. Tony Ulascewicz's team was dispatched to Martha's Vineyard, not as law enforcement officers, but to dig up further scandal for Nixon's private use. The same team followed Kennedy, questioned his associates, planned at one point seduction of putative "girl friends" who might be blackmailed to inform against him. It was the sordid beginning to all Nixon's later "dirty tricks" — the break-ins, the name-blackenings, all that scurrying in back alleys to bring down the shining Kennedy name. Charles Colson, who knew what would please his master, had Howard Hunt forge cables that would link Kennedy directly to the assassination of Ngo Dinh Diem. (Johnson, too, dwelt at times on the gruesomely satisfying thought that Kennedy might have assassinated another ruler just before his own assassination.) Nixon was at least as obsessed with Kennedys as Johnson had been.

And, like Johnson's, Nixon's admiring resentment of the Kennedys combined with earlier grievances against "the establishment" and various aspects of Washington. Nixon's service under Eisenhower had been a demeaning one. Respectable Republicans treated the Vice-President's "low road" tactics as a homeopathic medicine against McCarthyism's deadlier poisons. Washington circles were Nixon's feared enemies long before he reached the White House. Later, his defenders would say he resorted to private teams of lawbreakers because the official lawbreakers — the FBI, the CIA — had resisted his attempts to use them. But H. R. Haldeman hired private "investigators" just after the inauguration — long before there was a chance for the bureaucracy to oppose his master. Nonetheless, it is fitting that Haldeman — and brighter observers as well, like Nicholas von Hoffmann — should think the CIA, which overthrew foreign governments, overthrew Nixon's as well. He was governing *against* the government from the outset.

Nixon's inability to trust even his own government became a kind of blessing for the nation. He was brought down by his own drive to supplement the government's illegal taps and bugs, break-ins and smear operations. He felt more embattled in office than Johnson had, a counterinsurgent President distrusted by the establishment and under siege from the counterculture. He governed from a mental foxhole, with official enemies at his back as well as hostile "kids" out front. His attitude was expressed in the odd outburst he allowed himself when Charles Manson was on trial for the cult murder of Sharon Tate and others. Speaking extemporaneously in Denver, on the way back from his summer White House, Nixon denounced the press for glamorizing a mass murder, and contrasted this with the values in a John Wayne movie he had seen the night before (*Chisum*), where Wayne took the law into his own hands and rid the community of undesirables.

To be a hired gun for good, to ride in and rescue where there is no sheriff — that is the outsider's dream. But Nixon was the appointed sheriff when he reveled in that dream. And he was not talking of a man who "got away with" murder. Manson had been apprehended, and was standing trial as Nixon spoke. (Manson's lawyers moved for a mistrial when the President called their man guilty before his conviction.) Manson would be legally convicted. But that did not seem enough for Nixon. The hatred of the lawbreakers had not been expressed vigorously or directly enough by the press. The head of lawful government publicly entertained the desire for remedies outside the law, for a press lynching — the very thing sheriffs are supposed to prevent. (Earlier that summer, Nixon had spoken well of Lieutenant Calley, another mass murderer, because he was a lyncher of sorts, not a potential lynchee.)

Nixon fascinated the press and others by his ability to reveal his fantasy life so directly. At the time he launched the Cambodian invasion, he watched the movie *Patton* several times, but not to indulge vicarious bloodthirstiness. *Patton* was not about male aggression satisfied, but about the baffling of a good man's energies — and by Eisenhower! Nixon was not bracing himself with vicarious aggression, but with shared rejection. He was stiffening his spine with the surest medicines for it — resentment of his critics, and self-pity. Even as he wheeled vast forces of destruction to their work half a world away, he was the outsider, the despised one. The loyalty of his followers, their protectiveness, came from this vulnerability of the man hastening to hurt because he had been so deeply hurt himself. Nixon's was called an Imperial Presidency; but it was a backstairs presidency. He plotted against his own throne, and brought it down. Hating John Kennedy even more than Lyndon Johnson had, he felt even less worthy of that man's oval office, and carried on a personal guerrilla campaign against the traditional and legal governments of Washington.

Gerald Ford, it is true, did not seem obsessed with the golden family. But the acting president for foreign affairs during Ford's administration, Henry Kissinger, had been rejected by his Harvard peers of Camelot, and adopted many of Nixon's devices of secret government — tapping his own underlings, leaking, manipulating the press, governing *against* the State Department from the White House and by a purely personal reign when he went over to State. He believed in "back channels," and resented the bureaucracy.

Jimmy Carter ran more openly "against Washington" than any candidate before Ronald Reagan. The Hamilton Jordan memorandum of 1972, which planned the campaign of 1976, established Carter's basic theme: "Perhaps the strongest feeling in this country today is the general distrust of government and politicians at all levels." By riding that feeling into power, Carter confirmed and amplified it, denigrating the very power he had won. Arrived at the summit, he could not let himself be contaminated by close relations with the rest of his administration. Hoping to bestow decency on the presidential office from his own store of personal integrity, he forswore the trappings of office, and asked to be thought of as President *Carter* not *President* Carter. He was insistent on his personal concern, outrunning mere obligations of place. He encouraged people to think that one could be a good man only by keeping his personal characteristics daintily aloof from the dirtied center of power.

In fashioning a charismatic countergovernment, Carter — the student of James David Barber — absorbed the State Department not only into the White House but into his own person. Anwar Sadat and Menachem Begin were invited to Camp David, where the President shuttled back and forth between them, praying with each, assuring them he loved them. The Camp David Accords were hatched in his very own nest, under his warming breast. When Carter could not go to others in person, he sent surrogates, friends who would express his esteem — Andrew Young to African nations, Rosalynn Carter to speak Spanish to Latinos, Hamilton Jordan to meet with Omar Torrijos over the Panama Canal treaties or with Sadegh Ghobtzadeh over the Iranian hostages. Like other critics of the bureaucracy, Carter tended to *add* special envoys or experts to the "useless" machinery — a new office for Alfred Kahn to cope with inflation, a special Mideast mission for Sol Linowitz. And, all the while, distrust of official Washington led to disproportionate reliance on a "Georgia Mafia" — Charles Kirbo, Bertram Lance, Hamilton Jordan, Jody Powell — whose only credentials were their proximity to Carter and their total dedication to him.

Like other charismatic leaders, Carter found crisis necessary to enhance "emergency" powers. When he sank to a record low in public opinion polls during the summer of 1979, he withdrew into a ten-day retreat at Camp David, canceling speeches and summoning spiritual as well as political leaders to meetings shrouded in mystery. When he came down from the mountain, it was to proclaim a national affliction with "malaise," a moral and spiritual "crisis of confidence," for which the solution was announced: "We simply must have faith in each other." This meant: Have faith in me to lead you out of this newly discovered darkness. Carter reached for the emphases of the "active-positive" Roosevelt type in his speech of July 15: "And above all I will act . . . I will listen and I will act."

It didn't work. The machinery for cranking up the artificial crisis was too visible. Carter's real problem was too obviously his own slippage. The polls continued unfavorable, and Kennedy entered the race. But then national trouble became a political blessing. The capture of diplomats in Iran gave Carter a real crisis, one he nurtured for months, exploiting it all through the primary season, fashioning a "Rose Garden strategy" which kept him off the campaign trail tending a crisis too dangerous to be left alone for a single minute. If this mood could have been sustained for a whole year, Carter might have been reelected on the strength of it. But as urgency was dissipated, month after month, so were Carter's powers.

Like other successors to John Kennedy, Carter fashioned his charismatic presidency as a fearful attack on the former President's family. His most significant departure from the Jordan memo of 1972 was his failure to cultivate Edward Kennedy. On the contrary, he took the occasion of a 1974 Law Day address in Georgia to upstage and alienate Kennedy. When the family heir removed himself from the 1976 race, Carter wrote to let him know this was no relief to him: "Let me say quite frankly that as one who has considered becoming a candidate myself, I've always viewed you as a formidable opponent . . . and I certainly take no pleasure from your withdrawal." During the campaign he boasted that he did not have to "kiss Kennedy's ass" in order to win. Once in office, Carter showed no favor toward one of the most powerful Senators of his own party. On the contrary, he failed to consult him, gratuitously insulted him by omission (e.g., from the first invitations to a party at the Kennedy Center for representatives of the People's Republic of China), treated with suspicion such friends of his as Joseph Califano, and made sure that the newspapers carried his boast, on the day after Kennedy announced his own health plan, that he would "whip his ass" if Kennedy ran in 1980. It would have been easy for Carter to forestall any Kennedy race that year, simply by recruiting him to his own administration's efforts early on. But he sought an opportunity for defeating Kennedy. Later Presidents have not considered themselves fully legitimate until they prove they can deal with the heir presumptive.

Perhaps Ronald Reagan has broken the Kennedy spell over the White House — he awarded the medal Congress had struck in Robert Kennedy's honor and President Carter had "sat on." Of course, Reagan won in a year when Edward Kennedy finally did run. And he was not awed by the fake-Hollywood glamour of the Kennedys — he is (as they say) "real tinsel." Also, as the last of the Roosevelt-era politicians to win the presidency, he had a very different view of Neustadt's and Schlesinger's hero. His views were formed before "Camelot" occurred. Though he has been hailed as introducing a

new politics to the White House, he is still fighting our century's
oldest electoral battle, the fight over the New Deal.

Time plays tricks on us all. Reagan as the oldest President to be
elected, and Kennedy as the youngest, will be frozen in their images,
ages apart. Yet they were born only six years from each other. If
Kennedy had lived, he would have been sixty-three when the sixty-
nine-year-old Reagan was sworn into office. It is odd to remember
now, but Kennedy was also speaking for Army Lieutenant Ronald
Reagan when, at his inauguration, he said that "the torch has been
passed to a new generation of Americans, born in this century, tem-
pered by war, disciplined by a hard and bitter peace, proud of our
ancient heritage, and unwilling to witness or permit the slow undoing of those human rights to which this nation has always been
committed, and to which we are committed today at home and
abroad." In one sense, Reagan just came to fulfill that messianic
view of America's place in the world.

With the exception of Jimmy Carter's short intrusion, America
has been ruled for nearly four decades by politicians who served in
World War II. The men who appeared in a long succession had
been rivals and contemporaries. Kennedy, Nixon, and Johnson
fought over the prize in 1960. Reagan entered the fray in 1968, just
as Johnson dropped out. After Eisenhower, our last President born
in the nineteenth century, the new generation came onstage represented by its youngest member, then its oldest — first Kennedy,
then Johnson (born three years before Reagan). Nixon (born two
years after Reagan) and Ford (Nixon's exact contemporary) preceded Carter, the exception — the first President in almost half a
century not to have seen active military duty in the war (he was still
at Annapolis when it ended).

So, even if Reagan has escaped the Kennedy obsession, it is not
surprising that he retains a fondness for the war President, Roosevelt, on whom Kennedy tried to model his performance. It has been
considered odd for a right-wing Republican, the enemy of "big government," to admire the New Deal President. But if that is strange,
it should be put beside its sister paradox, that Kennedy, who considered himself the successor to Roosevelt, was also scathing in his criticism of "the bureaucracy," of big government as a set of procedures
resisting the will of a great leader. Ronald Reagan's promise to "get

the government off the backs of the American people" is a culmination of the anti-Washington "counterinsurgent" tendency that was launched by Kennedy and continued by his rival-imitators. The puzzle in both Reagan's and Kennedy's attitude is this: How could they admire so heartily a man who, more than any other, helped create the huge bureaucracy both men expressed such contempt for?

Roosevelt presided over the two-stage "takeoff" of big government in America. The first stage, the New Deal, doubled the government's budget over a period of eight years. This is the achievement the right wing has always criticized. It does not seem bothered by a second stage, though it was more important in bureaucratic terms. After the nascent welfare state had doubled the size of government in eight years, the warfare state doubled that larger government in half the time. In both cases, the expansion responded to emergency; and in both cases it refused to go away when the emergency had been met. Roosevelt built in terms of long-term size and continuing expansion. He did not see big government as a necessary evil. If anything, the emergencies supplied an opportunity for developments desirable in themselves. Yet those who admired this man had become, by 1960, critics of the large structure that was his most lasting bequest to the nation. In the eyes of Neustadt and Kennedy, the vigor of Roosevelt's will somehow discredited the sluggish huge bodies that will had called into being. It is hard for charismatic leadership to prolong itself, even in its own most intimate products.

16

Veralltäglichung

"Don't, Boris! You are such a diplomat that it is really tiresome,"
said Natasha in a mortified voice that trembled slightly. She used
the word "diplomat," which was just then much in vogue among
the children, in the special sense they attached to it.

— *War and Peace*

FRANKLIN ROOSEVELT HIMSELF could not have been a post-
Rooseveltian President. Those who wanted to apply his techniques
to a world which those techniques had shaped were mistaking their
own and Roosevelt's historic moments. Neustadt tried to teach
Kennedy how Roosevelt had circumvented the bureaucracy. But
Roosevelt did not circumvent that apparatus; he invented it in the
first place.

Presidents since Kennedy have conceived their task as a David-
and-Goliath struggle with the vast machinery of government. Control from within of all those cogs and wheels is impossible — they
would just churn the President up. So a series of raids from the outside was called for, hit-and-run tactics, guerrilla government. But
Roosevelt had been Goliath, not David, proliferating agencies outward from him, not sending raiders against them. The initiator of
programs is not a prisoner of their past record, of precedent and procedure. He controls them by setting their goals, choosing their first
personnel, presiding over their authorization. All new systems have
energy and focus, from the very effort that brought them into being.
The dead hand of the past is not yet felt, since the new department
has no past, just a bright unindictable future.

The very pressure of events gave the early welfare state and warfare state sharp definition. Roosevelt did not have to induce a sense of crisis to get his programs accepted. The Depression was real enough; Congress begged the President for *more* bills during the busy first three months of his administration. People yearned for him to do something, anything, to meet the crisis — and the demands of that crisis, rather than any ideological program, dictated what measures were taken. Some of these were makeshift, some mistaken, some illegal; but all were aimed, supported, desired. Spontaneity and resourcefulness were given a free hand — but only to create measures soon translated into programs, with set procedures.

There was the same virtue of definition in war measures. Roosevelt was free to override not only ordinary procedures but basic rights. The public supported the most irregular means of guaranteeing national security — a secret decision like that to build nuclear weapons, or an arbitrary punishment like the imprisoning of Japanese-Americans, or unilateral fiat like the unconditional surrender demand. The Manhattan Project was a spectacular success because, in time of peril, the President could commandeer men and talent, site and materials; he could assign tasks, and cloak the whole matter in secrecy, and use the weapons without consulting the citizenry. In all these ways, war gave Roosevelt quasi-charismatic powers —powers most Americans would shudder to see granted in peacetime. After the war, the spontaneous and arbitrary yielded to settled ways again. Security procedures, for instance, may have been unfair after the war, but they were not arbitrary and secret — Congress reviewed and regularized them. If agencies called up in wartime were to justify their continued existence, they had to do so by standards different from those applied at their inception. The one great exception was the CIA, whose funding was kept unconstitutionally secret, and whose mandate had a wartime character. It is no accident that the presidential itch to use charismatic power to overthrow foreign governments, or spy on Americans, or come up with criminal weapons, found its readiest outlet in the CIA's activities.

Crisis enables the charismatic leader to launch, unchallenged, projects that must *meet* challenge in a postcrisis atmosphere. Charisma, that is, must give its own products continuity by submitting to an "everydayizing" of its claims (*Veralltäglichung* in Weber, normally translated "routinizing"). The successful routinizer of charisma solves the successor problem by presiding over the dissolution of his own unique first claim. Thus George Washington's authority was lent, in diluted and diffused manner, to the constitutional procedures he affirmed by his resignation of power. The alternative to this is a jealous retention of crisis powers when the crisis is abating. Then the charismatic leader will not surrender his reign to anyone else, nor submit to the least cutback in his authority — the course of Napoleon, of Stalin, of Mao. The problem of routinizing charisma is presented, in parable form, by the formulaic Western movie. A gunfighter is called in to handle problems too great for the doddering sheriff. If the gunfighter, having got rid of the evil gang, tries to stay on and rule the town with his gun, then getting rid of *him* becomes the problem. Nixon's extraordinary musings on the movie *Chisum* show that he conceived his own task as charismatic, not regular — as the gunfighter's, not the sheriff's. If bureaucratic "big government" gets defined, permanently, as a doddering old sheriff, then each presidential election becomes a call for some new gunfighter to face the problems "government" cannot solve.

Kennedy's successors have drifted, steadily, toward this conception of their role. But their appeal to Roosevelt as a model is unjustified. It is true that crises gave Roosevelt quasi-dictatorial power, and that dictatorship in the old Roman sense became respectable again in the thirties. A widespread disillusionment with parliamentary procedures, combined with a fear of the radical Left and with economic breakdown, led to the call for strong leaders — for Hitler and Mussolini, Franco and Salazar. This mood even gave a momentary glamour of menace to American figures like Huey Long and Father Coughlin or an Englishman like Sir Oswald Mosley. But Roosevelt's achievement, like Washington's, was to channel his own authority into programs and institutions. In that sense, Roosevelt resisted even while exercising "charisma," *re*legitimating institutions at a time when other strong leaders were *de*legitimating them. This made Roosevelt differ not only in historical moment from the Kennedy period, but even more basically from Kennedy's conception of power. Theorists of "deadlock" in the Eisenhower fifties felt that the lethargy of the public, the obstructionism of Congress, the external menace of communism made it imperative for a President to seize every margin of power available to him: he was facing so many hostile power centers that only the glad embrace of every opportunity could promise him success. No internal check upon one's appetite for power was needed; the external checks were sufficient — were *overwhelming,* in fact, unless the President became single-minded in his pursuit of power. But Roosevelt did not have this ambition of seizing power to be used against his own government. He sought power *for* that government, and set up the very agencies and departments that Neustadt and his followers resented. He created subordinate power centers, lending them his own authority. He began that process of "routinizing" crisis powers that is the long-range meaning of the New Deal. There is something perverse about the "liberal" attack on Eisenhower's bureaucracy in the nineteen-fifties, which simply revived the Republicans' first response to the New Deal.

For Max Weber, charismatic power must always yield in time, either gracefully or by violence, to the everyday order of kingship (traditional rule) or contractual "modern" government (legal rule). And if the course taken is toward *legal* rule, then it will tend, of necessity, toward bureaucracy, toward patterns of accountability, predictability, oversight, and record-keeping. By contrast with a swift and arbitrary charismatic rule, this kind of government will seem to many "inefficient." In the same way, due process in criminal law is slower than arbitrary justice. But, outside crisis circumstances, the arbitrary soon becomes indefensible. Everyday conditions call for a regularization of procedures. Reinhard Bendix breaks down Weber's concept of bureaucracy into five main notes.

1. *Continuity.* Crisis-oriented government assembles itself for the moment; and, between crises, tends to dissolve. Its actions are sporadic, ad hoc, responsive to immediate challenge, following the leader's "inspiration." A bureaucracy, by contrast, assembles itself, nine to five, every working day. Its normal arena is the normal; it resists crisis-mobilization. This is a fatal reduction if, in fact, apocalypse is just around the corner. But the opposite error is to inflate every apparent crisis into the apocalypse, to think the continuing mandate of government is, as Kennedy said at his inauguration, "the role of defending freedom in its hour of maximum danger." Kennedy's indictment of Eisenhower was that he treated the Soviet

menace as a new form of the old struggle between nations, not as a "twilight struggle" with the enemy of all freedom everywhere. Others think that was Eisenhower's best contribution to a nation he took over at the height of its McCarthyite Cold War period.

2. *Regularity.* The charismatic leader is not bound by precedent, informed by meetings, submissive to advisers. But the bureaucracy works on lines set by "what we have always done." This blunts initiative, though it lets people know, whenever they enter a program, what lies down the road for them in future years. New Deal programs like Social Security gave much of the population an "entitlement" over society's future resources, and that limits the society's freedom of maneuver. The government is tied down by long-term commitments, which check the hand of those who want to refashion government from administration to administration. But the same bonds *free* the "entitled" from uncertainty about what is owed them. Daniel Patrick Moynihan, of New York, sidling over toward Richard Nixon in 1968, attacked "big government" this way: "The next President of the United States, as I write, will not be Lyndon Johnson [who had just withdrawn from the 1968 race]. It could be George C. Wallace. How much public money would American liberals be willing to see President Wallace expend for the purposes of increasing the participation in public affairs of those elements in the population he regards as simultaneously deprived and underorganized?" But the discretionary funds of one President are severely limited — precisely the complaint of activist Presidents like Kennedy. The truly "big government" spending is on entitled programs, passed by Congress, that are hard for Presidents to cancel or curtail (a fact of life Ronald Reagan had to learn in the White House). A society becomes unwieldy to the extent that it lays itself open to lasting claims from its subjects. In that sense, "big government" is not despotic, not Big Brother free to do what it likes with the populace. It is not "innovative" to the extent that it has ceased to be arbitrary. Mere size does not make for "inefficiency." Accountability does.

3. *Delegation* of authority. Bureaucracy sets up many loci of authority relatively impervious to a single superintending will. In a bureaucratic order, large government is by definition *not* centralized government. Thus when Kennedy sent his managers out to tame the

bureaucracy, they often found the only way to assert their will was to create new programs responsive to new needs, programs that were superimposed on the old, and became a further obstruction to Kennedy's successors. Robert McNamara is the finest example of this process. Appointed to whip the military into line, he doubled the military budget in seven years, created counterinsurgency teams that drew the regular army into Vietnam, then departed from government horrified at what he had accomplished.

McNamara resembled many of Kennedy's people, and Kennedy himself, in having been formed during the war years of governmental expansion. That was a time of administrative creativity, when McNamara's planning group multiplied exponentially the production of American airplanes. But such freedom to create left a cumbrous legacy behind, an air force so large that it sought separate status and, by its very extent and expense, limited the choices for a nuclear strategy in the postwar period. By that time McNamara and his Whiz Kids had moved on to the Ford Motor Company, where, again, they were given a comparatively free hand at a time of massive postwar conversion to peacetime production. The opportunity would not easily (if ever) come again for "starting over." The responsiveness of the entire company to his hand on the tiller called up illusions of control that only McNamara's second time of Pentagon service would dispel, at great cost to him and to the nation. The man Kennedy praised for "controlling" the Pentagon at last embraced a war that controlled — and broke — him.

In other areas of government, a similar tale unfolded itself. For special reasons, Robert Kennedy could not control J. Edgar Hoover, and so he built a separate investigative and enforcement machinery at Justice, adding to the bureaucracy rather than "taming" it. The New Frontier's National Security Council became a second State Department, which clashed with the original one throughout Kennedy's and subsequent presidencies. The civil rights and poverty initiatives left behind a machinery of "affirmative action" that became a target for later critics of regulation. In all these cases, the refusal to delegate just created further centers of delegated authority. Unwilling or unable to use what was at hand, Kennedy thought he could avoid procedure by using special teams — but each special team created a whole new book of procedures. The Peace Corps, born as a brilliant improvisation, soon had to cope with rules and was mired in its own bureaucratic battles.

4. *Separation of office from the person of its holder.* The charismatic ruler must act directly on all parts of his government — or act, at the least, through surrogates who have a close personal tie with him. In a bureaucracy, by contrast, job security is defined irrespective of the particular jobholders. This involves a loss of the personal touch, a loss regretted, for instance, in the contrast between bureaucratic social services and the ministration of personal "bosses" in the city machines. But this loss is balanced by a freedom from whimsical directives not subject to appeal. A bureaucracy carries to its logical extreme the principle of "a government of laws and not of men." It would reduce even the highest officeholder to powers granted *all* Presidents. Its emphasis lies on the title: *President* Kennedy, not President *Kennedy.* The Neustadt school maintained that the presidency is only what each President makes it, that the office is defined by the man, not vice versa. This has led to the intense personalization of the institution. We talk of the Kennedy years, the Johnson era, the Nixon regime in a way that people did not think of the Coolidge era or the Wilson years. This personalization creates charismatic expectations in noncharismatic times, to be followed by inevitable disappointment.

5. *Documentary record.* The bureaucracy, in the accusatory phrase, "shuffles paper." It leaves an inky trail. Bureaucrats, according to their critics, build a record "to protect their ass." If they did not act with greater resourcefulness, it was because a *regulation* (proper number supplied here) did not admit personal initiative. This aspect of bureaucracy especially galls those who see attractive shortcuts toward an immediate goal. The awareness of always acting "on the record" limits the bargains that can be struck, the informal arrangements that break logjams. For Presidents in the Kennedy mood, the CIA became the most appealing arm of action precisely because it keeps no public record (and, in the person of Director Richard Helms, destroyed much even of the secret record).

Both Kennedy and Reagan, from their different vantage points, won applause with their attacks on governmental obstructionism and bureaucracy. Both were praised as raiders against big and unresponsive governmental structures. There is a nostalgic streak in

American history that makes its citizens want to run a large empire on the values of the small town. Even as its citizens ask for security, in the sense of guaranteed status, they hymn unconfined opportunity. The market myth makes us think that spontaneity will sort out things according to their merits, without the need for planning and regulation. The individual is supposed to forge his or her own "environment," unfettered by prior social arrangements. More and more the governmental workings of America have come to reflect the necessities of national size and ambition, while the Presidents express a romantic rejection of that machinery, a denial of the rule of necessity, a promise to escape "back" toward remembered freedoms. For Kennedy's managers, these freedoms were the take-off opportunities of a burgeoning military establishment in World War II. For Ronald Reagan, the freedoms are those of the Chamber of Commerce's imagined past, when "enterprise" built character. With both men, however, there was a business model for the resentment toward big government. Kennedy's ideal was the raider style of his freewheeling father's rise. For Reagan, it is the corporate talk of opportunity within the confines of "big business." This lends a different tone and style to the Kennedy Democrats and Reagan Republicans; but this should not hide from us how they both betray the hero they appeal to. They delegitimate government in different ways — but each way is far removed from Roosevelt's gift for legitimating government by routinizing charisma.

17

The Prisoner of Charisma

As a principle of domination, familial charisma has generic
problems of its own, especially in regard to succession. . . . In
any case, the whole meaning of charisma is changed in the
process. From a quality that authenticates and ennobles a person through his own actions, charisma becomes an attribute of
the forefathers through whose deeds a man's authority and
privileges become legitimate.

— REINHARD BENDIX

LYNDON JOHNSON THOUGHT he had a legitimacy problem with respect to Robert Kennedy. But Robert had an even more acute problem of succession. As the designated heir, he had to demonstrate
charisma in revalidating exercises, day by day. The more charismatic
have expectations become, the more difficult is the problem of succession, even within the family. For charisma cannot simply be
handed on to a successor, for the same reason that it cannot be fully
delegated to a subordinate. It is a unique power to handle crises, and
both power and crisis must be fitted to each other, repeatedly, by the
original charismatic figure — and even more urgently, against the
disappointments of substitution, by any successor.

Johnson tried to solve his legitimacy problem by developing his
own "countergovernment" of cronies, to defeat the obstruction of
Kennedy loyalists. Robert Kennedy had to move even farther out
from "everyday" government to make new charismatic claims. His
was not only a government in exile, but also a kind of revolution in
the hills, his own personal Sierra Maestra. John Kennedy had radical-

ized others inadvertently; Robert Kennedy had to keep up with the forces his brother had loosed.

Civil rights was a prime example. During the 1960 campaign Kennedy criticized the President for failing to move aggressively in this area — though Eisenhower had passed the first civil rights bill since Reconstruction, and backed up the school desegregation decision with bayonets in Arkansas. Kennedy helped free Dr. King from jail during the race, and he promised to move around congressional obstruction by executive order. He would, for instance, desegregate government housing "with the stroke of a pen." But, once in office, he delayed that move for nine months, while civil rights leaders vainly sent him pen after pen for the magic stroke. Kennedy was wooing Congress after his disabling "victory" over Judge Smith's Rules Committee.

The difference between Eisenhower and Kennedy was less one of private disposition than of the stages of black militancy. Kennedy came to office as the movement was accelerating. He asked Dr. King to call off the freedom rides; the Attorney General said protection could not be provided unless a "cooling off period" intervened. King said no, which so angered Robert Kennedy that he telephoned Harris Wofford, asking him to intervene and end the rides: "This is too much! I wonder whether they have the best interest of their country at heart. Do you know that one of them is against the atom bomb — yes, he even picketed against it in jail! The President is going abroad and this is all embarrassing him." At this point in his own development, Robert Kennedy not only identified the good of the country with his brother's reputation but with the sanctity of nuclear weapons.

Robert Kennedy also considered the Civil Rights Commission, chaired by the Reverend Theodore Hesburgh, too activist; it would cause political trouble for his brother in the South. "You're second-guessers," he told the commission. "I am the one who has to get the job done." When the commission planned hearings in Louisiana and Mississippi, Kennedy called Berl Bernhard of the staff and told him to call them off, without letting anyone know he had made the demand. "Remember you never talked to me." In all this, Robert was following the lead of his brother, who had earlier told Wofford to end the freedom rides: "Stop them! Get your friends off those buses!" The President's insensitivity to black problems astounded Wofford. When the first Peace Corps class was being sent off to foreign countries, Warren Wiggins briefed the President before he addressed the group in the Rose Garden. In that conversation Kennedy casually assumed that black people in the corps had been trained at Howard Universtiy — i.e., that young people sent out to cross cultural and national boundaries had begun their government training in segregated facilities! Kennedy also astonished Angier Biddle Duke, the head of protocol, who was disturbed at the refusal of restaurants on the highway between New York and Washington to serve UN diplomats from Africa. Kennedy's solution: "Can't you tell these African ambassadors not to drive on Route 40? It's a hell of a road — I used to drive it years ago, but why would anyone want to drive it today when you can fly? Tell these ambassadors I wouldn't think of driving from New York to Washington. Tell them to fly!"

Kennedy's encouragement of the civil rights activists was largely inadvertent, when it was not the result of good public relations work by people like Wofford. The administration tried to cancel the 1963 March on Washington; when that failed, the White House took charge of the arrangements to keep them peaceful (and screened speeches to make sure they were not too militant). The government that tried to stop the march received credit for being its sponsor.

But Robert Kennedy's slow entanglement in the civil rights cause became a serious commitment by the time of his brother's death. At first he was forced to create special squads to protect federal marshals in the South, and then to protect the two students he could not warn away from the universities of Mississippi and Alabama. (In the early stages, he was naive enough to think pro quarterback Chuck Conerly, who had starred at Ole Miss, could walk James Meredith into the university). But as he gained experience of southern justice, Kennedy's first hopes hardened into grim skepticism. He began to understand black militancy, and knew why Dr. King had been unable to call off rides and marches — he had to work to maintain his credibility with younger SNCC types becoming angrier every day. Soon Kennedy was in the same position, running to keep up with the rhetoric his brother had loosed on the nation. But Robert came to feel the bitterness himself, and was criticized for saying that he would be a rebel too if he were a black. At the outset, like his brother, he had just opposed "the system" of lawmaking and bureaucratic administration as narrow and obstructive, not as malevolent. But by the time he reached the Senate, he listened respectfully to those who hated the system because they felt it was out to kill them.

Wofford, who helped Sargent Shriver set up the Peace Corps, tells how they worked to keep the President from turning it into an anti-Communist propaganda operation. Their resistance to this heavy-handed approach (meant to disarm congressional objections to the program) finally made Kennedy tell his own policy offspring to fend for itself. At this juncture, Shriver got needed support on Capitol Hill from Vice-President Johnson, whose aide, Bill Moyers, had become a Peace Corps official. John Kennedy, the cool and pragmatic leader, used the young without sharing their passion. But Robert Kennedy was easily infected with it. The resistance of the young eventually did as much to change his views on Vietnam as did reversals on the battlefield. He sought out radical leaders in 1967 as he had cultivated black leaders five years earlier. When Jack Newfield wrote his book on Kennedy as the "existential" politician, the term was more apt than when Arthur Schlesinger used it of John Kennedy: "He defined and created himself in action, and learned almost everything from experience. . . . When his brother died, he passed through a night of dread and learned about the absurd. He had the capacity to trust his instincts and become authentic. He was always in a state of becoming."

Admittedly, this was "kid talk," of the sort Tom Hayden had used in his Port Huron Statement on "finding a meaning in life that is personally authentic." But the point is that Kennedy began to like, in some measure, this assessment of his later role. He was becoming a kind of genteel outlaw-rebel, giving a muted performance of the Abbie Hoffman claim: "The revolution is where my boots hit." Where his brother had been tailored and aloof, he became tousled, shirt-sleeved, surrounded by longhaired guitar-playing aides who were his liaison with the Haydens and Chavezes. These people were praising Kennedy for educating himself by acting. It was a code that Abbie Hoffman liked to quote from Ché Guevara: "The best way to educate oneself is to become part of the revolution."

There is nothing stranger in our recent history than the way this puritanical Catholic became, in his final months, a hero to people whose earlier heroes were Ho, Mao, Fidel, and Ché. To appreciate the reversal involved, we have to remember that Kennedy had dutifully read the works of Ho Chi Minh and Ché Guevara when his brother first took office. It was part of the "counterinsurgent" mania — know your enemy, the better to beat him with his own weapons. Later, after the Bay of Pigs, Fidel Castro became a personal obsession of Kennedy's — the man who had defied his brother, made him look ridiculous. The CIA plotted to humiliate Castro, to "unman" him with drugs or depilatories; at last, to kill him. Castro brought out every combative instinct of the Kennedys. He was a hero to the young and a charismatic leader in both the superficial and the profound sense. John Kennedy was attempting a "charismatic" but very limited raid on certain aspects of America's bureaucratic legal order. Castro was charismatic in the fullest, most authentic way — he overthrew the old regime entirely and instituted a revolutionary order based on his personal authority. His "little brother" Ché was a rebel himself, off in other countries fomenting revolution. They had an all-out dash and vigor the Kennedys could only imitate in covert or surreptitious ways.

But by the rule that you begin to resemble the enemies that haunt you, Robert Kennedy toward the end of his life was taking his brother's charismatic tendencies farther out from the center of government, flirting with language that was framed in the hills of Cuba, becoming a mini-Fidel. He could only solve the successor problem by being more deeply charismatic than his brother — not in the superficial sense, not as a Prince Charming, but in the Weberian sense, as a rebel against the system. The more he tried to become a successor to the charisma of his brother, the less likely became his inheritance of power in the legal order. He was being "radicalized" just as the country was showing its revulsion against campus disorders, war protest, and civil rights militancy. Some of Robert's admirers felt that he could win over the "longhairs" and get the blue collar vote as well in 1968. They relied on some polls that showed George Wallace supporters — of all people — speaking kindly of the "mean" kid brother. But that was a protest reaction that would wilt under the realities of electoral alignment.

Richard Nixon narrowly beat Hubert Humphrey in 1968, but

only because George Wallace and Curtis LeMay won thirteen percent of the electoral votes. The combined Nixon-Agnew–Wallace-
LeMay vote was one for silencing "the kids." The proof of that is not
only Nixon's landslide reelection of 1972 after Wallace's shooting,
but the fact that Nixon, at the peak of popular dismay over Watergate, could not be impeached for his repressive acts — not for the
mass arrests of May Day, the violations of civil rights, the illegal suppression of Black Panthers and "Weathermen." Those acts were still
too popular for House members to include them in the articles of
impeachment.

The attempt at charismatic succession within a legal order is self-
defeating, a thing Lawrence O'Brien realized when he wept that
Robert was senselessly killed because "he didn't have a chance." He
didn't have a chance, not because he lacked his brother's charisma,
but because he embodied its next stage, the only stage he could have
embodied, given his place in succession and his own fierce character.

If Robert took the charismatic protest against legal system too far
for the politics of the late sixties, his younger brother has always
seemed to err in the opposite direction. He lives easily with the
everyday. He alone of the brothers liked and worked within the Senate system. He joined the establishment; he did not make waves. He
respected his elders, deferred to the rules, worked his way up. His
whole Senate career has been an enacted rejection of the Neustadt
scorn for governmental machinery as obstructive. In fact, by 1980 he
was under attack as the last New Deal liberal, a defender of the bureaucracy his brothers derided. He represented a *Veralltäglichung* so
drastic as to mean the dissipation of charisma rather than its routini-
zation.

Yet the trappings of charisma, or residues of it, were also present.
Memories of his brothers were stirred by the accent, the gestures. He
presided over a large and talented staff, attracting people with the
promise of his future presidency. He had to reach beyond his "ordinary" status if only to solidify that status. He was such a good Senator in large part because he was perceived as on the verge of becoming something more — this won him special treatment from his
Senate peers, special attention in the press, the brightest and best
speechwriters and legislative assistants. Even if he never aspired to

the presidency, he had to keep up a shadow campaign for it, to remain powerful in the Senate.

And then, the worst thing of all, he had to use his charisma, his exemption from the rules, to defend the indefensible after Chappaquiddick. Those who rushed to protect the Kennedy legacy contained in his person (as in some unworthy vessel) made the maximum claim for charisma on a minimum of performance. At this stage, charisma degenerates to mere totemism, protecting the sacred object as an endangered relic, not rallying to it as a center of active leadership. The way people rushed to tend his person, to remove the evidence of any wrongdoing, to hurry the bodies away (his and Ms. Kopechne's, along with those of the partygoers) looks like a farcical replay of the Dallas tragedy. There, too, a frantic "saving" of the body made loyalists bunch around their fallen leader and defy the world of legal order. Surrounded by aliens, Kennedy's people ignored the hospital official who said they would break the chain of evidence if they removed the President's body. Dave Powers and Kenneth O'Donnell told Dr. Earl Rose to get out of their way. Dr. Rose was expressing the legal rejection of charisma: "There are state laws about removing bodies. You people from Washington can't make your own law." Manchester, who completely agreed with O'Donnell in this confrontation, tells the story:

> As O'Donnell and O'Brien were shouldering their way toward Rose they were stopped by Burkley and McHugh, who proposed another solution. They explained that a local justice of the peace was present. He had the power to overrule the medical examiner. Everyone waited while the judge was summoned; then he arrived and disappointed them. He could do nothing, he said. If a JP suspected homicide, it was his duty to order an autopsy. There were plenty of grounds for suspicion here, and he couldn't overlook them. *Ergo* — he guessed the procedure wouldn't take more than three hours.
>
> O'Donnell asked that an exception be made for President Kennedy.
>
> Although the din was atrocious, both he and O'Brien heard the justice of the peace say, with what they regarded as a distinctly un-

sympathetic inflection, "It's just another homicide case as far as I'm concerned."

The effect on O'Donnell was instantaneous. He uttered a swart oath recommending monogenesis. Thrusting his head forward until their noses nearly grazed, he said, "We're leaving."

The policeman beside Rose pointed to the medical examiner and the justice of the peace and told O'Brien, "These two guys say you can't go."

"One side," Larry said cuttingly. Jerking his head, Ken said, "Get the hell over. We're getting out of here. We don't give a damn what these laws say. We're not staying here three hours or three minutes." He called to Dave, who had backed Jackie into a cubicle. "We're leaving *now.*" To Kellerman he snapped, "Wheel it out!"

At this juncture, in O'Donnell's words, "It became physical — us against them." Kellerman, who hadn't even heard Ken, had begun to pull the church truck on his own, butting flesh with his shoulders; the agents and Dugger were pushing.

There could not be a more clear-cut confrontation of the legal with the charismatic order. Law, procedure, the orderly preservation of a record, these mattered to officials, who are taught to think of each case as "just another homicide" for the record's purposes. But it was unthinkable to the Kennedy people that such orders could dictate the movement of their leader's body, which had been given into their keeping to be protected from violation by the "everyday."

Dr. Rose, as it turns out, was right. All the confusions caused by an autopsy in Washington, away from the doctors who first worked on Kennedy's body, created a disorderly record rife with targets of opportunity for conspiracy theorists. A later critic like David S. Lifton quotes Dr. Rose with approval, arguing that the chain of custody over the body *was* broken, leaving discrepancies of reporting at either end of the journey. Robert Kennedy later compounded the problem by giving the Warren Commission only limited access to the autopsy photographs, taking the photos and the medical remains (including the elusive brain) into his personal custody, allowing others to see them only after five years and then by application to the Kennedy crisis-manager Burke Marshall.

Many later misunderstandings — including the whole Manchester affair — could have been avoided if the grieving Kennedy people had not taken the presidential plane back with Lyndon Johnson. One must sympathize with the shocked mourners, whose reactions showed a charismatic set of expectations. They held on to the White House as their man's personal shrine. It is impossible to imagine them acting otherwise under the pressure of their sorrow.

The charismatic protection of Edward Kennedy at Chappaquiddick was less defensible, but also understandable. To contain problems within the family, to cover up, to arrange appearances, was the instinct built into real and honorary Kennedys. They made up, in their own minds, a world within a world, a government within (and over against) the "regular" government. The weaknesses of that position did not seem obvious while Kennedy held the presidency, or even when the life had gone out of his body. The dead end of charismatic leadership within a legal order was not finally revealed until Burke Marshall came to contain, arrange, and cover up for the least charismatic of the Kennedys, the one who most wanted to be ordinary, the man to whom loose talk of charisma has been an almost unmixed bane, not a blessing. If it is hard to be an American prince, it is even harder to be an ordinary politician treated part-time as a prince.

V
POWER

It was, after all, Greeks who pioneered the writing of history as what it has so largely remained, an exercise in political ironics — an intelligible story of how men's actions produce results other than those they intended.

—J. G. A. Pocock

18
Bulldog! Bulldog!

When the reading [of the battle plan] which lasted more than an
hour was over, Langeron again brought his snuffbox to rest and,
without looking at Weyrother or at anyone in particular, began to
say how difficult it was to carry out such a plan in which the
enemy's position was assumed to be known, whereas it was perhaps not known, since the enemy was in movement.

— *War and Peace* (the eve of Austerlitz)

MANY JOKES, and some serious comments, were devoted to the Harvard presence on Kennedy's Potomac. But the first team to move
out aggressively on the New Frontier came largely from Yale. Its
captain was Richard Bissell, class of 1932 — class of 1928 at Groton,
where his best friend was Joseph Alsop. Bissell stayed at Yale for his
doctorate, and to teach economics. Two of his students were the
Bundy brothers. Two of his colleague-followers were the Rostow
brothers. Walt Rostow was a teaching assistant for one of the Bissell
courses McGeorge Bundy took. Even at that time, Bissell was an in-
novator, introducing mathematical economics to an old-fashioned
department. For special students he offered an "underground" seminar — guerrilla teaching; he gave the course pacing a small room,
overpowering his awed students.

Even President Kennedy felt some of that awe before his own
bright aides' brightest teacher. When Chester Bowles (Yale '24)
tried to recruit Bissell for the State Department, Kennedy said
no — he meant to keep Bissell at the CIA, to replace Allen Dulles as
its Director. Bissell had directed two of the most successful opera-

tions in CIA history — development of the U-2 reconnaissance plane and launching of the "spy satellite" in space. Now he was working on a plan worthy of the legendary Dulles himself; and his deputy on this project was Tracy Barnes, who had followed a year behind him at Groton and Yale. Great excitement traveled through what Peter Wyden calls "the Yale-OSS-old-boy-network connection between the holdover CIA operators and many of the incoming New Frontiersmen."

Bissell had not shared the OSS experience of Dulles and other old-timers — including Barnes, who observed Dulles directing resistance inside Hitler's Germany from the famed house in Berne, Switzerland. But Dulles, who knew of Bissell's brilliant record in running Marshall Plan programs, recruited him in 1953 to save, if that was possible, resistance-building behind the Iron Curtain. In 1947, as soon as the CIA came into existence, its covert action counterpart — euphemistically named the Office of Policy Coordination — began to drop agents, supplies, and weapons in countries occupied by Russia after the war. Frank Wisner, who had worked with Dulles during the occupation, getting German intelligence on the Russians, ran the new resistance, recruiting heavily in refugee camps, spreading American money around to make up for a late start in the intelligence game.

The massive recruiting alerted Russian agents and developed what Thomas Powers calls a whole new class of espionage entrepreneurs. The supply of money created a demand for resistance centers and proliferating governments in exile. Guerrillas equipped with American gadgets were dropped into the waiting arms of Russian agents in Albania ("killed or arrested with eerie efficiency," says Powers), the Ukraine, Georgia, Yugoslavia, Poland. One of the most promising programs was the Home Army in Poland, which sent back encouraging reports as supply drops increased. But then, in 1952, General Eisenhower was elected; so Russian intelligence officers, afraid that a Republican might believe his own party's propaganda about freeing the captive nations, revealed that they had been running the fictitious Home Army all along. Eisenhower folded the resistance-building program his first year in office.

Allen Dulles hoped something could be salvaged from the scheme. What, after all, was America to do when exiles and refugees came to them bringing information, promising contacts behind the Iron Curtain? Even if most of the agents were sent to their death, resistance networks of any sort could be a nuisance to Russia when World War III broke out (as Dulles was expecting it to), and then they might breed *true* resisters of the sort Dulles used in World War II. Dulles would like to find some scaled-back way of continuing the work for resistance centers. Bissell was brought in as an outside efficiency expert to study the program. It was Bissell's first experience with the CIA, with the dream of running far-flung governments-within-governments. While going over the records, he came upon a plan for escalating guerrilla war in Albania to the point where a full invasion could be supported from within that country. He concluded that America could never mount a secret assault halfway around the world; but the plan bears a striking resemblance to one he came up with, seven years later, for invading a country in our own hemisphere.

After finishing his report, Bissell joined the CIA and, at once, had his first experience in overthrowing a government. Frank Wisner, who ran the unsuccessful operations Bissell had been studying, made the Guatemalan coup look easy. Bissell would later use directors of its various parts to help him overthrow Castro — Tracy Barnes, for instance, and David Phillips, and E. Howard Hunt. In Guatemala, Jacobo Arbenz had been accepting Soviet support, so the CIA came up with a handpicked successor for him, one trained like other Latin American military men at Fort Leavenworth, Kansas — Colonel Carlos Castillo Armas, who was given a little army in Honduras, provided with American air cover, and hailed as Guatemala's savior from radio stations at fake exile centers. Arbenz, uncertainly supported, grounded his whole air force after one pilot defected. Listening to CIA broadcasts as a nonexistent uprising tightened around his capital city, Arbenz resigned in panic before the broken-down trucks of Castillo Armas could drive all the way to Guatemala City.

Coming soon after the 1953 coup that returned the Shah of Iran to the Peacock Throne, Guatemala bred in the CIA an illusion that it could make and unmake governments around the globe. Even the coldly efficient Bissell, who as a child made toy and imaginary trains run accurately on complex schedules, shared this exhilaration. The beauty of the coup in Guatemala was that it could be held so secret.

No great army had to be recruited; no exile communities tingled with rumors; no governments in exile competed for future leadership. The "bugs" of the resistance movement in Europe had been eliminated. An operation could be improved as it was trimmed back. Less was more. "Psywar" had replaced real war. Armies could be routed with radios expertly used. Modern technology and expertise could undo fumbling large administrations, brains defeating brawn.

These were the lessons Bissell took to heart. He ran his own major projects for the CIA — the U-2 and the spy satellite — out of his own hat. Secrecy became his passion; no other parts of the CIA itself should know what he was up to — or as few as possible. He was beginning to run a secret government within the secret government, a guerrilla intelligence force in the counterguerrilla service. Sticklers for orderly procedure — mainly Richard Helms — resented the way Bissell cut them out of his growing personal sphere. Even before Kennedy arrived on the scene, Bissell had created a proto–New Frontier operation — relying on the intelligent shortcut, on impatience with bureaucracy, on the brilliance of a few amateurs and "generalists," on contempt for company men and committees and the military.

And so the Bay of Pigs was born. Kennedy legend put this failure down to the incompetence of Kennedy's predecessor. Nothing could be farther from the truth. Neither the military nor the bureaucracy misled Kennedy into the invasion of Cuba. Bissell cut all of them out, and convinced Kennedy *because* he embodied the ideals of the new administration. Bissell was proposing just what Kennedy had dreamed of doing from the White House. Peter Wyden describes early days on the New Frontier:

> Soon Mac Bundy told [Robert] Amory that the President had said, "By gosh, I don't care what it is, but if I need some material or an idea fast, CIA is the place I have to go. The State Department takes four or five days to answer a simple yes or no." This was music to the ears of Amory and his [CIA] colleagues, and they reciprocated: "People were willing to come in at three o'clock in the morning, because they knew damn well that what they produced was read personally by the President immediately." Eisenhower's cumbersome coordinating committees were scrapped. The intelligence business was fun again. And for Bissell, in particular, the stakes

were suddenly soaring. . . . Unlike the military and the State Department, the CIA got things done without so many committees, concurrences and pyramiding delays. It did not shirk tricky, nasty jobs. It didn't bellyache and constantly say that something was too audacious or couldn't be done.

The distinctive note of the Bay of Pigs invasion was that it was a military operation run *without* the military's control, an invasion force created specially by the CIA itself, a combination of every weapon in Bissell's private arsenal — assassination of a leader, propaganda war, guerrilla uprising, and coup from outside. Its success depended on a coordination of all these things in the mind of the master train-scheduler. Later, the plan would look so crazy that people could not credit its acceptance in the first place. But it made sense to a James Bond fan.

The origins were comparatively simple. Emigrés from Cuba presented the CIA with the same set of problems and opportunities that European refugees had. Some exiles brought valuable information about the Castro regime; rumors of resistance had to be confirmed; agents planted by Castro in Miami had to be smoked out. Hotheads needed controlling — the men who wanted to rent a single fishing boat and "invade" their homeland. The wilder sort could make more trouble for America if left alone than if the CIA harnessed their energies to some larger purpose. Howard Hunt, who thought that anything opposed to Castro must be praiseworthy, regretted the CIA effort to check extremists: "Jimmy [pseudonym for an agent] charged the Cubans with being inefficient and insecure, said giving them boats and ordnance was tantamount to letting them kill themselves. I replied that much as he might be right, our policy was to help the exiles do what they thought they themselves could do. Jimmy said the exiles were needed in the training camps, not floundering around in the Florida Straits."

Bissell's job, then, was to take a situation like that which led to the inefficient resistance-building program in Europe and turn it into another Guatemala. No long buildup of internal resistance could be attempted; Castro would track agents down and kill them as the Albanians had. A short quick elimination of the whole regime was called for, using surgical tools of modern psywar. Bissell was engag-

ing Fidel Castro in a mental game of chess, a test of comparative so-
phistications. That is why the first thing Bissell asked for was propaganda experts. Radios send out the first waves of attack in a modern
war of the minds.

Since David Phillips had run the Guatemalan radios, he was called
in, during the spring of 1960, to set up a studio for bringing down
Castro. A fifty-kilowatt transmitter was rushed from Germany to
Swan Island, off Honduras, for this purpose. Forty Cubans were
trained as radio operators, twenty at Useppa Island off the Florida
coast and twenty on the plantation of Robert Alejos in Guatemala — the plantation that would become a training camp for the
invading army.

The propagandists began with great confidence, and expended sophisticated hours making the project look unsophisticated enough
to be authentic — they removed rugs from the Great Swan studio so
chairs could be heard scraping the floor, as in some crude hideout. A
Madison Avenue advertising firm was hired to produce mimeo-
graphed releases with an amateur look. While this elaborate playact-
ing went on in Phillips's Washington apartment and New York offices, Castro's own propaganda operation ridiculed the American
tricks. This was just one of the differences between the Cuban and
the Guatemalan projects, differences the CIA resolutely ignored.
Propaganda unbalanced Jacobo Arbenz because he was teetering already. Not a revolutionary, Arbenz was a reformist trying to keep his
original military backing — the arms he got from the Soviets had to
be wielded, after all, by rightist colonels in his own country. Working to placate both sides, he formed no comprehensive program or
aggressive propaganda of his own; the distrust among his own followers could be exploited. But Castro was the master of a revolutionary regime with its own propaganda strength. Phillips did not
radio his "disinforming" messages into a vacuum but into a country
with the high morale of a revolution in its moment of success,
where resistance was easily branded as treason (when genuine), or as
United States aggression (when false).

In such a situation, the American propaganda operation's only
success was in persuading itself that resistance to Castro existed on a
scale sufficient to cause an uprising with only a little encouragement
from the outside. That is always the danger with propaganda, that it

becomes at last more credible to its disseminators than to its targets. This was increasingly true of the Cuban effort, as handling the fractious exiles became more difficult. The propaganda was used to convince the refugees, though the refugees were supposed to be the operation's own source of information! Exiles and agents drifted, without realizing it, into a relationship that involved constant fooling of each other — a pattern that would be repeated, up the rungs, into the White House itself.

If Cuba was not Guatemala, Castro was even more emphatically not an Arbenz. Eisenhower approved the Guatemalan operation when he was convinced that Arbenz was weak and could easily be toppled. But the CIA put Castro in its sights precisely because he was strong; he had not only created a discipline for Cuba, but had revived the failed hopes of Latin American Communists for a wider revolution. The campaign against Cuba was personal from the outset. Castro's jaunty defiance of the United States had made him a great villain to the American public — more resented, according to the polls, than Khrushchev himself. When Howard Hunt went to Havana to scout the possibilities of a coup, he came back with one overriding recommendation: the revolution was Castro, so Castro must be removed. Hunt later chafed and fumed that his recommendation was being neglected. But it wasn't. Acting on a suggestion from Colonel J. C. King, Bissell and Barnes made their first overture to potential assassins in July of 1960. When that failed, they got Colonel Sheffield Evans to approach underworld figures as "hit men." Meanwhile, the CIA's technicians were working on strange new devices to humiliate Castro if they could not kill him — make his beard fall out or garble his speech. Sophisticated "psywar" was the magic new destroyer of the opposition's chessmen.

Allen Dulles was relying on the power of such dirty tricks when he approached Eisenhower on the subject of Cuba. In February of 1960, early in the primary season of that election year, he suggested that Castro's sugar crop be sabotaged. Eisenhower, as usual, wanted a "program" within which such isolated acts could be judged; so the CIA framed one in a matter of weeks. On March 10, the President approved a four-point program setting up a government in exile (Eisenhower's own first priority — a moderate leadership was to be found, excluding veterans of Castro's revolution *and* Batista's regime), launching a propaganda campaign (the CIA's darling scheme), encouraging internal resistance, and training guerrillas outside American territory.

This initial agreement was rich with possibilities of future misunderstanding. The CIA was counting on its own tricks to unseat Castro before the election, despite what Bissell considered Eisenhower's lack of real interest in the plan. The President would be saved despite himself. Thus longer-range planning was given low priority; it served merely as a cover for Bissell's quick-fix approach. Two bunglers were assigned the important task of forming a government in exile: Gerry Droller (known to the exiles as Frank Bender) was a German with no sympathy for Cubans, and Howard Hunt was a right-winger with no sympathy for anti-Batista reformers. Far from seeking out moderate leadership, the two men exacerbated political conflicts in the exile community, and made noises that advertised the CIA plot. By neglecting long-range aspects of the plan he had given to Eisenhower, Bissell sabotaged his own quick "surgical" kill of Fidel.

Guerrillas were sent to the Guatemalan plantation where radio operators had been trained — first fifty, then a hundred more. While the search went on for resistance centers where they could be dropped, the secret army grew and its secrecy evaporated. Political differences among the exile fighters led to greater effort at control by the Americans, with decreasing success. Finally, when mutiny broke out and split the camp in two, the CIA rounded up a dozen "troublemakers" and held them in a prison camp till after the invasion. The political side of the operation was even messier. When Miami's Cuban leaders continued their feuding, the CIA appointed its own leaders, moved them up to New York (away from the squabbling in Miami), held them in the dark about the invasion, and issued statements in their name. If the Cubans would not act like Castillo Armas, voluntarily, they must be forced to.

By the end of the summer, it was clear that Castro would last through the American election. In August, Bissell sought authorization from Eisenhower for spending thirteen million dollars to train more guerrillas. There was still no talk of an invasion; and Peter Wyden argues, in the best history of the operation, that Eisenhower "thought the operation was in its infancy." The CIA had been disturbed all along that "Eisenhower was wary" when he was not bored: "He never gave Cuba high priority." But if Castro could not be overthrown by CIA tricks, Bissell felt sure that the next President would have the enthusiasm to give him whatever he needed. Vice-President Nixon had been the strongest supporter of the scheme within the White House, and Senator Kennedy issued a campaign statement promising support for freedom fighters in Cuba.

When John Kennedy won in November, Bissell pushed forward with his plans, certain of the support that Kennedy did, in fact, give him during the interregnum. But Bissell "sold" the plan to Kennedy by stressing its clandestine and "surgical" aspects. He was given a free hand on the assurance that a guerrilla operation would lead to a rapid coup — neither a long-run resistance, nor a full-scale invasion. The CIA had been saved from the "wariness" of Eisenhower, only to fall victim to Kennedy's romanticism about technological guerrillas. Eisenhower, the organizer of D-day, who as President approved the massive amphibious landing in Lebanon, would have put the military in charge of invasion troops — something Bissell resisted, making the whole operation depend on CIA funds and planning. But Kennedy, precisely because he wanted the plan restricted to CIA scale, cut the program back at the very time when even Bissell saw that more was needed, not less. Kennedy, unaware of the difficulties of an amphibious landing, insisted that the "raid" take place at night and in an obscure place, not at Trinidad, the obvious site for a countercapital to be set up. Kennedy was still thinking of guerrilla troops that would bring Castro down invisibly. The logic of invasion called for seizing a communications center; the logic of resistance called for secret drops that would "fade into the hills." The invasion of a remote area — the Bahía de Cochinos — fit neither scheme; it had remained remote, after all, because coral reefs and dangerous swamps made it hard to reach (or break out of) by sea or land.

Bissell was put in the position of having to expand his plan and cut it back at the same time — expand it to cope with new obstacles facing him every day, and cut it back to keep the President's support. Air cover was restricted, naval support held back from the shore. Meanwhile, striving to keep control, Bissell withheld information at the top — from the CIA's own Board of Estimates and from the

Joint Chiefs of Staff — while news of the invasion was leaking out around its periphery. Kennedy, aware only of the secrecy at the center, was taking steps to guard a secret that no longer existed. Castro knew the landing would occur; only Adlai Stevenson was kept in the dark. If the site of the invasion surprised Castro, that was only because it made no military sense.

Having denied himself the advantages of military precaution, while taking on all the dangers of a military invasion, Bissell ended up with ships crashing onto unexpected coral reefs off a lonely spot that Castro knew intimately as his favorite fishing retreat. Since control of the operation was held in Washington, reaction time to all these problems was slow — five or six hours to report the need of air support to the CIA and sue for presidential approval. Bissell's attempt at total control led to total breakdown. Not only were the military branches insufficiently informed and involved; they were not supportive, since they had been excluded from the planning. Bissell had exercised such personal control over all aspects of the U-2's construction that the resulting fleet of planes was known as the Bissell Air Force. But he could not personally check the manifests of every landing boat at the Bay of Pigs, to discover that the communications equipment was — against normal military procedure — stuffed into a single boat, which sank. Ordinary military procedure was what the CIA daredevils had transcended. That is why two hired captains of "freelance" ammunition ships fled from the shelling and had to be chased back by American planes — too late.

For many, the puzzle of the Bay of Pigs is how a brilliant planner like Bissell could have convinced himself and so many others that it would succeed. But the first thing we must remember is that "it" was never a single thing. It changed character constantly, often without Bissell himself noticing what had happened. The propaganda-cum-assassination-coup gave way, first, to a large-scale raid meant to set up a rival center of government at Trinidad. Then this was cut back to a covert raid again, but now on the scale of a small invasion. By the time this confused sequence came to the point where it must be launched or called off, Bissell seems to have taken a "cap over the wall" approach to the matter — Castro had to be attacked now, with whatever was at hand, or never. If the exile army was disbanded, to roam free telling its tale, America would lose without even trying. It would get blamed for assembling the force in the first place, and blamed even more heatedly for not using it. The Cuban political leaders would air their grievances against the CIA. Castro would have a propaganda victory fixing him more securely in the affection of his people. Russia would feel freer to move in on Latin America.

Eisenhower would have called off an amphibious invasion unless it became clear a *real* invasion was needed. But Kennedy would approve a raid on the scale of an invasion — and, having done that, Bissell thought he would have to follow up with whatever military assistance was needed to defeat Castro. The CIA would cause a crisis that America could not walk away from. In that sense, the one-man operation would succeed. A country that could not be invaded by following normal channels of military preparation *would* be invaded in order to rescue a desperate band of American-led patriots trapped on the beaches of "Pig Bay." Bissell would throw our cap over the wall, and Kennedy would have to follow. What else could a President do who had begun his reign with the promise to "pay any price, bear any burden, meet any hardship, support any friend, oppose any foe to assure the survival and the success of liberty"?

By the time of the invasion, a certitude of Kennedy's support — whatever was called for — pervaded the CIA team. Many shared Howard Hunt's feeling: "Everything seemed ready. So ready, with success so inevitable, that when President Kennedy on April 12 declared the United States would never invade Cuba my project colleagues and I did not take him seriously. The statement was, we thought, a superb effort in misdirection." The propaganda experts not only believed their own propaganda by this point, but thought the President was taking his cue from them. Clayton Lynch, the guerrilla trainer who went ashore with his Cuban pupils, could not believe it when the President canceled a second air strike — it was, he said, "like learning that Superman is a fairy." The ballsy President had betrayed the James Bonds whom he admired, and who admired him. The agents who took it as implicit that the President would back them up conveyed this certitude to the Cubans as an explicit promise — when Peter Wyden interviewed veterans of the invasion, they still felt betrayed, sold out after pledges of support.

Even Bissell had some reason to feel betrayed. If he was trying to "force the hand" of the military, draw them into a situation they would not have relished had they been given the choice, wasn't that what Kennedy's ideal of guerrilla government called for? The inventive and unorthodox agents of the President *should* cut across channels, defy normal procedure, get the bureaucracy moving despite itself; should welcome crises, not avoid them; should precipitate trouble, and then improvise; throw the cap over the wall, and then follow. That is what Kennedy had encouraged — and then, having loosed his unorthodox warriors, he failed to back them up. The President might claim he was misled into thinking this was less an invasion than a raid. But sophisticated men talked in signals, out on the Kennedy basketball court, not by way of long reports in triplicate. Bissell had only to wink among his peers, and he had taken Kennedy as a peer. How did he think a guerrilla raid in the hills could overthrow Castro in a matter of days? Kennedy had first trusted Bissell to know what he was doing; and then, at the crunch, he would not follow Bissell's recommendation to widen the war.

Kennedy apologists would later say the New Frontier was itself betrayed in this episode, misled and lied to by the government in place — overborne by the military, who took too narrow a view of the problem; awed by experts dealing with a team of novices in the fledgling administration; told that ongoing procedures could not be broken off; reminded that Eisenhower's authority stood behind the plan.

But the Taylor Report concluded, after investigating the invasion, that the military mindset was excluded from planning; that the Joint Chiefs of Staff rather acquiesced in the project than approved of it — precisely because it was kept outside their bailiwick. What was needed was more procedure and bureaucratic checking: "Top level direction was given through ad hoc meetings of senior officials without consideration of operational plans in writing and with no arrangement for recording conclusions and decisions reached." Taylor concluded that Kennedy, by instantly dismantling Eisenhower's National Security Council apparatus, removed the machinery that could and would have spotted the plan's inadequacies.

Far from being awed by military types, Kennedy trusted Bissell because he so openly expressed contempt for them. And Eisenhower's approval of the project — so far as any existed — was no recommendation to Kennedy, who tried to contrast his administration in every way possible with his predecessor's. He did not revere a man of whom he could say, when his own popularity increased after the invasion's failure: "It's just like Eisenhower, the worse I do, the more they like me." No, the Cuban invasion was taken to heart because it was so clearly marked with the new traits of Kennedy's own government. It had for its target the man who obsessed Kennedy. It had for its leader the ideal of Kennedy's "best and brightest." It was a chess game backed by daring — played mind to mind, macho to macho, charisma to charisma. It was a James Bond exploit blessed by Yale, a PT raid run by Ph.D.s. It was the very definition of the New Frontier.

19

The Midas Touch

Oh, I am fortune's fool! — *Romeo and Juliet*

A FAVORITE WORD in the Kennedy administration was "options." Eisenhower, it was contended, never heard the whole range of possible choices. By the time he was asked to decide, committees had sifted the possibilities, winnowing out the unusual or daring. Kennedy, by engaging in the decision process at every level from the outset, would consider even risky or bold new courses.

Yet it was precisely by seeking options, with regard to Cuba, that Kennedy hemmed himself in, making Schlesinger call him "a prisoner of events." Schlesinger means that there was a concatenation of pressures forcing the President toward the Bay of Pigs. Sorensen and others make Kennedy the prisoner of Eisenhower, whose plan he inherited. But Eisenhower told Maxwell Taylor, during the investigation of the Bay of Pigs disaster, that he had never even heard of an amphibious invasion of Cuba until it was in the news. What he authorized was the training of a few guerrillas, an action on the scale of Guatemala, small enough to remain covert, the kind of thing the CIA had been doing. Bissell wanted to do something much grander; and though he probably had some of the final plan shaping in his head while Eisenhower was in office, the "takeoff" in terms of scale occurred when Kennedy was elected and gave Bissell the go-ahead at a November briefing. The invading troops were almost doubled in the two months that followed, and that larger number was redoubled by the time of the landing.

It is true that Eisenhower recommended a continuation of the CIA operation against Castro; but he meant the small-scale one he had authorized. As Peter Wyden concludes: "To him, nothing called a 'program' was fully hatched. When he insisted in a September 10, 1965 interview that 'there was no tactical or operational plan even discussed' with him while he was in the White House, he was technically correct." For Eisenhower, military terms had technical meanings.

If Kennedy, inheriting an Eisenhower plan, was forced to go ahead with it despite misgivings, why did he not question Eisenhower about the operation after he took office? Make the master answer his doubts? Explore the possibilities of failure with the man who supposedly stood behind the plan? Kennedy did nothing of the sort. And even when he called Eisenhower in for a face-saving "conference" after the invasion's failure, Eisenhower noted in his diary that "the President did not ask me for any specific advice" — though Kennedy later claimed, before reporters, that he had sought Eisenhower's counsel.

When William Pawley, the conservative diplomat who had advocated an assault on Castro, gave Eisenhower some details of the operation (including the loading of the heavy signal equipment in one ship, and that ship carrying ammunition), Eisenhower wrote in his diary: "If this whole story is substantially correct, it is a very dreary account of mismanagement, indecision, and timidity at the wrong time." The right time for timidity would have been when Bissell gave the CIA the task of making an amphibious assault in force. Eisenhower was notoriously cautious when considering romantic options of that sort. Murray Kempton summed up the General's rules of action this way: "When a situation is hopeless, never listen to counsels of hope. Fold the enterprise. Do nothing unless you know exactly what you will do if it turns out to have been the wrong thing."

Before the Guatemalan coup was launched, Eisenhower asked his advisers if they were *all* absolutely *sure* it would succeed. They were. Then, when trouble developed and Allen Dulles asked for more airplanes, Eisenhower asked what were the chances of this making the difference. "About twenty percent," Dulles told him. The President later said that if Dulles had given him an inflated estimate, he would not have got the planes. For Eisenhower, only a realism verging on pessimism inspired confidence in the discussion of military matters.

By contrast, Kennedy asked his principal advisers, not if they were sure of success, but if they thought the mission worth trying. When the Joint Chiefs were asked to estimate the chances of a successful landing at Trinidad (the site chosen by the CIA before Kennedy overruled it), General David Gray wrote a report describing the chances as "fair," a term suggested by General Earl Wheeler. Wyden reports their conversation: "When they discussed what 'fair' meant, Gray said he thought the chances were thirty to seventy. 'Thirty in favor and seventy against?' asked Wheeler. 'Yes.' " Gray used no figures in his report for the White House, and President Kennedy never asked what "fair" meant. Gray thought it obvious that a "fair" rating would not imply chances were "very good" or even "good" — much less "certain." And this, remember, was the estimate for a landing site that had advantages lacking to the Bay of Pigs.

The truth is that Kennedy went ahead with the Cuban action, not to complete what he inherited from Eisenhower, but to mark his difference from Eisenhower. He would not process things through the military panels, let them penetrate Bissell's secrecy. He would be bold where he accused Eisenhower of timidity. He would not send in the Army, Navy, and Air Force, but only Bissell's raiders. In all this he was the prisoner of his own rhetoric. As Sorensen admits, "his disapproval of the plan would be a show of weakness inconsistent with his general stance."

Kennedy's campaign had promised strong action against Castro, a man, says Sorensen, who made Kennedy lose his normal "cool": "He should never have permitted his own deep feeling against Castro (unusual for him) and considerations of public opinion — specifically, his concern that he would be assailed for calling off a plan to get rid of Castro — to overcome his innate suspicions." Kennedy had "run scared" from accusations of softness on Castro in the campaign itself. When Harris Wofford was called in to produce a campaign book of Kennedy speeches (*The Strategy of Peace*), he wrote that Castro's revolution stood in the tradition of Simón Bolivar's fight against colonialism. That passage soon came under fire, and Kennedy told Sorensen to draft a strong statement against the Cuban government. Richard Goodwin wrote the release, which said: "We must attempt to strengthen the non-Batista democratic anti-Castro forces in exile, and in Cuba itself, who offer eventual hope of overthrowing Castro. Thus far these fighters for freedom have had virtually no support from our government." On the eve of the Bay of Pigs invasion, Kennedy reminded Goodwin of that statement: "Well, Dick, we're about to put your Cuban policy into action."

Schlesinger says that Kennedy had some misgivings about taking a hard line on Cuba and blaming its loss on Eisenhower. But campaign advantage won the day:

> Cuba, of course, was a highly tempting issue; and as the pace of the campaign quickened, politics began to clash with Kennedy's innate sense of responsibility. Once, discussing Cuba with his staff, he asked them, "All right, but how would we have saved Cuba if we had the power?" Then he paused, looked out the window and said, "What the hell, they never told us how they would have saved China." In that spirit, he began to succumb to temptation.

Began to? Adopting the method of McCarthyites in their assault on Truman is not merely flirting with temptation. But the important thing in this place is not the moral justification of Kennedy's campaign tactic, but the fact that his lunge toward immediate advantage inhibited his freedom later on. He would have to live with Goodwin's language if he disbanded the freedom fighters he had called for, had criticized Eisenhower for not raising up and "loosing" on their homeland. He narrowed his range of future options by stigmatizing ahead of time the one that might prove the most sensible. A man who has to be tough in each response is not free; his very professions of control put the matter beyond his choice:

> Weyrother evidently felt himself to be at the head of a movement that had already become unrestrainable. He was like a horse running downhill harnessed to a heavy cart. Whether he was pulling it

or being pushed by it he did not know, but rushed along at headlong speed with no time to consider what this movement might
lead to. (*War and Peace*)

As if he knew the decision was out of his hands, Kennedy cut off
criticism of the CIA's plan. Sorensen, considered "liberal" (i.e., soft)
in the early days of the administration, was not told of it; when he
heard something and sounded Kennedy out, the President quashed
any expression of disapproval by using "an earthy expression that
too many advisers seemed frightened by the prospect of a fight, and
stressed somewhat uncomfortably that he had no alternative."
Whether he had an alternative or not, he wanted to hear of none.
Wofford — whose patron, Chester Bowles, was one of those Kennedy considered "frightened by the prospect of a fight" — tells us
what "earthy expression" Kennedy was using to cut off criticism: "I
know everybody is grabbing their nuts on this."

Criticism of the plan was considered cowardice. Bowles and Rusk
and Stevenson were counted too "ladylike" to be consulted on the
manly scheme Bissell was outlining. Robert Kennedy wrote, just
after the failure: "A critical time was on D plus one, when the CIA
asked for air cover. Jack was in favor of giving it. However, Dean
Rusk was strongly against it." Maybe the "chickens" caused the failure. That is why, in the immediate aftermath of the landing, the fury
of the people responsible was directed against those who had opposed the scheme. Pierre Salinger stopped Harris Wofford in a
White House hallway and said: "That yellow-bellied friend of yours,
Chester Bowles, is leaking all over town that he was against it.
We're going to get him." Robert Kennedy confronted Bowles himself, poked his finger in his chest, and said: "So you advised against
this operation. Well, as of now you were all for it."

Despite his campaign promise to hear all sides of an issue, Kennedy showed resentment when forced to hear less than comforting
words about the future landing. After inviting Senator Fulbright to
fly with him to Florida, Kennedy read through a critique of the
CIA's plan which Fulbright brought along, put it down, and did not
discuss it with Fulbright, either on this flight or the return one.
Schlesinger was told by Robert Kennedy: "I hear you don't think
much of this business. . . . You may be right or you may be wrong,

but the President has made his mind up. Don't push it any further. Now is the time for everyone to help him all they can." It was the advice Edward Kennedy later gave Schlesinger on the subject of Robert's presidential campaign. Don't make him lose his nerve; rally round; keep up morale. The question was one of guts, and to back off was to show a lack of guts. Sorensen captures the atmosphere: "Unfortunately, among those privy to the plan in both the State Department and the White House, doubts were entertained but never pressed, partly out of fear of being labeled 'soft' or undaring in the eyes of their colleagues. . . ."

When Schlesinger took to the President a white paper he had composed on Cuba, he asked, "What do you think about this damned invasion?" Kennedy answered wryly: "I think about it as little as possible." Thinking was not the problem. Thinking might take away one's nerve. Schlesinger admits his own criticisms were checked by Kennedy's obvious unwillingness to hear counsels of caution. He tried an indirect approach when he spelled out the unpleasant tasks that would await the President if he failed:

> When lies must be told, they should be told by subordinate officials. At no point should the President be asked to lend himself to the cover operation. For this reason, there seems to be merit in Secretary Rusk's suggestion that someone other than the President make the final decision and do so in his absence — someone whose head can later be placed on the block if things go terribly wrong.

He was telling a man proud of his courage to hide, to skulk.

Kennedy was a prisoner of his own taste for crisis, for being in the midst of the action. The CIA told him he had to move fast, before Russia supplied Castro with jet planes (actually, there were already jet trainers in Cuba, which were used effectively against the invaders). Besides, the Guatemalan government wanted the growing army, whose presence was no longer a secret, moved from its territory. And the troops were anxious to go. And the rainy season was about to begin. The basketball team had to call its signals in the rush of events, if it was to keep control — which meant that events were controlling *it*. A similar taste for instant decision came into play during the missile crisis, when a dubious estimate on the arming

date of Castro's missiles led Kennedy to impose a deadline on the
Russians, forcing them to act in an atmosphere of panic.

The growing size of the invasion army — 1,400 men — made the
administration hostage to its own agents. Their visibility made them
an "asset" that had to be used immediately or moved in a way that
would waste the asset. And then there was the disposal problem if
they were *not* used — all those hotheads wandering around in loud
denunciation of a government that promised to back them and then
reneged. Once again, acquiring a "capability" chained one to its use,
so that decision became a kind of resignation to the inevitable. Confronted with the "disposal problem," says Schlesinger, "Kennedy
tentatively agreed that the simplest thing, after all, might be to let
the Cubans go where they yearned to go — to Cuba." The simplest
thing, the nondecision, was the surrender of power to one's own instruments of power. They were acquired so the President might have
the option of using them; but, once acquired on this scale, he had no
option *not* to use them.

The ironies multiply. Tracing the justifications for invasion,
Schlesinger wrote, "If we did in the end have to send American
troops to Laos to fight communism on the other side of the world,
we could hardly ignore communism ninety miles off Florida." In
order to have a future (hypothetical) option, one denies oneself a
present (real) option. Since one *might* have to go into Laos, one *must*
go into Cuba. Thus do options bind, making "freedom of maneuver" a straitjacket for the mind. The so-called domino theory, explaining enemy tactics, was — seen from the other end — an option
theory, testing the will of America: if we were going to stay free to
be tough anywhere else, we had to be tough everywhere. It was a
hard doctrine in terms of its result — Cubans died and were imprisoned. But it was the simplest doctrine so far as decision-making
goes. Every decision came, in fact, pre-decided: the "toughest" course
is the only one that can be followed, unless one wants to "grab one's
nuts" and look like a bum.

The last irony of all is that Kennedy failed because he had always
succeeded. He was a prisoner of his own luck. As Schlesinger put it:

> One further factor no doubt influenced him: the enormous confi-
> dence in his own luck. Everything had broken right for him since

1956. He had won the nomination and the election against all the odds in the book. Everyone around him thought he had the Midas touch and could not lose.

It is not mystical or perverse to say that good luck is bad luck; Machiavelli offered that as the very essence of his realism. Arguing that *fortuna* could undo even the man of greatest virtuosity (*virtù*), he gave Valentino (Cesare Borgia) as his example. Valentino was the type of *virtù* at its highest reach, a model for all who want, at once, "immunity from foes and attractiveness to friends, victory by force or stratagem, the love and the fear of one's people, the obedience and respect of one's soldiers, the destruction of those who can or might oppose one, innovative measure within an ancient system, harshness joined with charm, the disbanding of old armies to reassemble better ones, the perpetuation of friendly relations with other kings or princes, so that they welcome alliance and shy from opposition."

That sounds like a description of the Neustadt President, of the Roosevelt whom Burns called lion and fox. Such a range of skills, joined with favoring chance, would seem unbeatable. But Machiavelli lists all these skills to emphasize the fact that good luck made Valentino fail — it made his *virtù* the means of his undoing. Introduced to a spacious area of action by his papal father, Valentino both commanded and enlarged that sphere — in fact, enlarged it *in order* to command it. Only his skills could keep so many opponents off balance, and he could do that only by introducing so many new aspects to the game that his opponents were befuddled. Only by reaching for three other things could he grasp the first thing given him. But because everything depended on his superintending intelligence and will, any lapse in either of those qualities would bring the whole enterprise crashing down around him. The attempt at total control led to total collapse if one thing went wrong — in Valentino's case, an illness that immobilized him at a crucial moment. For this kind of juggler, so deftly keeping dozens of balls in the air, if one drops they all fall. Luck worked his destruction by giving him so many in the first place.

John Kennedy had neither the ruthless character nor the restless skills of a Valentino. And no President can aspire to the everyday powers of a Renaissance prince (though the modern powers of destruction far outreach anything dreamed of in the Renaissance). Nonetheless, the euphoria of the New Frontier, the ideal of the activist President always seeking more power, did make Kennedy think he could break free of normal restraints. His experience to date had been one of risks defied, of personal control, of unconventional activity backed up with the conventional might of his father's money. He was nothing if not confident — changing plans for the Bay of Pigs invasion on his personal authority, redirecting the invasion to a hidden cove, rescheduling it for night landing. He brought his own ideas to the matter, gave it his personal stamp, without seeking express military guidance from Eisenhower, from White House military experts, from the Department of Defense. He never suspected that he was out of his depth. Critics simply lacked his nerve, or were hidebound "experts," paper-shuffling "bureaucrats." They did not see how magically he had defied the odds before, how lucky he was. Wyden's interviews with participants in the control-room direction of the landing show how inadequate Kennedy was to this kind of operation:

> Fascinated, [Harlan] Cleveland watched a "stricken look" cross Admiral [Arleigh] Burke's face when the President picked up one of the little magnetic destroyer models and moved it over the horizon. It clearly pained the admiral to see the President bypass all channels of command — and all tradition. As a student of managers coping with crisis, Cleveland was chagrined to see how obvious it was that the President's only executive experience had been as commander of a PT boat.

> Throughout the day in the Cabinet Room, Kennedy did not ask enough questions, Harlan Cleveland thought. And the President failed to ask about situations in context; he would ask a "very specific question about some little piece of the jigsaw puzzle and you had to sort of guess what the rest of the jigsaw puzzle was in his mind."

> [Walt] Rostow was struck by Kennedy's deep personal concern about the fate of the men on the beaches. The President had a "small unit commander's attitude toward these people" . . . Rostow was chagrined that the President "really didn't have a very good visual picture of the whole thing."

The student of Neustadt had come to acquire power, not question it; to enjoy it, not fear it. The possibility that the very reach for power might, with luck, take one into situations beyond the measure of one's skill would not occur to a reader of Neustadt's book. James Reston rather fatuously called that book America's version of *The Prince*. But Machiavelli warns against the mindless reach for power — the victory that drains one's resources, the conquered people that are more dangerous under one's dominion than outside it, the mercenaries added to one's troops while crippling them, the added fortresses that delude a ruler with a sense of false security. For him fortune was a tricky friend when not a beguiling enemy — better held at arm's length in either case. When dealing with the subject of power, he did not say, "Enjoy! Enjoy!" but "Suspect! Suspect!" These are the real lessons to be learned from Machiavelli, and some of Kennedy's friends rejoiced that he had learned them in his bruising experience at the Bay of Pigs. But had he?

20

"Learning"

ACCOUNTS OF THE BAY OF PIGS READ like one of the "bad news,
good news" jokes. The bad news is that the disaster was complete.
The good news is that President Kennedy learned so much from the
experience. The Kennedys, Schlesinger has been saying ever since
1960, are late learners, and we may have to pay for their education
with the lives of a few hundred Cubans. Roger Hilsman put it this
way:

> If some extra-galactic observer with a wisdom and insight un-
> dreamed of on earth were asked to comment on the Bay of Pigs af-
> fair, he might well say that it was through this comparatively small
> disaster, though disaster it clearly was, that President Kennedy
> learned the lessons that enabled him to avoid a much greater, nu-
> clear disaster a year and a half later by managing the Cuban missile
> crisis with such a sure and steady hand. If so, the price may have
> been cheap.

Writers are always suspect when they introduce an imaginary being
"with a wisdom and insight undreamed of on earth" to say just what

the writer is saying. But many wise men on this earth have repeated this line of thought, making it a kind of orthodoxy. One of these, astonishingly, is Theodore Sorensen: "In later months, he [Kennedy] would be grateful that he had learned so many major lessons — resulting in basic changes in personnel, policy and procedures — at so relatively small and temporary a cost." I say astonishingly because, from the Sorensen account, Kennedy learned nothing at all. If the history of the invasion sounds like a "bad news, good news" joke, Sorensen's account of his learning process reads like the movie line, "Round up the usual suspects." Kennedy failed, according to Sorensen, because "John Kennedy inherited the plan." But he did not. He inherited a growing invasion force which he let grow at an even faster rate. Sorensen says the matter was out of his hands before the presidency was securely in those hands: "Unlike an inherited policy statement or Executive Order, this inheritance [of a plan] could not be simply disposed of by presidential recission or withdrawal." But presidential directive was the only thing that could stop the plan — or, for that matter, launch the invasion; and the very man Kennedy appointed to teach him the lessons of the invasion — General Maxwell Taylor — concluded that such cancellation was the proper course.

For the rest, Sorensen just repeats the Neustadt dicta. Kennedy was done in by experts and the bureaucracy. The planning "permitted bureaucratic momentum to govern instead of policy leadership. . . . He [Kennedy] did not yet feel he could trust his own instincts against the judgments of recognized experts. He had not yet geared the decision-making process to fulfill his own needs." Kennedy, who had been too confident, is called too diffident. He who broke the rules is called their victim. Is this what Kennedy learned from his own task force of postdisaster teachers?

The Taylor report has never been released; but its principal author has said enough in various places to show that the Sorensen account of Kennedy's education has little to do with that report's conclusions. General Taylor believed — and he says that his fellow investigators concurred — that it was a *lack* of bureaucratic procedure and expertise that doomed the landing. The military was blamed for an operation it did not control. It was asked to advise from the sidelines

with only partial glimpses of the total plan (which Bissell kept as
secret as possible from those above him, while it leaked out all over
the place below him). Taylor wrote in his memoirs:

> [The Joint Chiefs of Staff] felt that they had been obliged to work
> under circumstances which made it very difficult to carry out even
> these duties. In the interest of secrecy, there was no advance agenda
> circulated before the meetings and no written record of decisions
> kept during them [only bureaucrats "shuffle paper"]. Furthermore,
> the plan prepared by the CIA was always in process of revision so
> that the Chiefs never saw it in final form until April 15, the day of
> the first air strike.

In a White House that was proud of its lack of structured meetings
and orderly reporting, even the expressed doubts of the Joint Chiefs
were either misunderstood (e.g., the rating of chances at the Trinidad landing as "fair") or did not get a hearing (e.g., the rating of
chances at the Bay of Pigs as even less than fair). Taylor says:

> By mid-March, the President's growing dissatisfaction with the
> Trinidad plan caused the CIA authorities to propose three alterna-
> tives to the Trinidad site, one of which was the Zapata area [con-
> taining the Bay of Pigs]. Asked to comment on these alternatives,
> the Chiefs in a memorandum to the Secretary of Defense [McNa-
> mara] expressed a preference for Zapata from among the three but
> added that none of the alternatives was considered as feasible or as
> likely to accomplish the objective as Trinidad. Our investigation
> revealed the fact, never accounted for [accountability is a bureau-
> cratic priority], that neither the Secretary of Defense nor any other
> senior official appeared to have been aware of this clearly stated pref-
> erence and hence the views of the Chiefs never influenced the deci-
> sion on this point.

Arthur Schlesinger, given access to Robert Kennedy's notes from
the Cuban Study Group investigation, quotes this astonishing one:
"Evidently no probability of uprisings written up or put in memo
form. No formal statement of opinion was given *or asked for*" (italics
added). There were many experts who could have told Kennedy that
an amphibious landing is recognized, in every school of military
thought, as an exceptionally difficult maneuver, and that making

such a landing at night on an inadequately mapped beach would stretch the skills of a trained army properly staffed (most Cubans had been given only a few months' training). Yet Taylor found an incredible insouciance in the White House team:

> A final defect was the jerry-built organization improvised to run this complex operation extending from Washington to the beachhead. There was no permanent machinery in Washington designed to deal with such an undertaking, so one had to be improvised. When the action heated up, communications quickly broke down, and the Washington leaders were soon without the information necessary to guide their decisions.

After General Taylor submitted his report, Kennedy asked him to join the White House staff as its Military Representative, where Taylor found that the style of the Bay of Pigs operation was the style of the entire White House:

> As an old military type, I was accustomed to the support of a highly professional staff trained to prepare careful analyses of issues in advance of decisions and to take meticulous care of classified information. I was shocked at the disorderly and careless ways of the new White House staff. . . . I found that I could walk into almost any office, request and receive a sheaf of top secret papers, and depart without signing a receipt or making any record of the transaction. There was little perceptible method in the assignment of duties within the staff, although I had to admit that the work did get done, largely through the individual initiative of its members. When important new problems arose, they were usually assigned to ad hoc task forces with members drawn from the White House staff and other departments. These task forces did their work, filed their reports, and then dissolved into the bureaucratic limbo without leaving a trace or contributing to the permanent base of governmental experience.

This attitude toward orderly method had been derived from the President himself who, "like his subordinates, had little regard for organization and method as such." If these were the lessons Taylor was trying to teach the President, then, according to Kennedy's own alter ego, he did not learn them: Sorensen claims Kennedy went

away from the Bay of Pigs determined to push his own antibureaucratic methods even *further*, in order to protect him from the experts
(whose advice had not been solicited).

But Kennedy was not really seeking to learn new things from his
investigation of the Bay of Pigs. That is obvious both from the
formal instruction he gave to the Cuba Study Group, and from the
people he appointed to that group. He wrote to General Taylor:

> It is apparent that we need to take a close look at all our practices
> and programs in the areas of military and para-military, guerrilla
> and anti-guerrilla activities which fall short of outright war. I be-
> lieve we need to strengthen our work in this area. In the course of
> your study, I hope that you will give special attention to the lessons
> which can be learned from recent events in Cuba.

Taylor himself wondered at "the almost passing mention of the Bay
of Pigs" in this plan for *expanding* guerrilla warfare, with the Bay of
Pigs used only as a cautionary tale for that purpose. An investigation of the meaning of the Cuban invasion might have called into
question the very notion of paramilitary assaults on other governments. Kennedy's instructions precluded that. The assignment was
not to ask whether Americans should acquire a guerrilla warfare
capability but how America might do so most efficiently.

The choice of General Taylor was dictated by Kennedy's determination in this matter. Taylor had been a critic of the Eisenhower
doctrine of "massive retaliation." When he retired from office (an
act later regarded as a resignation in protest), he wrote *The Uncertain
Trumpet* to plead for a new doctrine of "flexible response," enabling
America to counter "wars of liberation" with limited-warfare tactics.
Senator Kennedy read this book during his campaign, and wrote a
letter of enthusiastic approval to its author. Theodore Sorensen echoed one phrase from the book in the inaugural address. Taylor concluded his argument by saying: "All the foregoing actions should be
taken to the sure notes of a certain trumpet, giving to friend and foe
alike a clear expression of our purpose and of our motives." Taylor
criticized Eisenhower for cutting back military expenditures and for
allowing a missile gap to develop. All this was useful to the 1960

candidate, even though Taylor's missile gap evaporated when Secretary McNamara began looking for it.

General Taylor, despite his own minimal support of a military staffing system (certainly more orderly than Kennedy's), was also a critic of the military bureaucracy. He said: "The Joint Chiefs of Staff have all the faults of a committee in settling important controversial matters. They must consider and accommodate many divergent views before action can be taken." That was the kind of general Kennedy wanted for his Cuba Study Group — and Taylor did not disappoint. The "jerry-built" operation of the CIA was criticized only because operations of that scale should go to the Department of Defense — which, in turn, should be trained to meet paramilitary and covert-action challenges too big for the CIA to handle. Bissell's agents should be replaced with Special Forces in the Army itself — with the Green Berets. Taylor, like most critics of bureaucracy, also suggested that a new bureau be added to run the old ones — in this case, a Cold War command center. The President rejected this idea, which challenged the State Department too directly, but then set up two secret boards to perform analogous tasks; and the leading figures on these boards were the commanding personalities of the Cuba Study Group — Maxwell Taylor and Robert Kennedy.

The simplest proof that Kennedy learned nothing from the Bay of Pigs invasion is that his own solution was to make Robert Kennedy the Director of the CIA. He told Arthur Schlesinger: "I made a mistake in putting Bobby in the Justice Department. He is wasted there. Byron White could do that job perfectly well. Bobby should be in CIA. . . . It's a hell of a way to learn things, but I have learned one thing from the business — that is, that we will have to deal with CIA. McNamara has dealt with Defense; Rusk has done a lot with State; but no one has dealt with CIA." Though Robert turned down the directorship, he added the CIA's business to his crowded schedule at Justice. Robert would "deal" with the CIA, exactly as McNamara dealt with Defense. Both men spurred their organizations on to new excess.

The President did not even know the CIA well enough to realize that the best critics of the Bay of Pigs operation were within the Agency. Richard Helms, leery of covert activity anyway, resented the

way Bissell had isolated himself from internal review. Robert
Amory, head of the bureau's own intelligence, had been excluded
from planning the invasion, along with the Agency's Bureau of Estimates. The most critical report on the Cuban performance would
come from the Agency — Lyman Kirkpatrick, the Inspector General, had fought for review rights over all operations, and had won
them at one of Eisenhower's regular meetings, where Dulles could
not override his own Inspector General before the President. When
Kirkpatrick completed his report on the Bay of Pigs, friends of Bissell considered him a traitor, much as similar agents would feel
about William Colby when that Director cooperated with the
Church Committee years later. Although the Inspector General's report has never been declassified, Kirkpatrick's later comments give
the gist of it. Kirkpatrick not only listed technical reasons for the
military operation's failure; unlike the Taylor group, he derided the
whole project: "If there was a resistance to Fidel Castro, it was
mostly in Miami. . . . All intelligence reports coming from allied
sources [which Bissell did not consult] indicated quite clearly that
he was thoroughly in command of Cuba, and was supported by most
of the people who remained on the island."

Now *there* was a lesson Kennedy could have learned from the Bay
of Pigs; but he made that impossible when he told his brother to
"deal with CIA," since the Bay of Pigs just increased Robert Kennedy's determination to "get Castro." His emotional response to the
defeat of his brother was intense. Peter Wyden describes his first reaction:

> As the planners in Washington tried to come to terms with defeat
> on Wednesday, Walt Rostow was concerned about Robert Ken-
> nedy, whom he hardly knew. The Attorney General, who had not
> attended any of the pre-invasion planning meetings, showed much
> more than the President how distraught he was. He refused to ac-
> cept the debacle and was needlessly upsetting the other advisers. On
> Tuesday, RFK had warned the presidential circle harshly in the Cab-
> inet Room that they were to make no statements that didn't back
> up the President's judgments all the way. In midafternoon Wednes-
> day, with the President absent from the room for a few minutes,
> Robert spoke, Rostow thought, "in anguish." He called on the ad-
> visers "to act or be judged paper tigers in Moscow." They were not

just to "sit and take it." With all the famous talent around the table, somebody ought to find something to do. Everybody stared. They were "absolutely numb."

Even after the failure, Robert Kennedy thought of the Cuban problem in purely military terms; he told Taylor that "the President would have gone as far as necessary for success had he known in time what had to be done."

Robert Kennedy endorsed the Taylor group's request for a command center to wage the Cold War; and, when that was rejected, Robert became a moving force in the secret committees set up to oppose Communist-inspired regimes or rebellions. These new boards were added to a prior one, the Special Group, which oversaw covert activities. General Taylor was put in charge of this, with a mandate to turn a harsher eye on CIA proposals. The first *new* group was also chaired by Taylor, but included Robert Kennedy — Special Group CI (for counterinsurgency). This group looked to the development of guerrilla warfare skills within the Special Forces of the regular Army. The Green Berets were its pampered baby, and Vietnam is its legacy. Robert Kennedy became an ardent reader of Mao and Ho, and held seminars on guerrilla tactics at Hickory Hill. The President himself insisted on the green berets as a badge of distinction, against the Army's reluctance to set men off from others except by rank, and a green beret became a fixture on Robert's desk at the Justice Department. Whenever this President saw a wall, he started throwing caps over it.

Robert's enthusiasm for counterinsurgency made him push and prod the CI Group, enforcing his brother's belief that America's future power would depend on its guerrilla capacity. William Gaud, who served on the CI Group, said in his oral history report at the Kennedy Library that the President and Attorney General "gave a hell of an impetus to the study of counterinsurgency and to setting up schools to indoctrinate our own people in this subject. And also, as a result of what they did, our own public safety programs, police programs, have been greatly enlarged." After observing Robert at the CI meetings, Gaud said: "There wasn't any question about the depth of his interest or the depth of his understanding of the problem. He was a pretty tough customer to face if he took one point of view and you took another, or if he felt that your agency had not been doing what it should be doing in respect of some problem. I developed a very healthy respect for his ability to get things done."

The things Robert got done included training Latin American officers in methods for putting down popular unrest. Why, after all, wait till a Diem is in trouble to come to his rescue? The pro-American governments should share America's expertise in *preventing* rebellion. Though there is no evidence that torture was taught in the American schools, there is no doubt that torturers were among their alumni, further embittering some Latin Americans against the United States.

For President Kennedy, Vietnam offered an invaluable opportunity to try out counterinsurgent devices and train American personnel. According to General Taylor:

> The President repeatedly emphasized his desire to utilize the situation in Vietnam to study and test the techniques and equipment related to counterinsurgency, and hence, he insisted that we expose our most promising officers to the experience of service there. To this end he directed that Army colonels eligible for promotion to brigadier general be rotated through Vietnam on short orientation tours, and he was inclined to require evidence of specific training or experience in counterinsurgency as a prerequisite to promotion to general officer rank. He looked to the Special Group to verify compliance with his wishes in these matters, a duty which we fulfilled by means of recurrent spot checks on departmental performance.

There was no reluctance to be "drawn into" Vietnam — we welcomed it as a laboratory to test our troops for their worldwide duties.

Fort Bragg was already the center for training America's corps of antiguerrilla guerrillas. The New Frontier philosophy of counterinsurgency had been enunciated in a famous speech Walt Rostow delivered at Fort Bragg in April of 1961. Rostow's academic reputation rested on his theory of the stages of economic development. In the early stages, emerging nations are vulnerable to opportunistic "scavengers of the process" — the Communists. It was America's historical role to protect the integrity of the development process by eliminating those scavengers. The counterinsurgents were technicians of progress: "I salute you, as I would a group of doctors, teachers, economic planners, agricultural experts, civil servants, or those others who are now leading the way in the whole southern half of the globe in fashioning the new nations." America was history's midwife, nursing freedom in numberless cradles. There could be nothing more enlightened or liberal than the learning of "dirty tricks" to undo the scavengers who specialize in them. Roger Hilsman in the State Department was another enthusiast for counterinsurgency: "The way to fight the guerrilla was to adopt the tactics of the guerrilla." New Frontiersmen traded maxims from the handbooks of the twentieth-century revolutionaries, then visited Fort Bragg to see how these heroes could be undone in their own backyards. The White House press corps was taken there in October of 1961 to watch Green Berets eat snake meat, stage ambushes, skip over ponds with back-pack rockets that let men literally walk over water. The Americans were coming — savvy as the Viet Cong, and with fancier gadgets.

Robert Kennedy was ardent about the Green Beret projects of the Special Group CI; but he was even more intense in pursuing the program of the second secret body set up in the wake of the Taylor report, the Special Group Augmented (SGA). This handled high-priority plots, and the highest priority of all was given to the downfall of Castro. At the very time when General Taylor, presiding over the Special Group, was supposed to curb the CIA, the Attorney General was using the SGA to increase its anti-Castro operations. The importance of this project can be seen from the fact that Robert Kennedy commandeered for its prosecution the "star" most in demand during this high season of counterinsurgent fever. Edward Lansdale was a man of mystery and glamour on the New Frontier, the man who had taught Ramon Magsaysay and Ngo Dinh Diem how to put down rebellions against their regimes. Lansdale, who opposed the Bay of Pigs operation, was now given a textbook assignment: show the CIA how it *should* have been done. Kennedy was ready to back him up with all the resources he might need. Operation Mongoose, the anti-Castro project, became the CIA's most urgent clandestine operation. Its base in Miami was the Agency's largest, with six hundred case officers running three thousand Cuban agents, fifty business fronts, and a fleet of planes and ships operating

out of the "fronts." Lansdale was told to act quickly, and he promised to bring Castro down within a year. Robert Kennedy did not
want the man who had humiliated his brother to gloat long over his
triumph.

Far from checking CIA excesses, Robert Kennedy forced reluctant
officials to undertake things they had resisted in the past. That was
signally true of Richard Helms, an espionage man who had always
opposed covert activity. Only after being "chewed out" by both
Kennedys for Operation Mongoose's lack of success did Helms, a
man temperamentally and historically opposed to assassination, revive the plot to use Mafia hit men against Castro's life. Defenders of
the Kennedys naturally deny that their heroes commissioned the assassination plots; and, naturally, there is no record of a direct
order — the CIA's lack of record-keeping about "sensitive" matters
was one of its attractions for the antibureaucratic Kennedys. But
what else are we to make of the fact that Helms, of all people, took
over the assassination plot for the first time after his meeting with
the Kennedys, *and that he canceled it as soon as Johnson came into office?*

Besides, Robert Kennedy was working in the closest collaboration
with Edward Lansdale all through this period, and that "enlightened" guerrilla leader asked William Harvey, who ran Task Force W
(the CIA program meant to implement Operation Mongoose) to
draw up papers on "liquidation of leaders" in Cuba. Harvey, a high-
handed CIA veteran, told Lansdale it was stupid to put such things
in writing — which does not mean that removal of it from their
pages removed it from their plotting.

The evidence that the Kennedys directly ordered Castro's death is
circumstantial but convincing. When Robert Kennedy was told of
the Mafia's use against Castro, on May 7, 1962, he blew up at the
man briefing him, but expressed neither surprise nor anger at the
plot against Castro, only at the killers being used. Lawrence Hous-
ton, the CIA general counsel who briefed Robert, told Thomas
Powers: "He was mad as hell. But what he objected to was the possibility it would impede prosecution against Giancana and Rosselli.
He was not angry about the assassination plot, but about our involvement with the Mafia." Kennedy, who was calling CIA people
at all levels to urge on Operation Mongoose, made no protest to
Helms or any other CIA officer about the plan to kill Castro. That

did not excite or upset him, and he did nothing — though he was by
office an enforcer of the law — to make sure it was not resumed (as
in fact it was). That is inconceivable unless he approved of the plan,
had in fact been part of its authorization.

Lyndon Johnson, when he took office, did not continue the attempts on Castro's life. When he directly asked Helms about them
and was given a full answer, Johnson was certain that President
Kennedy had authorized the assassination attempts, that he was
running "a damn Murder Incorporated in the Caribbean." He told
Howard K. Smith: "Kennedy was trying to get Castro, but Castro
got to him first." Johnson believed the gangland hit had backfired in
Dallas. One does not have to accept that inference to doubt what
Johnson was in the best position to know — how and whether a
President directs the CIA "unofficially."

Furthermore, how did Robert Kennedy expect Lansdale to bring
down Castro within a year, absent outright invasion or overt American participation, without a palace coup to go with the popular uprising? The *prevention* of palace coups had been Lansdale's specialty in
the Philippines and Vietnam; he was brought in to exercise his skills
in reverse, so far as Castro was concerned; and his highest contact
inside Cuba had insisted that such a coup, *preceded by execution of the
President,* was necessary to any plan for overthrowing the government. Rolando Cubela, a major in Castro's army, was given various
weapons for killing Castro, and was actually picking up one of these
in Paris on the day President Kennedy was shot. At a time when
Robert Kennedy was calling Lansdale and others incessantly, charging them with inactivity, would Lansdale withhold from him the
key to his whole operation? And if he did so, how could Robert, intent on discussing the "nuts and bolts" of guerrilla war, expect him
to overthrow Castro? Kennedy certainly knew about various sabotage efforts — he checked frequently on the attempt to destroy the
Matahambre copper mines — which involved the death of Cubans in
the area. In that sense, he authorized the killing of Cuban civilians
and soldiers. Why not the killing of the soldiers' commander-in-
chief?

I referred earlier to Robert Kennedy's extraordinary lack of interest in the motives or mechanics of his own brother's death. This
man, once the pursuer of those who merely humiliated his brother,

showed no such vindictiveness, or even curiosity, about Lee Harvey Oswald (whose name he garbled in referring to him) or any accomplices Oswald might have had. Harris Wofford argues that this reluctance came from disgust over his own knowledge about the plot to kill Castro. Robert Kennedy did not want any investigation if it would lead to the plans made against Castro, to his own involvement and his brother's. The deep change in Robert's character seems to have come from a genuine recoil against such violence and scheming. From that point on, he would seek out those for whom Castro was a hero, not a villain. Such a change did not come from any gradual learning process. In fact, the harshness of this shock indicated Robert's *failure* to learn from the Bay of Pigs experience. That episode made him rely on counterinsurgency more fanatically, which opened the way to Vietnam. It made him ignore the lesson taught by the CIA's own Inspector General's report — that the overthrow of Castro should not have been undertaken in the first place — and seek that goal even more single-mindedly, forcing previously reluctant CIA officers into the effort. His response to failure at the Bay of Pigs was not detachment and a calm review of the CIA's murderous activities. The response was anger, and a call for greater efficiency in those activities.

But if the Kennedys learned nothing from their first crisis with Cuba, how did they respond so wisely in the second Cuban crisis, when Russian missiles had to be removed? The orthodoxy is that such wisdom could only have been derived from lessons of the earlier mistake. But the orthodoxy assumes that the missile crisis ended in a triumph for America, and that assumption needs some looking at.

21
"Triumph"

When a man concludes that any stick is good enough to beat
his foe with — that is when he picks up a boomerang.

— GILBERT CHESTERTON

FOR ALL THE TALK of "learning" from the Bay of Pigs, and for all
the earlier talk of seeking options, there is one option the Kennedys
considered neither before *nor after* the failure of the Cuban invasion:
leaving Castro alone. Some people — notably William Fulbright —
tried to raise that option before the landing: Castro, said the Senator, is a thorn in America's side, not a dagger through the heart.
After the landing, the CIA's own Inspector General had the same
advice — which was not seriously considered. Perhaps the best lesson was presented gnomically by Clayton Fritchie, on Adlai Stevenson's staff at the UN. He told the President, "It could have been
worse." Kennedy wondered how. "It might have succeeded."

Suppose the invaders had overthrown Castro's army, killed or
imprisoned Castro himself, and ushered home the "government in
exile." America would have produced José Miró Cardona, like a
rabbit out of Uncle Sam's hat. Would he have commanded popular
support in Cuba? He was opposed even by some of the exile invaders, even by some of the CIA organizers. No matter what his own
qualifications, which were impressive, anyone would be tainted by
the treatment he was given in America. The way he was shuttled
from New York to Florida, after being kept ignorant of the invasion, would be an affront to Latin pride. That might not have been

true before the revolution; but after it, his presence would have been a living sign of American imperialism. He would have been our puppet, and keeping him in power would have become a full-time American task — like propping up Thieu or Ky in Saigon. At a time when even the fading colonial regimes found it impossible to retain their former possessions, how could revolutionary Cuba submit to a new round of imperialism from America? Even if we succeeded in Cuba itself, the blatant effort involved would be feared and resented throughout Latin America and the Caribbean.

Robert Kennedy discovered that no serious estimate of the chances for a popular uprising had been asked for. Needless to say, the further chance of keeping an American surrogate in power could not have been considered, three or four steps further down the road from a hypothetical uprising. Hard as this is to credit, the Kennedys saw the elimination of Castro as a thing so obviously desirable in itself that no serious thinking went into the aftermath of that blessed event. The same thing continued true during the period when exotic poisons and sporadic sabotage and thousands of agents were used against Castro. For the New Frontier team, power meant doing what one wanted — and the team wanted to remove Castro.

The Kennedys thought power had only two components — ample resources, and the will to use them. In the Bay of Pigs affair, Kennedy was assured by Bissell that we had ample resources, so he concentrated on toughening his will. Then, when things began to go wrong, Robert Kennedy supplied the will and demanded that people in the control room come up with the mental and other resources: with all the famous talent around the table, *something* could be done. I once heard Eunice Kennedy say almost exactly the same thing at the head of her dining table. It is obviously a favorite line with the Kennedys. Nothing can withstand the direction of great talent by a will to win.

It is this attitude toward power that explains the frustrating, the almost literally maddening, impact of Castro on John and Robert Kennedy. Cuba obviously had fewer resources, of every sort, than America possessed. Yet Castro continued successfully to defy the giant — which meant that, being inferior in the one component of power, resources, Castro must have a compensatory superiority in the other component, force of will. The Kennedys were winners, yet *he* kept winning in his contest with them — proving that he was an even more determined winner. It was macho to macho, and he came off manlier, "ballsier," his charisma as intact as that beard the CIA scientists had tried to hex.

This Kennedy attitude was simply an exaggeration of a basically American attitude toward the postwar world. It would show up again during the Vietnam war — the fury that a "third-rate" nation could successfully defy us. Earlier, we had instituted a security program more stringent than the one imposed during the war itself, to retain our nuclear monopoly. Given that overwhelming resource, we could dispose of the world benignly, without resistance. As Philip Marlowe told the doctor, "When a man has a gun in his hand, you are supposed to do what he says." We had the nuclear gun in our hand — and, to our amazement, people still refused to do what we told them to. We had all the resources, so the failure must be in our will. McCarthyism was a great national search for the conspirators, the enemies within, who had sapped our will. That *had* to be the deficient component, since our resources were so great.

But the best students of power — Machiavelli and Hume, Clausewitz and Tolstoy — have always placed the source of power in the will of the commanded not of the commanding. Political power is the ability to get others to do your will. If they refuse, you may have the ability to destroy them; but that is not political power in any constructive sense. We can, at present, blow up the world with our nuclear weapons; but that does not mean we can rule the world. Conquest is not, automatically, control. Machiavelli is constantly teaching the difference between those two concepts: "Anyone comparing one of the countries with the other will recognize a great difficulty of conquering the Turks, but great ease in governing them once conquered. . . . But it is just the reverse with realms governed like that of France." The difference lies not in the resources of the conqueror, but in the disposition of the conquered. The docile Turks resist well, but easily conform; the French are easily divided by their conquerors, but rarely if at all united by their rulers. As Tolstoy wrote in *War and Peace:* "Power, from the standpoint of experience, is merely the relation that exists between the expression of someone's will and the execution of that will by others," and the second factor is more determinative than the first.

Because of the tremendous modern powers of destruction, those who look only to the resources and will of America's rulers are astonished at the impotence of power as they conceive it. The Russians, Cuba, any "third-rate nation" can refuse to obey us, even though we are able to obliterate them. Given the "realities" of the force-equation, we have tended to dismiss "world opinion" as something outside the calculus of coercion, though it is at the very center of power as a reality. People obey, said David Hume, *only* because of opinion — what he called opinion of right (one should obey) and opinion of interest (it will pay one to obey). Insofar as quantum-of-force theorists took opinion into account, they thought only of interest — obey us or we'll blow you up; obey us because we have economic advantages to bestow. Vaguer forces like anticolonialism were dismissed as mere sentiment. But Hume would have recognized in them the "opinion of right" that gives stability to political power (opinion of interest can shift as the "bribes" on either side are altered). So the project for getting rid of Castro was seen simply in terms of ability to kill him, disrupt his regime, remove his person. The will of the Cuban people was never taken seriously as a factor in the power situation. How they would be ruled after we had conquered their leader — whether power to influence was coordinate with, or at odds with, power to disrupt — never entered into the Kennedys' calculations.

From the time of *Why England Slept,* John Kennedy had not thought of power as the recruiting of people's opinion, but as the manipulation of their response by aristocrats who saw what the masses could not see. Relying on his own talent and will, the leader prods them, against their instincts, toward duty and empire. Thus, in the secret war on Castro, the American people were not informed of their government's activities — those "in the know" performed these services for people who could not understand the necessities of power. But this benevolent censorship left Americans unprepared to estimate the situation when Castro accepted Russian missiles onto his territory.

To the American public, this step looked unprovoked, mysteriously aggressive, threatening because it added resources to a side that clearly had a strong will already. There was no way for Americans to know — and, at that point, no way Kennedy could bring himself to inform them — that Cuban protestations of purely defensive purpose for the missiles were genuine. We did not know what Castro did — that thousands of agents were plotting his death, the destruction of his government's economy, the sabotaging of his mines and mills, the crippling of his sugar and copper industries. We had invaded Cuba once; officials high in Congress and the executive department thought we should have followed up with overwhelming support for that invasion; by our timetable of a year to bring Castro down, the pressure to supply that kind of support in a new "rebellion" was growing. All these realities were cloaked from the American people, though evident to the Russians and to the Cubans.

In this game of power used apart from popular support, the Kennedys looked like brave resisters of aggression, though they had actually been the causes of it. Herbert Dinerstein has established, from study of Russian materials, that the Soviet Union considered Latin America not ripe for large Communist influence until the Bay of Pigs failure. That gave them an opportunity, as continued American activity against Castro gave them an excuse, for large-scale intervention in this hemisphere.

The Russians were aiming at influence, by their support of the Cuban David against a Goliath too cowardly to strike in the daylight. Americans, unaware of all this, did not bother to ask themselves hard questions about the real intent of the missiles in Cuba. The President said the purpose of the missiles was "to provide a nuclear strike capability against the Western Hemisphere." But why would Castro launch missiles against even one of our cities, knowing that would be a suicidal act? Just one of our nuclear bombs on Havana would have destroyed his nation.

Well, then, if Castro did not have the missiles to conquer us (and how would he control us afterward, presuming that he could conquer us), was he making himself a willing hostage to Russia's designs? Would he launch his missiles in conjunction with a larger Russian attack — again, knowing that we could incinerate his island as a side-blow in our response to Russia? Even if Castro had wanted to immolate his nation that way, his missiles would not have helped the Russians — might, rather, have been a hindrance, because of the "ragged attack" problem. If missiles were launched simultaneously from Russia and Cuba, the Cuban ones, arriving first, would confirm the warnings of Russian attack. Or, if Cuba's missiles were to be launched later, radar warning of the Russian ones' firing would let us destroy the Cuban rockets in their silos.

Then why were the missiles there? For defensive purposes, just as the Cubans said. We refused to accept this explanation, because President Kennedy had arbitrarily defined ground-to-ground missiles as "offensive" after saying offensive weapons would not be tolerated. Yet we called our ground-to-ground missiles on the Soviets' Turkish border defensive. Deterrence — the threat of overwhelming response if attacked — is a category of defense when we apply it to our own weapons; but we denied the same definition to our opponents. Which meant that we blinded ourselves to the only reason Castro accepted (with some reluctance) the missiles over which Russians kept tight control. He wanted to force the Kennedys to stop plotting his overthrow, by threatening that, if worse came to worst and we were ready to crush him, he would take some of our cities down with him.

Americans watched this drama, as it were, through a glass pane, unable to hear the dialogue. Even after the crisis, we read Khrushchev's defense of his motives for placing the missiles, and considered it mere Communist propaganda:

> Cuba needed weapons as a means of containing the aggressors, and not as a means of attack. For Cuba was under a real threat of invasion. Piratical attacks were repeatedly made on her coasts, Havana was shelled, and airborne groups were dropped from planes to carry out sabotage. . . . Further events have shown that the failure of [the Bay of Pigs] invasion did not discourage the United States imperialists in their desire to strangle Cuba. (Speech of October 12, 1962)

Now we know that every factual statement in that list is true. But then we were unable to credit the rationale for Russia's advance to the defense of a Latin American country:

> What were our aims behind this decision? Naturally, neither we nor our Cuban friends had in mind that this small number of IRBMs, sent to Cuba, would be used for an attack on the United States or any other country. Our aim was only to defend Cuba.

It might be argued, now, that even if we knew about our own clandestine war against Castro, and admitted that the missiles were placed for deterrence, we could not tolerate their presence so near us. After all, accident or crazy leadership might launch them. The same thing is true of Russian missiles, of course. As Robert McNamara said at the time, a missile is a missile, whether fired at us from Russia or from Cuba. If mere proximity was the threat, we are in greater danger now than during the installation of those missiles, since Russian submarines cruise closer to our shores than the ninety-mile distance to Cuba. And the Kennedy administration knew that would soon be the situation.

In extraordinary interviews for *The New Yorker*, William Whitworth heard Eugene Rostow, part of Lyndon Johnson's war administration, defend the Vietnam commitment in terms of America's psychic needs, rather than outright military threat. Looking back to the Cuban decision his brother Walt took part in, Rostow admitted there was no direct danger from the missiles:

> "But during the Cuban missile crisis," I said, "were we more threatened from a technological standpoint than we had been before the missiles were installed?"
> "No, I think we were just touching a nerve of concern. . . . The missile crisis was a situation that I think is important for us to think about, because we were ready to go."

Rostow talks of America as feeling psychically crowded and on the edge of panic. To our citizens, uninformed of the American campaign on Castro, the Cuban provocation seemed unmotivated and therefore eerie. President Kennedy had to do something to reassure the frightened populace. His toughness calmed a people "ready to go."

That last phrase is a key one for Rostow in defending the Vietnam war. We could feel "crowded" even by forces halfway around the world. And when that happens, we become "ready to go" —leaving our rulers with only one pressing problem: how to channel our aggression into a limited expression. "The Cuban episode is worth studying because we were ready to go then. There was a rage in the

country and a sense of threat, and these were extremely dangerous."
In the same way, if the North Koreans had added one more insult to
the capture of the *Pueblo* in 1969, the American people would have
been unrestrainable: "There was a lot of rage in the country about
that. And my guess is that if the Koreans acted up the Americans
would hit very hard. Very hard. That would be natural, and human,
but it might be dangerous." In the same way, if South Vietnam fell
to the Communists, we would feel crowded. The problem, Rostow
admits, is not one of immediate military threat, but of a sense of insecurity:

> I think that if we faced that situation we would have to become a
> garrison state on a scale we can't even imagine now, and be con-
> cerned about threats from every quarter of the compass — be
> hemmed in. We couldn't be the kind of society we want to be.

> The trade that counts for the United States is with Canada, West-
> ern Europe and Japan. That's the bulk of it. And we could survive
> without most of that trade, I suppose. It isn't that. It's the sense of
> being hemmed in that becomes so dangerous.

By this reading, President Kennedy had two dangerous situations
to deal with simultaneously — the missile emplacements, and
American panic over those emplacements. Robert Kennedy implicitly agreed with Rostow when he told the President he had to remove the missiles or be impeached. In other words, the President
was a captive of his own people's panicky emotions. Options were
denied him by the American people — he could not even think of
leaving the missiles in place. That avenue was sealed from the outset.
Yet Kennedy had himself stirred up the feelings that limited his
freedom. He had called the missiles offensive and exaggerated their
range. It is understandable that he would not reveal all the American
provocation that explained the presence of the missiles. But why did
he have to *emphasize* the unprovoked character of their placement?
He told the nation that the Russians had lied to him in promising
not to send offensive weapons to Cuba. He said in his address on the
crisis: "The greatest danger of all would be to do nothing." If he was
chained to a necessity for acting, he forged the chains himself.
In this he was renewing a cycle that has bound all our postwar
Presidents. In order to have freedom of maneuver, a sense of crisis is

instilled; but once that sense is instilled, it commits the leader to actions he did not have in mind when he excited the fears. The most famous instance of this is Harry Truman's use of Senator Vandenberg's advice — if he wanted to rally support for anti-Communist aid to Greece and Turkey, he would have to "scare hell out of the country." But once Truman had raised the spectre of communism as an immediate threat to America, he had to calm the people by imposing a security program, establishing the Attorney General's List, setting up the machinery in 1947 that McCarthy would use in the 1950s.

Henry Kissinger assured his old academic friends, during the Vietnam war, that such a war must be prosecuted to the end, lest a new McCarthyism arise to ask "Who lost Vietnam?" as it had asked "Who lost China?" War became a homeopathic cure for American bellicosity — a little war taps the aggressiveness that, bottled up, might break out in a larger war. By a kind of devilish symmetry, the contemptuous manipulation of public opinion leads to a slavishness toward public opinion. Kennedy thought he could wage a war out of sight of the American people, for the people's good; but when the Cubans responded in open ways, he could not explain their effrontery, and had to ride the wave of public fear. All the talent and willpower of the best and brightest could not manipulate away the emotions they had aroused.

Kennedy thought of himself and Castro in charismatic terms — the two leaders using skill and will against each other, fencing over the heads of their respective peoples. But Castro was openly recruiting his people to a revolutionary cause while Kennedy was secretly scheming at assassination. The difference extends to more than tactics. The mere removal of Castro would not have dissipated the revolutionary élan. An "indispensable man" fallacy was at work in Kennedy's approach to Cuba. Meanwhile, by failing to recruit the will of the American people in an open way, Kennedy was put in the position of lying to his citizens at a time when Castro was telling the truth about American intentions and schemings. Having fooled the people in order to lead them, Kennedy was forced to serve the folly he had induced.

22

"Restraint"

If Khrushchev wants to rub my nose in the dirt, it's all over.

— JFK TO JAMES WECHSLER

That son of a bitch [Khrushchev] won't pay any attention to words. He has to see you move.

— JFK TO ARTHUR SCHLESINGER

IN DEALING WITH THE CUBAN MISSILES, John Kennedy displayed a restraint that has become legendary. It made Arthur Schlesinger rather weak in the knees:

> It was this combination of toughness and restraint, of will, nerve and wisdom, so brilliantly controlled, so matchlessly calibrated, that dazzled the world. Before the missile crisis people might have feared that we would use our power extravagantly or not use it at all. But the thirteen days gave the world — even the Soviet Union — a sense of American determination and responsibility in the use of power which, if sustained, might indeed become a turning point in the history of the relations between east and west.

Undoubtedly there was restraint exercised in the White House, most laudably when a U-2 plane was shot down during the tensest moments of the quarantine, before Russia had agreed to pull back. Although "ExCom," the ad hoc Executive Committee assembled to cope with the crisis, had earlier agreed to take out one of the surface-to-air (SAM) missile sites if this happened, the President wisely said he would wait for Khrushchev's response to the principal point of contention.

There was also restraint, of a sort, in the quick rejection of a plan for outright conquest of the island — though no one was very serious about proposing that. The option that did get serious consideration, and toward which the President at first inclined, was a preemptive air strike to destroy the missile launching pads. If the military had not suggested technical difficulties in this procedure, it would have been given even more serious attention — though Robert Kennedy's first reaction to the idea was to slip his brother a note saying, "I now know how Tojo felt when he was planning Pearl Harbor."

Though the air strike was rejected as a first step, it was prepared as the next step in case the blockade failed. Sorensen puts among the signs of Kennedy's restraint his use of the politer term quarantine instead of blockade — but this ranks rather with the counsels of prudence than of restraint. A blockade is, in international law, an act of war — the reason the administration had earlier given for not intercepting the shipments of SAMs to Castro. Kennedy was cautious in enforcing the blockade. But, with credit given for that, we have exhausted the evidences of Kennedy restraint. It is on the basis of these acts that he claimed, to his brother: "If anybody is around to write after this, they are going to understand that we made every effort to find peace and every effort to give our adversary room to move. I am not going to push the Russians an inch beyond what is necessary." That claim is demonstrably untrue, on at least five counts.

1. Kennedy could have explained to Americans that Castro was the object of secret warfare on the part of the CIA. This was something that would have been hard, and no doubt seemed impossible, to do. But the course was "unthinkable" only because Kennedy's search for "options" imprisoned him in the lies told to cover those options; and refusal to admit that his own acts caused the missile crisis in the first place makes it impossible to claim that *every* effort to make peace was explored and *every* possible chance for maneuver allowed to the other side.

2. Kennedy ruled out, instantly and without discussion, open diplomacy as a means of settling the crisis. When he learned of the

missiles' presence, he kept the knowledge secret — in the first place, to preserve the option of a sneak attack on the sites, what Robert Kennedy called "a Pearl Harbor." No attempt was made to negotiate with the Russians until an ultimatum had been secretly devised, then publicly delivered. This not only prevented prior diplomacy with the Russians, and forced them to capitulate; it excluded our allies from prior consultation, along with Congress and the UN. It is known that General de Gaulle's resentment of this act — the risking of nuclear war without consulting those endangered — confirmed him in the determination to carve out a separate nuclear role for France. Walter Lippmann quickly identified the weakness in Kennedy's approach. During the quarantine itself, he wrote:

> When the President saw Mr. Gromyko on Thursday [two days before the ultimatum], and had the evidence of the missile build-up in Cuba, he refrained from confronting Mr. Gromyko with this evidence. This was to suspend diplomacy. If it had not been suspended, the President would have shown Mr. Gromyko the pictures, and told him privately about the policy which in a few days he intended to announce publicly. This would have made it more likely that Moscow would order the ships not to push on to Cuba. But if such diplomatic action did not change the orders, if Mr. Khrushchev persisted in spite of it, the President's public speech would have been stronger. For it would not have been subject to the criticism that a great power had issued an ultimatum to another great power without first attempting to negotiate the issue. By confronting Mr. Gromyko privately, the President would have given Mr. Khrushchev what all wise statesmen give their adversaries — the chance to save face.

Later, of course, Kennedy would claim he *did* give Khrushchev every chance to save face. Lippmann, even before the crisis was over, proved that was not so. Later examples of preemptive strikes — Nixon's invasion of Cambodia, Israel's raids on an Iraqi power plant and Beirut — would invoke Kennedy's action in the Cuban crisis as a justification for neglecting diplomacy. In this respect, at least, the lesson conveyed by Kennedy's actions was not one of restraint but of unilateral boldness.

3. The decision-making body Kennedy set up was one that con-

duced toward boldness, not caution. When, in the spring of 1963, Theodore Sorensen gave a course of lectures at Columbia University celebrating the missile crisis as a model of decision-making, he praised the President for his lack of "preoccupation with form and structure" — proving he had learned nothing from the Bay of Pigs invasion. The "ExCom" was an informal body in more-or-less permanent session, without any order for screening and discussing advice. Its participants dropped in or out as they maintained prior commitments in order to keep the crisis secret. The President himself went off to Cleveland and Chicago while the ExCom debated life-and-death matters. Orderly inquest was at the mercy of separate schedules and improvised security. Roger Hilsman writes: "Everyone tried to keep up social engagements, although they sorely needed both the time and the rest that social engagements cost them. At one stage, nine members of the ExCom piled into a single limousine, sitting on each others' laps, to avoid attracting the attention that the whole fleet of long black cars would have done."

This hasty coming and going, in the back corridors, of men starved for sleep and rubbing against each other in different combinations, led to a blow-up when Adlai Stevenson joined them and suggested a diplomatic trade — removing the Marines from Guantanamo, or our missiles from Turkey, in exchange for Khrushchev's taking the missiles out. He was savagely denounced; even the President, according to Hilsman, showed his anger — and punished Stevenson through a friendly journalist, as he had done with Arthur Krock. Charles Bartlett was allowed to quote him as a "high official," in the *Saturday Evening Post,* saying, "Adlai wanted a Munich." The same pressures toward "macho" talk, the same inhibitions on any sign of weakness, were at work as in the Bay of Pigs sessions. Robert McNamara, after expressing his view that "a missile is a missile," was talked out of the recommendation to do nothing. For two days the President pushed for assurance that an air strike would work, and no one of sufficient weight was opposing him — no one but Robert. Though Sorensen later tried to credit the President's *procedures* with the happy outcome of the missile decision, that outcome — to the extent that it was happy — was the single accomplishment of Robert Kennedy.

What brought about this new restraint in the "bad Bobby" who was, even at the time of these sessions, urging Castro's overthrow? The explanation is almost surely the very fact that he *did* know how much the crisis owed to prior provocation on the CIA's part. The "mean altar boy" always had a lively moral strain in him — not enough to urge the admission (or even the suspension) of assaults on Castro, but enough to make him see that the Russians were not acting out of sheer malevolence, that they had some case, and were probably open to sensible bargaining. Mad as the President had been when Adlai Stevenson brought up the idea of trading Turkish missiles for the Cuban ones, Robert quietly assured Anatoly Dobrynin that America intended to remove the missiles from Turkey. Other ExCom people knew of the efforts being directed at Castro — Taylor and Helms and the President — but they do not seem to have felt this made it inappropriate to treat Russia as the aggressor. Only Robert Kennedy showed a dawning awareness that America might have been somewhat in the wrong. It would be a while before he began to sense the same thing about our course in Vietnam. But the "receiving equipment" for such moral signals was already in place; and that alone — plus Robert's influence with his brother — saved the ExCom from acting as recklessly as the Bay of Pigs advisers had. The veterans of the later sessions would make exaggerated claims for their own restraint — in part because they could easily have taken less prudent steps, but for one man. Against the background of other courses forcefully urged, the outcome did look so magnanimous as to seem self-denying.

4. Nonetheless, the course pursued was reckless. President Kennedy did not give the Russians the obvious opportunity to "save face." In the matter of the Turkish missiles, he humiliated them gratuitously, though the missiles had no military importance for us. Sorensen says the trade-off was one of the first things suggested as the ExCom began its considerations, but that "the President had rejected this course from the outset." His anger at Stevenson for proposing the trade seems to have come in part from the "nerve" he showed in raising again a possibility the President had ruled out. Some have said the President did not want to insult our allies by withdrawing the missiles without consulting them. But the secret sessions were an odd place for punctilious consultation of allies to become a great concern; and, even if this argument were made sin-

cerely, the hurt feelings of allies were little compared with the danger we put them in by serving an ultimatum rather than offering a deal. Besides, the argument is clearly not sincere. Kennedy had already ordered the Turkish missiles removed, and mere procedural delay had kept them in place to this point. Not only were they of no value; they were a source of possible trouble. Hilsman notes that they were "obsolete, unreliable, inaccurate, and very vulnerable — they could be knocked out by a sniper with a rifle and telescopic sights."

Though the Turkish missiles meant nothing to us, they were a symbolic grievance to the Soviet Union — in fact, exactly the kind of affront we were complaining of. We felt "crowded" by missiles ninety miles from our shore. The Russians had to live with the ignominy of hostile missiles right on their border. If Kennedy's first and only concern was the missiles' removal from Cuba — as he and his defenders proclaimed — then a trade was the safest, surest way to achieve that goal. But Kennedy clearly had other priorities in mind — he wanted to remove the missiles *provided* he did not appear forced to *bargain* with the Soviets to accomplish this. He must deliver the ultimatum, make demands that made Russia act submissively. He would not, as he put it, let Khrushchev rub his nose in the dirt. Which meant that he had to rub Khrushchev's nose in the dirt; and that Khrushchev had to put up with it. Kennedy would even risk nuclear war rather than admit that a trade of useless missiles near each other's countries was eminently fair. The restraint, then, was not shown by Kennedy, but by Khrushchev. He was the one who had to back down, admit his maneuver had failed, take the heat from internal critics for his policy.

It was not known at the time that Robert Kennedy informally told Dobrynin that the Turkish sites would be dismantled. Since that detail was published (after his death) in Kennedy's own account, it has been taken as a further sign of restraint on America's part. But the secrecy of the assurance is what mattered — along with its late informal relay to a secondary figure in the chess game. Removing the Turkish missiles had been part of the open trade proposed in the famous "second letter" of Khrushchev — the letter Robert Kennedy said should be ignored. When, one day before the President's deadline ran out, Robert Kennedy told Dobrynin that he thought the missiles would be removed, he expressly "said that there could be no quid pro quo or any arrangement made under this kind of threat or pressure." In short, the missiles would be removed so long as the Russians got no credit for their removal, could make no plausible claim that they were bargaining with an equal, not submitting to an ultimatum. It should be remembered that Robert Kennedy wrote his account of the missile crisis in the summer of 1967, five years after the event and when he was rethinking his own hawkish position on Vietnam. If all he could do to emphasize his own dovish behavior in the missile crisis was suggest that last-minute secret assurance to Dobrynin, there is no reason to think this represented a significant act of restraint on the part of the Kennedy administration itself. Kennedy still insisted on Russia's public humiliation over a symbol that had no real military importance for us — an insistence that faced us with a real military threat if the Russians did not accede to the harsh demand we made. Macho appearance, not true security, was the motive for Kennedy's act — surely the most reckless American act since the end of World War II.

5. To add injury to insult, Kennedy — with his insistence on crisis — sent his brother to Dobrynin to enforce the twenty-four-hour deadline for Russia's response. This further "crowded" the Russians, made panicky response possible. It rubbed their noses a little deeper into the dirt. The justification for this hasty act was the possibility that some missiles might be armed and launchable within forty-eight hours. But what was the probability that Cuba would use a few short-range missiles, in a kamikaze attack, when America was in a state of alert, its SAC bombers in the air, its Polaris missiles prowling the waters around Cuba? It was surely less than the probability that Russia, backed into a corner and given a deadline, might make some hasty decision — perhaps to attack American troops in Germany — that could trigger World War III. Neither course of action made much sense. But the *less* probable was made the basis of our deadline, which threatened to trigger the *more* probable of two horrible possibilities. Kennedy, in other words, increased our danger by the deadline, on the chance that this would increase our victory, make it more total.

If the Russians had made even a *limited* attack in Europe or elsewhere, the Kennedy buildup of crisis rhetoric would have made it hard to refrain from nuclear response. After all, he felt unable to refrain from exaggerated response to the nonthreat in Cuba. He would have been *less* free to defy American "panic" if Khrushchev had imitated his bellicosity.

So the reaction to missiles in Cuba was not a model of restraint, of rational decision-making, of power used in peaceful ways. That it turned out "well" for us is a tribute to Khrushchev's restraint, not ours. And was the glorious victory so total after all? We have seen that it helped push de Gaulle farther down his independent path. Khrushchev's loss contributed, or appeared to contribute, to his own later downfall — depriving us of a leader who was easier to deal with than his successors. Besides, what was the lesson of the missile crisis for the Russians? That one should not back off in further confrontations over that island? When Jimmy Carter declared, in 1979, that the presence of Russian combat troops in Cuba was "intolerable," there was no sign of accommodation from Russian leaders. They have only two or three enthusiastic allies outside their own satellite system and Cuba is the most important one — one they cannot afford to fail again; one no Russian leader, with the example of Khrushchev before him, will abandon. We purchased submission at the price of later intransigence, which is often the case after gratuitous humiliation.

Praise of Kennedy for his conduct in the missile crisis often reaches the conclusion that he learned pacific ways in this "restrained" success. On the contrary, he must have learned that his own and his party's popularity soars when he can make an opponent visibly "eat crow," even if the only way to serve up that menu is to risk the national safety. But the argument for Kennedy can be put in a more persuasive way if we say that the totality of his victory gave him room to be more magnanimous in other areas, to make pacific overtures without looking dangerously weak or "dovish." The Kennedy literature makes his American University speech, in favor of negotiation and arms limitation, the fruit of the missile decision's outcome.

But if that is so, what lesson is taught? That one must never negotiate but in the wake of humiliating an enemy? Surely that is the lesson applied year after year in Vietnam. We must never negotiate from weakness, went the slogan; so, after sedating the war during elections, there was a heavy bombing schedule every November and December of the even-numbered years, culminating in the "Christmas bombing" of 1972. Negotiation, which should mean the achievement of mutual benefit by diplomatic means, has become for Americans the negotiation of the other side's surrender after a defeat. We could never go to the negotiating table as equals — that would look like trading missile for missile as equals in 1962.

Some critics, notably Ronald Steel, have accused Kennedy of pushing for a knockout blow late in October of 1962 in order to affect the congressional elections. Put so crudely, the charge is unfair. Rather, an eye on domestic response locked Kennedy into the cycle which makes it impossible for American leaders to make peaceful moves except in the aftermath of bellicose ones successfully carried out. Steel notes that even Sorensen quoted a Republican ExCom member (probably Douglas Dillon) during the crisis:

> Ted, have you considered the very real possibility that if we allow Cuba to complete installation and operational readiness of missile bases, the next House of Representatives is likely to have a Republican majority? This would completely paralyze our ability to react sensibly and coherently to further Soviet advances.

Roger Hilsman, too, admits that domestic pressures affected Kennedy's judgment during the crisis. To some extent, he was still the prisoner of his rhetoric, making an apparently "soft" attitude toward Cuba impossible:

> The fact of the matter was that President Kennedy and his administration were peculiarly vulnerable on Cuba. He had used it in his own campaign against Nixon to great effect, asking over and over why a Communist regime had been permitted to come to power just ninety miles off our coast.

Furthermore, in order to restrain the calls for interdiction of SAMs to Cuba, Kennedy had exaggerated the danger of ground-to-ground missiles (thinking they would not be installed):

Thus in trying to meet the opposition's charges and to reassure the public without actually saying why it was so confident, the administration fell into the semantic trap of trying to distinguish between "offensive" and "defensive" weapons.

Kennedy was soon stuck with his own claim that ground-to-ground missiles were offensive: "If the missiles were not important enough strategically to justify a confrontation with the Soviet Union, as McNamara initially thought, yet were 'offensive,' then the United States might not be in mortal danger but the administration most certainly was." When Ronald Steel quoted that sentence to show that Kennedy was affected by electoral pressures, Hilsman replied with the claim that he had larger issues of political support in mind: "I meant that the administration would be faced with a revolt from the military, from the hardliners in the other departments, both State and CIA, from not only Republicans on Capitol Hill but some Democrats too." Kennedy, who boasted that McNamara had brought the military people under control, had to please them, or they would "revolt."

Over and over in our recent history Presidents have claimed they had to act tough in order to *disarm* those demanding that they act tough. The only way to become a peacemaker is first to disarm the warmakers by making a little successful war. And if the little war becomes a big one, it must be pursued energetically or the "hawks" will capitalize on the failure. War wins, either way. If you are for it, you wage it. And if you are against it, you wage it. So Kennedy is given credit for making overtures to lessen the threat of nuclear weapons only after he risked nuclear war to get the "capacity" to make a mild disarmament proposal. That was the obvious lesson of the missile crisis. Even Sorensen had to admit it was the moral many people derived: "Ever since the successful resolution of that crisis, I have noted among many political and military figures a Cuban-missile-crisis syndrome, which calls for a repetition in some other conflict of 'Jack Kennedy's tough stand of October 1962 when he told the Russians with their missiles either to pull out or look out!' Some observers even attributed Lyndon Johnson's decision to escalate in Vietnam to a conviction that America's military superiority could bring him a 'victory' comparable to JFK's." Sorensen thinks that was not the lesson that *should* have been learned. But it is the lesson that *was* learned. Assertions of power rarely teach what the powerful intended.

23

Charismatic Nation

His success was the immediate cause of his destruction.

— GIBBON, of the Emperor Maximus

THE KENNEDYS RIGHTLY DAZZLED America. We thought it was our own light being reflected back on us. The charismatic claims looked natural to a charismatic country. America, we like to think, has been specially "graced." Set apart. The first child of the Enlightenment, it was "declared" to others as the harbinger of a new order. Yet this rationally founded nation was also deeply devotional, a redeemer nation. Reason and religion, which should have contended near our cradle, conspired instead. If we kept ourself isolated from others, it was to avoid contamination. If we engaged others, we did so from above, to bring light into their darkness. To deal with others as equals would betray our mission.

So, in the missile crisis, some asked why we should resent missiles near our shores more than Russians were allowed to resent missiles on their border. But to most Americans the answer was obvious. We are not like other nations. We can be trusted to use our power virtuously. Our missiles were not offensive because they were *ours*. As Hanson Baldwin wrote, after the crisis, in the New York *Times:* "The real measure of the overseas base therefore is its purpose. The United States contention, shared by its allies, has always been that its overseas bases were established solely in answer to Communist aggressive expansionism and at the request of the countries concerned." The distinction between missiles depended less on their structure and range than on the character of the country producing them. And who could doubt our good character?

If we refuse to "negotiate from weakness" (i.e., from parity with the negotiating partner), that is because we are not simply one more member of the community of nations scrambling for narrow advantage. It is our task to think for all those involved, to keep scavengers away from the world's developing nations, to uphold freedom around the globe. Charisma exempts from normal process. The sense of a "graced" country lay behind our dispatching of Peace Corps youths to dazzle the world with our virtue. The implicit message, underneath the laudable desire to serve, was anti-Communist even when crude propagandizing was excluded. The message was: Be like us.

The sign of grace is luck, and who could be luckier than Americans? Given a vast continent to explore and exploit in comparative isolation from the rest of the world, we entered the game of the great powers only when we were ready to — on our own schedule, for our own purposes. Our first major intervention in this century was for the rescue of democracy; but the old system of power relations thwarted us at Versailles. A whole generation of rising leaders vowed that would not happen next time, and the "lesson of Versailles" made us conduct our very own war to a conclusion that left us masters of the world. In 1945, America — which had entered the war still reeling from the Depression — stood at the pinnacle of power, with resources no other nation ever possessed. Our enemies had been defeated by a policy of total war carried through to unconditional surrender. Our allies had been invaded and weakened. Our military apparatus was the greatest ever assembled; and nuclear weaponry was added to it in the climactic last act of our Pacific campaign.

Total war was waged to insure the totality of our control afterward. Those defending the unconditional surrender policy, against military and intelligence people who said it would prolong the war, maintained that only this would give America a "clean slate" for building a world order of peace. The fascist philosophy had to be destroyed, erased, removed from the world like a cancer. This was not simply a war for trade rights, or ports, or access to material resources. The American *vision* had to prevail.

Our power had created expectations which alone can explain the panic of America in 1947. We were still the economic and military master of the world. No one could threaten our shores. We had a nuclear monopoly. Our prosperity continued. No other country could impose its will on us. Yet in an extraordinary series of moves, President Truman followed Senator Vandenberg's advice and scared the hell out of the country. Solidifying new prerogatives from this sense of crisis, he instituted the security system, established the CIA (which began building resistance centers for World War III), and opened a campaign to avoid "losing" Turkey and Greece as we were losing China.

Why this panic in the very heart of power? We were hostages to our own broad claims. By attempting total control, we felt imperiled *anywhere* when *anything* went against our will. We were illustrating a truth that Gibbon taught in various ways. The expansion of one's rim of power diffuses internal resources, stretches the thin periphery ever farther out, so that a small concentration of hostile force can burst the bubble of empire. Since "the increasing circle must be involved in a larger sphere of hostility," the entirety is risked at each isolable point along the rim.

The Eisenhower years represented a tacit acceptance of limits, at odds with this aspiration toward universal control. That is what Senator Kennedy complained of when he said the country must get moving again (Walt Rostow's phrase). A new generation must take up again the torch that had guttered out. Massive retaliation had become an excuse for inaction. Little challenges around our periphery of influence were being neglected, cumulative losses not redressed. Maxwell Taylor complained of the cuts in defense spending. Space did not command any enthusiasm on Eisenhower's part, even after Russia's Sputnik "victory."

We now know that Eisenhower let Allen Dulles initiate secret coups or coup attempts in Iran and Guatemala, Indonesia and the Congo. But, despicable as these were, they were kept secret precisely because there was no public policy of engagement everywhere, no mystique of countering any guerrillas who might pop up. The Dulles operations were small enough, and tailored to the individual situation, for "success" (as in Iran) to cause no widespread outcry against the United States and failure (as in Indonesia) to let us cut our losses with no great public humiliation. Eisenhower's attitude toward intervention in a colonial war was made clear when he overruled all the advisers asking him to rescue the French at Dien Bien Phu.

Eisenhower admitted there is a "tyranny of the weak," an ability of massed little forces to trouble the thin-drawn periphery of American concerns, for which there is no properly "calibrated" response. The gnats could be smashed, but only in ways that made the giant look worse than its challengers. Short of obliteration, no intimidation was credible for most of these enclaves of defiance. Recruiting their will was either impossible or would be made impossible by military threat. There was nothing to do but ignore what could not be controlled in any useful way. That was the advice of a man who understood power, its meaning and limits.

But John Kennedy had different teachers on the nature of power. They thought any recognition of limits signaled a failure of nerve. For them the question was not *can* you do everything, but *will* you do everything? The American resources were limitless — brains, science, talent, tricks, technology, money, virtuosity. The only thing to decide was whether one had the *courage* to use all that might — and John Kennedy, in his inaugural address, assured us that he had. In his first major speech on defense, he said: "Any potential aggressor contemplating an attack on any part of the free world with any kind of weapons, conventional or nuclear, must know that our response will be suitable, selective, swift, and effective." Anywhere along the outmost sweep of our vast reach, we would strike if provoked.

It might not have been possible for the Romans to protect an expanding perimeter of power, one thinned by its extension to enclose the known world. But America could protect the whole world, because we had things the Romans lacked — jet planes, helicopters, napalm, defoliants, one-man water-walking rockets, computers, and theoreticians of the strategic hamlet. We could do everything, it was believed, so long as we never did, in any one spot, more than was absolutely necessary. That is where Robert McNamara's computers came into play — for dispatching the exactly right-sized teams to troubled spots. Admittedly the computers could not measure things like the strength of anticolonial feeling. But that was considered an advantage by Kennedy's "pragmatic" nonideologists. For them, the hard facts of cash and firepower spoke louder than sentiment.

The Americans would come with "clean hands," as Pyle says in the Greene novel — not apostles of capitalism, like Eisenhower's big businessmen; not preachers of world ideals, like Wilson. We were just technicians of development in the age of Rostow; producers of what mankind wants, said McNamara of Detroit. This was the policy Arthur Schlesinger had proclaimed, as part of the "end of ideology," in his book *The Vital Center:* World War II veterans who had "learned the facts of life through the exercise of power" realized that life "is sometimes more complicated than one would gather from the liberal weeklies."

For men holding such views, Vietnam was an ideal place to try out new tools of power — a place to prove that development could be encouraged without colonial exploitation; a place where mobility and concentration of firepower could do more than massive armies and huge weapons; a place where infiltrating North Vietnamese could be interdicted. Jungle and swamp would train our new guerrillas to all kinds of conditions. Despite later talk of a "quagmire" that sucked us in, Americans actually charged into Vietnam — thinking, as we did of Cuba, that a few men brilliantly directed could wrap the whole thing swiftly up. Officers were cycled through to observe the process because the opportunity would not last forever.

A speech written for Kennedy's delivery on the day he died boasted that he had "increased our special counterinsurgency forces which are now engaged in South Vietnam by 600 percent." The administration was still presenting Vietnam as a symbol of Kennedy's success in the books written just after his death. Hugh Sidey, for instance, puts this in his list of breakthrough achievements:

> A deep pride in the state of our armed forces really was the biggest factor in the underlying serenity. Our superiority in missiles, our improved conventional fighting capability and the new emphasis on guerrilla warfare, all carefully tailored by Robert McNamara, reestablished confidence in our strength. In Southeast Asia the enemy had been engaged on his own terms, and though there still was no victory in Vietnam or Laos, we were no longer losing.

William Kaufmann, celebrating the success of *The McNamara Strategy,* wrote in 1964:

In fact, the war in South Vietnam, if it has done nothing else, illustrates how the Military Assistance Program and an American military advisory group can produce an indigenous combat force of significant power with a relatively small commitment of American manpower. But the real test of South Vietnam is less of the Military Assistance Program than it is of the ability of the United States to deal effectively with all the related aspects of subversion and guerrilla warfare.

The unhappy later progress of the Vietnam war made Kennedy's defenders claim he would have withdrawn from the contest after committing 16,500 troops to it. The only positive evidence that is offered for this view is Kennedy's assurance to Senator Mansfield that he would have to get out of Vietnam sometime after the 1964 election. But the year intervening between his death and that election would have involved further commitments of the sort that President Johnson (despite his initial distaste for the idea of a larger war) made, on the advice of Kennedy's most trusted counselors. And Kennedy's "commitment" would have been even more binding. Not only was he the initiator of the process Lyndon Johnson took over; it was an initiative formulated in the terms of the "flexible response" by which Kennedy hoped to justify his whole military program and foreign policy. Was he going to let Green Berets, too, learn "that Superman is a fairy"? Any withdrawal would have been a confession that his overarching strategy — with Rostow's rationale, and Taylor's strategy, and McNamara's reorganization — was feckless: it could not deal with precisely the kind of problem it was framed for.

Not only Kennedy's advisers, but the Kennedy brothers, supported the Vietnam war for years after John Kennedy's death. As late as 1966, Robert was still applying the wrong "lesson of the missile crisis" to Vietnam: "As a far larger and more powerful nation learned in October of 1962, surrender of a vital interest of the United States is an objective which cannot be achieved." This was said to assure people that his proposal for negotiating with the Communists did not mean a surrender — though that proposal was itself no guarantee of a quick solution, as Richard Nixon and Henry Kissinger would find to their sorrow. If it took so long for Robert

Kennedy to disengage, even under President Johnson, whose skill at conducting his brother's policy could be blamed for its mishaps, it would have been impossible to disengage with his brother still in charge and hoping to "win."

John Kenneth Galbraith has suggested that Kennedy was about to change his policies because he had expressed a desire to get rid of Dean Rusk after the 1964 election. But that desire signals the opposite of any withdrawal from Vietnam. The man he wanted in Rusk's place was McNamara, than whom there was no more "hawkish" adviser in 1964. Rusk, despite his hawkish line under President Johnson, was unacceptable to the Kennedys because he seemed too *timid* and irresolute.

That Kennedy would have started disengaging from Vietnam, at the very time when he had hope of building a new administration there in the wake of Diem's overthrow, is unlikely. Though America did not engineer Diem's assassination, we allowed it, hoping for better things. As Roger Hilsman wrote in 1964: "The downfall of the Diem regime gave Vietnam and the United States a second chance to carry out an effective program to defeat the Communist guerrillas and win the people. Ambassador Lodge and whomever Kennedy might have chosen to replace General Harkins, whose tour of duty was coming to an end, might well have done the trick — if Kennedy had lived." It should be remembered that Hilsman was considered a "dove." There was no dove position in Kennedy's administration that stood for withdrawal. The doves were for winning the war by gentler methods. If Kennedy had wanted to make withdrawal possible, he would have had to invent a new position out of thin air — against all the forces unleashed by his own rhetoric and planning, conveyed through his network of advisers.

The principal division between Kennedy's advisers just before his death pitted the "political solution" people against the "military solution" people. But the political solution was for further intervention, more central American command, and increased activity. Hilsman, for instance, thought that more men rather than more bombs were needed:

Our proposal was to put a division of American ground forces into Thailand as a warning and couple it with communications to

North Vietnamese representatives in the various Communist and neutral capitals. If the warning was not heeded, that division could be moved right up to the Laos border, and a second division could be introduced into Thailand. If that set of warnings was also ignored, a division could be introduced into Vietnam, and so on — not to fight the Viet Cong, which should remain the task of the South Vietnamese, but to deter the north from escalating.

Meanwhile, our "advisers" would direct an illegal "Bay of Pigs" operation into Laos, keeping our involvement clandestine:

> To help protect the more northern portions of South Vietnam, it might be necessary to do the ambushing in Laos. But there was a world of international political difference between a black-clad company of South Vietnamese rangers ambushing a black-clad unit of Viet Cong infiltrators on a jungle trail in Laos and American jets dropping bombs in Laos.

The "political" solution promised more for less, but involved an even more complete control of the situation. We needed better puppets in Saigon, to be treated as José Miró Cardona had been in New York. Hilsman's own hope was for the strategic hamlet approach ("clear and hold" rather than "search and destroy"), which had only failed because of a lack of the central discipline Americans must supply: "The major weakness of the program under the previous [Diem] regime [R. K. G.] Thompson reported, had been the lack of overall strategic direction and Nhu's policy of creating hamlets haphazardly all over the country."

The "lesser" option actually involved greater interference in the entire life of the country — we would build it up from scratch in hamlets we sited and ruled — and a great arrogance about America's ability to dispose of all things sweetly with minimal violence. The "doves" had decided that the Ngo family could not shed the taint of collaboration with the French colonizers (something America was not guilty of), so they had to go. But Arthur Schlesinger, in his life of Robert Kennedy, points out that the Ngos were showing a willingness to negotiate with the North, rather than allow America to take away the rule of their country, just at the time America helped topple the Ngos. Bad as their family's record had been, in the eyes of their countrymen, they were at least Vietnamese, and did not want to accept de facto dictatorship by American proconsuls:

> The Ngo brothers were, in their anachronistic fashion, authentic Vietnamese nationalists. They were reluctant about American troops and resistant to American interference. "Those who knew Diem best," Robert Shaplen of the *New Yorker* wrote after twenty years in Vietnam, "felt that neither he nor Nhu would ever have invited or allowed 550,000 American soldiers to fight in their country and to permit the devastation caused by air attacks." Diem may also have felt, as Bui Kien Thanh has suggested, that massive American intervention would provoke massive Chinese intervention and deliver Vietnam to its historic enemy. In May 1963 Nhu proposed publicly that the United States start withdrawing its troops. In the summer he told [Michael] Forrestal in his "hooded" way that the United States did not understand Vietnam; "sooner or later we Vietnamese will settle our differences between us." "Even during the most ferocious battle," Nhu said to Mieczyslaw Maneli, the Polish member of the International Control Commission established in 1954 to supervise the Geneva agreement, "the Vietnamese never forget who is a Vietnamese and who is a foreigner."

Maneli was a go-between in the diplomatic feelers the Ngos had put out to Ho Chi Minh just before Diem was killed. It was to prevent more negotiating of that sort that General Khanh engineered an anti-Minh coup after the anti-Diem coup had succeeded.

The self-styled doves were drawing us deeper in while they thought they were getting us out. This corresponds to the general pattern of Kennedy's administration. It was not the military that caused most trouble, but the civilians; not the bureaucrats but the "best and brightest" who thought they were beating the bureaucracy; not the Joint Chiefs of Staff but their "tamer," Robert McNamara; not Curtis LeMay, whose thirst to bomb was self-defeating because self-caricaturing, but Rostow and Taylor, who promised that we could get into Vietnam and never feel the urge to bomb. The advocates of "lesser" action envisioned the possibility of greater control — which always (just) slipped their grasp. Attempts at total control always do.

We have seen that Hilsman wanted to introduce one, or two, or three divisions as a buffer, so his pacification program would have a chance to be tried. The real story of Vietnam is not that of counterinsurgency yielding to regular troops. From the outset, the counterinsurgents needed regular troops to scale the fighting down to a point where the counterinsurgents could be effective. Guerrillas need water to swim in, or an umbrella for their actions. Regular troops were, from the outset, that umbrella. Schlesinger says:

> As for counterinsurgency, it was never really tried in Vietnam. Taylor and Rostow, for all their counterinsurgency enthusiasm in Washington, roared home from Saigon [in 1961] dreaming of big battalions. . . . The Special Forces were sent to remote regions to help peripheral groups like the Montagnards. At the end of 1963 there were only one hundred Green Berets left in South Vietnam.

The other "advisers" sent in were regular troops; partly because the Special Forces training program was still in its infancy, but mainly because the circumstances for using the Special Forces had to be *created* — Diem had to be "controlled," we had to give him reinforcements for his army, stiffen his morale, while trying to refashion his regime.

So much for the lesson of the Bay of Pigs. We were still trying to find a situation that would not call for heavy military commitment, and using heavy military commitment in order to create that situation. The whole mystique of flexible response was that it would fit each contingency with the appropriate force. But rather than adapt to reality, we ended up trying to make reality adapt to our preconceptions.

At home, the Kennedy people thought they could apply "surgical" control to problems while ignoring the bureaucracy. Problems were isolable, to be removed from prior context and given a neat technical solution. That was a questionable approach even in our own country. "Break the Rules Committee" and you have not solved the problem of congressional recalcitrance — you have only embittered congressmen, who will resist more stubbornly. To think we could go into an alien culture and manipulate the "hearts and minds" of its inhabitants by technical skill — remove a Castro here, put up a strategic hamlet there — was always a delusion. Once again, confidence in our resources and will had made the complex interplay of millions of other wills seem irrelevant. Even the guerrilla experts who talked of winning the hearts of other people thought this could be done by image-manipulation on a level with American campaign tricks. General Lansdale, the most respected of the "hearts and minds" school, ran Operation Mongoose on the assumption that he could woo the people of Cuba from Castro by a religious indoctrination program that presented him as the Antichrist. Other Green Berets naturally reverted to the saying, "If you have them by the balls, their minds and hearts will follow." The Kennedy pursuit of power never got far away from balls.

There is no way of knowing what President Kennedy might have done had he lived. Could he have withdrawn from Vietnam without losing face? He thought he could not trade Turkish missiles for Cuban without being impeached, so necessary was it to keep America's hawks happy with his toughness. Would he have disowned his own policies and advisers in Vietnam, and done it in time to leave him any choice in the matter? Perhaps; there is no knowing. But he did not live — and the lessons of power, the men of power, the examples of power he left behind him gave us the war in Vietnam. Even when a Republican President, after four years of negotiation and bombing, disengaged from Vietnam, some of his critics blamed America for the bloody turmoil in Vietnam and Kampuchea. We never consider that other countries, freed from a colonial framework, must work out their own tribal and historical grievances without regard for us. If anything happens in the world, America must get the credit or the blame — we did not act, or we did not take the right actions. It never occurs to us that we are not all-important in the long-range tides of particular peoples' histories. Kennedy, though he might eventually have freed himself from these illusions of total American control, helped to strengthen them in other Americans. His real legacy was to teach the wrong lesson, over and over. The attempt at total control does not merely corrupt, as Acton said; it debilitates. It undoes itself.

24

The Prisoner of Power

Those whom the splendour of their rank, or the extent of their
capacity, have placed upon the summit of human life have not
often given any just occasion to envy in those who look up to
them from a lower station.

— SAMUEL JOHNSON, "Life of Richard Savage"

HARRY TRUMAN ESTABLISHED for ex-Presidents the embarrassing
custom of building libraries to themselves (Truman used to act as
guide through his own shrine, signing things in the imitated Oval
Office, or playing the piano). President Kennedy did not live to
preside over his library's construction or arrangement; but one hopes
he would have eliminated the more grandiose touches. The worst
aspect of the exhibits is an illuminated dateline that runs over some
cases of memorabilia. Below a dividing line are important family
dates (from the landing of the first Kennedy on America's shore),
correlated, above the line, with events in world history. So, for
1917, we read "John F. Kennedy born in Brookline," conjoined
with "Russian Revolution," as if Clio viewed history stereoscopi-
cally with a Kennedy always in one slide.

The pairings suggest, in places, more than coincidence — as
when, late in 1963, we read below the line "President and Mrs.
Kennedy arrive in Texas for political tour" just after reading, above
the line, "Diem government in South Vietnam is overthrown."

The events in Edward Kennedy's life march side by side with history's major happenings. The Kennedy family's importance is asserted through this equal billing with World History. But it is hard

to shine when one is sharing the stage, always, with Historical Events. Edward Kennedy enters the world, in 1932, partnered with "The New Deal comes to Washington." Some think he is fading from our politics in the same company. And, even aside from such particular chimings, it must be unsettling for one's life to be measured out on such a macroscopic scale — to have wars for playmates, manifestos shuffled with the dance cards, weddings woven into the rise and fall of nations. No man's life should be drawn across the rack of Everything Important supplied by this schedule.

Even if the exhibit were not there, I suppose, people would construct something like it in their minds. Edward Kennedy lives with two great growth charts traced behind him in the air. In every situation, whomever he is meeting, the implicit question hangs there: How does he measure up? Has he got the stuff to be another John F. Kennedy? Somehow Edward acquired, through his late twenties and early thirties, the reputation of being "the family's best politician"; but the 1980 race seems to have destroyed that claim. He lacks the John Kennedy flair, the knowing suggestion of familiarity with ideas, the witty aside that reinforced his poised air of dignity. When Edward poses as an intellectual, he looks uncomfortable. He is not dumb, by any means; but his political feel is for people — preferably other politicians — not for books. His "deep" speeches tend to be delivered woodenly. My wife and I saw that at a 1978 meeting in Philadelphia, where Kennedy addressed a group launching "Project '87" to prepare for the bicentennial of the Constitution's drafting. The audience was made up of fat cats and scholars. For the scholars he met (James MacGregor Burns pointing them out to him), he ran a tape recorder in his head, the importance of the Constitution today, a perfunctory recital for which he had been programmed.

That night's speech was well researched and well written — a timely argument against calling a new constitutional convention. But the audience was cool, made up of conservative Philadelphia money types (some at our table spoke well of the town's pistol-packing mayor, Frank Rizzo). Those who knew Edward Kennedy only from political rallies full of his supporters were dumbfounded when he spoke so poorly in the 1980 campaign. I was partly prepared for that by his failure to reach out to a skeptical audience in Philadelphia, even with good material prepared for him.

The demands to live up to the President's memory make Edward alternate exaggerated efforts at seriousness with collapses into rowdy relaxation; one minute Peck's Bad Boy, the next an Elder Statesman. When, for instance, he went to a reunion of his Virginia Law School classmates, the same year as that Philadelphia speech, his fellow alumni came to rib him about his school days and his presidential chances. The university president, Dr. Hereford, introduced him by remembering how, as a young faculty member, he rented his home during a sabbatical year to Kennedy and John Tunney. Hereford had some misgivings about turning his house over to students, but these were mollified when he heard that the Kennedy son was bringing a family maid to care for the place. The misgivings revived when he came back to town and heard, from the cabbie who picked him up at the airport, that his address was famous now for the parties thrown, the bands hired, the jolly crowds. As jocular reminiscences were exchanged, Kennedy rose and gave a stiff recital on the privilege of legal training. Just as he is invisibly manacled in the public company of women, so reports of his Charlottesville speeding tickets made him almost a caricature of sober responsibility when he went back to that scene. His name and his past imprison him. It is hard to cross every stage escorting History on your arm.

If Edward is not another poised John Kennedy, he is even less a rumpled and plunging Robert. Robert was a prematurely serious child and he aged into even more childlike earnestness. His haste to be with Cesar Chavez breaking a fast seemed to reflect a desire to make up for lost time, for the vigils in southern churches that Robert had not shared with Dr. King. In the Senate, Robert, the elder, was defiant of custom and lacking in respect for ancient colleagues. Edward, the younger brother, went around picking up Robert's broken crockery. Edward is temperamentally a joiner — Robert was a resigner. I remember speaking just after Edward Kennedy, in 1972, at an antiwar protest held in the Senate caucus room. Kennedy was one of only two Senators who showed up, and he spoke earnestly against the war. But the group, which was petitioning for redress of the constitutional grievance of undeclared war, got no encouragement from him in its determination to commit civil disobedience. That is not Edward's way. If Robert had been there, he would have made it clear he shared the group's gut feelings, even if he did not agree with their tactics. Edward Kennedy is a dutiful liberal, not a natural radical. He will be courageous in his choice of goals, but conventional in his pursuit of them. He stands true to old positions — not breaking into new territory, like Robert. His health plan, for instance, is an old measure adopted in most industrial democracies, and he has maneuvered for it in the accepted Senate ways. But in a period of economic retrenchment and noisy "antigovernment" rhetoric, this essentially centrist politician is thought of as the leftwardmost major figure in our politics, the principal target of right-wing political action committees. With a compromise abortion stand close to the majority position, he is considered a villain by antiabortion groups, in part because of his religion. The gun lovers love to haunt his campaigns. He *is* the Left to much of the Right, and his downfall would signal the permanent fall of the Left. It is interesting to see how, as his own position has been eroded, the stature of people scheming against him has diminished. At first it was Lyndon Johnson, who tried to oust the Kennedys and establish his own legitimacy. Then it was Richard Nixon, a President hiring gumshoes to pad around Chappaquiddick. Then Jimmy Carter devoted disproportionate time and effort to the project of "whipping his ass." Now it is John Dolan of the National Conservative Political Action Committee who thinks he holds Kennedy's fate in his hands. Just by bearing his name, Kennedy has come to resemble the aging gunfighter of western movies, the one every young punk wants to beat as a way of making his reputation.

I asked him, in his Virginia home, if he ever thought of his family legacy as a burden, something that hampers him, by now, more than it helps. "I can't think of my brothers that way. I'm just grateful for all the things they taught me, all the experiences we shared. For the rest, you just have to take that." It was mid-February of 1981, and defenders of the new Reagan administration had claimed *they* were heirs to whatever was good in the Kennedy presidency — leaving the actual Kennedy to take blame for all that was bad. Arthur Laffer, the prophet of Reagan's "supply side" economics, continually invoked the 1963 tax cut as the cause of America's last spurt of prosperity. Kennedy laughed at that: "It is one thing to have a tax cut while maintaining inflation at less than 3.6 percent for three years. It is another matter to impose one with double-digit inflation."

Columnist George Will, who threw a party for the incoming Reagan administration, said that the Republicans now uphold President Kennedy's tough stance against the Russians, the determination to close a defense gap. Edward Kennedy tries to recapture his own name, but is resigned about the prospects of success: "President Kennedy believed the nation must be strong; but he was willing to take imaginative steps like the nuclear test ban." When I press him on the differences between John Kennedy in 1960 and Robert Kennedy in 1968, he says that naturally both men changed with the experience of new things. But Robert underwent especially deep changes in his last years? "He certainly did." One is to presume that John Kennedy would have taken the same course — though it is hard to imagine him at a Cesar Chavez rally.

Edward Kennedy has to keep living three lives at once — or keep giving an account of the lives the other men lived for him. Walking through his empty house, crammed with pictures of the family, one realizes how much of his life has already been lived for him, off in directions he can neither take, anymore, nor renounce. At one time, the same-and-different Kennedy smile coming from so many faces clustered on mantel or shelf must have intensified his presence, replicating every aspect of family influence he could bring to bear. Now they seem to drain him — he seeps off into their fading images.

His divorce proceedings have been announced. Only one son is living with him at the moment, and he is at school. Today the Senator's press secretary, Robert Shrum, has come out for lunch with us. Otherwise Kennedy lives here alone. But his family is never far from his conversation. He has just come back from a visit with his mother in Florida, where the February rain and cold kept most people from swimming — but not the ninety-year-old Rose. "When she took me to church, there was no one at the altar with the priest, so she said, 'Teddy?' You would have been proud of me, Bob, serving mass." I said I would not know how to serve Mass in the new liturgy, not since Latin went out. *"Ad Deum qui laetificat juventutem meam,"* Kennedy rattles off, in schoolboy tones. Shrum takes up the next response, and I the third. We all agree the *"Suscipiat"* was the toughest response, and prove our point by variously misremembering it.

It was an unnaturally warm day in February: I had seen three chairs lined up before the front door when I parked my car — like deck chairs on a liner, each with its own giant blanket. I went in through the open door and found Shrum, who said, "The Senator likes to be outdoors every minute he can." We sat down like a silly version of the three leaders lined up at Yalta, to talk about nuclear disarmament. Kennedy favors a comprehensive test ban (CTB): "President Kennedy took the initiative which led to the first test ban. We need to have some of that imagination."

Is CTB feasible? "In 1974, I explained my proposal to Brezhnev in Moscow, and he said, 'If you had that in your pocket, I could sign it right now' — which surprised me. When I went back in 1978, I asked him why the Russians were opposing our CTB proposal. He said, 'You have changed the terms, from five years to three years. You have added to the number of on-site inspections' — the agreement to have any on-site inspections was a breakthrough that we wasted. 'You have changed from no explosions allowed to none above three kilotons.' "

Why did Kennedy think these changes had been made? "Brzezinski told me we had to get SALT II first, and go for CTB later." In fact the Carter administration, like the Nixon administration before it, resented Kennedy's dealings with Russian leaders as an infringement on their own power to make foreign policy. Kennedy is one of the few men who can be welcomed by foreign leaders as a kind of surrogate President — which infuriates real Presidents. He can hurt his own proposals simply by advancing them in his own name. He continues to live inside the pressures that made Robert fear the cause of peace would be hurt with President Johnson if a Kennedy carried its banner. When Edward Kennedy took up the cause of wage and price controls in the 1980 election, he guaranteed that President Carter would never consider that course. Such power to initiate is easily translated into a powerlessness to conclude.

I asked Kennedy if his belief that wage and price controls were needed had been dispelled by the election. "No." Will you continue to call for them while President Reagan actually takes off controls? "I believe in deregulation. We deregulated the airlines and that was even more successful than it appears — part of the savings were eaten up by the increase in fuel costs. But there are forty or so more areas where we can deregulate." Why beat one's head against a wall? If the mood is for deregulation, then deregulate — something, at least, gets done.

Did Kennedy feel the liberal cause was badly damaged by Reagan's triumph, by the loss of so many of Kennedy's liberal colleagues in the Senate? He denies that any overwhelming mandate was won. After all, who can expect an incumbent to win with thirteen percent inflation? "Twelve Democratic Senators lost by less than four percent." A few votes here or there and the Senate would still be Democratic. Yet Kennedy is a centrist politician. He says President Reagan should be given a chance to show whether he has a cure for the nation's economic troubles. "I hope he does. We are looking for grounds of agreement. Maybe President Reagan can bring about voluntary price restraint." He does not sound very hopeful. "Well, I guess it can be done; but that would take a tremendous investment of the government's time and energy. I asked Helmut Schmidt how he controls prices in Germany. He said it takes two hundred hours of his personal time during the working year, to keep after labor and business — I wonder how he keeps track of the exact hours?"

Attempts at accommodation with the Reagan people are part of Edward Kennedy's temperament. But a man who could not elicit cooperation from the preceding Democratic administration is unlikely to get much from a White House stocked with right-wing types who think of him as the personification of the Left, or as the heir to certain historical stands — the defense-gap shrillness, the tax cut — they want to *detach* from him and claim as their own. Besides, any chumminess with them would offend his own constituency, labor and blacks and the tattered remains of the New Deal generation. Kennedy shows no desire or design for forging an entirely new coalition. In fact, Gary Hart — one of the few liberal Senators to survive the 1980 election — expressly excludes Kennedy as "old fashioned" when he talks of forming a new Democratic program in the Senate. He thinks Kennedy's appeal is based on nostalgia, something that does not stir young politicians trying to build new careers.

If the Right transfers irrational grudges against this or that Kennedy to Edward, the Left nurses an intermittently hopeful disappointment at his failure to live up to its dreams for him. A few liberals are continually running him for President, and he must encourage them (mildly) to protect his eroding position in the Senate. His problem, for a long time, was how to keep running for President without actually having to *run*. In 1980, that difficult juggling act became an impossible one. President Carter gave him no "out" of loyalty or partnership with the Democratic incumbent. And Carter's disastrous personal polls left him no excuse to be drawn from party discipline. All those who had waited for years to see Kennedy run told him, in effect, that it was time to put up or shut up. I saw how these converging pressures worked during the summer of 1979 (that period of "malaise" when President Carter retreated to his mountaintop and consulted every important person in his party except Kennedy). In May, I rode from Washington to Baltimore with Douglas Fraser of the United Auto Workers, Kennedy's principal noncongressional ally in the campaign for governmental health insurance. Kennedy was announcing his health plan, to put it in competition with the President's — and he expected Fraser to be with him in the Senate caucus room when he answered press questions. But Fraser said he could not come unless Kennedy was a declared candidate for President. "If you are not going to take on Carter, I may have to live with him for another four years." Carter was cultivating Fraser with phone calls and White House meetings, which gave labor access and leverage. Fraser would sacrifice that to stand with a *campaigning* Kennedy, but not to help a mere Senator promote this bill with a slim chance of passage. At some point, even to advance his Senate projects, Kennedy had to say yes to all those begging him to run.

Fraser was dutiful, rather than begging; he still doubted Kennedy could live down Chappaquiddick. But he joined with Kennedy when he announced. Others were less calm in their advocacy. Multiply the kind of pressure Fraser was exerting a thousandfold, and one sees that Kennedy really had no choice to make in 1980 — he had to run for President. He was not free *not* to. His own lack of enthusiasm for the task showed in the poor preparation he had made. He was only running because everyone assumed Carter had to lose; why prepare for a rough race? Kennedy wants the presidency, if it comes to him by the pressure of events; but he does not have the fire in his belly to rule, like John Kennedy, or the determination of an underdog, like Robert in 1968. Edward rented a private "Air Force One," early in the fall of 1980, and campaigned as an incumbent. The same forces that left him no real choice about running debilitated him when he began the campaign. He was trapped in a race he could not win because he would only undertake a race he thought he could not lose.

It is hard for some to realize that Edward Kennedy is hobbled by his own apparent power. They saw him deliver a stunning speech to the 1980 Democratic convention, and watched the crowd on the floor go crazy with affection for the man and his heritage. Many of those who merely accepted Jimmy Carter as a candidate almost fanatically desired Edward Kennedy. He speaks to them with a voice no one else can equal. That was apparent not only at the party convention of 1980, but at the midterm meeting of Democrats in Memphis two years earlier. Kennedy stole that show with a single speech, in some ways a more powerful one than the televised 1980 address.

President Carter, fearing a mini-convention revolt in 1978, dispatched his entire White House operation to Memphis; then came himself, to sit meekly in two "workshops" while people criticized his record ("Can you imagine Lyndon Johnson sitting there letting others attack his performance?"); and gave a speech too fervent in its rhetoric and too tepid in its delivery. Jerry Rafshoon produced a presidential movie to awe the crowds. Eleven White House aides were given the job of countering Kennedy's single appearance at a health-care discussion. To an overflow audience in the largest hall off the convention floor itself, the moderator admitted the reality behind the discussion of various health programs: Governor-Elect Bill Clinton of Arkansas said there had been a change in the program, that they were really going to discuss "the relative merits of Georgia peanuts and Massachusetts cranberries."

Joseph Califano led off for the White House, arguing that the economy would not allow any more in health care than the administration was proposing. Kennedy, following, thundered against that timid position. His prepared text, distributed to the press, distilled all his long advocacy on the subject. Charts showed his plan's feasibility. And then, his voice rising, face reddening, Kennedy abandoned his text, stepped forward of the lectern, his voice booming out unaided to the back rows, shouting that every family has disabling illnesses, the Kennedys had, but Kennedys can pay, and Senators have illnesses, but Senators have ample health insurance, but what of people without these advantages, isn't what's good enough for Congress good enough for *any American citizen?* The audience was up with him, shouting too, euphoric, happily angry. All the exaggerated talk of Kennedy style seemed vindicated. All the memories of his family's suffering, and its sense of caring, all the happier times of social concern at the heart of Democratic politics, made Democrats feel good again — all but dour White House aide Stuart Eisenstadt, who glowered at this demonstration against his boss.

And then the convention went off to vote with Carter on the key measure before it. There had been a moment of rapturous nostalgia, outside the everyday world of political bargaining. They were happy to forget the price tag while Kennedy orated — and were careful to remember it when the vote came. Kennedy was gone from Memphis by the time the real action took place. He had done his job. He had kept alive some memories. The deals were cut without him.

A pattern is emerging. Kennedy is at his best when he is not in the running. That is true not only in Memphis, or at the New York convention; the reporters following him in 1980 noticed a sense of freedom growing on him as his chances faded. He performed best when he was showing his mettle as a survivor, not bidding to take over. Forced by fame, by his name, toward power, he tightens up. Allowed to back off, he relaxes. This is not surrender. He still takes a role, subordinate, one where he can maneuver against the pressures that would *make* him succeed. He seems to be acquiring a sense of power's last paradox — that it is most a prison when one thinks of it as a *passepartout.* When one thinks of it as a prison, one is already partway free.

Epilogue

Brotherhood

There are secret aspects, beyond divining, in all we do — in the makeup of humans above all; aspects mute and invisible, unknown to their own possessors, brought forth only under the incitements of circumstance.

— Montaigne

THERE IS SOMETHING TWISTABLE in the hand about power — something tricky and unpredictable, "amphisbaenic," backward-striking. And that is as it should be. Remember, after all, what power is — getting others to do one's will. There is something obviously unhealthy in the concept of a whole world ready to do one nation's will. Yet America has yearned toward that unnatural condition, trying to force on others the relation of children to a parent. The American mission preached by recent Presidents — most fetchingly by John F. Kennedy — would benignly coerce others "for their own good," freezing the exercise of their wills in a state of incomplete development.

Power, if it is just the mobilization of resources by one's own will, has no internal check at all. Economy dictates the best use of resources, and to have any identity at all is to will one's own good. Such power must push out endlessly — which means it is not free. It must spread ever wider its periphery of influence — which means it will be dispersed. But power as the interaction with other wills is fundamentally suasive, which means it must surrender in order to rule. This formulation sounds paradoxical, yet we all have intimate experience of its truth.

A parent can have every resource of coercion, along with the will to coerce, in dealing with a child; he or she can "ground" the child, spank, take away toys, allowance, privileges. But this combination of resources with will does not equal power, in the sense of getting another to do one's will, if the child keeps saying *no*. One can kill the beast in a frenzy of impotence brought on by the attempt to use power at its utmost reach of determination. But real power depends on the checking of such unilateral ferocity of purpose, such indiscriminate use of available physical resource.

The parent who exerts his or her power over children most drastically loses all power over them, except the power to twist and hurt and destroy. This power to destroy — to wound, to sever bridges, to end lives — is easily wielded; and we tend to call this real power since it has such an instant, spectacular effect, dependent only on our will. We can all smash a TV set, a computer, a friendship, a marriage. Few of us can build a workable computer or rewarding marriage. Any idiot can wreck what only a genius can make.

In the case of political order, obedience comes to a leader only if he shows the respect for his followers that encourages opinions of right and interest in them — i.e., the belief that they ought to follow him, and that it will help them to do so. Thus Machiavelli, celebrating the ruthless prince, said that his highest skill was in gaining a reputation based on the solid opinion of his subjects. Even when the prince inspires fear, it must be a respectful fear without hatred. Helots and mercenaries, like compelled allies or satellites, weaken the state they seem to aggrandize. "Therefore the best fortress there can be is not to be hated by the people; for if you have fortresses, but the people hate you, the forts cannot save you." American politicians, including the Kennedys, tend to remember these truths when recruiting domestic support. But the ideal of foreign power has been to approximate our assertiveness to our powers of destruction, to equate ability to destroy with right to control. There, *our* will is being tested, not *other* wills recruited.

If sheer assertion of power results in its abdication, the reverse of that is also true: real power is gained by yielding one's own will in the persuasion of others. As Tolstoy said, "The strongest, most indissoluble, most burdensome and constant bond with other men is what is called power over them, which in its real meaning is only the

greatest dependence on them" ("Words About *War and Peace*").
The best witness to this truth is the real source of American power
in the Kennedy era. The 1960s was a period obsessed with power —
the power of the American system, or power to be sought by working outside it; the power of insurgency, or of counterinsurgency;
the power of rhetoric and "image" and charisma and technology.
The attempt to fashion power solely out of resource and will led to
the celebration of power as destruction — as assassination of leaders,
the sabotage of rival economies, the poising of opponent missiles.

The equation of real power with power to destroy reached its unheard refutation in the death of our charismatic leader. As children
can wreck TV sets, so Oswalds can shoot Kennedys. The need to believe in some conspiracy behind the assassination is understandable
in an age of charismatic pretensions. The "graced" man validates his
power by success, by luck. Oswald, by canceling the luck, struck at
the very principle of government, and it was hard to admit that he
was not asserting (or being used by) some *alternative* principle of
rule. Oswald was a brutal restatement of the idea of power as the
combination of resource with will. Put at its simplest, this became
the combination of a Mannlicher-Carcano with one man's mad assertiveness. Power as the power to *conquer* was totally separated, at
last, from ability to control.

Robert Kennedy's assassination gave lesser scope to conspiracy
theorists — no one knew, beforehand, his route through the
kitchen. With him, the effect of sheer chaos was easier to acknowledge (though some still do not acknowledge it — they think purpo-
sive will rules everything). What was lost with Robert Kennedy was
not so much a legacy of power asserted as the glimpse of a deeper
understanding, the beginnings of a belief in power as surrender of
the will. He died, after all, opposing the caricatures of power enacted
in our wars and official violence.

But another man was killed in the 1960s who did not offer mere
promise of performance. He was even younger than the Kennedys —
thirty-nine when he was shot, in the year of Robert's death at forty-
three. There were many links between the Kennedys and Martin
Luther King — links admirably traced in Harris Wofford's book on
the three men. Together, they summed up much of the nobler purpose in American life during the 1960s. Yet there was opposition,

too — Dr. King, more radical in his push for racial justice, was far more peaceful in his methods. Robert Kennedy, however reluctantly, used the police powers of John F. Kennedy's state to spy on Dr. King, to put in official hands the instruments of slander. King was a critic of the space program and war expenditures. King, though more revolutionary in some people's eyes, was not "charismatic" in the sense of replacing traditional and legal power with his personal will. He relied on the deep traditions of his church, on the preaching power of a Baptist minister; and he appealed to the rational order of the liberal state for peaceful adjustment of claims advanced by the wronged. His death, as tragic as Kennedy's, did not leave so large an absence. His work has outlasted him; more than any single person he changed the way Americans lived with each other in the sixties. His power was real, because it was not mere assertion — it was a persuasive *yielding* of private will through nonviolent advocacy.

Since he relied less on power as mere assertiveness of will, mere assertiveness of will could not entirely erase what he accomplished. He had already surrendered his life to bring about large social changes, constructive, not destructive. He forged ties of friendship and social affection. He did not want to force change by violence or stealth, by manipulation or technological tricks. His power was the power to suffer, and his killer only increased that power.

The speeches of John F. Kennedy are studied, now, by people who trace their unintended effects in Vietnam and elsewhere. The speeches of Martin Luther King are memorized at schools as living documents — my son could recite them in high school. "Flexible response" and "counterinsurgency" are tragicomic episodes of our history. But the Gandhian nonviolence preached by Dr. King is a doctrine that still inspires Americans. My children cannot believe that I grew up in a society where blacks could not drink at public water fountains, eat in "white" restaurants, get their hair cut in white barber shops, sit in white theaters, play on white football teams. The changes King wrought are so large as to be almost invisible.

He was helped, of course — he was not a single mover of the charismatic sort. And he was helped not so much by talented aides as by his fellow martyrs, by all those who died or risked dying for their children or their fellow citizens. While Washington's "best and brightest" worked us into Vietnam, an obscure army of virtue arose in the South and took the longer spiritual trip inside a public bathroom or toward the front of a bus. King rallied the strength of broken men, transmuting an imposed squalor into the beauty of chosen suffering. No one did it for his followers. They did it for themselves. Yet, in helping them, he exercised real power, achieved changes that dwarf the moon shot as an American achievement. The "Kennedy era" was really the age of Dr. King.

The famous antitheses and alliterations of John Kennedy's rhetoric sound tinny now. But King's eloquence endures, drawn as it was from ancient sources — the Bible, the spirituals, the hymns and folk songs. He was young at his death, younger than either Kennedy; but he had traveled farther. He did fewer things; but those things last. A mule team drew his coffin in a rough cart; not the sleek military horses and the artillery caisson. He has no eternal flame — and no wonder. He is not dead.

We see in Bolingbroke's case that a life of brilliant licence is really compatible with a life of brilliant statesmanship; that licence itself may even be thought to quicken the imagination for oratorical efforts; that an intellect similarly aroused may, at exciting conjunctures, perceive possibilities which are hidden from duller men; that the favourite of society will be able to use his companionship with men and his power over women so as much to aid his strokes of policy, but, on the other hand, that these secondary aids and occasional advantages are purchased by the total sacrifice of a primary necessity; that a life of great excitement is incompatible with the calm circumspection and sound estimate of probability essential to great affairs; that though the excited hero may perceive distant things which others overlook, he will overlook near things that others see; that though he may be stimulated to great speeches which others could not make, he will also be irritated to petty speeches which others would not; that he will attract enmities, but not confidence; that he will not observe how few and plain are the alternatives to common business, and how little even genius can enlarge them; that his prosperity will be a wild dream of unattainable possibilities, and his adversity a long regret that those possibilities are departed.

— WALTER BAGEHOT, on Bolingbroke

Acknowledgments

The author is grateful to the following for permission to quote: *The Search for JFK* by Joan and Clay Blair, Jr., Berkley Publishing Corp., 1976. Reprinted by permission of Berkley, the authors, and Scott Meredith Literary Agency, Inc.

My Story by Judith Exner as told to Ovid Demaris. Copyright © 1977 by Judith Exner. Reprinted by permission of the author.

"For John F. Kennedy His Inauguration," from *The Poetry of Robert Frost* edited by Edward Connery Lathem. Copyright © 1961, 1962 by Robert Frost. Copyright © 1969 by Holt, Rinehart and Winston. Reprinted by permission of Holt, Rinehart and Winston, Publishers.

To Move a Nation by Roger Hilsman. Copyright © 1964, 1967 by Roger Hilsman. Reprinted by permission of Doubleday & Company, Inc. and The Lantz Office Incorporated.

Why England Slept by John F. Kennedy (Funk & Wagnalls). Copyright © 1961 by Harper & Row, Publishers, Inc. Reprinted by permission of Harper & Row, Publishers, Inc., and Sidgwick & Jackson Ltd.

Presidential Power by Richard Neustadt. Reprinted by permission, from *Presidential Power* by Richard Neustadt. Copyright © 1960, 1976, 1980 by John Wiley & Sons, Inc.

Robert Kennedy and His Times by Arthur M. Schlesinger, Jr. Copyright © 1978 by Arthur M. Schlesinger, Jr. Reprinted by permission of Houghton Mifflin Company.

A Thousand Days by Arthur M. Schlesinger, Jr. Copyright © 1965 by Arthur M. Schlesinger, Jr. Reprinted by permission of Houghton Mifflin Company and Andre Deutsch Limited.

Kennedy by Theodore C. Sorensen. Copyright © 1965 by Theodore C. Sorensen. Reprinted by permission of Harper & Row, Publishers, Inc., and Hodder & Stoughton Limited.

Index

Casals, Pablo, 141, 142, 146
Castiglione, Baldassare (quoted), 84
Castillo Armas, Carlos, 221, 226
Castro, Fidel, 34, 37, 95, 171, 211, 221,
 223–229, 233–238, 251–261
Cecil, David, 15, 24, 71, 73–74, 82
Chamberlain, Neville, 80
Chancellor, John, 157
Chavez, Cesar, 92, 288
Chesterton, Gilbert (quoted), 59, 125,
 242, 255
Childs, Marquis, 149
Churchill, Randolph, 74
Clark, Ramsey, 88, 92
Clausewitz, Karl von, 257
Cleveland, Harlan, 240
Clifford, Clark, 96
Clinch, Nancy Gager, 56
Clinton, Bill, 294
Coit, Margaret, 136
Colby, William, 248
Colson, Charles, 192
Commager, Henry Steele, 135, 156
Connally, John, 109
Conerly, Chuck, 209
Coolidge, Calvin, 182–183
Corry, John, 109, 121
Coughlin, Father, 201
Cowles, Michael, 109
Cox, Archibald, 88, 164
Crimmins, John, 116
Cubela, Rolando, 253
Cullinan, Elizabeth, 65
Cushing, Richard, Cardinal, 84–85, 95, 128

Daladier, Edouard, 79
Daley, Richard, 92, 95–96, 102
Davids, Jules, 135, 136
Davis, Sammy, Jr., 28
de Gaulle, Charles, 266
Dickenson, Jim, 10
Dickenson, Molly, 10
Dickinson, Angie, 24, 113
Diem, Ngo Dinh. See Ngo Dinh Diem
Dillon, Douglas, 85, 89
Dinerstein, Herbert, 259
Dinis, Edmund, 159
Dinneen, Joseph, 128, 154
Doar, John, 85
Dobrynin, Anatoly, 268, 269, 270
Dolan, John, 289
Donovan, Robert, 132
Douglas, William, 85, 112, 129
Drake, Elizabeth, 18

Droller, Gerry (a.k.a. Frank Bender), 226
Duke, Angier Biddle, 209
Dulles, Allen W., 36, 219–221, 225,
 233–234, 248, 277
Dutton, Fred, 93

Edelman, Peter, 91
Eden, Anthony, 74
Eisenhower, Dwight, 105, 144–145, 163–
 164, 166–167, 175–178, 183, 186,
 220, 232–234, 277
Eisenstadt, Stuart, 295
Enthoven, Alain, 191
Evans, Roland, 85
Evans, Sheffield, 225
Exner, Judith Campbell, 22–24, 29, 31,
 34–35, 37, 103

Fairlie, Henry, 170
Farley, James, 76
Fay, Paul ("Red"), 86, 113, 154
Ferguson, J. D., 137
Fitzgerald, John ("Honey Fitz"), 63
Ford, Gerald, 181–182, 194
Forrestal, James, 21, 134
Franco, Francisco, 201
Frankfurter, Felix, 129
Fraser, Douglas, 293
Friedrich, Carl J., 130–131
Fritchie, Clayton, 255
Frost, Robert (quoted), 140
Fulbright, William, 236, 255

Galbraith, John Kenneth, 90, 91, 101,
 140, 175, 281
Gallagher, Edward, 64–65
Gallucio, Anthony, 30
Gargan, Ann, 114
Gargan, Joseph, 55, 114–121, 158
Gaud, William, 249
Giancana, Sam, 29, 34, 37, 103, 252
Gifford, Dun, 8, 121, 158
Gobbi, Tito, 41, 43
Goldman, Eric, 190
Goodwin, Richard, 101, 108, 109, 121,
 140, 235
Gorey, Hayes, 85
Graham, Philip, 85
Gray, David, 234
Greene, Graham, 141
Greenfield, Jeff, 85, 91, 93
Greenwood, Arthur, 81
Gromyko, Andrei, 266
Guevera, Ché, 210, 211
Guthman, Edwin, 91, 107

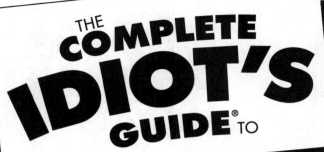

THE COMPLETE IDIOT'S GUIDE TO

Drawing Basics

Illustrated

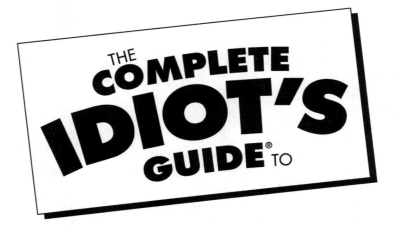

THE
COMPLETE IDIOT'S GUIDE® TO

Drawing Basics

Illustrated

*by Frank Fradella for Idea +
Design Works LLC*
(www.ideaanddesignworks.com)

ALPHA

A member of Penguin Group (USA) Inc.

This one's for my mom.

ALPHA BOOKS

Published by the Penguin Group

Penguin Group (USA) Inc., 375 Hudson Street, New York, New York 10014, U.S.A.

Penguin Group (Canada), 10 Alcorn Avenue, Toronto, Ontario, Canada M4V 3B2 (a division of Pearson Penguin Canada Inc.)

Penguin Books Ltd., 80 Strand, London WC2R 0RL, England

Penguin Ireland, 25 St Stephen's Green, Dublin 2, Ireland (a division of Penguin Books Ltd.)

Penguin Group (Australia), 250 Camberwell Road, Camberwell, Victoria 3124, Australia (a division of Pearson Australia Group Pty. Ltd.)

Penguin Books India Pvt. Ltd., 11 Community Centre, Panchsheel Park, New Delhi—110 017, India

Penguin Group (NZ), cnr Airborne and Rosedale Roads, Albany, Auckland 1310, New Zealand (a division of Pearson New Zealand Ltd.)

Penguin Books (South Africa) (Pty.) Ltd., 24 Sturdee Avenue, Rosebank, Johannesburg 2196, South Africa

Penguin Books Ltd., Registered Offices: 80 Strand, London WC2R 0RL, England

International Standard Book Number: 1-59257-547-1
Library of Congress Catalog Card Number: 2006925729

08   8   7   6   5   4

Interpretation of the printing code: The rightmost number of the first series of numbers is the year of the book's printing; the rightmost number of the second series of numbers is the number of the book's printing. For example, a printing code of 06-1 shows that the first printing occurred in 2006.

Printed in the United States of America

Note: This publication contains the opinions and ideas of its author. It is intended to provide helpful and informative material on the subject matter covered. It is sold with the understanding that the author and publisher are not engaged in rendering professional services in the book. If the reader requires personal assistance or advice, a competent professional should be consulted.

The author and publisher specifically disclaim any responsibility for any liability, loss, or risk, personal or otherwise, which is incurred as a consequence, directly or indirectly, of the use and application of any of the contents of this book.

Most Alpha books are available at special quantity discounts for bulk purchases for sales promotions, premiums, fund-raising, or educational use. Special books, or book excerpts, can also be created to fit specific needs.

For details, write: Special Markets, Alpha Books, 375 Hudson Street, New York, NY 10014.

Publisher: *Marie Butler-Knight*
Editorial Director/Acquiring Editor: *Mike Sanders*
Managing Editor: *Billy Fields*
Development Editor: *Lynn Northrup*
Production Editor: *Megan Douglass*
Copy Editor: *Krista Hansing*

Book Designer: *Trina Wurst/Kurt Owens*
Cover Designer: *Frank Fradella for Idea + Design Works LLC*
Indexer: *Heather McNeill*
Layout: *Becky Harmon*
Proofreader: *Aaron Black*

Contents at a Glance

Contents

Foreword

You probably don't know me, and that's all right; you don't have to. If you're reading this, then I'm assuming that you and I are one and the same: two folks learning how to draw. I've been learning how to draw my whole life, and I will continue learning up until its end. I'm no authority on art, and I have no right to tell you the proper way to draw. I'm just another person with a passion for drawing who is trying to improve his craft with every passing day.

If you, too, have been engrossed in the learning process for your entire existence—or even if you're just starting out—you already know the importance of the basics. The foundations of art cannot be shirked. To exploit an overly exploited metaphor, "Without a sturdy foundation, the supported structure will crumble." Composition, perspective, proportion, and so on are but a corner of the foundation. The "foundation" of art is composed of so many different fields of study that you could build a palace on it (yeah, okay, I'm through with that analogy). You might see a drawing with great rendering or some other form of gorgeous effect, but if there are any problems at its core, you'll quickly see through the gloss as it turns into an ugly, ugly thing. No matter how much the artist plays dress-up, the picture will never look right.

Some of the "greats" have such a different way of producing works that it seems they skipped over the beginning stages of learning how to draw. Take Picasso, for example. When I was younger, I thought Cubism was all he could produce and that he was a lazy person who chose to take the easy way to making art (I guess I was a pretty cynical kid). But one day, I took a field trip to a museum that had some of his earlier works on display. I was surprised to see that his sketches and paintings showed someone very adept in traditional styles and media. He had a solid grasp on principles such as proportion and space, and he produced lovely rendered drawings. Once he understood and practiced the essentials of art, he branched out into different methods of expression.

Things such as anatomy, design, movement, and negative space are such specific areas of study, yet they offer an inexhaustible wealth of knowledge. Merely training your hand to draw a somewhat straight line or a decent circle can take ages. I personally don't think it's possible to master any aspect of art. That might sound bleak, but I'm actually a "glass is half-full" type of guy. If it's impossible to obtain perfection in art, it means there's always room to grow and there are always new ideas to be had.

Practicing art is a never-ending feast of knowledge. If you're studying from this book, it means you're nowhere near full. So I raise my glass to you and make a toast. Here's to an eternity of stuffing our faces! Oh, and pass the salt.

Casey Maloney

Casey Maloney is an illustrator whose work has appeared in such award-winning venues as *Shooting Star Comics* and *Cyber Age Adventures*. He is half of the team, with Tom Waltz, responsible for the critically acclaimed *Children of the Grave* comic, soon to be released in a deluxe trade from IDW. Casey, again with Waltz, is part of Studio Eye Five. Their new series, *The Last Fall*, is due out in late 2006. Casey lives in Ventura, California, with his wife, Shelby.

Introduction

I grew up in a sleepy little suburban Long Island town called Hauppauge that, were you to blink on your way to Smithtown, you might easily miss. I spent a good portion of my childhood in the basement of that cookie-cutter house, playing with my action figures and losing myself in the four-color worlds of my favorite superheroes. I discovered, quite by accident during a trip to the bookstore with my mother, that the covers of certain novels really caught my eye. (I later discovered that they were too often better than the books they appeared on.) Not long after that, and much to my surprise, I learned that the great fantasy artist Ken Kelly lived just two blocks away, in sleepy little Hauppauge, New York. Who would have thought?

One day I knocked on his door. He lived across the street from my sister's boyfriend, and although we had been introduced and he was always kind enough to wave, I don't think I'd ever been in his house before. Don't ask me what gave me the courage that day. I honestly don't know. But Ken Kelly invited me in and showed me a whole new world. He showed me the world of art.

Up until then, I had been a doodler, a penciller of pretty nothings. But there, lining the walls, there on the canvas, there in the closet, there was art of real power. Breathtaking power. Not just in the poses or the often-barbaric scenes depicted, but in the reality of the work. I was standing in the studio where fantasies happened and dreams were made real.

Ken showed me how it happened, from the initial thumbnail sketches to the final brush stroke. It should have been one of those moments when the curtain was pulled back and the Great and Powerful Oz was revealed to be a feeble old man. But it wasn't. It was just the opposite. It didn't detract from the magic of that creation: it made it bigger. In the paperback novels I'd begun to collect, I was always looking at these images in terms of inches. Now I saw them as they had been. As a child, they seemed bigger than I was. In retrospect, I suppose they were. They were, quite literally, larger than life.

Since that day, I've had the great pleasure to make the acquaintance and occasional friendship with some of the greatest artists in the world. Justin Sweet, Don Maitz, Dan Brereton, Georges Janty, David Mack, Andy Lee, … the list goes on. And, of course, this includes the amazing Charles Keegan, whom I was fortunate enough to see paint the cover to my own debut novel not long ago.

When I was approached to do this book, I almost balked. I'm not primarily an artist. I've seen the work of real artists, and I don't yet have the hubris required to count myself among them. Oh, sure, I've got dozens of sketchbooks filled with thousands of drawings. But an artist? Me? Nah.

Still, perhaps I've learned a thing or two from all these years of being around other artists. Maybe some of that stuff has sunk in through osmosis. As I look back over the book you're about to read, I see that I knew more than I thought I did. If that teaches me anything, it teaches me that I learned what I was capable of by throwing myself off a cliff and trying to build a pair of wings on the way down.

Now it's your turn. Let's fly.

How This Book Is Organized

Ready? Set? Draw a brontosaurus!

No? Okay, maybe that wasn't fair of me. We should probably build up to prehistoric lizards. Lucky for you, this book is organized into bite-size pieces. You won't be asked to draw anything you're not well prepared for. (Well, not *again*, anyway.) Let's have a look at what you can expect as we move forward.

Part 1, "Getting Started," is where it all starts, friend. We're gonna take you on a little shopping spree (on your dime, I'm afraid) and teach you a bit about where some of the masters came from. Then we're gonna limber you up and get you doodlin' and scribblin', and before you know it we'll be on to the next part.

Part 2, "From Simple to Solid," is the fun part, where all the action happens, kids. This is the good stuff right here. We're going to start you off with the basic shapes and then show you how to make them come off the page. Little things like perspective and shading? They're all right here.

Part 3, "Drawing Things That Sit Still," starts you drawing things beyond the simple geometric shapes. We look at plants and flowers, take a little trip to a rock garden, sketch some clouds and waves, and see how drapery does more than just hang around. (And, oh yes, there will be plenty of puns on this journey. You have been warned.)

Part 4, "Drawing the Human Animal," teaches you all about proportion, gesture lines, simplified skeletons, Bubble Boys, and the kooky craft of caricature.

Part 5, "Drawing Other Animals," wraps up the book with a sampling of everything that swims, walks, gallops, sheds on your furniture, or ate prehistoric plankton.

To top it all off, I'm going to throw in a list of recommended reading and a glossary, absolutely free. Plus, if you act now …! Just kidding.

Extras

As we go along through this book together, you'll see three different kinds of sidebars peppered throughout the lessons. Here's what you can expect from them:

Layman's Lingo

Every now and then, you might come across a term that you haven't heard before, or a word that's being used in a context other than the norm. When this happens, the Layman's Lingo boxes will give you the skinny, the low-down, the straight dope, and keep you in the loop for all that follows.

Masters' Musings

Nothing inspires me quite the way the masters do. Sprinkled generously throughout this book you'll find fantastic quotes and candid remarks from great artists down through the ages. Because nothing is quite as sobering as hearing Michelangelo say, "I am still learning."

Staying Sharp

These suckers pop up all over the place! These are the invaluable tips, tricks, timesavers, and pearls of wisdom that will be an invaluable aid to you as you master the basics.

Acknowledgments

Ultimately, all the thanks and blame for this thing goes to Tom Waltz. They're going to have to invent a new unit of weight measurement for all the love and respect I have for this guy.

Thanks must also go to Kris Oprisko at IDW for being a joy to work with. I'd also be remiss if I didn't give a tip of the hat to Ken Kelly for opening that first door, for Charles Keegan for being so darned mythic, and to the amazing artists who have graced the pages of *Cyber Age Adventures* magazine. I have learned so very much from you all.

Trademarks

All terms mentioned in this book that are known to be or are suspected of being trademarks or service marks have been appropriately capitalized. Alpha Books and Penguin Group (USA) Inc. cannot attest to the accuracy of this information. Use of a term in this book should not be regarded as affecting the validity of any trademark or service mark.

In This Part

Part 1

Getting Started

This is where the road begins. Right here. This is where you and I come face to face with your biggest enemy and spit in its eye. We're also going to teach you a little history lesson, as well as give you the low-down on the kinds of materials you'll need to do this right. This very first section here? This isn't about your hands. This is about your brain. And if you can develop a mental understanding of the path ahead of you, walking that path will be scads easier.

In This Chapter

- Learning from Michelangelo and Leonardo
- The camera obscura
- The usefulness of failure
- Drawing your first lines
- Understanding relative distance
- The wisdom of FDR

     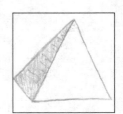

Chapter 1

Baby Birds and a Belly Full of Worms

Okay, here we are. Just the two of us, and the "white bull." That's what Ernest Hemingway called a blank piece of paper whenever he'd sit down to start a new story. That's because it's intimidating, that stark white canvas. Anything can happen, and right now, between you and me, what's probably going to happen is that you're going to draw something you don't like very much. But that's okay. I'm going to walk you through it. Right now you're like a baby bird, all naked and featherless. Me? I'm momma bird, swooping in with a mouth full of worms.

Mmmm, worms. But before we talk about my diet, let's meet a few other folks who have done this before, and who have done it pretty well. Maybe you've even heard of them.

High in protein, low in saturated fats!

Da Vinci and Michelangelo: A Long Road to Greatness

Leonardo da Vinci sucked. Michelangelo, too. Man, they both just stunk on ice. Later, of course, they did some things you could stand to look at. After a while, they did a few paintings that might find a place on a bathroom wall, but not at first. No, not at first. Because nobody (correct me if I'm wrong here, and I'll call the *Guinness Book of World Records*) comes out of the womb with a pencil in their hand knowing how to draw well.

Staying Sharp

Remember how mad your mother got when you drew on the wall in permanent marker or crayon? Imagine how mortified the cavemen must be. Our need to draw is so inherent in our being that some of the earliest drawings date back more than 32,000 years. That kid is never gonna live that down.

"Hmmm, a hand. Maybe I'll do something with that someday …."

Leonardo, Michelangelo, Picasso, Waterhouse … they all started off drawing things so ungodly bad that if we were to stumble across them now, they would come back from the dead and snatch them out of our hands in a panicked effort to protect their reputation. But that's the process. (Not the rising from the dead thing—that's just creepy. The other bit.) We all start off as baby birds. And let's face it, baby birds are ugly. But then they get feathers and wings, and they stop hopping around with their mouths open like that, and they get cool. Then they do that thing where they fly, and we're down here on the ground wishing we could do it, too.

One of da Vinci's lost sketches? Not.

The important thing to remember here is that everyone we refer to as a master was once as inexperienced and clueless as you. And while there's something to be said for raw, natural talent, the real secret to their success is that they didn't quit.

Masters' Musings

"If people knew how hard I worked to get my mastery, it wouldn't seem so wonderful at all."

—Michelangelo (1475–1564)

Even the Masters Cheated (the Camera Obscura)

Historically speaking, it may be fair to say that the old masters had it easier where art was concerned. It wasn't like kids had televisions or video games to distract them. Well, okay, they had to avoid the plague, but I don't think that counts. The point is that maybe they had countless idle hours in which to practice their art. Maybe when they weren't washing clothes down by the river or tending the fields or, you know, inventing flying machines, they were hunkered down over a pad of paper letting their imagination find its feet.

When we think of the old masters, we have a tendency to romanticize their process. Like everything in their lives existed in this kind of glorious sepia tone, and that their studios were cluttered with scraps of masterpieces gone awry. And you know, that's a nice fantasy. I'm not going to screw with that. But the notion that I am going to divorce you from is the one that lets you think that these folks drew everything by eye.

The fact is that there were a number of famous painters—and I'm not naming names

here (Vermeer)—who had a little help from a clever gadget we know today as the *camera obscura*. This forerunner of photography was a prime example of how people back in the day were a lot more clever than we gave them credit for.

Staying Sharp

The camera obscura and the modern-day camera … any relation? In fact, yes. The word *camera* comes from this device.

The most rudimentary form of this device was just a box with a small hole in one end. The light coming through the hole carried with it one part of a scene and got projected, through the miracle of physics, onto a canvas or wall on the other side. Of course, the image was inverted along the way, just like the lens of our eyes inverts things (it takes our brains to put them right). Some of the fancier camera obscuras had an additional mirror inside to flip the image right side up. Then the artist just traced the image there. That's right, I said "traced." But before we call them a bunch of no-talent cheaters, let's have a look at what sort of benefits the use of that tool yielded them.

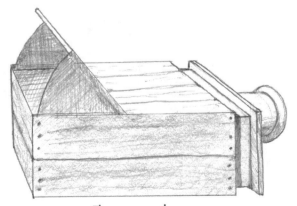

The camera obscura.

Trying, Failing, Trying Again, Failing Better

Got your pencils ready? We're going to try drawing a little something here. If you've got a piece of tracing paper (a semi-opaque, usually thin piece of paper, used for, well, tracing!) handy, that's swell, but I'm sure we'll get along fine without it if you don't. First, have a look at the following image.

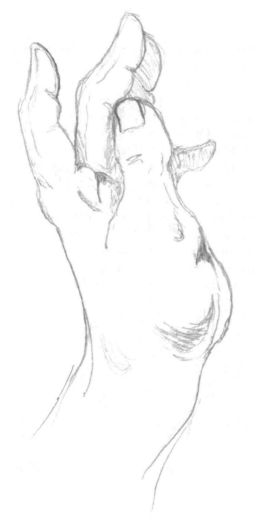

The hand is one of the hardest things to draw. Don't panic.

Now I want you to pick up your pencil, grab a piece of paper, and do your level best to draw the hand I've drawn here. Don't spend an hour on it: you're not being graded on this. As you draw, I want you to keep your hand loose and your pencil light, and just give it your best shot. Put down the ruler. Don't get fancy. Just draw.

Okay, how'd you do? My bet is that your first effort on one of the hardest subjects in the world won't be seeing the inside of the Louvre anytime soon (unless you sneak it in on a field trip in your back pocket). Now grab a piece of tracing paper (or if you don't have that, plain paper will do), and place it on top of the hand drawing that I did. Try it again. I'll wait.

Here's my traced version of the same thing.

Masters' Musings

"Life is pretty simple: You do some stuff. Most fails. Some works. You do more of what works. If it works big, others quickly copy it. Then you do something else. The trick is the doing something else."

—Ascribed to various sources, among them Leonardo da Vinci (1452–1519)

Staying Sharp

A lot of tools out there will help you get an image exactly the way you want it: tracing paper, projectors, light boxes, and more. (I discuss these and more in Chapter 2.) Although they're all useful tools, don't become dependent on them. Your art will suffer for it!

Now you've got two images drawn from the same source sitting side by side. Which do you like better? If you're anything like me, you're probably saying, "Neither." Why is that? Technically, the one you traced should be miles better, shouldn't it? So what's wrong? The problem is that it lacks soul. It's got no heart. You can mimic the length of a line. You can even refine it to match the varying width. But what you can't duplicate is the raw energy that I used when I drew the original. So what do you do? You tried. Maybe you failed. The trick is to keep trying and to fail better with each try.

So let's take a stab at this one more time. No tracing this time, but instead, try to remember the details of the hand as you just drew it. What did you miss the first time that you caught with the tracing paper? In what area did you screw up the proportion? Although the tracing method will suck the life out of a drawing, it's great for showing you where you went wrong with the original. So come on, give it one more try. I think you'll be amazed at the progress you've made in just the last two efforts. When you're done, think a little more kindly of the nameless masters who cheated (Vermeer). Using the camera obscura may have given them a starting place, but mostly they just used it to be sure of their perspective. The real act of drawing is a lot harder than just tracing, wouldn't you agree?

Drawing a Single Line

I want to prepare you for the biggest cliché you're going to hear as you walk this road toward drawing mastery. It's the phrase "I couldn't draw a straight line." You're going to hear that a lot as you make progress, showing people your early efforts. People, wanting to be nice, will take a look at your work and invariably say, "That's pretty good. Better than I could do. I couldn't draw a straight line." So let's just get this out of the way, shall we?

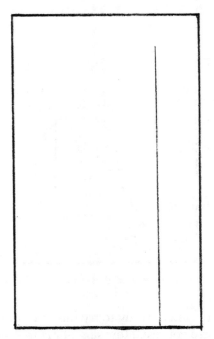

In a box, no less. If I knew you were coming, I would have wrapped it.

That's a (roughly) straight line. Notice how the line doesn't quite reach to the top of the box? Notice that it's not exactly centered? Notice how I keep using the word *notice*? (Sorry. I was on a roll.) Go ahead and duplicate the drawing, box and all. Got it? Good! Now we're ready for the next step. Oh, and now when people tell you, "I couldn't draw a straight line," you can tell them that's one of the first things you learned.

Two Lines! Now We're Cookin'!

I'm going to take a quantum leap forward here and add a second line to the box. ("Two! Two lines! Ah! Ah! Ah!") And yes, I did add a little curve to that one. How nice of you to have noticed.

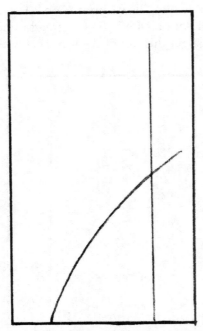

Now calculate the area under the hypotenuse ....
Just kidding.

Think you're ready to try this one yourself? Of course you are. How silly of me to even ask.

Take a few seconds to really look at the contents of the box before you move forward. Look at where the top of the line stops. Judge the distance on the bottom of the box from the first line. Study that curve. Now draw it.

Shapes and Relative Distance

Think this is easy so far? Good. Because you're already drawing. I know it seems like a few paltry lines, but trust me, if your box looks close to my box, you're going to be just fine. But now's the time to stop looking at it like a box. Stop looking at the lines. Let's define the shapes.

The two lines create a curved triangle.

In this illustration, I've extracted the triangular portion of my two-line drawing. Have a look at the triangle created by your lines. How close did you come? If you were a little off, you might find it easier to see where you went wrong, not by looking at the lines that you drew, but by examining the shapes those lines created. This is an important exercise. It may seem a far cry from the art you really want to do, but these are the worms, kids. Eat 'em up.

Masters' Musings

"Great things are done by a series of small things brought together."

—Vincent van Gogh (1853–1890)

Everything you've done with this line exercise has taught you some very important fundamentals, and it has probably done so without you even knowing it. It's like that scene in the movie *The Karate Kid* when Ralph Macchio finally understands that the whole "wax on/wax off" thing was more than just an opportunistic Japanese guy forcing the kid into indentured servitude. As we go forward, I want you to look at every drawing with these lessons in mind. Lines aren't just lines: they make shapes. Not just in the things you draw, but in the space around them. Look at everything and don't be afraid to get it wrong! Your best lessons will come from your own mistakes.

So what have you learned? By judging the distance from the top of the box to the top of the line, and the side of the box to the line itself, you've had your first taste of judging things by their *relative distance*. It's a basic but very important concept. By drawing things in their relative shape and distance to things around them, you'll have a better chance of mastering perspective later (see Chapter 6). Here's one more example before we move on:

Layman's Lingo

Relative distance is a way of measuring space without a ruler. Judging relative distance is accomplished by comparing the space between multiple objects. The distance from one eye to another, compared to the distance from one eye to the tip of the nose, for example.

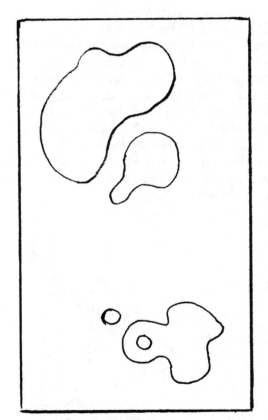

There's something to be said for asexual reproduction.

This is just two random blobs in a box, but if you can get their relative distance correct in relation to each other *and* the bounds of the box, you'll be drawing your *Mona Lisa* in no time. Which reminds me ….

"Nothing to Fear But Fear Itself"

You have heard of the *Mona Lisa*, right? I mean, you have a pulse, don't you? Okay, then. There's a little-known piece of information about that painting that I want to share with you right now: the *Mona Lisa* wasn't finished.

A family (their name is lost to us) commissioned Leonardo da Vinci to paint a portrait of their daughter. We don't know how much he got paid for the job, but we do know that he never delivered it. How do we know this? Because the painting was with him when he died. As astonishing as it may sound, Leonardo da Vinci worked on the Mona Lisa virtually every day for *17 years*. No, that's not a typo. He worked on it relentlessly for nearly two decades, right up until the day he died. Had he lived another two decades, I still don't think he would have been done.

How many mistakes do you figure he made on her in that time? How many times did he try that smirk and wipe away the paint, unsatisfied? Countless, I'd imagine. But where we are now, you and I, is a very disposable place in our learning. You're going to try things. You're going to fail. You're going to try again. You're going to get better. But sometimes you'll just crumple up the paper and throw it in the recycling bin.

You want to know what your biggest hurdle is going to be getting through this book? It's you. Go look in a mirror and accept the fact that you will be your own worst enemy. Your doubts, your fears, and your feelings of inadequacies will all but cripple you. You're going to spend a lot of time looking at the things I want you to draw and saying to yourself, "I can't do that." But you can. You really can. I promise. I wouldn't lie to you. (Well, I would, but not about this. And not until I knew you better.)

AFTER SHOUMATOFF

The 32nd President of the United States.

So why am I showing you a picture of Franklin Delano Roosevelt? Because he said something that I want you to remember: "The only thing we have to fear is fear itself." And luckily for you, I've already looked through the rest of the book. I didn't put any fear in it. You've got only yourself to blame if you bring it with you. So leave it at the door, huh?

The Least You Need to Know

◆ The great masters took time to become great.

◆ Love your failures! They're the surest way to get better.

◆ See lines in terms of the shapes they create.

◆ Learn to look at how far things are from each other. The power of relative distance will take you far!

◆ Fear is the enemy—you *can* learn how to draw!

In This Chapter

◆ Getting to know the tools at your disposal

◆ Why not all paper is the same

◆ Erasers: an artist's best friend

◆ Work surfaces

◆ The very best accomplices for taking a shortcut

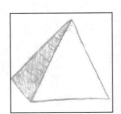

Chapter 2

Tools of the Trade

Up until now, you've probably been drawing with whatever you had handy. Maybe a no. 2 pencil and a sheaf of lined notebook paper. Maybe you'd even gone so far as to pick up a sketch pad at the local Wal-Mart. But there's a lot of stuff out there. A lot of it, quite frankly, you don't need. As with any hobby, a slew of companies out there will gladly help you out of your hard-earned cash. And hey, shopping is fun. No doubt about it.

What you'll learn in this chapter is not just what you need, but what you ought to take a chance on and why. At the very least, you're going to need a decent pencil or two and a nice pad of paper. What kind? Let's find out.

So many choices, so little cash!

Pencils

On your first trip to a decent art supply store, walking down the pencil aisle (and, yes, they'll probably have a whole aisle for pencils, or a good portion of an aisle, at any rate) will seem a lot like a visit to a candy store where all the wrappers have been peeled off. What do you need? What will work best for you? What should you avoid? The answer to that last one is the easiest: don't avoid any of it. Most of the better art stores keep out little pads of paper so you can try the different pencils. And try them you should—all of them. But we don't want your experience to be all about trial and error, do we? No. So let's have a look at what you're likely to find there.

> **Staying Sharp**
>
> We owe a lot to the Romans, and we can almost surely tack the pencil onto that long list. Some historians think that the earliest version of this implement was the stylus, a thin metal stick (usually made of lead) that was used for scratching on papyrus, an early form of paper that was made from the papyrus plant.

Nearly all of the pencils we're going to talk about were made by the same method. Somebody took two halves of a wooden cylinder, hollowed out the middle, filled it with an oil- or wax-enhanced graphite, and then glued it

back together. This isn't a far cry from the way we've been making pencils for almost 500 years now, ever since we found that huge deposit of graphite in Seathwaite Fell near Borrowdale, Cumbria, England. (Interesting historic fact: graphite was once so rare that people actually smuggled it to make pencils. I kid you not.)

The making of a pencil: complete the next image in this sequence ….

So now you know where pencils come from and how they're made. There's a lot of interesting history there, but let's press on. What we really want to know is, "What do those numbers and letters mean near the end of the pencil?"

All the pencils you'll find will have these codes. Pencils are graded in H's (for *hardness*) and B's (for *blackness*). You'll also spot a few F's in there (for *fine point*). The pencils are numbered from 9H (the hardest) to 9B (the softest and blackest). Smack dab in the middle is my personal favorite: the HB.

> **Staying Sharp**
>
> While we're on the subject of pencils, I want you folks to be careful. The points of these things can be plenty sharp, and if you're ever foolin' around, reenacting a scene from *West Side Story* with a pal and your favorite 6H pencil … well, I'm here to tell you that you just might be stuck with a piece of graphite in your hands for the rest of your days! Not that I'm speaking from experience or anything ….

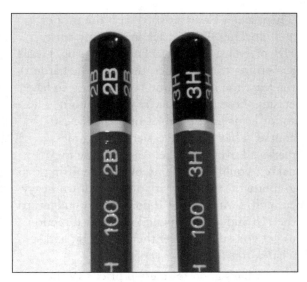

2B or not 2B? That is the question!

My advice to you is grab one of everything. At about a buck a piece, you may just find that it's the best $21 you're going to spend. A month from now, you'll be able to look in your pencil box and know, by sight, which pencils work best for you. How? Because the ones you use most often will get sharpened. And shorter. The ones you don't use will look pretty much the same as the day you bought them.

Not hard to see which one's my favorite, is it?

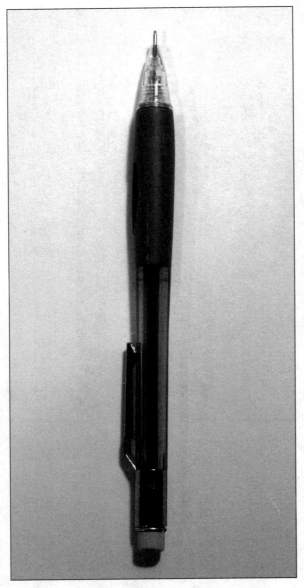

Of course, every rule has an exception. The mechanical pencil never needs sharpening—just refilling.

Beyond trial and error, how can you tell which pencils are likely to work best for you? That will depend on your style. For the longest time I would use a 6H pencil to rough in my figures, using very light, very quick strokes.

Then, when I was satisfied with the proportion and blocking, I'd go back in with my trusty HB, or even a 2B, just to finish things up. Here's something to remember, though. The harder the lead, the harder time you're going to have erasing those lines. They're just stubborn! Those softer leads have troubles of their own, of course. They smudge easier, leaving messy marks all over the page. And because they're darker, you'll have plenty of trouble lifting that graphite off the paper if you lay it down heavy enough. Bottom line? If you're on a budget, try the HB and a single pencil in either direction to get you started. Feel them out a bit and see what works for you.

So what's good for a good price? Without signing any endorsement deals, I've always found my Staedtler Mars and Faber-Castell pencils to give me a great bang for my buck. Beware of any pencil that's too inexpensive; these tend to crack and split when sharpened.

Colored Pencils

In your travels down the wondrous pencil aisle, you'll also find that pencils come in all the colors of the rainbow and beyond. Teaching you how to master the complexities of color is beyond the scope of this book, but if you're determined to try drawing in color, I suggest you remember the following hard and fast rule: "You get what you pay for." This is more than just common wisdom. In the world of art supplies, this borders on law. Don't skimp on your tools. I did that for years, picking up lousy papers and awful pencils, thinking that I'd upgrade when my talent warranted it. You know what I found out? That my "talent" was being severely hindered by inferior tools. The second I got a decent pencil and a nice toothy paper beneath it, I reached a new plateau in my studies.

You'll notice right away that you can get some things pretty inexpensively. And then there are the massive, overwhelming, kaleidoscope-of-colors, monstrous collections, like those put out by Prismacolor. You sit there and tell yourself that if you just had the right colors, you could draw like that, too! But despite my earlier statement, remember that you can't buy your ability to draw. You have to work at it.

Watercolor Pencils

An interesting quasi-medium for you to explore is the world of the watercolor pencil. The watercolor medium itself is deceptively hard. Controlling the flow of drying water is not nearly as easy as it looks, but watercolor pencils give the illusion of that control by allowing you to put color down exactly where you want it, and then brushing over it with clean water. The result, while not on par with real watercolors, can still be impressive.

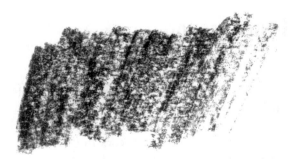

Use the pencil as you ordinarily would ...

... and when you've painted over it with clean water, it softens the lines. You can even blend colors this way.

Charcoal

Prepare to get messy—like, a lot. And be prepared to hate everything you do for a little while.

Charcoal is an extremely challenging medium. The lines go down so dark, so final, that there's not a lot of room for erasing. But charcoal isn't about erasing—not at first. Charcoal is about experimentation. It's about fluidity and being in the moment. Your hands are going to get dirty. Your fingers are going to be black with it. And then, as sure as the day is long, you're going to get an itch on your nose. Mark my words. And then you'll be standing there with a room full of people, one of them stark naked, and you'll be wiggling your nose like Samantha on a rerun of *Bewitched*.

Okay, maybe that was just me.

You'll want to do a few things when trying charcoal:

◆ Work big. Get a nice, large pad of newsprint paper.
◆ Use your whole arm to draw.
◆ Keep a paper towel handy.
◆ Draw standing up.

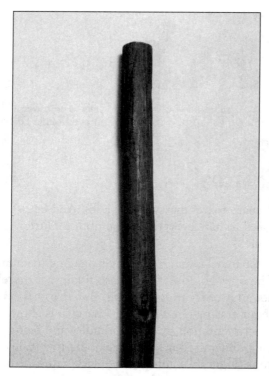

Charcoal can be bought in sticks. It's not recommended for barbecuing, however.

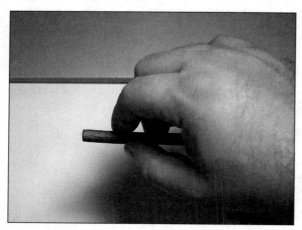

Hold your charcoal stick between your forefinger and thumb, like this. Don't just use your wrist to draw!

More so than any other medium, charcoal has impressed me as more of an *experience* than the others. Whenever I work in charcoal,

there's this sense that I'm following in a time-honored tradition—of sucking really, really badly. I'm not the first person to suck this badly. Many others have paved the way. But if you can get the hang of it, there are rewards to be earned here that can't be gotten any other way.

Masters' Musings

"I work in whatever medium likes me at the moment."
—Marc Chagall (1887–1985)

As for why I recommend working standing up, it's got everything to do with energy. When you sit down, you tend to rest your elbow on something and let your forearm and wrist do the work. When you're working larger, however, you're going to want your arm to have its full range of movement. Don't just swivel your hand on this stuff. Really be a part of the drawing. Get yourself into it. Throw your passion for the line into the drawing. Because it's not just a line anymore. It's not just charcoal and paper. It's a living, breathing thing that you're trying to represent. Even if you're trying to draw a tree, that tree has got life in it. Stand up when you do your large charcoal drawings, and you'll stand a much better chance of translating the pulse of life around you into art.

Conté Crayon

Conté crayon (invented in 1795 by Nicolas Jacques Conté, if you're curious) is a good charcoal substitute. The charcoal is combined with wax or clay, so it's less dusty than its counterpart, but it doesn't blend quite as well. The Conté crayon does its best work in the earth tones, ranging from browns to blacks; the white crayon does a great job on highlights.

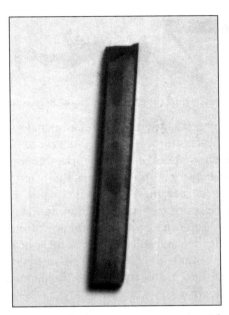

Like charcoal, Conté crayon comes in sticks.

Conté crayon has a good hardness, making it excellent for detail work.

Pastels

Pastels are a lot like charcoal in the way you'll use them, but their vast array of colors makes them a great tool for expressing yourself. Pastels can be chalky or waxy, depending on the manufacturer and price. The chalky ones blend better, so consider that when making your purchase. I've seen some mind-blowing work in pastel. If your city has an annual street painting festival, I suggest you make it a point of going out to see it. I guarantee there will be a pastel purchase in your future shortly thereafter.

Pastels are made of pure pigment, the same stuff that goes into fine artist paints, and is mixed with gum or some other fixative to keep it from being a gooey mess to work with. Pastels keep their colors amazingly well. Some sixteenth-century works done in pastels look like they were drawn yesterday!

Pens

You know what I've never understood? I've never understood when artists state their work as being done in "pen and ink." What else would it be? Pen and guacamole? A sharpened grilled cheese sandwich and ink? The mind boggles.

Pens come in a few different types. On one hand, you'll find a staggering variety of pens that work pretty much the same way your writing pen does: it has a reservoir of ink built right in. Most of these are meant to be disposable, but some of the fancier ones can be refilled. You'll find that the tips range from very fine to quite broad. Some pens allow you to simulate a calligraphy pen, a *Sumi-e* brush, and more.

Layman's Lingo

Sumi-e is the Japanese art of brush painting. It was actually developed in China during the Tang Dynasty (618–907 B.C.E.) and got introduced to Japan in the mid-fourteenth century by Buddhist monks. There's no underlying drawing. It's just brush, ink, and paper. It is, essentially, drawing with ink and brush.

And then, of course, there are the other kinds of pens—the ones that nearly belong in a museum. These pens come in two parts: the holder (handle) and the nib. The nib is usually made of metal and is similar to the very fine calligraphy pens you'll probably find in the same shopping aisle. The two parts are attached, and you dip the nib into an inkwell (sold separately) and apply it to the page. You've got to be careful when you use these pens because changing the angle of your stroke alters the weight of your line. If you can get the hang of that variance, you can do some really nice stuff.

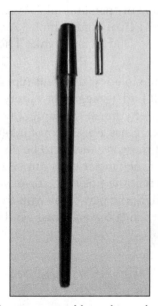

These nibs are removable and interchangeable.

Change the angle, and the line changes, too.

Many artists use these (and all pens) for an after-the-fact finish on a penciled piece. The entire comic book industry works this way. But many people will grab a pen as their first tool and just start laying black on the paper. The key here is not to get wrapped up in making it perfect. You can't erase ink, and any attempt to lift it off the page will only muck up your paper. And who wants mucky paper? So just get in there and do it. Put the pen on the paper and keep moving.

A quick drawing in pen and ink.

Even if you decide that pen and ink won't be a mainstay of your drawing diet, it's something you should do now and then to keep loose—like eating a bran muffin.

Staying Sharp

When you dip your nib into an inkwell, resist the urge to scrape the metal tip against the side of the container. Instead, tap it against the side once or twice to shake off the excess. Then draw.

Paper

We have to thank Ts'ai Lun for the stroke of genius he had in inventing paper. (Actually, we'd need to invent a time machine and take it back to the year 105 B.C.E. to thank him, but the thought is there.) He boiled down some tree bark, and set it on a screen to dry; the next thing you know, the whole universe was using the stuff. Truly an idea whose time had come!

But what do you, as an artist, need from your paper? If you're walking around in that art supply store right now, you're probably saying, "Great googly moogly! There are so many different kinds!" And then you'll feel your cheeks redden when you realize that the salesperson has overheard you talking to yourself. But then … then all kinds of magic happens. Paper is one of the most wonderful things in the whole world. Well, that and my mother's rice balls. But paper you can get anywhere. Momma Fradella's rice balls are available only through Momma Fradella's kitchen. And no, you can't come over.

Let's start with what you need as a beginner. The first item I want you to add to your shopping list is a good sketchbook. For the moment, don't worry about the acidity of the paper or its pH balance. Save that for your shampoo shopping. (If you really must know, the acid-free papers are suggested for those of you who have created a true masterpiece and want it to survive the test of time. It's the acid that will slowly eat away at your work. And yes, that includes the acid from your own skin, so quit eating potato chips while you're drawing; you're getting grease all over the page.)

For now, I just want you to get a decent-size bound sketchbook. Nothing less than 8 × 10 inches. You can pick the perfect bound or the spiral bound. It doesn't much matter.

The other thing that I want you to watch for when you buy your sketchbook is what we call *tooth*. A smooth finish is fine for your pencil work, but charcoal, inks, and pastels all benefit from a little tooth. (Personally, I like some tooth for my pencil work as well.)

Layman's Lingo

The **tooth** of a page is how rough it is, how much it "bites back" on the tool you're using.

The same Conté crayon dragged across smooth (on the left) and toothy paper (on the right).

Papers also come in different weights. You'll see these listed as 50 lb., 100 lb., and so on. What does this mean? Well, it's pretty obvious that the heavier papers will be thicker, but what those numbers really correspond to is how heavy a 500-page ream of that stuff will be. Most sketchbooks use a standard-weight paper—about 50 lb., or 105 grm (grams)—nothing you'll need a hand truck to get around. But when you stop sketching and start *drawing*, you may want to find something a little toothier and heavier. And lose the acid.

Erasers

Oh, eraser! How I adore thee! And you will, too. I promise, the eraser shall undoubtedly become your best friend. No other tool can make you look as good as the one that lets you make all your errors disappear.

But I can hear you now. You're saying, "Bah! I know all about erasers! I have a small pink one on the end of my pencil right now!" First, let me caution you that saying "Bah!" like that makes you sound like a supervillain from the former Soviet Union. Next, throw that pencil away or save it for your SATs. Is that the pencil I told you to buy? No. Your pencil should not have an eraser. Because what I'm about to show you will make all other erasers obsolete.

This is my best friend. I call him Bob.

My favorite kind of eraser (because, as I said, in the art world you've always got choices) is the kneaded rubber eraser. You can squish this thing in your hand and mold it into any shape you want (handy for those fine lines), and it leaves no residue when you rub the graphite off the page. Those little pinky things? They work by ripping off layers of paper. And they're self-destructive little buggers, leaving pieces of themselves all over the place. No more. The kneaded rubber eraser makes those grade-school memories a thing of the past. And let me tell you something: these little gray rectangles will take an awful lot of graphite off the page before you'll need to replace them. Just don't carry them around in your pocket: they suck up lint like they do graphite, and that's not good.

Another choice you have is the vinyl eraser. It works much like the kneaded rubber eraser, in that it lifts the graphite off your page, but you won't get to mash it up like a fist of Silly Putty. Of course, you may be one of the three people who don't like Silly Putty, in which case this might just be the eraser for you. (And seek help. Who doesn't like Silly Putty?)

This eraser's made of vinyl, for artists who like a little kink.

Staying Sharp

For the truly lazy among you, there are (you guessed it) electric erasers. Most of these keep you tethered to a wall outlet, but if you're going to be erasing whole pages of graphite, then it might be worth a few bucks.

Rulers

Is there really any difference between professional-grade art-store rulers and the ones you used in school? Very little, actually. The few notable differences are that your pro ruler will likely be made out of metal or plastic, it will be significantly longer, and it may include a right-angle tool on the end. Other than that, a ruler is a ruler. So why do you need one? Because when we get to Chapter 6 on perspective (deep breaths), you're going to need a handy straight edge with which to guide your pencil. So tramp down those Catholic school flashbacks with the nuns smacking your knuckles with a ruler, and pick yourself up one. Okay?

Drafting Tables and Other Flat Surfaces

Sooner or later, somebody's going to want to eat on the dining room table where you've got all your newly acquired art supplies strewn about. So what are your options? Well, there's always the kitchen table, but that's just asking for trouble. So where do you go? I'm glad you asked. You've got options.

Optimally, you'll get yourself a nice drafting table. These are miles better than your kitchen table because these are specifically designed to allow you to adjust the height of the table as well as the angle of the surface. If you haven't already, you'll soon find that drawing against an inclined surface does wonders for your back and neck, as opposed to laying the pad flat on a table. Plus, you can get a nice swing-arm lamp like mine and direct the light exactly where you need it. These drafting tables (also called "artist tables") will run you upward of $200. Check your local classifieds, though, or browse www.craigslist.com. You might be able to pick one up from a frustrated artist for half that.

But maybe a drafting table isn't in your budget. Maybe you don't have the room for one. Apartment living can be tough. So what's an aspiring artist to do? You can get yourself a large artist clipboard, available at art supply stores for about $20. It's like a portable easel. You rest the bottom in your lap and leave one hand up top to control the angle. The clip holds your paper in place, and you're on your way!

A clipboard like this one is perfect for traveling and drawing on the couch.

When you're using a clipboard like this, I want you to defy gravity. How? Turn your paper upside down or sideways, if you need to. Don't think of that clip as something that locks your paper in place. It's a tool. Use it to your advantage.

Drafting tables usually come in white, but I found a rare black one.

Because the board is so mobile, you won't have to bend over as much to draw. Bring the board to you!

Staying Sharp

Speaking of changing the direction of the page, if you're going to draw using reference photos, try turning them upside down when you're drawing them. It will force you to stop looking at the image as whatever it is and start seeing it as a collection of highlights and shadows. More on this later.

Viewfinders, Lightboxes, and Projectors

I'm always amazed at the lengths some people will go to in order to take a shortcut. The following items, purchased from most art supply stores, can be useful tools, but you'll have to go pretty far with your studies before they'll do anything but hurt your progress. A viewfinder, for example, allows you to visually cut up an image into smaller squares. Then you're not really drawing a face, you're drawing a few squiggly lines and a dark blotch. Like so.

While you can get some pretty decent results this way, it is just one step removed from tracing paper. It's a good exercise to try one of these, though, if only so you can learn to separate your brain from the object it's seeing. You'll do this in Chapter 10.

Another really handy tool is the lightbox. This is a … uh … box … um … with a light in it. No kidding. You've got yourself a light bulb in a frame, usually with a frosted piece of Plexiglas covering it. This is for industrial-strength tracing, kids. Now, despite my admonishments about tracing, there are times when it's not only helpful, but it's necessary. Say you've spent a few hours on a piece in your sketchbook, and you just adore how it came out. What now? What if you want to get this thing into a frame or transfer it to heavier paper so you can try your hand at coloring it? You lightbox the thing. Take your sketchbook page and the page you want to transfer it onto and tape them together. That will prevent any slippage. These things are notoriously hard to line up again once they've come apart. The tape will prevent that. Then you just have to lay the taped pages onto your lightbox, flip on the light, and trace away!

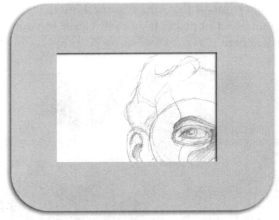

It's like a Rorschach test, isn't it?

Lightboxes come in varying sizes. This one's pretty small, and it was still kind of pricey.

Last but not least, there's the projector. This is a distant cousin to the camera obscura (see Chapter 1) and is not an uncommon way for artists to get their rough sketches onto a canvas for painting. As you'll see in later chapters, a small, rough sketch can have a lot of energy and emotion that a bigger piece doesn't. So artists will sometimes work small at first and then project their loose scribbles onto a canvas, choose the lines they want there, and paint like there's no tomorrow.

The Least You Need to Know

◆ From pencils to charcoal and more, there are many drawing tools to choose from.

◆ Paper is measured by weight; the "tooth" of the paper is also important.

◆ Because nobody's perfect … erasers and rulers are your friends!

◆ Get yourself a drafting table or a portable drawing board. Not only are these more comfortable than the dining room table, they help get you in the right frame of mind.

◆ Lightboxes, projectors, and the like can help you get a more accurate drawing, but they can also hinder your progress. On the other hand, tracing an image can show you things you may miss on your own. Find a balance!

In This Chapter

- ◆ Get your hands and fingers loose and limber
- ◆ Using office supplies to further your goals
- ◆ Start small with simple shapes and shading
- ◆ Drawing inspiration from your environment

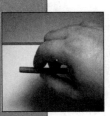

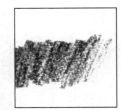
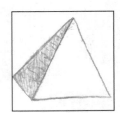

Chapter 3

Doodles and Scribbles and Sketches, Oh My!

Start small—that's my advice to you. Before you start painting the local church's ceiling or a gargantuan thing that's going to eat Tokyo when you're done, it's best to scale back and remember the little things. In this chapter we focus on beginnings, on the seeds of ideas. In later chapters we pour water on them and watch them grow into bigger things. But not now. Not yet. You gotta start at the beginning.

And while we're at it, let your wrist and fingers get a little exercise. Stretch 'em out. Get 'em limber! We want them loose as we doodle our little doodles. How small are we talking? Like the animals on the ark, I'm talking two by two (inches, that is).

There had to be rules.

Warming Up

One of the first mistakes you're likely to make is to try to squeeze too much detail into your early work. It's only natural. Details are all around you. But drawing is like any other exercise: you've got to limber up first. You wouldn't try to run a marathon without stretching, would you? Likewise, you wouldn't attempt a marathon the first time you decided to take up running. You'd do a few laps around the house first. Then, when you could breathe again and assured your spouse she didn't need the defibrillator, you'd try something a little bigger. The key is to start small and prepare yourself for the battles that lie ahead.

Masters' Musings

"A man paints with his brains and not with his hands."

—Michelangelo (1475–1564)

("Maybe so, but something's gotta hold the brush, pal." —F.)

To warm up, make sure you've got all your tools ready. No, not the pencils and erasers. I'm talking about your mitts, your paws, your hands and fingers. You gotta limber 'em up and get some blood flowing to those extremities! So how do we do that? Simon says, follow me:

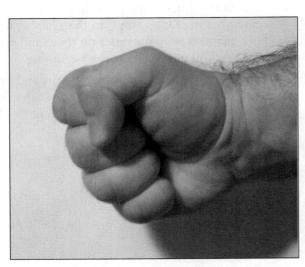

Clench your hands into fists. Hold 'em good and tight. Count to five, then release.

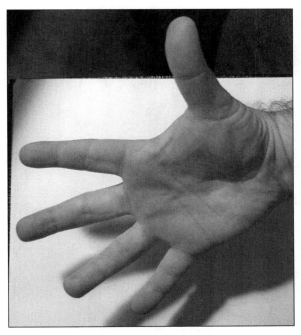

Open your hands as wide as you can. Gimme a five-count there, too.

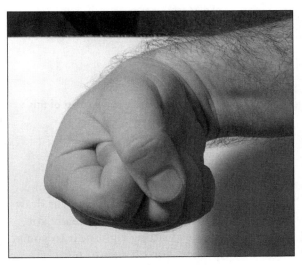

Close your hands and roll your wrists in slow circles without using your forearm. You want the motion to come solely from the wrist.

Repeat this a few times to let the blood start flowing. While you're drawing, you may find that your hand or wrist becomes fatigued, especially during marathon sketching sessions. When this happens, put down your pencil and pad and repeat these exercises. Your hands work in cooperation with your eyes and brain when you draw. (Well, they do on the good days ….) If you don't take a break now and then, you'll find that the quality of your work will slowly deteriorate.

Take care of your body, and it'll take care of you!

> **Staying Sharp**
>
> As with any endeavor that causes you to sit in one place for a lengthy period of time, you'll want to be sure to get up and walk around at least once an hour. There's also some great sit-in-your-chair yoga you can do. But don't take my word for it—consult your physician before starting any exercise program.

The Power of the Post-It Note

We use these little beauties to jot down phone numbers, take messages, and maybe, just maybe, create little micromasterpieces. You can hang these little guys wherever you sit and let your eyes fall over them throughout the day. As you look at them, you'll begin to recognize where you went wrong and where you should start feeling the first swellings of pride.

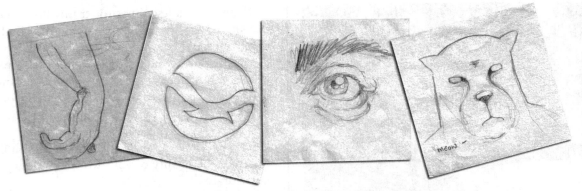

The walls around my desk are plastered with colorful squares.

Chances are, you're already doodling on the edge of your legal pad and the corners of your blotter, and filling the dates on your personal planner with inky scribbles. With a Post-It note, that little square becomes your canvas. The best part? We're used to thinking of them as disposable. That's the perfect mindset to have when you're just starting out. In fact, Charles Keegan, a good friend and famous fantasy artist, once told me, "The first nine canvases you put up on your easel, I don't want you tryin' to do nothing. Don't try to make a picture. You gotta spend some time just screwin' around. See what works for you and what doesn't." Now, Charles was obviously talking about oil painting, but the same principle applies for any type of drawing. You've got to do this for the fun of it. And what's more fun than doodling? (Well, yes, there's poking badgers with a cricket paddle and running for your life, but you can doodle at your desk. Badgers are a bit scarce around the office.)

No badgers were harmed in the writing of this book.

Doodling at Your Desk

You needn't carry around a field sketchbook and an arsenal of pencils to exorcise your drawing demons. Chances are, you've already got everything you need sitting right next to you at the office. And hey, don't forget to recycle! Though you won't see them here (for privacy reasons), most of my sketches are done on

Post-It notes that already have something written on them. We all have this bad habit of jotting down one thought, one phone number, one reminder, and then reaching for the pad again when we have a separate thought. We don't want to get the thoughts confused, so we usually just end up throwing away that first note. So why not start your doodling there? It was headed for the trash bin anyway. (And when am I going to learn to write people's names above their number when I write it down? I always think, "Oh, I'll remember." But I never do. Consequently, if you're waiting for a call from me and it's been a while, it's probably because your number is in a stack of unidentified digits.)

Making Time to Draw

There's no doubt that our lives are a metric ton busier than they used to be. Where did all that time go? I've checked the lost and found at Wal-Mart. It's not there—although I did find one half of a pair of mukluks. How do you get anywhere with just one mukluk? (If you've lost a mukluk, see me after class.)

All kidding aside, one of the most common excuses I hear for aspiring artists not doing as much drawing as they should is the often-imitated, "I just don't have the time." But come on. How many minutes pass you by throughout your day while you're waiting for a meeting to start, a document to print, or a tech support guru to answer your call? Would it be fair to say that you spend a healthy 30 minutes a day doing things that are, essentially, waiting for other things to happen? If you answered in the positive, you can use that time to draw.

> **Masters' Musings**
> "There is no greater harm than that of time wasted."
> —Michelangelo (1475–1564)

"Thank you for your patience. You are the next caller in line. Please continue to hold."

Draw while you're waiting. Scribble, doodle, make random lines, but put that pencil on the paper and keep it moving. You will surprise yourself at the little gems that come out of your subconscious in those moments. Sometimes these *roughs* can inspire you in larger pieces.

> **Layman's Lingo**
> **Roughs** is a term that means, you guessed it, any unfinished drawing, or something that's left deliberately ragged. Many artists will fill pages of roughs before they sit down to do a more detailed drawing.

Starting Simple

Let's do a few warm-up exercises, shall we? Now that your hand is limber and you have a few minutes to kill, let's start with something ridiculously easy. There's going to be a whole chapter on basic shapes later (see Chapter 5), but I want to do a few now to get you started.

Circles and Shapes

Forget your rulers. Don't worry about straight lines. And hey, you with the protractor—put down the hardware and back away slowly, and nobody gets hurt, okay? Now follow me.

The three shapes you see here will be the basis for almost everything you draw.

Squares, circles, triangles, and polygons. Easy peasy, right? Well, if you can get these down, you, too, can draw like the masters. In later chapters, I show you how to turn these humdrum shapes into things that look like, well, other things—but more interesting things. For now, though, let's just add a little depth to a few of these.

A little shading can turn a flat object into something three-dimensional.

Depending on where you put the shadow, you can make this sphere look like it's floating.

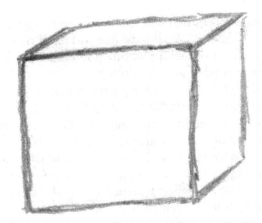

Add just a few lines, and you've suddenly got something with depth.

Once again, the addition of shading makes the sketch come alive.

Shading

We touched on shading a little in the previous section, but let's take a moment and explore the difference in a few more drawings. Here are a few scribbles, before and after shading. This is kid's stuff. Easy, right? Well if it's so easy, *you* do it. That's right! Just looking at the pretty pictures won't help you get any better. Don't think that just because this is so easy you shouldn't waste your time on it. Put that pencil on the paper and repeat after me.

Is this an isosceles or a scalene triangle? I can never remember.

And with just two lines, we have something that has depth.

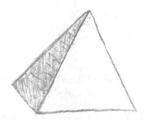

Shade one side of the triangle like so.

Add some small details, a few wavy lines, and violà!

This exercise may seem easy, but trust me when I tell you that if you can do this, there are greener pastures within your reach. Every great artist started just like this: with the basics.

Picking Random Objects

Right now, right this very second, there are probably a dozen objects sitting nearby waiting to be drawn. Unless, of course, you're in solitary confinement in one of the bigger penitentiaries, and then I imagine they've taken your pencils away, too. But assuming that you're not doing 8 to 10, you have within your view a plethora of common items that will happily model for you.

Masters' Musings

"When it came to my art, I went my own way and did not follow the trends."

—Frank Frazetta (1928–)

That pencil? The one with the pink eraser on the end? Perfect. (And I thought I told you to throw that away!)

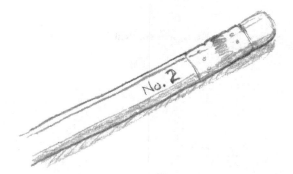

At least it's good for something.

Rough Sketches of Nearby Items

Got a drink nearby? A glass or a soda can? Draw it. Don't worry about complex reflections or flashy logos. What we want right now is the simple shape of the thing. Keep that hand loose. Don't worry about getting the drawing perfect. Just put a vague outline of the thing on the paper. Then move forward. If you're using a pencil, I want you to put down your eraser for now. We're not trying to make a finished drawing yet. This is just another bit of playtime. C'mon.

Note the oval at the top. Just another circle!

Draw in the sides, like so. Watch your proportion.

Another oval, and you're almost done!

What you've got right now is the basic shape. It's probably not perfect, and that's okay! Don't be afraid to redraw some lines. Don't erase—just keep that pencil moving. And don't try to draw any part of this in one smooth line. The goal at this stage is to get sketchy. Now let's add some finishing touches.

It doesn't take much to make a flat cylinder into a real object.

Very good! You're doing fine. Now try this again with another nearby object—a stapler, perhaps, or a magic marker.

Your Co-Workers: The Unwitting Models

You're likely to end up with today's special in your hair if you walk up to a co-worker and ask if he or she would be willing to model for you. Don't ask me why, but people automatically put the word *nude* in front of *model*, and the next thing you know, you've got HR asking you to report to the security desk—oh, and bring the entire contents of your desk with you.

Staying Sharp

All joking aside, "sexual harassment" and "hostile work environment" are two terms you never want thrown in your direction, especially when your intent is innocent. If your intentions aren't honorable, you probably deserve to be picking corned-beef hash out of your hair all day.

It won't take you long to realize the importance of drawing from life. No matter how many rules and guidelines I give you about how to draw the human face, there's no substitute for looking at one. There are basic rules that every face follows (well, almost every face), but the thing you'll learn firsthand is that every face defies those rules in at least one way. This person's eyes are closer together, that person's nose is affecting the tides … you can't predict these things. So let your co-workers be your unsuspecting allies. Keep that Post-It note and a pen handy, and seize the opportunities as they arise.

His neck is actually that big. I had to draw him.

Oh, a word of sincere caution here: merely by being alive, the people whom you're drawing possess the copyright on their distinctive likeness. Generally, that means you shouldn't draw someone without their permission, and you absolutely must not, under any circumstances, in any form, publish those sketches without getting the subject to sign a model release form. And yes, posting those sketches to your online blog counts as publishing. Don't do it. The U.S. Copyright Law makes some small exception when such drawings are done as a parody or if the person in question is a public figure, but do your homework before you start putting this stuff out there in the world.

Okay, enough talk. Start drawing! Your co-workers are going to go home sooner or later, and they're not going to sit still all day. So how can you do a complete portrait? Most times you can't. But you can take a mental snapshot of a nose or an ear, and do your best to quickly reproduce it.

I'm also a big fan of noting hairstyles. Hair is one of the trickiest things to draw, and your imagination is no substitute for the wide variety of styles that pass by you every day. Note where the hair starts on the forehead. How much can you see behind the ears? Generally, hair moves like a loose body rather than individual strands. You shouldn't try to draw every hair you see.

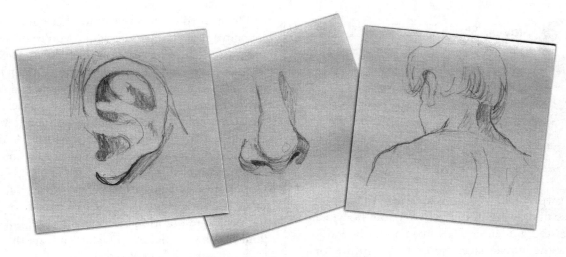

It's like a sign for a doctor's office.

"… shinin', gleamin', streamin' flaxen waxen!"
(That's from the musical *Hair*. And yes, I am that
old, thankyouverymuch.)

You've got more than enough in your every-day surroundings to keep you motivated and inspired. There will be plenty of time for fleshing out ideas and for serious study when you get home, but don't waste the precious minutes you can find for yourself to draw every day!

The Least You Need to Know

◆ Stay loose and do your warm-up exercises. Keeping your hands limber will allow your internal energy to come through. It's what keeps your drawings from feeling lifeless!

◆ It's best to start small. Even if you've been at this a while, it never hurts to take the time to doodle. Even oak trees started off as acorns!

◆ Your desk is filled with inspiration. Staplers, pens, telephones, mouses (mice?) ... take time throughout your day to keep your creative juices flowing.

◆ Co-workers are great for reference, and because they're always moving, it forces you to move fast. You've got to think on your feet!

In This Chapter

- Using your thumbnails as a springboard
- Transferring a rough to larger paper
- Basic composition
- The Law of Thirds

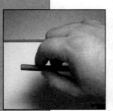

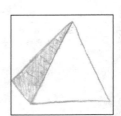

Chapter 4

Diamonds in Your Roughs

It's a rare artist who is so competent, so talented that he or she can forego any sort of thumb-nail sketch and go directly to the final-size painting or drawing. That's a lot easier to do if you're working on an abstract or surreal piece, obviously. Nobody but you will ever know that you didn't mean for that nose to be in the middle of that harpsichord. For the rest of us, we've got to start with something that speaks to the fundamentals. Look at it this way: some folks believe that the first kiss will tell them everything they need to know about a prospective mate.

Pucker up, buttercup.

A thousand kisses may follow it, but the passion and spontaneity of that first kiss are what they base everything on. This isn't far removed from that. Those little note-pad sketches you were working on in the last chapter? Those are perfect for building larger drawings. Of course, it doesn't have to be *that* small. Let me show you what I mean.

Using Small Thumbnail Sketches to Plan Larger Drawings

Every year, I attend a major popular media convention (sci-fi, fantasy, comics, movies, and more) in Atlanta. I've usually got a table there, schilling my wares, but my favorite part of the show is taking a walk down Artist Alley. Dozens of famous (and not-so-famous) artists sit behind their 6-foot folding tables, pencils in hand, banging out quick sketches for $20–$50 a pop. I have to limit myself to one sketch a year or I'll go nuts. I already don't have enough wall space for the art I've got. But even just being there, just watching these guys and gals scribble away, is all the inspiration I need.

A sample of what your $20 will get you.

The new artists will draw you anything for a dollar. They're eager, they're hungry, and the only thing they lack from their veteran counterparts is a little snow on the roof and a few miles of road on the odometer. For $20 you'll get your role-playing game character in excruciating detail. But those aren't the guys to watch. You want to watch the guys who have been in the trenches for a few years. For the same $20, these guys will give you a sketch. No details. No glitz. And you'll be glad to have it. Why? Because these guys (and I say that in the most genderless way possible) are doing the hard stuff. One of these artists (who must remain nameless) will do a sketch and show it to his wife, and if she likes it enough … he won't give it to the customer. He does another one, almost as good, and sells that. The first sketch? The one that's just a loose collection of lines and shading? That one gets turned into a painting.

Masters' Musings

"Drawing is like making an expressive gesture with the advantage of permanence."

—Henri Matisse (1869–1954)

It doesn't have to be a masterpiece. Those thumbnails, once you begin to see past the lines and into the spirit of them, are just like that first kiss. They tell you everything you need to know. It's about concept. It's about conception. Eventually, you may, like me, develop a love of artists' sketchbooks that surpasses their finished work. That's where the genius is!

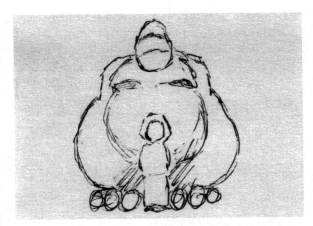

In a flash of inspiration, I jotted this down on a Post-It note one day at work.

When I got home that evening, I did this.

Even this "finished" version isn't finished. I'll play with this for hours. Eventually, I might even look at a picture of a gorilla, just to make sure I've got the hair right. For the ape here, I was strictly working from imagination and memory. And it's been a long time since I've seen Roddy McDowell. (Please tell me somebody gets the classic *Planet of the Apes* reference—please.)

Here are a few more before-and-after shots.

You can already see the figure coming to life.

And here he is refined—well, as refined as barbarians get, anyway.

I don't worry about the furniture yet.

I may throw in a couch later. Maybe not.

If you look at these two examples, you'll see how the process goes. I didn't use any light-boxes or projectors (see Chapter 2). I just kept the original sketch nearby to use as a guideline. Then I worked bigger. It doesn't have to be a lot bigger, mind you. These "finished" works are pages out of my sketchbook. But I did all the really hard work in the first sketch. Looking at them side by side, I know that's hard to believe, but it's true. Figuring out where to put those arms, trying to suss out what part of the leg gets *foreshortened* … that's the hard part. Especially when you don't have a model handy.

Layman's Lingo

Foreshortening is the act of drawing things larger or smaller to give them the illusion of distance. This is an important topic, and we cover it in greater detail in Chapter 6 on perspective.

When I was working with my publisher on my book *Swan Song* (New Babel Books, 2005), we went back and forth about what to do for a cover. I've got a pretty strict rule about not doing the cover art for the novels that I write, but in this case, I needed to convey to the cover artist a few essential facts, like what the main character looked like. And the mask he wears? I saw it very specifically in my head. I wanted to make sure the artist got it right. So I did a little sketch first, just to try out the pose and the angle, and see how that might look on a cover. Then I did a rough portrait of the main character and sent it off to the artist to use as a guide.

The finished "unfinished" piece.

It was very important to me to leave the work undone. I wanted to give the artist a direction, not draw him a map. In the end, he just took my pencils, brought them into Photoshop, inked it, colored it, and, voilà, we had a cover.

Doesn't look like much, does it?

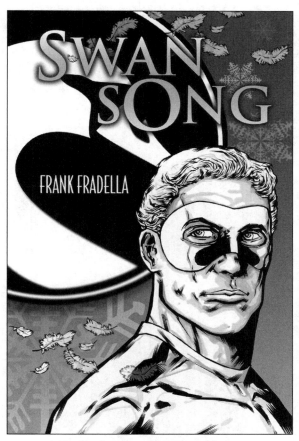

The final cover, with title and logo.

(Courtesy of New Babel Books.)

My initial sketch on this one was less than inspiring, wasn't it? After all my talk of how I prefer rough thumbnails to finished pieces, I had to go and prove that there's an exception to every rule, didn't I?

Keeping the Energy Alive in the Transition

The biggest problem any artist faces when transferring a thumbnail sketch to a full-size drawing is that very often the energy of the piece dies in the translation. Don't believe me? Let's try a few and see what happens.

I saw this on the highway one day. No, really.

It's not easy to capture that grace in a line.

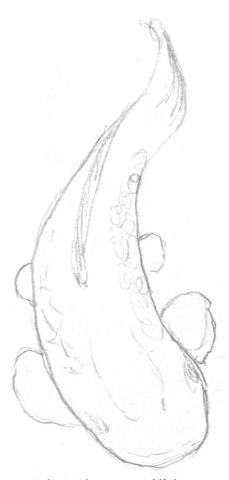

That's a koi, not a goldfish.

Masters' Musings

"He can who thinks he can, and he can't who thinks he can't. This is an inexorable, indisputable law."

—Pablo Picasso (1881–1973)

First things first. Get your pencil and your sketchbook, and try to reproduce these rough sketches on the page. Keep them small. Think of these as actual size. Find the flow of the line, and let your pencil do the work. Don't force it.

Good. Now let's try to reproduce those at a larger scale. Try to duplicate each of these images just as you see them, but this time fill the page. Much harder, isn't it?

I'm sure you did pretty well, but here are a few tips for how to keep that energy alive from thumbnail to full drawing.

Note the direction of the action here.

What you're looking for is the "action line." It's the imaginary line that flows through your sketch. It's indicated in a second color to make it easier for you to spot. That's usually where a good portion of the energy lies. Chances are, when you did the larger-scale drawing, you flattened this line a bit. You took some of the spunk out of its stride and maybe straightened its back a bit. This drawing isn't intended to be photorealistic. What we're looking for right now is an exaggerated dynamic. Have a look at the others.

The action line isn't always straight!

Staying Sharp

If you've been paying attention (and you *have* been paying attention, right?), then you've probably noticed that I've compared art to a lot of different things, from baby birds to kissing. That's because art is life. There are lessons to be learned in every aspect of your existence. Look around you and be open to the possibilities!

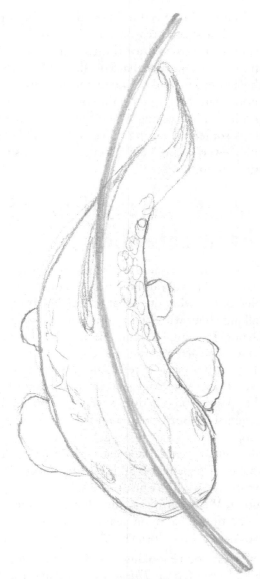

Consider the environment: it's fluid. Make the action line fluid, too!

Don't kid yourselves, folks. If you can get this part down, you'll enjoy a much more rewarding success in your artistic endeavors. Action lines aren't just there to direct traffic. It's an exercise in seeing the omnipresent motion in the universe. (Deep, huh?)

Why do you need to know this "action line" stuff? For several reasons. The first is that when you start to draw things that are actually in motion, knowing that you should look for the action line will help you enormously. But more than that, if you train yourself to find the motion in everything, when the time comes to draw somebody sitting down, you won't bore the viewer. There's a difference between still life and no life.

Layout, Composition, and the Law of Thirds

As we move forward, you're going to want to start thinking about how best to compose your pieces. But what does that mean? What are we talking about when we mention composition and layout? Put simply, composition is the manner in which you arrange the elements on your page. (Layout is a broader term, and can refer to everything from page size to orientation of that page. Composition is what you do on the page itself.) Sure, you could keep putting the subject of the drawing smack dab in the middle, but that lacks the creative eye that you're so clearly capable of. So how do artists do it? Trust me, we don't just make this up as we go along. We experiment, sure, but that experimentation is based on years of learning what works and what doesn't.

What you're looking at is a simple grid, but it's also the *Law of Thirds*. Let's say that the rectangle this grid is in is your page. Where should you put your subject? If you follow the Law of Thirds, you should put the main focus of your art on one of the places where those lines intersect.

Layman's Lingo

The **Law of Thirds** is the rule for placing the subject of your drawing on one of the intersecting lines that divides your page into thirds, both vertically and horizontally. On a blank sheet of paper, this would look like a tic-tac-toe board.

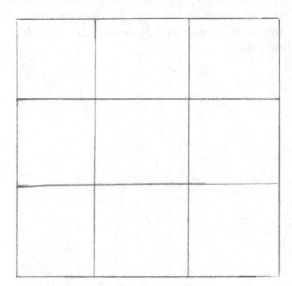

No, it's not a game of tic-tac-toe.

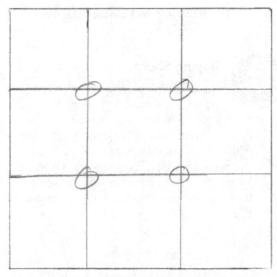

The Law of Thirds. You should place your subject where the lines intersect (noted here by cute little circles).

Here's an example of that law in action.

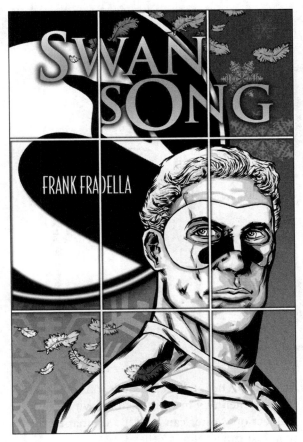

Here's that *Swan Song* cover again, with the grid overlaid on it.

You can see here that rather than just drop the face in the dead center of the page, the cover artist placed it on one of the intersecting lines. Why do this? Doesn't this leave a gaping white hole on the rest of the page? In some cases, yes. And many times, that's a good thing. The concept of "white space" or "negative space" is one we explore in greater detail later, but the long and short of it is that the fewer distractions you have on the page, the easier it is for your viewer to focus on your subject. Are there people who defy this thinking successfully? You bet. But it's a tool that you'd do well to have in your toolbox: the tool of leaving things uncluttered.

Sumi-e (the Japanese art of brush painting) wouldn't work without empty space.

Beyond the Law of Thirds (which is only ever something to be considered, not slavishly obeyed), the conception and layout phase is where the power of the thumbnails shines through.

Let's say that I wanted to draw a picture of a crow on a cold winter's night. What would that picture look like? You probably got a quick mental snapshot just from my description, didn't you? There was probably a sudden, immediate flash behind your eyes of what that picture might look like. That's where you should start. But don't end there. Take a few minutes (and I mean just a few—10, at the most) and give me a half a dozen thumbnails of that picture.

What are we looking at here? If you go back and look at the description, I never mentioned what that crow was doing. He could be sitting, flying, landing … heck, if I was morbid, I could have sketched a dead bird. But looking at the eight thumbnails I came up with, I think I like option 2 the best. After that Sumi-e exercise, I want something that's stark and bold. Here's where that took me.

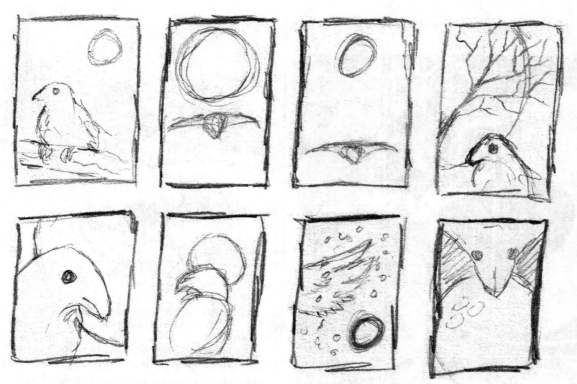

I took the same 10 minutes, and here's what I came up with.

When you're about to sit down to do a drawing, take that extra few minutes and bang out a series of thumbnails. You could find a view or perspective that you didn't think of in your initial conception. Even if you're working from reference, take a moment to frame that picture mentally in your head. Moving your subject off-center can lend it a dramatic effect you just can't get any other way.

Is this what they mean by "As the crow flies ..."?

The Least You Need to Know

◆ Thumbnails are an easy way to test different compositions without spending hours on a finished drawing.

◆ It's vital to maintain that energy when you increase the size of the piece. Keep the energy alive!

◆ Don't be afraid to leave large areas of your drawing stark white. While your first instinct may be to fill every square inch of the page, a lot of empty space can really draw the viewer's eye right where you want it.

◆ At the end of the day, whatever works for you is the law of the land. No matter what any book says. Even this one.

In This Part

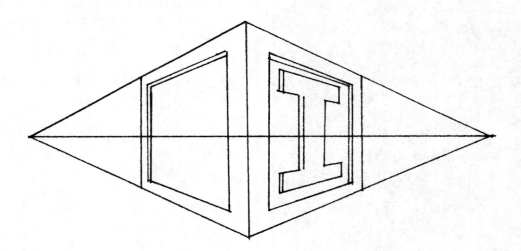

From Simple to Solid

You're not going to believe this now, but this section is the meat and potatoes of the whole book. And not just this book, but drawing as a whole. If you can master these concepts and put them into practice, there won't be anything you can't draw. In the steps ahead, you're going to tackle the all-important step of giving a simple geometric shape some dimension and weight. After this, my friends, all bets are off.

In This Chapter

◆ Circles, squares, and cylinders

◆ How basic shapes make up everyday objects

◆ Combining two or more simple shapes to make more complex items

 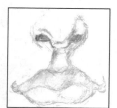    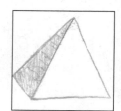

Chapter 5

Geometry Lessons

We've been moving forward at a pretty good clip here, but now's the time to stop, take a deep breath, and learn a few fundamentals. (Don't breathe *that* deep. You'll sound like Darth Vader.) We're going to learn about basic shapes and how they make up the world around us.

Seeing Simple Shapes in Complex Things

Almost everything you see—nearly everything you're ever going to try to draw—can be simplified into one of the following basic shapes.

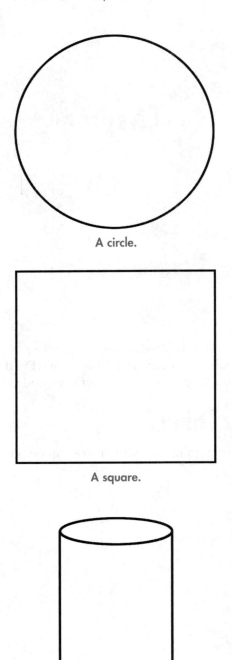

A circle.

A square.

A cylinder.

Right about now you're sitting there looking around the room and thinking to yourself, "When was the last time I dusted in here?" But housekeeping aside, in that room are various and sundry items, most (if not all) of which can be drawn by using one or more of these three basic shapes as a starting point. Squares and rectangles are obviously part of the same family, but would you believe that a circle is also part of the square family? It's true!

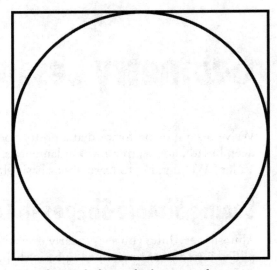

A perfect circle fits perfectly in a perfect square.

Yes, that's right. I'll say it again: a perfect circle fits perfectly in a perfect square. This is one of the most valuable truths you'll learn in art. Why? Because drawing a circle in perspective is devilishly hard. Drawing a square in perspective is almost sinfully easy. Now, you could go out and get yourself a protractor. It's probably not a bad idea. But quite honestly, the number of times you're going to draw a perfect circle is pretty rare—at least, it has been in my experience. Mostly you'll be drawing ovals. Those ovals will first come from a carefully measured rectangle, like so:

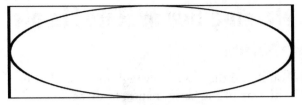

As the box narrows, the circle collapses.

In Chapter 3, I talked about drawing the stuff on your desk: pencils, soda cans, and the like. Let's take a new look at them and see what they're really made of.

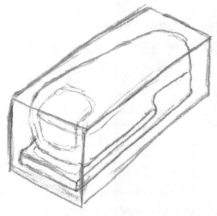

Look! The stapler's a rectangle!

The soda can is just a cylinder in disguise!

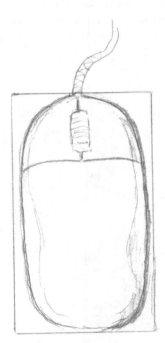

A mouse is just a rectangle with rounded corners.

Take a look around the room. It all becomes clear. Coffee mugs? Short cylinders. Your computer monitor? A square. Almost everything in your environment falls into one of these basic shapes. This is a great tool for when you're trying to draw something but you don't have the item handy for reference. Find the image in your mind, build it up from its basic shapes, and you're on your way!

Staying Sharp

Patience, grasshopper! As easy as this looks, it's going to take you some time before you can turn these simple geometric shapes into living, breathing art. Just stick to your guns and don't get frustrated! Even the masters had these difficulties early on.

Even the human body (which we've got a whole part on later) is made up of simple shapes. They don't all fall into the simple circle/square/cylinder model, but they come really close. Here's a quick sketch done of one of those little wooden art dummies. These things are great because they force you to see the human form in its most basic terms.

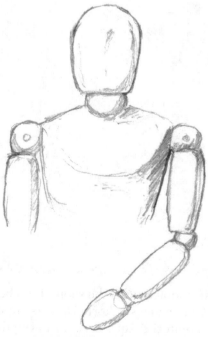

"Maybe someday I'll be a real boy …."

Merging Two or More Simple Shapes

You'll find that you can rough in most objects with one of the basic shapes, but what about the details? "Surely," you say, "the world is not so simple as all that." No. But it's not far off. Within each item, you're bound to have to adapt and modify it with one more of the basic shapes. You'll overlap them, cut them in half, do the hokey pokey, and turn yourself around. That's what it's all about. Come on, follow me through this progression.

Start with a simple box.

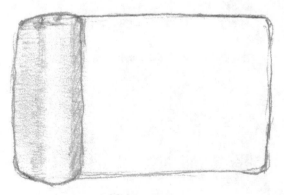

Add the cylinder.

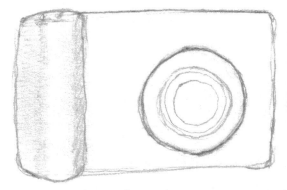

A few circles.

Refine a bit and ...

... voilà! It's a camera!

You did pretty well, didn't you? I can tell. (Well, no, I can't actually *tell*, but I have faith in you.) The whole process becomes much less mystifying once you've got the underlying structure of these things in your head. It's like pulling back the curtain in Oz and seeing how

the whole thing is done. When you start to rough things in from now on, try starting with these basic shapes, these building blocks, and see the difference. It may seem like it's an extra step, and it is, but nobody said this was going to be a walk in the park.

Masters' Musings

"Mistakes are almost always of a sacred nature. Never try to correct them. On the contrary: rationalize them, understand them thoroughly. After that, it will be possible for you to sublimate them."
—Salvador Dali (1904–1989)

Come to think of it, there *will* be a walk in the park, but it's not until Chapter 10. Until then, keep plugging away!

The Least You Need to Know

◆ Almost every object is comprised of three basic shapes: circles, squares, and cylinders.

◆ Most everyday objects can be drawn using one or more of the three basic shapes as a starting point.

◆ Basic shapes can be combined and modified to make more complex objects.

In This Chapter

◆ Why do things look smaller at a distance?

◆ Identifying horizon lines and vanishing points

◆ One-, two-, and three-point perspective

◆ How foreshortening can help you make a flat drawing more realistic and dynamic

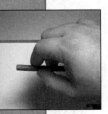

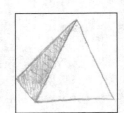

Chapter 6

Understanding Perspective

There's no doubt about it, kids. The stuff we're about to delve into is one of the most daunting subjects in all of art. But try not to panic. I'm here to lend some … perspective … on the matter. (Ouch. These are the jokes, folks. Don't forget to tip your waitresses.)

But seriously, what is perspective? Not the textbook definition, but the real application. Put simply, perspective is what makes your buildings look tall, your mountains look far, the ocean seem deep, a football field seem long. Perspective is the absolute need-to-know information for giving things length, height, depth, and breadth. No small task, eh? But for an artist like you? Piece of cake.

Why Things Look Smaller at a Distance

After learning the basic shapes in Chapter 5, there's really only one thing left to do with them: make them look real. There's no other way to do that than to put them into a three-dimensional world. But how do we go about doing that? It's not just adding a few lines at odd angles. Those lines have to mean something. More important, those lines have to go somewhere. They even meet someplace. (Usually just for drinks and a few laughs, but when the lights go down, who can say?)

Folks in hilly San Francisco think roads like this are a myth.

Look at it this way: when you're driving down a long, straight highway, those cars in the distance look smaller than the closer ones because of … you guessed it … *perspective*. Just don't pay any attention to those mirrors warning you that the "objects may be closer than they appear." The person who designed those mirrors obviously didn't read this chapter.

Layman's Lingo

Perspective is how objects appear to the eye, with depth being perceived by an object's relative size according to its distance.

A Simple Perspective Primer

Perspective has several common elements, regardless of how complex a drawing gets. Usually, you'd be worried about me throwing some complex terms at you, but these are pretty self-explanatory. The terms in question are *horizon line* and *vanishing point*. The horizon line is, well, the horizon. And the vanishing point is the point at which your lines, uh, vanish. (Thank you! I'm here all week!) The combination of these things is very powerful. These two simple concepts, when coupled with a judicious application of a ruler, can take you places you've only dreamed of going before. And no, I don't mean Topeka.

I'll give you just one guess which is the line and which is the point.

This illustration could easily be a knot in a string, but it's not. That's your vanishing point in the middle of your horizon line. But what does that *mean*? Come on, I'll show you.

One-Point Perspective

What we're actually looking at up there is a basic one-point perspective. One-point perspective is when there's just one vanishing point. Easy, right? The viewer's eyes are even with the horizon line, and the vanishing point is dead ahead. This is the same foundation that I used for the car in my illustration of the long road. But let's simplify that some more. Let's start with one of our basic shapes and see if we can use the one-point perspective to give it depth.

At this point, the square has no depth. That's where perspective comes in.

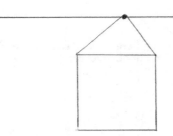

Extend lines from the corners of the cube out to the vanishing point.

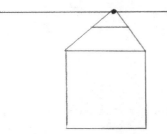

Draw another horizontal line to give it a back wall.

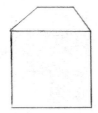

Now use your trusty eraser to get rid of the unwanted lines, and you're done! You've just drawn a box in perspective. By giving it depth, you've also given it the illusion of solidity. That's half of what drawing is all about.

What if we start thinking outside the box? (I can't believe I just went there.) The vanishing point and horizon line remain the same, but instead of having our focus in the center, we put objects on either side. Say, a street with buildings.

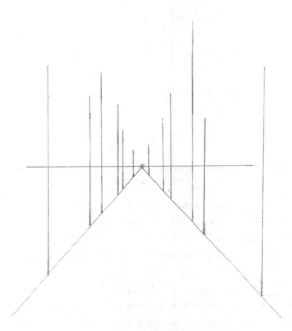

It's just a bunch of lines, isn't it?

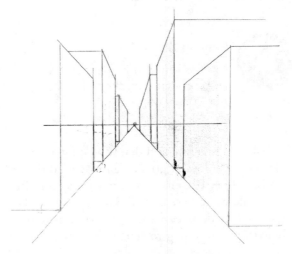

Add those horizontal lines, though, and it starts to take shape.

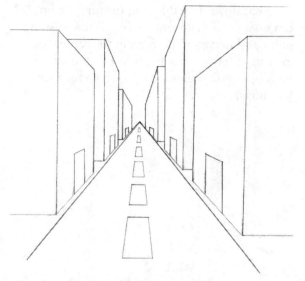

The rest is details! (Which will take you roughly for-ever. Be patient.)

That street scene is one I've been drawing since I was a kid. My brother, who has no artis-tic aptitude whatsoever, came home from school one day and shared the technique with me, which he had presumably traded a Tom Seaver rookie card for. Kids in the 1970s were weird. Nowadays you've got to worry about drugs and cyber predators. Back then kids were trading baseball cards and art tricks. The world never ceases to amaze me.

 Staying Sharp _____
Don't have a ruler handy? Improvise! Grab an extra pencil and use that as your straight edge.

All of this is fine and dandy as long as the viewer's eye doesn't go above or beyond the horizon line. Because that'll never happen. But, uh, while we're here and all, I might as well show you what to do in case the need ever arises. As before, you're going to start with your horizon

line and your vanishing point, but this time we're going to place the two boxes on the stage, one above the horizon line and one below.

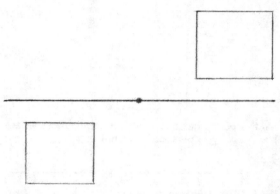

Nothing too daunting here. In fact, color this and you've got abstract art.

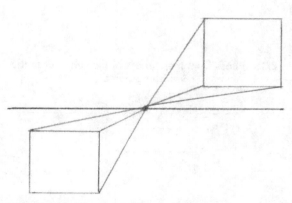

Extend lines from all corners out to the vanishing point.

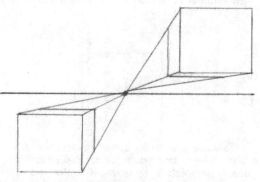

Draw in those secondary lines, horizontal and vertical …

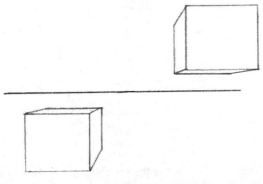

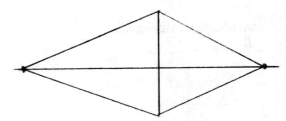

Extend your lines from the top of the "corner" and let them meet the dual vanishing points.

... and then erase what's left! You're left with two three-dimensional boxes, one on the ground, and one floating in the sky. Good job!

Two-Point Perspective

If you've managed to keep up with this so far, the rest will be a breeze for you. Where we go from here is into the daring realm of (gasp!) two-point perspective. I'm sure you're way ahead of me already. You've already figured out that this means we've got two vanishing points instead of one. In fact, you're just looking at the pictures, aren't you? You've stopped reading altogether. Fine. Be that way! I'll be over here, sulking with my Cheerios.

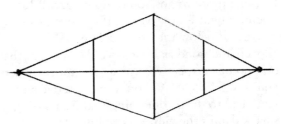

Drop in the vertical lines ...

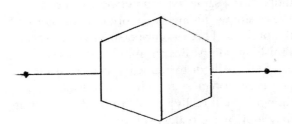

... and erase what you don't want. How easy can it get? This gives you another box, but the angle changes dramatically with that second vanishing point.

You're doing great so far. Just be aware that there will be times when those vanishing points will be pretty far off your paper. Like in Anchorage. Don't be afraid to use another piece of paper behind the one you're actually drawing on to get these angles right.

Start with two vanishing points on a line.

Instead of starting with the box face, we start with the corner of the box. I know, it just looks like a line. Trust me.

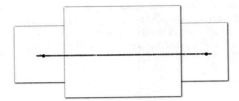

You can just eyeball it, but using a second sheet of paper is always another option.

Three-Point Perspective?

Just one more to go. You're doing great! Remember before how we did those two boxes above and below the horizon line? Well, that's all well and good as long as you've just got that one-point perspective. But what happens when you're working in two-point perspective and you need to draw something that isn't sitting smack dab in the viewer's eye line? You go to three-point perspective, that's what. This is just more of the same for you perspective pros. We're simply adding one more dimension to the process. Three-point perspective has three vanishing points. Bear in mind that this stuff can look really distorted when your vanishing points are too close together. At a distance, though, you'll really be able to render things as they look in the real world.

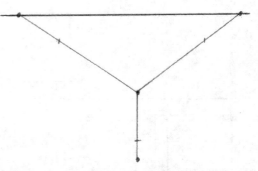

Draw your lines out to the vanishing points. Now is a good time to decide how long the box is going to be.

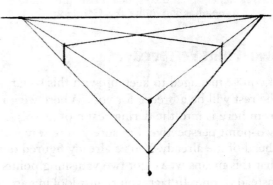

Add the lines for the additional sides and back.

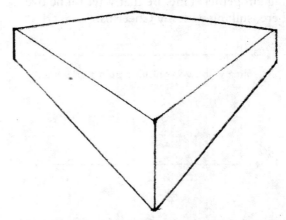

Get rid of those guide lines, and you're golden. Yet another box rendered through the power of perspective!

Start with the usual suspects, your vanishing points and horizon line. This time, we add two more to the equation. One is a new vanishing point. The other is the point for the corner of our box.

Staying Sharp

With perspective and foreshortening, you've got to forget everything you ever learned about angles and spatial geometry. Technically, a square should have corners that are 90°. But when you start dealing in perspective, adhering to that law will only make your drawing flat and unrealistic.

Take a walk down any street in a major metropolis, and you can see this stuff in action. Architects have to know this stuff like they know breathing. But, hey. While we're talking about skyscrapers, let's reverse the angle a bit and put that third vanishing point somewhere skyward. I'm even going to drop that horizon line below the picture's edge to really give it some height. Follow along, kiddies!

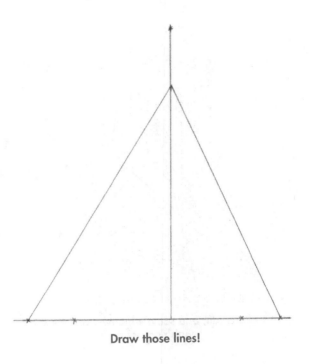

Draw those lines!

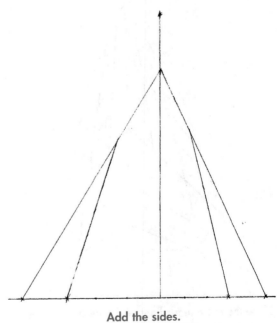

Add the sides.

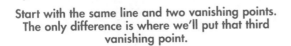

Start with the same line and two vanishing points. The only difference is where we'll put that third vanishing point.

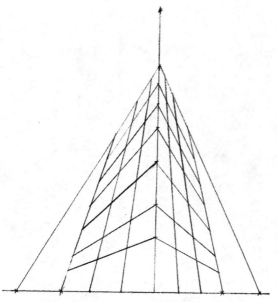

For extra credit, add some windows. Use the same vanishing points.

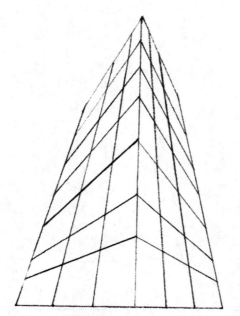

Erase the extraneous lines and take a bow! You've got a shiny skyscraper to call your very own.

No kidding, folks, if you can get your gray matter around this, there's no stopping you. The whole world is yours—all three dimensions of it.

The Power of Foreshortening

As you might recall from Chapter 4, in its most simple terms, foreshortening is when closer things look bigger and farther things looks smaller (just as with perspective). This is also what happens when one part of an object is hidden from view because of its angle. Think of Uncle Sam pointing his finger at you. You don't see the whole finger because it's coming right toward you. Let's use a cylinder to illustrate this a little better.

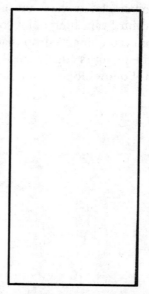

At this angle, it doesn't even look like a cylinder. Think of it like a tree trunk, cut off at the top and bottom.

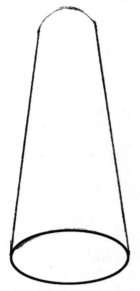

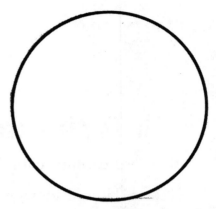

Tilt it just a little, and its shape becomes apparent. Now you see the curve of the trunk's shape!

Tilt it some more, and it almost seems to shrink. This is perspective at work!

Lying flat on its back, it's now a circle. Cool, huh? Looking straight on at the bottom of the "tree trunk" all that length vanishes. All that's left to do is count the rings.

These are killer concepts. Many artists have come up against these things and put down their sketchbooks, never to draw again. It can be a little daunting, sure, but once you've seen the process broken down, it's not quite so terrifying. Also, it's not important that what you're jotting down in your pages looks exactly like what you see here. Your proportion may be off. Your lines may be crooked and broken. None of that matters. What's important is that you develop a mental understanding of these principles. If you can do that, the physical thing will follow later. You can bet on it!

The Least You Need to Know

◆ Close objects appear bigger than further ones. That's not just in art. That's life, friend. Remember this when drawing and your sketches will really come to life.

◆ Perspective is made up of a horizon line and vanishing points. One vanishing point per kind of perspective (one for one-point perspective, two for two-point ... you get the idea).

◆ An angle change can hide part of your subject. This is called foreshortening, and it's one of the most powerful tools in your toolbox. You can't see all of every object all the time.

◆ Once you get the hang of these basic concepts, you'll be able to twist and turn any object you can imagine and make it exist in a three-dimensional space. Just remember that everything boils down to basic shapes, and take it from there!

In This Chapter

- ◆ Learning about light
- ◆ How shadows add depth and establish mood
- ◆ Secondary light sources
- ◆ Getting shady with rendering, cross-hatching, and smudging

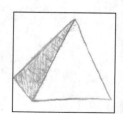

Chapter 7

Working with Light and Shadow

In the end, drawing is a just a bunch of lines on a page. That's it. It's like algebra that way, in that a simple equation such as 2 + 2 = X can become something so much more complicated when there's a lot of it. It's easy to get overwhelmed, to look at another artist's work and think, "I can't do that!" But you can. By using the basic shapes you learned in Chapter 5, you're going to start to make some art. All we need to do is shed a little light on the subject.

Identifying the Light Source

Take a look at the following two drawings. With your keen sense of deduction and newly acquired artist eye, can you tell me the difference between them?

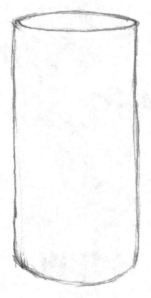

Just another basic cylinder.

The same cylinder, but this one got dressed up 'cause it knew
you were coming.

Side by side, the effect of light and shadow makes all the difference in the world, doesn't it? The first cylinder is flat, lifeless. It's got no substance. But once we add a little shadow, it takes on definition. It's got some weight. We put a little meat on its bones. It didn't take much: just a little shading, some rendering, and a few fine meals at Mama Fradella's.

This isn't magic. Looking at this right now, you're probably saying to yourself, "Hey, that's easy!" And you're right. But this is all drawing ever is. You draw a basic shape, identify the *light source*, render in some shadows—and the next thing you know, they're booking you on *Letterman* to pull hats out of rabbits. (Errr … strike that. Reverse it.) Like I said before, art is like algebra. No matter how complex it seems later, it all boils down to a basic 2 + 2 = X kind of deal.

Layman's Lingo

The **light source** is just what it sounds like: the place where your subject's illumination is coming from. It could be anything that sheds light, from sunlight to candles. There might even be more than one light source, as I discuss a little later in the chapter.

Come on, give it a try. Let's see if you can spot the light source in the following three drawings.

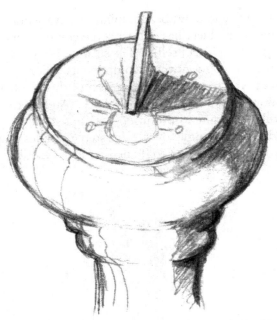

Here we are at 3:00 in the afternoon. We know it's the afternoon because the sun doesn't shine at night. The light source is almost exactly flush left from the sundial itself.

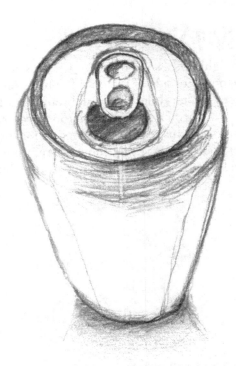

And sometimes the light's directly overhead.

These are some pretty obvious examples. Most of the time, you'll be dealing with more diffused light sources. You'll have to contend with ambient light, which tends to make shadows harder to find. (Ambient light is also called indirect lighting.) As you're starting out, try to find subjects that have a good contrast; you'll find them easier to draw.

So, okay, there's light. And there's an object. It seems like this is a perfect time to talk about …

Masters' Musings

"Some painters transform the sun into a yellow spot; others transform a yellow spot into the sun."

—Pablo Picasso (1881–1973)

If I had a kid sister, this would scare the heck out of her. Here the light source is coming from underneath and slightly in front. If you ever want to find the light source, look opposite the direction of the shadows.

Casting Shadows

When light hits a solid object, it casts a shadow on the opposite side of the object. This is one of those Golden Rules that you'll want to tattoo on your forearm. (Henna works, too, if you're opposed to permanent body alteration for the sake of your art. But hey, I thought you were serious about this.) When looking at something you'd like to draw, bear in mind that every drawing of an object has at least three components: light, the object itself, and its shadow. Now, note that I said *at least* three components. I don't want you to blame me later when I throw a few more straws on your camel's back. (And there will be a camel, I promise.) Let's get started. Here are a couple of step-by-step examples that you can sing along to. Pencils ready? Good!

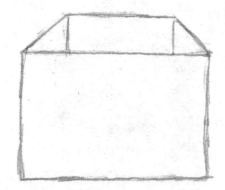

Start with a simple three-dimensional box.

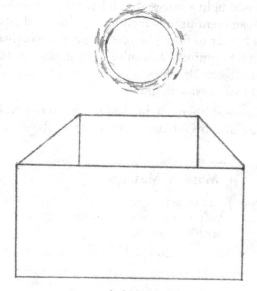

Drop a light behind it.

Add those shadows!

That's not a moon! Well, it could be, if you want.

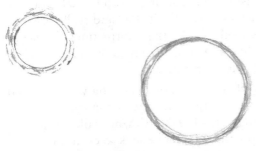

Add a sun. Flashlights and tennis balls make great models for this.

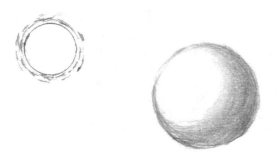

Tricky shadows these spheres have!

If you don't want a moon, add a shadow for your floor. The distance of that shadow from your object will determine its distance from the floor.

Awesome. Good job. As I talk about light and shadow, it bears mentioning that the darkness of your shadow depends entirely on the brightness of your light source. Got a spotlight on a vase? That sucker's gonna cast a long, dark shadow. Drawing an apple outside on a hazy day? Your shadows will be soft and sparse.

But shadows do more than just add depth. They can also establish a mood. Sparse shadows not only convey a sense of brightness, but they can also speak of joy and happiness. A face set in deep shadow can add mystery or bring an aura of depression. Darkness and light: try to think about these terms beyond the values and tones of your pencil.

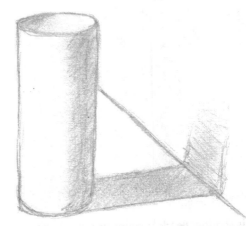

Shadows, like the one here, can create a sense of mood and atmosphere. They can also subconsciously tell you the time the scene takes place. Longer shadows occur closer to sunset.

Staying Sharp

Drawing with the very tip of a sharp pencil will give you a thin, fine line. That's just the kind of thing that might come in handy when fading out a shadow. All you have to do is play with the angle at which you're holding the pencil against the paper. Hold it nearly vertical and the only thing touching the page is the point.

When adding depth to your art, you'll find that shadows change their depth and shape according to what they're cast upon. Throw a shadow onto a white wall, and, depending on the strength of your light source, you might get a nice silhouette of your object. That same shadow cast onto a wrinkled fabric, however, will warp and bend to accommodate its unwitting canvas. As always, it's best to work from reference on this kind of thing.

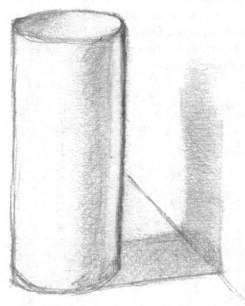

This shadow bends upward as it meets a vertical surface.

Reflections

Another thing you'll notice as you draw more regularly from life is that you're often confronted with more than one light source. These secondary light sources are usually a product of your original light source reflecting off a nearby object. It takes a little while to train your eyes to see these diffused shadows, but once you've found them, adding them to your art can make all the difference.

Staying Sharp

If you're using professional photography as your reference, be aware that most professional photographers set up multiple lights and reflectors to wash away the stronger shadows.

Light bounces off solid objects according to their angle, solidity, and color. There's a lot to consider when sitting down to make a realistic drawing. Just take it slow and really look at your subject. All the information you need is right there. You already know how to see it. The key is patience!

Of course, no one is saying you have to draw in a photorealistic way. Get crazy! Distort things. Bend reality to your will. But if you apply these fundamentals to even the craziest drawing, you just might find yourself with a masterpiece on your hands.

A crazy camel. Just because I like you.

Types of Shading

You have a few options at your disposal when you get past the initial line work. Some of those options, such as smudging, depend on the medium you're working in. You'll have some limited success with smudging your pencil drawings, but that technique really finds its legs with softer materials, such as charcoal and pastels (see Chapter 2). Let's take a look at the three most basic types of shading. Try each one for yourself; you may find that you prefer one over the others. Then again, you might end up with an eclectic mix of all of them. There's no wrong way; whatever gets the image out of your head and onto the paper is the way to go.

Rendering

Rendering is the most common form of shading done with a pencil. It's also the most intuitive. Rendering is, put simply, altering the pressure you put on the pencil to change the density of the graphite. Here's an example: this is just a horizontal bar, but I've decreased the pressure in the middle to make the tone a little lighter.

Change the pressure and you change the appearance.

Oh, and remember what I said before about keeping your pencil sharp? This is one of those times when you can feel free to hit me in the face with a lemon meringue pie. A duller, smoother tip can help you lay in shadows in a way that a fine point won't. And don't be afraid to switch pencils. I have a special fondness for the HB pencils, but I'll pick up a softer lead (a 2B or a 4B) if it's what I need. Know your toolbox and what your tools can do, and you'll have an easier time of it.

Let's do one that's a little more in context, shall we? Boxes and spheres and squiggly lines can take us only so far. Let's have a look at something more organic and see how the rendering style can help it come alive.

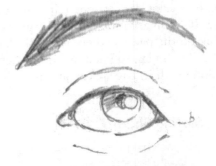

Here's the basic line work.

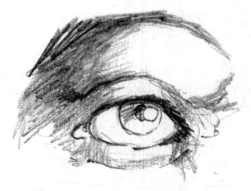

And here we are with a little graphite mascara.

As you can see, in the deep corner to the left of the eye, the area that's closest to the nose, you'll have a deeper shadow. That's where I applied a little more pressure and laid in a little extra lead. At the center of the eye, where the sphere of the eyeball itself would push out the lid (more on this in Chapter 13), I eased off. If there's a direct light source, you can even leave the highest points white.

Cross-Hatching

With cross-hatching, you've got to alter the whole way you see the picture. This approach can lend clarity to your drawing, and it's good practice if you ever want to ink your work later. Why is that? Because ink doesn't have the option of being lighter or darker depending on your pressure. It's a binary mode of drawing: there's either ink on the page or there isn't. Black or white. So if you plan to ink a drawing when you're done with it, pay special attention here.

> **Staying Sharp**
>
> Cross-hatching is one of those times when you'll need to keep that pencil razor sharp. You'll be laying a lot of lines down right next to one another, and you'll want those lines to be clear.

The basic principle of cross-hatching is very simple. You draw a series of lines. Then you draw other lines that cross them. Like so.

The direction doesn't matter right now, but note the spacing.

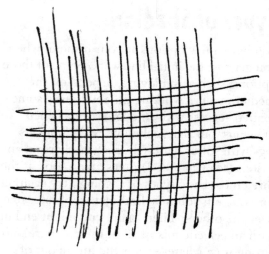

Now draw the lines going against the grain.

See where the lines intersect? That's your shadow area. If you want that shadow to fade, you increase the distance between the lines. If you want to deepen that shadow, don't be afraid to throw in another set of lines going in a third direction.

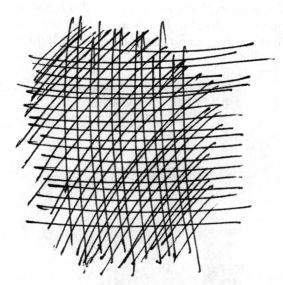

This horizontal addition really darkens the area.

When cross-hatching, it's a good idea to let your lines follow the contour of the object they are shading. Here's an arm in profile. The shoulder muscle is shaped like an inverted teardrop, so we lay in the lines to match the natural flow. Adding the horizontal set of lines gets trickier in cases like this, so use it sparingly.

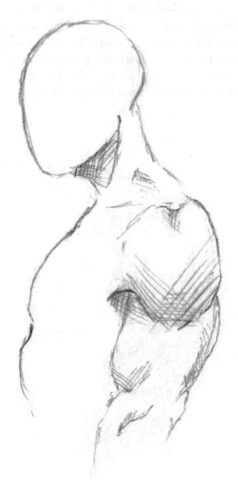

You, too, can have a manly shoulder! Just send $9.95 to ....

Albrecht Dürer did some great work with cross-hatching back in the late 1400s, but if you want to see some mind-boggling, savant-level cross-hatching, pick up the book *Bernie Wrightson's Frankenstein: Or the Modern Prometheus*, by Mary Shelley and Bernie Wrightson (Underwood-Miller, 1995). Wrightson spent years on the project, and any words I could say here would pale beside the savage mastery of that work. Go check it out. Seriously, go. I'll wait.

Staying Sharp

A lot of the old masters used cross-hatching when it suited them, but there are modern masters of the technique appearing monthly. Because comics are inked, comic book artists need to cross-hatch everything.

Smudging (Charcoal)

Nothing could be more opposite to cross-hatching than smudging. Whereas the former requires forethought, patience, and a sharp pencil, smudging is almost like regression finger-painting therapy. You'll need a softer tool to work with here. HB-grade pencils and softer will work, but a few of my artist friends continue to work solely in charcoal and pastels just for the freedom of smudging. Let's try that eye again, but this time I'm going to use the tip of my middle finger to smudge the charcoal a bit. Be sure to start smudging from the darkest areas to the lightest. Keep a paper towel handy when using your hands to smudge charcoal: the stuff gets messy. And watch where you put those hands! It's funny only until somebody loses an eye.

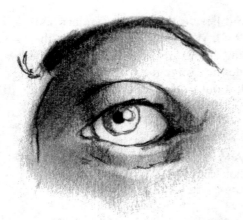

Remember to work from dark to light.

Charcoal and Conté crayon (see Chapter 2) can be a little frustrating to work with at first, but smudging is definitely one of the advantages to sticking with it.

So why should you cross-hatch instead of render? Why smudge instead of cross-hatch? Each of these methods has its own advantages and liabilities. Cross-hatching often gives you a cleaner look when it's done well. Rendering can give you a gradation of tone that the other two can't match. But smudging ... well, smudging is just fun. And working in a smudgeable medium such as charcoal can give you shadows so deep that it'll swallow planets and starships. My advice to you? Experiment. Get your hands dirty. There is absolutely no substitute for getting in there and doing it. So get going!

The Least You Need to Know

- ◆ Shadows fall opposite the light source. This is not only helpful when identifying your light source in a model, but essential when trying to figure out where to place shadows in your drawing.

- ◆ Light reflects off solid objects. This gives you lots of things to watch for, such as highlights and reflections off nearby objects. Pay attention!

- ◆ Shading can be rendered, cross-hatched, or smudged; experiment to find which technique works best.

- ◆ Light is more than just a way to illuminate your subject. It's a way to convey mood. Experiment with sparse light, strong shadows, and light sources. The same subject will look completely different from dawn to dusk.

In This Chapter

- ◆ Seeing the shapes, not the objects
- ◆ Tricking your brain
- ◆ Working with negative space
- ◆ Finding a technique that works for you
- ◆ An exercise that puts it all together

     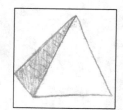

Chapter 8

Training the Artist's Eye

No matter how old you are, you've had a lifetime of training in seeing things the way they are. When you're walking down the street, you don't see each individual slab of concrete or pebble in the road. Your mind takes in all that information and turns it into an amalgam that is given the label "street," and you go on your merry way.

Likewise, when you look at a person's face, unless you're really dissecting it, you're not seeing that person's features as separate elements. Your brain does some work for you and allows you to see that face as a single unit. In this chapter, we're going to try to make your brain go on vacation—well, one side of your brain, anyway.

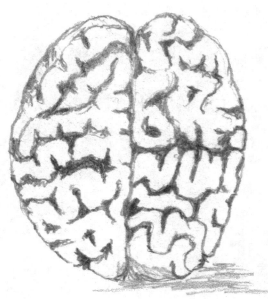

This is your brain.

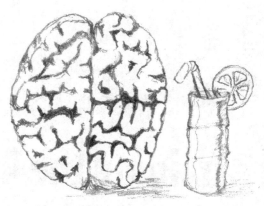

This is your brain on vacation.

Looking Past the Object

Take a look at this picture and tell me what you see.

There are no wrong answers.

Now, it could be that you see two faces looking at each other. It's also entirely possible that you see a pedestal. Which one's right? Without context, there's no way to tell. There are no wrong answers. Whichever you see is absolutely right. This tells us that the brain is often of two minds about things. Rarely is that more true than in art. You're not trying to draw the slabs of concrete and the rocks and the sidewalks; you're trying to draw "the street," something that will, at first look, be immediately recognizable to the viewer. As I've said before, that doesn't mean that we need to strive for photorealism. Not at all. But if you want to represent things in your art that people can identify, a good way to do that is to find a new way to see them.

 Masters' Musings

"Art is not what you see, but what you make others see."

—Edgar Degas (1834–1917)

This could be a lot of things, like a bow.

Add something to it, and it becomes something else.

Add some lipstick and other details, and it's
"Gimme a kiss, baby!"

Staying Sharp

You want a good exercise for that other half of your brain? Find a nice cow-free pasture, lie down in the grass, and spend a few hours looking at the clouds. Even if you're only half trying, you're bound to find shapes in there that flex that big gray muscle in your cranium.

"You must love the little birds to give them this to
perch on ...."

When you look at a person's mouth, chances are that you're not really seeing it the way you think you are—unless you're staring at it, in which case you're probably making some people uncomfortable. Stop that.

What I've drawn here is a "standard" set of lips. These things don't come off the rack, though. If you start looking at them (but please, not in a creepy, stalkerish way), you'll find that mouths (like noses) come in a nearly endless variety.

We live in a world of almost endless variety: trees, plants, flowers, shag carpet, three-legged dogs, and people of every shape and color you can imagine. Don't imagine that you'll just someday "know how to draw people." The truth is often stranger than fiction, and you're going to need to keep those eyes peeled for the diversity around you. Most of all, you're going to need to stop looking at the objects themselves. Stop looking at a nose like it's a nose. That's going to hold you back. You've got to look at it like it's a shape. Just a shape. If you think of it as a nose, you're going to have a prejudged notion of what you think a nose ought to look like.

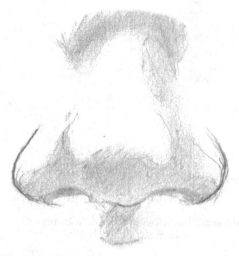

This nose belongs to a guy I work with. I'm gonna bring it back, I promise.

In Chapter 13, I show you the basic construction of a human nose. For right now, I want you to just look at this thing and remember it. We're gonna draw this together later.

Masters' Musings

"The pain passes, but the beauty remains."

—Pierre Auguste Renoir (1841–1919)

Don't Draw What You Think You See

Everyone has problem areas when they learn to draw. Certain things just make you balk, as if some kind of roadblock for it was thrown up in your mind and sent you detouring through old algebra homework. For me, one of those things used to be noses. Geez, those things used to bug me. I tried cheating it. I tried doing that washed-out look so you can see only the nostrils, you know? Finally, I turned a corner. I started to see some real progress. You know

how? Practice. (You saw that coming, right?) But the other thing that turned on the light bulb over my head was the concept that I had to stop trying to draw a nose. I needed to start drawing the shape I was looking at—which might not look like what I think a nose looks like at all. Here, let me show you something.

See this? It doesn't look like anything, right? Well, maybe Albania.

How 'bout this? See anything familiar?

Now let's play a little "Where's Waldo?" Take a look at the following drawing. Can you find those two shapes in the photo? Have a look.

I'll give you a hint: horses win races by it ....

Find them? I'm sure you did. Now the question is, can you draw the two shadow shapes I just drew? If you can, you're going to be a better artist than me in no time at all. How about this ....

This looks familiar, right? Maybe upside down?

But it's really just the shape of the shadow and eyebrow for this eye.

Why do I keep showing you shadows? What's up with that? Well, one of the most powerful tools you'll acquire during your artistic journey is the ability to spot highlights and shadows. Ultimately, maybe you'd like to get to the point that you stop drawing the shape of a thing and start drawing the shadows it makes. Maybe you'd like to be able to see something and not draw the object, but fill in those places where the object is not.

I'm sure you're sitting there scratching your head right now and wondering what the heck I'm talking about. But before you throw up your hands, have a bowl of Cheerios and follow me into the magical land of negative space.

Negative Space

About a million different methods can help you get the image from your head onto the page. As an artist, you'll need to see more than just the curve of the line. You're going to have to see the world in a whole new way. *Negative space* can help you do that. What's more, drawing in the negative space can help you establish mood or bring a brighter object into the foreground. As I explained in the previous section, negative space is the area of the picture that is *not* your subject. When you start to train your eye to see past the thing you're looking at and into the shapes that the subject creates, you take your art to a whole new level.

Layman's Lingo

Negative space is the area between and around the objects you want to draw. That's usually the background, but not always. For example, imagine someone standing with a hand on the hips. The negative space is the triangle made by the inner part of the arm and the side of the body.

Another great use of negative space comes up when you're trying to draw a really complex group of items. Whether that group is a bunch of pencils or a bunch of people, you'll find the composition easier to do if you take the time to explore the negative space created by their placement.

Here are the pencils ...

This portrait might be just fine on its own ...

... but filling in some of the negative space really makes it pop!

... and here's the negative space they create.

This all goes back to what I told you in Chapter 1: don't try to make a drawing based solely on lines. You've got to see the shapes those lines create, even the ones you didn't mean to make. As the great Zen saying goes, "Even an empty cup is full of space."

Masters' Musings

"I don't paint things. I only paint the difference between things."

—Henri Matisse (1869–1954)

The fact is that you've been acquainted with negative space all your life, even if you didn't realize it. Ever seen something in silhouette? That's a prime example of a drawing done in a negative space, even if the subject is the lighter part. The focus here is on drawing the thing that is not your subject. Come on, give it a try.

Don't draw the person. Draw around the person.

(Just so you know, the word *silhouette* was named after a fellow by the name of étienne de Silhouette. He was the finance minister under King Louis XV. Go forth and win at Trivial Pursuit.)

Finding the Method That Works Best for You

There's going to come a time when you find a nice, comfortable way to do things in your art. You'll find a method that works reasonably well, and you'll pretty much devote all your energy to that. But before you get there, you're going to have to do what all good scientists do: experiment. Get in there and try different things. I talked about shading and cross-hatching in Chapter 7. Which did you prefer? Now take that answer and throw it away. I want you to think about what's best for the drawing. Is it smudging? Cross-hatching? Drawing the negative space? Find the method that works best for you, but don't discount the possibility of using several techniques in one drawing.

Smudged, cross-hatched, and a little negative space thrown in for good measure.

Your sketchbook is going to be a remarkable repository for the progress you're making. Look back through the pages: if you've been filling just one page a day, in just a month or two, you're going to see progress. Six months from now, you'll barely believe how far you've come. But don't shackle yourself to any one medium or technique. You'll be surprised how much you can learn about drawing by trying watercolor. Or skydiving. You never know where that inspiration is going to come from. So get out there and live a little. Then put it in your sketchbook.

Driving Home the Point

So now that you know a little more about how an artist sees things, let's do a little drawing together and try to apply what you've learned. You're not being graded on this, so relax.

Some more shapes and shading. Keep going.

A few curved lines and shapes with some shading.
Now you try it.

And a few more shapes to round it out. Now flip it
upside down!

When you're doing stuff like this, the thing that I *don't* want you to do is draw the outline of a shape and then fill it in. Sketch in the area first, but if you leave that outline there, your drawing will look stiff and unnatural.

The Least You Need to Know

◆ Your object is made of individual shapes. Draw them. Notice how they connect and interact. Just do your best to separate them in your brain.

◆ Don't draw what you think you see. Draw what's there! That lump of gray matter in your skull will do its best to mesh everything into one recognizable thing. You'll have to resist that training!

◆ Negative space can help block in a drawing. Look at what's around your subject and use that negative space to help you find the shape.

◆ Remember that there is no one right way. Get that pencil on the paper and find out what works for you!

◆ Practice! Use the exercises in the book, even the ones that seem so easy you think you've already got it down. The only way to get better is to do it!

In This Part

Part 3

Drawing Things That Sit Still

Time to practice what you've learned! We are endlessly surrounded by things that don't move. Fruit, laundry, your Aunt Mildred's false teeth, whatever. The point is that you can use these things to practice some of the principles you have so recently acquired. And then, while we're talking about stuff that doesn't move, I'm going to show you how to make this stuff come alive. Not in a Dr. Frankenstein kind of way, but in a passionate, inject-your-art-with-a-little-soul kind of way. This is good! Come on!

In This Chapter

- ◆ A fruitful exercise
- ◆ Putting it all together
- ◆ Bringing emotion to your work

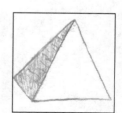

Chapter 9

Angry Bananas: Emotion in Art

Let me paint a picture for you (not literally, silly). You walk into a room and see a fruit basket on the table. You've got your sketchbook with you (because you always carry it these days, right?) and you have an immediate reaction. Now, some of you are thinking, "Kinky!" But the rest of you are thinking, "No. Please, no. Don't make me draw a fruit basket. Please!" Well, I'm afraid your cries have fallen on deaf ears. Because this is no ordinary fruit basket, my friends. Oh, no. In fact, this chapter's lessons aren't about fruit at all—not really. This chapter's lessons are about passion!

Applying What You've Learned

You've done a great job if you've gotten this far in the book. Of course, you may be somebody who's browsing in the bookstore, and you just happened to open to this page. In that case, take this book to the register and buy it immediately. You think this is a library? (For those of you who are actually *in* a library … umm … as you were.)

But I was talking to the folks who have managed to claw their way through the last eight chapters without taking out their own eye with a pencil. Bravo! You probably won't believe me when I tell you this, but right now you have most of the fundamentals that you'll need to be a successful artist. You've probably got a long road of practice ahead of you, but that's often as rewarding as it is frustrating. In the meantime, we're going to take everything you've learned so far and apply it to this fruit basket.*

(*Fruit basket sold separately. Some restrictions apply. See store for details. Part of this complete breakfast.)

This is what I had handy. I ate the rest. An apple a day, you know?

Okay, if you've got your own fruit, now's the time to get it out. You don't actually need the basket. Just put the fruit on a table and let's get to it. If you've got a bowl, that works, too.

Staying Sharp

Back when pirates were more prevalent on the high seas, the sailors kept crates of oranges, lemons, and limes on board because the citrus warded off scurvy. English sailors used to eat so many limes that they were called "Limeys." Yes, that's really where that comes from.

Finding the Simple Shapes

Okay. You've got your models. You've got your pencil, your eraser, and your sketchbook. There's nothing left to do but get to work. Let's start by roughing in the simple shapes. Circles, ovals, cylinders, squares—you know the drill. Right now, we're just looking for placement. Don't get fancy. Don't refine anything. Don't *draw*. Right now we just want to get the proportions right. Take a look at the shapes you're creating in the negative space as well (see Chapter 8). That will help you get the rough outline right.

It's a little off here and there, but that's okay. We're not looking for perfection.

Got it where you want it? Good. Now put down the sketchbook and go check your e-mail or something. I don't want to see you back here for at least 15 minutes. When you get back …. Oh. Back already? You totally cheated. Don't think I didn't notice.

> **Masters' Musings**
>
> "Where the spirit does not work with the hand, there is no art."
>
> —Leonardo da Vinci (1452–1519)

Anyway, when you've had a chance to get away from the drawing for a few minutes, you'll have an easier time seeing where you went wrong. This is the time to go back in there and fix those little trouble areas. Get it where you want it, and then erase those rougher lines that you don't want to appear on the final drawing.

Cleaned up a bit.

Don't go too far yet. Don't shade or render. This is where all the hard work is, right here. If you can get this part, the proportion and perspective, to a point that you're happy with it, then the rest of the drawing will go much easier for you. Let's find out.

Identify the Light Source

Now it's time to identify the light source. Your first reaction is probably the right one, but don't discount those ambient light sources. If you've got a strong light coming from the kitchen, don't overlook the sunlight (or moonlight or streetlights) coming in from the window. In my photo of the fruit basket, I've got light sources coming in from both places. I don't need to do anything about this yet, but it's imperative that I recognize where this is coming from because I'll need to use it later.

You know what goes hand in hand with identifying your light source? Spotting your shadows. They're not hard to see here, but take a moment and stop seeing the fruit. I want you to unfocus your eyes and look for just two things: the brightest spot in the picture, and the darkest spot. Yours will be different from mine, but rest assured that those spots exist. Of course, you may have multiple spots of equal lightness or darkness. And that's good, because we're going to lay in those dark spots now.

Adding the darkest shadows—and things that are just plain black to begin with.

Your drawing should look something like what I've got here. Already you can see this taking shape. The image is right there, just waiting for us to take it into the land of the living.

Staying Sharp

Because you're probably drawing on a white piece of paper right now, you don't really have a way to show off those highlights without leaving the highlights blank. However, for a few dollars more, you can get a hold of some tinted paper and then use a white Conté crayon or colored pencil to add those bright spots. Give it a try.

Refining and Rendering

Okay, I've taken you as far as I can. It's time to hunker down and finish this puppy—er, fruit basket. Drawing puppies doesn't come until Chapter 19. So let's do it. Here are some things to keep in mind as you go forward, though:

◆ You can use different pencils to convey darker or lighter areas. You're not locked into using one pencil.

◆ Pick one method of shading for the fruit and stick to it.

◆ Don't press down too hard, or you'll have a tough time erasing those mistakes.

◆ There's no order to this. Feel free to jump around to whichever area grabs your interest. You can always go back and retouch an area.

The final work.

Bringing Attitude and Emotion to the Work

Now what did I tell you at the beginning of this chapter? That this wasn't about fruit, right? So let's talk about passion.

Masters' Musings

"Great art picks up where nature ends."
—Marc Chagall (1887–1985)

No matter how technically proficient you get, a fruit basket, at its best, is going to look like a basket full of fruit. And, hey, I like fruit. I really do. But nothing about oranges gets me really excited. (I'm going to hear from the Florida Orange Growers Association on this, I can feel it already.) If you do it really well, and I was really hungry, you might be able to make me want a piece of fruit with a good drawing. But then I'm going to leave and go get food. Which takes me away from your drawing. Really, there's no upside. So how do you win here? The answer is *you.* You've got to put some of yourself into the drawing. I don't mean drawing something that isn't there (no adding little cherubs until much later in your career), but you can add some emotional component to your drawing that it didn't have before. Come on, pick up one of the pieces of fruit in your basket. Any one will do. Now draw that piece of fruit while giving it some feelings. I want an apple in love! I want depressed oranges! I want angry bananas!

Note the finer lines and the stylized touches on this apple.

Light source plays a big part in conveying the mood of this orange.

You do *not* want to make this banana angry. Everything about this banana says "go away": the jagged, thick lines, the rough appearance. It's a far cry from the apple.

Half an hour ago, you probably thought that drawing fruit was one of the least challenging things you'd do in art. But now? Uh uh. Now it's a challenge—and not just for fruit. As an artist, you have the opportunity to bring a piece of yourself to everything you do. If you take a look at the work of someone like Alphonse Mucha, you'll see that much of his personality and personal aesthetics went into design elements in the background. Vincent van Gogh went through a whole "blue period." There's no shortage in history of artists who brought their emotion to their art, and did so with great effect. So maybe your thing will be vicious vegetables. Maybe you'll even illustrate a great children's book called *War and Peas*. Who's to say?

"We have a report that the carrots have staged a coup on the rabbits, sir."

The Least You Need to Know

◆ Get the rough shapes right before you move on.

◆ Find the deepest black and whitest white in your drawing before you render.

◆ Emotion in your art can make even inanimate objects come alive!

In This Chapter

- ◆ Taking your art outside the studio
- ◆ Using a viewfinder
- ◆ Using your pencil as a measuring tool

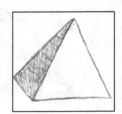

Chapter 10

Field Trip!

It's easy to forget what sunlight looks like when you go on those marathon drawing sessions. You might curl up on the couch with a good sketchbook, or maybe you've got a little studio set up with a drafting table and all the trimmings. Either way, chances are, you'll probably spend the majority of your time drawing indoors. It happens. But it doesn't have to stay that way. Drawing is not painting or sculpture. This is something you can do beyond the confines of your home. So get your sketchbook, a few of your favorite pencils, an eraser, and maybe a bottle of water, and let's hit the road.

Taking Your Sketchbook to a Park or Garden

Your geography will undoubtedly be different from mine, unless we're neighbors. But no matter where you live in the world, chances are, you've got some willing subjects for your art not too far from where you're sitting now. It doesn't matter what your local area affords you. Anything is good: beaches, mountains, parks, gardens … no matter where you go, nature will offer up some unexpected treasure for you to draw.

One of the major differences between drawing at home and drawing in the field is lighting. You're forced to rely on natural light for your subject, and that light changes the longer you stay outside.

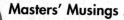

![Masters' Musings icon] **Masters' Musings**

"The dignity of the artist lies in his duty of keeping awake the sense of wonder in the world. In this long vigil, he often has to vary his methods of stimulation; but in this long vigil he is also himself striving against a continual tendency to sleep."

—Marc Chagall (1887–1985)

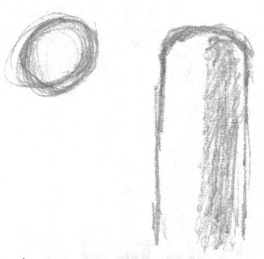

A rock at 3 P.M.: sometimes that hour won't make a huge difference.

A rock at 4 P.M.: and sometimes it will!

Yet another reason why this exercise is so important is that Mother Nature waits for no man. Nor woman. Nor pygmy goat herders.

Nobody. So you've got to find your subject and get right to it. Oh, a couple of other things you'll want to consider when you go exploring:

◆ Seat yourself in a place that won't kill your back. Good back support is vital!

◆ Make sure you're not sitting on an ant hill.

◆ A cushion for your tooshie isn't a bad idea, either.

◆ You're out in nature. Don't be surprised if you find yourself joined by something that crawls, wiggles, or slithers.

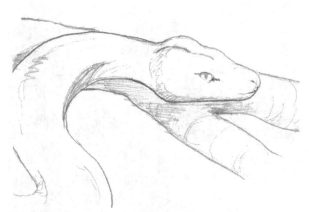

Most of these things look like something else, so be careful!

◆ If you live in South Florida (like me), steer clear of any body of water that's not the ocean. You just might find an alligator in there.

◆ Don't forget that all-important sunblock and insect repellent. Some of those critters get positively prehistoric in size down here.

◆ Watch out for poison ivy. If you're going to be out in the woods, steer clear of any plant that comes with leaves in clusters of three. The stuff in poison ivy that makes you itch is called urushiol oil. And it's strong, too: put that gunk on the head of a pin, and you've got enough to make 500 people itch.

So there you are, in the Congo, wondering what you should draw. There's an awful lot to choose from, isn't there? So how can you get the best picture into your sketchbook before you lose the light? Here's one way …

Using a Viewfinder to Choose Your Subject

Take a piece of cardboard, any kind will do, and cut a rectangle in the middle about an inch tall. This is obviously not a professional-grade viewfinder, but it'll do the job you need to get done. Plus, it's a great way to recycle. Before you throw away your next empty box of macaroni and cheese, cut out that back panel and make yourself a viewfinder. (There's one pictured at the end of Chapter 2.)

Staying Sharp

Oddly enough, it seems that the term *viewfinder* comes from the camera, not some earlier artistic predecessor. Speaking of this, if you can get your hands on an empty 35mm slide holder, they make excellent viewfinders for your art.

Hold the viewfinder a little bit away from you and look through the hole you made. You can adjust the distance from yourself to change the focus. Obviously, the size of your hole makes a big difference in the scope of your drawing. But all we're trying to do here is get rid of the distractions. Using the viewfinder lets us do what the brain sometimes can't on its own. By looking through this little window, we get to see our picture, already framed. So take a few minutes. Look around. When you see something you might like to draw, use your viewfinder to create the most dynamic composition (remember the Law of Thirds from Chapter 4!). Got what you want? Good. Now let's start drawing.

Use the viewfinder to help you compose the picture.

A subtle shift can make a big change in your composition. I'll leave it to you to decide which you like better!

Drawing in Nature

I've got a favorite outdoor spot not far from where I live. It's the Morikami Japanese Museum and Gardens. I grew up in New York, where I thought that the word *gardens* was limited to plants and flowers. And then somebody came up to me and said, "Hey, pal. Your ignorance is showing." That's when I discovered the quiet elegance of a Japanese rock garden. Yeah, that's right. Rock + garden = really cool. So when I feel like drawing outdoors, that usually where I

go. They've also got some little trees there called bonsai that are megacool. (You can see one in Chapter 11, if you'd like. As a matter of fact, there's a whole tour of nature waiting for you later on in the book. But first things first.)

For my outdoors experiment, I settled on one of the larger rock gardens and took a seat against the wall on one of the wooden benches they supplied. Added bonus to the benches? Fewer creepy-crawlers.

Here's what I was looking at. Cool, huh?

I settled on a composition I liked (not hard, with the beauty at hand) and got started. Notice how my subject matter is off-center. There's that Law of Thirds hard at work!

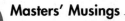

Masters' Musings

"I learned that landscape by drawing it, and I came to care for it with a lover's devotion."

—Philip Pullman (1946–)

Spotting the Lights and Darks

This time around, instead of starting with my basic shapes, I decided to do things a little backward. I spent a while looking for the darkest and lightest areas in the picture. Why? Because if I had those locked down, the position of the sun wouldn't matter much later. Then I could sit there as long as I needed to in order to get the details right. It's almost like trying to draw the negative space first, in a way. Once you've found your subject, try sketching in the darkest areas to use as guideposts later. Mark off the highlights with light pencil so you'll remember where they are. Option B? Do a quick thumbnail sketch to use for reference. Either way works.

Working at about one third the size of my drawing, this thumbnail sketch was almost as good as a snapshot for reference purposes.

Armed with quick guides to use for shading later, I started back at square one laying in the rough shapes.

Roughing in Your Picture

Boy, I really have my work cut out for me, don't I? That little stone statue has got a few different shapes going on there, huh? But that's okay. It's good that you can see it. You can see it, right? The cylinders, the ovals, the square at the base— it's all there. Trying to get this right by just drawing it would leave me with a mess. Don't forget the fundamentals. I don't care how many times you've built a house. You always put down the foundation first. The harder part is the organic stuff, such as the bushes in the background. Roughing those in with geometric shapes will get you only so far before you've got to just cut loose and go it alone. Luckily, there's nothing vital or specific about where those bushes lay, so when I do my roughs, I all but make them up as I go. This is the time when *persistence of vision* will work for you. In static drawing, the brain's subversive ability can work for you, too. Many times your subject will include a million separate components (such as grass). Try to remember that "less is more" and give the viewer just enough for the brain to do the rest.

Layman's Lingo

In animation, the term **persistence of vision** refers to your brain's ability to fill in frames in between those you've drawn so that you don't have to render everything.

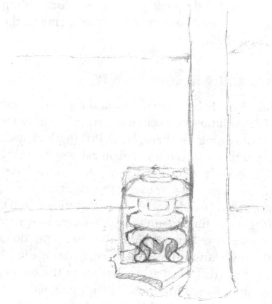

Remember, we're just trying to get the composition right.

I mentally overlay the shadows from my thumbnail and add them here.

It doesn't take me long to rough in these shapes. My subject is very forgiving, and I'm working almost entirely with geometric shapes. Your mileage may vary, of course. The key here is to get the basic shapes onto the paper. And don't forget that almost everything you're looking at is comprised of overlapping shapes. Trees are often just cylinders, with smaller cylinders branching out from them. Sure, they bend and twist a bit, but block them in first and you'll have an easier time later.

Once I got the proportions on the roughs to a place where I was comfortable, I took a look at my shadows thumbnail and started applying the dark areas that I'd noted before.

Masters' Musings

"From this drawing, the treasure secretly gathered in your heart will become evident through your creative work."
—Albrecht Dürer (1471–1528)

As I sat there, the sun passed overhead, changing the highlights and shadows as it went. My little thumbnail really helped me to cheat time. Adding the details on a drawing like this can take hours, depending on how in-depth you'd like to go. Just remember that the human brain will fill in a lot of details for you. You don't need to draw every leaf or blade of grass. You just need to give the mind enough information to work with so that it recognizes your drawing for what you intended.

All but done!

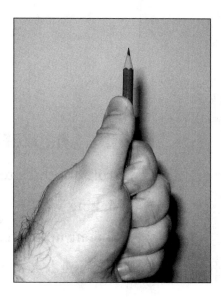

Hold the pencil like this.

Using Your Pencil to Gauge Depth and Distance

Did you ever notice how movies and sitcoms portrays painters? They always do this weird squint and hold their thumbs up. I never understood what that was all about. They didn't look overly happy when they did it, so it didn't seem to be a congratulatory sign. It baffled me. It wasn't until years later when I was having trouble getting the proportion right on a drawing that the light bulb came on over my head. What those painters were doing, and what I'm about to show you how to do, was using a handy tool to gauge the relative size of things so that you can get them onto your page more accurately. But this isn't just for judging the size of objects. This is also a great tool for determining the distance between objects. Instead of using your thumb, though, we're going to use our pencils. Here's how to do it:

Hold the pencil upright in your hand and line up the tip of the pencil with the object you want to measure. Next, use your thumb to mark the bottom of that object. Slide your thumb up and down on the pencil for objects of differing size. Then, when you go back to your sketchbook, you've got a relative guide to use for your drawing. Honestly, it's such a useful technique that I'm sorry I didn't add it to my arsenal earlier. But here I am, giving it you. I'm not doing that Shaolin kung fu master bit where I teach you everything but my deadliest technique. No, sir, you get the whole package. Except for … oh, wait.

Just kidding.

The Least You Need to Know

◆ Because your light source is always changing outdoors, it's a good idea to draw thumbnails of your highlights and shadows.

◆ Framing a picture using a viewfinder allows you to decide on the best composition.

◆ You can use a pencil to judge proportion and distance.

In This Chapter

- From foothills to mountain peaks
- Making waves
- The air up there: clouds
- Drawing leaves and trees

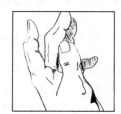

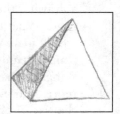

A Primer Course on Nature's Basics

In case you haven't noticed by now, the planet is a pretty big place. We've got about four gajillion types of trees, for starters. You say you want to draw water? What kind? Waterfalls? The ocean? The shoreline? Ponds? Streams? Rivers? Whirlpools? The variety is endless. But every journey has to start somewhere. There are paths up to those mountains and ships to take us out to sea. Nature is calling, so let's get started.

As Confucius said, "The journey of a thousand miles begins with a single step."

Foothills and Mountain Peaks

Like water, earth comes in a plethora of shapes and sizes. You've got hills, valleys, peaks, trenches, caves, and, oh, let's not forget the mountains that will do their level best to kill you if you try to climb them. Luckily, we're not going to do any climbing today. We're just going to draw them instead. First, let's understand some ground rules (hey, nice pun!). Take a look at the following two drawings.

In this drawing, these two images are actually about the same height. So how do you know which one is the hill and which one is the mountain? You know the answer, of course, but knowing it and being asked to articulate it are two different things. Hills are lower to the ground and they've got rounded tops. Mountains don't. Why is that? Because of a little thing called erosion, my friend. There's every possibility that a few million years ago, that low-lying hill was a high-flying mountain. But you pour enough water on anything, and it'll shrink.

Staying Sharp

There is no such thing as something being water*proof* (water *resistant*, yes). Water is the ultimate universal solvent. Given enough time, water will wear down anything. It's something you'll want to keep in mind when drawing old hills and valleys.

Let's start with some easy, gentle shapes: just a couple of foothills to get us started, nothing too complicated. Follow me.

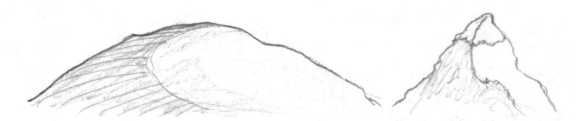

The bunny slope and the Widowmaker.

Overlapping the hills helps give this a sense of distance.

Draw a *C* shape on each hill.

Then shade the back side of each *C* to give the hills depth.

Easy, right? Good! That trick with the *C* will serve you well in other places, too. It won't be as gentle a curve on a mountain peak, but it's still a good guideline for laying in that shadow. Of course, if the sun is coming from the other direction, you'll need to reverse that. For now, though, let's keep the sun coming from the same direction and draw a small mountain range. For extra credit, and if you really want to express the jagged peaks that these monster mountains are capable of, try drawing the next set of lessons with your off hand. (That's your left hand if you're right-handed, and your right hand if you're left-handed.)

Drop these in right behind your foothills. No sense wasting paper.

Draw that *C* shape on each peak.

Shade the back side of the *C*, and you're in business. If you decide to shade the front side a bit, be sure to leave the peaks white to indicate snow. I've also shaded the mountains a little lighter to denote the distance.

You can go into the slopes and add details such as deep crevices or outcroppings, if you want. At this distance, I'd steer clear of adding trees; though, they'll only look fake.

Masters' Musings

"It had long since come to my attention that people of accomplishment rarely sat back and let things happen to them. They went out and happened to things."

–Leonardo da Vinci (1452–1519)

Seascapes

It covers more than three quarters of the planet and if you get some stuck in your ear, you're miserable for a week. Water. Our bodies are about 78 percent of the stuff—some people say as much as 90 percent. But let's not quibble, huh? It's a lot.

But that's not the water that we want to draw. We want the awesome rushing waves and the cool waterfalls. If you've ever taken a few minutes to look at water with the hope of drawing it, you've probably had the same thought that I had. "This would be great to draw … if only it would stop moving!" No doubt about it, right about now you're wishing for the fruit basket again. Ah, happy days. But I can show you a few things that will demystify the ways of the watery world for you. (Say that five times fast!) If you're used to working in harder pencils, now might be a good time to try out a nice 6B, or maybe some Conté crayon. Our first exercise is a bit of a science lesson in the anatomy of a wave. Follow along.

First there's a swell of the wave ....

Next there's a crest ....

Then the bough ... uh, wave ... breaks ....

At this point, your wave is usually met by a returning wave, which is what makes it churn.

This is Wave Basics 101. Seeing it simplified like this might make it easier for you to draw it yourself. Also notice how I used the negative space to show the whitecaps. You can't draw whitecaps on a white piece of paper, so you've got to do the reverse and draw around them.

Staying Sharp

Unless you're drawing on a toned paper and have a white Conté crayon or colored pencil, you'll have to adjust your thinking to realize that "white" is really just the absence of color. When you're scouting your subject for the highlights and shadows, remember to leave the brightest spots blank and you'll do fine.

Now that you've got the basics down, let's give them a try. Pencils ready? Begin!

On the wave face, keep those lines going in the direction of the water flow.

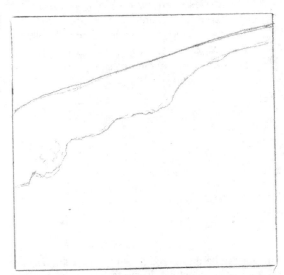

That top edge is going to slant a bit. It's never flat.

Deepen the shadows under the crest and drop in your background. Surf's up!

Send in the Clouds

I'm not a meteorologist, nor do I play one on TV, so let me be the first to tell you that on a clear day, I don't know the difference between stratocumulus clouds and cumulonimbus clouds. More important, although feeding your brain is always a good thing, this is not stuff you need to know. More than anything, when you're drawing clouds in your sky, I want you to remember your angry banana from Chapter 9. Bring some emotion to it. Let the clouds help set the mood for your piece. For now, I'm going to take a page out of the Bob Ross playbook and draw some happy little clouds. Join me, won't you?

While we're at it, let's do a little of Column A and a little of Column B. How about a shot of mountains *and* clouds? What's interesting about this picture is that, although we usually think of clouds as these wispy, insubstantial things just floating out there like … like … like other wispy things that float, the fact is that they have enough substance to block sunlight. They do cast shadows! Let's give it a go.

Staying Sharp

Sooner or later, you may want to put together a field kit, a collection of art supplies intended for going outdoors and drawing or painting in nature. You might get a bag or case that's specifically designed for the purpose, with plenty of places to store pencils, erasers, sketchbooks, the works!

Start by roughing in your shape. Big and puffy = happy clouds.

On clouds like these, you'll want to add the accents in the "corners."

Shade the bottom a little to give the clouds some solidity, and darken the sky behind it just enough to make the white pop.

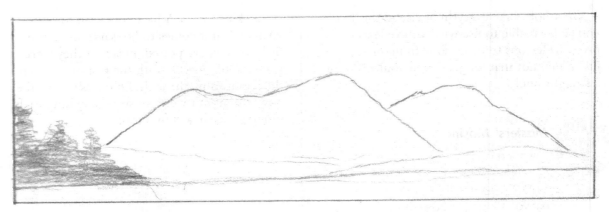

Rough in your foreground and your mountains.

Note that some clouds fall behind the mountain.

Add those shadows.

Great job. Like everything else in this book, you've been able to use what you've learned in previous lessons to make something new. And just think, not that long ago you couldn't draw a straight line!

> ## Masters' Musings
>
> "Do not quench your inspiration and your imagination; do not become the slave of your model."
>
> –Vincent van Gogh (1853–1890)

Trees, from Acorn to Oak

No matter where you live, you've probably got some trees that are unique to your region or climate. In Florida, we've got palm trees. They're very nice. It's always a little scary to watch them fly by your window during hurricane season, but even then they have a kind of charm.

I happened to be lucky enough to find a few trees around here that had managed to survive the last round of named storms. I bring them to you now so that we can immortalize them together. I feel a bonding experience coming on. Come on, group hug.

Scary! And yet, charming.

Luckily, we don't have to search for survivors when it comes to bonsai trees. These little suckers are potted, meaning they were inside watching TV with the rest of us when the winds came through. Of course, once the power went out we were stuck watching each other, but that was fun, too.

Like always, I start with a rough outline of my subject.

Don't try to draw each individual leaf on every branch. That way lies madness!

Try not to overdo the branches. Just think like a tree
and let it happen.

Notice that I drew the branches after I did
the leaves. In some cases, you'll want to reverse
that, but it depends on your instincts and the
tree involved. Then again, there are trees that
have the equivalent of male pattern baldness,
so they have no leaves to draw. We do not
mock these trees. We simply love them the
way they are.

See how these shapes seem to intersect? It's almost
like fabric, isn't it?

Lay in some shadow, add a few details. It's much
easier without the leaves!

The Least You Need to Know

◆ When drawing hills and mountains,
remember to treat them like any other
solid object and cast shadows according
to the light source.

◆ For waves and water, keep it at the front
of your mind that your subject is fluid.
Let your pencil strokes be fluid, too!

◆ Clouds are wispy things! They also make
great use of negative space. You'll have
more success there leaving things out as
you will putting them in.

◆ Use the viewer's persistence of vision
when drawing leaves and trees. Let their
brains do your work for you!

In This Chapter

- ◆ Getting to know the different types of folds
- ◆ Seeing the figure beyond the fabric
- ◆ Fun with laundry

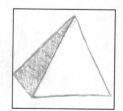

Chapter 12

Drapery and Folds: It's Not Just Laundry Anymore

It would be easiest, I suppose, if we drew fabric only from photographs or live models. That would be a foolproof way of making sure that we're getting it right. Because, let's face it, it all looks pretty random, doesn't it? Why does clothing move this way around the arms and that way around the knees? Why does it dip, dangle, zig, zag, fold, lock, or just lay there? Believe it or not, there are reasons. They're not even hard reasons. Most of all, there's a predictable pattern in which fabric will interact with things.

If you can get the hang of these rules (that was an unintentional pun, I swear!), you'll be able to draw convincing fabric without reference. C'mon, let me show you.

Learning the Different Types of Common Folds

If the old masters are to be believed, there are seven different kinds of folds: the diaper fold, the zig-zag, the half-lock, the pipe fold, the spiral, the drop, and the inert fold. And why shouldn't we believe them? They are the masters, after all!

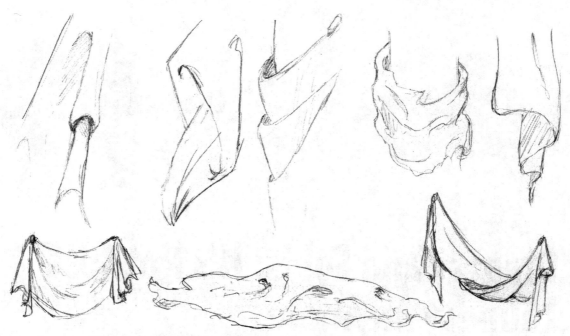

The seven folds. Clockwise from top left: pipe, zig-zag, spiral, drop, half-lock, inert, and diaper.

Masters' Musings

"To finish a work? To finish a picture? What nonsense! To finish it means to be through with it, to kill it, to rid it of its soul, to give it its final blow, the coup de grace for the painter as well as for the picture."

—Pablo Picasso (1881–1973)

Looks pretty simple, right? Right? Come on! This is a piece of cake! Quit shaking your head like that! Look, I'm not going to make you draw them all at once. That thing is there just for future reference. We're gonna take this one step at a time. You and me. You're gonna have fun, too. You'll see.

Let's start off with baby steps. The diaper fold. (Ha! Diaper … baby … ahem. Work with me here, folks.)

Just two pegs in a wall.

Okay, we've got two pegs sticking out of a wall. Nothing scary about that, right? Good. Now let's drape some fabric over them.

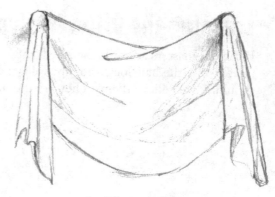

And then we drape.

See that? It really is that easy. You've just learned the diaper fold. (And yes, if you look at the outside folds, those are actually drop folds. Good eye!)

The hidden drop fold, for you observant few.

Besides learning the way that a diaper folds (who actually folds their own diapers anymore?), the important lesson that these illustrations teach us is that folds are the product of what lies beneath them, behind them, and beyond them. The diaper fold occurs because it's being pulled on equally from three directions. Three? Yeah, three. Can't forget about gravity.

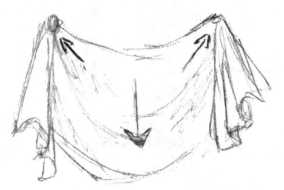

Gravity pulls the fabric down, but the opposing pegs also provide resistance.

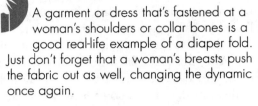

Staying Sharp

A garment or dress that's fastened at a woman's shoulders or collar bones is a good real-life example of a diaper fold. Just don't forget that a woman's breasts push the fabric out as well, changing the dynamic once again.

That drop fold? What's that thing doing over there? Where's the pull? Where's the resistance? Let's have a look.

Just a dishrag hangin' on a peg.

This is the simplest, most basic fold there is. Here you've got one point of resistance: the fabric hangs from it. If you look at the lines, it's a little like that peg is a "vanishing point," isn't it? All the lines seem to radiate from that single area. Well, that's not far from the truth. Fabric has weight. It has a solidity to it. So although it will drop from a single point, it will also fan out a bit at the bottom.

Zig-Zag Folds

Unlike the gentle, sweeping motion of the diaper or pipe folds, the zig-zag fold is a bit jerkier, with sharper angles. Let's have a look.

The zig-zag fold.

How do folds like this come about? Well, any number of ways, but let me give you a mental picture to carry with you. Imagine that you rolled some fabric into a tube shape. Now bend that fabric. You can already see it in your head, can't you? The sharp twist, the resultant gap at the other side. These things don't happen by accident. Next time you see somebody sitting down in a crisp, fresh pair of pants, watch the way it folds.

Masters' Musings
"I'll never have enough time to paint all the pictures I'd like to."
—Norman Rockwell (1894–1978)

Another example of the zig-zag fold.

Spiral Folds

Hey, while we're talking about pants here, let's talk about how fabric reacts in tubular form when there's an object inside it that bends and moves—you know, like human limbs.

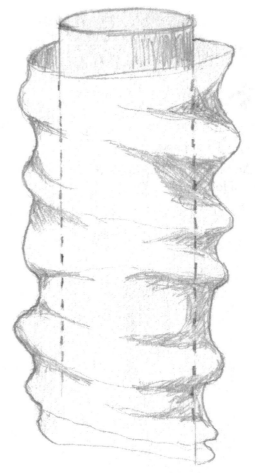

And it bunches just like this.

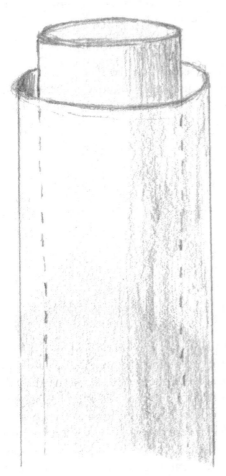

Imagine a piece of wood inside a fabric tube.

Here's a simple piece of wood put through a sleeve of fabric. What happens when you roll up your sleeves? What kinds of folds are created? Why, spiral folds, of course. If you imagine this piece of wood as your arm, and the fabric as your sleeve, you'll see just how common this fold is!

This isn't all too different from the way it twists when you bend your arm at the elbow. Now, depending on the tightness of the fabric and the extent of the bend, you may find that the back of the arm, near the triceps down to the elbow, doesn't show the opposite side of that fold. It's pulled so taut that it's actually smooth.

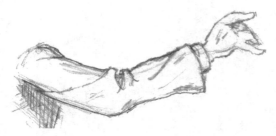

It's all about where the resistance is.

And hey, the same holds true of pants. Let's have a look.

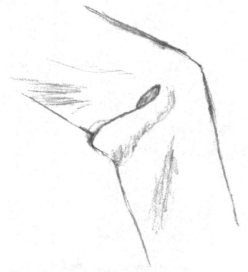

Note that the fold at the corner of the knee is not a spiral fold, but a half-lock.

Other Common Folds

It's going to take more than a few pages of practice in a book like this to get you good at drapery and folds. But if I can get you to start looking at those folds in terms of how they're created, you'll be 10 steps ahead of the game. You just have to remember that folds are created by resistance and the lack of resistance. Some of them are pulled taut. Others, like the drop fold and the inert folds, are literally created by the lack of support.

Staying Sharp

Here's an exercise you can do on the cheap: before you lug that basket of clothes down to the laundry room, dump it on the floor and draw the folds you see. That's the best way to learn the unpredictable art of inert folds!

Now, before I cut you loose to wreak havoc on an unsuspecting laundry room, let's take a closer look at just one more of these fold types: the half-lock.

Not quite a diaper fold, the half-lock is a close cousin.

Hold up a dishtowel or a small rag from two points, generating a diaper fold. Now lower one of those points while bringing the other point slightly inward. See what happened? Does it look like the fold in the previous drawing? (If not, try again. It will!) The point here is to illustrate that these folds are like waves. They're organic, growing out of the circumstances that form them. All these folds will meld one into the other. They'll morph, twist, bend, and gel from one fold to the next. But now those twists and turns won't shake you! So get to practicing! Start filling those sketchbooks with drapery. A good exercise is to draw *just* the clothing on people. If you do it right, you should be able to see the figure beneath it just by the folds in the clothes.

It's like the Invisible Man met the Invisible Girl.

The Least You Need to Know

◆ Folds in fabric are created by resistance and the lack thereof.

◆ Folds do not exist in a vacuum; they meld into other folds in a dynamic fashion.

◆ You can practice with everyday objects, such as your laundry!

In This Part

Part 4

Drawing the Human Animal

People. People who need people—uhh, draw people, I mean. And that's you. Now don't go getting scared on me now. The human body is nothing more than a collection of basic shapes: circles, cylinders, the whole kit and kaboodle. All you've gotta do is learn the basic proportions. See how it all fits together. Then we'll take all that and make it move. Heck, we'll even make it fly!

In This Chapter

◆ Learning the individual components of the human head

◆ Combining elements to make a face

◆ Seeing the head at different angles

◆ Expressing yourself and seeing the importance of mirrors

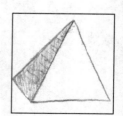

Chapter 13

Launching (or Sinking) a Thousand Ships: Drawing the Face

Take a moment right now and picture your best friend. Now how about your boss at work? Got any siblings? Parents? Close your eyes and visualize them in your head. Chances are, the first thing you saw behind your eyelids was a face, not their hands or their thighs or their shapely buttocks. Odds are pretty good that faces populate the glossy photographs gathering dust in a drawer somewhere.

Beyond a fingerprint, there's no more common identifying feature than a person's face. Let's take a look at what makes the face what it is and spend a little face time with a mirror to see how expressions are made.

Eyes

On nearly every other page in my sketchbook, you'll find a single left eye. It's a habit I got into to get my juices flowing. Whenever I sat down to draw, the first thing I did was limber up by drawing an eye. I usually did the left eye because I'm right-handed, and the eyebrows gave me the chance to do a sweeping kind of gesture with them.

A few of the quick warm-ups in my journals.

None of these was a serious effort, obviously. But they did get better as time marched on. (Practice and all that.) My early efforts with eyes were marred by the fact that I was drawing what I thought an eye should look like instead of what an eye *actually* looked like. Biggest mistake that newbies make? They forget that eyes have a lower lid, too.

This eye loses some of its depth without the lower lid.

Okay, by show of hands, who wants to learn how to draw these things? One … 2 … 10 …. Good! The "eyes" have it! (Ouch. That was so bad it could only be a reality TV show next year: *Puns Gone Wild!*) Alright, down to business. Let's start with the basic shape of the eye.

The basic eye shape. Don't forget that little tear duct thingie on the inside!

What you're looking at here is the eye's most basic shape. This differs drastically depending on any number of factors, not the least of which are age, gender, race, and angle of view. But that's okay. We're not trying to draw every eye on the planet right now—just the one you see here.

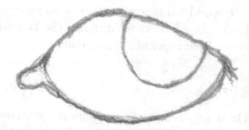

Unless the lids are open very wide, the eyeball itself will be partially hidden.

So far, so good. At first glance, you've already got something that's recognizable as an eye. That's harder than you think. In fact, there's a chance that you couldn't do this when you first picked up this book. Great job! But, hey, where are you going? We're not done yet!

Staying Sharp

Remember those spheres and circles you were drawing earlier in the book? The eyeball is a perfect example of how you can apply the most basic shapes to real-world objects.

You've got the outline for the eye, which is fine as long as the person you're drawing has a bad case of glaucoma, but you're going to need an iris and a pupil to make it real. Oh, and notice that I add the reflection first before I add the pupil.

Now we're getting somewhere.

This next step of adding the eyelids will take a little practice on your part. You can just mimic what I'm doing, but spend a little time looking at people's faces in magazines and on TV to see how wildly different this can be. Also, a low eyebrow can cause that upper lid to behave differently.

Add those upper and lower eyelids.

For women, children, and the surgically enhanced, you can go a lot easier on that lower lid. The elderly, some men, and your basic college undergrad on an all-night study session might have some luggage beneath those eyes.

Bags this deep should have handles!

Before we go any further, let's take a quick look at the varying depths of the human eye. Getting a handle on this now will help you later when you try to rotate the head and show the eye from different angles.

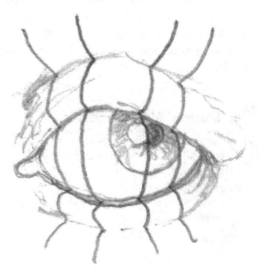

The eyes aren't flat—don't draw them that way! These are features that have depth. If you follow the contour lines on this eye, you'll see the relative depths of the eye.

Looking good, but there's something missing. Can anybody put their finger on it? Anybody? Anybody? Bueller?

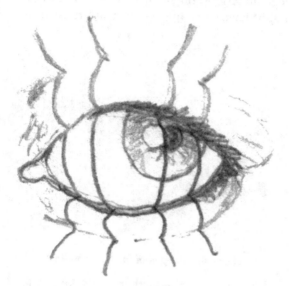

Eyelashes!

Unless you've managed to burn those suckers off in a cigar-lighting frenzy, chances are, you've got eyelashes. When drawing these things, you want to avoid trying to draw each lash individually. In this instance, you're going to want to lay in the overall shape of the collective group of lashes. Got that? Good. Now you try it.

Masters' Musings

"The secret of life is to have a task, something you devote your entire life to, something you bring everything to, every minute of the day for the rest of your life. And the most important thing is, it must be something you cannot possibly do."

—Henry Moore (1898–1986)

Finally, feast your eyeballs on these eyeballs and do your best to draw them. These are different angles you may be called upon to draw someday, so it's best to start warming up now!

Up, down, all around.

Oh, one more thing: the eye in profile. You'll do a full-face profile in a little while, but right now I want to show you the drastic difference between an eye seen from the front and one seen from the side.

Note that this looks nothing like the "almond" shape of the eye seen from the front.

The eye in profile is actually a triangle with a bowed edge. Note that the lower lid is slightly recessed from the upper one. Eyelashes are (almost) always more pronounced on a woman.

Layman's Lingo

In the coming pages, you'll hear me mention the term **drawing through** a lot. What that means is that when you've got something like a circle (such as an eyeball) that is partially hidden from view, you should draw through the offending object as though it weren't there. You can always erase the part of the circle you don't need later, but this is the best way to ensure that your proportions are right.

Nose

Nothing gives me quite the problem that noses do. I never quite "got it." Then I took some time, as we're going to do right now, and I took it step by step. Here you learn the simple basics that apply to almost every nose. Some will be wider, some shorter, some longer, some thicker. But barring any industrial accidents or unfortunate gene splicing, the human nose is comprised of the same elements on everyone: the bridge and length of the nose, the bulbous tip, and the nostrils. Sounds easy enough. Let's do it!

Starting at the top, remember that all noses connect to the eyebrows in their way.

You may end up erasing those diagonal lines that connects the nose to the eyebrows, but I usually draw them in at first so that I'm aware of their connection and symmetry. From there, the nose meets the bridge and often bows out a little. There's a bone structure underneath this part of the nose, so you need to be aware of it!

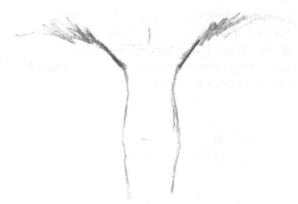

Don't forget that bridge!

From there, it's a short shot down to the bulbous area of the nose. I'm drawing it a little more angular here than it might appear on the average face because I want you to see the anatomy involved.

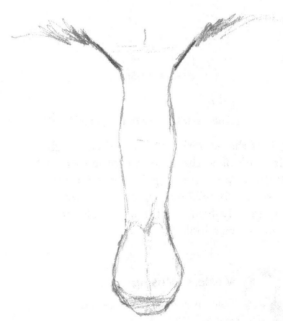

It almost looks like that thing on *Star Trek* that … nevermind.

Finally, we add the nostrils. From this angle, the symmetry makes it easy to accomplish, but these buggers will drive you a little crazy when you tilt and rotate the head a little. At this stage it's important to remember that those two small black ovals aren't just graphite on paper; they represent deep shadows created by holes in a person's head.

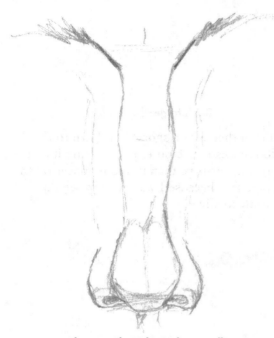

The nostrils. What's that smell?

Got that so far? Not too difficult, right? Have a look at the nose in profile to see how all this fits together. Again, remember that these are "base" samples. Actual noses will vary greatly. Still, the fundamentals are the same. Have a look.

Masters' Musings

"Faith in oneself is the best and safest course."

—Michelangelo (1475–1564)

That which we call a nose, by any other name, would smell as sweet.

See how the nostrils take on an entirely different shape at this angle? It's vital that you're able to visualize that as the head tilts to different angles. Now might be a good time to get that mirror and watch the changes that your features go through as you turn your head side to side and up and down.

Mouth

What are we really thinking about when we talk about drawing the mouth? It's the lips, isn't it? More than a handful of muscles and such go into the mouth, but let's start with the obvious.

This is the mouth in repose: neither smiling, nor frowning, nor puckering.

Have a good look at your own lips, and they'll likely look a lot like this. Perhaps they're more or less full, but the basic mechanics stay the same. The lips, as it turns out, are made up of the same five ovals on everybody. Have a look.

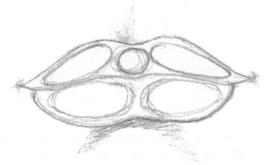

You'll be able to spot these on just about anybody's mouth.

The lower lip is made of two long ovals that narrow and connect at the corners to the two outside ovals in the upper lip. In the middle of the upper lip, a smaller, nearly circular shape dips down lower than its neighbors. These shapes have been there all the time, but we very often don't think of them. But the next time you see a photo of Angelina Jolie, notice how her bottom lip has a deep groove in it. That minor crevice is caused by the two ovals meeting.

As with all the other facial features, the basic shapes that comprise the mouth undergo a startling transformation when seen in profile.

Looking at the mouth from the side, note that (unless the person in question has a severe underbite) the lower lip is slightly recessed from the upper one. Also look at where the light hits the lips and where the darkest parts are: out in the corners and in that space where the lips meet.

And hey, when it comes to drawing teeth, don't overdo it, huh? We don't need to see every groove and plaque stain. Just give us the general shape and call it a day.

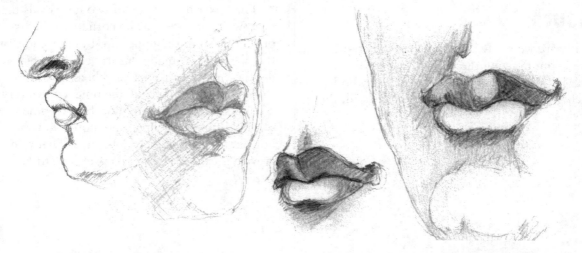

Lips and mouths are among my favorite features on people. Here are some at various angles. Good stuff!

> ### Staying Sharp
> Remember that the features on the face are not drawn on a flat surface. Even when seen from the front, be aware that the face curves backward toward the ears. When you turn the subject's head, parts of it will recede.

Last, here are a few examples of the mouth that you can practice to gain a better understanding of its depth and dimension.

Ears

There's a story that the famous artist Vincent van Gogh once cut off his own ear and sent it to a woman he was fond of. Although one can admire the kind of obsessive dedication that took, I tend to think there are easier (and less frightening) ways to get the attention of someone you love. Besides, what kind of card do you include with that? "Can't wait to hear from you?" That's just not right.

Not the most pleasant surprise she ever got, I'll wager.

Ears are convoluted things, aren't they? Call them what you want, "shell-like" or whatever, but they're a little intimidating. If you can remember just the two letters *S* and *C*, though, you'll find them much easier to draw.

Just remember the *S* and *C*.

Look at somebody in profile, and you'll be able to pick out these two major shapes. Obviously, people's ears, like their noses, change from one head to another, but this is a good rule of thumb … er, ear … to follow.

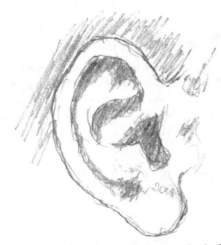

Add some depth with the shading method of your choice, and you're done!

Here's another example to perk up your own ears. Get those pencils ready and draw!

The ear from behind is a tricky thing. Watch that light source!

Masters' Musings

"It is not the language of painters but the language of nature which one should listen to, the feeling for the things themselves, for reality is more important than the feeling for pictures."

—Vincent van Gogh (1853–1890)

Framing the Face

So you've got all the ingredients for a fine quiche, but you need a bowl to mix them in. That's what the head is, in its way. It's a blank canvas. It's the place where all these things come together to make their home. Unless you're Picasso. And then you can just put the nose wherever you want. Inside guitars is good, too. Don't ask me why.

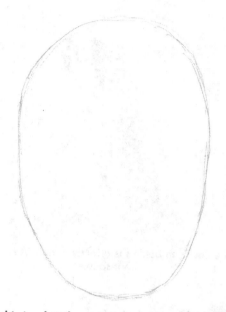

So this is what they mean by someone having a "blank look" on their face ....

You might hear that a head is like an inverted egg, but the fact is that … well … it can be, but it isn't always. Some people have square heads. Or rectangular ones. Or nearly round noggins. The shape of the head varies almost as much as the features that populate it. But for argument's sake, yeah, it's sometimes like an inverted egg, like the previous illustration. But sometimes it looks like this:

This variety extends across gender lines. On the whole, though, women have chins that are slightly less broad, and the whole shape of the thing has softer edges.

Make a Face

Now you've got everything you need. You know the basics for drawing eyes and noses and ears and mouths. You know the basic shape of the head. So how do you combine all these elements into something that looks like a human being? As luck would have it, the human face was put together pretty symmetrically. Things balance out, and there are some basic rules to help you put stuff in the right place. It's not unlike using a Mr. Potato Head. There are slots where these things go. All you have to do is plug them in.

First things first. Take that roughly oval shape that represents the head and draw a *center line* cutting it in half.

Layman's Lingo

The **center line** is an imaginary line that runs down the middle of the human body, starting at the top of the head and running down through the torso.

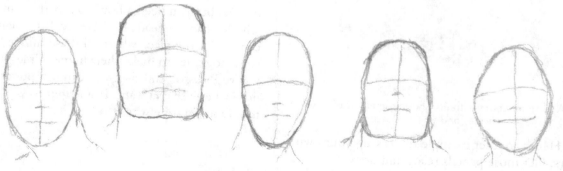

Heads, in all their endless variety.

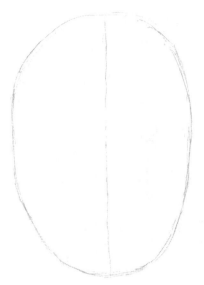

This is called the center line.

Some of your face's features, such as the nose and mouth, will need that center line as a guide. The next step is to divide the head in half horizontally.

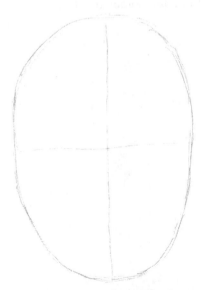

This is the eye line. (Not eyeliner—that's something else.)

Halfway between that line and the bottom of the face, you're going to add another line. This one represents the bottom of the nose. You

don't need this to go across the whole head; a short dash will do just fine.

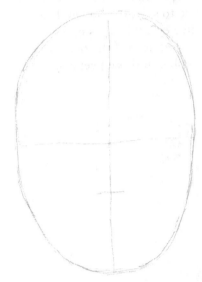

We don't have a term for this, but you can call it the "nose dash" if it makes you happy. And you thought noses only ran.

Last, halfway between the bottom of the nose and the chin, you'll add another line to represent the mouth.

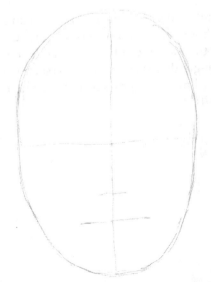

When drawing this line, don't make it any longer than half the width of the whole head.

So now you've got this thing divided like a birthday cake. What now? Well, for starters, you'll want to mark off the width of the eyes. From side to side, the human head is approximately five eyes wide. Using your best guess, go ahead and tick off the place where you're going to plug in those peepers.

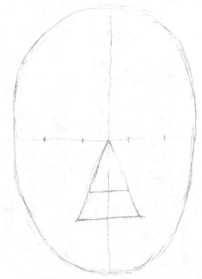

You weren't expecting this much geometry, were you?

Okay. Triangles drawn? Center lines, uh, centered? Good deal. Now you'll find that the rest of the face really is just as simple as plugging everything in. Come on, let's start with the eyes.

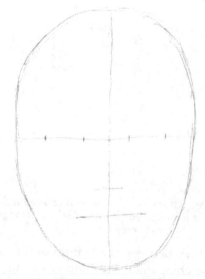

Notice that the width of the nose line is equal to the width of one of the eyes.

Oh, and while we're measuring stuff and talking about basic proportions, note that the width of the mouth can be estimated by creating a triangle that starts at the intersection of the center lines and goes out past the line for the nostrils.

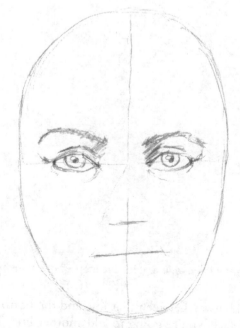

The center of the eyes falls on the center line. You shouldn't have any problem remembering that.

The rest of it is just what you'd think. Knowing the basic shapes of the nose and mouth, add them in. It's always a good idea to draw these in lightly at first and then darken the lines you really want later on. Then we follow with the other details, like ears and hair.

Think we're done? Oh, foolish mortal! Actually, we're really close. You need to add those ears, for one. Hair is good, too. And if you want, you can add little details throughout. But the basics are there. Everything else is up to you!

Staying Sharp

When drawing hair, remember that less is more. Don't draw every strand of hair; instead, find the direction that the hair is going and try to let your lines suggest that movement. And here's a little trick, from me to you: you can use the eraser to create your shine for you. Just erase the areas where the highlights should appear.

The Profile

Arguably, the profile of the face is a lot easier than the full-frontal view. For one thing, you have to draw half the eyes and nostrils. But easier is not "easy," so let's take a stab at this, huh? Let's start with these basic profile shapes.

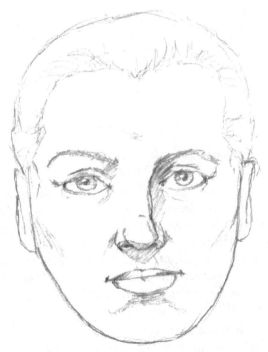

Here's the finished product. Don't forget to erase your guidelines—it's easy to forget they're there.

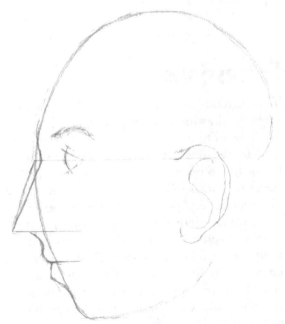

Notice how the nose can be represented as a simple triangle at this point.

If you did your homework in the earlier parts of this chapter, you'll find this a walk in the park. All we're doing, as in the full-face exercise, is plugging things into our Mr. Potato Head. A good guideline to notice here is that the corners of the mouth are on the *plumb line* with the front of the eyes.

Layman's Lingo

The **plumb line** is an imaginary vertical line that exists between two points. The term comes from carpentry, in which a string is weighted with a ball and hung from an object to make sure that something lines up properly beneath it. That means the plumb line doesn't just connect any two points; it's a straight drop down from one point to see where that line intersects. Often you'll find that the line meets in the middle of another object, but it's a great way to gauge depth and distance.

Expressions

The exercises we've used in this chapter will be great for drawing faces in profile or full on. You'll need to do a little supplemental studying if you want to tackle the three-quarter view (allow me to recommend *The Complete Idiot's Guide to Drawing People Illustrated*, by Brenda Hoddinott; see Appendix A). But the other thing we can do before you go traipsing off to nearby chapters is explore the idea that not every face will be this passive. People have been known to smile—even cry. The human face is capable of some pretty amazing expressions. Just about every emotion that we're capable of makes its way to the face in some form. Actually whole books are devoted to this subject, but let's take a look at someone smiling, just to see what we're up against.

The same generic face as before, but now he's happy!

Take that artist's eye we've been training and set it on the previous image. Take a look at the mouth, yes, but also notice that the eyes change. A person's emotional state doesn't change just one aspect of appearance: it affects many muscles. The cheeks here become more prominent. Creases appear at the corners. We can see teeth. What else can you spot?

When the time comes to start drawing expressions on people's faces, you'll have no better ally than a mirror. Sitting on a couch at 2 A.M. is a great, quiet time to sit with your sketchbook. It's also a lousy time to call on friends and family and ask them, quite casually, to look forlorn. On the bright side, wherever you go, your face goes with you. So get used to looking at your own mug in the looking glass and see what's looking back.

In this self-portrait, I went straight past forlorn into miserable.

You can find great reference books to help you master drawing the face. Just don't overlook the obvious resource you have in your own visage! Of course, it could be problematic to keep running to the restroom every time you need to check your progress. Many professional artists use one of those light-up vanity mirrors, or a full body-length mirror, and they keep it right next to their drafting tables. You might not have that kind of set-up just yet, but there are alternatives. Got one of those nifty cell phones that has a camera in it? Snap a picture of yourself and refer to it as necessary. Or you can always buy a little face-size mirror. Either way, start polishing your acting skills. You're gonna be a star, baby!

The Least You Need to Know

◆ The face is made up of several definable elements, but you've got to know the overall structure to put them together right.

◆ All these features can vary wildly, but certain basic rules apply to them all.

◆ Mirrors are an invaluable ally in getting an expression right.

◆ These features have depth! Don't be afraid to use some light contour lines to help you gauge their relative distance.

In This Chapter

- ◆ A look at a simplified skeleton
- ◆ The major muscle groups of the body
- ◆ Basic proportions: the eight-heads rule
- ◆ Exceptions to the rules
- ◆ Draw from life!

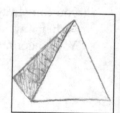

Chapter 14

The Body

Beyond the portrait, which I cover in Chapter 18, no subject is more dear to the artist than the human form. From women in repose and men fighting dragons, to warrior queens and socialites at tea, the body remains a focal point for our wildest fantasies and most artistic day-dreams.

I've often wondered whether we would have developed the same urge to draw and paint if we had invented the camera sooner. But I think that, no matter what advances we make in technology, we will always return to pencil and paper and a desire to make something beautiful and permanent. Of course, at this stage, I'd settle for something we won't be ashamed to hang on the refrigerator, but, hey, that's just me.

The Simplified Skeleton

Remember what I was saying about how fabric drapes in Chapter 12? How the ultimate form the folds will take depends on what's underneath it? The human body follows the same rules. Underneath those clothes are muscles and skin, but underneath it all is the skeleton. Now, another art book might take you on a guided tour of *Gray's Anatomy*. I'm not that guy. I spent a good long time looking at and studying the bare bones of the skeleton only to realize that unless you're drawing a scene from the *Seventh Voyage of Sinbad* or *Pirates of the Caribbean*, you're rarely, if ever, going to be called upon to draw a human skeleton.

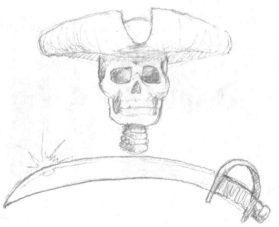

Arrr, matey!

So, look, there's an easier way. Knowing the foundations for the forms you're drawing is a good idea. We just need to simplify the skeleton. Consider the ribs, for example. You don't need to draw each and every one of those things. I can spare you that. (Spare. Ribs. Spare ribs. Get it? When this is over, I'm going to have to change my name and enter the Witness Protection Program to save me from the anti-pun organizations.)

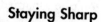

Staying Sharp

There are roughly 400 ribs on either side of the ribcage—or, at least, it feels that way. When roughing in the chest area, you can use any number of shapes, from bubbles to barrels. Experiment. See what works best for you.

Likewise, the arms and legs, which have multiple bones in their lower halves, can be simplified into a single cylinder. And geez, don't get me started on the hands. Or the feet. Those are topics for another chapter; for your simplified skeleton, all you really need is right here.

Hi, Mom!

Go ahead and draw this a few times. Change the pose, if you want. Lower that arm. Raise the other. Do what you like, as long as you get a sense of the thing. It's nothing you don't already know: it's a lot of spheres and cylinders, and you mastered those ages ago. But, here. Look at the profile and try it for yourself.

If there was ever a time to stop dieting ....

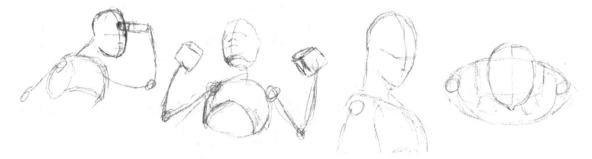

Nothing hard about this. It's just like posing mannequins.

So what are you supposed to do with this thing? Well, for starters, instead of leaping straight to the rendering stage, you'll find the simplified skeleton a huge tool for blocking out your drawings. They're also essential for getting poses just right before you start laying in the musculature. Try a few of these. There's nothing overly dramatic here, but if you can get the hang of posing your little stick-figure guy, all the stuff that follows will be much easier.

Major Muscle Groups

You're going to drive yourself crazy if you try to memorize every muscle in the body. The simple fact is that unless your subject is a green, gamma-irradiated, steroid-laden freak, you will never need to draw all those muscles. Even the muscles you do see on people are usually covered in a thickish layer of skin and fat, softening their appearance. So when you start to lay the muscles on your simplified skeleton, don't worry so much about defining the separation between those muscles. Let me show you an example.

This reminds me of that Invisible Man model kit I had as a kid.

On the left, we've got the actual musculature of the neck. On the right, you can see what it really looks like once you've added normal human tissue on top of it.

Masters' Musings

"When I've painted a woman's bottom so that I want to touch it, then the painting is finished."

—Pierre Auguste Renoir (1841–1919)

See how those really detailed lines go away? All you're left with is the really pronounced muscles that support the head. Let's take a look at a relaxed arm and see what's what.

You don't need a lot of lines to convey something.

Let's take a look at that arm from a different angle. You'll see that from both angles, even though literally dozens of muscles are at work here, you just need to know the basic shapes of the arm.

The long muscle on top is the bicep; the shorter, fuller one on the bottom is the tricep.

You can spend a lot of time getting to know the official Latin names of all the muscles. Biceps, triceps, latissimus dorsi, and so on—but remember that you probably have at least one of everything you're trying to draw. Keep that mirror handy and don't be afraid to ask friends or family members to roll up their sleeves to

help you out. It's the same thing with the legs: there are a ton of interconnecting muscles. Take a few minutes to draw them. Then you can all but forget about them.

> **Staying Sharp**
>
> Don't get the impression that a knowledge of anatomy isn't helpful! Find yourself a good reference source, and keep it handy. (I recommend *Atlas of Human Anatomy for the Artist,* by Stephen Rogers Peck; Galaxy Books, 1982). Knowing what's underneath the skin can only make your drawings more realistic. Just understand that not every drawing needs that level of detail.

Here's a side-by-side look at the leg. The one on the left shows you the underlying musculature. The one on the right is how it actually appears. Unless it's my leg, in which case it's a lot hairier. Because, hey, as much as I like you, I'm not about to shave my legs for you. They don't call me Fradella Gorilla for nothin', you know.

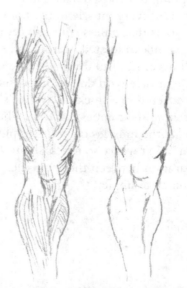

Knowing the major underlying muscles helps, but you don't have to draw them every time.

Hey, while we're on the subject of muscles, let me throw a little-known fact at you. Those bodybuilders go through quite a bit to make their muscles pop like that at a show. They go through a pretty serious regimen of sodium-loading and dehydration to make their bodies look that defined; it doesn't just happen by working out. Think about that the next time you try to Herculize somebody!

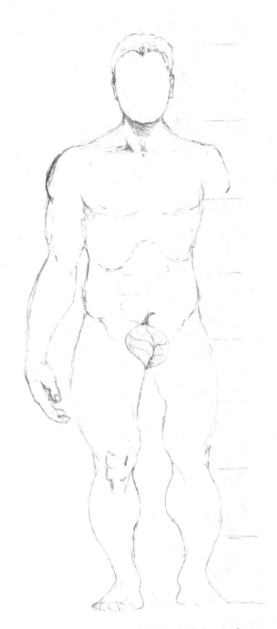

Yeah, I've got six-pack abs. A six-pack of beer, maybe ….

Learning Proportions

The hard and fast rule for the proportions of the human body is that we all stand approximately eight heads high. That is, if you take the size of a person's head and stack seven more head-heights beneath them, that's the total height of the person's body. This is a measurement system that goes back to the Renaissance era. If it was good enough for Michelangelo, it's good enough for me!

Note that the palm of the hands falls at about midthigh. If you're a man and you've ever worn a suit jacket, you already knew that.

And here are those same proportions from the side.

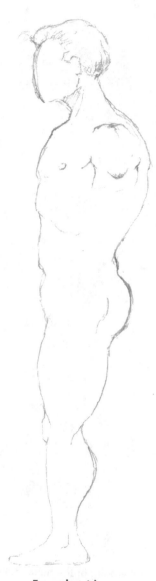

From the side.

The eight-head measurement is a good guide, but I'll let you in on a little secret: Michelangelo often drew his divine and mythological figures at eight and a half heads tall. That extra half-head of height alters the proportions just enough to give them a more "epic" scope. That theory worked well. In fact, in the best-selling tome by the late John Buscema and the ever-popular Stan Lee, *How to Draw Comics the Marvel Way*, Big John advises all Marvel hopefuls to follow suit.

> **Masters' Musings**
>
> "After four tortured years, more than 400 over life-sized figures, I felt as old and as weary as Jeremiah. I was only 37, yet friends did not recognize the old man I had become."
>
> —Michelangelo (1475–1564)

Different Rules for the Young and Old

Of course, the rules that I'm giving you here are just like the new shows of a season on FOX: they're subject to change without notice. For example, kids and elderly folks don't follow the whole eight-head rule. Especially not kids. Have you ever seen the size of a kid's melon in relation to the rest of the body? It's a miracle that we ever develop neck muscles strong enough to get our noggins off the pillow.

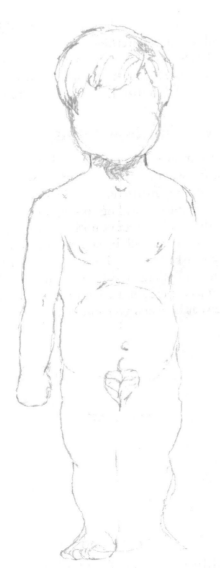

It's either a kid or one of those alien races with a telepathic brain.

Another weird thing that you ought to know about kids (and people in general, for that matter): the size of our eyes never changes. Didn't know that, did you? It's true. You're born with your peepers at actual size. The rest of your body just takes a while to catch up. As for older folks (not pictured here), they actually do tend to shrink a bit as they age. You could lose as much as two heads in height by your 80th birthday!

Drawing from Life

You're going to get tired of hearing me say it, but there's no substitute for drawing from life. Whether it's a potted plant or a human being, you'll learn more in an hour with a live model than you will in 10 hours just using your imagination. Muscles, proportion, drapery, light, shadow, texture—you can't begin to imagine the difference it's going to make. Don't believe me? Here, let me show you the difference. Following you'll find two images. The first one is a *self-portrait* based solely on memory. There couldn't be an easier subject, right? I mean, I've been looking at this face all my life. If anybody should be able to draw it, it should be me.

Me. And yet, not me.

Even without looking in a mirror, I know I'm a good ways away from any actual likeness. Some of you out there might possess a photographic memory and can do this in your sleep. Of course, if that's the case, why draw? Just kidding. But now that we've got the distorted self-image onto the page, let me try this again with a mirror handy.

I don't know if it's "better," but it's more accurate.

Okay, your turn. Put away the pictures. No cheating. Just pick up your sketchbook and do your level best to draw your own face. It's not going to be perfect, so just relax. The *point* is not to be perfect, so get to drawing.

> **Layman's Lingo**
>
> A **self-portrait** is any work of art (drawing, painting, photography, and so on) that uses the artist as the subject. It's often done with the help of a mirror or some other outside assistance.

So, how'd you do? Probably not as good as you're about to do. It's time to go get that mirror and take a real look at the hills and valleys that make up your face. We get into this in greater depth in Chapter 18, but for now, I just want you to take your best stab at it.

Now put those two drawings side by side and look at the difference—not just in quality, either. Really look at all the things that are in there that your memory and imagination can't account for. With that in mind, let's go forward.

Where to Find Nude Models

Let's face it, even if you've got a live-in significant other, whether it's a husband, a wife, a boyfriend, or a girlfriend, that person is not always going to be willing to strip out of his or her clothes at a moment's notice and then, you know, not move at all for several hours just because you asked nicely. (For the record, asking any other way than "nicely" will often result in blunt objects being hurled at one's head. Just a little caveat between you and me.)

Don't say I didn't warn you.

But barring a willing friend, where can you go to find perfect strangers who have no qualms about showing you some skin? First stop, check your local college. Over in the art departments, they often have message boards with notices from kind folks who are willing to get naked for a few bucks. I got lucky with such a message board, in fact. On Monday nights, for just $10 I can draw from a live nude model for three solid hours. That's not a typical scenario, but they do exist. Keep your eyes peeled. Another avenue worthy of exploration is the local free newspapers. They've always got some great esoteric stuff in there. Look for "open drawing" or the like. If that doesn't work out for you, check with the professors at the local college. They have access to the nude models and might be willing to put you in touch with one of them. If you can make it worth his or her time (read: pay enough), a model might be willing to come pose for a group of artists at your location. Good luck!

Contour Drawing

When you've secured yourself a nude model, there are roughly four billion ways that you can start drawing him or her. I'll tell you that the first time I stood behind an easel with a stick of charcoal in my hand, I was almost paralyzed. I had spent years working in smaller sketchbooks, in pencil. Suddenly, I had an unfamiliar tool and a canvas that was as big as me from belt to bowler. My drawings were not what I had hoped they would be. Chances are, yours won't be, either. Part of my problem, though, was that I wasn't taking any formal instruction. I just found my way to an open drawing and set up shop. I had no idea what I was doing. So before you panic and throw up your hands in frustration, let me give you a starting place. Instead of sketching, I want you to do a *contour drawing*.

Layman's Lingo

Also known as "taking a line for a walk," a **contour drawing** is a technique wherein the artist draws a line of varying thickness to represent only the outline of the subject.

During your first attempts at contour drawing, your proportions more than likely will be a little off. That's okay. If you were able to do all this stuff right the first time, you wouldn't need this book and I'd be out of a job. Let's just be glad we found each other, huh?

This woman's back was drawn with almost a single line.

What you're looking for is the basic shape and proportion of the subject. You can always go back later and do the shading after you've fixed your proportions. What's the importance of doing a contour drawing? Well, there are a few reasons. First among them is that a contour drawing can be done fairly quickly. In a live-model session, the model often starts the session by doing several 30-second poses. Then a minute. Then 5 minutes, and so on. By combining contour drawing with a judicious application of gesture lines, you're more likely to put something on the paper that actually looks like what you're trying to draw. That's no small feat, and you should pat yourself on the back if you can get there.

Quick Sketches in a Café

A lot of emphasis is put on the nude in art. That's fine, but I have to tell you that I get really jazzed by the opportunity to draw people with clothing on. No, seriously. Clothes fit differently on small Asian girls than they do on strapping Nordic men. Like anything else, your ability to imagine this will never be as awesome as your ability to simply draw what you see. The best part of this? You don't need to pay people to wear clothes. The law requires it—well, in most places.

Take your sketchbook and head out to one of the larger bookstores. Most of them have a built-in café these days. Get yourself a cup of java, find a nice corner with decent lighting, sit back, and let your models come to you. These are not people who are going to sit in one pose for very long, though, so get what you can *while* you can.

The setting sun gave me nice shadows to work with here, but the guy got up and left before I could lay in any real details.

It has been my experience that, 99 times out of 100, the people who notice you sketching them don't mind. They might become a little self-conscious, but if somebody is ever honestly bothered by the attention, stop right away. Pick somebody else. Draw the salt and pepper shakers for a while. And never, ever publish your drawings of these people without their express permission! These folks are providing you with an endless supply of free models. Show some respect.

I was glad this guy sat in the café as long as he did!

Getting Help from Family or Friends

Although you might get a fight over asking people to drop their drawers in the living room, you'll find that folks won't mind standing still and posing while you rough in the details you need. For example, let's say you've decided you want to draw a gladiator marching forward, sword in hand and ready for battle.

I roughed this in pretty quick, but I needed reference for the hands.

The gladiator drawing was done in less than 20 minutes while sitting on the couch watching TV. For the most part, I really liked where it was going. It's a long way from done, but one

of the things that really irked me was his right hand. I tried it a few times, but it just wasn't gelling for me. So I asked my girlfriend (who, incidentally, looks nothing like the gladiator in the picture) if she would grab a wooden spoon from the kitchen and hold it a certain way for me.

A little help from my sweetie, and I was able to add the details I needed here.

The resulting drawing turned out much better for her participation, and nobody had to get naked. This is especially good if you're asking someone like your father. Just thinking about that makes me want to take out my eyes with a 9H pencil.

We covered a lot of ground in this chapter. There's a ton to absorb here, so take a little extra time and go back over the lessons. If you've already drawn everything once, draw it again. If you've drawn it more than once, good for you! Now get a cup of coffee and do it again! Go!

The Least You Need to Know

◆ You don't need to know every bone and muscle in the body.
◆ A stick-figure skeleton is a handy tool for posing your drawings.
◆ The human body is approximately eight heads tall.
◆ Contour drawings can help you get a pose onto paper very quickly.
◆ It's essential to draw from life!

In This Chapter

- ◆ The hand in basic shapes
- ◆ Getting to know your own palm
- ◆ The hand's many emotions

     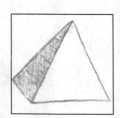

Chapter 15

Hands Down

Ask some artists out there, and they'll cite a few areas of the human body that filled their hearts with fear and their sketchbooks with pages of near misses. The hands are one of those things. It's entirely possible that the last time you drew a decent hand, you were in Ms. Biernbach's art class in first grade, and you'd just traced your own hand onto a piece of construction paper and then transformed it into a turkey.

Okay, maybe that was just me. But the fact remains that hands are tough to draw. They have attitudes. They have emotions. Like the features on the face, the hand can transform as it rotates. But in this chapter, we're going to make all this a lot less scary. No kidding. C'mon. Let me show you how.

Examining Your Own Hands

Drawing the hands would be a lot harder if it wasn't for the simple fact that you've got a pair of them right in front of you. Take a minute now and look at your hands. Really look at them. What do you see? Sure, there's a little dirt beneath the fingernails, but we'll keep that between us. What else? Raise your hand if you said you saw a collection of cylinders connected to a polygon. No? Have a look.

Masters' Musings

"I think a painter looking at a painting sees the image, but they also see how the image was constructed."
—Chuck Close (1940–)

Believe it or not, it really is this easy.

Of course, the second you change the position of the hand, that polygon alters dramatically. If you think of that box as having depth, though, you'll be much better off. For example, here's what that box looks like slightly rotated.

You already know the rules of perspective. All you have to do is apply them.

Rotate that box far enough, and you'll see that, lying on its "side," it's just another rectangle!

Imagine that this is palm down.

So now you're thinking, "Great. I already knew how to draw a box. I want to draw a hand!" You're probably also thinking, "Did I leave the gas on?" But let's move forward until you smell smoke.

Staying Sharp

Now's a good time to loosen up again. Take a few minutes to clench and stretch those hands. During these next few exercises, I want you limber. Your ability to draw will be much improved if you're relaxed and able to focus your energy without having your drawing hand cramp up. And don't forget to breathe, Daniel-san!

So you've got this flat box, which had a lot more corners on it just a few minutes ago. How do you turn this into a hand? Well, for starters, let's add some circles and cylinders.

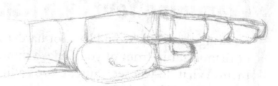

Already you can see the hand taking shape.

Now, although cylinders are good guidelines for the fingers, you're going to want to soften those shapes before you're done. We're talking about an organic object here. The top side of the fingers gets a little knobby around the knuckles, and the bottom is fleshier between the joints. If you take a look at your own hand in this position, you'll immediately see where the real work needs to be done.

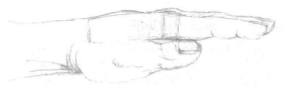

Just a few more strokes of the pencil—give yourself a hand!

From here, it's just a matter of adding depth through shadow. Luckily, you're working from a model (you!) and you can more easily identify the light source(s). You don't need me to hold your hand on this one. Go ahead and finish it up!

Erase your guidelines and you're done!

Of course, unless you plan to draw people solely as they try to judo-chop each other, you'll need to get a handle on the hand from all angles. This isn't as hard as you might think, but let me walk you through another flat view before you get on with the hard stuff.

Masters' Musings

"The attitude that nature is chaotic and that the artist puts order into it is a very absurd point of view, I think. All that we can hope for is to put some order into ourselves."

—Willem de Kooning (1904–1997)

Start with the palm open.

This is the left hand with the palm facing toward you. In no time at all, you'll be able to see that for yourself without me having to tell you. Always remember that you should keep your drawings loose and rough until you've got your basic shape on the paper in the proper proportion. Also, because most of these lines will be erased anyway, there's no sense in pressing down yet.

If you look closely, you can see that I used action or gesture lines to give myself a guide for the fingers.

Geez, would you look at that? Step 2 and we're almost there already. Who said this drawing hands stuff was hard? Oh, right—that would be me.

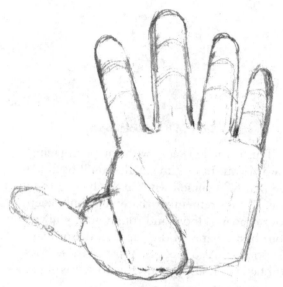

Erase a few lines, add a few more ....

From here, it's all over but the shouting. Then again, what you have here is a blank canvas. That hand has no story to it. No soul. No mystery. Sure, we could add some shadows, but what it's really missing are the palm lines that give it character. Let's do that now.

Drawing Your Palm's Fortune

Whether or not you believe in the art or mysticism surrounding *palmistry*, the truth of the matter is that the palm of a person's hand does tell a story. At first glance, there is the world of difference between the hand that has spent the past half-century with a shovel clutched in its grasp and the smooth, serene lines of the concert pianist. (I'm guessing on the smooth and serene part. I don't actually know any concert pianists. If you do, draw his or her hand for me and send it to me, okay?)

Layman's Lingo

Palmistry is the art of divining a person's future through the study of the lines on the palms. A lesser known fact is that the left hand is your "destiny hand," the hand that shows your life as it should have been. The right hand is the "hand of action," and it shows the life you actually lead. I suppose you would switch this if you're not right-handed. Why I know this stuff is anybody's guess.

You don't need a fortune teller to explain where these lines come from, though. Over the course of your life, the activities you've engaged in, the way your skin has folded when your fist clenches, the weight you've gained and lost—it all has contributed to the grooves in your hand that are simply there out of habit. Take a look at both of your palms side by side. You'll see that they're ever so slightly different. Why? Well, one of them was probably more active. One of them got delegated certain tasks, such as writing and drawing, and the other one didn't. Over the course of a few decades, that makes a difference.

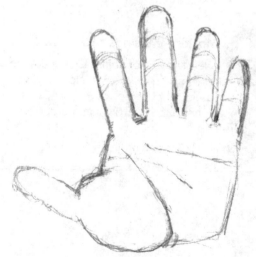

I see a long life ahead of you ....

All I did here was draw in the four most prominent lines on my palm (can't forget that opposable thumb). Your lines will vary. But before you start drawing yours in, hold up that left hand again, palm toward you. Now slowly bend your fingers toward the center, thumb included. Watch what happens. Certain lines deepen immediately. You'll also notice that little microlines crop up, but all we're looking for right now are the obvious ones.

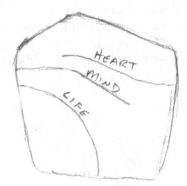

Because I know you were dying to know.

When you bent your fingers toward you, did you notice how that fleshy bar right beneath your fingers puffed up a bit? What about how the ball of muscle around your thumb got more prominent? Of course you did. Good. That might come in handy later!

Masters' Musings

"What is one to think of those fools who tell one that the artist is always subordinate to nature? Art is in harmony parallel with nature."
—Paul Cezanne (1839–1906)

Drawing the Hand in Repose

As I said in Chapter 9, art is emotion. That's never more true than with the human hand. The hand in repose, relaxed, can tell a story of rest, of peace, of grace and beauty. The clenched fist can speak of determination, of victory, and, of course, of violence. You've got the basic tools at your disposal to draw the hand. You know the component parts. But let's draw them both ways so you can see what its like. As you go through this section, note that the fingers block each other. Some parts remain hidden. You can follow along with these examples, or you can draw your own hands. Either way, let's have some fun.

Start with the rough shapes.

Like before, as with anything else, I start by roughing in. Light sketching. Nothing is set in stone at this stage. Just draw what you see, and don't be afraid to draw through nearer objects to get your proportion right. This is the stage when you should identify any major problems that will plague your drawing later. Put the sketch down and walk away if you have to. I know it's hard to break that artist's trance, but a few seconds away now could save you an hour of redrawing later.

Refine the shapes, correct small errors.

When you know what the basic construct of any object is, it's really like pulling back the curtain at Oz, isn't it? All the scary bugaboos of drawing just vanish. Kind of like when you see how they cut a woman in half. No mystery, no magic.

Tighten it up. Just keep it loose when you do!

Tell you what, I'm going to give you one more quick one of the hand in repose, this time from the pinky side. I'm not going to give you the step-by-step on this one. You can fly solo. I have faith in you.

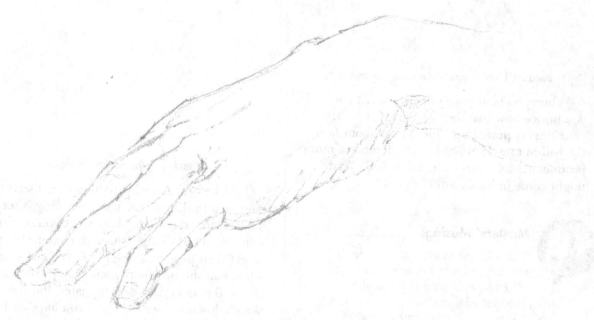

Don't just copy the drawing—build it up from basic shapes.

Staying Sharp

Practice! There's simply no substitute for it. If you find any part of this book difficult, I challenge you to open your sketchbook to the first empty page and spend just a half-hour a day practicing that one thing. Look at your progress over a week. Two weeks. A month. A year. There is *nothing* you can't draw if you practice it!

Drawing the Clenched Fist

Back in the old days, they called this a "knuckle sandwich." They probably served that on wry. (Groan.) The special challenge of drawing the clenched fist is that most of what you've become accustomed to drawing has vanished. There are no extended fingers, no wiggly-lined palm to draw. It's like a hunk of concrete on the end of a stick.

These are more similar than you'd think.

Now, before we start using our own hands as models, I'm going to give you a few simple gesture drawings. I want you to spend some time copying them. Draw them more than once.

These loose, simple gesture drawings will help you keep a sense of energy in the closed fist. It's too easy to let that clenched feeling penetrate the drawing.

Why, you—I oughta …!

From there, it's not a far jump to where we want to be. The fist can be hard at times because of the position of the thumb, but you can do it. Let's take it one step at a time and see what happens.

Not too far from the gesture drawings we did a minute ago.

The thumb lays on top of the closest two fingers.

Refine and render.

And voilà! You're done! As you draw this, be sure to check your own fist for discrepancies. Oh, and while we're comparing stuff, notice what happens to your forearm muscle when you clench that fist. Every part of the body is connected to another part. Be aware of those relationships.

Flex it!

If you made it this far, you've got a lot to be proud of. Pat yourself on the back! The human hand is incredibly complex, but like anything else, if you break it down to simpler shapes, it's not quite so intimidating. Good job! Now go check on that gas. Something smells in here.

The Least You Need to Know

◆ Just like everything else, the hand is made up of basic shapes.

◆ A relaxed hand and a clenched fist are different animals. Treat them that way.

◆ Clenching your fist has visible effects on other body parts. Don't ignore them!

In This Chapter

- ◆ Getting familiar with your own tootsies
- ◆ Basic structure of the foot
- ◆ See the feet at different angles

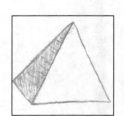

Chapter 16

Two Feet Below

I've been a fan of superhero comics since before I could read. My earliest doodles were of Batman and Robin, complete with starbursted sound effects. As time went on, my drawings got more sophisticated. The musculature got better. The eyes, that feature that I always used to warm up, got a lot better. But if you look through those old pages, you'll find that most of my character studies end at the calf. I hated drawing feet. Even when I did it, the heroes looked like they were wearing feetie pajamas that were too big. They were flat and baggy and messy and awful.

Then I realized that feet weren't any different from anything else I was trying to draw. A foot was just another object. It had a unique shape, yes, but I could simplify those shapes into boxes and rectangles and circles and the like. So can you. Let's get to it.

The Infamous "Draw Your Own Feet While Watching TV" Exercise

All right. Are you ready? Get that sketchbook ready, grab a cup of your favorite tasty beverage, plop yourself in front of the TV, and get ready to work. Got a coffee table? A footstool? Good! Put your feet on it. Cross your legs, if you'd like. For this exercise, you're going to draw your own legs and feet. This is a time-honored tradition, dating back to the early Phoenicians, who … uh … also drew feet. But, hey, they had papyrus and a stylus. They've got nothing on us! Let's get jiggy with it!

Let's start off with bare feet. Get comfy and rough in those shapes.

By this time, you could probably teach me the procedure! Rough in the basics. Tighten them up, like so ….

Don't rush through this part. Really take a close look at what you're drawing.

The feet are a challenge, sure, but you already made it through the lesson on hands. This is a walk in the park! Now that you've got that drawing tightened up a bit, let's just take it that extra step and finalize a few details.

You want extra credit? Draw what's on the TV, too!

Nice job! Keep in mind that you're not trying to *jury* your work into a gallery just yet. An exercise like this should be loose, fun. It's nothing more than a little sketch time on the couch.

Layman's Lingo

Before an artist can show his or her
work in a show or gallery, very often
the owners of that gallery will ask you
to **jury** your work—that is, allow them to
judge its quality. Jurying is often a stressful
ordeal, but if you manage to make your
way past the judges into the show, there's a
big ol' basketful of pride waiting for you on
the other side.

We've got time for another quick exercise.
Got your pencil ready? Got it nice and sharp?
Awesome! I want you to take off your shoes, if
you're wearing them. If you're not wearing shoes,
go ahead and grab a pair. Now take them and
toss them a few feet away. Don't arrange them.
Don't pose them. Just toss them onto the floor
and let them lie where they fall. If you had a
pair of sneakers handy, don't worry about the
laces right now. For starters, we're not going to
just sketch like we did last time; let's try another
approach. Remember way back toward the
beginning of the book when we talked about
using the most basic shapes to represent things?
Well, good. Let's start there. The advantage of
using shoes apart from the feet is that we can
view them as just three-dimensional boxes.

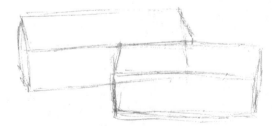

Simple geometric shapes!

See how easy that was? It's like going back
to your ABC's. You know this stuff. So let's
take it further.

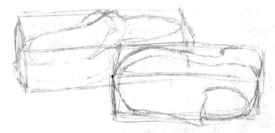

**Add a few gentle curves to denote the tops or
arches.**

Even as you begin to refine the shapes, don't
lose that mental picture of them as three-
dimensional objects. Round out the corners for
the toe and the heel. Carve out that area where
the arch is. Don't worry about shading yet, but
open up the window and let some reality in. It's
time to refine this a little more.

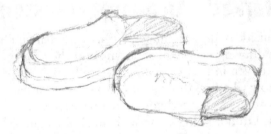

**Start getting rid of the extraneous lines to show the
true image.**

We're just a hop, skip, and a jump from the
end of this thing. Go ahead and make a dash
for the finish line!

Take it home!

These are just a couple of warm-up exercises. How finished you make these drawings is up to you. As always, the goal here is two-fold: learn a little something, and a have a whole lot of fun doing it!

"This Little Piggy Went to Market": An Anatomy Lesson

Outside of drawing nudes, chances are that you'll be drawing people in shoes most of the time. But even in footwear, it's going to help you to know what's *in* those shoes. Now, the foot has more bones in the body than anywhere else, but I'm not going to draw them all for you. That would be silly. Still, a basic outline of what's in the foot might do you some good. Let's have a look, shall we?

How about a dead-on shot? You might not have much need to draw it this way, but those little piggies have to get to the market somehow.

Toes aren't round. Don't draw them that way!

Finally, let's take a look at the foot from the inside. Not like an x-ray machine, but your foot looks completely different from the arch side than it does from the outer edge. Have a peek.

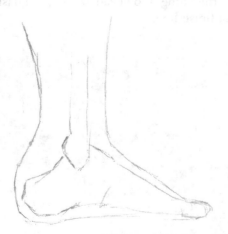

If you can visualize this when you draw, it'll help your foot take form.

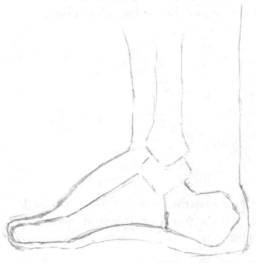

Don't overdo it on that arch—you'll only make it look fake.

These simplified bone diagrams should give you enough to work with, but never hesitate to check one of your handy reference books if you're seeking authenticity.

Draw Those Feet!

Alright, enough pussy-footing around. These boots are made for walkin' … er … drawin'!

Staying Sharp

When the opportunity arises to draw the soles of someone's feet, you'll get a first-hand (or first-foot) look at how a person's lifestyle can alter their physiology. I once had the unique experience of meeting a woman who never wore shoes. Like, really. Except where required by law, this woman would not wear shoes. She had feet like a Hobbit. I'm still not a good enough artist to convey the leathery texture of those things. Yeesh!

It'll help if you've got a model for this next part. We're going to draw the feet from an angle that you can't manage on your own, although if your eyesight is good and you can position a mirror just right, you may be able to manage. Ready? Go!

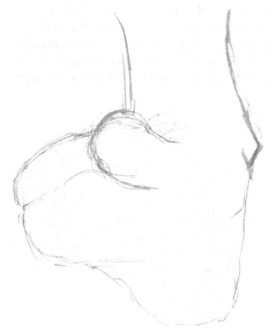

The angles here can be a little tricky!

Starting with the rough, just do your best to convey the overall shape of the feet. If using boxes works for you in this case, do it. There is no wrong way.

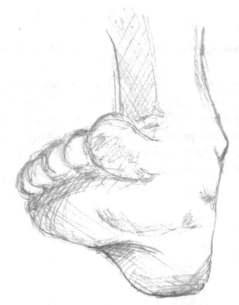

Hey, those are actually starting to look like something.

Try to keep that pencil hand loose. Just keep it moving, going over shapes that feel right again and again. Squiggle, sketch, doodle … do it all. Find the unique style that is yours alone. You can get in there with an eraser later.

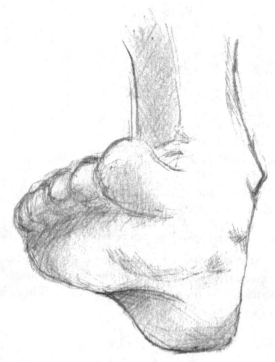

Amazing what those kneaded rubber erasers can do, ain't it?

After you've cleaned it up a bit, you'll be a lot closer to where you want to be. Now all that's left is to darken the lines you want and finalize the piece. Note how I'm making the lines on the darker side thicker. Not a bad habit to get into.

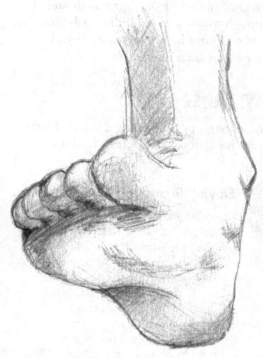

Done!

Good job! Not only can you kick butt, but now you can draw the feet doing the kicking!

The Least You Need to Know

◆ Feet have personality, just like any feature. Give them some character.

◆ The bone structure of the foot is different on the arch side than it is on the outside.

◆ Drawing shoes is just as important as drawing feet themselves.

In This Chapter

- ◆ Using gesture lines to denote movement
- ◆ Showing the body in various stages of motion
- ◆ Tilting the "camera" for more dramatic views

     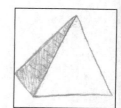

Chapter **17**

The Body in Motion

You've been doing an awesome job so far, no doubt about it. At this point in the book, you've got all the fundamentals you need to go off on your own, but stick around for a few more chapters, huh? I might have a trick or two up my sleeve that you wouldn't immediately arrive at through experimentation alone.

Like this chapter, for example. I know we talked about "action lines" in another chapter, but those suckers are also known as "gesture lines." They're gonna come in really handy for the stuff that comes next. So limber up your drawing digits and let's get to work.

The Importance of Gesture Lines

Before you ever start employing that simplified skeleton, and years before you want to delve into photo reference, you've got to get comfortable with *gesture lines*. These are the first, essential building blocks for any drawing that's going to denote any sort of action. So before we start talking about how to make the human figure walk, run, and fly, let's take a few minutes and get to know gesture lines and what they can do. Step 1? Gimme two lines, going in any direction. They can run parallel, perpendicular, criss, cross … anything you want. Don't just ape me on this one. And don't overthink it! Just put the pencil on the paper and do the first thing that comes to mind.

Layman's Lingo

Gesture lines are the quick, loose lines that will help you define the direction of the action in your drawing.

Random. Tandem!

Take a look at what you drew. Now look again. Pretend it's a Rorschach test. What do you see? If those lines are the basic directions of an object or objects in your finished drawing, what would they be? There's no wrong answer here, so just draw whatever comes to mind. Rough in a shape. This is just for practice, so don't go spending an hour on this.

This is just one direction I could have gone.

Notice how I'm using quick, rough sketches here. I know we spent a good long time teaching you all about rendering and shading techniques, but put them on the back burner for a while. There's a time for hunkering down and doing a more finished piece. That time is not now. We're going to be working in sticks and bubbles. Ah, if your mommy could see you now!

Staying Sharp

This wouldn't be the worst time in the world to try using a different-weight pencil for the early stages. You can start off with a good mechanical pencil or something in the 6H range, and then switch to the trusty HB later. Give it a try.

Ready for step 2? Of course you are. You were born ready. You're a step 2 drawin' maniac. So what is step 2? Easy. I want you to do the exact same thing you just did. But I want you to do it differently. Yeah, you heard me right. I want you to take the same two gesture lines you just drew and draw a different image out of them. Bear in mind that you don't have to draw human beings. You can draw a ship, a bird, a telephone ... anything that works with the lines you've put on the page. Get to it!

Same lines, different end result.

Walking

To draw the figure in motion, it'll help for us to have a vertical guide to judge the angle by. So let's start there. In this exercise, we're going to draw a walking figure. Not jogging or sprinting or crouching or knitting a scarf—just walking. So step 1 here is to start with a light vertical line.

This is your figure's center of gravity.

When you've got that line sketched in, you can add the second, more important gesture line. This is the one that will determine the speed at which your figure is moving. Tilt the gesture line off the center line just a little, and you've got somebody walking, like so.

The angle here determines the speed of the figure.

Now, you might be thinking that this doesn't look like much of anything. Of course, you might be thinking about the crossword puzzle you were trying to solve earlier, and you've just remembered that a 13-letter word for a person who likes to have sex with trees is a dendrophiliac. I can never tell. But assuming that your focus is here, let me add a few sticks and bub-bles to the lines you see here and show you where this is all going.

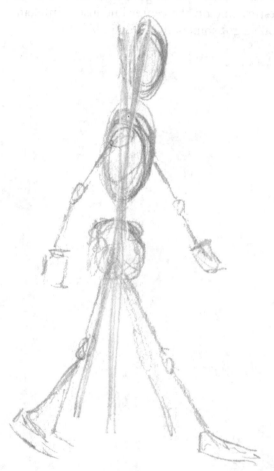

And now, the amazing adventures of Bubble Boy!

And in about 10 seconds flat, you can see the basic structure of the figure. You do an oval for the head, a larger oval for the chest area, another one for the hips, and then wee little tiny ones for the joints, hands, and feet. None of this is meant to do anything but give us a blueprint for the motion of the figure. Try to get the proportions right, of course, but that's mostly just to keep you in the practice of it.

Masters' Musings

"The function of muscle is to pull and not to push, except in the case of the genitals and the tongue."

—Leonardo da Vinci (1452–1519)

You wanna see how this is really going to play out? Alright, let's take it a step further.

Using a darker pencil, I added a few major muscle groups.

The rest I leave up to you. As we move forward with more aggressive forward motion, remember to keep your post-gestures drawings down to simple stick-and-bubble figures. This is all you really need to get the hang of using gesture lines for motion, and it's a technique that will serve you well in other places, too.

Running

Starting with that same vertical guide, let's tilt the gesture line a little further into the wind. The faster your figure is running, the more drastic that tilt will be. You wanna get really drastic just to prove a point? Have a look.

Okay, you've had your fun. Back to work! Let's see what that running gesture line should really look like.

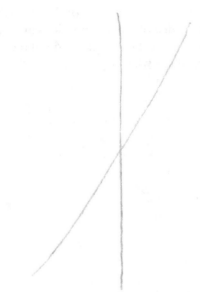

This is more like it.

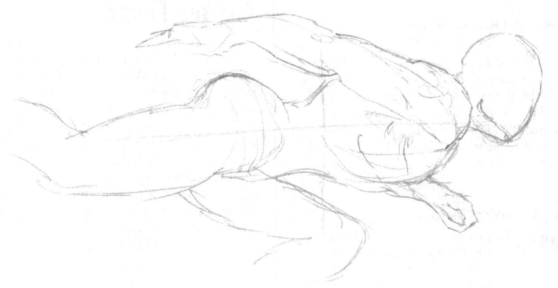

This is an extreme angle, exaggerated to illustrate the point.

Now that we've done one of these, you've got a better idea of what you're looking at, yeah? So let's get those sticks and bubbles working and see what we've got.

He walks! He runs! He misses the bus! Yes, it's Bubble Boy!

Oh, hey. While we're at it, let's practice our foreshortening. In fact, let's go all out with the Bubble Boy. Let's take him running down a corridor, using foreshortening to give it some excitement and depth. And we'll rotate the "camera" while we're at it. This adds another dynamic element.

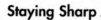 **Staying Sharp**

What's all this talk about a camera? Well, I'm actually not talking about the camera obscura, which you learned about in Chapter 1. Many artists refer to the view in their drawings as though it were a camera's view. It gives you a whole language of terminology to help you describe what you're doing. Almost anyone can follow along.

Look! It's a cheesy 1970s cop drama!

Okay, your turn. Bring on da funk.

And Yes, Flying

As I've mentioned a few times throughout this book, I've had a long relationship with the comic book. And it's probably obvious by now that I've got utter gobs of respect for the folks who draw those things. I know I make a big deal out of drawing from life, but what are you supposed to do when you have an urge to draw something for which there is no reference? How do these guys and gals draw people flying? Well, the truth is that it's done through a process of gesture lines, perspective, foreshortening, and a hard-earned knowledge of anatomy. Here's a quick sample.

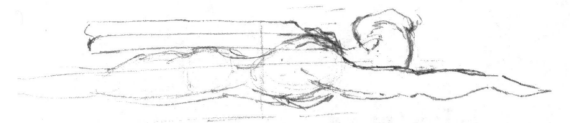

That short line in the center of the drawing is still the center of gravity.

Even though our hero is flying, it doesn't mean that things like wind and gravity don't touch him. Check out that cape: totally a product of the speed that he's flying. If he were to stop moving forward ….

I'd hate to be on the receiving end of that charge.

There aren't a lot of places you can go to learn about the muscles at these odd angles. On the other hand, there are about 14 billion comic books out there. Either way, you already know everything you have to do for these things. Start with your gesture lines. Move on to stick figures and bubbles. Use cylinders and other shapes as needed. Tighten, revise, refine. Now take to the skies!

The Least You Need to Know

Look, Ma! No hands!

The cape hangs the way it does because even though the character is not affected by gravity, his costume is. One of the other great things about drawing a flying character is that you get to do extreme foreshortening shots like this one.

- ◆ The angle of the gesture line suggests the figure's speed of motion.
- ◆ Use simplified skeletons to block in your figures and define their range of motion.
- ◆ Rotate that camera angle to create a more dynamic picture.

In This Chapter

- ◆ Using a model to draw a likeness
- ◆ Getting to know the grid method
- ◆ Fun with photos and Photoshop
- ◆ Exaggerating features to do caricature

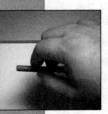

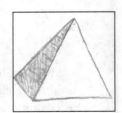

18

Portraiture

In Chapter 13, you learned the fundamentals of drawing the human face. We took a little time to talk about the commonalities among features, regardless of race or age. But now we need to re-examine those concepts. Not because we're going to turn them on their ear, but because, if you're going to draw a person's portrait, you need to also see where people are different.

The challenge in drawing a portrait is not in being able to draw a person's face, but in the skill with which you can draw *that* person's face. And hey, they say that everyone has a twin, right? Well, considering that there are a few billion people on the planet, if only one other person looks just like you, think about how many different faces don't!

Drawing Likenesses: A Special Challenge

Drawing a person's distinct likeness presents a unique challenge for an artist. If people are familiar with the subject, any imperfection in the picture will leap off the page, grab them by the throat, and slap them silly. It's a lot of pressure, so don't get discouraged if you don't get this right the first, oh, few hundred times. This is such a difficult field of study that I've actually heard some instructors recommend including a secondary object such as a plant or a vase in the drawing so that when the portrait goes bad, you'll still have a piece of the drawing that you can be proud of! This could well be the most challenging part of this book, so keep your chin up, keep your eye on the prize, and be prepared to fill your sketchbook with a lot of failed efforts. Unfortunately, there's no easy way to get good at this. It's just going to take practice!

Staying Sharp

Painters in the Renaissance era counted themselves lucky if they could land a gig as the court's official artist. Most of their duties involved painting the royal family, often in a more flattering light. It's very possible that the term "warts and all" referred to a painter offering up a portrait with the lord's imperfections immortalized in oil!

When you decide to try your hand at portraiture, allow me to make a suggestion. Open your daily newspaper and thumb through until you hit the movie show times. On those pages, you'll find at least half a dozen quarter-page ads for your theater's current offerings. The quality on these things is just about what you'd expect from newsprint. It's a little muddy, a dirty kind of gray. But it's also a perfect place to start. All of those images are in stark black and white. You can readily see the shadows, the highlights, the composition. And there's none of that pesky color to distract you!

If that's not your cup of tea (and it's not everyone's), you're left with just four options:

1. Using a mirror to draw self-portraits
2. Having someone sit for you
3. Drawing from photographs
4. Trying to draw from memory

As I showed you a few chapters back, there's a world of difference between your memory of a face and the reality of that face, even when that face is your own. So although option 4 on the list is a legitimate option, let's assume for the moment that you're going to take another avenue here. We've already discussed using a mirror to get features right, so let's look at those other two options.

Having Someone Sit for You

If you can wrangle a family member or friend to sit still for an hour or two, having someone offer a likeness for your studies is an enormously powerful tool in your education—especially if it's someone you know! American illustrator Norman Rockwell often spent quite a bit of time talking to his subjects while he sketched them so that he could get their personality into the paintings. Let that be a lesson to you! A portrait is not strictly a collection of lines in the proper configuration; it's a representation of a person.

Masters' Musings

"I talk as I sketch, too, in order to keep their minds off what I'm doing so I'll get the most natural expression I can from them. Also, the talking helps to size up the subject's personality so I can figure out better how to portray him."

—Norman Rockwell (1894–1978)

It's vital to have a comfortable place for your model to sit for the process. Don't make people stand—that's just cruel. Also, be careful of any pose that makes subjects tilt their eyes or neck at an unnatural angle for any length of time. Ouch!

Luckily, this one came from a photo. No model would sit in this pose for hours.

So, since we're going to show some common courtesy where the comfort of our model is concerned, what's the best way to make use of your subject's time? It's not having the person change poses a hundred times before you find an angle you like, that's for sure. Before your model ever takes a seat, you'll be doing both of you a favor if you do a few thumbnail sketches to try to get a handle on what you're after.

As you start to plan your portrait, throw away any sketch that takes a full-face view. We're not drawing a passport photo here. There's very rarely anything interesting in drawing someone from that angle. (Not never, just rarely. There are exceptions.)

Not the best angle for a winning portrait.

Look to your sketches for something that adheres a little better to the Law of Thirds (see Chapter 4). Also, when placing your model's face in the frame, keep more space in front of the person than behind. Otherwise, you'll end up with an unbalanced portrait.

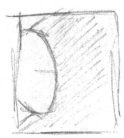

Fifteen minutes of sketches can spare your model hours of discomfort.

Too much space behind the head!

Again, there are exceptions here. For that *Swan Song* book cover pictured in Chapter 4, for example, having the character look backward made that negative space work in my favor. Then again, I didn't have a model straining the optic nerves to make that portrait a reality. So what does that leave you with? Lots of things, actually, but here's a classic.

The classic portrait pose.

This is a pose that has worked for everyone from Napoleon Bonaparte to presidents of the United States. Might be a good place for us to start, too. So, okay, let's say we've settled on a pose for our first portrait. We can get funky with angles and poses later. For now, we've got everything we need to get started with our model. Using your thumbnail sketch as a guide, have your subject take a seat and get comfortable in the pose you've chosen.

I'm fortunate to have such a good-looking subject.

Staying Sharp

Depending on whom you have access to, you'll find that the elderly make fantastic subjects for portraits. Their faces are so full of character (and lines!) that it's often easier to get their likeness right.

When your model is seated and has stopped scratching his or her nose, you can get to work. The process here will be much the same for you, no matter what medium you decide to use. Charcoal portraits can be very nice, as can pastels. For now, though, let's stick with pencil.

Rough in the basic shapes.

Without pressing too hard, do your best to get the basic shape of the person onto the page. Loose, rough shapes will serve you well here. A contour drawing is a great tool for overall body drawings (see Chapter 14), but it's often ill-suited to portraiture.

Make minor adjustments as needed.

This is really the place where you want to make any proportion adjustments. You'll be

much less likely to want to do so later, when you've started to lay down harder lines. It's especially distressing to have rendered and shaded an area only to realize that your once-beautiful model is starting to look like something seen through a funhouse mirror. So take a step back, get a beverage for you and your model, and make your minor corrections now.

Masters' Musings

"I paint self-portraits because I am so often alone, because I am the person I know best."
—Frida Kahlo (1907–1954)

Oh, while we're talking about beverages, and although it's important to keep your model happy, try to keep the influx of liquids to a minimum. Poses are like lightning; they never strike the same place twice. A model who gets up and sits back down again will not be the same model you were drawing a minute ago. The curve of the hair will be different, the sitting angle will alter slightly, and so on. Do your best to get the foundation of your portrait down before you have to let the model up.

Start to refine the features.

Now that you've got the fundamentals of your drawing on the page, it's time to start looking at the specifics. What is it that makes a portrait look like the subject? Where do our faces differ from one another? Obviously, that question has a lot of answers—many, many answers. But here's a quick checklist that might help (see Chapter 13 for more specifics):

◆ Shape of the face

◆ Shape of the eyes and eyelids

◆ Distance of the eyes from each other

◆ Distance of the eyes from the eyebrows

◆ Width and shape of the nose

◆ Shape of the nostrils

◆ Curve of the mouth

◆ Proper distance from eyes to nose to mouth

Looking at the face dead-on, you'll see that a kind of square gets created by the area comprised of the eyebrows, nose, and mouth. If you can nail the elements within that square, you'll be well on your way to mastering the difficult world of portraiture.

Erase extraneous lines and start to polish.

When you've got the features down and you're happy with the results, you can start to attack the hair. Now, don't fool yourself: hair is one of the hardest things to draw. There's no one right way to do it. There are, however, a lot of wrong ways, first among them being trying to draw every single strand of hair individually. You're better off identifying the areas where the hair shines and building around those areas from light to dark.

> **Staying Sharp**
>
> Look to the masters! Having trouble with a particular feature? Find a book on your favorite artist and look at how he or she does it. Ape your favorites until you've got bananas growing out of your nose. Every master you've ever studied has done the same thing. We have all stood on the shoulders of giants!

It takes some practice to master drawing a portrait from a photograph, but you can do it!

To be honest (and perhaps you can tell from this drawing), portraiture has never been my strongest suit. I keep practicing, though, because, like you, that's the only way I'm going to get better!

The Grid Method

There are easier ways to draw a portrait, of course. Some methods will work better for you than they do for other people. Keep experimenting until you find the one that works best for you. One way that might help is the grid method. By dividing your portrait into smaller, more manageable chunks, you're able to focus all your attention on getting just one square right at a time. Have a look at this.

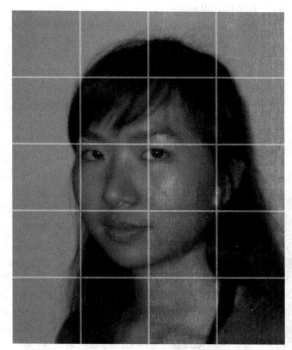

Slice it up!

Now, instead of using just your eyes to measure the proportions and such, you've got a series of guidelines to use. All you need to do now is draw a corresponding number of squares

on your page and then fill them with the images you see on the portrait.

Make sure you get the same number of squares in your sketchbook.

Let's take that on a smaller scale to show you how this relates to what we've been saying all along.

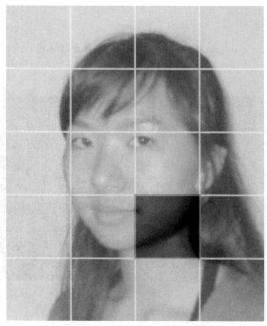

Isolate just one of the grid squares for study and copying.

Remember way back in Chapter 1 when I drew two lines in a rectangle and asked you to duplicate it? Remember how it was important to be mindful of the distance from the edges, to watch the shapes created by the intersection of lines? That's all you're doing here. Heck, that's all we've been doing the whole book! But this is a direct example of that exercise put into practice. Look:

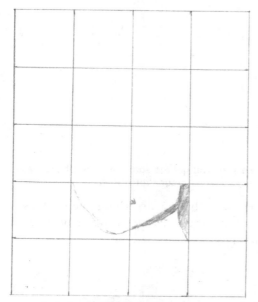

It's a whole lot easier when it's just a little area at a time, isn't it?

From here on out, it's just more of the same. Take each square one at a time. Go into as little or as much detail as you like. In no time at all, you'll be drawing flawless portraits! Well, maybe not flawless, but pretty darned good. So get to it!

Working from Photographs

There are *tons* of advantages to working from photographs. When you're working with a live model, you're limited by your subject's ability to hold a pose comfortably for a decent length of time. Not so with a photograph. You can play with angles, get more daring with light and shadow, and have your subject assume a pose that someone might not be able to hold for more than 10 seconds. As long as you've got that camera ready, you're good to go.

Let me show you a few examples of the kind of shots I mean. These are poses or angles that are simply too hard to do logistically.

A series of hard poses.

In some of these shots, the difficulty is not that the model can't hold the pose, but that the angle for me is too hard to draw from. I'd have to sit on the floor with my sketchbook in my lap and tilt my head back to get the angle. Why put my poor neck through that kind of torture when a simple snapshot does the job for me? Here, let's take one of these and use it for a drawing.

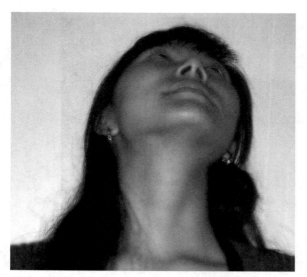

This shot from below is an atypical portrait pose, but that's part of what makes it work.

The process here is much the same as it was in the other examples. We're going to take this from basic shapes, through roughs, into tighter pencils and finally finished shading. Follow along!

I'm just roughing in basic shapes. I pay special attention to the blocking of the nose and other facial features because they overlap in interesting ways here.

Lay in a few details.

Clean it up a bit.

In no time at all, we have a finished portrait.

I've got one more trick up my sleeve where photos are concerned, but it warrants its own section. Follow me.

A Useful Trick in Photoshop

Okay, this one is not for everyone. You need the following special equipment to tackle this exercise:

- A digital camera, or a photo you'd like to work with and a scanner
- Adobe Photoshop (any version will do)

If you've got these things, then by all means, press on! If you don't, you can skip ahead to the next section.

Bear in mind that some of the other photo-editing software out there will probably do you in a pinch, but I don't know them well enough to talk you through them. If you can apply what I say here to that program, more power to you!

First things first. Let's select a photo to manipulate. I browsed through some of the shots I snapped in the earlier photo session and selected one to modify.

Nothing special about this photo, but I wanted something that needed a little more contrast.

Convert the picture to a grayscale image (if it isn't one already) by going to the menus at the top and selecting Image, Mode, Grayscale.

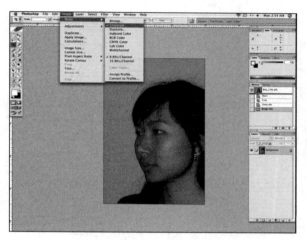

Change to grayscale.

From there, the process is pretty simple. We're going to play around with Levels a bit. There are a few ways to do this, but for the neophyte, here's the simplest: Image, Adjustments, Levels.

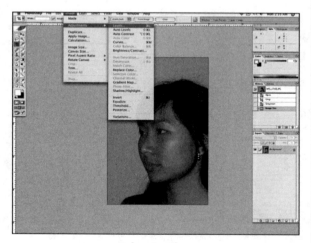

Select Levels.

From here, it's pretty simple. We're going to drag the two sliders on the outside edges of the graph toward the center. You don't want to smack them into the middle; bring them gradually

inward until the picture has an exaggerated contrast. We don't want to blow it out to pure white, but we want to create some shapes that are easier to mimic.

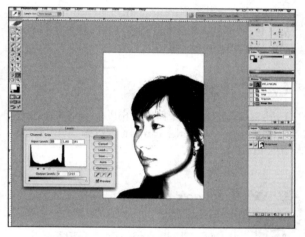

Bring the sliders in toward the middle.

The whole point of this exercise is to use the program to force us to see the image differently. When you jack up the contrast like this, you can see clearly defined shapes where before there was only a smooth gradation of tone.

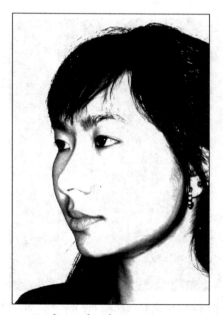

Duplicate the shapes you see.

I've always found it easier to draw from a drawing of a hand than a photograph of a hand. That's because someone else has taken the guesswork out of it. With this little trick in Photoshop, it's much the same. If you find yourself struggling with a certain aspect of a drawing and you're working from a photo, give this trick a try. It might make all the difference for you.

Caricature

Let's do a *caricature!* Some folks, such as political cartoonists, make quite a decent living at this kind of thing.

Layman's Lingo

A **caricature** is a portrait done in which the subject's features are exaggerated, often to comedic effect.

You ready over there? Let's give it a try together. First, let's start with me making a funny face.

My mother always warned me my face would stick like this.

Okay, it's a goofy face. Back off. But hopefully the goofiness will make it a little easier to exaggerate.

Geez, this almost drew itself.

You know, back in school they used to call me Fradella Gorilla.

You might find that doing a caricature of someone makes it easier to draw that person in a more traditional fashion. The exaggeration of the more obvious features will help train your eye all the more.

The Least You Need to Know

◆ Drawing portraits requires extra attention. You're not just trying to draw a nose anymore; now that nose belongs to a specific person. That makes it unique in all the world. Be patient with yourself and use that artist's eye!

◆ Don't choose any pose for your subject that would prove difficult to maintain unless you've got a camera handy.

◆ Dividing your portrait into grids can really help focus your eye.

◆ A caricature can get you to see your subject's obvious features.

In This Part

Part 5

Drawing Other Animals

The final part already? Man, you just flew through this book! Well, lucky for you, there are a few exercises inside so you can draw other things that fly, too. In these final pages, we'll take a little tour through various stages of the animal kingdom. But don't think that when you get through these last few pages you're done. Far from it. There's still a whole world out there waiting to be drawn. Let's see a little more of it before we're done. Follow me!

In This Chapter

- ◆ Basic anatomy of dogs and cats
- ◆ Drawing the hair
- ◆ Taking your sketch to the next level

     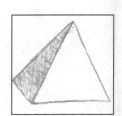

Chapter 19

Starting with Household Pets

Hey, you made it! You passed all that pesky human being stuff. Now it's time to venture forth into the animal kingdom. Before we get ourselves a pith helmet and head out on safari, let's take a stab at some of our domestic pets: dogs and cats. And, uh, I don't mean a literal "stab," people. Keep the pointy pencils and pens away from the pooches and pussycats. M'kay? Groovy.

Spot and Fluffy: Loose Drawings

Have you got a dog or a cat handy? For the next few exercises, it'll help to have access to something that walks on four legs. I suppose you could substitute a hamster or a ferret in a pinch, but let's steer clear of any kind of lizard for now. There's a whole chapter on those creatures later, and I don't want you to have nothing to do when we get there. Of course, if you don't have a dog or cat, an option is to go to your local pet store and take your sketchbook with you. You won't need a chair or anything. We're just going to start off doing loose sketches right now. Like so.

Each of these sketches took me less than five minutes.

These really aren't much different than the ball and stick figure drawings that I did for human beings. Some of them are closer to contour drawings, but the principle is the same. All I'm looking for here is rough sketches. I want the gesture of the animal on the page: the basic curve of the spine, the position of the paws. All we're doing right now is learning the anatomy.

The canine anatomy, courtesy of Sticks & Bubbles, serving your art needs since 40 million B.C.E.

And, just to give them equal time …

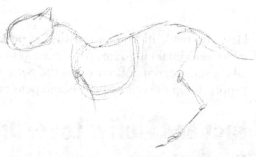

The feline anatomy. Not all that different, is it?

Now obviously, if you want to know the precise bone structure of these wee beasties, you'll have to refer to another book. There's not a lot of call for drawings of skeleton cats, but if that's your thing, who am I to judge you?

Anyway, unless you've never seen one of these animals, much of this will be intuitive for you. Then again, you've been looking at yourself and other human beings all your life, and how well do you know their anatomy?

Kind of weird the way their knees bend backward, isn't it?

One of the first things you'll have to get used to when drawing *quadrupeds* is that their hind legs have knees that bend in the opposite direction of ours. There are very few exceptions to this rule (we'll get to one of them later). And of course, they can do things with their hind legs that we can't.

Layman's Lingo

Quadrupeds refers to anything that walks on four legs. Folks like you and me who walk on two legs are called bipeds.

You can't say they're not clean.

How else are dogs and cats different? Well, yeah, they've got paws. Have a look at their paw prints. The dog's is on the left, and the cat's is on the right.

Book 'em, Dano.

Ultimately, I suppose, you could make the argument that our pets have much the same stuff going on that we do. They've got the same number of eyes, same number of ears, a nose, a mouth, a tail … wait, no tail. Sorry.

And thereby hangs a tail!

Another thing that's worthy of some of your sketching time is the ears. Like tails, ears are almost as diverse and unique as the personalities of the animals themselves. My dog, Max, for example, can speak volumes with a raise of his ears. It's really kind of amazing! The ears have a kind of triangular shape on cats, but on dogs, that triangle shape is coupled with a kind of half-lock drape fold on some breeds.

The ears of a cat.

My dog's ears. Your dog's might be different.

Sketch in the outline.

Draw the eyeball itself.

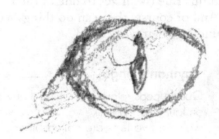

Lay in that iris.

Watch what happens to your cat's eye when light hits it. That iris in the center utterly collapses.

Bright light! Bright light!

Staying Sharp

There's not much chance of learning how to draw a dog's ears without seeing a whole bunch of them. A Doberman's bobbed ears are radically different from the ears on a basset hound or a cocker spaniel. They might as well be different species. Still, if you decide this is an area of study you'd like to pursue, check your local newspapers for dog parks in the area. You can go there on a weekend and sketch a wide variety of dogs to your heart's content.

Hey, what about those eyes, huh? The cat's eyes, in particular, are worthy of attention: they don't have a round iris. Come on, give it a try.

Say, remember when I said that it's sometimes easier to draw a drawing of something than to draw the something that it represents? (Does that make sense?) Well, let's put that theory to the test. I'm going to do a quick, simple study of a sleeping kitty. What I want you to do is draw the study I've drawn. Just do your best to mimic the energy of the sketch. I don't want you to copy me, per se. Just do a rough sketch of my rough sketch. Got that?

Just a couple of circles and a triangle or two!

Why did I want you to do that? Because when you're looking at a live animal, you've got the brain working overtime trying to identify the edges, the light source, the shadow, the hair, the spine … it never ends. Now and then you need to see the thing as the simple object it really is. Now take a few minutes and sketch your own kitty!

Drawing your pets while they're sleeping is obviously a lot easier than drawing them in motion. Except for the occasional paw twitch as they dream, you've got a basically motionless model. Of course, if you get really good at gesture lines and contour drawing, you might do pretty well if they're standing at the water bowl for a few long seconds.

Masters' Musings

"I can't work without a model. I won't say I turn my back on nature ruthlessly in order to turn a study into a picture, arranging the colors, enlarging and simplifying; but in the matter of form I am too afraid of departing from the possible and the true."

—Vincent van Gogh (1853–1890)

Remember the most important lesson of all: have fun!

Getting the Hang of Hair

You can't look at dogs and cats for any length of time without noticing the hair. I mean, there's a lot of it. If you live with these creatures, you know this to a level I don't have to explain. It's everywhere. You can't escape it. I still don't know how it gets in the ice cubes. But, hey, if you want to learn how to draw animals, you're gonna have to get the hang of hair sooner or later. Might as well do it now.

Go with the flow.

The key to drawing hair on anything, from your cat to your Aunt Gertrude, is to find the flow of the hair and use as few lines as possible to suggest that movement. You've heard me say this before, but you don't want to draw every single strand of hair.

Here you need to concentrate on only the bottom fringe.

One of the most important tricks you'll learn in regard to drawing hair (and this works in other places, too) is to use your eraser to lift off the graphite after you've covered an area. This helps create that shine of the hair. You might also use that when doing the reflections in eyes. The applications are endless.

I used the tip of the eraser to lift out the shine in this guy's hair. He doesn't seem all that happy about it.

Pet Portraits: Refining a Rougher Work

Ready to take all this to the next level? Sure you are. Your fingers are almost literally itching to take this to the next level; I can feel it from here. So look back over the quick sketches you've done or draw a new one, and we'll get started.

Here's a quick sketch of my doggie.

There's nothing different here about this sketch. I used a combination of techniques, from contour lines to gesture lines to quick scribbling—anything to get the basic gist of it onto the page before he moved. Unless they're sleeping, animals aren't exactly prone to long periods where they'll just sit perfectly still and let you draw them. No, it's more like, "So you thought I would sit still and let you draw me,

Mr. Bond? Ha ha! You fool! This has all been part of my elaborate plan to drive you mad!" Or maybe only *my* pets sound like Ernst Stavro Blofeld. Hard to say.

Cleaned up a bit.

I was kind of all over the place with my rough sketches, so before moving on, I decided to erase some of the lines I knew I wasn't going to use. Erasing is drawing, too!

Adding some features.

Before you start laying in that mountain of hair, make sure you've got all your proportions right. If you're happy with the progress on that score, add some details and step back to see where you're at.

Staying Sharp

Some folks say you should spend just as much time on the hair in your drawing as you do the whole of the face. This applies to both humans and animals! Your mileage may vary, of course.

Finally, one of the obvious advantages to drawing domestic pets is that you don't need their permission. You can ask them, sure, but cats are particularly finicky when you do. Oh, and if you have pets of the feline variety, be prepared to have them do their very best to get between you and your sketchbook. This is why most of my sketches are of cats while they're asleep! Good luck!

Takin' it home.

The Least You Need to Know

◆ Dogs and cats have similar skeletons. A few differences exist, but they're mostly external.

◆ When it comes to hair, go with the flow. Find the contour of the hair's movement and let your pencil strokes follow it.

◆ Before you start adding the animal's hair, make sure you've got all your proportions right.

In This Chapter

- ◆ An introduction to basic equine anatomy
- ◆ A passing glance at pachyderms
- ◆ Using toys to substitute for live models

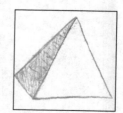

Chapter 20

Other Things That Walk on Four Legs

Given the size of our planet, I'd need a book roughly the size of Montana to cover every animal that walks on four legs. I mean, think about it. Dogs and cats we've covered in the previous chapter, but what about raccoons? Opossum? Rabbits? You can't forget about lions and tigers and bears (oh, my!), either.

But aside from the fact that we don't have the room to cover every animal, and the indisputable fact that my hand would literally fall off if I tried to draw all of them, I think you'll find (if you were to do the research) that many animals are more similar than they are different. You'll notice a symmetry in their construction that defies the borders of species. There are always two legs out in front. Two legs behind. The head? Always on top. Sure, there's the odd mutation or two here and there, but far and away, the four-legged animals of this blue marble follow much the same principles—even the cranky badgers.

Okay, so there are exceptions to the rule.

In this chapter, we take a look at one of the most popular and beloved animals: the horse. We also have a quick run around the elephant and see what makes his anatomy so unique.

Horses, of Courses

Horses! Boy, that brings back memories. Say, did I ever tell you about that summer I spent learning to ride horses? Well, I did. Of course, that was … uh, geez … like 25 years ago. So not really relevant. But it does give me a little firsthand knowledge about horses. Not much, but any real-life connection you have to something you're trying to draw can only be helpful.

![Staying Sharp]

Staying Sharp

When it comes to finding references for animals, nothing will be easier for you than the horse. People have a love affair with horses, and finding inspiration to draw from is never farther away than your Web browser. Badgers, not so much. Just be sure to keep your child-safe options turned on. There are some images from Tijuana that nobody should have to see.

What constantly amazes me about horses is that their massive body weight is supported by these really scrawny-looking legs. So first, let's have a look at the basic shapes that make up that body.

The basic wedge shape.

This area sits right behind the horse's head and neck. This area represents the section the front legs play into.

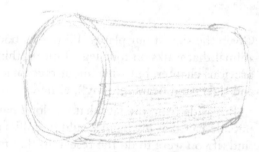

Your basic cylinder.

This is the horse's belly and midsection. But you probably figured that out already. Just one more.

A "saddle" shape.

And here we've got the hind quarters. Looking at these three things, you might be able to put them together in your head and get the sense of a horse, but let's put it into actual practice and see where that gets us.

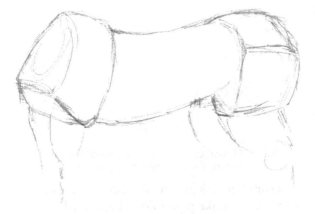

The basic shapes assembled.

Here's a perfect example of why it's important to "draw through" your object. By lining up these shapes and keeping their perspective consistent, you'll be able to draw the horse from almost any angle you want.

A page ripped from my sketchbook.

This sketch was done in about two and a half minutes. When you understand the basic shapes involved in the creation of an object, turning that thing upside down or sideways gets that much easier. So let's try that together, shall we? Let's turn these three shapes in a direction so that we've got some foreshortening and see what that yields us. (Don't remember what foreshortening is? Check back to Chapter 6 for a refresher.)

Masters' Musings

"My mother said to me, 'If you are a soldier, you will become a general. If you are a monk, you will become the Pope.' Instead, I was a painter, and became Picasso."

—Pablo Picasso (1881–1973)

You can add the head, neck, and legs, if you want.

How about one more? This one from behind.

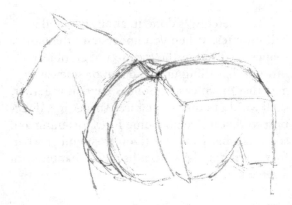

Easier than you thought it would be, yes?

I'm just roughing in the head here, so let's take a few minutes to really get a look at the construction of the thing.

Masters' Musings

"For me, an object is something living. This cigarette or this box of matches contains a secret life much more intense than that of certain human beings."

—Joan Miro (1893–1983)

It's not nearly as tough as you think it is. What we're looking at is a tapered cylinder with a diamond shape in the upper quadrant.

Like I said, just a tapered cylinder.

Add that diamond shape. You can already see where the eyes are going to go.

From here it's just details, isn't it? Those ears are a lot like pipe folds—kind of like tulips, if you're a flower lover.

Adding ears and other details.

Good job! Now let's have a look at that head from the side. This one's even easier, although we do add a circular shape to the mix for the horse's jaw. Have a look.

Staying Sharp

When you start to draw horses and other animals from reference, try to forget that you're looking at a horse. You need to short-circuit that portion of your brain that is interpreting the image for you so that you can see what's really there. Ultimately, you'd like there to be a direct conduit from your eyes to your hand.

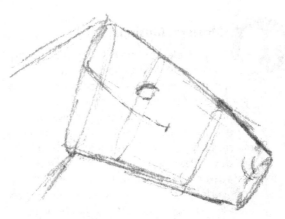

There's that line I was talking about.

The rest is just details. That line we drew in earlier provided the base line for the ears. Also note that the ear on the opposite side of the head is still visible, even though it's partially hidden.

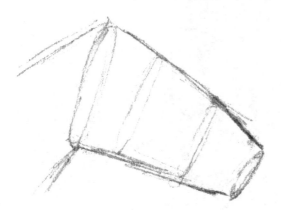

Just another tapered cylinder!

See how I keep breaking up the head into three parts like that? Draw a line from the upper middle of the head down to the center of that middle area. That's where your jowly section will go.

Don't exaggerate that jaw too much!

Great job on this. From here you should have a good foundation for drawing our equine friends. Use your gesture lines, build up your shapes, and have fun with it!

Masters' Musings

"My whole life has been spent walking by the side of a bottomless chasm, jumping from stone to stone. Sometimes I try to leave my narrow path and join the swirling mainstream of life, but I always find myself drawn inexorably back towards the chasm's edge, and there I shall walk until the day I finally fall into the abyss. For as long as I can remember, I have suffered from a deep feeling of anxiety which I have tried to express in my art. Without anxiety and illness, I should have been like a ship without a rudder."

—Edvard Munch (1863–1944)

Elephants and Those Crazy Knees

Where elephants differ from nearly every other quadruped is the fact that all their knees bend the same way. Horses, lions, dogs … they've all got their hind legs reversed in the knee department. Not so our gentle giants!

Just a quick anatomy sketch.

I feel that I should come clean at this point. I don't want to mislead anyone. You see, I don't have a pet elephant. Nor was I able to find one at the local Wal-Mart (and I thought they had everything!). I checked the parks, the ice cream parlors, the nut factories—all to no avail. Luckily, though, while I was at the toy store, I found a very lifelike replica of an elephant. That's what I'll be drawing from for these lessons.

You can get more than just elephants at your local toy retailer. Want to practice proportions and anatomy? Try the action figure aisle. Snakes? They've got them in rubber. Want to practice hair or fashion? Most of these places have a whole Barbie aisle. You'll be amazed what you can find in a toy store.

They sure are wrinkly.

When refining the details of your sketch, the number-one thing you need to be aware of is that an elephant's skin drapes over its body. It bunches, it folds, it wrinkles, almost like fabric does. If you approach an elephant from this point of view, you'll have an easier time spotting the creases.

The elephant's trunk is really versatile. It can rise up, double back on itself, spray water, pick up nuts, and hug people. Imagine if your nose could do that; the industry for facial tissues would go nuclear!

Another signature feature of the elephant is their ears. Have a go at the following drawing and note the sharp edges.

The basic shapes of an elephant's head.

Okay, forget the knees for a minute. When somebody says the word *elephant*, you don't yell, "Knees!" No, usually you say, "Where?!" But after they've explained that there isn't actually an elephant nearby, you realize that your first thoughts of elephants are usually about their ears and their trunks.

A closer look at the elephant's ear.

A few trunk studies.

Bear in mind that the elephant I'm drawing here is of the African variety. Asian elephants have much smaller ears. And they're okay with that.

Toys as Models

If you're of a mind to draw animals, there's a few places you can go. Zoos, of course, are an option, but don't discount your local shopping mall. Not that you're likely to find any free-range lions there, but you might find some good models lurking in the toy store.

I'm going to do a few quick sketches of my toy elephant now. You can follow along, or pick one that you like and turn it into a more finished piece. The choice is yours.

The Asian elephant.

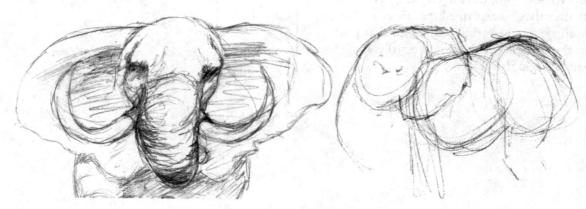

My little toy elephant.

The Least You Need to Know

◆ Horse bodies have three major shapes in them.

◆ Unlike in most other quadrupeds, an elephant's knees all bend in the same direction.

◆ Use toys as reference for hard-to-find subjects.

In This Chapter

- ◆ Understanding a bird's anatomy
- ◆ "Drawing through" the bird to visualize its far wing and other tricks
- ◆ A closer look at a bird's wing

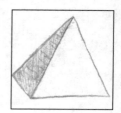

Chapter 21

Birds of a Feather

I'm sure you've heard this about a zillion times, but since the day when man first stood erect (which was a Tuesday, I think), nothing has quite captured our imagination like the power of flight. There's a little bit of jealousy on our parts, isn't there? Sure, none of us would ever want to have to live outside during a hurricane, or smack beak first into a sliding glass door that somebody cleaned too well. But on the whole, being a bird looks pretty cool. Okay, not the worms. But think about your commute to work: no traffic!

In reality, we think of movement within our worlds on only two axes: forward and backward, left and right. Our whole system of movement is based on this. Think about any place you've ever gone by car, boat, scooter, skateboard, or foot. Now add a third dimension to that travel. Imagine if, on your morning gridlocked commute, you could lift yourself up and over that three-car pile-up a few miles ahead. Do birds have midair collisions? I honestly don't know, but I've never seen one. It is, after all, a pretty big sky up there.

The thing that I find most utterly absorbing about birds is the sheer endlessness of their variety. There are some huge birds, some really massive beasts, such as the ostrich. Then there are finches, hummingbirds, and sparrows. Think about the size difference between these species and just take a moment to imagine humans being so varied. Can you imagine if our biggest people were 50 to 100 times the size of our smallest? That would be like *Attack of the 50-Foot Woman*—but bigger! So look, I'm not going to have time to show you how to draw every species of bird on the planet. No book could do that without coming complete with a motorized hand cart to help you get it around. So let's start off with a look at the basics, shall we? Good!

A Quick Look at Our Feathered Friends

For the sake of consistency, let's restrict our studies to the birds that can fly. Sorry, penguins.

Masters' Musings

"For once you have tasted flight, you will walk the earth with your eyes turned skywards, for there you have been and there you will long to return."

—Leonardo da Vinci (1452–1519)

A hummingbird.

Just as all human beings have some common equipment, the same holds true for birds. Consider our hummingbird sketch. We've got a head, a beak, two wings, little bitty legs and feet, and tail feathers. Come on, you try.

Star with a few circles.

Add the roughly triangular wings.

Lay in the details.

Erase your guides.

Your last step should be to further refine and render the drawing. If you can find a piece of reference to work from, you'll be better off, of course. This drawing of the hummingbird shows the hummingbird with its wings frozen in flight. In reality, the wings of these things beat like a million times a second. They're an absolute blur—but we can worry about that at another time. I certainly wouldn't be helping you learn how to draw if I just scribbled in some blurry lines where the wings ought to be!

 Staying Sharp

Really interested in birds? There are a ton of bird-watching organizations in the world. Chances are, you'll find one near you!

When drawing birds, unless you catch them at just the right angle, you're going to only see part of one of the wings. Get used to doing that draw-through!

Note how the back wing is partially blocked.

You can always erase lines later, but if you don't draw through the objects that obstruct your view, sooner or later you're going to be sorry—very, very sorry. But, hey, what about birds that aren't flying?

Draw through that top wing.

I chose this angle so that you could see how a bird's wings interact when they're at rest. They fold over one another, but don't let that hidden one just end at the top wing. Draw through it so that you can retain a sense of depth. Trust me, your drawings will show the benefit of this effort.

Rough in the features a bit.

A bird at rest has always impressed me as something like a squat bowling pin in shape. Or, oh! I know! Like this:

A martini shaker! Look familiar?

When you get the basic shapes on the page, you need to spend quite a bit of time getting the details right. Feathers are like leaves, though: you don't need to draw each and every one of them for someone to know what you're drawing.

Sometimes the suggestion of feathers is enough.

You could ignore that advice, you know. From the very first page of this book to the last, you could ignore it all. You could strike out on your own and make up the rules as you go along. I wouldn't wish that kind of torture on my worst enemy, but perhaps it's best if you look at these lessons as a kind of buffet. Take what you want. Leave the rest. And don't forget to tip your waitress; she does more than keep that water glass filled, believe me.

Masters' Musings

"What I am looking for … is an immobile movement, something which would be the equivalent of what is called the eloquence of silence, or what St. John of the Cross, I think it was, described with the term 'mute music.'"

— Joan Miro (1893–1983)

If you want to spend hours building in the most minute detail, do it! But get here first. Walk before you run. Get the hang of sketching and drawing basic shapes and the like. Learn perspective. If, after you've mastered all these things, you want to start putting women's noses in the middle of guitars, who am I to stop you?

Just another wavy line? Not quite.

It's not often that you get to watch a bird fly in slow motion—or, better yet, stop motion. But if you have a look at the following figure, it might just help you with the basic motions that some birds go through when they soar through the air.

The flight path.

Anatomy of a Bird's Wing

At the end of the day, what fascinates us about birds is their wings. We've taken a few stabs at roughing in the basic shapes, but what we really need to do right now is get a better grip on the three parts of a bird's wing. You ready? Let's fly!

Don't forget this part!

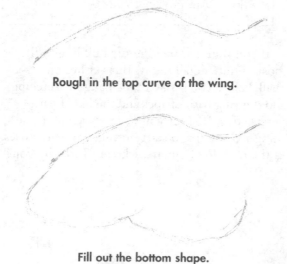

Rough in the top curve of the wing.

Fill out the bottom shape.

These feathers on the outside are very much like fingers.

I didn't include running commentary on this last bit because I think the pictures speak for themselves. That being said, take a closer look at that last illustration. Those shorter feathers right beneath the bone structure are all kinds of important. Feathers don't spring out in one long spray from the upper section. They kind of waterfall down in a cascade effect. Remember that!

Staying Sharp

You want to sketch birds in the wild? You're gonna need to be fast! These suckers won't sit still for very long, which makes them perfect target practice for your gesture lines.

The Least You Need to Know

◆ Birds, like everything else, can be broken down into simpler shapes in order to draw them.

◆ Drawing through the body of the bird will help you get the partially hidden wings right.

◆ A flying bird's wings have certain parts, including a tiered feather system.

In This Chapter

- ◆ Using wavy gesture lines
- ◆ Seeing the common *S* shapes
- ◆ Drawing things that no longer exist

 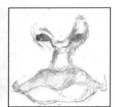    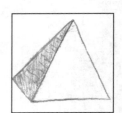

Fish and Reptiles

There's a pretty convincing argument for the fact that dinosaurs once walked the earth. Now, whether or not you buy into that theory is irrelevant; it's still a cool concept. I know that everybody gets hopped up on the T-Rex, but I dig the brontosaurus, man. Those things were *huge*, and they were vegetarians. I find that whole thing rather amusing. So for this, our last chapter together (*sniff*), let's have a look at things that slither, things that swim, and gigantic things that once left footprints roughly the size of Texas.

Things That Swim

Here's another one of those species that ranges in size from the miniscule to the immense. All the way from minnows to blue whales, fish are the occupants of the oceans, rivers, streams, and, and, uh, some other wet thing! One of my favorite kinds of fish to draw is koi. These are Asian goldfish, and they can get pretty big. They'll actually grow to accommodate the body of water they occupy (within reason), and they come in a variety of fruit flavors—err, colors. I've always enjoyed the treatment of these things within Chinese brush paintings, so let's do a project that kind of emulates that style. First things first: let's create the stage where our little scene is going to take place.

Masters' Musings

"In printmaking, I essentially use the same process as in painting: with one important exception to try, with sensitivity to the medium, to emphasize what printing can do best ... better than, say, painting or collaging or watercolor or drawing or whatever. Otherwise, the artist expresses the same vision in graphics that he does in his other work."

—Robert Motherwell (1915–1991)

Don't spend a lot of time trying to get this frame exactly right. Don't use a ruler or anything now; I just want you to rough it in. We'll go back over it later with a heavier hand.

Staying Sharp

Creating the frame first forces you to adjust the scale of your drawing to accommodate the given area. Comic book artists have to do this all the time. In fact, each comic book panel is its own little canvas.

Now that we've got our frame roughed in, let's drop in a couple of wavy lines to use as gesture lines. Fish are naturally designed to work with the existing currents in a river or stream. It only makes sense that a wavy gesture line would serve our purposes very well here.

A long, narrow frame is the perfect canvas for this picture.

Looong, wavy lines. These will be your gesture lines.

Believe it or not, the really hard part is already over. No, seriously. Not only have you created the space in which your scene will occur, but you've also created a rhythmic flow within that picture. Now all you need to do is place two or three koi within the scene, using the gesture lines to define their posture. At this stage, I'm not worried about the scales or the fins. I just want to rough in the basic teardrop shape of these critters.

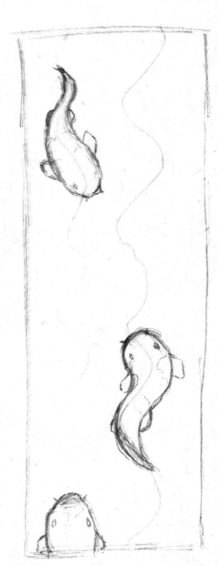

The koi have two sets of fins. Be sure to get them both.

Okay, before we go any further, let's clean up a bit, eh? Let's start by erasing those gesture lines so we can see the empty space that exists within the frame.

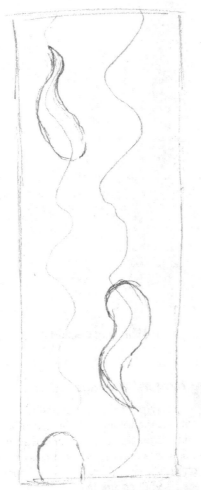

Just lay your shapes on the existing gesture lines. That's what they're there for!

Look at that! You're almost there! Now we can start laying in some details.

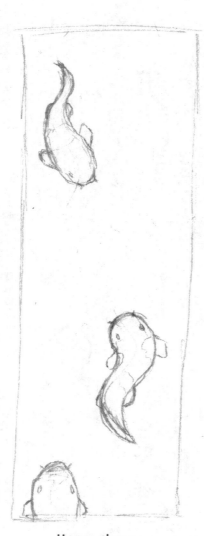

Hmmm, cleaner.

Ahhh, that's better!

Good job. Now that we've got a clear shot at these things, let's finalize those last remaining details, such as the eyes, whiskers, and color splotches. While we're at it, we can show a few scales here and there to add a little realism to the illusion.

Masters' Musings

"Never permit a dichotomy to rule your life, a dichotomy in which you hate what you do so you can have pleasure in your spare time. Look for a situation in which your work will give you as much happiness as your spare time."

—Pablo Picasso (1881–1973)

Depending on how big or small you made your koi in the picture, you may decide to add a lily pad or two to fill in some dead areas. Either way, you may want to shade in that negative space with a little tone to help the koi pop more. Don't be afraid to use your eraser to give it some variance. Water isn't static!

Fill in that negative space!

Great job! Oh, but before we move on, let me show you a quick trick for getting realistic scales. First, lay down a row of small circles

that are all roughly the same size. The sides of the circles should butt right up against one another. Do *not* press down hard at this stage.

The size of the circles will, of course, depend on the size of the fish they're going on.

Next, we want to create a second row that overlaps that first one. On this row, however, we want the circles to shift just a little bit to one side so that the center of the new circle is lined up with the ends of the circles above it.

Offset the second row by half a circle's width.

Good job, good job. Just one more.

Second verse, same as the first!

This is good enough to illustrate the point (that was an unintentional pun, I swear). What we want to do now is erase what we just did. No, really. Not completely. We want enough of it to remain so that we can use it for guides. If you feel confident that you can erase only those areas you don't need, feel free. At some point, though, the size of your drawing will prohibit that kind of detail work. After you've erased your lines, now's the time to go back in and draw in only those lines that you need to make the scales. Like so ….

Scales!

Things That Slither

As I've mentioned, I live in South Florida. Yes, hurricanes are a problem here, but the other thing they don't mention when you're crossing into the state with all your worldly belongings in a U-Haul is that they've got two snakes here that look virtually identical. But one of them will *kill you* if it bites you—kill you dead.

So imagine my surprise and concern when I'm walking my dog one night and I come across this snake that is ... well ... he could be either one. I have no idea. There's this stupid rhyme you're supposed to know to help you identify this thing. Something like, "If black touches red, you're better off dead; if red touches yellow, you're a lucky fellow," or some such. And, of course, while I'm standing there trying to remember how the verse goes, the snake is looking at me as if to say, "Look, mate, are you almost done? Not to rush you or anything, but I am on a bit of a schedule, you know? People to bite, places to see, and all that." (Why he was talking with a British accent I'll never know.)

Staying Sharp

Before I inadvertently get somebody killed, the *real* rhyme goes like this: "Red touches yellow, kill a fellow; red touches black, good for Jack." Know it. Learn it. Live by it.

You probably noticed in the koi exercise that the gesture lines were little more than modified and extended *S* shapes. You'll find that pattern a lot in the gestures of snakes and fish. But instead of just drawing a snake lying flat on the ground, let's get one that's raising his head to say, "Hello." Follow me, and step where I step.

Rough in the shape of the head.

What is a snake's head? It's really just an exaggerated tapered cylinder. Draw yourself a smaller shape in the lower center of your head and let that serve as your "snout."

The "snout."

Good! Now let's rough in the eyes and start to get the rest of the body going. Don't forget the nostrils.

Eyes, body, nostrils.

And last but not least, let's flesh out the rest of that body, shall we?

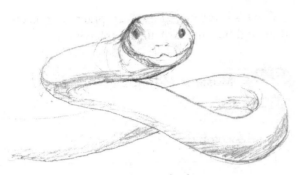

Finishing the body.

Okay, one more quickie with these forked-tongue devils and then we've gotta hit the time machine. Ready?

Think of it like a spiral fold.

Snakes like to hang out in trees sometimes. The trick here is to get the hang of wrapping them around the branch itself (another unintentional pun). Remember to draw through! Don't just copy what I've done. Build the snake!

The rest is just shading!

Really, once you got the snake wrapped around the branch in a realistic fashion, there was simply nothing left to do but lay down some graphite and add depth. Sssssssssspectacular!

Things That Are Extinct

Here we are, the last exercise in the book. You've made it! And it was worth it. The sleepless nights, the messy apartment, the ulcers, the fights with loved ones. No, wait—that was me. But you, my friend, you have done the impossible and that makes you mighty. (Bonus points if you can name the movie.) So how do we end? Why, at the beginning, of course. Not down at the single-celled organism stage, but just a few short million years later. We end with the noble brontosaurus. Ach, laddie, we hardly knew ye!

Hey! There's that S shape again!

Once again, my mail-order brontosaurus didn't show up as promised, so I'm flying without a net. On the plus side, if this is not what a brontosaurus looks like, who's going to know?

Refine a bit. Note the creases at the back of the neck.

And one last bit of scribbling ….

That's it for me, kids. Keep practicing, keep drawing, but, most of all, keep having fun!

Masters' Musings

"I never achieved what I set out to do as fully as it filled my mind."

—Leonardo da Vinci (1452–1519)

And we're done.

The Least You Need to Know

◆ There's a common *S* shape in many fish and reptiles.

◆ Scales overlap—draw them that way.

◆ Don't forget to draw through your hidden parts!

Appendix A

Recommended Reading

Here you'll find a bunch of books, names, and websites that I recommend you peruse at your leisure. This list is *highly* subjective. These are the things I like, the stuff that has helped me. Pick up any one of them, and you might see the direct influence of what I learned.

Far and away, the best way to learn to draw is to draw. You can read about art all you want, but there's just no substitute for doing it. That being said, find a bunch of artists whose work you just adore. Study it. Then copy it. Ape it down to the last line and freckle. Do this with one artist, and you'll come off as a fake. Do it with a dozen of them, and you'll see them meld into an amalgam style that's all yours.

Here's what switches me on:

◆ *The World of Art*, by Sandra Forty (Collins & Brown, 2000). I found this monster hard-cover on sale for pennies at my local Barnes & Noble, or you can look for it online at www.amazon.com. It's a full-color opus on art from the dawn of time to present. Grab it if you can find it.

◆ *Bernie Wrightson's Frankenstein: Or the Modern Prometheus*, by Mary Wollstonecraft Shelley and Bernie Wrightson (Underwood-Miller, 1995). This must be seen to be believed. It's the most astonishing work of cross-hatching done in the last 50 years or more.

◆ *Icon*, *Legacy*, *Testament*, by various authors (Underwood Books, 2001). This three-book series shows the amazing work of fantasy art master Frank Frazetta. Visceral and amazing. Real ground-breaking stuff.

- *Bridgman's Complete Guide to Drawing From Life: Over 1,000 Illustrations*, by George B. Bridgman (Sterling, 2001). This is the master who the masters learned from. Look through Frazetta's sketchbooks, and you'll see him aping Bridgman.

- *Kingdom Come*, by Mark Waid and Alex Ross (DC Comics, 1997). Pick up this graphic novel to see Alex Ross turn gods into real people. An astonishing work of art. The story by Mark Waid is original and compelling. The two of them together add up to something extraordinary.

- The works of Alphonse Mucha. The undisputed master of nouveau art. Breathtaking simplicity of line and form.

- *The Complete Idiot's Guide to Drawing People Illustrated*, by Brenda Hoddinott (Alpha Books, 2004). Another great book in this series, this one focuses solely on drawing people. Worth your time and money.

- *Facial Expressions: A Visual Reference For Artists*, by Mark Simon (Watson-Guptill Publications, 2005). This is one of the bibles in my own studio. I met the author at a convention once, and he's a super nice guy.

- *Spectrum 1–12* (Underwood Books, 2003 and on). This series of full-color books edited by Cathy and Arnie Fenner features the most jaw-dropping talent extant. An essential part of your library.

- *Kabuki*, by David Mack (Image Comics, 2005 and on). David Mack is the creative force behind this series, and his presence is felt on every page. Masterful storytelling.

- *Cyber Age Adventures* (iHero Entertainment). This quarterly magazine of superhero fiction features some of the best up-and-coming talent in the world.

- Google (www.google.com). Need a reference for something you're drawing? Click on the image link, type in what you're looking for, and get to sketching. I don't know what people did without the Internet.

- The amazing world of Charles Keegan (www.keeganprints.com). Both a friend and a mentor, the man's work is inspiring. Be sure to watch as newer works are added; he's experiencing a personal Renaissance right now.

Appendix **B**

Glossary

camera obscura   An instrument used by early artists to transfer sketches onto a canvas. Predecessor to the modern camera.

caricature   A portrait done where the subject's features are exaggerated, often to comedic effect.

center line   The imaginary line that runs down the middle of the human body, starting at the top of the head and running down through the torso.

composition   The manner in which objects are arranged within a piece of art.

contour drawing   Also known as "taking a line for a walk," this is a technique wherein the artist draws a line of varying thickness to represent only the outline of the subject.

drawing through   When you've got something like a circle (such as an eyeball) that is partially hidden from view, you should draw through the offending object as though it weren't there. You can always erase the part of the circle you didn't need later, but this is the best way to ensure that your proportions are right.

field kit   A collection of art supplies intended for going outdoors and drawing or painting in nature. The field kit is usually held in a bag or case that's specifically designed for the purpose. It usually has plenty of places to store pencils, erasers, sketchbooks, and other tools.

foreshortening   The act of drawing things larger or smaller to give them the illusion of distance.

gesture lines Quick, loose lines that help you define the direction of the action in your drawing.

jury Before artists can show their work in a show or gallery, very often they'll ask you to "jury" your work—that is, to allow them to judge its quality. Jurying is often a stressful ordeal, but if you manage to make your way past the judges into the show, there's a big ol' basketful of pride waiting for you on the other side.

Law of Thirds The rule for placing the subject of your drawing on one of the intersecting lines that divides your page into thirds, both vertically and horizontally. On a blank sheet of paper, this would look like a tic-tac-toe board.

layout A close cousin to composition, layout is the broader term that also includes the dimensions of your work.

light source The place where your subject's illumination is coming from. It can be anything that sheds light, from sunlight to candles. There might even be more than one source.

negative space First and foremost, negative space is the area between and around the objects you want to draw. That's usually the background, but not always. For example, imagine someone standing with a hand on the hips. The negative space is the triangle made by the inner part of the person's arm and the side of the body.

palmistry The art of divining a person's future through the study of the lines on their palms.

persistence of vision In animation, the term refers to the brain's ability to fill in frames in between those you've drawn so that you don't have to render everything. Many times in static drawing, the brain's subversive ability can work for you, too. Sometimes your subject will include a million separate components (such as grass). Try to remember that "less is more" and give the viewer just enough for the brain to do the rest.

perspective How objects appear to the eye, with depth being perceived by an object's relative size according to its distance.

plumb line The imaginary vertical line that exists between two points. The term comes from carpentry, in which a string is weighted with a ball and hung from an object to make sure that things are lined up properly beneath it. That means the plumb line doesn't just connect any two points; it's a straight drop down from one point to see where that line intersects. Often you'll find that the line meets in the middle of another object, but it's a great way to gauge depth and distance.

quadrupeds Anything that walks on four legs. Folks like you and me who walk on two legs are called bipeds.

relative distance A way of measuring space without a ruler. Judging relative distance is accomplished by comparing the space between multiple objects. The distance from one eye to another, compared to the distance from one eye to the tip of the nose, for example.

roughs A term that refers to any unfinished drawing, or something that's left deliberately ragged. Many artists will fill pages of roughs before they sit down to do a more detailed drawing.

self-portrait Any work of art (drawing, painting, photography, and so on) that uses the artist as the subject. Often done with the help of a mirror or some other outside assistance.

silhouette The outline of a person or thing. It was named after a fellow by the name of étienne de Silhouette. He was the finance minister under King Louis XV. Go forth and win at Trivial Pursuit.

Sumi-e   The Japanese art of brush painting. This was actually developed in China during the Tang Dynasty (618–907 C.E.) and was introduced to Japan in the mid-14th century by Buddhist monks. There's no underlying drawing; it's just brush, ink, and paper. It is, essentially, drawing with ink and brush.

tooth   The tooth of a page is how rough it is, how much it "bites back" on the tool you're using.

Index

American Foreign Relations Reconsidered, 1890–1993

This major new textbook brings together twelve of the leading scholars of US foreign relations. Each contributor provides a clear, concise summary of an important period or theme in US diplomatic and strategic affairs since the Spanish–American War. Michael H. Hunt and Joan Hoff provide an overview of the traditions behind US policy and a preview of things to come. Together, the contributors offer a succinct explanation of the controversies and questions that historians have grappled with throughout the twentieth century. Students will find these essays a reliable and useful guide to the various schools of thought that have emerged. Although each of the scholars is well known for their detailed and original work, these essays are new and have been specially commissioned for this book.

The articles follow the chronological development of the emergence of the United States as a world power, but special themes such as the American policy process, economic interests, relations with the Third World, and the dynamics of the nuclear arms race have been singled out for separate treatment.

American Foreign Relations Reconsidered, 1890–1993 represents essential reading for upper-level undergraduates studying modern American history. The book has been designed and written exclusively to meet the needs of students, either as a major course text, or as a set of supplementary readings to support other texts.

Gordon Martel is Professor of International History at Royal Roads Military College. He is the editor of *The Origins of the Second World War Reconsidered* (1986) and *Modern Germany Reconsidered, 1870–1945* (1992).

American Foreign Relations Reconsidered, 1890–1993

Edited by Gordon Martel

London and New York

First published 1994
by Routledge
11 New Fetter Lane, London EC4P 4EE

Simultaneously published in the USA and Canada
by Routledge
29 West 35th Street, New York, NY 10001

Typeset in Times by
Ponting–Green Publishing Services, Chesham, Bucks

Printed and bound in Great Britain by
T.J. Press (Padstow) Ltd, Padstow, Cornwall

British Library Cataloguing in Publication Data
A catalogue record for this book is available from the British
Library

Library of Congress Cataloging in Publication Data
American foreign relations reconsidered, 1890–1993 / edited by
 Gordon Martel.
      p.   cm.
   Includes bibliographical references (p.   ) and index.
   1. United States–Foreign relations–20th century.
   2. United States–Foreign relations–1865–1898.
   I. Martel, Gordon.
  E744.A5327   1994
  327.73–dc20   93–36339

ISBN 0–415–10476–9 (hbk)   0–415–10477–7 (pbk)

for:

Eric, Jim & Maurice

– who know great power when they see it

Contents

Notes on contributors

Russell D. Buhite is Professor and Head of the Department of History at the University of Tennessee. He is the author, in addition to other works, of *Patrick J. Hurley and American Foreign Policy: Soviet–American Relations in Asia, 1945–54*; and *Decisions at Yalta: An Appraisal of Summit Diplomacy*.

J. Garry Clifford is Professor of Political Science at the University of Connecticut, Storrs. He is the author of *The Citizen Soldiers: The Plattsburg Training Camp Movement, 1914–1920*. He has co-authored *The First Peacetime Draft* with Samuel R. Spencer, Jr, and *American Foreign Policy: A History* with Thomas G. Paterson and Kenneth J. Hagan. He is currently working on a study of Franklin D. Roosevelt and American entry into World War II.

John W. Coogan is Associate Professor of History at Michigan State University. He is the author of *The End of Neutrality: The United States, Britain, and Maritime Rights, 1899–1915* and is currently at work on a sequel, *"The Practical Joke on Myself": The Doctrine of Freedom of the Seas in Anglo-American Relations, 1915–1921*.

Joseph A. Fry is Professor of History at the University of Nevada, Las Vegas. He is the author of *Henry S. Sanford: Diplomacy and Business in Nineteenth-Century America* and *John Tyler Morgan and the Search for Southern Autonomy*.

Thomas N. Guinsburg is Professor of History at The University of Western Ontario. He is the author of *The Pursuit of Isolationism in the United States Senate from Versailles to Pearl Harbor* and of several articles on isolationism between the wars, and is the editor of *The Dimensions of History*.

James G. Hershberg is Coordinator of the Cold War International History Project at the Woodrow Wilson International Center for Scholars in Washington, D.C. He is the author of *James B. Conant: Harvard to Hiroshima and the Making of the Nuclear Age*.

Joan Hoff is Professor of History at Indiana University, Bloomington, and wrote the essay in this collection while the Mary Ball Washington Chair in American History at University College, Dublin. She is the author of *American Business and Foreign Policy, 1920–1933*; *Ideology and Economics: United States Relations with the Soviet Union, 1918–1933*; *Herbert Hoover: Forgotten Progressive*; and *Nixon Without Watergate: A Presidency Reconsidered*.

Michael H. Hunt is Professor of History at the University of North Carolina at Chapel Hill. The best known of his early work on Sino-American relations is *The Making of a Special Relationship: The United States and China to 1914*. His most recent book is *Ideology and U.S. Foreign Policy*.

Walter LaFeber is the Noll Professor of History at Cornell University. He is the author of *America, Russia, and the Cold War, 1945–1992*; *The American Age: U.S. Foreign Policy at Home and Abroad Since 1750*; and *Inevitable Revolutions: The United States in Central America*, among other works.

Melvyn P. Leffler is Professor of History at the University of Virginia. He writes on economic foreign policy and national security issues. He is the author of *The Elusive Quest: America's Pursuit of European Stability and French Security, 1919–33* and *A Preponderance of Power: National Security, the Truman Administration, and the Cold War*.

Dennis Merrill is Associate Professor of History at the University of Missouri-Kansas City. He is author of *Bread and the Ballot: The United States and India's Economic Development, 1947–1963*, and co-editor of the forthcoming edition of *Major Problems in American Foreign Relations*. He has twice visited India on Fulbright Fellowships and sits on the editorial board of *Diplomatic History*. He is currently working on a history of US foreign aid programs and development policies in South Asia during the Cold War.

Emily S. Rosenberg is DeWitt Wallace Professor of History at Macalester College. She is the author of *Spreading the American Dream: American Economic and Cultural Expansion, 1890–1945*; *World War I and the Growth of United States Predominance in Latin America*; and co-author (with Norman L. Rosenberg) of *In Our Times: America Since 1945*.

Preface

This is the third collection of "Reconsiderations," the first of which dealt with A. J. P. Taylor's *Origins of the Second World War*. The aim of the present book, like the first one, is fairly simple: to serve undergraduate students taking courses in the history of US foreign relations. The origins of the first book reveal how this ambition was conceived and, hopefully, realized: in an attempt to demonstrate R. G. Collingwood's concept of "secondary history" to a class of first-year history students, I had them first read Taylor's *Origins* and then a series of reviews, articles and books written on the subject since he wrote. This experiment proved to be a great success, as students were challenged by his provocative interpretation and eager to see how professionally trained historians reacted to it. Thus, both the nature and the value of historical debates were demonstrated to students who could also test Collingwood's hypothesis that it was the secondary history of a subject with which one should begin.

What I found to be difficult and frustrating was the process of putting together a coherent and accessible set of readings for my students to consider; the best that I could do was to collect a miscellany of materials that varied considerably in size, scope, and style, and which were cumbersome to use. With this in mind I approached a number of leading historians of the subject to see if they would be interested in writing essays on various aspects of Taylor's interpretation and to talk about the responses to it and the "state of the art" of the debate today. Simultaneously, I found a receptive and enthusiastic editor in Jane Harris-Matthews of Allen & Unwin, who was convinced of the utility of such a book. Her assessment has proved accurate, and that first book is now used regularly in undergraduate history courses around the world.

The original formula was expanded upon for the next book, *Modern Germany Reconsidered*, which was not tied to any one historian or interpretation. But the aim remained similar: to provide students with clear and accessible summaries of the most important controversies and developments in the interpretation of German history from 1870 to 1945, and thus to enable both instructors and students to overcome the limitations imposed by reliance upon a single-author survey of the period, a form which usually leaves little room for a discussion of debates.

The essays in *American Foreign Relations Reconsidered* are not intended to be "original" in themselves, and I am indebted to the distinguished contributors who were willing to forgo originality for the sake of producing a book that would be useful for students. They apparently share my conviction that there are some important gaps in the literature between the textbook and the monograph. If this book proves to be a useful one it will be owing to the commitment of these scholars to their craft, and I sincerely thank each of them.

Gordon Martel
Royal Roads Military College
March 1993

1 Traditions of American diplomacy: from colony to great power

Michael H. Hunt

The foreign policy of the United States between independence and World War I has attracted the attention of several generations of historians, each intent on relating that early era to the policy of their own time. At first historians saw a predestined, triumphal march toward world power by a virtuous people. Accounts shifted for a time to a decidedly less celebratory mode, stressing the lapse into national isolation and passivity after the heroic era of the struggle for independence. Long free-loaders, dependent on the British fleet for their security, Americans entered the twentieth century (so this version of the rise to world power went) unprepared for its challenges. Most recently, historians have drawn attention to the strains of arrogance and anxiety that ran through the first century and a half of American foreign relations. Oppression of native Americans, deceit and manipulation by political leaders, and a seemingly insatiable hunger for land and foreign markets top a long list of disagreeable features defining nineteenth-century expansion.[1]

Today the whiff of decline is in the air. The American military giant faces distracting, perhaps even disabling, social and economic problems at home as well as uncertainties about its future role in the world.[2] Now more awake to the fact that great powers cannot forever sustain their predominance, we are perhaps ready to look afresh at the beginnings of the great cycle – the period during which the United States rose with astonishing swiftness from vulnerable new nation to a place of international prominence. In our fin de siècle mood, this extraordinary transformation invites sober contemplation and serious analysis for what it may tell us about how we have reached our present, problematic position and where we may go from here.

THE GROWTH OF AMERICAN POWER

The obvious starting point for explaining the rise of the United States as a great power is the base of material wealth that Americans were able to build in a relatively short time. Seizing the opportunities created by the British-dominated international economy, Americans profited from a flourishing foreign trade, primarily in agricultural products and raw materials. Accumulated capital went into a domestic industry whose growth had by 1830 established the United States in sixth place among industrial powers. By the 1890s American industrial output was second to none. In 1900, for example, iron and steel production roughly equalled the *combined* figure for Britain and Germany.[3]

By the early twentieth century the United States had, judging by the usual indices, largely completed its ascent. A population of only three million in 1783 and thirty-two million in 1860 had climbed to ninety-eight million by 1914. The people of the United States by then occupied a continent secure from any proximate military threat and rich in natural wealth. By 1914 the United States had far outstripped all the major powers in national as well as per capita income: Britain, the closest competitor, had only one-third the national income ($11 billion vs $37 billion) and two-thirds the per capita income ($244 vs $377). Indeed, on the eve of World War I the national incomes of all the European powers combined (including Russia) exceeded that of the United States by only a small margin ($4 billion).[4] By then the US navy stood third in the world, just behind the British and the German fleets.

While internal developments were critical to the American success story, changes in the international setting were also important. The prolonged Anglo-French struggle for international hegemony placed major obstacles in the way of American expansion between 1776 and 1815. First as a colony, then as a nominally independent state, Americans sought to make good on their claim to independence, protect their commerce, and secure their territorial control in the face of British imperial pretensions and recurrent international crises. Even after abandoning formal control of the Thirteen Colonies, British policymakers tried to keep the new state weak by containing the United States within a narrow coastal strip, by maintaining its commercial dependence on the British Isles, and by monopolizing its maritime and natural resources during wartime.

Even so, from the beginning Americans were able (in the memorable and telling phrase of Samuel Flagg Bemis) to draw advantage from Europe's distress.[5] Locked in competition with each other, the European powers were constrained in their dealings with the United States by the broad Atlantic, limited budgets, and war-weary populations. If American policymakers exercised patience, they would find the moment when those powers, distracted by problems close to home, could be driven to settle on terms advantageous to the United States. Where diplomacy failed, even when backed by a growing population of Americans in disputed territories, policymakers could try stronger medicine: threatening an alliance with one European power against its rival, grabbing weakly defended territories of distant European antagonists or, in extremity, resorting to armed force – and thereby exploiting the advantage of fighting on home ground.

The British were the first to give way, conceding independence in 1783 after discovering that their rebellious subjects, backed by the French, were difficult to defeat on their own soil. But London persisted in its bullying after 1783, setting off a second war with the Americans in 1812. This time the

British were forced to recognize that even their vaunted sea power was not enough to overcome the formidable difficulties of waging war across the Atlantic, and that they would have to accept Canada's status as a hostage to American good will. Slowly, the British were forced to concede the dominance of the American republic on the continent. In 1846 London accepted a compromise division of the Pacific Northwest (the Oregon territory) and showed a general deference through the balance of the century in handling a series of potentially explosive maritime cases and disputes over the US–Canadian border. Indeed, so formidable had the United States become that, even when Americans found themselves engaged in a civil war between 1861 and 1865, neither Britain nor any other major European power dared risk the lasting American enmity that intervention would bring.[6]

Other powers also gave ground. Napoleon sold France's Louisiana territory in 1803 to make ready for a renewal of his struggle against Britain. A weakened Spain gave up Florida under duress in 1819, a prelude to its expulsion from all but a fragment of its holdings in the Americas. Mexico failed to pacify expatriate Americans who had taken control of its northern territory (Texas), and then watched helplessly as they joined their land to the United States in 1845. With the American army occupying its capital in 1848, Mexico again had to submit, this time surrendering almost half of its territory as the price of peace. In 1867 Russia liquidated the last of its holdings in the Americas by selling Alaska. In 1898 Spain's turn came again, giving up Cuba, Puerto Rico, and the Philippines to American control.[7]

The resistance from native Americans entrenched in pockets across the continent proved even easier to overcome than the imperialism of the Europeans. Diminished by diseases borne by the European intruders, outmatched by their technology, and overwhelmed by their burgeoning population, native Americans put up a long and stubborn resistance. But the resulting battles ended ever more frequently in defeat of native forces, while alliances with Britain or France against their common enemy repeatedly collapsed as the European powers staged their own reluctant but inexorable retreat. Native attempts at accommodation with Washington ended in political betrayals that were no less disastrous. Whatever their choice, the ultimate outcome was a loss of land and relocation to distant, barren "reservations."[8]

The turning points in the subjugation of native Americans roughly coincided with the European withdrawal. By 1815 the United States had begun to establish military dominance over indigenous peoples, and the last spark of their resistance flickered out in the 1890s, just as Spain surrendered the final vestiges of its empire and British policymakers came to terms with US supremacy in the hemisphere as a whole. Approximately two to ten million people lived north of the Rio Grande before the first European settlements; by 1900 they were a defeated, dispirited remnant.[9] No longer a troublesome foreign policy problem, native Americans could now be quietly set aside as wards of the federal government.

The cumulative effect of these developments on American expansion was impressive. The territorial extent of the United States had quadrupled in the first half century of independence. The settlements hugging the Atlantic coast, augmented by lands acquired in the 1783 peace, carried the country to the Mississippi River. The Louisiana purchase doubled American territory by adding a vast expanse west of the Mississippi. The succession of acquisitions between 1845 and 1853 rounded out the continental base. The total cost of expansion was three wars and the payment of $48 million.

From this position of continental strength and security, the United States advanced additional claims which, before long, became global. In 1823 President Monroe had decreed limits on the European role in the Americas, and in the latter third of the century American presidents enforced those limits. In 1898 the McKinley administration humbled Spain in war and seized its remaining Caribbean possessions. Washington annexed Puerto Rico, imposed a protectorate over Cuba, and proceeded to make the Caribbean an American lake, launching repeated interventions over the following two decades in order to block European interlopers or keep order among the "natives."[10]

At the same time that Americans were establishing hegemony in the Caribbean they were extending their influence across the Pacific, which they thought of both as a road to Asia and as a moat guarding the United States. This thinking prompted naval expeditions to open Japan and Korea to trade, the acquisition of Midway Island in 1867, and the seizure of Hawaii, Guam, Wake Island, as well as portions of Samoa and the Philippines at the close of the century. With these Pacific way-stations in place, Washington demanded of the other powers a voice in the economic and political future of China, and backed those demands in 1900 by sending troops to restore order in north China.

Just as the United States was becoming a Pacific power, it was also taking the first tentative steps toward involvement in European politics. The seizure of colonies and the creation of dependencies set Americans on the same imperial road on which the Europeans were already well embarked, and began to entangle the United States in European rivalries and alliances through the colonial periphery. With earlier reservations concerning involvement in European affairs partially compromised already, President Theodore Roosevelt took the next cautious step in 1905 when he offered himself as a mediator in a crisis between France and Germany over Morocco and in Russia's losing war against Japan. This interest in European diplomacy, however roundabout or tentative, had by the turn of the century begun to create a commonality of outlook between Washington and London just as it injected tensions into dealings between Washington and Berlin.[11] While Washington consistently disavowed any step that might directly implicate the country in an alliance system, the United States had nevertheless become a factor in the thinking of European foreign offices. They well knew that to ignore or alienate the United States would be at their own peril.

Fed by a strong economy and strengthened by a long string of successful foreign policy exercises, the American state in the 1880s began to put on muscle as presidents sought to assert and defend extra-continental interests. From that decade can be traced the rise of a professional military and naval force trained for expeditionary duties. At the same time, the executive began to cultivate international affairs expertise (the beginnings of a foreign affairs bureaucracy) and to accumulate foreign policy powers in its own hands (the first steps toward an imperial presidency). In William McKinley the American state found the first strong chief executive bent on turning palpable national power to a variety of international ends. What McKinley began, his immediate successors, notably Theodore Roosevelt and Woodrow Wilson, would continue.[12]

Rapid economic development, territorial predation on a widening scale, mounting foreign policy pretensions and capacity – all this does much to explain the rapid American ascent from a vulnerable new nation seeking to overcome its colonial dependency to a great power with its own colonies and dependencies and the means to control and defend them. But it does not tell the full story. Notably, it does not tell us why the American international position ultimately took the particular form it did: dominance on the continent and growing influence overseas. It is possible to imagine other, quite different outcomes. Americans could, at critical points, have chosen other national paths that would have carried them toward quite different destinations in foreign affairs.

Most fundamentally, Americans might have resisted the lure of industry and international commerce, counted the social costs of technological innovation, and obstructed the flow of an immigrant work force, thus holding down the overall rate of economic growth. A less rich United States might have proven a much less formidable presence in the world. However, Americans rejected this course, a decision that needs to be added to our explanation of the international ascent. Rather than maintaining a domestic environment friendly to simple republican civic values and stable communities, Americans placed their faith in the unconstrained marketplace – the most efficient arbiter for a society that they regarded as a collection of self-interested individual buyers and sellers whose economic behavior was to be only lightly fettered by social, political, or moral constraints.[13] Individualism unleashed personal ambition and energy, encouraged the use of new technologies, helped sustain a dynamic (if crisis-prone) economic system, and fueled the relentless process of urbanization, industrialization, and immigration-driven population growth that was the concomitant of territorial expansion.

There were other, more discrete choices to be made in the realm of foreign policy. The decisions made in the first decades may have been the most consequential. The Federalist administration of George Washington might have resisted rather than accommodated British hegemony on the high seas, or the Republicans who followed might have been less prickly in their response to continuing British maritime pressure. Either way, policymakers would have paid a price. Federalist defiance would have divided the country politically, damaged trade, and enfeebled the new state, which was dependent on the revenue from trade. On the other hand, quiescent Republican leaders would have found themselves vulnerable to charges of passivity and dependence and watched their party lapse into a deadly malaise.

Subsequent policymakers also discarded alternatives that might have pointed the United States in quite a different direction. Washington might have adopted a policy of greater accommodation toward native Americans and respected the constraints embodied in treaties negotiated with them. A humane live-and-let-live approach might, in turn, have imposed a measure of restraint on national expansion toward the Pacific. Americans might have resisted presidential incitement to war against Mexico in 1845–6. In the peace that followed they might have either settled for minor territorial adjustments in Texas that were the ostensible cause of the conflict, or alternatively seized all of Mexico. Later still, some means of resolving the quarrel with Spain short of war might have been found in 1898, the quarrel avoided altogether at its inception in 1896, or the peace treaty in 1899 framed in non-territorial terms.

Certainly some voices were heard in support of each of these alternative policies at points between the 1790s and the 1890s. But they did not prevail. Why? The answer can be found in one critical element missing in the discussion to this point: the ideas that guided American policymakers as they contemplated their choices and made the decisions that carried the United States from success to success and ultimately to eminence as a global power. Those ideas constituted a powerful and enduring tradition within which US policy was made, and which linked the early era to the later.

FORMAL POLICY DOCTRINES

In thinking about the role of ideas in relation to policy, it is helpful to draw a distinction between formal policy doctrines and informal policy ideology. The formal doctrines arose as responses to particular policy problems in one of the three regions of the world that commanded the attention of Washington and the foreign policy public: Latin America, East Asia, and Europe. Often no more than a pious hope or vague preference when first broached, these doctrines gained authority as generally accepted axioms through repeated invocation by policymakers.

The two doctrines that proved to be the most influential, the Monroe doctrine and the open door, provided guidance for US policy in Latin America and East Asia – the two regions that offered the young American republic the broadest field for asserting national will and developing markets. By contrast, American influence was sharply circumscribed on the European stage, and thus the United States had to proceed more cautiously there. Europe could not be ignored altogether, however, as it remained a center of global economic and military power. The complex American relationship with that region spelled an uneven career for the doctrines devoted to trans-Atlantic dealings.

The longest-lived of the doctrines, indeed one still central to US policy, bears the name of President James Monroe.[14] In 1823 European powers seemed ready to intervene in Latin America to restore Spanish colonial dominion. Monroe responded by asserting that Europe and the Americas had distinct interests pointing those two worlds toward different destinies. Although his warning against European interference in the New World had little teeth at the time, it did establish a basis for a US claim as the leader and protector of this hemisphere.

By degrees the Monroe doctrine acquired teeth. Soon after the end of the Civil War, Secretary of State William Seward linked Monroe's doctrine to a successful drive to eliminate a French presence in Mexico. The doctrine received strong affirmation again in 1895 when Secretary of State Richard Olney, speaking for the Harrison administration, forced Britain to withdraw from a Latin American territorial dispute and, in effect, to accept the United States as the hemispheric hegemon. And the doctrine was expanded in 1905 when Theodore Roosevelt used it in arrogating to the United States the role of policeman in the hemisphere, as much concerned with the good behavior of Latin Americans as with the intrusion of outsiders.

In East Asia, second only to Latin America as an overseas stage for national expansion, the open door emerged as the guiding doctrine. It had its formal birth in 1899 when William McKinley's Secretary of State, John Hay, used it to claim equal treatment for American commerce in China, which was vying for a place in a market of supposedly enormous potential but seemingly threatened by European imperial ambitions. A year later, in the midst of a crisis in north China, Hay restated the open door in broader terms: to the previous concern with access to China's market, he now added a commitment to safeguard Chinese independence. The open door thus linked equal trade opportunity to long-term American political and cultural influences. It also elevated China, the weak Asian giant whose future development seemed to hold the key to long-term American influence throughout the region, to a place of importance in US policy.[15]

The ideas behind the open door were, however, older than Hay and broader in application than China. Concern with access to markets and competition on equal terms had, for example, been expressed by Americans in the 1850s when dealing with Japan, and later in Korea. In the twentieth century the open door would be applied virtually on a global basis.[16] The all-purpose nature of the open door – its mix of economic, political, and cultural concerns – made it applicable to a wide variety of circumstances but at the same time rendered it increasingly diffuse and contributed to its ultimate decline as a formal doctrine. It has nonetheless remained influential as a background idea, where it became interwoven with the informal ideology.

When dealing with Europe, Americans adopted a more cautious approach.

Unlike the countries of Latin America and East Asia, the European powers
were strong enough to define the terms of their trade with the United States
both in the metropole and in their colonies. Declarations of an open door
would have had no effect. Similarly, European military strength, established
political patterns, and cultural self-confidence combined to discourage the
projection of an American nationalist dream to that region – indeed they
posed a potential threat to American security and national identity. The two
policy doctrines that were developed in dealing with Europe were consequently governed by conflicting impulses: to hold the Old World at a safe
political and military distance while simultaneously protecting access to the
continent that provided the most important market for American goods and
the indispensable source of capital for American economic development.

The doctrine of the freedom of the seas reflected the importance of Europe
in American economic life. It was intended to assure unimpeded access to
European markets in time of conflict among European powers. As a neutral,
the United States claimed the right – subject to minimal restrictions and
responsibilities – to carry goods on the high seas safe from harassment,
seizure, or interference by the belligerents. In this way business would
preserve its regular trade and perhaps even add markets that were normally
closed to the United States in time of peace.

The American claim to freedom of the seas, couched in terms of international law, reflected early US naval weakness and hence an inability to
defend commerce in any way but through abstract appeals. Not surprisingly,
Britain, with its well endowed naval force, respected neutral claims only when
it was convenient. Equally unsurprising, when American naval strength grew
to the point that it could not only effectively protect US maritime interests but
advantageously command the trade of others, the doctrine of freedom of the
seas was soon eclipsed. Suspended during the Civil War when the Union
sought to break the Confederacy's economic lifeline to Europe, the doctrine
thereafter enjoyed a revival but also faced a growing challenge from big-navy
advocates who argued that might – not law – was the best and ultimate defense
of American commerce. The outbreak of the First World War rallied the
Wilson administration to the cause of free trade and neutral rights (at least as
the president understood them), but thereafter freedom of the seas faded
rapidly as the US navy moved toward mastery of the world's oceans.[17]

The doctrine of isolationism was generated by fear of European power.
While freedom of the seas sought to keep the Atlantic an open highway for
American commerce, isolationism tried to make that ocean a great divide
separating the Old World from the New. The United States was a peaceful
republic with nothing to gain by entanglement with Europe's rapacious, war-
prone, and oppressive monarchies. Thus, isolationism was a conceptual twin
to the Monroe doctrine, building from the idea of two spheres. Just as
policymakers committed themselves to resisting European interference on
their own side of the Atlantic, so too they should resist any temptation to get
caught up in Europe's alliances and wars.

This notion of isolation developed out of the American colonial experience with Anglo-French imperial rivalry between 1688 and 1763. During this period Americans had suffered from European quarrels, been deprived of a voice in the critical questions of war and peace, and were often forgotten when the spoils were divided. Once independent, Americans searched for a policy that would remove them as far as possible from the European maelstrom generated by the French Revolution and Napoleonic conquests. In 1796, on the eve of his retirement from the presidency, George Washington urged on his countrymen the wisdom of maintaining a "detached and distant position" from European quarrels. His successors in the White House consistently echoed his sentiments throughout the nineteenth century.[18]

Growing American strength and the temptation to meddle in European quarrels killed off isolation as a doctrine in much the same way that these developments undermined freedom of the seas. But the ideas behind the doctrine proved tenacious through the first half of the twentieth century, repeatedly inspiring opposition to policymakers imprudent enough to want to throw the weight of American might and ideals into European struggles. The anti-interventionists lost, and the victors took their revenge by constructing a caricature of their former foe. Advocates of direct participation in World War II and then cold warriors preoccupied with the defense of Western Europe blamed the earlier era of isolation for what they saw as their countrymen's deplorable passivity, woeful ignorance, and lamentable inexperience in world affairs. According to this critical, latter-day view, isolation carried a curse for twentieth-century Americans trying to adjust to the nation's transformed position in the world – a lack of preparation, even an aversion, to playing the role of a world power.

But isolation as a doctrine deserves to be understood historically. To do so requires moving beyond the pejorative, anachronistic, and distorting use of that term that had developed, by the middle of the twentieth century, out of heated public debates over European policy and that even today dominates both popular and elite discussions of policy issues. Isolationism itself was, to be sure, a doctrine of denial, but it was applied to only one region – Europe – and only to forms of political and military entanglement deemed dangerous or irrelevant to American interests. Americans could, in this sense, be isolationist and yet, at the same time, trade avidly with the Old World, borrow large amounts of its capital, travel to look with awe on its monuments, read its literature and philosophy, accept its poor, and mix socially with its prominent families.

Isolation was, moreover, not *the* doctrine of early US policy but rather one of several, and the caution and prudence that characterized it should not obscure the more assertive and aggressive aspects of the other doctrines. The application of those doctrines, taken together, endowed American policymakers with a rich and varied experience in international affairs. Hardly inactive, they could boast an overall record of stunning success.

Finally, isolationism was not (as its critics have charged) shallow and thoughtless. "Isolationists" raised serious questions about the wisdom of involvement in European rivalries. Such involvement, they contended, made the United States hostage to developments beyond its control while imposing real domestic costs: increased national debt, lives lost and disrupted, and the concentration of power in what would come to be called the "national security state."

INFORMAL POLICY IDEOLOGY

Underpinning these four major policy doctrines, and providing support for them, was an informal ideology that constituted the other intellectual tradition of early US foreign policy. Studies on US policy have often depicted ideology as a rigid and misleading view of the world or, alternatively, as a narrow set of marketplace calculations that has led Washington to pursue an open-door world for American goods and capital. But ideology can be understood in a third way: as a coherent, mutually reenforcing body of ideas that gives structure and meaning to the way policymakers and the broader public concerned with international affairs see the world and the American place in it. This informal system of ideas is grounded in cultural values and practices that subtly shape foreign policy. It is intellectual baggage that policymakers carry into office. Its contents reflect their personal, class, regional, and ethnic backgrounds as well as their socialization into the dominant myths of American nationalism. As such, ideology is the fundamental starting point for explaining how and why policymakers make their critical decisions. It is also just the beginning, and thus room needs to be left for a variety of influences from the pressures imposed by the international system to the personality quirks of particular leaders.[19]

In practical terms this informal ideology takes us another step closer to an explanation of why American leaders made certain choices in the conduct of foreign relations, rejected others, and in the process created an expansionist, outwardly oriented country. Ideology gave American leaders the confidence and shared purpose to get through the difficult first decades, while the harvest of successes after 1815 did much to validate and deepen the beliefs that were at the core of their thought. Ideology also infused early policy doctrines with meaning and then provided continuity when policymakers shucked off the old doctrines and replaced them with new ones such as collective security, containment, and development theory. Finally, this approach to ideology helps us to see that early US foreign policy was not exceptional but "normal" in the sense of being comparable to that of other major powers: Britain, Germany, and Japan have also sought – at one time or another – to define their nationalism in terms of an activist foreign policy.[20]

Foremost of the elements in this informal ideology was a commitment to the pursuit of national greatness, cast in terms of the promotion of liberty abroad. Americans conceived of themselves as a people engaged in a political

experiment of historical and global significance. As the patriot and pamphlet-
eer Thomas Paine declared at the outset of the struggle for independence,
Americans had it in their power "to begin the world over again." However,
this sense of self-importance, so central to American nationalism, contained
an ambiguity that was brought sharply into focus in the 1790s at the very
outset of US foreign policy in a heated and far-ranging exchange between the
ruling Federalists and the emergent opposition party, the Republicans.[21]
Echoes of that first encounter sounded throughout the next two centuries and
can still be heard today.

①
Original
Debate of
Federalist
Papers

Alexander Hamilton, the architect of Federalist foreign policy, was the first
to articulate the activist vision of national greatness with its emphasis on the
promotion of American power in the world and the exercise of that power in
the interest of freedom. Hamilton conceived of the United States as a dynamic
republic, committed above all to the vigorous promotion of liberty abroad as
a good in its own right, but also as a stimulant to a vigorous liberty at home.
This vision committed Hamiltonians to the building of a strong federal
government and to the exercise of American power overseas – the scope and
scale of which would broaden as national resources grew.

Hamilton

✓,

Thomas Jefferson, the foremost Republican, offered during his time as
Washington's Secretary of State and then in the political opposition a more
cautious, alternative vision. Jefferson was critical of Hamiltonian foreign
policy because it ignored, even endangered, the primary obligation of a good
society: to see to the welfare of its own people and to protect and perfect a
fragile experiment in democracy. He regarded imperial aspirations and
commitments as poisonous to republican ideals, and he rejected a forceful
policy of global transformation as a destructive illusion. The appropriate
American role in the world, Jefferson and fellow Republicans argued, was as
a model for – not a guarantor of – others seeking freedom.

Jefferson

The debate continued as the United States became a continental power. In
the 1840s, proponents of the nation's "manifest destiny" such as President
James K. Polk contended that the addition of new territories was consistent
with the US role as a special agent of freedom and progress and as a special
country with boundless possibilities. Passivity would, expansionists argued,
doom the American experiment to stagnation and failure, while the acquisition
of new lands would revitalize the American spirit and extend the sphere of
liberty. Expansionist schemes roused critics who decried above all the danger
that a war of conquest would pose to liberty and to republican virtue; they
warned that the United States could not champion liberty and at the same time
pursue empire.[22]

The debate was rejoined in the 1890s as the United States established its
hemispheric dominance and entered the competition for overseas empire.
Echoing the liturgy of earlier foreign-policy activists, McKinley claimed for
the United States a right and duty to establish colonies, help "oppressed
peoples," and generally project its power and influence into the world.
Americans would benefit, and so would all humanity. On the other side,

critics with a pristine and self-limiting vision of the American future made the familiar claims for the incompatibility of liberty with the exercise of dominion over others. They predicted that the net effect of foreign adventures would soon be seen at home in the form of a burgeoning state apparatus that would dispense patronage and control a large military establishment. Factions would contend for this concentrated power, inexorably corrupt republican virtue, and ultimately overthrow liberty.[23]

By the turn of the century the Hamiltonian conception of national greatness was predominant, having triumphed in each of the earlier confrontations with its Jeffersonian alternatives. Even so, the voice of the doubters could be heard as the Wilson administration moved toward entry into World War I and, later, proposed American participation in a League of Nations; later still, on the eve of American entry into World War II, they raised familiar doubts about the wisdom of entanglement in European quarrels. On each occasion the doubters sought to counter the appeal of an assertive foreign policy by stressing the costs to republican ideals and to the welfare of the common man. In their view the national interest might be better served by focusing on domestic welfare rather than channeling American energy and treasure abroad in the delusion that the United States could control events in a dangerous world. While the Cold War silenced the debate, the classic questions concerning the purpose of foreign policy and the costs attached to it have again moved to center stage in the last decade: critics from both the Left and the Right, alarmed by the portents of national decline, have attacked the course of Ronald Reagan and George Bush.

The second element making up the informal ideology of early US foreign policy was a conception of racial hierarchy that served as a check to expansionism, but also as a goad and a justification. American views on race, derived initially from Europe, gained additional form and force through the subjugation of native Americans, the enslavement and repression of African-Americans, and the reaction to millions of immigrants arriving from China and Japan as well as Europe. The essence of these views, which came to exercise a grip on the imagination of policymakers and the influential public (largely white Americans of old stock), was the conviction that skin color was closely related to innate worth, whether measured in terms of individual virtue or the capacity of a people. Whites in general and Protestants of English descent in particular were at the top, blacks at the bottom, and other peoples arrayed at intermediate and sometimes changing points between the poles. This hierarchical notion easily applied to the world outside as well. It required no more than an understanding of easily grasped polarities and superficial characteristics. Races were different and unequal. Some were more civilized and progressive, others were more barbaric and backward.

In the structure of American race thinking, Anglo-Saxonism – the belief that Americans and the British were one people united by uncommon qualities and common interests – came to occupy a central position. By the first half of the nineteenth century some influential Americans had begun to take pride in proclaiming their place in a trans-Atlantic community of English-speaking people. By the end of the century the Anglo-Saxon spell had further strengthened its hold. The predominant racial characteristics of both peoples, as they were now defined, included industry, intelligence, a keen sense of moral purpose, and a talent for government.[24]

Seen in global terms, the Anglo-Saxons were dominant. The Germans came next: they had the same qualities as their racial cousins save one – they had lost their love of liberty. This single serious defect set Germans just beyond the Anglo-Saxon pale, making them a formidable people and a threatening global competitor that would have to be watched closely; by the turn of the century, Americans increasingly pictured them as latter-day Huns, prone to the aggressive, even brutal behavior characteristic of a militaristic and autocratic system. The Slavs, half European and half Asiatic, were also seen as formidable racial competitors on the international stage. Highly regimented and of rugged peasant stock, they had displayed great endurance, patience, and strength (but not intelligence and a knack for innovation) as they had slowly but irresistibly extended their control over much of the Eurasian land mass.

Lower down in the hierarchy were the Latin peoples of Europe (defined to include the French as well as Italians and Spaniards) and of the Americas. They lacked vigor; they were sentimental, undisciplined, priest-ridden, and superstitious; consequently, they were of small account in international affairs. Latin Americans figured prominently as somewhat child-like or brutish inferiors in need of the benevolent hand of the more mature. The peoples of East Asia, sometimes designated "the Mongolian race" but more popularly referred to as "orientals," also stood somewhere near the middle of the racial ladder. They were construed as a disturbing, even dangerous, bundle of contradictions. Inscrutable and somnolent, they were also a people of promise, on the verge of shaking off a stagnant cultural tradition and improving their position in the hierarchy of race. They were subhuman, yet cunning; unfeeling, yet boiling inwardly with rage; cowardly and decadent, yet capable of great conquests. Predictably, on the lowest rung of the ladder were the peoples of Africa, a continent that, above all others, invited white dominion.

Racial notions had helped Americans to rationalize the drive to expel Spain from North America and then to push south the border of Mexico, an enemy denounced as "ignorant, prejudiced, and perfectly faithless."[25] Those notions again made themselves felt in the 1890s. They supported the ripening claim of the United States to the role of natural leader and policeman of an American system of states, inspired cries to rescue a ravaged Cuba from Spanish atrocities, and bolstered demands for the annexation of the Philippines. But at the same time those same notions gave rise to opposition to overseas colonies, especially in the Philippines. Ruling in tropical climates and mixing with lesser peoples would undermine the racial vitality of the Anglo-Saxon stock.

Accepted by the turn of the century as an important ingredient in a demonstrably successful foreign policy no less than in the established domestic order, race thinking would pass to subsequent generations as a wellnigh irresistible legacy. American policymakers would continue to look to race as an essential category for understanding other countries and peoples and as a fundamental basis for judging them. While the civil rights movement in the United States would, by degrees, put a taboo on overtly racist expressions, policymakers continued to think of other peoples in terms of the characteristics previously associated with the hierarchy of race and to assign other nations a rough ranking that bore a striking resemblance to earlier estimates.

The final element rounding out the informal American foreign policy ideology was an ambivalent attitude toward revolutionary change. That attitude was strongly influenced by memories of the American revolution, fixed in nationalist lore as a model of moderation and wisdom. Against that model all struggles for freedom were to be judged, whether directed against foreign masters or home-grown tyrants. Revolution was a solemn affair, to be conducted with a minimum of disorder, led by respectable citizens, harnessed to moderate political goals, and happily concluded only after a balanced constitution – essential to safeguarding human and property rights – was securely in place.

Foreigners who embarked on revolution almost never measured up. Their revolutions had a deplorable tendency to self-destruct. Revolutionary leaders stumbled because of their personal failings: despotic habits, selfish ambitions, and simple ineptitude or weakness of character. The inability of foreign peoples to meet the test of revolution and liberty was explained most often in the familiar terms of the hierarchy of race. Where Anglo-Saxons succeeded, all others struggled. The lower down the hierarchy, the more rapid and disastrous would be the revolutionary failure.

Once unleashed in one land, the infectious spirit of revolution could spread, for better or worse, to other lands with important consequences for the American political experiment itself. The achievement of ordered liberty by others would confirm for Americans their leading role in a secure world of free peoples. Revolutions gone astray, on the other hand, would leave Americans feeling repudiated, isolated, and anxious. All fresh revolutionary outbreaks, even distant ones, bore careful watching. This anxiety that came to mark early US foreign policy was confirmed through confrontation with three waves of revolutionary change.

The first wave of revolution struck in France and Latin America between the 1790s and the 1810s. In 1789, just as Americans were bringing their own seminal struggle for liberty to a successful constitutional conclusion, an upheaval in France held out the promise that Europe would soon recast itself along American political lines. But as the revolution in France took a more radical and violent turn after 1793, increasing numbers of Americans set it beyond the bounds of legitimacy – and roundly condemned its sympathizers in the United States. If Americans needed another bitter lesson in the dangers of the revolutionary contagion, then they soon got it in Santo Domingo, where in 1791 an underclass of black slaves and freedmen had taken the doctrines of the French Revolution seriously and massacred their French masters to gain freedom. Might the southern United States be next?

Latin America's struggle for freedom from Spanish control, following the crest of revolutionary activity in France and Santo Domingo, served to confirm and extend the darker view. If those outbreaks of the 1790s had conclusively established the danger of social revolution, the revolts against Spain suggested the limits of even moderate anti-colonial struggles. Peoples long oppressed by foreign rule were bound to want liberty, but the conditions that had held them down, including the burden of race, might also leave them incapable of either winning or maintaining it.

The second wave of revolutions was confined to Europe at mid-century, sweeping across its entire face. From the heights of hope in 1848 that a community of youthful republics were about to replace the tottering old monarchies, American observers sank by 1871 into a slough of despair as mobs took over the streets of Paris. Before its violent suppression in late May, the Paris Commune had yielded a full catalogue of radical transgressions that ranged from systematic pillage of private property to unreasoning violence.

The third wave of revolutions witnessed by Americans began to build in the 1890s, and by the 1910s girdled the globe. In both the Philippines and Cuba, revolutions against Spanish colonial authority were cut short by American military intervention. Washington decreed that tutelage was the correct course for "natives" not yet ready for liberty and full independence. Thereafter, China, Mexico, and then Russia would become the scenes of revolutionary dramas that commanded close American attention. In all three countries the old order crashed with such speed and resounding finality that Americans were tempted to entertain those old sweet dreams of freedom's advance. But not for long. As each of these revolutions "went astray," old American prejudices again rose to the surface. The Bolshevik seizure of power in Russia gave rise to the greatest alarm. Policymakers and commentators found abhorrent a regime that denied political, religious, and property rights, advocated "free love" and atheism, and promoted class warfare not only at home but also abroad. American nativist and other conservative elements joined in a campaign to insulate their own country from a fever that was spreading into the heart of Europe.

By the early twentieth century a deep ambivalence about revolutionary change had become an important element in the thinking of policymakers, and it would shape their response to a fourth revolutionary wave that burst upon them in the middle of the twentieth century. Then as earlier, the terror and injustice spawned by revolutions raised the call for armed vigilance in Washington. Those same explosions of political heterodoxy abroad also served to strengthen the case for an American right to judge and instruct others less politically adept and to reenforce the assumptions about the greatness of a nation that could for so long maintain order within its own borders even as disorder raged in other lands.

TRADITIONS AND THE FUTURE OF US POLICY

The traditions that shaped early US foreign policy are multiple. Most obviously, they consisted of an impressive record of success in gaining control of a continent and then projecting power from that continental base overseas – into Latin America, across the Pacific into East Asia, and even tentatively into Europe. Americans entered the twentieth century acutely aware of and buoyed up by that record. Those early traditions also consisted of formal doctrines, concepts that emerged from the actual formulation and application of policy to one or another of the three regions that stood foremost in the concerns of Washington. Some of those doctrines, such as Monroe's, would remain potent while others, such as isolation, would lose their grip on policy.

Informal ideology was the most far-reaching and fundamental of the foreign policy traditions. It served as an indispensable compass for policy-makers as they moved from triumph to triumph, while the accumulating record of success in turn validated and made stronger the claims of that ideology. At the same time ideology provided the intellectual underpinning for the early policy doctrines, sustaining those that survived and outlasting those that faltered. The foreign policy ideology that guided the United States on its road to becoming a great power by the early twentieth century and a superpower by the end of World War II is now woven deeply into the fabric of the national culture and policy discourse. It is easily heard in celebrations of victory in the Cold War and in proclamations of a "New World Order."

The ideology that took form during the rise of the United States to its standing as a major player on the world stage is also a potentially serious obstacle to understanding and managing the affairs of a country now somewhat beyond the apogee of its might. Efforts to slow or reverse the process of decline will, at important points, collide with an informal ideology that endows Americans with a pervasive, unexamined conviction of national greatness, an impulse to judge the worth of others by the standards of America's own institutions and values, and a commitment to particular lines of political and economic development.

The challenges to traditional American ideological claims issue from four directions. First, the world is becoming increasingly fragmented into regions that are dominated by one or more centers of economic and military strength that are suspicious (if not intolerant) of meddling from outside. It is a world that will not prove hospitable to American attempts to impose its own solutions on regional problems. Yet the failure of policies that were built on a respect for spheres of influence, ranging from the initiatives of Theodore Roosevelt to those of Richard Nixon, does not augur well for any renewed effort toward limiting the American global reach. Even though American power may be less freely and effectively exercised today than in the recent past, any call to retreat from the accustomed "great role" in the world is likely to give rise to a profound and politically explosive sense of unease.

A second challenge can be found in the international economy. The system that the United States put in place and dominated in the wake of World War II has now reached into virtually every corner of the globe, and in the process has undermined even the old bulwarks of socialism. But the United States, itself palpably faltering, can no longer convincingly claim to stand as a model for or master of that economy. As the world's largest debtor with low rates of saving, slow productivity gains, and slow overall growth, the United States does not cut an impressive figure. Here too the United States faces unaccustomed limits and the need to address domestic problems that discredit the American model and undermine American capacity for leadership. A Jeffersonian program of economic and social revival will require American leaders to look inward and restrict the funds and attention that were previously devoted to international affairs. But is it possible for Americans to put on hold their outward-looking nationalism while they put their house in order?

Third, the United States faces a challenge to its old identity in a world still marked by profound differences in cultural values and aspirations. Resurgent nationalism in parts of Eastern Europe and much of the former Soviet Union, together with the revitalization of Islamic values, ought to remind us that the age of global diversity has not passed. That diversity is likely to be strengthened by the emergence of three global economic blocs, each with a distinct cultural orientation. The German-dominated pan-European market and the Japanese-dominated East Asian co-prosperity sphere are both likely to sustain ways of life quite different from that within the US-dominated North American bloc. As this culturally plural world increasingly intrudes into the lives of Americans through trade, immigration, and new technologies of communication, an understanding of other cultures will be essential to function effectively and live comfortably.[26] The maintenance of condescending assumptions about cultural superiority and simple stereotypes will not make the encounter with this complex and differentiated world either profitable, smooth, or enriching.

Finally, the most subtle but perhaps the most profound challenge to Americans is to respond humanely to the political, social, and economic aspirations that have, in other lands, given rise to revolutionary dreams and movements in this century. Hopes for a better life continue to animate peoples in the grip of military violence, political injustice, and dire poverty. But Americans have difficulty responding empathetically and effectively because they remain in the grip of an ideology that insists on the universality of the American way and at the same time begrudge tax dollars devoted to foreign assistance. Can the United States make a significant commitment to the welfare of foreigners not in order to confirm national greatness but in order to fulfill fundamental obligations of human solidarity?

One option for Americans is to leave the old ideology unexamined and uncontested. Perhaps fate will treat the United States kindly and little harm will come from clinging to familiar nationalist pretensions and policies. But it is more likely that such a course will steadily intensify the domestic malaise and diminish the ability to act internationally. One alternative – to seek to live apart from ideology – is to misunderstand the problem. Without ideology any people are left in limbo, wondering what values might give meaning and direction to their foreign policy.

The remaining alternative is to reflect on, debate, and perhaps reorient key elements of US foreign policy ideology in a way that helps meet these international challenges. It is an effort that will not come easily or quickly, and it may well take pain, even trauma, before Americans are prepared to set about the task with the requisite seriousness. To that process of trans-formation historical perspective will be essential, offering above all else a reminder that defining the United States as a nation and its role in the world is not the work of a day but merely the extension of an enterprise as old as the sense of nationhood itself. Americans of the 1990s would do well to recognize that they have inherited strong foreign policy traditions even if they do not fully recognize them, and that any effort to alter the direction of their policy must confront the constraints imposed by those traditions.

NOTES

1 On these different views of the early decades, see Jerald A. Combs, *American Diplomatic History: Two Centuries of Changing Interpretations*, Berkeley, Calif., 1983; Kinley J. Brauer, "The Great American Desert Revisited: Recent Literature and Prospects for the Study of American Foreign Relations, 1815–61," *Diplomatic History*, vol. 13, 1989, pp. 395–417; and Robert Beisner, *From the Old Diplomacy to the New, 1865–1900*, 2nd rev. ed., Arlington Heights, Ill., 1986, chap. 1. Anyone interested in this or any other era can turn for help to Richard D. Burns (ed.), *Guide to American Foreign Relations Since 1700*, Santa Barbara, Calif., 1983, a critical bibliography; to the journal *Diplomatic History*, which regularly carries historio-graphical surveys; and to Alexander DeConde (ed.), *Encyclopedia of American Foreign Policy*, 3 vols, New York, 1978.

2 For the most influential case for American decline, see Paul Kennedy, *The Rise and Fall of the Great Powers: Economic Change and Military Conflict from 1500 to 2000*, New York, 1987. Of all the critical responses to the decline thesis, none was more triumphal and more widely discussed than Francis Fukuyama's "The End of History?," *The National Interest*, no. 16, summer 1989, pp. 3–18. Richard Rosecrance, "Must America Decline?," *Wilson Quarterly*, vol. 14, 1990, pp. 67–85, surveys the debate.

3 Kennedy, *Rise and Fall*, pp. 94, 200.

4 Kennedy, *Rise and Fall*, p. 243.

5 This theme is central in Samuel Flagg Bemis, *A Diplomatic History of the United States*, 3rd ed., New York, 1955. Reginald Horsman, *The Diplomacy of the New Republic*, Arlington Heights, Ill., 1985, offers a recent survey of these early, difficult years.

6 Kenneth Bourne, *Britain and the Balance of Power in North America, 1815–1908*, Berkeley, Calif., 1967; Reginald Stuart, *United States Expansionism and British North America, 1775–1871*, Chapel Hill, N.C., 1988; and David Crook, *The North, the South, and the Powers, 1861–1865*, New York, 1974.

7 On territorial expansion see Robert W. Tucker and David C. Hendrickson, *Empire of Liberty: The Statecraft of Thomas Jefferson*, New York, 1990; Alexander DeConde, *This Affair of Louisiana*, New York, 1976; Norman A.

Graebner, *Empire on the Pacific: A Study in American Continental Expansion*, New York, 1955; Thomas R. Hietala, *Manifest Design: Anxious Aggrandizement in Late Jacksonian America*, Ithaca, N.Y., 1985; and Charles S. Campbell Jr, *The Transformation of American Foreign Relations, 1865–1900*, New York, 1976.

8 Richard White, *The Middle Ground: Indians, Empire, and Republics in the Great Lake Region, 1650–1815*, New York, 1991; Gregory E. Dowd, *A Spirited Resistance: The North American Indian Struggle for Unity, 1745–1815*, Baltimore, Md, 1991; Francis Jennings, *The Invasion of America: Indians, Colonialism, and the Cant of Conquest*, Chapel Hill, N.C., 1975; Dorothy V. Jones, *License for Empire: Colonialism by Treaty in Early America*, Chicago, 1982; Reginald Horsman, *Expansion and American Indian Policy, 1783–1812*, East Lansing, Mich., 1967; and Robert K. Berkhofer Jr, *The White Man's Indian: Images of the American Indian from Columbus to the Present*, New York, 1978.

9 Henry F. Dobyns, *Their Number Become Thinned: Native American Population Dynamics in Eastern North America*, Knoxville, Tenn., 1983; and John D. Daniels, "The Indian Population of North America in 1492," *William and Mary Quarterly*, 3rd series, vol. 49, 1992, pp. 298–320.

10 Robert E. May, *The Southern Dream of a Caribbean Empire, 1854–1861*, Baton Rouge, La, 1973; Louis A. Pérez Jr, *Cuba between Empires, 1878–1902*, Pittsburgh, Pa, 1983; and Thomas D. Schoonover, *The United States in Central America, 1860–1911: Episodes of Social Imperialism and Imperial Rivalry in the World System*, Durham, N.C., 1991.

11 Bradford Perkins, *The Great Rapprochement: England and the United States, 1895–1914*, New York, 1968; and Holger H. Herwig, *Politics of Frustration: The United States in German Naval Planning, 1889–1941*, Boston, 1976, Part 1.

12 Beisner, *From the Old Diplomacy to the New*; Lewis L. Gould, *The Spanish–American War and President McKinley*, Lawrence, Kan., 1982; John L. Offner, *An Unwanted War: The Diplomacy of the United States and Spain over Cuba, 1895–1898*, Chapel Hill, N.C., 1992; and Robert C. Hilderbrand, *Power and the People: Executive Management of Public Opinion in Foreign Affairs, 1897–1921*, Chapel Hill, N.C., 1981.

13 Steven Watts, *The Republic Reborn: War and the Making of Liberal America, 1790–1820*, Baltimore, Md, 1987.

14 John J. Johnson, *A Hemisphere Apart: The Foundations of United States Policy toward Latin America*, Baltimore, Md, 1990; and Dexter Perkins, *A History of the Monroe Doctrine*, Boston, 1941.

15 Thomas J. McCormick, *China Market: America's Quest for Informal Empire, 1893–1901*, Chicago, 1967; and Michael H. Hunt, *The Making of a Special Relationship: The United States and China to 1914*, New York, 1983, offer divergent perspectives.

16 William Appleman Williams, *The Tragedy of American Diplomacy*, first edition, Cleveland, Ohio, 1959; Williams, *The Roots of the Modern American Empire: A Study of the Growth and Shaping of a Social Consciousness in a Marketplace Society*, New York, 1969; and Walter LaFeber, *The New Empire: An Interpretation of American Expansion, 1860–1898*, Ithaca, N.Y., 1963, all make a strong claim for the importance of a global open door. For some thoughtful rejoinders, see William Becker, "American Manufacturers and Foreign Markets, 1870–1900," *Business History Review*, vol. 47, 1973, pp. 466–81; and William H. Becker and Samuel F. Wells Jr (eds), *Economics and World Power: An Assessment of American Diplomacy Since 1789*, New York, 1984.

17 Bradford Perkins, *The First Rapprochement: England and the United States, 1795–1805*, Philadelphia, Pa, 1955; Perkins, *Prologue to War: England and the United States, 1805–1812*, Berkeley, Calif., 1961; and John W. Coogan, *The End*

of Neutrality: The United States, Britain, and Maritime Rights, 1899–1915, Ithaca, N.Y., 1981.

18 Felix Gilbert, *To the Farewell Address: Ideas of Early American Foreign Policy*, Princeton, N.J., 1961.

19 For additional discussion see Michael H. Hunt, *Ideology and U.S. Foreign Policy*, New Haven, Conn., 1987, chap. 1; Hunt, "Ideology," and Emily Rosenberg, "Gender," both in "A Roundtable: Explaining the History of American Foreign Relations," *Journal of American History*, vol. 77, 1990, pp. 108–24; and Bradford Perkins, "The Tragedy of American Diplomacy: Twenty-five Years After," *Reviews in American History*, vol. 12, 1984, pp. 1–18.

20 The treatment through the balance of this section draws, directly at points, from Hunt, *Ideology*, chaps 2–4. I am grateful to Yale University Press for permission to make use of this material. For a pioneering study, see Albert K. Weinberg, *Manifest Destiny: A Study of Nationalist Expansionism and American History*, Baltimore, Md, 1935.

21 Jerald A. Combs, *The Jay Treaty: Political Battleground of the Founding Fathers*, Berkeley, Calif., 1970; Jacob E. Cooke, *Alexander Hamilton*, New York, 1982; and Drew R. McCoy, *The Elusive Republic: Political Economy in Jeffersonian America*, Chapel Hill, N.C., 1980.

22 Hietala, *Manifest Design*.

23 Robert Beisner, *Twelve Against Empire: The Anti-Imperialists, 1898–1900*, New York, 1968; and Stuart C. Miller, *"Benevolent Assimilation": The American Conquest of the Philippines, 1899–1903*, New Haven, Conn., 1982.

24 Reginald Horsman, *Race and Manifest Destiny: The Origins of American Racial Anglo-Saxonism*, Cambridge, Mass., 1981.

25 Quote from Hunt, *Ideology*, p. 60.

26 Michael Vlahos, "Culture and Foreign Policy," *Foreign Policy*, no. 82, spring 1991, pp. 59–78.

2 "They don't come out where you expect": institutions of American diplomacy and the policy process

J. Garry Clifford

The new British ambassador came to Washington in early 1941. A distinguished statesman, former viceroy to India, and foreign secretary for the previous three years, Lord Halifax nonetheless had little first-hand knowledge of the United States and even less "feel" for the vagaries of American politics. Gaffes soon occurred. The ambassador went fox-hunting in Virginia during the Congressional debates over lend-lease; he treated defeated presidential candidate Wendell Willkie as though he were the shadow prime minister; and he wrote long reports to London bemoaning the inefficiency and irrationality in the policy process in Washington. Halifax expressed amazement at the deference President Franklin D. Roosevelt seemed to pay to every ripple of public opinion. He was aghast at the distance and suspicion that separated the White House and Congress along Pennsylvania Avenue. Nor could he make sense of the institutional crosscurrents and personal rivalries among the various executive departments, "who might almost as well be the administration of different countries." Finally, Halifax used a favorite metaphor: "I suppose it is rather like a disorderly line of beaters out shooting; they do put the rabbits out of the bracken, but they don't come out where you expect."[1]

Lord Halifax was hardly the first foreign visitor to be perplexed by the American foreign policy process. Learning quickly, he became an accomplished wartime ambassador over the next six years, a sharp contrast to one of his predecessors, Sir Lionel Sackville-West, who had become *persona non grata* for accidentally intruding into the presidential election of 1888. The puzzles that most perplexed Halifax and other observers were the separation of powers and the intricate system of checks and balances, in short the constitutional and organizational limits upon the capacity of the chief executive to provide a bold and straightforward lead in foreign affairs. Notwithstanding the legendary juggling skills of a Franklin Roosevelt, political procedures in Washington were often byzantine in their complexity. A system of governance designed to protect the polity against King George III's supposed tyrannies (or those of a home-grown despot) has inevitably impeded innovation and diluted presidential dominance. As the historian Theodore A. Wilson has written, "the institutions, attributes, and

systemic constraints which Americans embraced differ in important respects
. . . from the systems of governance of other nation states. Those differences matter."[2]

Diplomatic historians who focus on the pluralistic and centrifugal dynamics of the American policy process tend to emphasize discontinuity,
accidental results, and intra-governmental conflict. Given the historiographical concerns of the present volume, scholars who elucidate the institutional interactions of the policy process practice, at least unconsciously,
what H. W. Brands has called "fractal history."[3] Intent on explaining the
mechanics and timing of particular episodes, illuminating proximate as
opposed to deeper causes of policy, and showing why outcomes were not
always what was intended, historians who scrutinize the policy process are
not trying to answer such grand questions as why the United States has
opposed revolutions and why hegemonic powers inevitably decline. More a
framework for analysis than a school of interpretation, this approach has a
narrower focus. The bureaucratic details of débâcles like Pearl Harbor and
the Bay of Pigs invasion are thus better understood than the evolution of
containment strategies over four decades.[4] In John L. Gaddis's categor-
ization of historians, those scholars who emphasize the policy process tend
to be "splitters" rather than "lumpers".[5] To use Isaiah Berlin's analogy, it
is one of the many truths the fox must understand as he competes with the
single-minded hedgehog.[6]

As such, this interpretive approach is best suited to sharply defined periods
(wars and their aftermaths, major transformations in the international system)
characterized by dramatic change and political realignments. Such a framework stands in contrast to the so-called "corporatist" and "postrevisionist"
schools in which scholars stress collective efforts by individuals and groups
to overcome inhibitions against cooperation.[7] These scholars suggest that
shared interests and common ideologies of generational elites regarding
national security or a liberal capitalist world order may transcend internal
checks and bureaucratic inertia over time.[8] By investigating the tugging and
hauling and trade-offs that occur within governmental institutions we learn
how the cooperative core values posited by the corporatists and neorealists
are actually formed. Both levels of analysis can be used profitably.

Looking inside the American foreign policy process is like eating sausage,
in that closer examination of the ingredients does not always inspire confidence in the finished product. Scholars who study institutional underpinnings usually reject the assumption that foreign policy is produced by the
purposeful acts of a unitary national government. Rather, policies emerge as
the outcome of battles between the executive and legislative branches, of
compromise and bargaining among various participants within the executive.
"Instead of unity," former Assistant Secretary of State Roger Hilsman has
written, "there is conflict. Instead of a majestic progression, there are erratic
zigs and zags. Instead of clarity and decisiveness, there are tangle and
turmoil; instead of order, confusion."[9]

LEGISLATIVE–EXECUTIVE STRUGGLES

Regarding the respective roles of Congress and the president in the formulation of American foreign policy, the historian Edwin Corwin once characterized the Constitution as an "invitation to struggle."[10] By giving Congress the power to "declare war" and the authority to raise and support armies and navies, while making the president commander-in-chief with the power to "repel sudden attacks" and to make treaties "by and with the consent of the Senate . . . provided two-thirds of the Senators present concur," the Founding Fathers established a system of separate institutions with shared and competing responsibilities.[11] The purpose, as Justice Louis Brandeis later noted, was "not to avoid friction, but, by means of the inevitable friction incident to the distribution of the governmental powers . . . to save the people from autocracy."[12] From the beginning, when George Washington refused in 1795 to release to the House of Representatives official correspondence pertaining to Jay's Treaty, the contest between legislature and executive over foreign policy has ebbed and flowed, at times assuming epic proportions. The political scientist John Rourke has compared the process to Edgar Allan Poe's "The Pit and the Pendulum" in which "the struggle between the first two branches of government cyclically swings the power pendulum to and fro while the captive *corpus americanus* watches from below."[13]

Most historians agree that presidents have won these struggles far more often than they have lost. Notwithstanding the tragic confrontation in 1919–20 between Woodrow Wilson and Senator Henry Cabot Lodge, wherein the president's refusal to compromise over reservations to the Versailles Treaty led to its rejection and the subsequent failure of the United States to join the League of Nations, the Senate has refused to ratify only a handful of treaties.[14] The precedent was set early, as Pinckney's treaty with Spain in 1795, the treaty of Ghent following the War of 1812, and the Adams–Onís treaty of 1819 with Spain were unanimously approved by the Senate. Thomas Jefferson established presidential initiative in acquiring territory when he swallowed constitutional scruples and persuaded Congress to approve the Louisiana Purchase in 1803.[15] James Madison and James Monroe learned to bypass the treaty procedure through less binding executive agreements, the most notable being the Rush–Bagot agreement of 1817, which regulated naval armaments on the Great Lakes for the remainder of the century. When President John Tyler could not obtain a two-thirds Senate vote for a treaty annexing Texas, he accomplished the desired goal in early 1845 by resorting to a joint congressional resolution, which required only simple majorities in both houses.[16] President William McKinley employed a similar tactic in annexing Hawaii in 1898.

On occasion, bitter personal and political disputes between Congressional leaders and presidents resulted in foreign policy setbacks for the White House. After the Civil War a series of expansionist projects proposed by

Secretary of State William Seward were rejected, in large part because of
Congressional opposition to President Andrew Johnson's Reconstruction
policies.[17] Ulysses S. Grant's scheme to acquire Santo Domingo foundered
because of scandal and what amounted to a personal feud with the powerful chairman of the Senate Foreign Relations Committee, Senator Charles
Sumner of Massachusetts. The Senate killed the treaty, but Grant eventually
stripped Sumner of his committee chairmanship.[18] John Hay's arrogant
personality so antagonized Senate leaders that they almost delighted in
rejecting and amending treaties during his seven-year tenure as secretary of
state under Presidents McKinley and Theodore Roosevelt.[19] Similarly, by his
call for a Democratic Congress in 1918, by his failure to include a prominent
Republican or Senator in the American peace delegation, and by his vow
that "the Senate must take its medicine," Woodrow Wilson unnecessarily
politicized peace-making after World War I and, in effect, kept the United
States from joining the League of Nations.[20]

The pendulum of Congressional influence reached its apogee in the mid-
1930s. With war clouds looming over Europe and Asia, and with little initial
opposition from the White House, Congress passed a series of neutrality
laws designed, it was often said, to keep the United States out of World War
I. No longer did Americans claim the right to travel on belligerent ships like
the *Lusitania*. Loans to belligerents were banned, as was the sale of arms
and munitions; all other trade was to be on a cash-and-carry basis with
American merchant vessels staying out of war zones. President Roosevelt
acquiesced because he needed isolationist votes for his New Deal programs.
He even encouraged Senator Gerald P. Nye of North Dakota to launch his
famous investigation of the munitions industry, which added impetus to
neutrality legislation.[21]

Not until after the Munich conference in the autumn of 1938 did Roosevelt
decisively alter course, adopting what Robert A. Divine has called a child's
"game of giant steps" in which the president moved "two steps forward and
one back before he took the giant step ahead."[22] All subsequent steps on the
road to Pearl Harbor – neutrality revision, selective service, the destroyers for
bases deal, economic sanctions against Japan, lend-lease, naval patrols, aid to
Russia, convoys, neutrality repeal – FDR justified as the best way for the
United States to stay out of the war. Relying on international events and his
own manipulative ability, he waited for the right moment to permit Congressional debate on such measures as conscription and lend-lease, both of
which eventually passed by substantial margins.[23] More often, he circumvented Congress in obtaining overseas allies and bases, in waging undeclared
economic and naval war, and in planning for coalition warfare against the
Axis. He discredited isolationist opponents by suggesting that they were
unwittingly aiding the Axis.[24] He moved circuitously, obliquely, successfully. Sometimes he went too far, as in his misrepresentation of an unprovoked
German U-boat attack on the destroyer *Greer* in September 1941. "FDR's
deviousness in a good cause," Senator J. William Fulbright later commented,

"made it much easier for LBJ to practice the same kind of deviousness in a bad cause."[25]

The subordination of Congress continued during World War II and through much of the Cold War. Roosevelt and Harry S. Truman made certain there would be no repetition of Woodrow Wilson's mistakes by consulting with key legislators, particularly the senior Republican Senator Arthur H. Vandenberg, and including them as delegates to international conferences. Vandenberg's notion of "bipartisanship" (a phrase as fuzzy as the mind of its inventor) seemed to promise Congress some influence. The idea, as Vandenberg put it, was that Republicans in Congress would be "co-pilots in the foreign policy take-offs as well as in the crash landings."[26] For Secretary of State Dean Acheson, however, "bipartisanship was a magnificent fraud . . . which ought to be perpetuated" because "you cannot run this damn country under the Constitution any other way except by fixing the whole organization so it doesn't work the way it is supposed to work. Now the way to do that is to say politics stops at the seaboard – anyone who denies that postulate is a son of a bitch and a crook and not a true patriot. Now if people will swallow that then you're off to the races."[27] The White House won most of the races through the 1960s. Even though Senator Fulbright's hearings helped to focus public opposition to the Vietnam War after 1966, Congress as a body supported the Kennedy/Johnson policy of gradual escalation, backed the Tonkin Gulf Resolution with only two dissenting votes, and consistently voted military appropriations until the 1973 peace settlement.[28]

The end of the Vietnam War and the Watergate scandal brought a revival of Congressional prerogatives.[29] Reacting to a weakened executive and re-asserting its own collective ego, Congress voted, over President Richard M. Nixon's veto, the War Powers Resolution of 1973, under which a president could commit American troops abroad for no more than sixty days, and after that period he or she must obtain Congressional approval. Congress also cut foreign aid to Turkey, Cambodia, South Vietnam, and Angola. The Jackson–Vanik amendment to the 1974 Trade Act blocked most-favored-nation status for the Soviet Union until Moscow relaxed its restrictions on Jewish emigration. In 1975 Senator Frank Church's Select Committee to Study Governmental Operations with Respect to Intelligence Activities uncovered shocking evidence of abuses by the Central Intelligence Agency (CIA), including assassination plots against foreign leaders. The Church Committee hearings spurred a series of reforms that gave Congress a statutory role in overseeing intelligence and covert activities.[30] Other reforms during the 1970s abolished the seniority system, limited the powers of House and Senate leaders, provided much larger staffs for individual members by adding more than a hundred subcommittees, and thus decentralized Congress. This asser-tiveness continued into the Jimmy Carter administration, as freshman Senator Dennis DeConcini nearly derailed the Panama Canal Treaty by attaching a crippling reservation and as Senate opposition to the Strategic Arms Limi-tation Treaty (SALT II) caused the White House to withdraw it in 1979.

26   *J. Garry Clifford*

Pundits spoke of an "imperial Congress," and the British ambassador asked: "Senator, do you think it's time for all of us to establish our embassies up on the Hill instead of going indirectly through the State Department?"[31]

Congressional ascendancy proved short-lived. The Iran Hostage Crisis, renewed tensions with Moscow after the Soviet invasion of Afghanistan, and the election of Ronald Reagan ushered in a decade of executive dominance. Military intervention against Grenada in 1983, air strikes against Libya's Moammar Gadhafi in 1986, and Operation Just Cause to topple Panamanian strongman Manuel Noriega in 1989 went forward with minimal Congressional consultation and even less dissent. Oversight gave way to what Thomas Paterson has called "afterview," as hawkish intelligence committee members openly approved, usually after the fact, covert operations which in earlier periods would probably have remained secret: aid to Nicaraguan Contras, Cambodian rebels, and Afghan insurgents.[32] When Congress did prohibit aid to the Contras in 1984 and officials of the Reagan administration circumvented the ban by illegal means, including the solicitation of funds from other countries and residual money from secret arms sales to Iran, the subsequent investigations into the Iran–Contra Affair stopped short of challenging a popular president and focused instead on subordinates who were characterized as "loose cannons" and "rogue elephants."[33] As Theodore Draper's penetrating study of Iran–Contra makes clear, "Congress was an easy, almost willing, victim of the administration's machinations."[34] The press, not Congress, discovered what Lt-Col. Oliver North and his associates were doing in Iran and Nicaragua in the president's name; yet the joint committee's final report virtuously upheld Congress's checking and balancing role in foreign policy without mentioning that it had failed to fulfill that responsibility.[35]

Perhaps the nadir of Congressional influence came with the Gulf War. When President George Bush unilaterally reacted to Iraq's invasion of Kuwait in August 1990 by rushing US troops to Saudi Arabia and pledging that the aggression "will not stand," and then in November doubled the number of forces to assure an "adequate offensive military option," he did so without approval or consultation with Congress. When United Nations Resolution 678 authorized member states to use force against Iraq if it did not evacuate Kuwait by 15 January 1991, the president went so far as to argue that he did not need Congressional approval to order American forces into combat against Saddam Hussein. The White House's eventual request for Congressional authorization to use force, which came after a short debate and close vote (250–183 in the House and 52–47 in the Senate) on 12 January, seemed to render the issue moot, but the victorious outcome of Operation Desert Storm caused an exultant Bush to proclaim that "I had the inherent power to commit our forces to battle after the UN resolution." According to Michael Glennon, a legal scholar, Bush's behavior "pushed the Constitution's system of separation of powers steadily backwards toward the monopolistic system of King George III."[36]

Defenders of Congress point out that there have always been enough tools in the legislative box to protect its constitutional prerogatives. Under favorable political circumstances, legislators can overcome parochial and partisan divisions by denying appropriations, voting against appointments, holding hearings, rejecting treaties or, in extreme circumstances, commencing impeachment proceedings. A powerful legislator can frighten the White House at any time, as perhaps most vividly illustrated by the chairman of the foreign aid subcommittee of the House, who once told a State Department official: "Son, I don't smoke and I don't drink. My only pleasure in life is kicking the shit out of the foreign aid program of the United States of America."[37] Even a strong president who is – as Woodrow Wilson was – committed to a particular foreign policy may challenge Congressional opponents and lose. When President Kennedy once complained to Nikita Khrushchev that dealing with Congress was a "time-consuming process," the Soviet leader shot back: "Well, why don't you shift to our system?"[38] More often, Congress is seen as part of the public opinion-building process, partly echoing and partly shaping that opinion. Occupants of the Oval Office usually try to avoid the kind of acrimony that detracts from the president's image as a national leader. Even in extending diplomatic recognition to foreign governments, an area of exclusive executive prerogative, presidents have often modified, delayed, or abandoned preferred courses of action in the face of real or anticipated criticism. Whether or not (according to the old adage) Congress disposes what a particular president proposes depends on the political skill and persuasion each participant brings to the process.

BUREAUCRATIC POLITICS

One of the ironies of the cold-war era is that the creation of a vast bureaucracy designed to strengthen executive control over national security policies actually diffused the process by adding competing institutional perspectives. The urban geography and the architecture of Washington and the surrounding vicinity reflect these changes. The ornate Victorian structure next to the White House once known as the State, War, and Navy Building is now the Executive Office Building and houses the president's National Security Council staff. A squat, modern State Department now holds quarters in Foggy Bottom, on 21st Street, along with the Arms Control and Disarmament Agency. Across the Potomac in Arlington sits the huge Pentagon Building, the seat of a defense establishment employing more than three million Americans and spending hundreds of billions of dollars per year. Occupying even more acreage in Langley, Virginia, is the Central Intelligence Agency, while twenty buildings at Fort Meade, Maryland, comprise the lesser known but larger and more expensive National Security Agency, where fifty thousand employees and underground computers monitor much of the world's communications. Along the interstate highway surrounding Washington are hundreds of think tanks and other "beltway bandits" under contract to do research, primarily for the military establishment. No longer a charming southern town, Washington has become, in Ernest May's phrase, "Yes, a city. But at heart a military headquarters, like the Rome of the Flavians or the Berlin of the Hohenzollerns."[39]

One result is clear: proliferating institutions bring more diversity and conflict to the policy process. Building on the seminal works of Harvard scholars Graham Allison and Ernest May, students of bureaucratic politics emphasize that there is no single "maker" of foreign policy.[40] Policy emerges instead from a mesh of large organizations and political actors who may have real differences on particular issues and who battle to advance their own personal and departmental interests as they attempt to shape policy. The president, despite his constitutional authority, is not omnipotent; he is only one chief among many. Not even strong executives like Lyndon Johnson and Richard Nixon can fully tame the bureaucratic beast. Policies become "political resultants," as Graham Allison has put it – "*resultants* in the sense that what happens is not chosen . . . but rather results from compromise, conflict, and confusion of officials with diverse interests and unequal in-fluence; *political* in the sense [of] . . . bargaining along regularized channels among individual members of government."[41]

Even when the president makes a firm policy decision, the process does not stop because decisions are often ignored or carried out contrary to the original intent. President Ronald Reagan may have envisaged his Strategic Defense Initiative (or "Star Wars") as a workable program to shield entire popu-lations from the threat of nuclear war, but hard-liners in the Pentagon saw it primarily as an antiballistic missile (ABM) defense that would offer a technological advantage over the Soviet Union and stifle public agitation for more substantial arms control proposals.[42] Because large bureaucracies operate according to set routines and standard procedures, familiar scenarios derived from experience form the basis for options furnished the president. Thus, when the Kennedy and Johnson administrations asked the US military to fight an unconventional war in Vietnam, it did what most organizations do in such circumstances: it followed established doctrines and procedures, modifying them only slightly in deference to different conditions and executive preferences.[43]

Proponents of presidential predominance often assert that 535 members of Congress cannot possibly micromanage foreign policy. In truth, neither can the White House much of the time. Even during a crisis when a skilled president personally monitors performance, as John F. Kennedy sought to do with the navy's "quarantine" during the Cuban Missile Crisis in 1962, bureaucratic routines and procedures are so complicated that things automatically happen without presidential volition. The former PT-boat commander was astonished to learn that antisubmarine warfare units were regularly forcing Soviet submarines to the surface, thereby precipitating the hair-trigger confrontations he was trying so hard to avoid.[44] Similarly, despite assurances by the Central Intelligence Agency that no pilot would ever be captured alive, President Dwight D. Eisenhower's personal approval of each U-2 overflight of the Soviet Union could not prevent Francis Gary Power's spy plane from being shot down on the eve of the Paris Summit in May 1960 – a diplomatic disaster that was compounded by Eisenhower's recitation and subsequent repudiation of the routine cover story about a US weather plane straying over Soviet air space.[45] The buck may stop with the president, but he can deal only those cards brought to the game by the relevant institutional participants.

Bureaucracies are notoriously resistant to innovation. General Leonard Wood liked to quote the US Army bureau chief who complained in 1898: "This is awful. I just had my office in the best shape it was ever in; and along comes this [Spanish–American] war and upsets everything."[46] FDR, who enjoyed the bureaucratic give-and-take as much as any president, once expressed exasperation with his favorite armed service. "To change anything in the Na-a-vy," he said, "is like punching a feather bed. You punch it with your right and you punch it with your left until you are finally exhausted, and then you find the damn bed just as it was before you started punching."[47] Just as the navy blocked plans to construct a battleship for the Soviet Union in the 1930s, the institutional aversion to giving warships to a foreign power nearly killed the destroyers-for-bases deal with Britain in the summer of 1940.[48] Only by getting eight bases in direct exchange for the destroyers could Roosevelt convince the chief of naval operations, Admiral Harold Stark, to certify, as required by law, that these vessels were not essential to national defense.[49] The president reportedly threatened to fire Stark if he did not support what nearly every naval officer opposed.[50] The navy's subsequent impatience to begin Atlantic convoys in the summer of 1941 and the air force strategy that autumn of reinforcing the Philippines with B-17s were designed in part to retain ships and planes that FDR might have given to the British or Russians.[51]

Inertia in the face of war was matched by bureaucratic bewilderment at the collapse of communism in 1989. "There are file drawers of contingency plans in the Pentagon for fighting all kinds of wars that can never be fought," Richard Barnet noted, "but the White House clearly had no contingency plans for what to do in the face of Cold War victory."[52] When government agencies do not know what to do, they do what they know. Clinging to the status quo, those institutions with a vested interest in combatting the Red Menace now saw Soviet weakness and new regional rivalries as sufficient reason to maintain current programs. "The challenges of this world," President Bush avowed in November 1991, "are as daunting as Stalin's army was menacing forty years ago."[53] "Getting the bureaucracy to accept new ideas," Ambassador Chester Bowles once said, "is like carrying a double mattress up a very narrow and winding stairway. It is a terrible job, and you exhaust yourself when you try it. But once you get the mattress up it is awfully hard for anyone else to get it down."[54]

Bureaucratic "leaks" punctuate the policy process as well, although as often as not these leaks emanate from the White House itself. Tips are given to favorite columnists: the latest intelligence about Soviet SS-20s in eastern Europe, or documentary proof that the Guatemalan government is purchasing arms from communist Czechoslovakia are provided for the purpose of furthering administration policies. Hawkish subordinates can sometimes prod a reluctant president by passing alarming information, as with the premature release of the Gaither Report and intelligence estimates about a "missile gap" in the late 1950s.[55] Most notorious, however, have been those leaks meant to embarrass the government for the purpose of reversing its policy. A high-ranking air force officer, possibly General Henry "Hap" Arnold, gave a copy of the Army's top secret "Rainbow Five" war plan to isolationist Senator Burton K. Wheeler, who in turn leaked it to the *Chicago Tribune* where it was published in full on 4 December 1941, just three days before the Japanese attack on Pearl Harbor.[56] Even more infamous was Daniel Ellsberg's leak of the Pentagon Papers to the *New York Times* in 1971, one of several damaging leaks that prompted President Nixon to organize an extra-legal "Plumbers Unit" to plug up further indiscretions, an innovation that resulted in the Watergate break-in and Nixon's eventual resignation.

The bureaucratic axiom "where you stand depends on where you sit" also skews the policy process. On one level, it suggests that an individual adopts the values, priorities, and mission of his or her departmental position within the government. Caspar W. Weinberger, for example, earned the sobriquet "Cap the Knife" for his fiscal orthodoxy as budget director under Richard Nixon, but as secretary of defense in the Reagan administration he eagerly supported a huge military build-up that eventually led to record budget deficits.[57] Prior to the Reagan years it was virtually automatic that anyone who headed the Arms Control and Disarmament Agency enthusiastically backed nuclear arms negotiations, which the Joint Chiefs of Staff invariably viewed with deep skepticism.[58] Similarly, diplomats stationed abroad can fall victim to "localitis" – that is, they come to reflect the views of their host government, just as Joseph P. Kennedy embraced appeasement as ambassador to Britain in 1938–40, and as Chester Bowles befriended Jawaharlal Nehru in his missions to India in the 1950s and 1960s.[59] Propinquity can also breed contempt, as a whole generation of Soviet experts recoiled from the Stalinist excesses of the 1930s and applied hard-line lessons from their collective experience during the cold-war era.[60]

Scholars dispute whether ideological core values shared by so-called national security managers count more in determining policy than do differences attributable to bureaucratic position.[61] For such "wise men" as Averell Harriman, Robert A. Lovett, and John J. McCloy, whose membership in the foreign policy establishment spanned nearly a half century and cut across bureaucratic and partisan lines, ideals of public service undoubtedly mattered more than any particular job.[62] Yet McCloy, for example, advocated early intervention and a full-scale military effort as assistant secretary of war during 1941–5, then championed the revival and reintegration of Germany as high commissioner to Bonn after World War II, and later pushed hard for arms control as President Kennedy's disarmament adviser.[63] More often than not, intramural struggles between hawks and doves during the Cold War reflected real institutional differences. Whether it was civilian theorists of limited war in the 1960s debating military professionals whose watchword from Korea was "Never Again," or Secretary of State Cyrus Vance resigning in protest after the abortive mission to rescue the hostages being held in Iran, or Assistant Secretary of Defense Richard Perle and Assistant Secretary of State Richard Burt warring for President Reagan's attention on nuclear policy, such battles along the Potomac produced flawed outcomes. Although the tugging and hauling may be over tactics more than strategy, over pace rather than direction, those differences matter significantly when the policy compromises are gradual escalation in Vietnam, humiliation in Iran, and a deadlocked disarmament process and disarray in NATO.

The more institutions involved in formulating a particular foreign policy, the more difficult it is to coordinate that policy. Consider recent diplomatic relations with Japan. For decades the main issue between Washington and Tokyo centered on American military bases in Japan and the collective effort to contain China and the Soviet Union. The State Department and Pentagon made sure that no trade disputes could disturb the security relationship. In the 1980s, however, when Japan's huge exports produced a trade imbalance that assumed threatening proportions, other Washington agencies jumped in. "Basically there was a small circle of players you could count on one hand," the head of the State Department's Office of Japanese Affairs recalled. "Now, because our interests are so interdependent and our foreign policy so intertwined with domestic economic issues, you have so many more players – State, Treasury, Commerce, the Trade Representative, Pentagon, Justice, Council of Economic Advisers all need to be in the room."[64]

In fact, three groups vied for control of the policies to be adopted in relations with Japan. The State Department, Pentagon, and National Security Council wanted to maintain the traditional relationship, that of subordinating trade issues to security cooperation. The Commerce Department and Office of the United States Trade Representative advocated sanctions to break down the formal and informal barriers that Japan had built to protect its domestic markets. The Treasury, Office of Management and Budget, and the Council of Economic Advisers were dominated by free-trade zealots who opposed any government attempts to manage trade, even with Japan. President George Bush, whose earlier experience as head of the American diplomatic mission in Beijing gave him an exaggerated view of China's importance in Asia, found it hard to focus on Japan. Instead of reconciling the competing wings of his own government, Bush lurched between supporting managed trade one week, free trade the next, and subtle Japan-bashing on other occasions. A zig-zag pattern persisted through the end of Bush's presidency.

Even the Iran–Contra imbroglio, often depicted as a struggle between the executive and the legislative branches, can also be seen as the unintended consequence of bureaucratic infighting run amok. Despite strong opposition from Secretary of State George P. Shultz and Defense Secretary Weinberger to trading arms for hostages with Iran, President Reagan encouraged such a dubious policy to proceed, and eventually to intermingle with the secret program of supplying the Nicaraguan Contras, by making the National Security Council staff responsible for both covert operations. Since clandestine activities required compartmentalization, secrecy, and deniability, National Security Advisers Robert C. McFarlane and John M. Poindexter were able to direct the operations in total disregard of Congress, almost completely outside the purview of State and Defense, and indeed of virtually the entire structure of government. The action officer in charge of both operations, Lt-Col. Oliver North, was a "can do" marine, a superpatriotic Vietnam veteran who found it hard to conceal his contempt for Congress, professional diplomats, and traditional bureaucrats. "Colonel North was given a very broad charter," Poindexter later commented, "and I did not micromanage him."[65] When North discovered a way to take profits from the Iranian arms sales and divert the monies to the Contras, Poindexter approved but did not tell President Reagan. In effect, the "buck stopped" with Poindexter because he wanted the president "to have some deniability so that he would be protected."[66]

In attempting to explain what went wrong in Iran–Contra, Secretary Weinberger blamed the fiasco on "people with their own agenda," a few strategically placed insiders who deceived the president by feeding him the wrong information and excluding "views that they suspected, quite correctly most of the time, differ from theirs."[67] Secretary Shultz also portrayed the president as an innocent dupe misled by his inner circle. Nonetheless, the record is clear that at all top-level meetings on Iran–Contra, President Reagan spoke more than any of his advisers, forcefully steered discussions, and made basic decisions, whether or not he subsequently approved every operational detail. Actually, Weinberger and Shultz were overruled on policies they regarded as ill-advised and probably illegal. They might have resigned in protest, as Cyrus Vance had done in 1980, but they chose to be good soldiers. They remained willfully ignorant of operational particulars in what amounted to a breakdown in the American system of government. It is almost an afterthought to note that the policy initiatives with regard to Iran and Nicaragua ended in failure.

CONCLUSION

The foregoing discussion of the American foreign policy process does not claim to be definitive. By highlighting interactions between Congress and the presidency and competitive dynamics within the executive branch, the essay slights what some political scientists consider the "outer circles" of the policymaking process. The effect of public opinion, the role of pressure groups and lobbies, the quasi-official influence of the press and media (the so-called fourth branch of government), shifting structures of socio-economic power within society, cultural and ideological values need to be taken into account by historians of American foreign relations, who must attempt to fit these additional pieces into the larger mosaic.

Nor does the emphasis on intramural conflict and accidental outcomes necessarily invalidate interpretations of American diplomacy that stress consistent patterns and purpose over the long run. Despite sharp breaks and reversals of policy, there has usually been general agreement throughout American history about essential national interests – a working consensus about the goals of foreign policy. The debates have been about tactics: how best to expand into what territories; whether to have formal or informal empire; how to create and maintain a favorable international order; how to protect democratic values at home and abroad without compromising those ideals. Viewed from a global perspective, sudden alterations in the international system, as in the aftermath of World War II and with the dissolution of the Soviet empire after 1989, can virtually compel policy changes, irrespective of internal debates, by eliminating adversaries and conditions that had justified previous policies. In short, the history of American foreign relations involves more than the workings of the policy process.

Franklin Roosevelt once wrote that he "had little sympathy with Copernicus" who "looked through the right end of the telescope, thus greatly magnifying his problems. I use the wrong end of the telescope and it makes things much easier to bear."[68] This whimsical statement suggests that presidents prefer to focus on the larger picture, to see themselves piloting the ship of state toward some clear destination, even as they tack according to the political winds of the moment, alter course because of bureaucratic or Congressional opposition, or turn 180 degrees in search of quick-fix solutions. Historians who take the trouble to chart a particular policy by looking inside the governmental process should not be surprised when it comes out in unexpected places.

NOTES

1 As quoted in David Reynolds, *The Creation of the Anglo-American Alliance 1937–41*, Chapel Hill, N.C., 1982, p. 177.
2 Theodore A. Wilson, *The First Summit: Roosevelt & Churchill at Placentia Bay, 1941*, rev. ed., Lawrence, Kan., 1991, p. xiv.
3 H. W. Brands, "Fractal History, or Clio and the Chaotics," *Diplomatic History*, vol. 16, 1992, pp. 495–510.
4 Roberta Wohlstetter, *Pearl Harbor: Warning and Decision*, Stanford, Calif., 1962; Lucien S. Vandenbroucke, "Anatomy of a Failure: The Decision to Land at the Bay of Pigs," *Political Science Quarterly*, vol. 99, 1984, pp. 471–91; John L. Gaddis, *Strategies of Containment: A Critical Appraisal of Postwar American National Security Policy*, New York, 1982.
5 Gaddis, *Strategies of Containment*, p. vii.
6 Isaiah Berlin, *The Hedgehog and the Fox: An Essay on Tolstoy's View of History*, New York, 1957.
7 See especially Michael J. Hogan, *The Marshall Plan: America, Britain, and the Reconstruction of Western Europe*, New York, 1987; and Melvyn P. Leffler, *A

Preponderance of Power: National Security, the Truman Administration, and the Cold War, Stanford, Calif., 1992.

8 For a convenient summary of the different historiographical and analytical approaches, see Michael J. Hogan and Thomas G. Paterson (eds), *Explaining the History of American Foreign Relations*, New York, 1991.

9 Roger Hilsman, *The Politics of Policy Making in Defense and Foreign Affairs*, New York, 1971, p. 8.

10 Edwin S. Corwin, *The President: Office and Powers 1787–1957*, 4th ed., New York, 1957, p. 171. For other major works on Congress, the presidency, and foreign affairs, see Cecil V. Crabb Jr and Pat M. Holt, *Invitation to Struggle: Congress, the President and Foreign Policy*, Washington, 1980; Robert A. Dahl, *Congress and Foreign Policy*, New York, 1950; I. M. Destler, *Presidents, Bureaucrats, and Foreign Policy*, Princeton, N.J., 1972; Thomas N. Frank and Edward Weisband, *Foreign Policy by Congress*, New York, 1979; Martha L. Gibson, *Weapons of Influence: The Legislative Veto, American Foreign Policy, and the Irony of Reform*, Boulder, Colo., 1992; Louis Henkin, *Constitutionalism, Democracy, and Foreign Affairs*, New York, 1990; John T. Rourke, *Congress and the Presidency in U.S. Foreign Policymaking: A Study of Interaction and Influence, 1945–82*, Boulder, Colo., 1983, and *Presidential Wars and American Democracy: Rally 'Round the Chief*, New York, 1992; Francis O. Wilcox, *Congress, The Executive, and Foreign Policy*, New York, 1971; Abraham D. Sofaer, *War, Foreign Affairs and Constitutional Power: The Origins*, Cambridge, Mass., 1976.

11 Article VI of the Constitution.

12 Ervin H. Pollack (ed.), *The Brandeis Reader*, New York, 1956, p. 134.

13 Rourke, *Congress and the Presidency*, p. xiii.

14 From 1789 to 1928 the Senate approved 86 per cent of the 786 treaties submitted to it. Royden J. Dangerfield, *In Defense of the Senate: A Study in Treaty Making*, Norman, Okla., 1933, pp. 91–2, 305–13; Denna Frank Fleming, *The Treaty Veto of the American Senate*, New York, 1930, pp. 50–1.

15 Alexander DeConde, *This Affair of Louisiana*, New York, 1976.

16 David M. Pletcher, *The Diplomacy of Annexation: Texas, Oregon, and the Mexican War*, Colombia, Mo., 1973.

17 W. Stull Holt, *Treaties Defeated by the Senate: A Study of the Struggle Between President and Senate Over the Conduct of Foreign Relations*, Baltimore, Md, 1933, pp. 100–20.

18 Charles C. Tansill, *The United States and Santo Domingo, 1798–1873*, Baltimore, Md, 1938.

19 Holt, *Treaties Defeated by the Senate*, pp. 177–95.

20 For Wilson and the Senate, see Lloyd E. Ambrosius, *Woodrow Wilson and the American Diplomatic Tradition: The Treaty Fight in Perspective*, Cambridge, Mass., 1987; Thomas A. Bailey, *Woodrow Wilson and the Great Betrayal*, New York, 1945; Arthur S. Link, *Woodrow Wilson: War, Revolution, and Peace*, Arlington Heights, Ill., 1979; Seward W. Livermore, *Politics is Adjourned: Woodrow Wilson and the War Congress, 1916–1918*, Middletown, Conn., 1966; Ralph A. Stone, *The Irreconcilables: The Fight Against the League of Nations*, New York, 1973.

21 For important works on Congress and foreign policy in the 1930s, see Wayne S. Cole, *Senator Gerald P. Nye and American Foreign Relations*, Minneapolis, Minn., 1962 and *Roosevelt and the Isolationists, 1932–1945*, Lincoln, Neb., 1984; Robert A. Divine, *The Illusion of Neutrality*, Chicago, 1962; John E. Wiltz, *In Search of Peace: The Senate Munitions Inquiry, 1934–1936*, Baton Rouge, La, 1963.

22 Robert A. Divine, *Roosevelt and World War II*, Baltimore, Md, 1969, p. 37.

23 For an important study that argues that Congress actually moved faster than FDR prior to Pearl Harbor, see David L. Porter, *The Seventy-Sixth Congress and World*

War II, 1939–1940, Columbia, Mo., 1979. My own research concludes that the president overestimated the strength and cohesion of Congressional isolationists in 1940. J. Garry Clifford and Samuel R. Spencer Jr, *The First Peacetime Draft*, Lawrence, Kan., 1986.

24 Cole, *Roosevelt and the Isolationists*, chap. 30; Richard W. Steele, "Franklin D. Roosevelt and His Foreign Policy Critics," *Political Science Quarterly*, vol. 94, 1979, pp. 15–32.

25 *Congressional Record*, 14 April 1971, p. 10355.

26 Quoted in Arthur M. Schlesinger Jr, *The Imperial Presidency*, Boston, 1973, p. 129.

27 Quoted in Thomas G. Paterson, *On Every Front: The Making and Unmaking of the Cold War*, New York, rev. ed., 1992, p. 160.

28 "In the early years, Congress was a willing, if usually silent, accomplice in the formation of Vietnam policies. Dissent developed slowly and assumed significant proportions only at the very end of the war." George C. Herring, "The Executive, Congress, and the Vietnam War, 1965–1975," in Michael Barnhart (ed.), *Congress and United States Foreign Policy*, Albany, N.Y., 1987, p. 176.

29 See especially P. Edward Haley, *Congress and the Fall of South Vietnam and Cambodia*, Rutherford, N.J., 1982, and John Lehman, *The Executive, Congress and Foreign Policy: Studies of the Nixon Administration*, New York, 1974.

30 Loch K. Johnson, *A Season of Inquiry: The Senate Intelligence Investigation*, Lexington, Ky, 1985.

31 Peter Jay, quoted in Rourke, *Congress and the Presidency*, p. 288.

32 Thomas G. Paterson, "Oversight or Afterview?: Congress, the CIA, and Covert Operations Since 1947," in Barnhart (ed.), *Congress and United States Foreign Policy*, p. 155.

33 See especially the Tower Commission Report, *Report of the President's Special Review Board*, New York, 1987.

34 Theodore Draper, *A Very Thin Line: The Iran–Contra Affairs*, New York, 1991, p. 596.

35 Joint committees, *The Iran–Contra Affair*, Washington, 1987, p. 426.

36 Michael J. Glennon, "The Gulf War and the Constitution," *Foreign Affairs*, vol. 70, 1991, p. 84.

37 Otto Passman, quoted in Wm Roger Louis, "Dulles, Suez, and the British," in Richard Immerman (ed.), *John Foster Dulles and the Diplomacy of the Cold War*, Princeton, N.J., 1990, p. 146.

38 Quoted in Michael R. Beschloss, *The Crisis Years: Kennedy and Khrushchev, 1960–63*, New York, 1991, p. 199.

39 Ernest R. May, "The U.S. Government, a Legacy of the Cold War," *Diplomatic History*, vol. 16, 1992, p. 270.

40 Graham T. Allison, *Essence of Decision: Explaining the Cuban Missile Crisis*, Boston, 1971; Graham T. Allison and Morton H. Halperin, "Bureaucratic Politics: A Paradigm and Some Policy Implications," *World Politics*, vol. 24, 1972, pp. 40–80; Ernest R. May, *The "Lessons" of the Past: The Use and Misuse of History in American Foreign Policy*, New York, 1973; and May, *The Truman Administration and China, 1945–1949*, Philadelphia, Pa, 1975.

41 Allison, *Essence of Decision*, p. 162.

42 Strobe Talbott, *Deadly Gambits: The Reagan Administration and the Stalemate in Nuclear Arms Control*, New York, 1984.

43 Leslie Gelb and Richard Betts, *The Irony of Vietnam: The System Worked*, Washington, 1979; Robert W. Komer, *Bureaucracy at War: U.S. Performance in the Vietnam Conflict*, Boulder, Colo., 1986; and Wallace J. Thies, *When Governments Collide: Coercion and Diplomacy in Vietnam, 1964–1968*, Berkeley, Calif., 1980.

44 Allison, *Essence of Decision*, p. 138.
45 Michael R. Beschloss, *Mayday: The U-2 Affair*, New York, 1986.
46 Quoted in John Garry Clifford, *The Citizen Soldiers: The Plattsburg Training Camp Movement, 1913–1920*, Lexington, Ky, 1972, p. 7.
47 M. S. Eccles, *Beckoning Frontiers*, New York, 1951, p. 336.
48 Thomas R. Maddux, *Years of Estrangement: American Relations with the Soviet Union, 1933–1941*, Tallahassee, Fl., 1980, pp. 87–8.
49 James R. Leutze, *Bargaining for Supremacy: Anglo-American Naval Collaboration, 1937–1941*, Chapel Hill, N.C., 1977, ch. 8.
50 John Callan O'Laughlin memorandum of telephone conversation with Herbert Hoover, 16 August 1940, Box 45, O'Laughlin Mss, Manuscripts Division, Library of Congress, Washington, D.C.; William R. Castle Jr, diary, 20 September 1940, Houghton Library, Harvard University, Cambridge, Mass.
51 Waldo H. Heinrichs, *Threshold of War: Franklin D. Roosevelt and American Entry into World War II*, New York, 1988, pp. 42–4, 144.
52 Richard J. Barnet, "Reflections: After the Cold War," *New Yorker*, vol. 65, 1990, p. 66.
53 Quoted in William G. Hyland, "The Case for Pragmatism," *Foreign Affairs: America and the World 1991/92*, vol. 71, 1992, p. 40.
54 Quoted in Arthur M. Schlesinger Jr, *A Thousand Days*, New York, 1967 ed., p. 627.
55 For evidence that intra-service rivalries and hawkish defense intellectuals pushed American nuclear strategy and force levels well beyond the objectives sought by presidents, see David Alan Rosenberg, "Origins of Overkill: Nuclear Weapons and American Strategy, 1945–1960," *International Security*, vol. 7, 1983, pp. 3–71, and "Reality and Responsibility: Power and Process in the Making of United States Nuclear Strategy, 1954–1968," *Journal of Strategic Studies*, vol. 9, 1986, pp. 35–52; Fred Kaplan, *The Wizards of Armageddon*, New York, 1983.
56 Thomas Fleming, "The Big Leak," *American Heritage*, vol. 38, 1987, pp. 64–71.
57 Caspar Weinberger, *Fighting for Peace*, New York, 1990.
58 Strobe Talbott, *Endgame: The Inside Story of SALT II*, New York, 1979.
59 Michael R. Beschloss, *Kennedy and Roosevelt: The Uneasy Alliance*, New York, 1980; Dennis Merrill, *Bread and the Ballot: The United States and India's Economic Development, 1947–1963*, Chapel Hill, N.C., 1990.
60 Hugh De Santis, *The Diplomacy of Silence: The American Foreign Service, the Soviet Union, and the Cold War, 1933–1947*, Chicago, 1980; Daniel Yergin, *Shattered Peace: The Origins of the Cold War*, Boston, 1977.
61 See especially Robert J. Art, "Bureaucratic Politics and American Foreign Policy: A Critique," *Policy Sciences*, vol. 4, 1973, pp. 467–90; and Stephen D. Krasner, "Are Bureaucracies Important, (or Allison Wonderland)," *Foreign Policy*, vol. 7, 1972, pp. 159–79.
62 Walter Isaacson and Evan Thomas, *The Wise Men: Six Friends and the World They Made*, New York, 1986.
63 Kai Bird, *The Chairman: John J. McCloy, The Making of the American Establishment*, New York, 1992.
64 Thomas J. Friedman, "America's Japan Policy: Fractured Vision," *New York Times Magazine*, 28 June 1992, p. 24.
65 Quoted in Draper, *A Very Thin Line*, p. 565.
66 Quoted in Draper, *A Very Thin Line*, p. 560.
67 Quoted in Draper, *A Very Thin Line*, p. 567.
68 FDR to Felix Frankfurter, 11 March 1943, in Max Freedman (ed.), *Roosevelt and Frankfurter: Their Correspondence, 1928–1945*, Boston, 1967, p. 692.

3 Economic interest and United States foreign policy

Emily S. Rosenberg

As the Soviet Union crumbled and the Cold War ended in the late 1980s and early 1990s, US policymakers and analysts increasingly articulated the country's national interests in terms of economic goals. Grim trade statistics, a declining dollar, and a spate of books examining the precipitous decline of American economic power promoted the view that America's revitalization within a global economy needed to take center stage in the formulation of foreign policy. With the end of the Soviet Union and the KGB, officials of the CIA spoke of recasting their cold-war mission to emphasize "economic intelligence." Similarly, in the first presidential election after the end of the Cold War (1992), most of the aspiring candidates emphasized international economic competitiveness as their foremost goal in foreign policy. President George Bush rushed to finalize the North American Free Trade Agreement to send to Congress just before the election. Democratic nominee Bill Clinton, in the first major foreign policy address of his campaign, promised to "elevate economics in foreign policy, [to] create an economic security council similar to the National Security Council."[1] Touting the importance of economic interests in foreign policy became so commonplace following the end of the Cold War that policy discourses of the early 1990s asserting the prominence of economics in foreign policy hardly seemed a remarkable, and much less a contestable, assumption.

Earlier in this century, however, scholarly accounts that elevated economic interest to a prominent role in foreign policy generated great controversy. The reason is not hard to divine: interpretations that stressed economics tended to be joined to radical critiques of American foreign policy and of America itself. Economic interpretations were hotly contested, often portrayed as subversive, and sometimes labeled Marxist, whether they were or not.

To clarify and make more concrete the historical debates related to the role of economic interest in foreign policy, it may be useful to focus on three interpretive traditions. Scott Nearing, though not a historian, helped formulate a socialist critique in the 1920s that emphasized revisionist views on World War I and an anti-imperialist analysis of US policy. Charles Beard, probably the most influential American historian of the twentieth century, popularized non-socialist economic interpretations of history during the 1920s and 1930s.

William Appleman Williams, a historian associated with the "Wisconsin school," built upon Beard's economic interpretation and dissenting tradition during the period of the Cold War. All three of these writers emphasized the role of economic interest in foreign policy as part of their critique of the existing order. They all had a vision of radical change for American society, were social activists, and presented controversial and influential formulations of American history. The positions that they articulated and the debates that they helped to generate significantly shaped the historiographical discourses of the eras in which they lived.

Especially since the end of the Cold War, however, it may be that interpretations stressing economic interest are becoming less contentious and increasingly dissociated from dissenting perspectives. After examining several of the traditions of economic interpretation in the history of American foreign relations, this essay will assess some reasons for the apparent decline of controversy over this issue.

SCOTT NEARING: SOCIALIST DISSENT AGAINST WAR AND IMPERIALISM

Scott Nearing was a major critic of "dollar diplomacy" in the 1920s. His writings and activities in that decade argued that US capitalist elites and their search for profits produced both imperialism and war. Nearing's radical views kept him out of academic life. He received his graduate training in economics at the Wharton School of the University of Pennsylvania, studying under the renowned Simon Patten. But unlike most economists of his time, he spent his summers on a communal farm – with Upton Sinclair and other unconventional thinkers – and was strongly influenced by the radical, egalitarian doctrines of Henry George and Edward Bellamy. After accepting a faculty position at Wharton, Nearing outraged many of the school's alumni by his critique of inequality in American life. One letter, which referred to Nearing, condemned teachers "who talk wildly and in a manner entirely inconsistent with Mr. Wharton's well-known views and in defiance of the conservative opinions of men of affairs."[2] Nearing was quickly dismissed from his job. Although his case was taken up by the newly formed American Association of University Professors (AAUP), who subsequently condemned the University of Pennsylvania for its actions, another short and stormy stint at the University of Toledo ended Nearing's academic career.[3] During World War I, Nearing formed a pacifist group and began to write pamphlets for the Socialist Party, expounding the thesis associated with V. I. Lenin, that capitalism's surplus profits and overproduction led to imperialism and then to war. For these writings, he was indicted under the Espionage Act.[4] As Nearing's case demonstrated, those who supported the "war to save the world for democracy" hotly opposed economic interpretations of America's entry into the war. Such interpretations seemed especially subversive after Lenin's new Bolshevik government in Russia in 1917 withdrew from the war, repudiated foreign property rights, and urged that class struggle within nations should replace elite-based conflicts between them. Although Nearing left the Socialist Party in 1922, he continued to frame his analyses of foreign policy around links between capitalists at home and imperialism (and consequent war) abroad. Drawing from both his domestic populism and from Marxism, he elaborated the view that government, operating closely with business elites, preferred to protect investment opportunities abroad rather than pursue economic policies that would alleviate class inequality at home. The dollar, and monied interests generally, guided diplomacy in the direction of imperialism, which led to exploitation of the lower classes at home and abroad. He was an important promoter of revisionist views on the causes of World War I and became even better known as a major critic of dollar diplomacy, the practice of using American private bank loans to "stabilize" areas deemed to be in the national interest.

Although Nearing had little standing in the historical (or economics) profession because of his activism and lack of a university appointment, his ideas nonetheless had a considerable impact. From 1924 to 1926 he served as president of the American Fund for Public Service, commonly known as the Garland Fund. Guiding the Fund's grant efforts, Nearing encouraged the circulation of dissenting publications through creation of the Vanguard Press and underwrote a new series of books called "Studies in American Imperialism." For the latter project he enlisted, as series editor, the well-known World War I revisionist historian Harry Elmer Barnes.[5] Although the series finally produced only a few books, most of them became widely read and cited in academic circles, and several remain standard works in the history of relations between Latin America and the United States.[6] Meanwhile, Nearing himself collaborated with Joseph Freeman on a famous book, published in 1925, called *Dollar Diplomacy*. Nearing and Freeman's study traced the political impact of the loans made by American bankers, charging that US foreign policy was increasingly guided by the investment decisions of capitalists and their subsequent demands for protection of their property interests abroad.[7]

Although Nearing's historical interpretations often corresponded to Lenin's formulations, his distrust of the international connections of bankers and of the close relationship between private bank loans and US foreign policy by no means fell outside of the mainstream of American attitudes in the 1920s and 1930s. His critique was part of a larger, quite widely held, view that World War I had been caused mainly by the greed of economic elites.

During the interwar period, many groups propounded the notion that economic competition among national business elites produced both international conflicts and social injustice. Jane Addams and Emily Balch, for example, worked from the same premises as they guided the Women's International League for Peace and Freedom – and both received Nobel Peace Prizes. The book and movie versions of Erich Remarque's *All Quiet on the Western Front* popularized the economic interpretation and revisionist view of the war. Revisionist histories, questioning Germany's culpability and Allied motives, became widely influential. Moreover, politicians nurtured on the long tradition of midwestern anti-bank populism, disaffected by the decline of farm prices during the 1920s and by the spreading international depression after 1930, also maintained a steady opposition to the influence of bankers in foreign policy. In Congressional hearings throughout the 1920s, these "anti-imperialist" members of Congress, often drawing on the Garland Fund's studies, opposed governmental efforts to assist in the collection of foreign bonds and dissented from supporting military action in countries controlled through American financial receiverships (Nicaragua, the Dominican Republic, and Haiti). In the most dramatic and influential Congressional hearing of the interwar period, the Nye Committee of 1934 concluded that a conspiracy of "munitions-makers" and bankers had been responsible for American entry into World War I. A critical economic interpretation of foreign policy probably had more popular acceptance in the period between the two world wars than at any other time in the twentieth century.

In the era before World War II, Nearing's work helped to promote an economic interpretation of foreign policy and stimulated both academic and public debate over "dollar diplomacy." But an overtly Marxist school of interpretation never became very dominant in the historiography of US foreign relations. Following Nearing's lead, later generations of Marxist-oriented historians – especially Philip Foner, Sidney Lens, Harry Magdoff and Gabriel Kolko – emphasized the inevitability of class conflict, the identification of imperialism as a stage of capitalism, the suggestion that the capitalist nation-state was a creature of the owners of the means of production, and the idea that social organization and ideas were mere "superstructure" to material relationships. According to their theoretical perspective, capitalist economic expansion, sponsored by business and government elites, led inevitably to international conflict abroad and class conflict at home. Rhetoric of morality, self-defense, promotion of liberty and other common justifications for policy couched real, material motives.[8]

Such Marxist-oriented histories reenforced the identification between political radicalism and an emphasis on economic interest in foreign policy. With Marxist scholars dwelling so often on economic topics, conservative historians tended to stress the strategic or moralistic dimensions of foreign policy and to emphasize evidence that questioned economic motivations or business influence. During the same period that nurtured Nearing's studies of US imperialism and the weak beginnings of a tradition of Marxist scholarship in the field of United States foreign relations, a less coherent and non-Marxist – though still fiercely critical – economic interpretation became far more influential. Yet, as will be seen, the widespread fear of Marxism in American academic life made even this interpretation hotly controversial. This other dissenting strain, one historian disparagingly called "history with a Beard."

CHARLES BEARD AND ECONOMIC INTERPRETATION

Foremost among those working from an economic interpretation in the interwar period was America's best-known and most influential historian, Charles Beard. Beard admired Karl Marx as a thinker, but, unlike Nearing, Beard did not operate from a Marxist perspective nor claim connections to a Marxian socialist tradition. Never a thoroughgoing historical materialist, Beard believed that ideas (especially his own) could influence policy, that class struggle was an inappropriate framework for American life, and that reform (not revolution) could bring a democracy of goods to the American people. His book *The Open Door at Home* described his vision of what the United States could become: a relatively self-sufficient, prosperous middle-class country, in which the excesses of private property-holders were checked by a system of strong, nationally based planning, designed to promote the common good.

Such an egalitarian society, he believed, could come only from a repudiation of economic expansionism abroad. Policies promoting greater trade and investment abroad, he suggested in *The Idea of National Interest*, provided the country with few economic benefits because foreign exports comprised such a small percentage of GNP. An economically expansionist foreign policy did, however, risk global conflicts that wasted enormous resources when they resulted in war.[9] Beard rejected the Wilsonian liberal view that world trade, openly pursued, promoted world peace. Global economic aspirations, he instead suggested, led to wasteful and quixotic extensions of "national interest" to areas that were difficult to defend and thus to ever-larger military build-ups and far-flung international conflicts. He urged that the term "national interest" once again be identified with the strength of a continentally-bound economy rather than being defined globally by business internationalists and other expansionists. A strong nation would maximize its self-sufficiency, concentrating on building profits and new opportunities at home.

Beard was part of the "New History" movement, a group of leading interwar historians who believed that history should be relevant to current problems and that it should contribute to social change. Distrusting "objectivity" and ivory-tower professionalism, Beard never reentered academic life after he left Columbia in 1917 to protest the violations of freedom of speech that were associated with World War I. Economically secure due to the royalties of his popular textbooks, he immersed himself in public life and reformist causes. By the late 1930s and 1940s, his greatest energy went into denouncing America's entry into World War II and the growth of executive-branch power that he knew would accompany an all-out war effort. He felt that a war against European fascism might, by centralizing political power at home, usher in an American-style fascism.

Beard's economic interpretation lacked consistent theoretical grounding. Sometimes he suggested a special-interest-driven economic determinism. In the late 1920s, for example, he wrote Harry Elmer Barnes that "Probably [the] Morgans will get the American boobs to lend fifty billions more to the European powers . . . to loose [*sic*] in the next war for liberty, democracy, and Christianity. But I am not going to have any more wool pulled over my eyes if I can help it."[10] At other times, however, he developed a more structural economic interpretation, arguing that bankers and politicians did not operate in a vacuum but at the behest of the public at large, which pressured politicians to create jobs, both by cultivating export markets and by awarding military contracts.

Beard was similarly unclear about the role of individuals. Did economic forces inexorably drive history or could particular individuals be held responsible for courses of action? His interwar histories featured socio-economic structures much more than individuals. But in the late 1930s, as he mounted his impassioned pleas for the country to avoid involvements that could lead to US participation in another world war, he became more and more focused on the role of a single, misguided or even malevolent person: President Franklin D. Roosevelt. Roosevelt, he charged, was deliberately and cynically maneuvering to prepare the country to enter a war, which was contrary to its national interests.[11]

As Beard's writings became more and more controversial during World War II and afterwards, many scholars attacked Beard's inconsistencies as a way of discrediting his work.[12] But Beard's most recent biographer, Ellen Nore, is no doubt correct in arguing that "he was less a theorist than an activist," less concerned with consistency than with asking probing, difficult and dissenting questions.[13] The influences that operated on Beard were eclectic: his Quaker heritage; his acquaintance with various traditions of European radicalism; and his involvement in the New History movement. He was a free-thinker who refused to apply any particular radical vision in a block-print manner. Beard elevated and stirred controversy around the role of economic interest in foreign policy, but he provided no theoretically con-sistent blueprint for an "economic interpretation." Beard's attention to the importance of economic interest, his belief in a usable past, his irreverent treatment of received wisdom and power, and his strident opposition to World War II and the growth of executive-branch power put him at odds with the intellectual fashions that dominated the United States in the 1950s. As postwar historians decried "ideology" and celebrated consensus, Beard's emphasis on commitment and on conflict seemed both intellectually old-fashioned and politically suspect. Probably the best known and most in-fluential American historian in the years leading up to World War II, by the 1950s Beard was widely dismissed by established, academic historians as a naive propagandist whose economic interpretation and relativism brought him dangerously close to Marxism.[14] As pressures for cold-war conformity mounted throughout the 1950s, younger historians insistently refuted, but seldom read seriously, Beard's works.

WILLIAM APPLEMAN WILLIAMS AND THE WISCONSIN SCHOOL

Although Beard's influence waned, another equally controversial historian, William A. Williams, reformulated many of his perspectives. Williams's work built on Beard's by emphasizing the centrality of economic expansionism in American foreign policy and the importance of developing dissenting perspectives. Williams, a graduate student at the University of Wisconsin from 1946 to 1950, worked under Fred Harvey Harrington, the intellectual mentor for a group of diplomatic historians who became collectively known as "the Wisconsin school."

The University of Wisconsin provided a unique environment for dissenting views in the 1950s. While many other history departments across the country celebrated cold-war orthodoxies, exiling economic interpretations from respectability and removing Beard from reading lists, Wisconsin maintained an attachment to economic interpretation and to independent, unorthodox thinking. Williams's first book after leaving graduate school, *American–Russian Relations* (1952), went against the cold-war grain by questioning the historical premises of America's newly minted "containment" policy.[15] After returning to Wisconsin as a faculty member in 1957, his work became even more controversial. *The Tragedy of American Diplomacy* (1959), Williams's most influential book, expanded his critique of American foreign policy. *Tragedy*, which was heavily indebted to Beard's work, argued that commercial expansion (what Williams called the "open door") was the driving force behind US foreign policy. Most Americans, he explained, believed that domestic prosperity was linked to market expansion overseas, and he criticized the search for economic markets and stability that resulted from this assumption as a "tragedy" that led to intervention and often undercut self-determination and the emergence of democratic societies abroad. Open-door expansionism, he wrote, had become such an intrinsic part of American thought and policy that "empire" had become a "way of life" – to paraphrase the title of one of his subsequent books.[16] *Tragedy* became one of the central historical works of the cold-war era. It was initially dismissed by established scholars for employing an "outmoded" economic interpretation; it was also pilloried as communist-inspired and undocumented.[17] Increasingly, however, it was read and acclaimed, especially a decade later, by younger scholars who began to search for historical explanations of their country's destructive involvement in Vietnam and its close alliances with dictatorships in the Third World.

The "open door" interpretation identified the pursuit of economic interests as the driving force of foreign policy, relegating other potential motivations (defense, morality, balance-of-power politics) to secondary status. It became the central theme of a generation of scholars, most of whom did graduate work at the University of Wisconsin. Williams provided the most sweeping development of the theme, but others of the so-called "Wisconsin school," such as Walter LaFeber, Lloyd Gardner, Thomas McCormick and others, elaborated it in narrower studies during the 1960s and 1970s.[18]

There were a number of reasons why the Wisconsin school's "open door" thesis sparked one of the most divisive controversies in American history-writing. Some critics seized upon any interpretation that highlighted economics as akin to Marxism, the same charge that had dogged Beard. Other critics noted the same ambiguity that had been present in Beard: was economic expansionism a structural necessity of American capitalism or simply a misguided policy that right-thinking people could reverse?[19] Still others, again echoing earlier critics of Beard, challenged the contention that trade expansion had been a paramount policy objective and pointed out the frequently detached, or even antagonistic, relationship between government and the business community.[20] Opponents of the Wisconsin school attacked both its logic and its evidential basis.

Moreover, by emphasizing the economic expansionism of the United States, the "open door" thesis was closely linked to "revisionist" scholarship on the Cold War. "Traditionalist" scholars, who saw the Stalinist state in the Soviet Union as being the primary cause of a divided and endangered postwar world, were incensed by the suggestion of US culpability. These historians attacked the idea of an "open door empire" as being imprecisely defined and perversely one-sided. The Wisconsin school, they charged, seemed attentive only to the domestic side of influences in US foreign policymaking, implicitly glossing over the misbehavior of other nation-states. The most extreme critic of revisionism, Robert Maddox, purported to find a deliberate pattern of falsification, though his charges were so scurrilous and overstated that he mostly undermined his own credibility.[21] By linking the emphasis on economic interpretation to the revisionist stance on cold-war issues, however, Wisconsin school historians became the principal academic critics of the cold-war verities that were still strongly rooted, both in American society and in the politics of the history profession.

Probably the most important element that fueled the controversy over the Wisconsin school involved the Vietnam War and the growth of "new Left" politics. Williams's *Tragedy* became a kind of manifesto for the growing antiwar movement during the late 1960s. Denouncing the failure of the United States to allow an "open door for revolution" against injustice around the world as a "tragedy," Williams spoke to a generation of activist scholars who believed that cold-war crusading had become a cover, especially in the Third World, for allying with pro-capitalist elites who suppressed movements for social justice. Vietnam provided a case in point, and Wisconsin school historians, who saw social involvement and dissent as scholarly virtues, tended to be outspoken in their opposition to the war. (Williams continued to oppose the war but left Wisconsin for Oregon State University because of his dislike for the growing militancy and cultural radicalism among members of the antiwar student movement in Madison.)

As was the case with most American institutions during the late 1960s and early 1970s, the historical profession was bitterly divided over the issue of the Vietnam War. The Wisconsin school, playing the dissenting role, allied with and provided a framework of analysis for the antiwar "new Left." And conservative scholars, laboring overtime to refute those works that may have been influenced by Beard and Williams, ironically helped to place the "open door" thesis at the very center of scholarly debates. By the early 1970s, controversy over an economic interpretation of US foreign policy had become what historian Bradford Perkins aptly characterized as "a battle, not a dialogue."[22] As both of the Vietnam wars – the one in Southeast Asia and the domestic one over foreign policy – waned after the mid-1970s, the controversies over "new Left" historiography also subsided. A growing number of scholars continued to write from perspectives influenced, in some ways, by the Wisconsin school's economic interpretation; others continued to refute the importance of economic interests. But, slowly, the context of historical debates shifted and began to undermine the long-standing discursive connections between attention to economic factors and dissenting or critical perspectives.

THE DECLINE OF CONTROVERSY

The gradual decline of controversy over the role of economics in US foreign relations may be related to three trends: new interpretive turns in histories of foreign relations; a shifting of focus in radical or dissenting scholarship; and changes in the economic and political positions of the United States and the Soviet Union in the world.

First, historians of foreign relations writing in the late 1970s and 1980s incorporated much of the Wisconsin school's scholarship but blunted its critical, dissenting edge. A new "corporatist" interpretation, for example, built upon the Wisconsin school's premise that government sought economic expansion. The corporatist view emphasized the coalescence of government bureaucracies working in tandem with organized functional groups – businesses, agriculture, labor, professionals – to spread economic, political, and cultural forms that were congenial to US interests. Corporatist scholars also drew upon the research of more conservative business and "organizational" historians who were studying the emergence of corporate and governmental bureaucracies. Viewed from this perspective, the new bureaucratic elites that began to emerge after the turn of the century worked together to stabilize the industrial order and extend their influence internationally.[23]

Michael Hogan, whose work on the interwar period and study of the Marshall Plan most fully elaborated this perspective, explained that a corporatist interpretation "focuses on the role of functional elites rather than governing classes, and traces the connection between foreign policy and ongoing changes in the industrial and political structure."[24] During the interwar period, he found an emerging cooperation among Anglo-American elites in such areas as international communications and finance.[25] In the case of the later Marshall Plan, Hogan showed how the joint efforts of similar European and American elites became institutionalized in new postwar agencies that worked to revive a strong, anti-communist Europe and to stabilize global economic patterns generally.[26] Corporatist interpretations were rooted in assumptions that state and private interests were alike in pursuing economic advantage, but, more importantly, stressed the complexity of both motivation and process in policymaking and avoided a thoroughgoing economic interpretation of history.[27]

Moreover, corporatist historians displayed little of the dissenting style of a Beard or a Williams, nor did they overtly push radical economic agendas through their histories. Hogan insisted that his interpretation was compatible, as a conceptual framework, even with the anti-revisionist, anti-Williams views that adhered to the primacy of geopolitics. For Hogan at least, corporatism offered a potential "synthesis" that could accommodate all sides of the fierce debates that raged over economic interpretation.[28] Whereas Beard and Williams had sought to stir controversy, Hogan advanced his corporatist synthesis in hopes of soothing it.

The subject of oil policy, once a part of this bitter controversy, became, during the 1970s and 1980s, a prime example of the more diffuse – and decidedly less radical – corporatist interpretation. In the 1970s, the conflicts between the United States and the Organization of Petroleum Exporting Countries (OPEC) stimulated much new study of the relationship between oil companies and foreign policy during the Cold War. Many of the studies, influenced by the Wisconsin school but recast to fit the emerging corporatist perspective, emphasized how access to key natural resources became a component of cold-war national security policy. Although scholars differed in the degree to which they saw big oil interests directly influencing government policy, most stressed that policymakers and oil executives often shared mutual interests in expanding global access to oil during the Cold War. The economic goals of private businesses often, but not always, ran parallel to the national security concerns defined by governmental elites.[29]

A second area of new scholarship that began to burgeon during the 1980s related to the growing visibility of economic foreign policy, particularly with regard to assistance programs to developing nations in the aftermath of World War II. In the postwar period, governmental agencies that directly extended loans, grants, and various kinds of technical assistance to foreign nations, flourished as part of America's cold-war policy to secure areas against Soviet influence. From the Marshall Plan and Point Four under the Truman administration to a wide variety of other programs (including the Agency for International Development, Department of Agriculture projects, regional banks, and the Alliance for Progress), economic assistance became integral to postwar definitions of national security. Some scholars, in the tradition of Beard and Williams, argued that particular business interests identified their own well-being with national goals and that they influenced government to accept the same equation. In *Bitter Fruit*, for example, Stephen Schlesinger and Stephen Kinzer emphasized the dominance of United Fruit in the shaping of President Eisenhower's policy to undermine the reformist government of Guatemala in 1954 – a policy that resulted in economic destabilization and was topped off with a coup (promoted by the CIA) against the government of Jacobo Arbenz.[30] Most studies of postwar economic policies, however, emphasized less the pursuit of particular economic advantages and more the context of simplistic cold-war faith in a bipolar contest between freedom and tyranny. Richard Immerman's study of the covert action in Guatemala, published in the same year as Schlesinger and Kinzer's, detailed the activities of United Fruit but emphasized the rigid cold-war ideological context in Washington to which the company was able to appeal.[31] Most other recent histories of postwar economic policies also emphasized the operations of cold-war bureaucratic and functional elites, but they did so in a way that leads economic interests to emerge as an important component of foreign policy, rather than the fundamental foundation of it, as in the older economic interpretations.[32]

Second, in the post-Vietnam era scholars associated with traditions of radical dissent themselves moved away from the emphasis on economic modes as determining historical change and began to look more carefully at the role of cultural production. Influential neo-Marxist scholars, such as Raymond Williams and Stuart Hall in Great Britain, elaborated theories that stressed mutual interactions between the realms of economics and culture. And non-Marxist, dissenting scholarship, especially in the United States, also focused increasingly on cultural questions such as racial and gender ideologies. These shifts increasingly pushed older debates over economic interest to the sidelines. Thus the "battle" over the economic interpretation of history became a mere skirmish in the new "culture wars" that racked academic life and historical interpretations after the mid-1980s.[33]

Although these culture wars were slow in breaking out in the field of US foreign relations, economics certainly no longer raised temperatures or prompted intellectual battles at podiums during historical conventions. Foreign relations went from being the historical profession's most divisive and contentious field during the era of the Vietnam War to being its most placid in the 1980s, when controversies were more likely to occur within the fields of social and cultural history.

Third, rapid changes in the international order during the post-Vietnam era also placed interpretations that stressed economic factors in a more favorable light. A spate of studies in the late 1980s argued that the United States was entering a period of economic decline. Although some explanations of decline extended the economic interpretation, others worked to undermine it. Some theories of decline tied the US economic slippage to open door expansionism and the resultant creation of a world system dominated by internationalized businesses. The "core economy" in the world system (which, in the modern era, had been first Britain and then the United States) was, according to this view, becoming less a geographic place than an internationalized socio-economic group. Business elites cared more about profits from international expansion than about national living standards and the public good in their own nation-states. America's decline thus seemed the ultimate result of the assistance that had been provided to multi-nationals by a succession of governments. Stagnation and growing inequality represented the "tragedy of American diplomacy" finally coming home, a confirmation of the basic critique developed previously by dissenting scholarship.[34] But probably a more dominant, and certainly a more publicly highlighted, theory of decline undermined such an economic interpretation. Books such as Vogel's *Japan as Number 1* and other popular investigations of Japan's rising economic power advanced the notion that Japan carefully planned and coordinated with business elites a strategy for global economic growth while the government and business community within the United States could not get their act together.[35] This view suggested that the United States was capable of mounting only weak and deficient policies to promote global economic expansion. Williams's trade expansion thesis or the corporatist interpretation of US policy looked flimsy indeed when set against Japan's even stronger promotional policies and corporatist organization. The preoccupation with the economic weakness of the United States in the aftermath of the Cold War fed pervasive popular images of clever foreigners beating America out of its rightful place as world hegemon. The implicit, and sometimes explicit, critique of American foreign policy from this perspective was that economic interest should have been central to recent US foreign policy but that it had not been. By 1990, leaders from nearly every shading in the political spectrum were calling for new government-business partnerships in expanding foreign trade. Criticism of US economic foreign policy after the 1980s, then, was no longer the terrain primarily of the Left or of radicals.

Along with the US economy, Marxist governments were also in decline. The collapse of the Soviet Union and the communist states of Eastern Europe, along with new disclosures about both the human and the ecological oppression that had been conducted in the name of communism, put Marxism increasingly on the defensive throughout the world. At the same time, there was an accompanying resurgence of free-market doctrines throughout the world in the late 1980s and early 1990s. In this context, filled with celebratory images of capitalism, few Americans worried any more that accentuating economic interest in foreign policy would give grist to the spread of "dangerous" Marxist ideas.

From World War I to the 1980s, then, economic interpretations of US foreign policy had been firmly joined to dissenting, radical perspectives. Highlighting the importance of economic interest in foreign policy, however, no longer seemed so radical or dangerous after the 1970s and 1980s, given the changes in academic interpretations and in global power balances.

NOTES

1 Speech to Los Angeles World Affairs Council, quoted in *New York Times*, 14 August 1992, p. A 11.
2 Quoted in Walter P. Metzger (ed.), *Professors on Guard: The First AAUP Investigations*, New York, reprint, 1977, pp. 138–9.
3 Stephen J. Whitfield, *Scott Nearing: Apostle of American Radicalism*, New York, 1974, pp. 1–145; Scott Nearing, *The Making of a Radical: A Political Autobiography*, New York, 1972; Ellen W. Schrecker, *No Ivory Tower: McCarthyism and the Universities*, New York, 1986, pp. 3–12.
4 "Trial of Scott Nearing and the American Socialist Society," New York, Rand School, 1919, in no. 825, Reel 141, Socialist Party Papers (microfilm edition).
5 Merle Curti, "Subsidizing Radicalism: The American Fund for Public Service, 1921–41," *Social Service Review*, vol. 33, 1959, pp. 274–95.
6 Margaret A. Marsh, *The Bankers in Bolivia: A Study in American Foreign Investment*, New York, 1928; Leland H. Jenks, *Our Cuban Colony: A Study in Sugar*, New York, 1928; Melvin H. Knight, *The Americans in Santo Domingo*, New York, 1928; J. Fred Rippy, *The Capitalists and Colombia*, New York, 1931; and Charles D. Kepner Jr and Jay H. Soothill, *The Banana Empire: A Case Study of Economic Imperialism*, New York, 1935.
7 Scott Nearing and Joseph Freeman, *Dollar Diplomacy: A Study in American Imperialism*, New York, 1925.
8 Harry Magdoff, *The Age of Imperialism: The Economics of US Foreign Policy*, New York, 1969; Gabriel Kolko, *The Roots of American Foreign Policy: An Analysis of Power and Purpose*, Boston, 1969; Sidney Lens, *The Forging of the American Empire*, New York, 1971; Philip S. Foner, *The Spanish–Cuban–American War and the Birth of American Imperialism, 1895–1902*, New York, 1972.
9 Charles A. Beard, *The Open Door at Home: A Trial Philosophy of National Interest*, New York, 1934 and *The Idea of National Interest: An Analytical Study in American Foreign Policy*, New York, 1934.
10 Beard to Barnes, June 24 192[7?], quoted in Richard Hofstadter, *The Progressive Historians*, New York, 1968, p. 320.
11 This position was fully articulated in Charles A. Beard, *President Roosevelt and the Coming of the War, 1941: A Study in Appearances and Realities*, New Haven, Conn., 1948.
12 For example, John Higham, *History*, Englewood Cliffs, N.J., 1965, p. 207.
13 Ellen Nore, *Charles A. Beard, An Intellectual Biography*, Carbondale, Ill., 1983, p. x.
14 Peter Novick, *That Noble Dream: The "Objectivity Question" and the American Historical Profession*, New York, 1988, pp. 290–2. Ironically, by the 1940s Beard had become more critical than ever of Marxist groups because of their internationalist, pro-war stance. On Beard and Marxism, see Nore, *Beard*, pp. 192–3.
15 William A. Williams, *American–Russian Relations, 1781–1947*, New York, 1952.
16 William A. Williams, *The Tragedy of American Diplomacy*, Cleveland, 1959 and *Empire as a Way of Life: An Essay on the Causes and Character of America's Present Predicament Along with a Few Thoughts about an Alternative*, New York, 1980.
17 Bradford Perkins, "'The Tragedy of American Diplomacy': Twenty-five Years After," in Lloyd C. Gardner (ed.), *Redefining the Past: Essays in Diplomatic History in Honor of William Appleman Williams*, Corvallis, Ore., 1986, p. 21.
18 Walter LaFeber, *The New Empire: An Interpretation of American Expansion, 1860–1898*, Ithaca, N.Y., 1963; Lloyd Gardner, *Economic Aspects of New Deal Diplomacy*, Madison, Wis., 1964; Thomas J. McCormick, *China Market:*

America's Quest for Informal Empire, 1893–1901, Chicago, 1967. For a complete bibliography of Williams's work and essays that suggest the direction and contributions of the "Wisconsin school" see Gardner (ed.), *Redefining the Past.*

19 See, for example, Robert W. Tucker, *The Radical Left and American Foreign Policy*, Baltimore, Md, 1971.

20 See, for example, John Braeman, "The New Left and American Foreign Policy during the Age of Normalcy: A Re-examination," *Business History Review*, vol. 57, 1983, pp. 73–104; William H. Becker, *The Dynamics of Business–Government Relations: Industry and Exports, 1893–1921*, Chicago, 1982.

21 Novick, *Noble Dream*, pp. 448–52; Robert Maddox, *The New Left and The Origins of the Cold War*, Princeton, 1973.

22 Perkins, "Tragedy of American Diplomacy," p. 34; Novick, *Noble Dream*, pp. 446–56.

23 Ellis W. Hawley, "The Discovery and Study of a 'Corporate Liberalism,'" *Business History Review*, vol. 52, 1978, pp. 309–20.

24 Michael J. Hogan, "Corporatism," in Michael J. Hogan and Thomas G. Paterson (eds), *Explaining the History of American Foreign Relations*, New York, 1991, p. 227.

25 Michael J. Hogan, *Informal Entente: The Private Structure of Cooperation in Anglo-American Economic Diplomacy, 1918–1928*, Columbia, Mo., 1977.

26 Michael J. Hogan, *The Marshall Plan: America, Britain, and the Reconstruction of Western Europe, 1947–1952*, New York, 1987.

27 Other studies in this tradition include Melvyn Leffler, *Elusive Quest: America's Pursuit of European Stability and French Security, 1919–1933*, Chapel Hill, N.C., 1979; Emily S. Rosenberg, *Spreading the American Dream: American Economic and Cultural Expansion, 1890–1945*, New York, 1982; and Frank Costigliola, *Awkward Dominion: American Political, Economic, and Cultural Relations with Europe, 1919–1933*, Ithaca, N.Y., 1984. See also Thomas J. McCormick, "Drift or Mastery? A Corporatist Synthesis for American Diplomatic History," *Reviews in American History*, vol. 10, 1982, pp. 318–30, and Joan Hoff-Wilson, "Responses to Charles S. Maier, 'Marking Time: The Historiography of International Relations,'" *Diplomatic History*, vol. 5, 1981, pp. 377–82.

28 Hogan, "Corporatism," *Explaining the History*, pp. 226–36.

29 Major recent studies of oil policy include Burton I. Kaufman, *The Oil Cartel Case: A Documentary Study of Antitrust Activity in the Cold War Era*, Westport, Conn., 1978; Aaron David Miller, *Search for Security: Saudi Arabian Oil and American Foreign Policy, 1939–1949*, Chapel Hill, N.C., 1980; Irvine H. Anderson, *Aramco, The United States, and Saudi Arabia: A Study of the Dynamics of Foreign Oil Policy, 1933–50*, Princeton, N.J., 1981; Michael B. Stoff, *Oil, War, and American Security: The Search for a National Policy on Foreign Oil, 1941–1947*, New Haven, Conn., 1980; Stephen G. Rabe, *The Road to OPEC: United States Relations with Venezuela, 1919–1976*, Austin, Tex., 1982; Stephen J. Randall, *United States Foreign Oil Policy, 1919–1948: For Profits and Security*, Montreal, 1985; David S. Painter, *Oil and the American Century: The Political Economy of US Foreign Oil Policy, 1941–1954*, Baltimore, Md, 1986; Daniel Yergin, *The Prize: The Epic Quest for Oil, Money, and Power*, New York, 1991.

30 Stephen C. Schlesinger and Stephen Kinzer, *Bitter Fruit: The Untold Story of the American Coup in Guatemala*, Garden City, N.Y., 1982.

31 Richard H. Immerman, *The CIA in Guatemala: The Foreign Policy of Intervention*, Austin, Tex., 1982.

32 Examples would include Gary R. Hess, *America Encounters India, 1941–1947*, Baltimore, Md, 1971, and more recent studies discussed in Gary Hess, "Global Expansion and Regional Balances: The Emerging Scholarship on United States Relations with India and Pakistan," *Pacific Historical Review*, vol. 56, 1987,

pp. 259–95; Robert J. McMahon, *Colonialism and Cold War: The United States and the Struggle for Indonesian Independence, 1945–1949*, Ithaca, N.Y., 1981; and Nathan Godfried, *Bridging the Gap between Rich and Poor: American Economic Development Policy toward the Arab East, 1942–1949*, New York, 1987; Stephen G. Rabe, *Eisenhower and Latin America: The Foreign Policy of Anticommunism*, Chapel Hill, N.C., 1988; Dennis Merrill, *Bread and The Ballot: The United States and India's Economic Development, 1947–1963*, Chapel Hill, N.C., 1990; Peter L. Hahn, *The United States, Great Britain, and Egypt, 1945–1956: Strategy and Diplomacy in the Early Cold War*, Chapel Hill, N.C., 1991.

33 For a perspective from a cultural conservative see, for example, Daniel Bell, "The Culture Wars," *Wilson Quarterly*, summer 1992, p. 34.

34 Such a world-systems perspective could be formulated from Marxist tenets, such as work by sociologist Immanuel Wallerstein, *The Capitalist World-Economy: Essays*, New York, 1979; by political scientist Fred Block, *Postindustrial Possibilities: A Critique of Economic Discourse*, Berkeley, Calif., 1990; by scholars associated with "dependency theory" discussed in Louis A. Pérez Jr, "Dependency," in Hogan and Paterson (eds), *Explaining the History*, pp. 99–110. It could also arise from the perspective provided by Beard and Williams, as in the work of economist Robert Reich or historian Thomas McCormick. Robert B. Reich, *The Work of Nations*, New York, 1991; Thomas J. McCormick, *America's Half-Century: United States Foreign Policy in the Cold War*, Baltimore, Md, 1989 and "World Systems," in Hogan and Paterson (eds), *Explaining the History*, pp. 89–98.

35 Ezra F. Vogel, *Japan As Number 1: Lessons for America*, New York, 1979.

4 Imperialism, American style, 1890–1916

Joseph A. Fry

In April 1899 Theodore Roosevelt exhorted his countrymen to meet the challenges and responsibilities of an imperial foreign policy: "If we are to be a really great people," Roosevelt asserted, "we must strive in good faith to play a great part in the world." His vision included building an isthmian canal, seizing the strategic bases necessary to decide the "destiny of the oceans of the East and the West," and subduing and ruling the islands acquired from Spain. Three years later, Republican Senator George F. Hoar lamented the nation's decision to follow TR's advice. Hoar charged the United States with converting the Monroe Doctrine from a policy of "eternal righteousness and justice . . . to a doctrine of brutal selfishness looking only to our own advantage." Even more tragically, by suppressing the Filipino revolution, "We crushed the only Republic in Asia . . . made war on the only Christian people in the East . . . [and] inflicted torture on unarmed men."[1]

These conflicting perspectives clearly foreshadowed the difficulty historians have had in "coming to terms" with American empire. Indeed both Americans generally and many influential scholars have been loath to acknowledge that the United States had joined the European powers in the practice of imperialism after 1890. In contrast to the British who justified and took great pride in their imperial exploits, Americans have persistently denied the existence of an American empire or have labored to demonstrate that it was more benign and more transitory than its European counterparts.[2]

This discomfort with the existence and nature of American empire lies at the heart of the differing interpretations of United States foreign relations from 1890 to 1916. Simply defining the term "imperialism" has generated intense disagreement and frustration. As early as 1919, Joseph A. Schumpeter pronounced "The word 'imperialism' . . . abused to the point where it threatens to lose all meaning." Conscious of this ambiguity or averse to linking the United States to imperialism, many historians of this period have avoided grappling with the definition or the substance of imperialism by employing the expression "expansion" or by interpreting the period in terms of America's rise to "world power." Still, given the acquisition of the Philippines, Hawaii, Puerto Rico, Guam, and Samoa; the establishment of protectorates over Cuba, Panama, and the Dominican Republic; and armed interventions in several of these countries as well as Mexico, Haiti, and Nicaragua, students of these years must acknowledge and confront directly the phenomenon of imperialism. And, they must define it. Although he was referring to jazz, musician Fats Waller has provided an applicable admonition: "Man," Fats warned, "if you don't know what it is, don't mess with it."[3]

Those most reluctant to acknowledge the existence of an American empire have defined imperialism narrowly. These scholars have essentially equated imperialism with colonialism, or the formal annexation of territory not meant to be integrated into the larger body politic. In so doing, they effectively limit American imperialism to the holding of Puerto Rico and the Philippines and separate these acquisitions from Hawaii and from previous territorial annexations on the north American continent. Thus American imperialism was a "great aberration," a temporary, almost accidental, loss of national direction, from which the United States quickly recovered after 1900.[4]

By contrast, those historians most disturbed by US actions abroad have defined imperialism more broadly. While citing the holding of formal colonies as imperialistic, they have also contended that the United States had begun establishing an "informal empire" by the 1890s. These scholars emphasize that imperial control may be exercised through economic means as well as political annexations or military interventions and that the United States built an "overseas economic empire." Because Americans had pursued commercial expansion abroad to solve internal problems since the 1780s and had expanded territorially at the expense of nonwhites throughout the nineteenth century, the imperialism of the 1890s was neither accidental nor transitory. Still other students add culture to the areas of imperial control. They define "cultural imperialism" as a stronger nation assuming the right to impose and disseminate its beliefs and values at the expense of a weaker, native culture.[5]

Given these widely varying definitions, one might be tempted to agree with the Australian historian Sir Keith Hancock, who pronounced "Imperialism . . . no word for scholars. The emotional echoes which it arouses are too violent and too contradictory. It does not convey a precise meaning."[6] But the centrality of imperialism to this period of United States foreign relations demands a working definition. The key considerations are power, control, and intent. Imperialism and hence empire exist when a stronger nation or society imposes or attempts to impose control over a weaker nation or group of people. This control may be formal (via annexations, protectorates, or military occupations) or informal (via economic control, cultural domination, or threat of intervention). The informal species of empire might involve businessmen, missionaries, and other non-state actors. Advocates of a stricter definition will protest the difficulty of measuring the degree of informal control or domination that constitutes imperialism. For example, where does normal commercial activity end and economic imperialism begin? Although absolute certainty of measurement may be unobtainable in such areas, the phenomenon of imperialism remains apparent. As Richard Graham, a historian of Latin

54   *Joseph A. Fry*

America, observed, "It may take a hydraulic engineer to measure the flow of water, but anyone can see it flows downhill."[7]

THE ECONOMIC PERSPECTIVE

A scholarly consensus on the motives for American imperialism in the period from 1890 through 1916 has been just as elusive as agreement on a definition of the phenomenon. Easily the greatest contention has centered on the influence of economic considerations. Observing the vast increase in American productivity and exports, turn-of-the-century critics of European and American imperialism cited the quest for markets and investment opportunities as the driving force behind United States foreign policy. Scholars such as Charles A. Beard and Scott Nearing subsequently developed these themes during the 1920s and 1930s; but it was not until the 1960s and 1970s that the "revisionist" or "new Left" school of American historians compiled the most comprehensive brief for the primacy of economic influences. Beginning in 1959 with the publication of *The Tragedy of American Diplomacy*, William A. Williams and a number of his former students emphasized the continuity of an aggressive, expansionist American foreign policy. Prior to the Civil War, the United States had constructed an empire on the north American continent; following Appomattox, the focus shifted to a "New Empire" of foreign trade with the final suppression of the native Americans serving as the crucial linkage between the two forms of empire. By the 1890s, the makers of US foreign policy sought markets rather than extensive new territories. Indeed, they practiced the "imperialism of anti-imperialism" by arguing for free trade and investment and against large colonies.[8]

According to the revisionist argument, the pursuit of this "informal empire" intensified during the Gilded Age as repeated depressions disrupted the economy and incited an alarming level of social protest. Both farmers and manufacturers traced the core problem to overproduction, hence the need for unobstructed access to foreign markets to dispose of the "glut" and to avoid explosive outbursts such as the Homestead Strike or the Populist Movement. This compulsive search for an "open door" for foreign trade, and the attendant practice of looking abroad to solve internal problems, became the essence of American foreign policy. Building on this theoretical grounding, on world systems analysis, and on dependency theory, several more recent studies have argued that the United States emerged as a core or metropole (industrialized, commercially and militarily developed) nation during this period and pursued a foreign policy designed to dominate and exploit peripheral (weaker, non-industrialized) countries economically and politically.[9] From this perspective of more than a century of empire building, the annexation of Hawaii and the Spanish islands was more a "culmination" than an "aberration" and more a product of the nation's political economy and place in the world capitalist system than a momentary, irrational act.

Several interlocking "chains of causes" had produced war and empire: the depression of the 1890s had solidified the consensus on the need for foreign markets; the potential for sales in China and the fear that the Europeans were about to close their spheres of influence to American trade left businessmen uneasy and the Far East second in importance only to Cuba among policy-makers; and the government, particularly in the person of McKinley, formu-lated a partnership with business in promoting foreign trade. Both McKinley and his business constituents had concluded in mid-March 1898 that only by restoring international order and preserving domestic tranquility could trade and particularly the development of US prospects in China be pursued. Although McKinley "did not want war, he did want what only a war could provide: the disappearance of the terrible uncertainty in American political and economic life, and a solid basis from which to resume the building of the new American commercial empire."[10] With the conflict came the annexation of Hawaii, Puerto Rico, Guam, and the Philippines, not as the first steps toward a great territorial empire but as strategic outposts for safeguarding an isthmian canal and as outposts en route to the China market.

According to the revisionists, both this partnership between business and government and the drive for international economic expansion remained central to the making of American foreign policy in the early twentieth century. Together with Williams, other historians have asserted that busi-ness and political leaders agreed on the need for the establishment of a liberal capitalist world order. This ideal world order would have replicated American representative government and private capitalistic enterprise, guaranteed the access of industrialized nations to the raw materials and markets of less developed countries, and instituted government action to maintain the order and stability necessary for economic penetration and growth and to protect overseas markets and investments. The practical pursuit of these objectives led the United States to oppose virtually all revolutions during these years.[11]

With business clamoring for aggressive government support through trade associations such as the National Association of Manufacturers and the American Asiatic Association, and establishing a worldwide presence in everything from Heinz ketchup to McCormick reapers, the "promotional state" was born. Most importantly, argue the revisionists, the United States promoted and protected American economic interests by working to exclude European influence and to suppress political and social disorder in Latin America and to enforce the open door policy of equal access for trade and investment in China. Government pursuit of these ends encompassed a broad range of actions. In Latin America, the United States threatened and carried out military interventions, established protectorates, administered customs houses, and applied political and economic pressures. The government also employed "chosen instruments" or groups of American bankers in efforts to counter Russian or Japanese influence in China or to promote order in the Caribbean through loans to favored clients. And, as the US government–business relationship solidified, the United States reformed the consular service, adopted "bargaining" tariffs aimed at forcing concessions from other nations, established the Bureau of Foreign and Domestic Commerce and the National Foreign Trade Council, and allowed American banks to establish branches abroad – all with an eye toward augmenting foreign commerce and investment.[12]

The revisionist critique of US foreign relations elicited one of the most bitter debates within the American historical profession. Opponents of the so-called "New Economic Determinists" charged them with misunderstanding and perhaps even consciously misrepresenting the history of the late nineteenth century. Rather than a period of panic and depression, the Gilded Age was, they argue, an era of growth and optimism. American business looked first to the home market, and Congress signaled its agreement with this focus by repeatedly enacting protective tariffs that impeded commercial expansion. Critics charged the revisionists with exaggerating the closeness of government–business relations. For example, there was no unimpeachable evidence that McKinley had acted principally from economic concerns. As Julius W. Pratt had argued in the 1930s, business had opposed war until the very eve of the conflict and had been "indifferent to imperialism or definitely opposed" until Dewey destroyed the Spanish fleet in Manila Bay. Official policy was hesitant and contradictory, and "tenuousness of the contacts . . . characterized the structural relationship between business and government."[13]

These critics further asserted that only by concentrating on the "rhetoric" of expansionists at the expense of "objective realities" could one make the economic argument. Business was far from unitary on the issue of commercial expansion, with larger, more concentrated companies providing the bulk of the exports and smaller concerns being the most solicitous of government aid. The most successful US exporters, such as the Singer Sewing Machine Company or Standard Oil, carved out foreign markets with little government assistance, and the value of exports and investments in Europe and North America far exceeded those in Latin America or China, the focus of most expansionist strategies. Indeed, the fabled "China market" was statistically a "myth," since it constituted only 0.3 per cent of American exports in 1890 and less than 1 per cent in 1910. Given these "realities," placing economic expansion at the center of US policy made the process unduly "rational" and "unitary" and helped make treatments of this period "the worst chapter in almost any book."[14]

Such cautions, especially those treating the structural relations of business and government, the most successful export companies, the geographic distribution of American exports, and the overly rational portrayal of policy, are well taken. However, these critics have not refuted the depiction of the liberal–capitalist ideology which, according to the revisionists, provided the essential intellectual context for policy formation. While "realistic" trade figures are useful, they did not prevent generations of Americans from coveting *potential* profits in China. Finally, the Gilded Age was not an era of optimism for farmers. Plagued by chronic hard times, both cotton planters and midwestern producers of livestock and grain clamored for expanded export markets throughout this period.

THE PRATT SCHOOL AND ITS ADHERENTS

Most of the remaining writing on the motivation for American empire has investigated alternatives to the economic interpretation. Building particularly on the work of Julius W. Pratt and Samuel Flagg Bemis, who responded to Beard and Nearing in the 1930s and 1940s, and on subsequent studies by Richard Hofstadter and Ernest R. May in the 1950s and 1960s, scholars emphasizing non-economic explanations have more often portrayed US actions in the twenty-five years after 1890 as humane and well-meaning rather than selfish and exploitive, as ad hoc and accidental rather than systemic and predictable, and as breaking with rather than continuing American foreign policy traditions.

Like the revisionists, Hofstadter and Robert Dallek linked foreign policy to domestic events; however, they contend that the American public's response can be understood best in psychological rather than material terms. Buffeted by the post-1893 depression, by the Populist Movement, by the growth and consolidation of big business, by urbanization and the changing nature of immigration, by the labor violence, and by the ostensible closing of the frontier, the nation experienced a "psychic crisis." Americans channeled their domestic frustrations and humanitarian concerns into a chauvinistic, jingoistic foreign policy; both the war and colonial empire "had more to do with relieving internal strains than with serving American interests abroad."[15] Extending this argument, other historians have decried the nation's failure to deliberately weigh "interests and responsibilities." Instead of acting from "political realism" (or economic self-interest), the nation had gone to war out of an "explosive combination of altruism and self-assertive national egoism" and acquired an "empire in a fit of absent-mindedness."[16]

The concept of national hysteria driving the nation to war raised the crucial question of how this overwhelming public pressure was translated into governmental action. If businessmen were reluctant followers in the decisions for war and empire, who provided the impetus for these momentous steps? Writing in the 1930s, Julius Pratt offered several seminal interpretations. First, he credited scholars and publicists such as Admiral Alfred T. Mahan, Congregationalist minister Josiah Strong, and Columbia University professor John W. Burgess with instructing the American public in the merits of a "new manifest destiny." Burgess and Strong assured Americans of the superiority of their Anglo-Saxon governmental institutions and Protestant Christianity and urged them to spread this superior civilization abroad. Mahan argued for a "large policy" featuring the construction of a great navy and an isthmian canal and the holding of key naval bases in the Caribbean and the Pacific for both strategic and commercial purposes. Therefore, when the American public sought an emotional, psychological release from the problems of the 1890s, they had before them a racial, religious, and strategic blueprint.[17] To these domestically-produced prescriptions, subsequent historians have added the influence of the contemporary example of European imperialism and the assumption that imperialism was a requisite of the great power status to which the United States aspired.[18]

Other historians, writing contemporaneously with Pratt, agreed that an aroused public had driven McKinley and the Republican Party into war; however, these historians cited the sensational reporting of the American press as primarily responsible for focusing American sympathy on the plight of the Cuban people. Drawing on their own reporters and information provided by the Cuban junta in New York City, the "yellow press" had inundated readers with a flood of biased stories depicting Spanish cruelty and Cuban suffering. The American public's intensely humanitarian response, when combined with its outrage over the sinking of the battleship *Maine*, dictated war.[19]

Pratt augmented these explanations by providing another ostensible point of linkage between the public outcry and the McKinley administration. Although Mahan was the principal popularizer of the "large policy," Assistant Secretary of the Navy Theodore Roosevelt and Senator Henry Cabot Lodge were the government officials most responsible for laying the "fruits of war" at the feet of this aroused public. Roosevelt and Lodge had adopted and advocated Mahan's ideas, had anticipated that war with Spain would afford the opportunity for its consummation, and had helped manipulate a weak McKinley (who was "clay" in their "hands") into the acquisition of empire. In sum, a skilled group of "large policy" conspirators had utilized their positions and the war brought on by a public convinced of its racial, humanitarian, and nationalistic mission to launch the nation on its imperial voyage.[20]

Regardless of the exact source of the stimulus, the concept of an overly-excited public forcing war on a resistant political and business establishment became common staple by the 1950s. Ernest R. May cited the "feverish emotion" and "mass passion" that gripped the nation, while providing the most forceful depiction of still another linkage between popular opinion and government action: "Overshadowing all other factors . . . was the domestic political aspect of the Cuban problem." May's study culminated a long tradition of portraying McKinley as weak and politically expedient. His "duty to the Republican party was much clearer than his duty to the nation," and he bowed to public opinion in order to avert the threat of Democratic victories in the mid-term congressional elections of November 1898.[21] If then, as the cumulative "Pratt approach" contended, the US decision for war and empire had been unplanned and accidental, manipulated by a few conspirators, or the result of sincere (if misplaced or misguided) humanitarian concern, the nation was absolved of the selfish, calculated, and exploitive motives ascribed to it by the revisionists.

The emphasis on idealistic and humanitarian objectives provided another alternative to the economic argument for explaining not only the onset of war and empire but also the essence of US foreign policy during the decade and a half after 1900. Pratt's treatment of the "imperialism of righteousness" had again anticipated this new trend when he contended that "the missionary minded" among Protestant religious groups had argued effectively that the United States had a "moral and religious responsibility" to spread Christianity and uplift mankind in Cuba, the Philippines, and the world over. Concentrating particularly on Asia, the missionary movement experienced its "golden age" from 1900 to 1915. As a group, missionaries had much greater exposure to Asia than other Americans. They and the domestic religious establishment had the greatest influence over general American perceptions of the Far East, and, according to some historians, exercised considerable control over general policy formation.[22]

Although the missionary movement provides the most obvious example of humanitarian motives, scholars have not confined this argument to organized religion. They have asserted that the benign impulse to aid others characterized US policy in general, within both the insular empire and the Caribbean. By promoting sanitation, furthering education, building public works, maintaining order, and instituting democratic institutions, the United States sought to prepare these less developed countries for material prosperity and self-governance. Within this interpretive framework, presidents from McKinley through Wilson are seen as acting to extend "civilization" to others, as promoting "progressive" societies abroad, or as practicing "missionary imperialism."[23] Working from this reform dimension of US policy, other historians have suggested that American imperial actions abroad were natural extensions of the progressive movement for honesty, efficiency, and expanded opportunity at home.[24]

Historians seeking to refute the "sinister and sordid motives" associated with the economic interpretation have also accentuated strategic considerations. Focusing particularly on the Caribbean region, these writers make "continental security" the essence of policy: the United States acted to safeguard the isthmian canal route and to prevent European nations from securing bases or threatening the safety of the continental United States. Following the nation's rapprochement with Great Britain at the turn of the century, both US civilian and military leaders feared German meddling in Latin America, and similar apprehensions over German intentions had prompted retention of the entire Philippine archipelago rather than a single coaling station. Maintaining the order and stability necessary to block European intrusions had required annexations, formal protectorates, administration of customs houses, military interventions and occupations, and the general suppression of revolutions. But these actions were undertaken reluctantly and for defensive purposes rather than to gratuitously dominate and exploit smaller, weaker nations. Termed by some "protective" or "preclusive imperialism," such ostensibly defensive, non-economic behavior has led others to dismiss "North American imperialism" during these years as a "myth."[25]

Accomplishing such strategic objectives required power or the "tools of empire." Foremost among these tools was the development of US military capacity and especially a modern navy. With increased strength came an enhanced institutional and professional role for the American military. From their positions on the Navy General Board and the Army General Staff, military leaders endorsed the antirevolutionary drive for order and stability in the Caribbean, favored the exclusion of Europeans from the western hemisphere, and sought additional resources and bases in the Far East. Significantly, historians have contended that these military spokesmen were motivated primarily by strategic concerns, and secondly by their desire to strengthen their own branches of the service.[26]

According to other historians, enhanced American naval power was part of the larger process of modernization by which the United States and Europe outstripped the rest of the world technologically. The resulting disparity in power, together with parallel differences in national coherence and purpose, undergirded empire. Making modernization the essential context, Richard H. Collin has portrayed a vibrant, materialistic, technologically advanced, conjoint, and Protestant United States confronting a less developed, comparatively inert, disparate, and Catholic Latin America. Against this background of cultural dissonance and of US strength and Latin weakness, both conflict and American predominance were virtually inevitable.[27] This analysis represents "imperialism as an objective process due fundamentally to the unavoidable impact of advanced western civilization on the comparatively backward native cultures of the third world." Objectivists also emphasize the necessity for advanced nations "to intervene . . . to impose order on chaotic conditions" and the interventions as "primarily a work of education and civilization."[28] If the process is inexorable and progressive, then selfish national or political interests are minimized or excluded.

Just as the economic analysis elicited stringent criticism, the "Pratt approach" has not gone unscathed. Students of American naval policy have discredited a central aspect of the "large policy" conspiracy by demonstrating that a group of navy officers, rather than Theodore Roosevelt, formulated the battle plan directing Admiral Dewey to attack the Spanish fleet at Manila Bay. Drafted before Roosevelt took office as assistant secretary, the plan had been personally approved by President McKinley prior to its implementation.[29] This portrayal of the president controlling strategic planning is part of the more recent depiction of McKinley as a masterful politician and adept manager of men who dominated his administration and its foreign policy. H. Wayne Morgan, Lewis L. Gould, and John L. Offner have argued convincingly that McKinley was neither manipulated by large policy conspirators nor overwhelmed by public pressure. Instead, he opted for war and empire based on a deliberate assessment of US interests. In the most recent and exhaustively researched of these volumes, Offner constructs a strong case for the influence of domestic political over economic considerations in McKinley's thinking.

But Offner's McKinley is a much stronger, more competent, and reflective leader than the man presented by Ernest May.[30]

Even with Offner's meticulous reconstruction of the political and diplomatic context, definitively proving that the reticent McKinley acted *principally* from humanitarian or political motives remains only slightly less difficult than demonstrating his primary economic aims. Similarly, determining the true nature of "public opinion" at the turn of the century, and linking such sentiment to the actual formation of policy has proven most difficult. Who constituted the public? In the absence of Gallup polls, how can public opinion be gauged? Were editorial opinions synonymous with and representative of public opinion? Other scholars have questioned the influence of intellectuals and publicists. Men such as Strong and Mahan, according to James A. Field, Jr, were more concerned with internal problems or strategic defense than with aggressive expansion or imperialism, and their decisive impact on American public perceptions remains unsubstantiated.[31]

More generally, the analytical approach of finding exceptions to the economic argument or comparing "rhetoric" to "reality" might also be applied to the humanitarian or strategic reasoning. For example, even the most ardent practitioners of the Pratt approach are embarrassed by Theodore Roosevelt's high-handed treatment of Colombia and his expedient response to the Panama "revolution"; nor were the fixing of elections in Nicaragua and Santo Domingo or the violent military rule of Haiti consistent with democratic doctrine. Similarly, Melvin Small has questioned the widely held view that Germany constituted a military and strategic threat in the Caribbean after 1903.[32] If the reality were not so menacing, then the rhetoric of contemporaries and those historians who justified US interventions in the Caribbean or Mexico must also be challenged. Such "exceptions" or discrepancies between rhetoric and reality raise the larger issue of American "innocence." Can such innocence and alleged devotion to principle and self-defense be reconciled with the uncanny promotion of US material interests by humanitarian and strategic policies?[33] And can the innocent and aberrant nature of US policy from 1890 to 1916 be sustained other than by narrowly defining imperialism and by ignoring the continuity of an acquisitive, domineering policy toward Mexicans, Indians, and other nonwhites?

DEVELOPMENT AND DEPENDENCY

Such questions demand an assessment of the impact of American imperialism on other nations and peoples. Generally, but not exclusively, those scholars working within the conceptual boundaries of the Pratt approach have positively evaluated the outcomes of American policies. They emphasize that the United States undertook imperialism with an "uneasy conscience" and a commitment to prepare others for self-government. This commitment distinguished American imperialism from the European variety and operated as a "safety valve" protecting the United States from "some of the temptations

– to abuse, to disillusionment, and to cynicism – of its great power." As the requisite first step to imparting respect for democratic processes, the United States imposed order and stability on the Philippines and the Caribbean. By subduing chronic banditry and suppressing revolution, Americans reduced the persistent violence in these societies and rescued them from the threat of European intervention.[34]

According to these historians, this greater domestic tranquility facilitated other positive achievements. American control in Cuba, Puerto Rico, or the Philippines improved public sanitation, eradicated disease, extended education, and transformed public facilities. The enhanced political and social order also attracted foreign investments for economic development, at least a portion of which trickled down to the general population. While acknowledging that US policies had kept some unpopular governments in power, that the lessons in self-government had not always been learned well, or that development had not brought general prosperity, these scholars concluded that "by the comparative standard, the United States had no reason to apologize for its record."[35]

Other students of US policy in the Philippines and Caribbean have been less complimentary, arguing that the costs of the US quest for order and stability have been far too high. Suppressing the Philippine revolution between 1899 and 1902 resulted in eighteen thousand Filipino battle casualties and contributed to at least another hundred thousand deaths from disease and starvation. Other interventions led to several hundred Mexican and more than two thousand Haitian deaths. Critics have also attributed deleterious social and economic developments to these military occupations. Louis A. Pérez, Jr argues convincingly that US intervention against Spain stifled the social portion of the Cuban revolution that had called for the distribution of land to the dispossessed. Similarly, the American military has been credited with extending discriminatory racial codes and opposing labor organization in areas under its control.[36]

This conservative bent has also been detected in the political realm where the order imposed by the United States repeatedly produced or sustained elitist, usually autocratic, domination rather than effectively promoting the adoption of democratic institutions. American-trained and armed national guards provided the bases for decades-long dictatorships, and catering to American wishes became more crucial than public service to successful office holding. Corruption and narrow personal and upper-class self-interest, in the absence of clear domestic accountability, too often characterized these distorted polities. Those emphasizing the negative aspects of US control have vigorously disputed the contention that an American presence benefitted smaller nations economically. They argue that increased US and foreign investment, better roads and ports, enhanced technology, greater productivity, and expanded exports failed to improve the standard of living for the great majority of Filipino, Caribbean, or central American peasants and workers. Instead, these countries developed export economies focused on agricultural or extractive products that were often controlled by foreign owners or local elites and were especially vulnerable to international economic forces. The poor repeatedly lost small, food-producing farms to large haciendas and were left as migrant workers subject to seasonal unemployment. The experience of Puerto Rico provides perhaps the most telling refutation of the "exaggerated claims" for the benign influence of US administration and economic presence. Despite orderly, honest, efficient government imposed by the United States, despite significant private investment in sugar, tobacco, and public utilities, and despite greatly expanded exports, the overall standard of living remained static between 1898 and 1930. As Daniel R. Headrick has perceptively noted, "growth" and "development" are not synonymous. The latter requires investment in human rather than physical capital – a process that seldom occurred under the imperial mantle.[37]

Dependency theory has provided one of the most provocative attempts to explain the developmental experience of smaller, poorer countries. In essence, this complex body of thought contends that the development and prosperity of the industrialized, technologically sophisticated "metropolitan" nations and the agrarian, non-industrialized, and poor "peripheral" countries have been incompatible. Using their wealth and technology, their control of markets, and their military might, metropolitan nations have forced the periphery to supply raw materials and consume foreign-produced industrial goods. According to dependency theorists, this relationship compels the poor countries to concentrate on a few exportable products, and leaves them with little control over economic decisions and with severely limited capacity to industrialize and enhance national welfare. Real power resides with the metropolitan nations: they determine the terms of trade and, together with local elites, derive the profits from the system.[38]

Dependency theory has evoked spirited rejoinders. Dissenters assert that this analysis gives insufficient weight to local conditions, such as the colonial history of elite rule, neglect of education, or lack of physical and human resources for industrialization in Latin America. Others complain that *dependencestas* fail to devote proper attention to non-pecuniary ideologies or to account for different rates of development among third-world countries.[39] Given these and other criticisms, dependency theory fails to demonstrate direct US responsibility for *all* the ills of its client states, but this analytical shortcoming does not refute the theory's accurate description of dismal conditions in the Philippines or Latin America.

While dependency theory has addressed the imperial relationship in economic terms, the concept of "cultural imperialism" encompasses ideas and beliefs. Once more differences over definition abound. Some scholars believe that the process must be forcefully imposed and promote political or economic ends. Others reject this "functional" approach for a "structural" theory that accentuates the discrepancy in power between two societies and the ability of the stronger one to provide the teachers and to define topics (ranging from religion to technology) worthy of study. The latter approach coincides most closely with the broad working definition of imperialism adopted earlier in this essay. Regardless of definition, the concept of cultural imperialism facilitates an examination of the roles of often-overlooked "non-state actors" such as missionaries, teachers, and medical personnel in US foreign relations and promotes a more inclusive assessment of the impact of US presence abroad.[40]

In the broadest sense, American insistence that others should adopt democratic and capitalistic institutions has been "profoundly imperialistic."[41] By pressuring Cubans to eschew political violence or Filipinos to prepare for self-government based on a US model, the United States demanded that these countries remake their societies according to American values. Clearly, the "reforms" aimed at stabilizing economies, or instituting honest, efficient, representative governments, or promoting improved sanitation or medical practices embodied a critical cultural dimension. To effect changes in any of these societal or political areas required alterations of cultural beliefs and practices.

Missionaries were the most prominent group of non-state actors propagating American cultural beliefs abroad from 1890 through 1916. Indeed, this era has been characterized as the most aggressive in American missionary history. Phrasing their goals in a language of conquest, missionaries went to China and the Philippines not as "passive cultural intermediaries" but as "conscious agents of change, of radical transformation. They came to Asia *to do something to* Asia and Asians." Missionaries sought to impose religious codes that they deemed to be superior; they also labored tirelessly on educational and medical projects.[42]

Education obviously provided a mechanism for disseminating western values and technology, but historians have also included western medicine among the "tools of empire." On an immediate and practical level, Americans instituted measures for improved sanitation to protect their administrators and soldiers in Cuba, Mexico, or the Philippines and to help prevent the spread of disease from the Caribbean to the mainland. But Americans also viewed medicine as a "superior form of propaganda for the benefits of western civilization and capitalism." Missionaries perceived medicine as a way to do good while at the same time making contacts with and acquiring influence over indigenous populations. Medicine, contends David Arnold, was a "celebration of empire itself," since it often involved massive exercises in state and military intervention and the reordering of indigenous societies along western lines.[43]

If US imperialism produced mixed economic results, what was the cultural impact? Historians once referred to tremendously "constructive activities" and "useful reforms and achievements" in the Philippines and other areas under American control.[44] More recent scholarship either questions the positive effects of the American presence or suggests that the impact has been exaggerated – both negatively and positively. Virtually all historians agree that efforts to transplant US political institutions were largely futile. Even if client states adopted an ostensibly representative government, they were invariably plagued by dictatorships, elite domination, politically related violence, inefficiency and corruption. In short, patterns that existed prior to US control persisted. The same was often true in education or medicine. For example, US efforts to promote education in the Philippines were well intentioned and aided tens of thousands of Filipinos, but by 1913 the average child spent only two years in school and the overall literacy rate had not improved. Similarly, the US occupation of Vera Cruz in 1915 produced a startling medical and sanitary transformation of the city into a much cleaner and healthier place; soon after the US departure, all had returned to "normal." Finally, missionaries in the Philippines and China contributed to a spirit of individualism promoting democracy in the former and revolution in the latter. The missionaries in China also furthered education and medical innovations on a scale similar to that in the Philippines, but they converted few Chinese to Christianity. Again, the native culture was tenaciously resistant to change. A. E. Campbell's observation concerning political transference seems more generally applicable: "They [subject peoples] cannot be made more civilized, and therefore fitter for self-government, if civilization is defined in alien terms."[45]

Both dependency theory and cultural imperialism raise the issue of collaboration between Americans and the people they sought to control. This, like the impact of the US presence more generally, has been a relatively neglected topic. But, as European scholars have emphasized, collaboration was an essential component of the imperial process. From the European and American perspective, it was directly related to the cost of empire. Without indigenous collaborators, the administration of either colonies or informal empire would have been prohibitive. Discerning the motives of local collaborators has proven more difficult. Politicians often cooperated with the United States or solicited US aid or intervention as a means of gaining or retaining control of their governments. Merchants who were well placed usually profited from US trade and investment. Elites in Cuba or the Philippines understood the US tendency to block revolution and thereby preserve their social and economic positions. Still, narrow self-interest was not the only motive for collaboration. Many politicians, merchants, or aristocrats also considered US political institutions, economic practices, and technology as the most viable route to modernization and general prosperity. Therefore, elite collaborators were often complex figures who pursued national as well as personal goals within severely constricted choices. For the masses in Cuba or the Philippines the reality of American power and the futility of resistance were probably more responsible for their acquiescence, if not active collaboration.[46]

IMPERIALISM, AMERICAN STYLE

What conclusions emerge from this welter of interpretations? First, the United States was neither so exceptional nor so innocent as scholars once contended. Like their European contemporaries, Americans possessed and

employed superior power to control others. After all the justifications have
been stripped away, the essential process remains one of "Big Dog eats Little
Dog."⁴⁷ Second, the economic, social, and political dislocation of the 1890s
provided an essential backdrop for a more assertive foreign policy, but
American imperialism was not the result of conspiracy, mass irrationality,
incompetent leadership, or national absent-mindedness. McKinley, Roosevelt,
and Wilson were competent leaders who dominated their foreign policies and
acted from considered assessments of national and international interests.

When evaluated from the perspective of long-term ideological and policy
patterns, the events of the 1890s were neither an accident nor an aberration.
American imperialism followed logically from a heritage of continental
expansion at the expense of Mexicans and Indians and from an ideology that
had long emphasized the inequality of races and the superiority of white
Anglo-Saxons, had linked US expansion to a "mission" extending liberty to
others, and had made economic growth central to obtaining national great-
ness.⁴⁸ The campaign after 1890 for a liberal world order featuring democratic institutions and capitalism was built on solid foundations.

Regardless of the specific motive or objective – whether economic expansion, strategic security, democratic reform, cultural uplift, or religious conversion – those who made policy in the United States, and those who
attempted to influence it, invariably sought order and stability and opposed all
revolutionary change they felt unable to control. Indeed, the pursuit of order
and stability and a predictable international environment open to American
ideals and interests provided the principal operational theme for US policy
from 1890 through 1916. Turn-of-the-century Americans were not, however,
completely cynical and selfish. Although variously interested in national
welfare and personal and economic fulfillment and certainly ethnocentric and
patronizing toward their supposed "inferiors," Americans sincerely believed
that US imperialism would benefit those being controlled. And the various
motives for American imperialism reinforced one another; they were not
mutually exclusive. National aggrandizement and altruistic motives coexisted
quite comfortably with one another; economic, strategic, racial, philosophical,
and religious influences fused imperialism and idealism.⁴⁹

Still, any assessment of American imperialism must not divorce even the
most benign motives from their impact abroad. The effects of American
policies have received much less scholarly consideration than the domestic
roots of imperialism, and greater attention needs to be devoted to the role of
the periphery and collaboration within the American empire. Interestingly,
the desire to prepare others for self-government and the conviction that these
clients should follow the developmental example of the United States has
persuaded many observers that their policies were less exploitive than those
of the Europeans; but these objectives simultaneously rendered Americans
more imperialistic, not less, because they were more ambitious in their
insistence upon instituting more fundamental changes in indigenous societies.
Moreover, the claims for the benefits of American control must not be

overstated. Order was imposed; education was promoted; sanitation and medical care were improved; roads, railroads, and ports were constructed; private capital was infused; productivity was enhanced. But such reforms usually proved transitory and did little to improve the lot of the majority of local inhabitants. Neither democratic institutions nor true economic development and general prosperity proved exportable to the Caribbean or the Philippines. This failure resulted in part from the tenacity of indigenous cultural, political, and economic forces. But the US presence also contributed to the deaths of thousands of Filipinos and Latin Americans, to elite-controlled and dictatorial politics, and to static or declining economic conditions for the masses. Only by ignoring such outcomes and the coercion involved or by attempting to narrowly define US imperialism out of existence can the image of American innocence and the fundamental uniqueness of imperialism, American style be sustained.

NOTES

1 Joseph A. Fry, "Theodore Roosevelt and the Rise of America to World Power," in Howard Jones (ed.), *Safeguarding the Republic: Essays and Documents in American Foreign Relations, 1890–1991*, New York, 1992, pp. 26–7; Robert L. Beisner, *Twelve Against Empire: The Anti-Imperialists, 1898–1900*, New York, 1968, p. 162.
2 Edward P. Crapol, "Coming to Terms with Empire: The Historiography of Late-Nineteenth Century American Foreign Relations," *Diplomatic History*, vol. 16, 1992, pp. 573–97; Robin W. Winks, "The American Struggle with 'Imperialism': How Words Frighten," in Rob Kroes (ed.), *The American Identity: Fusion and Fragmentation*, Amsterdam, 1980, pp. 143–77.
3 Schumpeter quoted in Arthur Schlesinger Jr, "The Missionary Enterprise and Theories of Imperialism," in John K. Fairbank (ed.), *The Missionary Enterprise in China*, Cambridge, Mass., 1974, p. 336; Waller quoted in David Hackett Fischer, *Historians' Fallacies: Toward a Logic of Historical Thought*, New York, 1970, p. xiii.
4 Samuel Flagg Bemis, *A Diplomatic History of the United States*, New York, 1950, p. 468; Dexter Perkins, *The American Approach to Foreign Policy*, Cambridge, Mass., 1962, pp. 30–4, 41–7; Ernest R. May, *American Imperialism: A Speculative Essay*, 1968; rept, Chicago, 1991, pp. xxx, 3, 14–16.
5 William A. Williams, *The Tragedy of American Diplomacy*, New York, 1972, pp. 47, 50–1, 55. See also: Walter LaFeber, *The New Empire: An Interpretation of American Expansion, 1860–1898*, Ithaca, N.Y., 1963; Thomas J. McCormick, *China Market: America's Quest for Informal Empire, 1893–1901*, Chicago, 1967.
6 Wolfgang J. Mommsen and Jurgen Osterhammel (eds), *Imperialism and After: Continuities and Discontinuities*, Boston, 1986, p. ix.
7 Graham quoted in Thomas G. Paterson and Stephen G. Rabe (eds), *Imperial Surge: The United States Abroad. The 1890s–early 1900s*, Lexington, Mass., 1992, p. xviii.
8 Williams, *Tragedy*; LaFeber, *New Empire*; McCormick, *China Market*; Crapol, "Coming to Terms."
9 Walter LaFeber, *Inevitable Revolutions: The United States in Central America*, New York, 1984; Louis A. Pérez Jr, *Cuba and the United States: Ties of Singular Intimacy*, Athens, Ga, 1990; Thomas D. Schoonover, *The United States in Central*

     America, 1860–1911: Episodes of Social Imperialism and Imperial Rivalry in the World System, Durham, N.C., 1991.

10   LaFeber, *New Empire*, p. 400.

11   Robert Freeman Smith, *The United States and Revolutionary Nationalism in Mexico, 1916–32*, Chicago, 1972, pp. 23–5; N. Gordon Levin, *Woodrow Wilson and World Politics: America's Response to War and Revolution*, New York, 1968; Emily S. Rosenberg, *Spreading the American Dream: American Economic and Cultural Expansion, 1890–1945*, New York, 1982, pp. 7–13.

12   Rosenberg, *American Dream*, pp. 38–86.

13   Paul S. Holbo, "Economics, Emotion, and Expansion: An Emerging Foreign Policy," in H. Wayne Morgan (ed.), *The Gilded Age*, Syracuse, N.Y., 1970, pp. 199–221; Julius W. Pratt, *Expansionists of 1898: The Acquisition of Hawaii and the Spanish Islands*, 1936; rept, Chicago, 1964, p. 257; William H. Becker, *The Dynamics of Business–Government Relations: Industry and Exports, 1893–1921*, Chicago, 1982, p. 184 (final quote).

14   Becker, *Dynamics*; David M. Pletcher, "Rhetoric and Results: A Pragmatic View of American Economic Expansionism, 1865–1898," *Diplomatic History*, vol. 5, 1981, pp. 93–105; Paul A. Varg, *The Making of A Myth: The United States and China, 1897–1912*, East Lansing, Mich., 1968, pp. 37–53; James A. Field Jr, "American Imperialism: The Worst Chapter in Almost Any Book," *American Historical Review*, vol. 83, 1978, p. 645.

15   Richard Hofstadter, "Manifest Destiny and the Philippines," in Daniel Aaron (ed.), *America in Crisis*, New York, 1952, pp. 173–200; Robert Dallek, *The American Style of Foreign Policy: Cultural Politics and Foreign Affairs*, New York, 1983, p. 4; Marilyn Blatt Young, *The Rhetoric of Empire: America's China Policy, 1895–1901*, Cambridge, Mass., 1968, pp. 1–4.

16   Robert E. Osgood, *Ideals and Self-Interest in America's Foreign Relations: The Great Transformation of the Twentieth Century*, Chicago, 1953, pp. 18, 27, 42; Norman A. Graebner, *Ideas and Diplomacy: Readings in the Intellectual Tradition of American Foreign Policy*, New York, 1964, p. 339.

17   Pratt, *Expansionists of 1898*, pp. 1–22.

18   May, *American Imperialism*, pp. 116–230; David Healy, *US Expansionism: The Imperialist Urge in the 1890s*, Madison, Wis., 1970, pp. 9–33.

19   Joseph E. Wisan, *The Cuban Crisis as Reflected in the New York Press, 1895–1898*, New York, 1934.

20   Pratt, *Expansionists of 1898*, pp. 242, 327.

21   Ernest R. May, *Imperial Democracy: The Emergence of America as a Great Power*, New York, 1961, pp. 82, 129, 143.

22   Pratt, *Expansionists of 1898*, pp. 279, 282; James C. Thomson Jr, Peter W. Stanley, and John Curtis Perry, *Sentimental Imperialists: The American Experience in East Asia*, New York, 1981, pp. 45–56; James Reed, *The Missionary Mind and American East Asia Policy, 1911–1915*, Cambridge, Mass., 1983.

23   Whitney T. Perkins, *Denial of Empire: The United States and Its Dependencies*, Leyden, 1962; Richard Collin, *Theodore Roosevelt's Caribbean: The Panama Canal, the Monroe Doctrine, and the Latin American Context*, Baton Rouge, La, 1991; Richard H. Abrams, "United States Intervention Abroad, The First Quarter Century," *American Historical Review*, vol. 79, 1974, pp. 72–102; Frederick S. Calhoun, *Power and Principle: Armed Intervention in Wilsonian Foreign Policy*, Kent, Ohio, 1986.

24   Jerry Israel, *Progressivism and the Open Door: America and China, 1905–1921*, Pittsburgh, Pa, 1971; Howard E. Gillette Jr, "The Military Occupation of Cuba, 1899–1902: Workshop for American Progressivism," *American Quarterly*, vol. 25, 1973, pp. 410–25.

25   Samuel Flagg Bemis, *The Latin American Policy of the United States: A Historical*

Interpretation, New York, 1943, pp. 140, 166; Dana G. Munro, *Intervention and Dollar Diplomacy in the Caribbean, 1900–1921*, Princeton, N.J., 1964, pp. 530–1; Lester D. Langley, *The Banana Wars: An Inner History of American Empire, 1900–1934*, Lexington, Ky, 1983, pp. 5–6, 8.

26 Richard D. Challener, *Admirals, Generals, and American Foreign Policy, 1898–1914*, Princeton, N.J., 1973, pp. 406–12; Kenneth J. Hagan, *This People's Navy: The Making of American Sea Power*, New York, 1991, pp. 228–47.

27 Winks, "American Struggle," p. 144; Akira Iriye, *Across the Pacific: An Inner History of American–East Asian Relations*, New York, 1967, pp. 54–5; Richard H. Collin, *Theodore Roosevelt, Culture, Diplomacy and Expansion: A New View of American Imperialism*, Baton Rouge, La, 1985, pp. 8, 103, 198; Collin, *Roosevelt's Caribbean*, pp. 9–11, 547.

28 Wolfgang J. Mommsen, *Theories of Imperialism*, New York, 1982, pp. 76, 78.

29 John A. S. Grenville and George Berkeley Young, *Politics, Strategy, and American Diplomacy: Studies in Foreign Policy, 1873–1917*, New Haven, Conn., 1966, pp. 269–76.

30 H. Wayne Morgan, *America's Road to Empire: The War with Spain and Overseas Expansion*, New York, 1965; Lewis L. Gould, *The Spanish–American War and President McKinley*, Lawrence, Kan., 1982; John L. Offner, *An Unwanted War: The Diplomacy of the United States and Spain over Cuba, 1895–1898*, Chapel Hill, N.C., 1992.

31 Field, "American Imperialism," pp. 646–50.

32 Melvin Small, "The United States and the German 'Threat' to the Hemisphere, 1904–1914," *The Americas*, vol. 28, 1972, pp. 252–70; David Healy, *Drive to Hegemony: The United States in the Caribbean, 1898–1917*, Madison, Wis., 1988, p. 289.

33 For American innocence, see Stuart Creighton Miller, *"Benevolent Assimilation": The American Conquest of the Philippines, 1899–1903*, New Haven, Conn., 1982, pp. 253–68.

34 D. Perkins, *American Approach*, p. 31; W. Perkins, *Denial of Empire*, pp. 343, 351; Munro, *Dollar Diplomacy*, pp. 534–43.

35 D. Perkins, *American Approach*, p. 47.

36 Pérez, *Cuba and the United States*, pp. 80–3, 97, 105–10, 117, 161; Schoonover, *United States in Central America*, p. 111; Brenda Gayle Plummer, *Haiti and the Great Powers, 1902–1915*, Baton Rouge, La, 1988, p. 124.

37 LaFeber, *Inevitable Revolutions*, pp. 5–78; Healy, *Drive to Hegemony*, pp. 260–74; Glenn A. May, *Social Engineering in the Philippines: The Aims, Execution, and Impact of American Colonial Policy, 1900–1913*, Westport, Conn., 1980, pp. 142–3, 146, 150, 166, 175; Daniel R. Headrick, *The Tentacles of Progress: Technological Transfer in the Age of Imperialism, 1850–1940*, New York, 1988, pp. 383–4.

38 Christobal Kay, *Latin American Theories of Development and Underdevelopment*, New York, 1989; Mommsen, *Theories of Imperialism*, pp. 121–37; Tony Smith, *The Pattern of Imperialism: The United States, Great Britain and the Late-Industrializing World since 1815*, New York, 1981, pp. 59–84.

39 Smith, *The Pattern of Imperialism*.

40 Schlesinger, "Missionary Enterprise," pp. 363–5; Paul W. Harris, "Cultural Imperialism and American Protestant Missionaries: Collaboration and Dependency in Mid-Nineteenth Century China," *Pacific Historical Review*, vol. 60, 1991, pp. 311–15.

41 W. Perkins, *Denial of Empire*, p. 342.

42 Thomson, *et al.*, *Sentimental Imperialists*, p. 45; Kenton J. Clymer, *Protestant Missionaries in the Philippines, 1898–1916: An Inquiry into the American Colonial Mentality*, Urbana, Ill., 1986; Jane Hunter, *The Gospel of Gentility:*

American Women Missionaries in Turn-of-the-Century China, New Haven, Conn., 1984.

43 David Arnold (ed.), *Imperial Medicine and Indigenous Societies*, Manchester, 1988, pp. 2, 10, 14–19.

44 Julius W. Pratt, *America's Colonial Experiment: How the United States Gained, Governed, and In Part Gave Away a Colonial Empire*, 1950; rept, Gloucester, Mass., 1964, p. 201; W. Perkins, *Denial of Empire*, p. 208.

45 Peter W. Stanley (ed.), *Reappraising an Empire: New Perspectives on Philippine–American History*, Cambridge, Mass., 1984, pp. 1–7; May, *Social Engineering*, p. 123; Robert E. Quirk, *An Affair of Honor: Woodrow Wilson and the Occupation of Vera Cruz*, Lexington, Ky, 1962, pp. 123–54, 170–1; A. E. Campbell, "The Paradox of Imperialism: The American Case," in Mommsen and Osterhammel (eds), *Imperialism and After*, p. 37.

46 All the articles in Stanley, *Reappraising an Empire*, address this theme, as does the *Pacific Historical Review*, vol. 68, 1979, pp. 467–591, entitled "American Empire, 1898–1903"; Peter W. Stanley, *A Nation in the Making: The Philippines and the United States, 1899–1921*, Cambridge, Mass., 1974, pp. 52, 268–75; Glenn A. May, *Battle for Batangas: A Philippine Province at War*, New Haven, Conn., 1991, pp. 198–201; Pérez, *United States and Cuba*, pp. 113–17; Gilbert M. Joseph, *Revolution from Without: Yucatan, Mexico, and the United States, 1880–1924*, New York, 1982.

47 Friedrich W. Horlacher, "The Language of Late Nineteenth-Century American Expansionism," in Serge Ricard (ed.), *An American Empire: Expansionist Cultures and Policies, 1881–1917*, Aix-en-Provence, 1990, p. 40.

48 Michael H. Hunt, *Ideology and U.S. Foreign Policy*, New Haven, Conn., 1987; Albert K. Weinberg, *Manifest Destiny: A Study of Nationalist Expansionism in American History*, 1935; rept, Chicago, 1963.

49 David L. Anderson, *Imperialism and Idealism: American Diplomats in China, 1861–1898*, Bloomington, Ind., 1985, pp. 2, 191; on the synthesis of motives, see also Robert L. Beisner, *From the Old Diplomacy to the New, 1865–1900*, 2nd rev. ed., Arlington Heights, Ill., 1986.

5 Wilsonian diplomacy in war and peace

John W. Coogan

President Woodrow Wilson left office in March 1921, a crippled, embittered man. His years in the White House had dramatically and permanently changed the relationship of the United States to the rest of the world. The actions of his administration, his motives, and the consequences of the changes he produced were a source of controversy from 1913 to 1921. Controversy has been a key element of the historical scholarship concerning his era ever since.

Perhaps the most striking aspect of this debate has been its range, as scholars have failed to agree on even the most basic points. Charles Seymour,[1] Charles Tansill,[2] Thomas Bailey,[3] George Kennan,[4] and other first-generation Wilson historians produced many volumes and great heat, but little consensus. Instead, they seemed to write about different Woodrow Wilsons: an impartial defender of American neutrality; an economically-driven dupe of the Allies and the house of Morgan; a martyred prophet of world peace; an unworldly idealist ignorant and contemptuous of the realities of power.[5]

Nor did this historical confusion end in 1951. In 1953 Robert Osgood published a long, well documented book arguing that Wilson was an idealist who paid little attention to balance of power considerations;[6] two years later Edward Buehrig published a long, equally well documented book arguing that Wilson was a realist whose policies were dominated by concern to maintain the balance of power.[7]

The 1960s saw Arthur Link's multivolume analysis of Wilson's "higher realism"[8] as well as N. Gordon Levin, Jr's picture of an ideologically driven anti-*Junker*, anti-Bolshevik "liberal–capitalist."[9] In the next decade Link re-emphasized the pervasive impact of Wilson's Christianity,[10] while David Trask described him as "a disciple of Clausewitz."[11] More recent scholarship has seen Wilson portrayed by Lloyd Gardner as a crusader against revolutionary nationalism,[12] as a willing tool of an aggressively expansionist business community by Sidney Bell,[13] and as a "liberal internationalist" by Lloyd Ambrosius.[14] The number of labels used to describe Wilson and his foreign policies over the past seventy years approximates the number of scholars who have written on the topic.

What has been missing is any significant integration of these disparate, often directly contradictory, interpretations. Historians have been so busy trying to prove that Wilson was a "realist" or an "idealist," a "progressive" or an "imperialist," a "liberal–capitalist" or a "liberal internationalist," a disciple of Christ or of Clausewitz, that they have missed one basic point: Wilson was all of those things, but none of them exclusively. Each scholar has identified and documented a legitimate aspect of the foreign policy of the Wilson administration, but only by ignoring or twisting lines of equally valid evidence that point in different directions.

The historical Woodrow Wilson, as distinguished from the one who appears in much of the historical literature, simply defies one-dimensional (e.g., "realist") or even two-dimensional (e.g., "liberal–capitalist") labels. He was a man of genius, of enormous inner complexity, of self-contradiction and, ultimately, with the capacity for self-destruction. He had to define and implement his foreign policies in a complex world in which the lives of millions of people depended on his decisions. As a result, he tended to be more concerned with consequences than with ideological or political consistency. Thus he could, simultaneously, be a disciple of Christ, as Link has maintained, and a disciple of Clausewitz, as Trask has argued. In the name of world peace he waged a world war; in the name of self-determination he ordered American troops into Latin America and Russia; in the name of western civilization he failed to provide food for starving German and Austrian children after the armistice of November 1918. He saw neither contradiction nor hypocrisy in these positions. Any attempt to find one label to describe his foreign policies inevitably falls short because he did not have one dominant, consistent motive and because his actions and statements often contradicted each other. Any attempt to find one label to describe the foreign policies of his administration inevitably falls short because he often failed to control the agents who claimed to act in his name or even to explain his ideas to them.

An understanding of American foreign relations during the Wilson era must begin with an acceptance of these complexities and contradictions. As a tenured professor at Princeton, Wilson – like the scholars who write about him – enjoyed the luxury of engaging in leisurely research and reflecting on his thoughts before he committed himself to publication. As president of the United States he depended on subordinates to do the research, and many of his most important decisions had to be made under intense pressure and rigid deadlines. While he certainly maintained long-standing, deeply-held principles such as respect for democracy and self-determination, he constantly had to integrate such abstractions with complicated, interrelated considerations of politics, economics, diplomacy, bureaucracy and personality. As a result, his policies were more ad hoc and less calculated than present scholarship acknowledges.

A second point to keep in mind is that Edwin Weinstein's brilliant work on Wilson's physical and mental health has forever changed the ground on which any understanding of the president's personal role must be based.[15] Wilson hardly was a disembodied intellect even before his stroke in October 1919: he was a human being who battled physical and emotional illness throughout his presidency – illness that grew gradually more severe and influenced both personal and policy decisions. His major stroke must be seen as the culmination of these problems, not as a sudden trauma that transformed overnight a previously healthy, absolutely rational man into the pitiful shell of one that he became in his last seventeen months in office.

The third point which must be understood is that "Woodrow Wilson" and "Wilson administration foreign policy" were not synonymous. Wilson himself acknowledged on his inauguration day that his primary interests were domestic and that it would be an "irony of fate" if he had to become deeply involved in the management of foreign affairs.[16] Yet if he came into office with little interest in events overseas, they quickly forced him to reassess his priorities. The Mexican revolution and a series of upheavals in the Caribbean drew the United States into political, economic, and occasionally military intervention in Latin America despite the president's deeply held and sincerely stated commitment to the principle of self-determination. Japanese imperialism at the expense of China and the festering imperial sore of the Philippines led to erratic but ongoing presidential concern about the Far East. Above all, World War I led him to believe that his program of domestic reform could be implemented only in a new international environment, one that could be created only by active American leadership of the world in war and peace. Wilson, in spite of these pressures, mastered foreign relations as quickly as any president in American history, on a level of understanding matched only by the most sophisticated of his predecessors.

The style that emerged was highly personal, and as brilliant and erratic as the president himself. This personalization of policy became particularly important because Wilson was never able to devise an effective mechanism to communicate his ideas and decisions to those who were institutionally responsible for implementing them. He never trusted his State Department. Wilson considered his first secretary of state, William Jennings Bryan, a political necessity but an intellectual and diplomatic embarrassment.[17] The president made no attempt to build a competent foreign relations establishment. Instead he bypassed the department and, on important issues, operated through private agents – the most important of whom was Colonel Edward House. As a result, the State Department often found itself acting in utter ignorance of major presidential initiatives in its contacts with foreign governments.[18]

Bryan resigned in despair after two years and his successor, Robert Lansing, proved to be a better administrator but no more able to secure the confidence of his boss. Wilson considered his second secretary of state a narrow-minded lawyer who became bogged down in technicalities and unable to understand any larger vision of international relations. The president continued to ignore or even deliberately mislead his own State Department.

Lansing lasted five frustrating years before being fired in 1920.[19] Bainbridge Colby, Wilson's last secretary of state, could do little more than hold the department together through a year when the White House could not lead but would not delegate.

This weakness at the State Department compounded the abysmal quality of Wilson's diplomatic appointments. The president himself characterized his ambassador to Germany as an "ass" and an "idiot," but chose to leave James Gerard as chief American representative in Berlin until 1917.[20] The ambassador to Britain was actively disloyal, not only to his president's instructions but to his country, to the point where he helped the Foreign Office draft its reply to a protest from his own government. Yet Walter Hines Page remained accredited to London until his health failed in 1918.[21] The president did recall his governor general from the Philippines, but only upon receiving evidence that Francis Burton Harrison ran Manila in the manner of Henry VIII, impregnating two teenage sisters and inducing nationalist leaders to pimp for him.[22] Scholars have attempted to blame such disastrous appointments on Bryan, but they were – including the appointment of Bryan himself – the president's responsibility. Wilson simply did not care enough about his State Department or his formal representation abroad to secure competent men to staff those positions.[23]

As a consequence, the United States from 1913 to 1921 often found itself communicating to other nations in multiple voices. One classic case in October 1914 saw the British government try to make sense of five contradictory explanations of American policy toward Allied interference with neutral commerce: the president's own conversation with the British ambassador, Sir Cecil Spring Rice; House's statements to Spring Rice, which were supposedly approved by Wilson; Bryan's statements to Spring Rice, which were supposedly approved by Wilson; Lansing's statements to Spring Rice, which were supposedly approved by Wilson; and Page's statements to Foreign Secretary Sir Edward Grey – which, once again, supposedly represented Wilson's own views.[24] In the midst of such chaos, even the most straightforward diplomatic communication would leave the British government mystified and frustrated. It also goes far to explain why historians have continued for seventy years to publish such diverse and even contradictory interpretations of the foreign policies of the Wilson administration: because the institutional chaos that produced those policies generated evidence to support just about any interpretation of administration actions or motives.

What then would constitute an interpretation of "Wilsonian diplomacy in war and peace" which took into account Wilson's genius, his lack of preparation in foreign affairs, his personal ad hoc style of policymaking, his physical and psychological condition, and his contempt for the State Department and diplomatic corps? While any answers must be tentative, some assessments are possible.

Both Wilson and his administration clearly ranked the regions and the races of the world in a hierarchical way. Europe was more important than Latin

America, which was more important than East Asia, which was more important than Africa; Anglo-Saxons were superior to other white races, which were superior to yellow, which were superior to brown, which were superior to black. Wilson might or might not like David Lloyd George or Georges Clemenceau or Prince Max of Baden on a personal level, but their nationality and race gave them an inherent credibility in his eyes that was automatically denied to Victoriano Huerta or Ho Chi Minh.

These hierarchies helped to determine many Wilson administration policies. The principle of non-intervention in Latin America was important to the president, but adhering to such an abstraction did not prevent him from applying economic, diplomatic and military pressures to destabilize the Huerta government in Mexico City. Nor did it prevent Wilson from first supporting Pancho Villa's revolt and then sending troops into northern Mexico to suppress it after the *Villistas* rejected his tutelage. In the same spirit, he lamented the need to intervene in the internal affairs of Haiti, the Dominican Republic, Panama, and Nicaragua – but he intervened anyway, justifying his actions by citing American national security and his self-proclaimed obligation to "teach the South American Republics to elect good men."[25] Wilson's Latin American policy began in 1913 with noble words about self-determination, but after years of being filtered through the racism and paternalism of the administration, and after being compared with the needs of American national security interests, those words had a hollow ring by 1921 – a ring punctuated by the tramp of American combat boots.

Many of the same themes appear in American relations with East Asia, although the distance involved and other priorities generally limited the willingness of the administration to use military force. Wilson, in 1913, had spoken vaguely in favor of independence for the Philippines, though he clearly lacked Bryan's personal commitment to it. By the time Filipino nationalist leaders began to demand that the administration's actions match its rhetoric, Bryan had resigned. The president continued to claim that he sympathized with the Filipinos, but insisted that he was unable to implement independence because of the war in Europe. The Jones Act of 1916 promised independence but set no date for it. When the war ended, Wilson refused to move toward independence because of the Paris Peace Conference; when the conference ended, he refused to move toward independence until the Senate had approved the Treaty of Versailles. The Philippines remained an American colony when Wilson left office. While there is no reason to doubt the sincerity of his pro-independence rhetoric, the failure to make more progress in eight years demonstrates that he gave its implementation a low priority.[26]

Much the same can be said of Wilson's support for the Chinese revolution. In principle, he supported democracy and self-determination for China; in practice, he maintained the unequal treaties which gave the United States special rights at China's expense. When Japan presented the Chinese government with the "21 Demands" in 1915, seeking to take advantage of the preoccupation of the warring European powers to establish predominance,

Wilson supported the efforts of his envoy in Beijing, Paul Reinsch, to encourage Chinese resistance. Bryan issued a formal statement, shortly before his resignation, that the United States would not recognize any Sino-Japanese agreement that compromised American treaty rights or Chinese integrity. When Beijing asked what practical support the United States would give, however, the administration made clear its unwillingness to consider economic or military sanctions. The Chinese then made the best deal they could with Tokyo, a deal Washington informally recognized two years later in the Lansing–Ishii agreement.

Wilson went to Paris in 1919 pledged to uphold the principle of self-determination, but ended up agreeing that the former German concessions in China should be transferred to Japan rather than returned to China. His rhetoric of international equality had raised hope throughout China, particularly among young intellectuals. The dashing of that hope in the Versailles Treaty led directly to the outpouring of outraged nationalist fervor which exploded into the 4 May Movement, which was central to the origins of the national revival led by Sun Yatsen. Ironically, Wilson's failure to uphold his own principles at Versailles proved to be his only lasting contribution to the rise of modern China.[27]

If the gap between Wilson's rhetorical support for self-determination and his practical accommodation with Japanese imperialism infuriated the Chinese, it failed to win the United States many friends in Tokyo either. The administration's pattern of publicly challenging Japanese actions then backing down and accepting them was hardly likely to earn respect. The ambiguous American role in the Allied military intervention in Siberia only confirmed this pattern. Perhaps Wilson himself knew whether he sent American troops to Vladivostok to maintain order and protect refugees, to meddle in the Russian Civil War, or to keep an eye on the much larger Japanese contingent. From the point of view of Tokyo, however, Washington's motives were less significant than the very presence of American troops in Northeast Asia. Continued discrimination against Japanese in California, which the president claimed was a matter of state law and thus beyond his federal authority, and his personal opposition to Japanese attempts to add a racial equality clause to the Versailles Treaty further poisoned Japanese–American relations.[28]

Wilson saw few attractive options for American policy in the Far East. He believed, sincerely, in the principles of self-determination and self-government. Yet he also believed, with equal sincerity, that the Philippines were not ready for self-government and that immediate independence would quickly lead to anarchy. He believed that China too was not yet ready for full national sovereignty, and that the unequal treaty structure would have to be dissolved gradually. He feared that Japanese imperialism would undermine China's progress toward national responsibility, and that it would injure American economic and missionary interests there. Yet Wilson also understood that the American people would not permit him to use military power, or even meaningful economic pressure, to oppose Japan; and although he believed in the principle of Russian autonomy, he also believed that the United States had a responsibility to protect Siberia from anti-democratic Bolsheviks at home and imperialistic Japanese abroad. His administration tried for eight years to balance these different principles, interests, and responsibilities. By the time Wilson left office, he had disappointed Filipino nationalists, infuriated Chinese nationalists, irritated Japanese nationalists, used American troops to shoot Russian nationalists on Russian soil – and generated several volumes of presidential speeches supporting nationalism and democracy in East Asia.

The major reason why the Wilson administration refused to become more deeply involved in the Far East and in Latin America was the European war that began in August 1914. First as leader of the world's most powerful neutral, then as a belligerent and as a peace-maker, and finally as a politician unable to win domestic support for his peace program, Wilson led the United States to play a central role in World War I. His map of the world was firmly centered in Europe. His definitions of culture, civilization and politics were centered in Europe – especially in his romantic view of English history and institutions. He understood that American overseas trade was primarily with Europe. He believed that the future of the United States was linked to that of Europe in a way it never could be linked to Asia, Africa, or even Latin America. He believed the United States had both a deep moral responsibility and a vital national interest to save Europe from self-destruction and to help rebuild it on a healthy, democratic foundation.

Wilson's decision to regard relations with Europe as his highest priority in foreign affairs has been reflected in the work of historians. The nature of American neutrality and the motives behind the declaration of war in April 1917 remain extremely controversial. Efforts to make peace both before and after the armistice on 11 November 1918 have sparked a similar degree of controversy. Intervention in the Russian Civil War remains among the most mystifying events in all of American history, while the Senate's rejection of the Versailles Treaty has become the classic case of legislative/executive rivalry in US foreign relations. Simply to list the major scholarly works on these topics would expand this essay far beyond reasonable limits.

The debate over the nature of Wilson's neutrality policy has tended to follow the outlines of positions originally staked out between August 1914 and April 1917. Some critics, the most notable of whom was Theodore Roosevelt, complained that the administration was too neutral, that it gave too much importance to the technicalities of international law and too little to the realities of national interest. Supporters of the Allies repeatedly criticized Wilson for violating neutrality in favor of the Central Powers; supporters of the latter criticized him with equal intensity for violating neutrality in favor of the Allies. The president often cited these attacks from partisans of both sides as the best possible evidence that he was, in fact, maintaining a rigorous neutrality.

The historical debate has focused on two questions: was the administration neutral, and should it have been? Those who argue that it was not neutral also tend to conclude that the United States favored the Allies at the expense of the Central Powers, and that a genuinely neutral position would have been in the American interest.[29] Those who maintain that the administration was neutral, on the other hand, are split into those who consider this to have been a wise policy[30] and those who believe that earlier and more generous support for the Allies would have worked to the benefit of the United States.[31]

The question of whether the American government was in fact neutral has been debated endlessly, with little resulting agreement. Those who argue that it was tend to emphasize Wilson's own statements, public and private, imploring others to remain neutral and promising that his administration would uphold the standards of neutrality. Those who argue that the United States was not neutral tend to emphasize that American trade and finance went overwhelmingly to the Allies rather than to the Central Powers and thus favored one belligerent camp at the expense of the other. Both positions are well documented, since there is ample evidence to demonstrate that Wilson did sincerely wish to remain neutral at least until early 1917, and simultaneously, that one-sided access to American economic resources did become a vital element in the ability of the Allies to carry on the war.

Unfortunately, this debate has been largely about semantics rather than the substance of American neutrality. Only Wilson's most embittered critics have doubted that he sincerely intended to be neutral; the president himself admitted that the effect of America's unbalanced trade patterns was to favor the Allies. Yet the first of these interpretations reduces neutrality to a matter of intent, while the second makes it a matter of effect. Neither intent nor effect was central to the definition of neutrality that existed in international relations in 1914. "Neutrality" was a status which a nation maintained by behaving in a certain manner toward belligerents and toward other neutrals. The rights and duties that constituted appropriate patterns of behavior had been established over more than a century of American history, in state papers and in court decisions. They had been collected by John Bassett Moore, the dean of American international lawyers, and published by the US Government Printing Office in 1906.[32] The overwhelming majority of scholars who have written about the period 1914–17 have confused the question of whether the administration was *impartial* – which is indeed a matter of intent and effect – with the question of whether it was *neutral* – which is a matter of law.

Once this semantic confusion is clarified, it becomes much easier to understand American policies during this period. It is clear that Wilson himself was not impartial in the attitude he took to the war: he favored the Allies, he hoped they would win and, aside from Bryan, his senior advisers on foreign policy (particularly House, Lansing, and Page) shared his bias.[33] This attitude undoubtedly violated the standard set in the president's message to the Senate of 19 August 1914, in which he urged Americans to be "impartial in thought as well as in action."[34] But it did not violate *neutrality*, which is determined by actions and not by private thoughts.

The evidence is also clear that Wilson sincerely tried to maintain what he perceived to be neutrality. Yet the fact that the president intended to be neutral does not establish the fact that the United States behaved as a neutral. Again, neutrality is determined by actions, not by intentions.

The same distinction applies to the argument that the American government violated the principle of neutrality because it permitted businessmen to sell munitions and provide loans to the Allies. This decision resulted in an unbalanced trade that clearly gave the Allies an enormous, perhaps decisive, advantage over their enemies. Yet, under international law, the private citizens of a neutral state had every right to sell any products or to make any loans they wished to belligerents. If superior seapower allowed one belligerent free access to such resources while denying them to its enemy, the trade imbalance that resulted was in no way the neutral's responsibility. The flow of American economic and financial resources across the Atlantic in no way constituted a violation of American neutrality: the law authorized neutrals to take certain actions, and it was indifferent to the effects of those actions – even when they favored one belligerent over another.

The question must ultimately be answered by determining whether or not the United States met the requirements of neutrality as defined by international law in 1914. And the answer is clear: the United States was not entitled to neutral status because it failed to meet those requirements. The American government was obligated to defend its neutral rights equally against violation by all belligerents. Wilson permitted the Allies to interfere in American commerce with the Central Powers and with European neutrals in ways that were flagrantly illegal, while he refused to permit a similar liberty to Germany in its illegal submarine campaign against Britain. The result of this difference in treatment of the two belligerents was precisely what James Brown Scott, a leading international lawyer and chairman of the administration's Joint Neutrality Board, had warned in September 1914 that it would be if the United States refused to act against the British blockade: "non-neutrality toward Germany."[35] The United States did not become a belligerent until April 1917, but it had ceased to be neutral after August 1914.

Why then did Wilson, if he was as sincerely committed to neutrality as he claimed to be, refuse to act within the existing definition of that status? That question can be answered only through an appreciation of the extent to which the president was unable to control the contradictory activities in which his subordinates engaged. The actions of Page, Gerard, House, and other official and unofficial agents of the administration were in themselves more than enough to undermine American neutrality, whatever the official position of the White House. Wilson knew of some of these indiscretions and suspected others, but made no effective effort to stop them by controlling or replacing those responsible.[36]

In the final resort the un-neutral acts of subordinates were possible only because of un-neutral acts by the president himself. If House and Page advised Wilson to challenge the German submarine but not the British cruiser, the decision was his and not theirs. The ultimate explanation for the failure of the United States to maintain its neutrality under law lies in the mind and heart of Woodrow Wilson.

The president himself never acknowledged, publicly or privately, that his actions failed to live up to the laws of neutrality. He admitted that the British blockade did violate some existing neutral rights, but believed that the violations were of a technical nature and resulted primarily from the need to adapt sailing ship precedents to modern warfare. The obligation of the United States as a neutral was met, as far as Wilson was concerned, when his State Department filed formal protests with the Foreign Office: to go beyond such paper reservation of American rights would actually violate the principle of neutrality, since it would hurt the Allied war effort to a degree far out of proportion with the seriousness of the original offense. The actions of the British, even if technically illegal, resulted in the seizure of property that could be restored through established diplomatic processes. The German submarine campaign was different: it resulted in the destruction of American lives that could not be restored by diplomacy. The belligerents violated the neutrality of the United States in different ways and, in Wilson's view, these differences dictated that he respond more severely to the more severe violations by Germany. He saw this distinction as the essence of neutrality, not a violation of it.

As the war continued into its third year, however, this line of argument came to seem increasingly thin, even to Wilson. There is ample evidence to demonstrate that he became increasingly angry and frustrated with British actions. As Robert Ferrell notes, this anger and frustration eventually grew so severe that it "drove Wilson almost to real impartiality."[37] Ironically, Wilson became most upset when the British chose to prosecute British firms doing business with American firms that the British government had black-listed for suspicion of trading with Germany. The blacklist was entirely a matter of British municipal law and quite unobjectionable under international law – in contrast with just about everything else the British were doing to neutral commerce by this time. But "impartiality" was a matter of attitude, while "neutrality" was a matter of action under law. The administration never took any action, or made a credible threat that it would take action, to force Britain to respect the rights of the United States as a neutral.

Wilson never understood that British violations of international maritime law were not legalistic technicalities growing from different definitions of how to adapt agreed principles to modern conditions. The British were violating, directly and deliberately, established legal principles. They were also violating the sovereignty of the United States by seizing American ships, cargoes and mail without legal justification. The foundation of the blockade was an Admiralty proclamation dated 3 November 1914, which announced that British mines had been scattered throughout the North Sea. German submarines had orders to spare American ships entering the war zone established by Germany around Britain four months later, although Berlin admitted that its captains might attack neutrals by mistake. Automatic contact mines in the British war zone threatened to blow up any ship that attempted to navigate the North Sea without sailing instructions – which the British provided only to ships that cooperated with Allied blockade authorities. Wilson sent an ultimatum in 1915 to protect the right of Americans, as citizens of a neutral state, to be free from submarine attack when sailing through the German war zone on munitions-laden Allied ships; two years later he went to war for the same principle. He simply ignored the danger that those same lives might be destroyed by British mines, although these were far more indiscriminate than German submarines. The real difference was not that the British blockade threatened property while the German blockade threatened lives: both German submarines and British mines threatened American lives. The difference in the president's mind was that one blockade was British and the other German.

Wilson did not understand the nature of the British blockade because he did not wish to. He believed that a German victory in Europe "would change the course of our civilization and make the United States a military nation."[38] He believed that Britain was a kindred democracy and a kindred spirit. He believed that blockade was one of the most formidable weapons the Allies possessed in the war against Germany. Surrounded by advisers who gave incoming reports a pro-Allied slant, convinced that a German victory would endanger the United States, Wilson was always able to find excuses to take no action against British violations of international law. To admit that Allied measures were as offensive to American rights, and as dangerous to American citizens as German measures, would have required Wilson to confront his own prejudices. It was easier to maintain that the British actions constituted only technical violations, quite different from those of Germany, and that true neutrality – as distinguished from empty legalism – required a strong stand against the latter and an understanding tolerance of the former.

Whether American interests might have been better served by more effective neutrality or by earlier belligerency cannot be determined by the historian. What can be demonstrated is that the policy of non-belligerent non-neutrality proved a tremendous boon for American political and economic interests. By permitting Allied access to American supplies and credit while helping to protect that access by insisting on restricted German use of submarines, Wilson enabled the Allied Powers to compensate for the exhaustion of their own resources and thus to continue the fight against Germany. At the same time, his refusal to challenge the British blockade hurt the Central Powers economically and encouraged the Allies to believe they could win a decisive victory by starving out their enemies.

Had the administration followed Bryan's policy of banning munitions sales and loans to the belligerents, the loss of Allied war orders would have severely damaged the American economy. Had Wilson refused to defend neutral rights against Germany as he refused to defend them against Britain, the Germans would have initiated unrestricted submarine warfare earlier and might well have won the war. Had Wilson insisted that both belligerents respect neutral rights, the Allies would have had to abandon the hope that economic warfare could win a cheap victory and would have had far more incentive to consider a compromise peace. Had Wilson followed the advice of Lansing, House, and Page by entering the war earlier, American forces would have taken a much greater role in the fighting and suffered much heavier casualties. By abandoning neutrality and tilting the United States toward the Allies, but not declaring war until 1917, Wilson helped to maintain the stalemate that encouraged both sides to continue pouring blood and treasure into what became a mutual suicide pact. All the while the United States grew stronger and richer by remaining at peace and filling Allied war orders. The effect of American policy, although not its intent, was to create a power vacuum in Europe that in itself dramatically increased the relative power of the United States in the world.

The same pattern is evident in Wilson's decision to enter the war after almost three years as a non-belligerent. He did not come into the war in order to save the Allies from defeat, since at the time he believed they were winning. He asked Congress for a declaration of war on 2 April 1917 because he considered the German submarine campaign an act of war against the United States. His attempt to negotiate abandonment of the campaign with Berlin had failed; his attempt to secure Congressional approval for armed neutrality had failed. Left with a choice between either going to war or retreating from his warnings to Germany over the past two years, he chose to go to war.

The result, ironically, was another boost for American power. The president fully intended to play an important role in the achievement of an Allied military victory, yet the administration's failure to mobilize its military and naval resources before intervention left the United States a spectator in the bloody campaigns of 1917 and very much a junior partner in those of 1918. The "Yanks" were in fact "coming" to Europe – a testimony to the American genius for improvisation. Their presence, in itself, helped inspire the Allies to keep fighting, which was fortuitous because, when the American Expeditionary Force arrived in Europe, it turned out to consist of a mob of untrained recruits equipped with few of the tools needed for trench warfare. During the last months of the war, units of the AEF fought bravely and with increasing effectiveness. But they flew Allied planes and fired Allied shells from Allied guns. Deficiencies in equipment, training and shipping – each of which was ultimately the responsibility of the president as commander-in-chief – ensured that Americans constituted only a relatively small percentage of the combat forces that broke the German army in the fall of 1918.[39]

This delay in effective military intervention resulted in short American casualty lists compared with those of Britain, France, or Germany. If the United States provided the financing and sustained the hope that was necessary to keep the Allied armies in the field in 1917 and 1918, the Allies continued to provide most of the blood. Wilson certainly would have been indignant at the suggestion that he delayed the despatch of an effective military force in order to spare American lives and wring the last drop of blood from his European "associates." There is no evidence that he had any such purpose in mind. Yet whatever his intent, his policy did minimize American casualties and thereby increase postwar American power relative to both the Central Powers and the Allies.

Much the same was true of intervention in the Russian civil war. Whether Wilson was an anti-Bolshevik crusader, a humanitarian protector, a confused man trying to muddle through an impossible situation – or all of the above – remains unclear.[40] But whatever the motivation behind American intervention and however reluctantly it was undertaken, it encouraged continuation of a civil war that devastated Russia. It encouraged Britain, France, and Japan to invest far more than did the United States in the futile effort to overthrow the Bolsheviks. It also ensured that Russia would remain an ideological pariah, isolated from the peace settlement. Whatever American motives may have been, the consequence was another enormous increase in the relative world power of the United States.

The fact that the United States had sacrificed relatively little compared to the European belligerents, and therefore possessed a fresh army and the world's strongest industrial economy, gave it a potentially dominant position in shaping the peace treaty. The president had outlined his ideas for a fair, healing peace in his Fourteen Points speech of 8 January 1918: an end to secret treaties, freedom of the seas, free trade, disarmament, self-determination, and a world organization to maintain peace. When the German government requested an armistice on those terms in October 1918, Wilson used the threat of a separate peace to force the Allies to accept the Fourteen Points. Aside from a British reservation on freedom of the seas and a French reservation on reparations, all the major powers went into the Paris Peace Conference in January 1919 formally committed to the American plan.[41]

That formal commitment did not mean that the Fourteen Points were without their critics. The French premier, Georges Clemenceau, privately compared them to the Ten Commandments: noble principles of little relevance to the harsh realities of the world. Scholars of the "realist" persuasion have followed his lead, citing Wilson's revolutionary program as evidence that the president was an idealistic crusader against a system he did not understand.[42]

This argument is largely one of semantics rather than substance. If it was "realistic" to revive the old balance of power system, which had just led directly to the death of millions of people, Wilson would have been the first to admit that he was not a realist. If it was "idealistic" to believe that nations could create a system that was better able than the balance of power to maintain peace, Wilson would have been first to claim that he was an idealist. He had seen millions die in a war in which civilization itself was brought to the brink of destruction. He believed there had to be a way to prevent such conflicts. The Fourteen Points represent the twentieth century's most brilliant attempt to identify the causes of international conflict and to remove or reduce them. Had Wilson's plan been implemented, the world would have been a more peaceful place.

The Fourteen Points were not implemented, however. What Wilson should have done in Paris, or could have done, will be debated as long as historians study the twentieth century. What he did do is clear. He helped the victors redraw the frontiers of Europe and redefine the norms of international relations without the participation of German or Russian representatives. He ignored freedom of the seas, explaining later that Point II had been a "practical joke on myself" because it was implicit in Point XIV, the League of Nations. He helped to disarm Germany, but failed to persuade the Allies to follow suit and launched a massive American naval building program. He sanctioned violation of his principle of self-determination from Syria to Silesia and from Shantung to South West Africa. He created a league of victors rather than a league of all nations, then failed to secure the consent of the Senate required for American participation.[43]

Historians who seek to explain Wilson's role in the peace-making process must begin by recognizing the enormous gap between his objectives and his achievements, between the Fourteen Points and the Treaty of Versailles. Why, given the power he possessed to impose his will on the Allies, did he compromise so many of his principles? Part of the answer clearly lies in his deteriorating health during the peace conference. A second part, perhaps even more important, lies in his faith in democracy, which would now be given the opportunity to exert itself through the League of Nations. Wilson acknowledged that there were flaws in the treaty. He regarded them as unfortunate but inevitable, given the bitterness the Allies felt after years of war. By creating the League and securing Allied participation in it, he believed he had created a mechanism to correct those flaws as the passions of war cooled. He could accept short-term compromises as the price to be paid for creating a viable League of Nations because he saw it as essential to lasting peace.

Oddly enough, the Treaty of Versailles and its subsequent rejection by the Senate produced yet another unanticipated increase in American power. By the time Wilson left office, Europe was weaker and more divided against itself than it had been for centuries. Russia, which was just beginning to emerge from its civil war – its second massive bloodbath in seven years – was still an ideological pariah. Eastern Europe was fragmented. Germany was crippled by its wartime losses, unstable in its new democratic government, economically devastated and utterly determined to overthrow the system imposed upon her at Versailles. Britain, France, and Italy were almost as crippled by victory as their former enemy was by defeat, staggering under political and economic instability and facing astronomical debts to the United States. They squabbled amongst themselves and, in an effort to maintain a status quo that was dissolving under their feet, committed resources that they could not afford.

The situation outside Europe was equally satisfying to the United States from the perspective of *machtpolitik*. Latin America was securely within the

American orbit. The expanded European and Japanese colonial empires already were showing the strains of absorbing the enormous acquisitions they had demanded so vociferously at the peace conference. Yet Wilson's ineffectual resistance to these demands had distanced the United States to some degree from the colonial powers. Over the next two decades America's potential rivals for world power would continue to squander precious resources in their efforts to solve colonial problems that had been created by the failure to implement Point V. The United States, behind its selective anti-imperialism and its selective open door policy, continued to forge ahead in comparative economic terms.

These consequences were completely unanticipated, of course, by the president who had negotiated the Treaty of Versailles but who had not been able to win Senate consent for its ratification. Wilson opposed those economic and territorial clauses that made the settlement so unstable. He did everything he could to get the Senate to approve the treaty as he submitted it, though he resisted fiercely every attempt to modify his text through reservations. He set out to build a functional world organization that would reduce or even eliminate the possibility of war. He ended up helping to plant the seeds of the bloodiest war in human history, which began twenty years after the signing ceremony at Versailles ended "the war to end all wars." Yet by his failure to achieve his goals at Paris and in the Senate he also planted the seeds of American preeminence in world affairs over the second half of the twentieth century.

Again, the pattern is complex and contradictory. Wilson certainly was not the dedicated crusader against the Left or against revolution that has been pictured by some historians. Nor was he a tool of American business expansionists. Wilson thought of himself as someone on the Left who advocated revolutionary change in international relations. If he opposed the Bolshevik government of V. I. Lenin in Russia, he supported the democratic socialist government of Friedrich Ebert in Germany. If he opposed revolution in the Caribbean, he supported it – however ineffectually – in China and practically demanded it in Germany.[44] Like every president since George Washington, Wilson believed that expansion of trade would benefit the economy of the United States and provide jobs for its citizens. But the suggestion that he would enter a world war to save the house of Morgan or that economic concerns dictated his foreign policy is not supported by the evidence. Instead, ideological and economic concerns were among the many factors that influenced his decisions; they were sometimes central but were often peripheral, or even negligible. It was not the success of his policies that built American political and economic power around the world, but their failure.

The single most significant result of American foreign relations from March 1913 to March 1921 was one the president never planned: the rise of the United States to a position of unrivalled world power. Wilson's neutrality policies helped to maintain an artificial strategic balance that encouraged both belligerent camps to exhaust themselves in pursuit of decisive military victory while the United States enjoyed three years of peace and prosperity. His war policies helped to secure the defeat of Europe's most aggressive power while ensuring that Britain, France, Russia, and Italy paid most of the blood price that victory over Germany demanded. His peace policies left the exhausted European allies struggling to control overextended colonial empires while simultaneously attempting to maintain a European status quo that Germany, the Soviet Union, and several smaller powers were determined to overthrow. His failure to win Senate support for his peace policies ensured that the Allies would have to do their controlling and maintaining without American support. Had the president of the United States deliberately set out in March 1913 to bleed the Great Powers of Europe to death over the next eight years and expand American influence to fill the vacuum, he could hardly have been more successful.

Since Woodrow Wilson was himself and not Cesare Borgia, there is not a shred of evidence to indicate that such was his intent. On the contrary, the pattern that emerges is of a brilliant, erratic, willful man, often meddling in affairs he did not understand through agents he did not control and producing results he did not anticipate. He came into office with little interest in foreign affairs, but quickly mastered the subject. By 1917 his analysis of the roots of international conflict was extraordinarily sophisticated. He was the first world leader to recognize that the old world order could not be rebuilt, that to restore the system of uncontrolled nationalism and the balance of power would condemn humanity to continue an endless cycle of conflict. He sought to create a new system of international relations, one based on a League of Nations united under the democratic, progressive leadership of the United States and the British empire. The fact that the League, in the absence of American participation, fell far short of Wilson's expectations does not detract from the genius of his vision.

By the same token, however, historians cannot allow the glory of the vision to distract attention from the consequences of Wilson's failure to achieve it. Noble failure in the highest cause remains failure, and Wilson ultimately achieved neither peace without victory nor a functional international organization. Instead, largely through the unanticipated consequences of his actions rather than by design, he achieved an enormous increase in American power relative to the rest of the world. The United States he turned over to Warren G. Harding in March 1921 had no rival in the western hemisphere and no potential European or east Asian challenger to the Monroe doctrine. Europe was weak and divided against itself, with the winners as bankrupt and exhausted as the losers and more in debt to the United States. Wilson's promise to guarantee the peace settlement and French security turned out to be empty. Japan's gains at the expense of China ensured that the two greatest powers of the Far East would be locked into a quarter-century of confrontation between the imperialism of Tokyo and the rising nationalism of Nanjing and Yan'an. A navy "second to none" was filling American bases, while merchant ships carried American goods to ports all over the world. As the United States geared up for the "Roaring Twenties," it stood in truly splendid isolation. The fact that Wilson achieved such a result while pursuing completely different objectives is simply the greatest "irony of fate" for an administration whose foreign relations resounded with ironies.

The past decade has been an exciting and productive time for historians of international relations during the Wilson years, with major works appearing in the United States and in Europe. The recent completion of editorial work on Arthur Link's magnificent multivolume edition of *The Papers of Woodrow Wilson*[45] can only accelerate this interest by enabling scholars to examine essential documentation in their own libraries without the need for prolonged archival visits. While existing work provides a solid foundation, however, much remains to be done. Systematic examination of attitudes on race, which has brought such valuable insights to so many areas of history in recent years, is a particularly promising topic for research. Surely it is no coincidence that Wilson and so many of his key foreign policy advisers were white southerners who grew up in the shadow of the Civil War and Reconstruction. More generally, scholars need to be more open to complexities and contradictions, to the multiple levels on which the president and his administration operated. There needs to be more integration of different perspectives, particularly the impact of Wilson's medical condition and the institutional confusion of his foreign relations establishment. Given the number of challenges that remain, there is every reason for the next seventy-five years of Wilson era scholarship to be as exciting and productive as the first seventy-five.

NOTES

1 For example, Charles Seymour, *American Neutrality 1914–1917*, New Haven, Conn., 1935.
2 Charles Tansill, *America Goes to War*, Boston, 1938.
3 Thomas Bailey, *Woodrow Wilson and the Great Betrayal*, Chicago, 1951.
4 George Kennan, *American Diplomacy, 1900–1950*, Chicago, 1951.
5 Convenient summaries of the state of historical debate on two major interpretive issues as of the early 1960s are Herbert J. Bass (ed.), *America's Entry into World War I*, New York, 1964, and Ivo Lederer (ed.), *The Versailles Settlement*, Boston, 1960.
6 Robert Osgood, *Ideals and Self-Interest in America's Foreign Relations*, Chicago, 1953.
7 Edward Buehrig, *Woodrow Wilson and the Balance of Power*, Bloomington, Ind., 1955.
8 Arthur S. Link, *Wilson* vols 3, 4 & 5, Princeton, N.J., 1960–5; further developed in *The Higher Realism of Woodrow Wilson*, Nashville, Tenn., 1971.
9 N. Gordon Levin, *Woodrow Wilson and World Politics*, New York, 1968.
10 Link, *Higher Realism*. The same religious themes are elaborated by Kendrick Clements in *Woodrow Wilson: World Statesman*, Boston, 1987, and in *The Presidency of Woodrow Wilson*, Lawrence, Kan., 1992.
11 David Trask, *Captains & Cabinets*, Columbia, Mo., 1972, p. 124.
12 Lloyd Gardner (ed.), *Wilson and Revolutions, 1913–1921*, Lanham, Md, 1976;

further developed in *Safe for Democracy*, New York, 1984, and "Woodrow Wilson and the Mexican Revolution," in Arthur S. Link (ed.), *Woodrow Wilson and a Revolutionary World*, Chapel Hill, N.C., 1982.

13 Sidney Bell, *Righteous Conquest*, Port Washington, 1972.

14 Lloyd Ambrosius, *Wilsonian Statecraft*, Wilmington, Del., 1991.

15 Elwin Weinstein, *Woodrow Wilson: A Medical and Psychological Biography*, Princeton, N.J., 1981. This highly technical issue is examined at much greater depth in Link *et al.* (eds), *The Papers of Woodrow Wilson*, Princeton, N.J., 1966–, vols 58 & 64.

16 John Milton Cooper, "An Irony of Fate," *Diplomatic History*, vol. 3, 1979, pp. 425–37, argues that Wilson was not so unprepared, but he does so mainly by challenging the foreign affairs credentials of other contemporary presidents. To prefer Cooper's assessment to Wilson's own seems a case of being more royalist than the king.

17 Kendrick Clements, *William Jennings Bryan*, Knoxville, Tenn., 1982, supersedes other work on Bryan as secretary of state, although its attempt to label Bryan as isolationist and Wilson as idealist (see especially p. 110) raises more questions than it answers.

18 Rachel West, *The Department of State on the Eve of the First World War*, Athens, Ga, 1978, provides the best analysis of State Department confusion and demoralization under Bryan. See also Larry D. Hill, *Emissaries to a Revolution*, Baton Rouge, La, 1973. There is as yet no adequate biography of House, the ultimate presidential agent, although Charles Neu's forthcoming work is eagerly anticipated.

19 Daniel Smith, *Robert Lansing and American Neutrality, 1914–1917*, Berkeley, Calif., 1958, remains the best account of Lansing's bizarre relationship with Wilson. Calvin Davis is currently working on a study of Lansing as secretary of state.

20 Quoted in Arthur S. Link, *Wilson the Diplomatist*, Baltimore, Md, 1957, p. 26.

21 On Page, see Ross Gregóry, *Walter Hines Page*, Lexington, Ky, 1970; John Milton Cooper Jr, *Walter Hines Page*, Chapel Hill, N.C.

22 W. Christopher Hamel, "The Illusion of Disinterest," draft Ph.D. dissertation, Michigan State University, chap. 4; J. Halsema, *E. J. Halsema: Colonial Engineer*, Quezon City, 1991. Not all scholars would agree with Clements, *Presidency*, p. xiv, that Wilson's administration was "without a significant scandal."

23 Clements, *Bryan*, pp. 60–5.

24 John W. Coogan, *The End of Neutrality*, Ithaca, N.Y., 1981, pp. 182–91.

25 Wilson, quoted in Ray Stannard Baker, *Woodrow Wilson: Life and Letters*, Garden City, N.Y., 8 vols, 1927–39; vol. 4, p. 289. On the Mexican revolution see the works by Gardner and Hill cited above, as well as Mark T. Gilderhus, *Diplomacy and Revolution*, Tucson, Ariz., 1977, and Peter Calvert, *The Mexican Revolution*, London, 1968. On the policy of the United States in Latin America generally, see Gilderhus and David Healy, *Pan American Visions*, Tucson, Ariz., 1986.

26 There is no adequate overall study of Wilson's racial views and their impact on foreign relations, but see Paul Gordon Lauren, "Human Rights in History . . . ," *Diplomatic History*, vol. 3, 1978, p. 261.

27 Roy Watson Curry, *Woodrow Wilson and Far Eastern Policy*, New York, 1957; Michael H. Hunt, *Ideology and U.S. Foreign Policy*, New Haven, Conn., 1987, pp. 108–9.

28 Burton F. Beers, *Vain Endeavor*, Durham, N.C., 1962.

29 For differing statements of this position see Tansill, *America Goes to War*, and Coogan, *End of Neutrality*.

30 Link, *Wilson*, vols 3–5, and *Higher Realism* remain the most complete and persuasive statements of this interpretation.

31 Kennan, *American Diplomacy*, and Osgood, *Ideals and Self-Interest* remain the classic statements of this interpretation.
32 *A Digest of International Law*, Washington, 8 vols. The law of neutrality is covered primarily in vol. 7. Among the more ironic aspects of an administration whose history was filled with irony is that Moore had been State Department Counselor, second only to Bryan, but had resigned early in 1914 because of his frustration at trying to work with Wilson.
33 Coogan, *End of Neutrality*, pp. 179–82, 249–52, and *passim*.
34 Quoted in Ray Stannard Baker and William E. Dodd (eds), *The Public Papers of Woodrow Wilson*, New York, 6 vols, 1925–7, vol. 3, pp. 157–9.
35 Quoted in Coogan, *End of Neutrality*, p. 173; on the specific British violations of international law which Wilson refused to challenge effectively, see pp. 209–15.
36 For example, the actions of House and Lansing described in Clements, *Presidency*, pp. 136–7.
37 Robert H. Ferrell, *Woodrow Wilson and World War I, 1917–1921*, New York, 1985, p. 10.
38 Quoted in House, diary entry, 30 August 1914, House Papers, Yale University.
39 Edward M. Coffman, *The War to End All Wars*, New York, 1968; Ferrell, *Woodrow Wilson and World War I*.
40 The anti-Bolshevik position is best stated in Levin, *Woodrow Wilson and World Politics*; Gardner, *Safe for Democracy*; and Arno J. Mayer, *Politics and Diplomacy of Peacemaking: Containment and Counterrevolution at Versailles*, New York, 1967. George F. Kennan, *Soviet-American Relations, 1917–1920*, Princeton, N.J., 1956–8 remains the best statement of the humanitarian argument.
41 Arthur Walworth, *America's Moment, 1918: American Diplomacy at the End of World War I*, New York, 1977. Inga Floto, *Colonel House in Paris*, Princeton, N.J., 1980, provides a devastating indictment of its subject but neglects the president's responsibility for his agent.
42 Kennan, *American Diplomacy*, remains the classic statement of this view. For a more sophisticated, updated version, see Lloyd E. Ambrosius, *Wilsonian Statecraft*, Wilmington, Del., 1991, and *Woodrow Wilson and the American Diplomatic Tradition*, New York, 1987.
43 Ambrosius, *Woodrow Wilson*; Arthur Walworth, *Wilson and His Peacemakers*, New York, 1986.
44 See Klaus Schwabe, *Woodrow Wilson, Revolutionary Germany, and Peacemaking, 1918–1919*, Chapel Hill, N.C., 1985.
45 Princeton, 1966–.

6 The triumph of isolationism

Thomas N. Guinsburg

The British statesman Lord Lothian, writing in 1929, underscored the ambivalence at the core of American international attitudes in the aftermath of World War I. The United States, he observed, "wants on the one hand to prevent war, and on the other to retain the right to be neutral in the event of war and to assume no obligation for maintaining world peace."[1]

For the first decade of the interwar years, plagued by this divided mind, the United States settled for what Richard W. Leopold has termed the "interwar compromise" and assumed a posture aptly characterized by Joan Hoff Wilson as "independent internationalism."[2] While pursuing a more stable world order primarily via economic diplomacy, the United States avoided any substantial collaboration with foreign powers in the mechanisms of international peace-keeping. Cautiously, it moved away from its isolationist moorings: first, there was the Pacific treaty system negotiated in the Harding years; then subtle cooperation began with the League of Nations (which it would not join); then there was the circumscribed (and ultimately abortive) adherence to the World Court; and finally, the United States initiated the Kellogg–Briand Pact, which outlawed war as an instrument of national policy (without establishing the means of enforcing that ban).[3] The following decade witnessed the disintegration of the policy of compromise, as the Great Depression and the force of external events undermined these gestures toward international collaboration and bolstered the credo conventionally known as "isolationism."

Confronted by a worldwide collapse, which might plausibly have demonstrated the need for international collaboration, most Americans, as Robert H. Ferrell has noted, found "only additional proof of the folly of participation in the World War of 1917–1918, and the desirability, indeed necessity, of detaching the United States from further vicissitudes of Europe."[4] As if Europe's debt defaults and political instability were not sufficient grounds for maintaining autonomy, it seemed reasonable for the nation to believe that to solve its domestic problems the United States should take refuge from international uncertainties. In the crisis at hand, Senator William E. Borah, Chairman of the Foreign Relations Committee, proclaimed in 1932, "Americans should look after our own interests and devote ourselves to our own people."[5]

In the 1930s, the high priests of American disengagement had a long heritage from which to draw. From George Washington's Farewell Address, through the irreconcilable manifestos of the years after the treaty of Versailles, influential leadership in the United States gave voice to isolationist aspirations, even as the nation never quite fulfilled them.[6] To avoid making the term a caricature of American foreign policy, "isolationism" must be carefully defined. It never signified a posture of hermit-like seclusion; for better or worse – the influential Senator Arthur H. Vandenberg acknowledged on the eve of Pearl Harbor – in the twentieth-century world "literal isolationism" was impossible. As William Appleman Williams and such "corporatist" interpreters of American diplomacy as Carl Parrini, Joan Hoff Wilson, and Michael J. Hogan have demonstrated, the quest for political non-entanglement and freedom from collective peace-keeping arrangements did not preclude active pursuit of conditions favorable to international economic expansion. Still, despite forceful attempts by Williams to suggest that isolationism might best be treated as a "legend," a pronounced isolationist tradition endured in the 1920s and gained strength in the 1930s.[7]

A useful definition comes from Charles Beard, a scholar who disliked the term but understood its meaning. In the postwar context, Beard wrote, isolationism signified:

> Rejection of membership in the League of Nations; non-entanglement in the political controversies of Europe and Asia; nonintervention in the wars of those continents; neutrality, peace, and defence for the United States through measures appropriate to those purposes; and the pursuit of a foreign policy friendly to all nations disposed to reciprocate. An isolationist may favor the promotion of goodwill and peace among nations by any and all measures compatible with non-entanglement in any association of nations empowered to designate "aggressors" and bring engines of sanction and coercion into action against them.[8]

The writings of corporatist historians have not vitiated this definition; by properly insisting that what we have called isolationism did *not* mean full-fledged international withdrawal or diplomatic abstention, they have, perhaps unwittingly, helped to demonstrate the allure and saliency of the isolationists' position.

Support for such a posture had many wellsprings, and historians and political scientists have spent much energy arguing over whether the most important were geographic insularity, ethnic predispositions, partisan politics, or ideological perspectives.[9] In early attempts to delineate the roots of isolationism, such scholars as Ray Allen Billington and Jeannette Nichols called attention to the strength of isolationism in the Middle West and suggested that the insularity, economic self-sufficiency, and cultural makeup of the region might account for a peculiar foreign policy orientation.[10] In fact, the importance once assigned to the Middle West as the bedrock of isolationism now seems exaggerated, as detailed analyses suggested that the differences between regions were those of degree, that midwestern fervor alone could not have provided isolationism's political strength, and that the Middle West was by no means monolithic in its stance nor always the most intransigent toward international cooperation.[11]

Pursuing Billington's contention that ethnic traditions might have prompted isolationist predispositions in the Midwest, Samuel Lubell concluded that regionalism itself was no key to explaining isolationism but rather that ethnic attitudes were *the* touchstone. In areas of pro-German or anti-British ethnic prejudices, Lubell asserted, isolationism flourished; in areas of predominantly Anglo-Saxon heritage, it did not.[12] This easy solution to the riddle of isolationism, however, also unraveled in the face of detailed analysis of the interwar years by Ralph Smuckler and myself, while assessments of the persistence of isolationism after World War II have as well failed to support Lubell's neat distinctions.[13]

Partisan politics, too, have been credited with fostering opposition to internationalist projects, and those who study the makers of foreign policy have long recognized that politics do not stop at the water's edge.[14] Still it is hard to make a case that isolationism was rooted primarily in partisan politics; its zenith, in fact, came at the point where the partisan opposition had reached its nadir. While isolationism could sometimes gain support from partisan consideration, true believers like William E. Borah and Hiram Johnson generally made a virtue of shunning the dictates of party loyalty.

Beyond regionalism, ethnicity, and partisanship, isolationism bespoke deeply held convictions about national destiny. Scholars such as Wayne S. Cole and Manfred Jonas, who led the way in taking the isolationists seriously rather than acceding to the mindless stereotypes of their foes, have amply demonstrated that isolationists, whether from "progressive" or "conservative" instincts, clung to a vision of their country in which the distinctive American heritage stood at risk. They feared an eclipse of political and economic liberty and democracy if the United States failed to separate its own interests and values from forces already threatening freedom and stability worldwide.[15]

No single force – regional, ethnic, partisan, or ideological – was, in fact, sufficient to explain the strength of isolationism in the 1930s. In the face of pointed challenges, all were essential to its power. Relentlessly, the champions of the isolationist persuasion shrewdly exploited whatever attitudes could be harnessed to their cause. For almost the entire decade anxieties at home, compounded by bewildering events abroad, provided a milieu conducive to their triumph – a triumph that was by no means foreordained. It resulted from the most concerted and effective sort of crusade on the part of those who propounded it, and the timidity and irresolution of those who sought to deter it.

How adamantly isolationist was the United States in the 1930s and what were the prospects for a more effective American effort at confronting the challenges to world peace? Answers to these questions are intimately related and together comprise a critical interpretive framework in which to depict the central path of American foreign relations in the turbulent years prior to World War II.

The first standard accounts of the foreign policy debates of those years depicted a Manichean contest: an enlightened, if perplexed, internationalist leadership in the White House and State Department was supposed to have been temporarily vanquished by overwhelming forces of reaction, as the power of isolationist sentiment among the American people was given focus and leverage by their tribunes in the Congress. Works by historians Basil Rauch and William Langer and S. Everett Gleason refined but did not challenge the broad contours of the argument documented in the State Department's compilation *Peace and War: United States Foreign Policy, 1931–1941*. That volume had contended that public opinion in the United States, accepting "the idea of isolation expressed in neutrality legislation," precluded the President and State Department from more vigorous response to mounting external dangers. Rauch wrote of a nation "bogged down in isolationist indifference for twenty years," which would surely have rebuffed earlier and more direct challenges to its assumptions. Langer and Gleason, documenting Roosevelt's convoluted "challenge to isolation," and questioning whether the opposition was always as powerful as the President believed, nonetheless conceded that isolationism was buttressed by a public that "steadfastly shrank from facing the issues."[16]

Early revisionism merely turned the tale on its head: clear-sighted non-interventionists strove, with initial success, to protect the national interest against a purposeful, scheming White House whose efforts would inevitably involve the nation in war. Charles Beard led the attack, contending that Roosevelt, at least outwardly, long adhered to isolationist policy as consistent with the best interests of the United States, only to embark subsequently on a disingenuous course in which he feigned support for non-entanglement while moving toward interventionism. Charles Tansill portrayed an administration quietly determined "to place America in the van of a crusade against aggressor nations," which ended up "moving down the road to war while talking loudly about the importance of peace."[17]

Neither interpretation has worn well. A subsequent generation of scholarship – benefitting from access to enlarged archival materials, greater distance from the emotion-laden debates of the 1930s, and perspective furnished by subsequent foreign policy debates in the United States – has generally come to shun simplistic portraits of heroes and villains. Though echoes of the old controversies persist, we now have the basis for a more subtle interpretation, wherein leaders on both sides of the 1930s debate were plagued by defective vision and flawed judgment and rendered the nation a prisoner of illusion as the world catapulted toward war. Assessing the contest over isolationism thus becomes a more interesting and complex task.

FDR AND ISOLATIONISM: THE CAPTAIN AS CAPTIVE?

The contest took form early in the decade. Even as the domestic economic crisis preoccupied the White House, international challenges demanded attention and presented alternatives. When the Japanese invasion of Manchuria broke the international calm in 1931, the response of the United States – "non-recognition" of Japanese territorial hegemony – while articulating concern for the crisis, showed a respect for isolationist sensibilities. Secretary of State Henry Stimson, who suggested the possibility of using economic sanctions as a diplomatic mechanism or making a collaborative effort to implement the Kellogg–Briand Pact, was held in check by President Herbert Hoover.[18]

This early episode reveals not that the United States was indifferent to challenges to the international equilibrium but that it continued to believe that symbolic gestures and the use of moral suasion were likely sufficient and all that could be prudently applied to the circumstances at hand. In retrospect, it is beguiling to see it as the first in a domino-like series of events that inexorably led to the breakdown of collective security and inaction in the face of aggression. Yet the triumph of isolationism was far from settled in 1932. When Franklin Roosevelt assumed the presidency, many hoped that the New Deal in domestic affairs would be accompanied by a new deal in foreign relations – in which FDR, the Wilsonian protégé, would soon redeem the promises made by his former chief after World War I.[19] That expectation was not to be, for reasons that historians continue to debate and that the remainder of this essay seeks to explore.

Franklin Roosevelt came to office confronting both a devastating socio-economic crisis at home and an international scene filled with uncertainty and potential peril. If the domestic crisis understandably dominated the headlines and the early political agenda, immediate and prospective threats to the stability of the broader international economic and political structure demanded attention as well. Those who have criticized the lack of clarity and effectiveness in American policymaking during the 1930s have the luxury of analyzing each issue separately and abstractly; those with the responsibility for governance had no such freedom from complicating interrelationships and formidable obstacles.

Included in the obstacles that confronted FDR were external events not always susceptible to American influence, domestic priorities that sometimes competed politically and substantively against would-be international stratagems, and opposing viewpoints that were articulated in powerful forums. Students of the era need to recognize the complex domestic and world environments in which the Roosevelt administration groped for a coherent policy, the bureaucratic in-fighting that inescapably accompanied so large and crowded a domestic and international agenda, and the dilemmas of leadership in a democratic society. In this context, the tasks confronting Roosevelt were daunting, errors unavoidable, and steadfastness not fully sustainable.[20]

Strong isolationist leadership, opposing what overall design Roosevelt did pursue, managed until the outbreak of World War II to circumscribe severely the nation's capacity to react politically and militarily to external aggression. Their beliefs and motivations, too, as recent studies have demonstrated, are both more complicated and more justifiable than was assumed by the early commentators who branded them "illustrious dunderheads." As suspicious and fearful of Roosevelt's power as he was of theirs, they understandably lacked a balanced view of their adversary and the advantages of twenty-twenty hindsight. If their successes in the 1930s do not seem worthy of historical celebration, neither do they warrant mindless vilification.[21]

Unquestionably, though, the centerpiece of all assessments of the era is the powerful if enigmatic figure of FDR. "Like a colossus," writes Frederick W. Marks III in a recent reappraisal, "he bestrode American diplomacy for twelve tumultuous years. Sphinx-like, he continues to baffle each generation of historians."[22] Controversies abound concerning FDR's principles and goals in foreign policy, about his consistency in applying them, his honesty in articulating them, and his judgment and leadership in confronting the obstacles to them.

"Most scholars would agree," Marks writes, "that Roosevelt could have done a good deal more than he did to combat isolationist sentiment, especially during his initial term of office."[23] Of course, he *could* have and probably in certain instances he *should* have, but at what risks or costs? Marks's analysis here and elsewhere in his provocative revisionist work begs the question of why Roosevelt shunned the possible alternatives and whether, in the context of the times, commentators then and since should reasonably have expected more boldness in presidential leadership.

Marks, though, goes even further, contending that "isolationism in the mid to late 1930s might have been less of a problem for Roosevelt had he not done so much to foster its growth."[24] Foster its growth? If so, FDR himself stands as a principal architect of isolationism's triumph, and familiar portraits of the era would be chromatically reversed.

Robert Dallek, in his comprehensive study *Franklin D. Roosevelt and American Foreign Policy, 1932–1945*, takes pains to explore "the constraints under which [FDR] had to work in foreign affairs" and generally sustains the options pursued by the President. But even his essentially admiring overview makes evident that the substance and style of Roosevelt's leadership were confusing: he lacked clarity, coherence, firmness, predictability and a consistent tempo.[25] Roosevelt himself, had he lived to write his memoirs, might have grudgingly admitted as much. When asked by an admirer early in 1934 to articulate long-range planning guidelines for American foreign policy, he conceded his inability to do so and added that even if he had known how to do it he probably would not have pursued such a policy because he had learned from Woodrow Wilson's experience that the public could not be attuned to the highest note in the scale without being discomforted.[26]

This explanation could be viewed as a rationalization by a leader who had himself retreated from an internationalist to an isolationist stance, seeking peace at almost any price.[27] Certainly Roosevelt's faith in the League of Nations had, by the time of his presidential campaign of 1932, withered to the point of his abandoning public support for its work. But it is going too far to conclude that Roosevelt and the isolationists occupied much of the same ground, apart from that which led them to seek a peaceable resolution of international tensions. Roosevelt's retreats, as Dallek suggests, were due less to philosophical conversion than to "calculation about what he could achieve at home and abroad," including the task of maintaining what Cole has delineated as an "uneasy alliance" between himself and the group of influential western progressives in Congress, many of whom supported isolationism.[28]

Recent scholarship, whatever its disagreements, shows a president who was, from the outset, actively interested in foreign policy questions.[29] If Roosevelt pursued "first things first," it was not that he set aside foreign policy goals. Rather he pursued those objectives in such a way as to avoid making a hostage of his important domestic initiatives. Given the importance of the New Deal agenda, and the isolationist fervor of the progressives in Congress whose support was necessary to its passage, Roosevelt shied away from boldly leading the United States in the direction of international collaboration. Dallek sees Roosevelt's strategy as a series of necessary and prudent trade-offs; Marks regards them as pusillanimous. Both are too fixed in their judgments.

It is impossible, even for Dallek, to rehabilitate Roosevelt's torpedoing of the London Economic Conference. FDR built up expectations only to dash them and exalted international collaboration only to sacrifice it abruptly to "intranationalism." In so doing he demonstrated a misplaced confidence that a residual effect of the Conference would be "continued international discussion of perplexing world problems," despite the bitterness that its failure had evoked. In reality, as the columnist Walter Lippman noted, he had "failed to organize a diplomatic instrument to express" his excellent purposes.[30] There were indeed instruments available to Roosevelt had he chosen to throw American influence behind collaborative efforts at maintaining peace. Roosevelt did make some use of these, but only in a manner that avoided the risk of a head-on collision with isolationist adversaries; he refused to jeopardize his domestic objectives or to escalate fears of American involvement in war.

To the consternation of more dedicated internationalists in the State Department, while Roosevelt made gestures of undertaking initiatives aimed at deterring aggression, he caved in when the going got tough. In 1933 the White House approved administration sponsorship of an arms embargo bill that would have allowed the president to designate particular countries to which the embargo applied. Shortly thereafter, FDR authorized a proposal promising that, if a general disarmament treaty could be arrived at, the United States would be willing to consult with other states in the event of an international conflict and, if it concurred in the designation of an aggressor, that it would "refrain from any action tending to defeat collective effort" to restore the peace. Together, these propositions marked a high point in the professed willingness of the United States to cooperate with the League of Nations in a peace effort.[31]

Immediately, isolationists sounded the alarm. Several members of the Foreign Relations Committee – notably Hiram Johnson of California, William Borah of Idaho, and Robert La Follette, Jr of Wisconsin – unfurled the argument that international consultations, coupled with the power to discriminate among combatants, provided the president with a catapult to further action that might lead to direct involvement; they amended the bill to require a mandatory embargo against all participants in a conflict. The State Department persuaded Roosevelt not to accept the amendment, and the bill died in committee.[32]

With Senate isolationists on the rampage at the same time that their support for the New Deal remained essential, and with disarmament foundering because of European insecurity, one can understand why Roosevelt backed away on this issue. But his quick capitulation signaled an exaggerated caution and a lack of willingness to use his fabled powers of persuasion. Most importantly, the triumph of the isolationists represented Roosevelt's failure to recognize that, without countervailing efforts on his part, isolationism would carry the day – not merely in 1933 but in the years to follow.

If isolationism were to be combatted, the White House would have to do more. As the prospect of disarmament collapsed and combustible problems smoldered, fears of an international conflagration began to grow. Apprehensions about a future world conflict were nourished by the sentiment, fed by popular revisionist accounts of World War I, that US intervention in 1917 had been a grave mistake. With only slight exaggeration, Senator Homer Bone of Washington exclaimed in 1935 that "everyone has come to recognize that the Great War was utter insanity . . . and we had no business in it at all."[33]

Focusing on such apprehensions and rhetoric, historians have tended to share Roosevelt's perspective that isolationist sentiment was too powerful to combat in any direct way. Recent studies, however, have begun to cast doubt on the intensity of isolationism in the nation at large and on the likelihood that isolationist leaders in Congress would have been successful *if* the proponents of internationalism had been as committed, energetic, and resourceful as their foes. Even the Middle West's commitment to isolationist orthodoxy appears to have been exaggerated. Furthermore, there was no omnipotent isolationist "bloc" in Congress or among opinion-makers, but rather a disparate aggregation of leaders – including many paragons of progressivism like La Follette and George W. Norris, as well as conservatives like Vandenberg and Hamilton Fish, old-fashioned nationalists as well as international-minded pacifists – who were able to band together effectively because they succeeded in donning the mantle of peace and security while their adversaries lacked effective leadership.[34]

Only in the fall of 1939 did FDR grasp what had happened when he declared: "Let no group assume the exclusive label of the 'peace bloc.' We all belong to it."[35] Ironically, by making this plea the president, perhaps unwittingly, recognized that the isolationists had successfully seized the initiative, captured public opinion and placed the administration in a position where its leaders felt unable to move purposefully either to deter aggression or to strengthen the forces opposing it.

The pivotal contest had been fought four years earlier, in 1935, over the proposition that the United States should enter the World Court. The isolationists began the contest by recognizing that the platforms of both political parties, as well as public opinion, favored US entry, that the Senate was more than 70 per cent Democratic and contained only a scattering of opponents who were known to be against the proposition. Hiram Johnson claimed, with some exaggeration, that he was practically "alone" when the debate started – but he and Borah dominated the debate and conducted a superb campaign. As FDR refused to send a message urging approval at the outset of the contest, and as he personally joined the fray only toward the end, senators on both sides of the aisle perceived a breakdown in leadership. Twenty Democrats joined sixteen Republicans in defeating the measure.[36]

Roosevelt afterwards complained about twelve or fourteen senators who would not commit themselves, and he blamed the abnormal times for making people "jumpy and very ready to run after strange gods"; he failed to acknowledge that his own stand might have made a difference.[37] Again, the argument can be made that there were critical battles ahead on the domestic scene and that Roosevelt's strategy enabled him to avoid alienating insurgent Republicans on whom he might have to rely for support. But since he did not disarm the progressive isolationists by his passive stance and since it is not certain that many of them would have taken vengeance against the reform measures of 1935–6, would it not have been better to have prevented the ensuing demoralization of the internationalist ranks, a strengthening of the isolationist grip on public opinion, and vastly increased prospects for intransigence on foreign policy in the Senate?

As it was, having failed to use his leverage and gain the advantage early, Roosevelt was now forced to yield center stage to the isolationists. By the mid-1930s the Special Committee to Investigate the Munitions Industry, headed by Senator Gerald P. Nye, riveted attention to the evils of arms sales and the virtues of neutrality.[38] FDR's prospects for acquiring discretionary powers worsened, even as the fears of conflict abroad mounted. The isolationists strove, with renewed intensity, to set the terms of the debate and seize the advantage, and on the issue of neutrality the president was persuaded to avoid a "head-on collision with the Nye Committee."[39]

Diversity and rivalry among the isolationists as to the wisest sort of neutrality legislation did not prevent them from uniting against the administration. Roosevelt preferred no legislation at all to a mandatory law that would tie his hands or to a vehement, protracted controversy that would impede his domestic agenda. But the isolationists were by then – with the aid of a filibuster – able to obstruct presidential conduct of neutrality policy either via discretionary legislation or the absence thereof. "We hold the whip hand," Nye boasted, "and we intend using it to the fullest."[40] So, indeed, they did, time and again. The neutrality legislation of the 1930s, as Hiram Johnson gleefully proclaimed, signaled "the triumph of the so-called 'isolationists'" who "stood firmly for maintaining America's pristine glory and keeping out of every foreign entanglement and every European war."[41]

Not until after the outbreak of World War II could Roosevelt reclaim effective leadership of the foreign policy of the United States in the midst of the conflagrations in Europe and Asia – and even then he often succeeded only by guileful indirection. Concerned with his own political fortunes and the fate of his domestic programs, frustrated by the collapse of the League of Nations and the indecisiveness of America's allies, Roosevelt capitulated time and again to isolationist sentiment. He was, moreover, himself uncertain of what politically acceptable steps the United States could take to influence events, and he was overconfident about Congress's willingness to alter the fundamentals of neutrality policy once in place. Efforts at changing neutrality policy to provide more opportunity for US leadership, despite intensive back-stage maneuverings by the administration, failed to withstand isolationist assault.[42]

THE LEVERS OF ISOLATIONIST POWER

The great advantage enjoyed by the isolationists was that they knew what they wanted. Part of the problem for FDR was that neither he nor anyone else knew precisely where the world was headed and what the appropriate US response would be. In this sense, "internationalism," especially within the foreign-relations bureaucracy, was too diffuse to provide a coherent policy, and those who espoused it could by no means agree on how it was to be put into practice.[43] Isolationism, on the other hand, whatever divergences there might be on particulars, had the much simpler task of upholding political and military non-entanglement, a time-honored tradition that one advocate likened to "a north star, constant and steady, which will hold us true to our course."[44]

Isolationism also derived strength from the very domestic circumstances that deterred more purposeful initiatives on the part of the Roosevelt administration. Tangible efforts abroad could be perceived as detracting from greater accomplishments at home: was entering the World Court more important, Huey Long asked, than putting clothes on people's backs?[45] Nor, as Wayne Cole and Ronald Feinman have shown, can progressive concerns about the political structure at home be dismissed as isolationist rhetorical camouflage.[46] Amidst the menace to liberty abroad, it was not unreasonable to ask whether the nation wanted to take the risk of delegating authority to the president – responsibilities that might tip the scales toward undue centralization of power at home. Early fears of Roosevelt's appetite for power gained reinforcement when he proposed to pack the Supreme Court and reorganize the executive branch. These initiatives did more than strengthen the determination of the isolationists to trammel Roosevelt in making foreign policy: they broadened distrust of the president to include many who were not necessarily opposed to his leadership in foreign affairs; and they bolstered, prior to World War II, arguments that Roosevelt the diplomatist had to be held in check.[47]

Comprehension of isolationism's strength in the 1930s can be clouded by emphasizing its regional and ethnic underpinnings. While it is true that it was strongest in the West and Middle West and that it gained significant support among Americans of German, Scandinavian, Irish, and Italian extraction, it is also important to note that these sources by themselves were insufficient to sustain the nationwide success of isolationism in the 1930s. Ethnic prejudices alone, bereft of a broader credo of American distinctiveness, certainly could not have mounted an argument as compelling as that offered by the isolationists. Furthermore, if the anti-Semitism and pro-Nazism had been as prevalent among isolationists as their foes charged, would their appeal have been as magnetic as it was? In any case, scholars like Cole and Jonas have demonstrated that, with occasional exceptions, anti-Semitic and pro-Nazi sentiments were confined to the extreme edges of the isolationist movement.[48]

What we find in examining the isolationist success is, in fact, the power of a dedicated and able minority, espousing a vision of the nation's destiny consistent with the popular reading of its past, fervently urging their program as vital to democratic liberty, and taking full advantage of the American political system to implant their position as policy. Within the legislative arena, the two-thirds rule for the passage of treaties, such as the World Court protocol, or for bringing closure to debate in the Senate, meant that isolationist leaders had the capacity to triumph despite their small numbers. Opportunity for protracted debate gave them the time they needed to trumpet their case and mobilize additional support; the threat of filibuster gave them the chance to exact concessions from an administration anxious to avoid battle or to pursue other priorities.

The Senate's Foreign Relations Committee provided a vehicle that enabled dedicated isolationists like Borah, Johnson, Vandenberg, and La Follette to enhance their following and build a stronghold, because those on the committee that supported the administration – including the chairman, Key Pittman – lacked a similar fervor. Isolationists succeeded in exploiting legislative hearings to boost support, bottling up a number of measures and intimidating the president into proceeding with great caution and making critical concessions. With the White House hesitant and with internationalist sentiment muted within Congress and across the nation, a determined minority continued to "hold the whip hand" and have their way.[49]

The triumph of isolationism in the 1930s thus depended less on the power of the abstract credo than on a complicated political process, about which facile judgments should be avoided. In examining Roosevelt's encounters with the isolationists, we should now phrase our central question more precisely: did *this* president, under *these* circumstances at home and abroad, faced by *these* adversaries, in *this* political system have a reasonable chance to move the country more purposefully toward collective security in the name of peace? Without indulging in the sort of "iffy" history that FDR himself justly derided, we cannot be at all sure.

FDR'S STEWARDSHIP: WHAT PRICE PRUDENCE?

We can speculate that greater resolution between 1933 and 1935 might well have altered the results of an early contest or two, especially that over the World Court. Yet there are no assurances that, ultimately, such a victory would have made much of a difference, or that the eventual ramifications on international affairs would have been more satisfactory.[50] Furthermore, earlier, more strenuous, exertions on Roosevelt's part might only have thrown the spotlight sooner on the issue of the expanding power of the president, with the consequent backlash that we now know emerged. Finally, with no guarantees of a more successful outcome, can we be sanguine about would-be initiatives that might have jeopardized Roosevelt's effort, in Dallek's words, "to meet worldwide attacks on democracy by preserving it in the United States," in maintaining the United States as a symbol of progressive change in a world desperate for such an example?[51]

Still, even as we avoid overly simplistic second-guessing of Roosevelt's stance in challenging isolationism, we can express some legitimate concerns. For if constraints on his leadership limited his ability to win the contests at hand, could he not at least have done more to encourage his countrymen to be more skeptical about isolationist dogma? A president who elsewhere showed a stunning ability to make the office what his cousin Teddy had dubbed it, a "bully pulpit," FDR left the American people to be educated first by the isolationist reading of events and then by the all-too-brutal reality of events.[52]

Roosevelt, with little circumspection, seems to have sloughed off any opportunities to educate the American public until at least 1937. Instead, though he groused privately, he accepted the isolationist victories from 1935 through 1937 with almost no public remonstration. Because it did no immediate damage, he could term the neutrality act that set the precedent of limiting his powers "entirely satisfactory." And in the midst of the 1936 election campaign, in which he would triumph overwhelmingly, he could not resist talking about his commitment to "isolate" America from war.[53] It was not until the fall of 1937, in the famed quarantine speech, that Roosevelt felt free to begin to launch a public education effort. But even then the isolationists, having severely limited his options, prevented FDR from moving confidently and steadily along the path of international responsibility.[54]

This failure to educate relates to another shortcoming of Roosevelt's leadership: lack of coherent planning. Again acknowledging that the kaleidoscope of circumstances abroad and at home could not have produced a fixed or consistent grand design, when one reads the presidential papers and the diaries and memoirs of a variety of State Department officials, one feels a little like Alice in Wonderland searching for stable moorings. The Roosevelt foreign policymaking apparatus, Justus Doenecke and John Wilz have concluded, "appeared to make an absolute virtue out of government by improvisation . . . The president moved by fits and starts; there was little cohesion."[55] That sort of leadership not only confounded the nation's allies and adversaries; it left a void in public comprehension that the isolationists were quick to fill.

Had Roosevelt made a greater effort earlier on in his administration to achieve consistency in foreign policy and to educate the public in the realities of international affairs, it is possible that he might have been able to lead the nation at least a little more effectively through the agonies of 1939–41. As it was, the dominance of isolation came to an end slowly and painfully. That phase of Roosevelt's leadership goes beyond the scope of this essay, and is itself fraught with controversy.[56] Here we can merely ask if, in ceding early some of the responsibilities of leadership, did Roosevelt not in some measure add to his difficulties in the period prior to American entry into the war?

Whatever our answer, we know that even after the outbreak of war, the foundations of isolationism did not suddenly crumble. Public opinion had shifted from strict neutrality to an aid-short-of-war sentiment, but FDR nonetheless struggled to find a politically acceptable means of satisfying that sentiment without inciting fears of intervention. Though willing to challenge the isolationists directly for limited objectives such as repeal of the arms embargo and passage of the selective service and lend-lease measures, Roosevelt had to resort, simultaneously, to a campaign to discredit the isolationists and secretive and deceptive overseas initiatives, both of which sometimes transgressed constitutional scruple.[57]

The isolationists, of course, had long warned of Roosevelt's abuse of power and that the effort to save democracy abroad would threaten it at home. In 1940–1 they believed their forecasts were coming true, without ever understanding the degree to which their earlier triumphs had helped to make their prophecies self-fulfilling.[58] For his part, Roosevelt, as even his admirers concede, "in his determination to save democracy from Nazism . . . contributed to the rise of some undemocratic practices in the United States."[59] Thus, while the great debate between isolationism and internationalism ended at Pearl Harbor, troubling residual issues endure, and the challenge of historical interpretation continues unabated.

NOTES

1 Quoted in Roland N. Stromberg, *Collective Security and American Foreign Policy*, New York, 1963, p. 60.
2 Richard W. Leopold, *The Growth of American Foreign Policy*, New York, 1962, chaps 31–5; Joan Hoff Wilson, *Herbert Hoover: Forgotten Progressive*, Boston, 1975, p. 168.
3 See, in addition to the previous chapter and Leopold, *Growth*, the incisive

synthesis by Warren I. Cohen, *Empire without Tears: America's Foreign Relations, 1921–1933*, Philadelphia, Pa, 1987.

4 Robert H. Ferrell, *American Diplomacy in the Great Depression*, New Haven, Conn., 1952, p. 18.

5 Borah to M. H. Brownell, 3 January 1932, William Borah Mss, Library of Congress, Box 332.

6 See Albert K. Weinberg, "The Historical Meaning of the American Doctrine of Isolation," *American Political Science Review*, vol. 34, 1940, pp. 539–47; Selig Adler, *The Isolationist Impulse: Its Twentieth-Century Reaction*, New York, 1957; Thomas N. Guinsburg, *The Pursuit of Isolationism in the United States Senate from Versailles to Pearl Harbor*, New York, 1982, chap. 1; and Wayne S. Cole, "Isolationism," in Otis Graham Jr, and Meghan R. Wander (eds), *Franklin D. Roosevelt: His Life and Times*, Boston, 1985, pp. 211–13.

7 Vandenberg to Irving Glasband, 18 November 1941, Arthur H. Vandenberg Mss, Clements Library, University of Michigan. Williams's influential re-interpretation is found in *The Tragedy of American Diplomacy*, Cleveland, Ohio, 1959. See also Carl P. Parrini, *Heir to Empire: United States Economic Diplomacy, 1916–1923*, Pittsburgh, Pa, 1969; Joan Hoff Wilson, *American Business and Foreign Policy, 1920–1933*, Lexington, Ky, 1971; and Michael J. Hogan, *Informal Entente; The Private Structure of Cooperation in Anglo-American Economic Diplomacy, 1918–1928*, Columbia, Mo., 1977.

8 Charles A. Beard, *American Foreign Policy in the Making, 1932–40*, New Haven, Conn., 1946, p. 17, n. 2.

9 The literature is summarized in Justus D. Doenecke, *Anti-Intervention: A Bibliographical Introduction to Isolationism and Pacifism from World War I to the Early Cold War*, New York, 1987, pp. 11–18, and critically examined in Guinsburg, *Pursuit of Isolationism*, pp. 9–14, 283–9.

10 Ray Allen Billington, "The Origins of Middle Western Isolationism," *Political Science Quarterly*, vol. 60, 1945, pp. 44–64; Jeannette P. Nichols, "The Middle West and the Coming of World War II," *Ohio State Archaeological and Historical Quarterly*, vol. 62, 1953, pp. 122–45.

11 William G. Carleton, "Isolationism and the Middle West," *Mississippi Valley Historical Review*, vol. 33, 1946, pp. 377–90; Ralph H. Smuckler, "The Region of Isolationism," *American Political Science Review*, vol. 47, 1953, pp. 386–401; Warren F. Kuehl, "Midwestern Newspapers and Isolationist Sentiment," *Diplomatic History*, vol. 3, 1979, pp. 283–306.

12 Samuel Lubell, *The Future of American Politics*, 2nd ed.; Garden City, N.Y., 1956, pp. 137–43.

13 Smuckler, "Region of Isolationism"; Guinsburg, *Pursuit of Isolationism*; and Robert P. Wilkins, "The Non-Ethnic Roots of North Dakota Isolationism," *Nebraska History*, vol. 44, 1963, pp. 205–11.

14 Julius Turner, *Party and Constituency: Pressures on Congress*, Baltimore, Md, 1951; George Grassmuck, *Sectional Biases on Foreign Policy*, Baltimore, Md, 1951.

15 Wayne S. Cole, *Roosevelt and the Isolationists*, Lincoln, Neb., 1983; Manfred Jonas, *Isolationism in America, 1935–1941*, Ithaca, N.Y., 1966.

16 US Dept of State, *Peace and War: United States Foreign Policy, 1931–1941*, Washington, 1943, pp. 2–3; Basil Rauch, *Roosevelt: From Munich to Pearl Harbor*, New York, 1950, pp. 22, 145; *The Challenge to Isolation, 1937–1940*, New York, 1952, pp. 13, 201.

17 Beard, *Foreign Policy in the Making*, especially chaps II and III; Charles C. Tansill, *Back Door to War: The Roosevelt Foreign Policy, 1933–1941*, Chicago, 1952, pp. 237, 349.

18 Elting E. Morison, *Turmoil and Tradition: A Study of the Life and Times of Henry L. Stimson*, Boston, 1960, pp. 382–98.

19 See F. H. Simonds, "A New Deal in Foreign Policy?," *Harper's*, vol. 166, 1933, pp. 514–20.

20 A superb examination of the challenges of assessing FDR's foreign policy leadership is J. Garry Clifford, "Both Ends of the Telescope: New Perspectives on FDR and American Entry into World War II," *Diplomatic History*, vol. 13, 1989, pp. 213–30.

21 Efforts to avoid pejorative stereotyping and to understand the isolationists include Cole's monumental *Roosevelt and the Isolationists*; Jonas, *Isolationism in America*; and Guinsburg, *Pursuit of Isolationism*. For the epithet, see Rex Stout, *The Illustrious Dunderheads*, New York, 1943.

22 Frederick W. Marks III, *Wind Over Sand: The Diplomacy of Franklin D. Roosevelt*, Athens, Ga, 1988, p. 1.

23 Marks, *Wind Over Sand*, p. 166.

24 Marks, *Wind Over Sand*, p. 20.

25 Robert Dallek, *Franklin D. Roosevelt and American Foreign Policy, 1932–1945*, New York, 1979. The quotation is on page 529.

26 Letter of 30 January 1934, cited in Edward M. Bennett, *Franklin D. Roosevelt and the Search for Victory*, Wilmington, Del., 1990, p. xxi.

27 Robert A. Divine, *Roosevelt and World War II*, Baltimore, Md, 1969, chap. 1, "Roosevelt the Isolationist."

28 Dallek, *Franklin D. Roosevelt*, p. 530; Cole, *Roosevelt and the Isolationists*, Part I, "An Uneasy Alliance." See also Arthur M. Schlesinger Jr, "Franklin D. Roosevelt's Internationalism," in Cornelis van Minnen and John F. Sears (eds), *FDR and His Contemporaries*, New York, 1992, pp. 3–16.

29 See Marks, *Wind Over Sand*, pp. 13–39, and Dallek, *Franklin D. Roosevelt*, pp. 23–58.

30 Dallek, *Franklin D. Roosevelt*, pp. 35–57, explains the delicate balancing act of Roosevelt's diplomatic and economic goals but without much persuasiveness. On the inherent self-contradictions of the administration's stance see Elliot Rosen, "Intranationalism vs. Internationalism: The Interregnum Struggle For the Sanctity of the New Deal," *Political Science Quarterly*, vol. 81, 1966, pp. 274–92.

31 Cordell Hull, *Memoirs*, New York, 1948, vol. 1, p. 228; Robert A. Divine, *The Illusion of Neutrality*, Chicago, 1962, pp. 43–51.

32 Robert A. Divine, "Franklin D. Roosevelt and Collective Security, 1933," *Mississippi Valley Historical Review*, vol. 48, 1961, pp. 56–9.

33 *Congressional Record*, 74th Cong., 1st Sess., p. 13779.

34 See the works cited in note 21, above, and Kuehl, "Midwestern Newspapers and Isolationist Sentiment."

35 *New York Times*, 22 September 1939.

36 The defects of administration handling of the World Court proposition have been analyzed in Guinsburg, *Pursuit of Isolationism*, pp. 155–76; and Gilbert N. Kahn, "Presidential Passivity on a Nonsalient Issue: President Franklin D. Roosevelt and the 1935 World Court Fight," *Diplomatic History*, vol. 4, 1980, pp. 137–60. "Roosevelt can bulldoze Congress and he can hypnotize the people," Chester Rowell had written earlier to his internationalist co-worker Esther Lape. "He will not need reason or logic for either of these purposes. But he will need intensity." Rowell to Lape, 2 January 1934, copy in Franklin D. Roosevelt Mss, Roosevelt Library, Hyde Park, Official File 202.

37 Roosevelt to Elihu Root, 9 February 1935, and Roosevelt to Henry Stimson, 6 February 1935, in Elliott Roosevelt (ed.), *F.D.R.: His Personal Letters, 1928–1945*, New York, 1950, vol. 1, pp. 450–1.

38 See John E. Wiltz, *In Search of Peace: The Senate Munitions Inquiry, 1934–36*, Baton Rouge, La, 1963.

39 Memorandum from Cordell Hull to Roosevelt, 14 March 1935, File 811.113/582,

Dept. of State Mss, Archives of the United States.
40 Divine, *Illusion of Neutrality*, pp. 97–114; Cole, *Roosevelt and the Isolationists*, pp. 166–79. Nye's statement is found in Cole, p. 179.
41 *Congressional Record*, 74th Cong., 1st Sess., p. 14430.
42 Cole, *Roosevelt and the Isolationists*, pp. 223–319; Dallek, *Franklin D. Roosevelt*, pp. 122–91.
43 See Howard Jablon, *The State Department and Foreign Policy, 1933–1937*, Lexington, Ky, 1983.
44 Ernest Lundeen, radio address, 6 April 1938, National Council for the Prevention of War Mss, Swarthmore College Peace Collection.
45 *Congressional Record*, 74th Cong., 1st Sess., p. 1047.
46 Cole, *Roosevelt and the Isolationists*; Ronald L. Feinman, *Twilight of Progressivism: The Western Republican Senators and the New Deal*, Baltimore, Md, 1981.
47 For the role of reactions to Roosevelt's "grabs for power" see especially Cole, *Roosevelt and the Isolationists*, pp. 211–22, and James T. Patterson, *Congressional Conservatism and the New Deal*, Lexington, Ky, 1967.
48 Cole, *Roosevelt and the Isolationists*; Jonas, *Isolationism in America*.
49 Guinsburg, *Pursuit of Isolationism*, pp. 143–217 and 289–92.
50 Gerhard Weinberg's penetrating studies conclude that Hitler's formulation of foreign policy was undertaken with remarkably little consideration of policies and initiatives emanating from Washington. Weinberg, *The Foreign Policy of Hitler's Germany: Diplomatic Revolution in Europe, 1933–1936*, Chicago, 1970; and *The Foreign Policy of Hitler's Germany: Starting World War II*, Chicago, 1980.
51 This point has been emphasized by Dallek (*Franklin D. Roosevelt*, p. 530), citing the eloquent contemporary views of the economist John Maynard Keynes and the philosopher Isaiah Berlin.
52 See James MacGregor Burns's *Roosevelt: The Lion and the Fox*, New York, 1956, whose assessment did not have the advantage of all that we know today about Roosevelt's dilemmas but which retains an eloquent persuasiveness, especially on p. 262.
53 Though Dallek rarely faults Roosevelt directly, his account itself points up instances where Roosevelt's attempt to placate the isolationists may have gone too far. Dallek, *Franklin D. Roosevelt*, pp. 108–22. See also Marks, *Wind Over Sand*, p. 20. Beard, *Policy in the Making*, cites more examples in order to demonstrate that Roosevelt's earlier isolationist-oriented exclamations were betrayed by his later interventionism.
54 Dallek, *Franklin D. Roosevelt*, pp. 147–52.
55 Justus D. Doenecke and John E. Wilz, *From Isolation to War, 1931–1941*, 2nd ed., Arlington Heights, Ill., 1991, p. 157.
56 For a thoughtful assessment of much recent scholarship, see Clifford's article "Both Ends of the Telescope," cited in note 20 above.
57 Roosevelt's devious maneuvers are discussed from widely different perspectives, in William Langer and S. Everett Gleason, *The Undeclared War*, New York, 1953; and Tansill, *Back Door*, Marks, *Wind Over Sand*, and Dallek, *Franklin D. Roosevelt*. The sometimes over-zealous efforts to discredit the isolationists and stifle debate are documented in Cole, *Roosevelt and the Isolationists*, chap. 30, and Richard E. Steele, "The Great Debate: Roosevelt, the Media, and the Coming of War, 1940–1941," *Journal of American History*, vol. 71, 1984, pp. 69–92.
58 Cole, *Roosevelt and the Isolationists*, pp. 409–55; Guinsburg, *Pursuit of Isolationism*, pp. 241–74, 293.
59 Dallek, *Franklin D. Roosevelt*, pp. 312–13.

7 The interpretive wars over the Cold War, 1945–60

Melvyn P. Leffler

The Cold War may be over, but the debates over its origins and evolution persist. The arguments between traditionalists, realists, and revisionists still simmer, and they have been enriched and refined by new interpretations such as those referred to as "postrevisionist," "corporatist," and "world systems." Historians want to know how the Cold War got started and why. Not content to look only at the personalities of Stalin, Roosevelt, Truman, and Churchill, they are studying the bureaucratic and political institutions as well as examining the impact of economics, ideology, geopolitics and strategy. Historians of US foreign relations now use not only the documents of the State Department and the personal manuscript collections of key officials but also the records of the Department of Defense and the Joint Chiefs of Staff, the Army, Navy, and Air Force, the Treasury Department and the Economic Cooperation Administration, the business community and labor unions, Congressional committees and political parties.

The debates among historians of the Cold War is no longer restricted to Americans: scholars outside of the United States have enlivened the controversy, often by utilizing the national archives of their own country. Hence some historians looking at British records attribute responsibility for important initiatives to Ernest Bevin, the Labour Foreign Secretary.[1] Likewise, writers using French and Italian records suggest that the international order created after World War II cannot be understood without studying how domestic politics in those nations influenced the actions of the great powers.[2] Similarly, students of Chinese and east European history have been showing how internal struggles and policy debates shaped foreign policy choices and options,[3] while those who examine the globalization of the Cold War have been demonstrating that the leaders of third-world nations were not simply the pawns of the Americans and the Soviets, but could also be manipulative, cunning, and shrewdly self-interested.[4]

So the history of the Cold War grows more exciting and sophisticated, even as the worries about great power confrontation and nuclear holocaust abate. Participants in the scholarly dialogue seem to want to distance themselves from some of the vituperative exchanges that went on in the 1960s and 1970s among traditionalists, realists, and revisionists, but they also know they cannot circumvent some of the critical questions that those controversies raised. Traditionalists claimed that the Cold War was the result of the relentless expansionism of the Soviet Union and the paranoid personality of Joseph Stalin; they maintained that presidents Franklin D. Roosevelt and Harry S. Truman reacted slowly and did so out of their concern for democratic values and individual rights. Revisionists retorted that the United States was not guiltless; they charged that American power, spurred by possession of an atomic monopoly and interacting with fears about another depression, pushed the United States into an expansionist mode of its own.[5]

The memoirs and diaries of American officials provided the grist for the traditional interpretation. President Truman, secretaries of state James Byrnes, Dean Acheson and many of their advisers crafted accounts of the early Cold War that exonerated themselves from any fault while attributing to the Soviets the responsibility for the breakdown of the coalition that had won World War II. They claimed that the United States sought to cooperate with the Kremlin at the end of the war, but Stalin tried to impose his rule over all of Eastern Europe. And his demands elsewhere were insatiable. Basically, he wanted to enslave all of Europe by taking advantage of the widespread economic and social distress that followed the war, and he aimed to rupture the great coalition because the specter of foreign encirclement was indispensable for maintaining communist totalitarian controls and his own dictatorial rule at home. George F. Kennan, the American *chargé d'affaires* in Moscow, presented these views in diplomatic dispatches in 1945 and 1946. He was recalled to Washington and articulated them again in a series of speeches and in a renowned article in *Foreign Affairs*. Subsequently, he qualified some of his original thoughts and altered many of his policy recommendations, but the image of a relentlessly expansionist Soviet Union bent on exploiting every opportunity and seeking ideological aggrandizement and imperial domination cast huge shadows over subsequent generations of cold war historical scholarship.[6]

These views were reinforced in a number of important books written by influential analysts of Soviet foreign policy. Adam Ulam, William Taubman, and Vojtech Mastny agreed that, although he had no blueprint for world domination, Stalin was a cunning, ruthless, and paranoid statesman who was moving cautiously, yet systematically, to grab control over Eastern Europe, lure Germany into the Soviet orbit, and capitalize on the success of communist parties in France and Italy.[7]

This traditional perspective still has many proponents. In a widely acclaimed study of *The Origins of the Cold War in the Near East*, Bruce Kuniholm portrayed an expansionist Russia hoping to seize parts of Turkey, gain control of the Dardanelles straits, foment unrest in Iran, and capitalize on communist strength in Greece. The United States, Kuniholm concluded, "was forced to act."[8] Hugh Thomas, a British historian, reached a similar verdict in 1987. In his comprehensive account of the beginnings of the Cold War, Thomas acknowledged that Stalin had limited short-term objectives and that he sought to avoid war. Yet Thomas insisted that historians should not neglect the "extreme subtlety of the Marxist–Leninist philosophy" and the "brute force of Communist methods." Stalin's aims were clear: "in the far distant future the establishment of a Russified world state; in the middle distance, a Soviet Union surrounded by a network of Communist-inspired republics . . ."[9] In their recent survey of the causes of the Cold War, Randall Woods and Howard Jones restated these views. They were more nuanced than Thomas and they attributed considerable importance to American public opinion and British pressure, but their major emphasis was on the intransigence of Soviet negotiators, the machinations of Soviet diplomacy, and Stalin's desires "to foster Soviet control of Eastern Europe . . . to expand Soviet influence in Western Europe, the Near East, and Asia; and to position the USSR for even greater gains when the next Western economic crisis struck."[10]

Some scholars, usually referred to as "realists," did not place quite so much responsibility on the Soviet Union: they did not think the Kremlin was motivated by ideological imperatives, nor did they believe Soviet goals to be unlimited. No one put the realist perspective more succinctly than did John Spanier. The post-World-War-II conflict, he wrote, "was not fundamentally due to the personalities of leaders or to the principal contestants' domestic political or economic systems; it was essentially due to the nature of the state system and the emergent bipolar distribution of power, which led each state to see the other as the principal threat to its security and to take the appropriate steps."[11]

Historians who were labeled "revisionist" disagreed with this stress on the international system. The most influential revisionist works were written in the late 1960s and early 1970s. Inspired by the writings of Charles Beard and William A. Williams, outraged by the war in Vietnam, and armed with the recently opened manuscript collections of many officials and the newly declassified documents of the Department of State pertaining to the mid-1940s, they emphasized the domestic sources of US policies and challenged traditional notions that the United States was restrained, naive, and innocent. They believed that the United States sought to create a peaceful and prosperous multilateral world order that would be conducive to the spread of American values and interests. Some (but not all) revisionists attributed narrowly economic motives to US officials. Most saw a complex interweaving of economic and ideological variables, fueled by a sense of overweening power and of stark fears that the nation might sink into another depression. In provocative, insightful, and well-researched books and articles, Barton Bernstein, Lloyd Gardner, Thomas Paterson, Bruce Kuklick, and Walter LaFeber showed how the United States sought to retain an open sphere of influence in Eastern Europe, erode the influence of communists in Western Europe, revive capitalism and liberalism in western Germany and forestall revolutionary nationalism in the Third World. They showed how plans to create postwar political and financial institutions like the United Nations, the

World Bank, and the International Monetary Fund were part of this attempt to establish a peaceful and prosperous international order along liberal and capitalist lines. This open, multilateral world order would insure that American business could have access to the markets and raw materials that were necessary to sustain a full employment economy.[12]

Revisionists also argued that the United States was neither naive nor hesitant about using its power to achieve its objectives and to dominate the postwar order – or the "American Century," as they liked to call it. Paterson, for example, suggested that Roosevelt, Truman, and their advisers were prepared to exact important concessions from the Soviets in return for a large postwar loan. But more important than the use of economic leverage was the availability of the atomic bomb. In one of the most controversial books of the revisionist genre, Gar Alperovitz maintained that Truman decided to drop the bomb on Japan in order to influence the postwar configuration of power between the United States and the Soviet Union. Relying heavily on the diaries of Secretary of War Henry L. Stimson, Alperovitz showed how discussions about the bomb almost always took place in the context of how to handle the Kremlin.[13] Not all revisionists agreed with the degree of importance that Alperovitz attributed to the Soviet factor in the decision to drop the bomb, but they all believed that the evidence unmistakably proved that Truman and Byrnes hoped that the dropping of the bomb would make the Soviets more malleable. They concurred that US officials assumed that the atomic monopoly would strengthen their hand in postwar diplomatic discussions and would evoke concessions from the Kremlin. They wanted Stalin to agree to free elections and non-discriminatory trade in Eastern Europe, to unified economic control of the four zones in Germany, and to Nationalist rule and the open door in China.[14]

The revisionists claimed that the Soviet Union was not unduly expansionist. They showed that Stalin was willing to make concessions over reparations from Germany and that he did not initially impose communist governments on countries like Hungary and Czechoslovakia. They suggested that Stalin was responding to demonstrations of American power, to probes of his sphere of influence in Eastern Europe, and to the deployment of US troops to Korea, China, and Japan at the end of the war. They stressed that the Soviets had legitimate security interests at risk when discussing the composition of governments on their borders and, even more so, when discussing the future of Germany and Japan.

Some of these revisionist claims have found support in an eclectic array of studies of Soviet foreign policy. Although based on the same meager set of Russian source materials that had been available to scholars like Ulam, Mastny, and Taubman, and relying heavily on the memoirs of European communist leaders and on documents from Eastern Europe, scholars like William McCagg, Gavriel Ra'anan and Robert Slusser have shown that the postwar Kremlin was racked by fierce bureaucratic, ideological, and personal rivalries.[15] These feuds sometimes assumed far more importance in the calculations of Soviet officials than considerations of foreign policy. Although these accounts often obscured the dominating position held by Stalin, other writers who acknowledged Stalin's preeminent place in the Soviet hierarchy nevertheless argued that he sometimes sought to restrain the efforts of foreign communists seeking to capitalize on favorable postwar conditions to win or seize power in their own countries.[16] He was certainly more concerned with thwarting the revival of hostile German and Japanese power than with promoting revolution in the Third World, and even in parts of Europe.[17]

Some recent literature emanating from the Soviet Union suggests that the revisionists who emphasized Stalin's circumspection and Soviet defensiveness may be right. Recollections by Soviet leaders like Nikita Khrushchev, V. M. Molotov, Andrei Gromyko and Nikolai Novikov underscore Stalin's respect for US strength and his fear that Americans were trying to exploit the power of the bomb to extract concessions from the Soviet Union. Molotov, an unrepentent Stalinist if ever there was one, notes that Stalin observed strict limits even while he sought to exploit opportunities. More illustrative of Russian perceptions at the end of the war are the memoirs of Novikov, wherein the former ambassador to the United States stresses the relentlessness of American imperialism and the threats it posed to the security of the Soviet Union.[18] Even in Dimitri Volkogonov's acclaimed biography of Stalin, perhaps the most representative Russian book of the glasnost era, the author insists that American and British behavior at Potsdam "gave Stalin justified grounds for concern." On virtually every page of the volume Volkogonov indicts Stalin's crimes, brutality, and cynicism, yet he also stresses Stalin's prudent cautiousness and non-provocative behavior in foreign policy. The Soviet dictator, Volkogonov says, was right to reject the Marshall Plan because it would have meant "virtual US control over the Soviet economy."[19]

The quest for American hegemonic control over a reformed world capitalist system was the key component of Gabriel and Joyce Kolko's massive history of postwar US foreign policy. This was unquestionably the most important revisionist work of the 1970s, and what was so noteworthy about the book was that the Kolkos played down the importance of the Soviet Union and insisted that "American policy merely fitted the Soviet problem into a much larger context, a framework which would have existed apart from anything Russia might have done." The overriding objective of US policy, the Kolkos claimed, "was to sustain and reform world capitalism." And this goal was dictated by "the expansive interests of American capitalism," an economy "with specific structural needs" that shaped the country's "global role."

According to the Kolkos, "the Great Depression defined Washington's wartime plans for the reconstruction of the world economy." The United States had to create an open international order conducive to the free flow of American goods and capital. Socialism, state ownership, and revolutionary nationalism in the Third World posed serious problems to the United States. The Kolkos spent a great deal of time focusing on US rivalries with Great Britain, on US efforts to break down autarchical arrangements in Western

Europe, on US attempts to reconstruct, integrate, and coopt Germany and Japan into a liberal–capitalist world economic order, and on US struggles to thwart revolutionary nationalist movements in Asia, Africa, and Latin America. The Kolkos grasped the centrality of the dollar gap problem – the shortage of dollars available to foreign purchasers of American goods – and the sophisticated mechanisms that Truman and Eisenhower administration officials devised to funnel dollars to Europe and Asia through economic and military aid packages. The Kolkos' book was a tour de force because it was so vast in its scope, because it scrutinized American behavior in all areas of the globe, and because it illuminated the complex interrelationships between military and economic policy, between the developed and underdeveloped worlds, between state and society. Yet its central themes were simple and straightforward: American policies were determined by the nature of its capitalist system and by recurrent fears of depression; American aims were to reform and sustain the international capitalist system; America's great challenge was to defeat not the Soviet Union but the revolutionary Left.[20]

The revisionists had a great impact on assessments of US foreign policy because they accurately demonstrated that American officials were not naive, simple-minded, and defensive. Marshalling considerable evidence, they showed that Roosevelt, Truman, and their advisers grasped the likelihood of a postwar struggle with the Soviet Union and sought to safeguard US interests. These interests were shaped by the tradition of expansion in American history, by the dynamics of the American political economy of liberal capitalism, by a sense of political and racial superiority, by a need to avoid the mistakes of political isolationism and economic nationalism that had plagued the interwar years, and by the futile experience of trying to appease totalitarian foes. These revisionist views were anathema to traditionalists and conservatives because they suggested that the United States shared responsibility for bringing on the Cold War.

Revisionist interpretations were gaining ascendancy in the early 1970s when John Lewis Gaddis published his prize-winning book *The United States and the Origins of the Cold War*. Gaddis did not deny that Stalin's objectives were limited and he did not dispute that economic and ideological variables played a role in the formulation of American foreign policy. Hence he sought to coopt elements of the revisionist critique. But, while acknowledging that these factors were worthy of historical attention and while agreeing that US actions raised Soviet suspicions, he contested the centrality of their importance. Instead, he stressed the profound significance of the domestic political system, of partisan politics, of ethnic voting blocs, and of legislative–executive rivalries. "The delay in opening the second front [in Europe during World War II], nonrecognition of Moscow's sphere of influence in Eastern Europe, the denial of economic aid to Russia, and the decision to retain control of the atomic bomb can all be explained far more plausibly by citing the Administration's need to maintain popular support for its policies rather than by dwelling upon requirements of the economic order."[21]

Subsequently, Gaddis labeled his views "postrevisionist," an interpretive genre that became highly influential in the early 1980s. Gaddis continued to claim that the Cold War was primarily the fault of the Soviet Union: "Stalin's paranoia, together with the bureaucracy of institutionalized suspicion with which he surrounded himself," made agreement impossible. There was simply nothing the West could do to allay Russian hostility, which "sprang chiefly from internal sources."[22] American officials were justified in believing that the United States needed to balance Soviet power, and that the way to accomplish this was to utilize American economic leverage to achieve geopolitical goals. Indeed, the focus on economic leverage as means rather than as ends became a key component of the postrevisionist critique. So did geopolitics. In *Strategies of Containment*, a book that made Gaddis famous in the 1980s, he declared "that American interest was not to remake the world, but to balance power within it." Sounding like a realist, he wrote that containment was designed to prevent the Soviet Union from using its power and position to gain ascendancy in the international system. And in thwarting Soviet designs, Gaddis argued, the United States did establish an empire, but it was an "empire by invitation," an empire that was created by the many governments who looked to the United States for protection against Soviet imperialism.[23]

By the time that Gaddis came to write *Strategies* he had been influenced by Geir Lundestad, a Norwegian historian, and by other scholars who were studying the internal dynamics of policymaking in European countries. These historians did not see the United States acting systematically to create an American world order in the immediate postwar years. Lundestad showed that American concern with Eastern Europe was often rhetorical and sporadic, that US policy lacked consistency of purpose, and that Washington's actions were frequently influenced by local factors and external pressures.[24] Some studies of British diplomacy reinforced these findings, showing that the Labour government of Clement Attlee viewed Soviet actions in Eastern Europe and the Middle East with even greater alarm than the Americans, and that British officials pushed and prodded the Truman administration to take a tougher stand. Although Churchill was no longer in power, his famous Iron Curtain speech at Fulton, Missouri symbolized British attempts to alert Americans to the Soviet threat and to harness American power on behalf of British interests, especially in the Balkans, the eastern Mediterranean, and the Middle East.[25]

This emphasis on the external sources of US foreign policy has resonated through some of the more thoughtful recent books and articles on US diplomacy in the late 1940s and 1950s. It was not pressure from the US government but domestic politics and the infighting among fractious political parties that prompted the Christian Democrats in Italy and the democratic Left in France to exclude communists from the postwar coalition governments; it was not Washington but London that inspired the North Atlantic alliance; it was not the Marshall Plan but French, German, and other

European initiatives that were responsible for the success of European reconstruction and for the subsequent course of European integration. Even small countries in the Third World were alleged to have manipulated American fears about communist takeovers and exploited great power tensions in order to elicit guarantees and aid from the United States that they otherwise might not have received.[26]

By the late 1980s, the postrevisionist critique, the regional and local studies, and the examination of the external sources of US diplomacy put the revisionists on the defensive. So did analyses of public opinion and bureaucratic behavior. In books and articles, Ernest May disputed the notion that the rational pursuit of national self-interest shaped the course of US foreign policy in the 1940s and 1950s. Looking at the course of US policy in China, he stressed the impact of public opinion and legislative politics, and he focused on the battles between military and civilian officials. He also saw organizational feuds and interservice rivalries influencing the course of US defense policy and the deployment of US troops to Europe.[27] Other studies of the US defense posture underscored the role of organizational self-interest and inept, if not irrational, presidential leadership. This was especially true of the work of David Rosenberg on the hydrogen bomb decision and the strategic arms race. Rosenberg showed how the Joint Chiefs of Staff, the Air Force, and the Strategic Air Command molded decisions that culminated in the build-up of a gigantic arsenal of atomic and nuclear warheads that made no sense in terms of the objectives of foreign policy and that were unwanted by Eisenhower himself.[28]

The size of the US defense budget and the relationship of the air–atomic strategy to diplomacy have become important topics in studies of the foreign relations of the Truman and Eisenhower administrations and in the larger debate over the causes of the Cold War. Traditionalists and postrevisionists have argued that the comparatively small amount of military expenditures and the limited size of the atomic arsenal prior to 1950 demonstrate the non-aggressive, defensive, and reactive nature of US policy. They maintain that the attempt of Secretary of State Byrnes to use the atomic monopoly to leverage the Soviets into concessions failed, and that thereafter the strategic superiority of the United States was not of great utility in the nation's diplomatic behavior. McGeorge Bundy, a national security adviser to President Kennedy, has argued along these lines in a thoughtful and wide-ranging analysis of atomic weapons and American diplomacy. The fear of mutual destruction deterred officials from pursuing a course of atomic diplomacy, and, he insists, Truman and Eisenhower eschewed nuclear blackmail in their dealings with the Russians and the Chinese.[29]

But these conclusions remain hotly contested. Although much information concerning the development and deployment of atomic weapons and strategic air power remains classified, Rosenberg, Gregg Herken, Roger Dingman, Robert Wampler, and Marc Trachtenberg have done pioneering work in this area. Trachtenberg, for example, has been studying the use of atomic diplomacy during and after the Korean War. At critical times during the 1950s officials used language and conveyed signals that were intended to intimidate the adversary and elicit concessions. More importantly, Trachtenberg argues that perceptions of the overall balance of strategic power continually influenced the diplomatic options chosen by US officials. Furthermore, he says, the deployment of tactical atomic weapons to Europe in the 1950s and the prospective nuclearization of America's NATO allies, especially West Germany, had enormous repercussions on both Soviet–American and Franco-German relations.[30]

Trachtenberg's conclusion regarding the relationship between the strategic balance and diplomacy might seem to buttress revisionist arguments about the use of military capabilities to support a pax americana, but it does not. This is because Trachtenberg has not spent much time yet examining the larger purposes of US foreign policy. One theme that resonates through some of his essays on the 1950s underscores Eisenhower's desire to bring US troops home from Europe. This reinforces a key traditional and postrevisionist idea that US officials after World War II were not eager to intervene politically in Europe and never wanted to keep US troops there on a permanent basis.[31]

In some recent studies (such as those mentioned above), students of US foreign relations can see a welcome trend to integrate military and diplomatic history. Indeed one cannot examine the policies of the Truman and Eisenhower administrations anywhere in the world without utilizing both Defense and State Department archival materials. This is evident in some pathbreaking work on the Middle East and South Asia. In his careful analysis of US and British relations with Egypt from the end of World War II to the Suez Crisis of 1956, Peter Hahn shows that British and American concerns were focused on maintaining western access to the great air base at Cairo–Suez. British and American officials counted on the use of this base to launch their strategic air offensive against the Soviets, in the event of a global war. Notwithstanding American sympathy for Egyptian nationalist appeals to regain control over their own territory, Truman and Eisenhower administration officials (prior to 1956) hesitated to exert commensurate pressure on the British to withdraw, lest this interfere with their future ability to use this strategic base. Similarly, Robert McMahon has found that the aim of locking Pakistan into a strategic alliance with the United States accounted for the chaotic pattern of US relations on the Asian subcontinent.[32] This concern with strategy departs from, but does not necessarily contradict, those earlier revisionist interpretations of US diplomacy in the eastern Mediterranean, the Middle East and Southwest Asia as being dictated by the need to control the oil repositories in those regions.

Indeed, the meshing of strategic and economic variables has been an important part of the agenda of the "corporatist" school of diplomatic history. Michael Hogan is the leading proponent of this interpretive model, and he has presented his ideas in his analysis of the formulation and implementation of the Marshall Plan. He contends that the Marshall Plan was not primarily a response to the communist threat in Europe or to Soviet expansionism – as traditionalists and postrevisionists claim – but part of "America's twentieth-century search for a new economic order at home and abroad." That economic order was a corporatist order, by which Hogan means "an American political economy founded on self-governing economic groups, integrated by institutional coordinators and normal market mechanisms, led by cooperating public and private elites, nourished by limited but positive government power, and geared to an economic growth in which all could share." The Truman administration, Hogan argues, "sought to restructure the world economy along lines similar to the corporative order that was emerging in the United States."[33]

Hogan does not closely examine the motives that prompted US officials to pursue this new order. Unlike Kolko, for example, he does not stress the underlying structural economic forces that pushed the United States in this direction. But his analysis of the complex linkages between the public and private sectors and his emphasis on establishing a multilateral international order while reforming capitalism at home and abroad underscore some of the important points in the revisionist critique. And, although he dwells on economic and financial arrangements, he does demonstrate the strategic implications of the Marshall Plan. He stresses that integration was a key thrust of the Marshall Plan from the outset and that "integration was the way to reconcile Germany's recovery with France's security and bring both together in a unit of sufficient scale to contain the Soviets."[34]

This theme of double containment, that is, containing both existing Soviet power and prospective German power, constitutes another important trend in recent historical writing. American officials were not simply worried about the Soviet Union. They were also fearful that an impoverished and disillusioned Germany might retard overall west European economic recovery and orient itself eastward. So Truman and his advisers chose to boost German industrial production, limit reparations, and unify the western zones. But at the same time they were fearful that a strengthened Germany might maneuver between the two blocs, act independently of the United States, and perhaps even provoke a full-scale war. Students of America's German policy, like Thomas Schwartz, have shown how Truman, Eisenhower, and their European experts worked diligently to coopt German power for the western alliance. They had to do so because Germans skillfully manipulated American fears about their future alignment to further German goals, like the relaxation of occupation controls and the reassertion of German sovereignty.[35]

While responding imaginatively to concerns about Germany, however, US officials had to be careful not to alienate the French. As was the case after World War I, the French remonstrated that Anglo-American attempts to cater to the Germans endangered their security and conflicted with their need to gain favorable access to German coal in the Ruhr. Franco-German rivalries posed major policy dilemmas, and some historians like John Gimbel and

Timothy Ireland have argued that the Marshall Plan and the North Atlantic Treaty were primarily attempts to overcome these traditional disputes.[36] Such claims are overstated because the magnitude of American concerns with these Franco-German controversies was certainly influenced by calculations about the advantages that the Soviet Union could reap from French disillusionment or German revanchism. But the focus on intra-European squabbles and on the attempts of Europeans to resolve these struggles has become an important subject of historical inquiry. During the Truman and Eisenhower administrations, the United States was not simply waging a bipolar struggle with the Soviet Union while other participants in the international system stood watching. Middling and small nations labored feverishly to pursue their own interests in the midst of this great power competition, and the Americans and Soviets could ignore them only at their own peril.[37]

Recognizing that the United States was grappling with a plethora of problems in the international system, another group of historians has found evidence supporting a "world systems" interpretation of US foreign policy behavior. This mode of analysis tries to integrate three critical variables: world position, state, and social situation. The United States, argues Bruce Cumings, "had real problems on its hands: the decline from empire of England, the intractability of the world economy, stagnant industrial allies, and at least one 'grand area' of the world now removed from capitalism: the Soviet sphere." American foreign policy, Cumings stresses, must be understood in terms of its "structural position in a distinct world system . . . .The world market system placed similar but unequal burdens on states and societies, with economic competition the driving force, but with the nation-state being a prime vehicle of conflict, and with society reacting to market penetration in different but always significant ways."[38]

Cumings and Thomas McCormick claim that US foreign policy was designed to revive and stabilize the world capitalist system and to preserve America's leading role in that system. The sophisticated framework designed by Cumings considers the factional struggles within the business community, legislative politics and organizational rivalries. Against a vast panorama of conflicting interests and political rivalries, Cumings illuminates how the state preserves its autonomy above individual and class interests, seeks to maintain the system, and guarantees "the field on which the bourgeoisie plays." To achieve these goals, American officials during the Truman and Eisenhower years often had to establish linkages with elites in other countries, help preserve them in power, and insure that their countries' economies were integrated effectively into the world market system.[39]

One of the great attributes of the world systems approach is that it incorporates ideas from the revisionist and corporatist literature, which tend to stress the domestic sources of US foreign policy, without slighting the evidence that US policy was continually buffeted by external pressures, local rivalries, and regional struggles. Cumings, of course, uses this approach to explain the origins of the Korean War. The world system, he claims, was in precarious shape in early 1950 as Western Europe, Germany, and Japan were still experiencing terrible dollar shortages, as the British pound was tottering, as the Chinese communists were triumphantly taking over the mainland, and as US policy was foundering in view of the Soviet acquisition of atomic weapons. The eruption of hostilities in Korea provided an opportunity for Acheson and his aides to go on the offensive and to launch a series of initiatives to grapple with these profound threats beleaguering the functioning and stability of the world capitalist system.

World systems can also help to explain the origins of the American embroilment in Indochina. Many recent studies trace the beginnings of the US involvement in this part of the world to American anxieties about the future of Japan. Acheson and John Foster Dulles did not think that Japan could support itself and maintain a stable democratic and capitalistic system without having access to markets and raw materials in Southeast Asia. Aware that Japan traditionally depended on extensive economic ties with Manchuria, north China, and Korea, and knowing that most of this area was now in the enemy bloc, Acheson and Dulles felt they had to link Japan and Southeast Asia. In this interpretation one sees the extent to which US officials believed that the industrial core of the world system had to be integrated with the underdeveloped periphery.[40]

But was economic competition the driving force behind this orientation, as most revisionist and world systems historians contend? In one of the exciting books that highlighted the Japanese–Indochina relationship, Michael Schaller was ambiguous about whether geopolitical, bureaucratic, or economic factors were most responsible for the integrated approach to the problems of East Asia.[41] And even in a monograph that more comfortably fits into the literature on world systems, William Borden wrote that "Balance of power considerations were paramount; the loss of Germany and Japan to the Soviets would irrevocably tip the balance in the Soviet favor."[42] In this rendition, one might see economic and military aid (to overcome the dollar gap) as moves to redress unfavorable trends in the balance of power rather than to buttress the world market system. Although this was not Borden's intent, some of his findings might add credibility to the postrevisionist emphasis on geopolitics and threat perception.

In analyses of US relations with East Asia, geopolitical factors have acquired a new saliency as historians have probed the policies of the Truman and Eisenhower administrations with the People's Republic of China. Earlier views that American policy was dictated by domestic interests, known as "the China bloc," and by ideological antipathy toward the Chinese communists have been replaced by closely textured analyses of the thinking and actions of Acheson and Dulles. The two historians most responsible for this reconsideration are Warren Cohen and Nancy Bernkopf Tucker. They show that the so-called "wedge strategy," the desire to split Beijing from Moscow, was on Acheson's mind from the outset.[43] Although the Korean War and Chinese intervention narrowed the options subsequently available to US officials, Eisenhower and Dulles recognized the possibility of a Sino-Soviet split, thought that a tough stance against the PRC might accentuate strains in the communist bloc, and pondered the prospects of living in a world with two Chinas.[44] Tucker has presented considerable evidence showing that US officials contemplated more flexible policies, but few historians believe that the United States actually practiced a policy of accommodation. Gordon Chang, for example, maintains that US antipathy toward the PRC grew during the 1950s, even as Eisenhower and Dulles explored possibilities of détente with the Soviet Union.[45]

These analyses of the Eisenhower administration's relations with the PRC highlight elements of pragmatism that earlier historians of the Eisenhower era did not see. Tucker's work, for example, underscores elements of the "revisionist" approach to the Eisenhower years, but this type of revisionism should not be confused with the revisionist approaches to the history of the Cold War discussed earlier. Eisenhower revisionism stresses that the president was active, thoughtful, and manipulative. In fact, much of the recent writing on the Eisenhower era has centered on questions of whether he was in command, whether he knew what was going on, and whether he was wise. Most writers have come to agree that the president exerted decisive control over his administration's foreign policies and that he was thoughtful, analytic, and intelligent. They do not agree that he carried out a wise set of policies.[46]

Aside from a number of sympathetic biographers, H.W. Brands has become one of the most prolific writers on the diplomacy of the Eisenhower era. In his stimulating book *The Specter of Neutralism*, Brands studies the response of the United States to neutralist and revolutionary nationalist regimes in Yugoslavia, India, and Egypt. Showing, for example, that Eisenhower and Dulles were willing to assist Tito's communist government, Brands argues that the president and his advisers acted "in a remarkably non-ideological fashion." Their diplomacy "reflected primarily a geopolitical interpretation of American strategic, military, diplomatic, and economic interests, and it demonstrated a shrewd weighing of the effects of the international balance of power of the particular activities of specific nonaligned countries."[47]

The emphasis on geopolitics, power balances, and external stimuli gives a postrevisionist appearance to much of Brands's work. He largely ignores the economic determinants of policy and fails to engage the world systems critique, while consciously posing an alternative to revisionist historians of the Cold War like Walter LaFeber, Richard Immerman, and Blanche Wiesen Cook, who had claimed that Eisenhower and Dulles were rigidly ideological, bent on fighting communism and revolutionary nationalism everywhere, and determined to retain open access to the world's natural resources and markets. Although Brands does show that there was nuance and flexibility in the tactics of the Eisenhower administration, he has not persuaded most of his colleagues that there was also wisdom and consistency. Eisenhower was aware of the potency of nationalism in postwar international affairs, was restrained in his use of force, was committed to limit military spending, was interested in arms control and intent on avoiding global war. He was shrewd, learned from some of his mistakes, and came to see that government economic aid could enhance his policy goals. But he was never able to escape from the view that the United States was locked in a zero-sum game of power politics with the Soviet Union – so he supported covert actions to overthrow unfriendly governments in Guatemala and Iran, bolstered unpopular regimes like that of Ngo Dinh Diem in South Vietnam, and disregarded the immense build-up in nuclear armaments. Even Brands acknowledges the validity of some of these criticisms.[48]

But what factors served to inspire the ongoing Cold War during the 1950s? Big interpretive foreign policy books on the Eisenhower era, like those by Gaddis, the Kolkos, Hogan, and Cumings on the 1940s, do not yet exist. Instead we have penetrating collections of essays, first-rate biographies, and astute analyses of crisis decision-making.[49] In some of these works we see Eisenhower and his aides demonstrating more and more concern with American credibility. The United States, they felt, had to show resolve in places like the Taiwan straits, Indochina and Lebanon, in order to bolster the confidence of wavering allies and in order to deter even more troublesome behavior from adventurous adversaries. This concern with credibility highlights how important perception and misperception became in the global competition with Soviet communism.[50] Historians are increasingly interested in how American officials saw their adversaries and allies, how friends and foes saw Washington, and how US policymakers thought their actions would affect prospective policies elsewhere. In order to evoke behavior that complied with the wishes of the United States, Truman, Eisenhower, and their successors believed the United States had to be credible. Notions of credibility, therefore, are critical to understanding deterrence, coercive diplomacy, and crisis decision-making.

But credibility was linked to interests as well as to threat perception. The important interpretive books on the Cold War have always tried to sort through this maze of complex interrelationships. Traditionalists, realists, and revisionists, as well as postrevisionists, corporatists and world systems historians have examined how US officials defined their fundamental interests; how they assessed the intentions of the adversary; how economics, geopolitics, public opinion, and ideology entered the policymaking equation; and how external pressures affected policy outcomes. And, although they still disagree on the question of primacy, one can see that historians who may be categorized as fitting into these different "schools" nevertheless borrow increasingly from one another and are influenced by one another's work. Hence, in truth, the categories that are used in essays like this one tend to suggest more rigid definitions than exist in practice.

In my own research on the Cold War I have found evidence that has forced me to integrate key elements from the different schools of interpretation.[51] As I have indicated earlier in this essay, it seems to me that the revisionists were right in stressing that the Soviet Union's initial postwar actions were limited. To acknowledge this is not to exonerate the Kremlin for its barbarous behavior at home, or on its periphery; it is simply to suggest that Stalin's focus was on protecting his immediate borders and on thwarting the recreation of German and Japanese power. American officials did have a more expansive conception of their security and did hope to establish a world order compatible with their interests and values. But as persuasive as is the revisionist and world systems critique in these respects, I do not share their penchant to discount Washington's preoccupation with Soviet strength. US officials were gravely worried about the Kremlin's capacity to exploit postwar economic dislocation, socio-political turmoil, and revolutionary nationalism in order to further its own self-interest and its totalitarian rule at home and abroad. The Kolkos and Cumings err when they minimize American apprehensions about the Soviet Union and when they dwell primarily on economic and capitalist imperatives.

My research suggests that Truman, Eisenhower, and their associates paid a great deal of attention to geopolitical configurations of power, as some realists and many postrevisionists argue. These policymakers were attuned to external stimuli, were aware of local rivalries, and, within certain limits, were subject to manipulation by weaker partners. But while acknowledging these strengths in the realist and postrevisionist literature, I do not always share their conclusions. What Truman, Eisenhower, and their advisers wanted was not a world of diversity but a world in which most nations accepted American values and comported themselves in ways that buttressed American interests. In other words, the United States wanted not a balance of power but a configuration of power in the international system that was preponderantly to America's advantage. And in pursuing these goals, US policymakers did grasp how the world capitalist system functioned: they did seek to integrate core and periphery; they did establish linkages with the private sector at home and with elites abroad; they did use covert action and strategic superiority to buttress their diplomacy; they did not believe that the configuration of power abroad would affect the political economy at home. But American diplomacy would not have assumed the characteristics it did and would not have garnered the resources and popular support it needed if it had not been designed to thwart a totalitarian adversary as well as to revive world capitalism – if it did not have, as its ultimate objective, a desire to foster free politics as well as free markets, liberalism as well as capitalism.

NOTES

1 Allen Louis Charles Bullock, *Ernest Bevin, Foreign Secretary, 1945–1951*, New York, 1983; Anne Deighton, *The Impossible Dream: Britain, the Division of Germany and the Origins of the Cold War*, Oxford, 1990.
2 Irwin Wall, *The United States and the Making of Postwar France, 1945–1954*, New York, 1991; David Reynolds, "The Origins of the Cold War: The European Dimension, 1944–51," *Historical Journal*, vol. 28, 1985, pp. 497–515; Josef

Becker and Franz Knipping (eds), *Power in Europe?: Great Britain, France, Italy, and Germany in a Postwar World, 1945–1950*, Berlin, 1986.

3 Sergei Goncharov, John W. Lewis, and Xue Litai, *Uncertain Partner: Stalin, Mao, and the Korean War*, Stanford, Calif., 1994; Charles Gati, *Hungary and the Soviet Bloc*, Durham, N.C., 1986; Antony Polonsky, "Stalin and the Poles, 1941–47," *European Historical Quarterly*, vol. 17, 1987, pp. 453–92.

4 Roger Dingman, "The Diplomacy of Dependency: The Philippines and Peace-making with Japan," *Journal of Southeast Asian Studies*, vol. 27, 1986, pp. 307–21; Robert J. McMahon, "United States Cold War Strategy in South Asia: Making a Military Commitment to Pakistan, 1947–1954," *Journal of American History*, vol. 75, 1988, pp. 812–40.

5 For an assessment of the debate between traditionalists and revisionists as it started to gain intensity, see Norman A. Graebner, "Cold War Origins and the Continuing Debate: A Review of Recent Literature," *Journal of Conflict Resolution*, vol. 13, 1969, pp. 123–32.

6 For key memoirs and diaries, see, for example, Harry S. Truman, *Memoirs: 1945, Year of Decisions*, New York, 1955 and *Memoirs: Years of Trial and Hope, 1946–1952*, New York, 1956; James F. Byrnes, *Speaking Frankly*, New York, 1947 and *All in One Lifetime*, New York, 1958; Dean G. Acheson, *Present at the Creation: My Years at the State Department*, New York, 1969; George F. Kennan, *Memoirs, 1925–1950*, New York, 1967. On Kennan, see David Mayers, *George Kennan and the Dilemmas of US Foreign Policy*, New York, 1988; for influential traditional views, see Arthur M. Schlesinger Jr, "Origins of the Cold War," *Foreign Affairs*, vol. 46, 1967, pp. 22–52; Herbert Feis, *From Trust to Terror: The Onset of the Cold War, 1945–1950*, New York, 1970.

7 Adam Ulam, *The Rivals: America and Russia Since World War II*, New York, 1971; William Taubman, *Stalin's American Policy: From Entente to Detente to Cold War*, New York, 1982; Vojtech Mastny, *Russia's Road to the Cold War*, New York, 1979.

8 Bruce R. Kuniholm, *The Origins of the Cold War in the Near East: Great Power Conflict and Diplomacy in Iran, Turkey, and Greece*, Princeton, N.J., 1980.

9 Hugh Thomas, *Armed Truce: The Beginnings of the Cold War, 1945–1946*, New York, 1987, pp. 102–3.

10 Randall B. Woods and Howard Jones, *The Dawning of the Cold War*, Athens, Ga, 1991, p. 30.

11 John Spanier, *American Foreign Policy Since World War II*, 7th ed., New York, 1977, p. 29; Norman A. Graebner, *Cold War Diplomacy: American Foreign Policy, 1945–1975*, 2nd ed., New York, 1977.

12 Barton J. Bernstein (ed.), *Politics and Policies of the Truman Administration*, Chicago, 1970; Lloyd C. Gardner, *Architects of Illusion: Men and Ideas in American Foreign Policy, 1941–1949*, Chicago, 1970; Thomas G. Paterson, *Soviet–American Confrontation: Postwar Reconstruction and the Origins of the Cold War*, Baltimore, Md, 1973; Bruce Kuklick, *American Policy and the Division of Germany: The Clash with Russia over Reparations*, Ithaca, N.Y., 1972; Walter LaFeber, "Roosevelt, Churchill, and Indochina, 1942–45," *American Historical Review*, vol. 80, 1975, pp. 1277–95.

13 Gar Alperovitz, *Atomic Diplomacy: Hiroshima and Potsdam*, New York, 1965.

14 Martin Sherwin, *A World Destroyed: The Atomic Bomb and the Grand Alliance*, New York, 1977; Barton J. Bernstein, "Roosevelt, Truman, and the Atomic Bomb, 1941–1945: A Reinterpretation," *Political Science Quarterly*, vol. 90, 1975, pp. 23–69.

15 William O. McCagg, *Stalin Embattled, 1943–1948*, Detroit, Mich., 1978; Gavriel D. Ra'anan, *International Policy Formulation in the USSR: Factional "Debates" During the Zhadonovschina*, Hamden, Conn., 1983; Robert Slusser, *Soviet*

Economic Policy in Postwar Germany, New York, 1953.

16 Paolo Spriano, *Stalin and the European Communists*, London, 1985; Fernando Claudin, *The Communist Movement: From Comintern to Cominform*, New York, 1975.

17 Michael MccGwire, "The Genesis of Soviet Threat Perception," Washington, 1987; Charles B. McLane, *Soviet Strategies in Southeast Asia: An Exploration of Eastern Policy under Lenin and Stalin*, Princeton, N.J., 1966; Steven I. Levine, "Breakthrough to the East: Soviet Asian Policy in the 1950s," in Warren I. Cohen and Akira Iriye (eds), *The Great Powers in East Asia, 1953–1960*, New York, 1990, pp. 296–316.

18 See the reviews of the memoirs by Novikov and Molotov, in *Cold War International History Project Bulletin*, vol. 1, 1992, pp. 16–22; Nikita Khrushchev, *Khrushchev Remembers: The Glasnost Tapes*, Boston, 1990, pp. 69, 100–1; Andrei Gromyko, *Memoirs*, New York, 1989, pp. 107–12, 138.

19 Dmitri Volkogonov, *Stalin: Triumph and Tragedy*, New York, 1991, pp. 501 and 531.

20 Joyce and Gabriel Kolko, *The Limits of Power: The World and United States Foreign Policy, 1945–54*, New York, 1972. The quotations are on pages 31, 11, 8, and 15.

21 John Lewis Gaddis, *The United States and the Origins of the Cold War, 1941–1947*, New York, 1972. The quotation is on p. 358.

22 Gaddis, *The United States*, p. 359.

23 John Lewis Gaddis, *Strategies of Containment: A Critical Appraisal of Postwar American National Security Policy*, New York, 1982, pp. 201, 204; for the postrevisionist critique, see also Gaddis, "The Emerging Post-Revisionist Thesis on the Origins of the Cold War," *Diplomatic History*, vol. 7, 1983, pp. 171–90.

24 Geir Lundestad, "Empire by Invitation? The United States and Western Europe, 1945–1952," *Journal of Peace Research*, vol. 23, 1986, pp. 263–77; *The American Non-Policy Towards Eastern Europe, 1943–1947*, New York, 1975; and *America, Scandinavia, and the Cold War, 1945–1949*, New York, 1980.

25 Fraser Harbutt, *The Iron Curtain: Churchill, America and the Origins of the Cold War*, New York, 1986.

26 Wall, *United States and the Making of Postwar France*; James E. Miller, *The United States and Italy: The Politics and Diplomacy of Stabilization*, Chapel Hill, N.C., 1986; Bullock, *Bevin, Foreign Secretary*; Alan S. Milward, *The Reconstruction of Western Europe, 1945–1951*, Berkeley, Calif., 1984; Robert J. McMahon, *The Cold War on the Periphery: The United States, India, and Pakistan, 1947–1965*, New York, 1994.

27 Ernest May, *The Truman Administration and China, 1945–1949*, Philadelphia, Pa, 1975; "The American Commitment to Germany, 1949–1955," *Diplomatic History*, vol. 13, 1989, pp. 431–60.

28 David Alan Rosenberg, "American Atomic Strategy and the Hydrogen Bomb Decision," *Journal of American History*, vol. 66, 1979, pp. 62–87; "Origins of Overkill: Nuclear Weapons and American Strategy, 1945–1960," *International Security*, vol. 7, 1983, pp. 3–71.

29 McGeorge Bundy, *Danger and Survival: Choices about the Bomb in the First Fifty Years*, New York, 1988.

30 Rosenberg, "Origins of Overkill"; Marc Trachtenberg, *History and Strategy*, Princeton, N.J., 1991; Roger Dingman, "Atomic Diplomacy During the Korean War," *International Security*, vol. 13, 1988/9, pp. 50–91; Robert Wampler, "Nuclear Learning and Nuclear Teaching: The Eisenhower Administration, Nuclear Weapons and NATO Strategy, 1953–1960" (unpublished paper), 1992.

31 Trachtenberg, *History and Strategy*, pp. 167–8.

32 Peter L. Hahn, *The United States, Great Britain, and Egypt, 1945–1956: Strategy*

and Diplomacy in the Early Cold War, Chapel Hill, N.C., 1991; McMahon, *Cold War on the Periphery.*
33 Michael J. Hogan, *The Marshall Plan: America, Britain, and the Reconstruction of Western Europe, 1947–1952*, New York, 1987, pp. 2–3.
34 Hogan, *The Marshall Plan*, p. 32.
35 Thomas A. Schwartz, *America's Germany: John J. McCloy and the Federal Republic of Germany*, Cambridge, Mass., 1991.
36 John Gimbel, *The Origins of the Marshall Plan*, Stanford, Calif., 1976; Timothy P. Ireland, *Creating the Entangling Alliance: The Origins of the North Atlantic Treaty Organization*, Westport, Conn., 1981.
37 Geir Lundestad, *The American "Empire" and Other Studies of US Foreign Policy in a Comparative Perspective*, New York, 1990; Reynolds, "Origins of the Cold War."
38 Bruce Cumings, *The Origins of the Korean War*, vol 2, *The Roaring of the Cataract*, Princeton, N.J., 1992, pp. 38 and 36.
39 Cumings, *The Roaring of the Cataract*, p. 20; see also Thomas J. McCormick, *America's Half-Century: United States Foreign Policy in the Cold War*, Baltimore, Md, 1989.
40 William S. Borden, *The Pacific Alliance: United States Foreign Economic Policy and Japanese Trade Recovery, 1947–1955*, Madison, Wis., 1984; Andrew J. Rotter, *The Path to Vietnam: Origins of the American Commitment to Southeast Asia*, Ithaca, N.Y., 1987.
41 Michael Schaller, *The American Occupation of Japan: The Origins of the Cold War in Asia*, New York, 1985.
42 Borden, *Pacific Alliance*, p. 11.
43 Nancy Bernkopf Tucker, *Patterns in the Dust: Chinese–American Relations and the Recognition Controversy*, New York, 1983; Warren I. Cohen, "Acheson, His Advisors, and China, 1949–1950," in Dorothy Borg and Waldo Heinrichs (eds), *The Uncertain Years: Chinese–American Relations, 1947–1950*, New York, 1980, pp. 13–52.
44 Nancy Bernkopf Tucker, "A House Divided: The United States, the Department of State, and China," in Cohen and Iriye (eds), *Great Powers in East Asia*, pp. 35–62.
45 Gordon H. Chang, *Friends and Enemies: The United States, China, and the Soviet Union, 1948–1952*, Stanford, Calif., 1990, pp. 143–217.
46 For an excellent review of the literature, see Stephen Rabe, "Eisenhower Revisionism: A Decade of Scholarship," *Diplomatic History*, vol. 17, 1993, pp. 97–115.
47 H. W. Brands, *The Specter of Neutralism: The United States and the Emergence of the Third World*, New York, 1988.
48 These generalizations are based on Blanche Wiesen Cook, *The Declassified Eisenhower: A Startling Reappraisal of the Eisenhower Presidency*, New York, 1980; Burton I. Kaufman, *Trade & Aid: Eisenhower's Foreign Economic Policy, 1953–1961*, Baltimore, Md, 1982; Robert J. McMahon, "Eisenhower and Third World Nationalism: A Critique of the Revisionists," *Political Science Quarterly*, vol. 101, 1986, pp. 453–73; H. W. Brands, "The Age of Vulnerability: Eisenhower and the National Insecurity State," *American Historical Review*, vol. 94, 1989, pp. 963–89; David L. Anderson, *Trapped by Success: The Eisenhower Administration and Vietnam, 1953–61*, New York, 1991.
49 See, for example, Richard H. Immerman (ed.), *John Foster Dulles and the Diplomacy of the Cold War*, Princeton, N.J., 1989; Richard A. Melanson and David Mayers (eds), *Reevaluating Eisenhower: American Foreign Policy in the 1950's*, Urbana, Ill., 1987; Stephen E. Ambrose, *Eisenhower: The President*, New York, 1984; Chester J. Pach and Elmo R. Richardson, *The Presidency of Dwight*

   D. Eisenhower, Lawrence, Kan., 1991; Melanie Billings-Yun, *Decision Against War: Eisenhower and Dien Bien Phu, 1954*, New York, 1988.
50 Robert J. McMahon, "Credibility and World Power," *Diplomatic History*, vol. 15, 1991, pp. 455–71.
51 Melvyn P. Leffler, *A Preponderance of Power: National Security, the Truman Administration, and the Cold War*, Stanford, Calif., 1992.

8 From Kennedy to Nixon: the end of consensus

Russell D. Buhite

In the first volume of his insightful *Democracy in America*, written in the 1830s, Alexis de Tocqueville observed that "it seems as if all the minds of Americans were formed upon one model, so accurately do they follow the same route."[1] Over the following century there were a great many occasions on which American minds did not pursue the same route; but during World War II and the first twenty years of the Cold War a remarkable consensus once again emerged: general agreement about American foreign policy. President Franklin D. Roosevelt was able to lead the United States through its most popular war because the overwhelming majority of the American people profoundly believed that the nation was fighting for vital interests – territorial, economic, political – as well as for ideals of universal validity. Among these ideals were not only the "truths" and rights incorporated in the Declaration of Independence and the first ten amendments of the American constitution, but basic human values as well. The onset of the Cold War brought a continuation of the consensus. Just as Hitler, Mussolini, and the Japanese military leadership had posed palpable threats to American ideals and interests so too, people thought, did Josef Stalin – a brutal tyrant who had killed millions of his compatriots in the Soviet Union: the kulaks who stood in the way of collectivized agriculture; military officers who might threaten his internal hegemony; loyal party members and former close associates who knew of his crimes; the executioners; the executioners of the executioners; etc., etc. He imprisoned millions of others out of paranoid fear or irrational whim. He also presided over a hostile, messianic ideology that promoted revolution in other nations and rejected many of the norms of international behavior.

To most Americans and, not insignificantly, most Europeans, Stalin's regime was as ruthless, as dictatorial, as expansionist, as Hitler's. To many, the argument that the Soviets had achieved a legitimate right to extend their empire over Eastern Europe because they had carried the heaviest burden in the defeat of Germany was like saying that a Mafia gangster who served the public good by killing a murderous rival suddenly became deserving of recognition and standing in the larger community. Stalin's death in 1953 and events of the late 1950s brought hope for an improved relationship but did not alter the basic presumption. If anything, the election of John F. Kennedy in 1960 signaled a clarion call to take up more vigorously the challenge against the Soviet Union and its ally, the People's Republic of China.

Although historians and political scientists are in general agreement that public opinion played an extraordinary role in defining American foreign policy in the 1960s – for part of the decade the World War II/Cold War consensus and for the remainder skepticism about American international commitments – they are not in accord in interpreting some of the most important events of the era. Both the Cuban Missile Crisis and the Vietnam War, for example, have generated heated historiographical controversies. This essay will address those controversies and others, but, on the assumption that students are not attracted to densely historiographical essays, will do so while focusing on the nexus of opinion and policy decision in the administrations of Kennedy, Lyndon B. Johnson, and Richard M. Nixon.

Public opinion is not an easy phenomenon for the diplomatic historian to assess. It is difficult to define, hard to measure, and, because archival evidence is usually inadequate, nearly impossible to gauge in its impact on policymakers. It is best understood if broken down into its major components: opinion-makers, among whom are editors of major newspapers, prominent journalists, television commentators, government consultants and officials, leading businessmen and an occasional scholar or other professional; an attentive or interested public, which would consist of 20 to 30 per cent of the American people, depending on the issue; and mass opinion, which will be 70 to 80 per cent of the people who are generally uninterested in foreign policy except on major issues of war and peace. The opinion-makers shape opinion and often policy itself through their access to the media and to policymakers. The attentive public may influence policy in any number of ways, including personal contact with government officials or through organizations formed for that purpose. Mass opinion usually makes an impact through polls and elections. Presidents and other top policymakers are usually much more concerned about and give more attention to the elites than to mass opinion, except in the presence of a presidential election.[2]

In the period down through the early stages of the Vietnam War the vast majority of Americans, as polled in George Gallup's interviews, saw foreign affairs generally and communism specifically as the most important problems that the United States faced. Both the attentive and the mass publics supported America's international behavior, the idea of a strong US military establishment, and those political figures, both Democrats and Republicans, who endorsed the standard cold-war line. Politicians who spoke up against US policies did not fare well. The historian will search in vain for any clear demarcation between liberal and conservative positions on basic foreign policy matters until after the major US build-up in Vietnam.[3]

That the World War II/Cold War consensus broke down after the mid-1960s is evident in the primary concerns of Americans from that time onward. Polls have shown that far fewer Americans identified foreign policy issues as being of overriding importance and far fewer members of the mass public believed that the United States should maintain the range of international commitments incurred in the previous twenty years. More importantly for this essay, a large segment of the attentive public came to regard as misguided American political, economic, and, especially, military intervention in the Third World.[4]

Convinced that the administration of President Dwight Eisenhower had not only allowed the nation's defenses to slip but had failed the test of competition in the developing world, John F. Kennedy brought to the presidency a commitment to global involvement on a grand scale. "We will pay any price, bear any burden, meet any hardship, support any friend, oppose any foe," Kennedy said in his inaugural address, "to assure the survival and success of liberty." And he brought with him to Washington a group of intelligent and confident advisers – "action intellectuals" – who would help fashion his new activist policies. Among the most prominent of these "action intellectuals" were McGeorge Bundy, a former Harvard dean who became National Security Adviser, Walt Rostow, an MIT professor who became head of the Policy Planning Staff of the State Department, and Robert McNamara, former president of the Ford Motor Company who became Secretary of Defense. That these men and Kennedy's brother, Robert, who became Attorney General, would overshadow Secretary of State Dean Rusk in the fashioning of policy was always the intention of the new president, although Rusk's credentials as Rhodes scholar, college professor, military officer, former Assistant Secretary of State for Far Eastern Affairs in the Truman administration and as head of the Rockefeller Foundation, were truly impressive.

Although President Kennedy's team became interested in third-world areas from Indochina to the Congo, it was in Latin America that they chose to challenge most forcefully the perceived communist threat. Their strategy was multi-faceted: economic development fostered through the Alliance for Progress, in which the United States would expend $20 billion to help Latin American nations modernize their economies – a plan usually cited as a failure but one that achieved some successes;[5] an educational effort carried forward through the Peace Corps in which young men and women would teach Latin Americans some basic technical skills; and military action through which the United States would seek to stabilize friendly governments, quell guerrilla uprisings and destabilize or overthrow unfriendly regimes.

No regime seemed more unfriendly than that of Fidel Castro in Cuba and none received as much attention from the Kennedy administration. Kennedy believed that both strategic necessity and American public opinion required that he get rid of the Castro government, which, by January 1961, had become a Soviet client. Accordingly, in that same month he gave his approval to a CIA plan begun under the Eisenhower administration, in which some fifteen hundred Cuban exiles trained in Florida and in Guatemala would land at the

Bay of Pigs on the coast of Matanzas province, draw support from Cubans disaffected with Castro and overthrow his government. A fiasco of embarrassing dimensions, the operation failed when the men were captured within forty-eight hours of their landing because the hoped-for Cuban uprising did not occur and Kennedy refused to authorize air power. To compound the embarrassment for the new administration, Kennedy then had to pay a $10 million ransom to retrieve the invaders.

Worried about the administration's credibility both at home and abroad, the Kennedy team over the next eighteen months redoubled its efforts to dispose of Castro. In October 1961 Kennedy authorized contingency plans for an invasion of Cuba and then, in November, approved the establishment of Operation Mongoose, the largest covert operation undertaken up to that time – an operation that would receive funding in the amount of $50 million a year and the participation of over four hundred CIA officers. Kennedy's plans for overthrowing Castro were thus two-dimensional: a military invasion if such action were required to get the job done and a series of plots to murder the Cuban dictator. The latter included agents giving him poison cigars, planting exploding sea shells in his favorite snorkeling area, and arranging with US mobsters to send "hit teams" to Havana. Many of these plans were extensions of secret operations already begun in the Eisenhower administration. One such plan had a female CIA operative, of whom Castro had already had carnal knowledge, insinuate herself into his bedroom and then, at an appropriate time, slip poison pellets into his drink – a plan that failed because the young woman had hidden these pellets in her cold cream, where they melted and became useless.[6]

Possibly to forestall an American invasion, assuming some Soviet knowledge of Kennedy administration plans and plots but almost certainly to redress the Soviet Union's enormous inferiority in intercontinental ballistic missiles, Premier Nikita Khrushchev decided in the spring of 1962 to place Soviet medium and intermediate range missiles in Cuba. Given its failure at the Bay of Pigs and its inability to respond to the Soviets' building of the Berlin Wall in the summer of 1961, not to mention the roughing-up Kennedy received from Khrushchev at the Vienna Conference of June 1961, the Kennedy administration held deep-seated fears of appearing inadequate in view of the prevailing consensus. The existence of missiles in Cuba was a challenge that Kennedy, for several reasons, not least of which was domestic political considerations, simply could not refuse.

Since 1962 was a Congressional election year and the Republicans, led by Senator Kenneth Keating of New York, had begun making charges as early as September about administration neglect of possible nuclear missiles in Cuba, Kennedy had to act as soon as he had hard evidence of their existence. Imagery intelligence quickly confirmed their presence to the president after U-2 air reconnaissance overflights of Cuba on 14 and 15 October.

Kennedy's initial move was to appoint a high-powered panel of advisers, the Executive Committee of the National Security Council (Ex Comm), to consider various policies that would result in the removal of the Soviet missiles. Among the options considered were private appeals to the Cuban and Soviet governments, taking the matter to the United Nations, a US air strike followed by an invasion, and a blockade or quarantine of arms shipments to the island. Leading military members of the Ex Comm, the Chairman of the Joint Chiefs of Staff General Maxwell Taylor and the Air Force Chief of Staff, General Curtis Lemay, among others, strongly urged the use of an air strike, but Kennedy was attracted to the idea endorsed by his brother Robert for a blockade – on the assumption that it left other options open.

On 22 October, Kennedy went on national television to announce the presence of the missiles and the decision to impose the quarantine, in support of which he quickly placed 180 US warships in the Caribbean, B-52 bombers loaded with nuclear bombs in the air and US ground forces on high alert. What followed was a week filled with almost unbearable tension for both policymakers and world opinion. "The smell of burning," Khrushchev said, "hung in the air." When, on 24 October, the Soviet ships bound for Cuba stopped dead in the water short of the blockade line, a ray of hope appeared for a peaceful resolution of the crisis – hope that was enhanced when a KGB agent in Washington, Alexsandr Fomin, contacted ABC news reporter John Scali on 26 October with a proposal that the two sides conclude a deal in which the United States would promise not to invade the island in return for Soviet withdrawal of the missiles. On the following day, when Khrushchev seemed to raise the stakes by insisting on US removal of its missiles from Turkey as well, Kennedy came back, using his brother Robert as envoy to the Soviet ambassador, Anatoly Dobrynin, with the proposal that the United States would promise not to invade Cuba if the missiles were withdrawn and would later take US missiles out of Turkey – an action that it was going to take anyway because of the obsolescence of these missiles. This part of the deal, Robert Kennedy reported, would have to remain secret. Khrushchev agreed, and the crisis ended on 27 October.

A series of meetings attended by many of those who had participated in the events, as well as by scholars who had studied the crisis, at Harvard University in October 1987, in Moscow in January 1989, and in Havana in January 1992 has revealed that the crisis was even more dangerous than people thought at the time. American officials in October 1962 assumed that the Soviets had stationed between 12,000 and 16,000 military personnel in Cuba; there were actually about 42,000. The Soviets had built twenty-four launchers for 1020 nautical-mile missiles and had loaded these missiles with nuclear warheads, the latter a fact not known by US officials during the crisis. They had built sixteen launchers for 2200 nautical-mile missiles but these missiles were cut off by the US quarantine. Most disturbing is the revelation that the Soviets had provided their forces in Cuba with six tactical rocket launchers and nine tactical nuclear warheads to use in the event of an American invasion, and that they had given the Soviet commander in Cuba,

General Issa Pliyev, authority to fire these missiles at his discretion. Moreover, it is now known that the KGB agent, Fomin, whose démarche was seen
at the time as coming from Khrushchev, was actually acting on his own.[7]

Given the danger inherent in a showdown of this nature, Kennedy's
motives for abjuring private diplomacy in favor of a public ultimatum deserve
further scrutiny. Among his motives were a desire to convince the Soviets
that aggression did not pay, to show that the United States was a credible
actor on the world stage, and to address the strategic threat posed by the
existence of these missiles only ninety miles from American soil. One other
possible motive, concern about domestic politics and American public
opinion, remains a matter of some contention – indeed it has emerged as the
focus of historiographical controversy.

Kennedy's defenders, most notably Arthur Schlesinger, Jr, Elie Abel,
Theodore Sorensen, McGeorge Bundy, David Welch, and James Blight, have
written books and articles praising the president's measured, unemotional
approach to the problem of the missiles. They argue that Kennedy was
motivated by strategic concerns and the need to demonstrate American
resolve both to the Soviets and to the larger international community, and that
he was not motivated by concerns with US politics. Sorensen has argued that
Kennedy and his advisers at the time believed the blockade would adversely
affect the administration's political standing, while Welch and Blight have
pointed out that Kennedy was prepared, as a last resort, to arrange a public
trade of the US missiles in Turkey for the withdrawal of the Soviet missiles
from Cuba – hardly a move designed to gain political points. Bundy and
others claim that the deliberations of the Ex Comm betray no evidence of
worry about domestic politics.[8]

Revisionists have interpreted Kennedy's motives in a diametrically opposite way. I. F. Stone has argued that the reasons Kennedy opted for a
confrontation were partly to assuage his "inferiority complex," partly to
prove his machismo, and mainly to strike a political blow before the
November elections. Quiet diplomacy, Stone argues, would have led to
protracted negotiations going well beyond November and would not have
provided the drama that the president required. Another revisionist, Ronald
Steel, has criticized Kennedy's obsessional concern with the removal of the
missiles before election day and has argued that a private back channel
overture to Khrushchev would have terminated the crisis without fanfare.
Barton Bernstein has advanced a more inclusive interpretation but likewise
stresses Kennedy's attention to his domestic political constituency.[9]

Recent scholarship, particularly an article by Richard Ned Lebow in the
fall 1990 issue of *Diplomatic History*, while noting the complexity of
Kennedy's motives, demonstrates that domestic politics and American public
opinion – opinion-makers, the attentive public and mass opinion – surely
played a part in his decisions. Because Kennedy had used the Cuban issue in
the campaign against Richard Nixon, charging that the Republicans had been
derelict for allowing the existence of a communist regime in the Caribbean,

he could not have it appear that he, the tough candidate, would permit the establishment of a Soviet military base in Cuba. As Roger Hilsman, a Kennedy adviser, put it: "President Kennedy and his administration were peculiarly vulnerable on Cuba."[10] According to Hilsman, Kennedy was mainly concerned with the opinion of the elites, the opinion-makers, if he did not reverse the Soviet move: he would be "faced with a revolt from the military, from the hardliners in other departments, both State and CIA, from not only Republicans on Capitol Hill but some Democrats, too."[11]

Remarks by John Kenneth Galbraith, Kennedy's ambassador to India, reinforce the Hilsman view: "The political needs of the Kennedy administration," Galbraith said of the Soviet missiles, "urged it to take almost any risk to get them out."[12] To Robert McNamara's comment in the midst of the crisis that "I don't think there is a military problem here . . . This, this is a domestic political problem," President Kennedy added his observation that if he had not acted, "I would have been impeached."[13] Whether he actually feared impeachment or was simply rationalizing his policy of confrontation, Kennedy certainly had serious concerns about the popular perception of his ability to perform adequately in the arena of the Cold War. Fortunately, in this instance, to quote Secretary of State Rusk, "the other fellow blinked" and Kennedy emerged from the crisis appearing strong and courageous.

Although the United States would never show assiduous restraint toward foreign intervention or foreign ideology in its sphere of influence, Kennedy's policy in the Third World, where possible, combined anti-communism with the promotion of democratic principles and economic stability; indeed, the Kennedy administration hoped that liberal democratic nation-building would prove a successful alternative to communism in all of the developing world, including Latin America. Thus, when citizens of the Dominican Republic in 1961 assassinated the execrable dictator Rafael Trujillo, who had plundered and misgoverned the country since 1931, Kennedy hastened to support his democratically elected successor, Juan Bosch, an anti-communist liberal, a poet and philosopher. When Bosch, who had been in exile for over twenty-five years, demonstrated a greater capacity to inflame than to govern and was himself removed from power in a military coup after only seven months in office, Kennedy did not like the result but accepted it. Kennedy's successor in the presidency, Lyndon B. Johnson, seemed to like the result, fearing the prospect of another Castro regime in the Caribbean. In any event, because he saw Juan Bosch as a woolly-headed, rather impractical intellectual, Johnson supported the regime of Donald Reid Cabral.

Another coup, launched on 24 April 1965 by followers of Bosch, frightened Johnson because they included some communists and admirers of Fidel Castro; four days later the president sent in the marines. "The last thing we want to have happen is a communist takeover in that country," Johnson proclaimed to a group of his advisers meeting at the White House just before the landing of a large American force.[14] At first announcing that the purpose of the intervention was to protect American nationals, Johnson sent only a small contingent of men, but as it became clear to him that assuring a pro-American outcome in that chaotic country would take a much greater effort, he dispatched over 22,000 troops. Not an incidental factor in his decision was his perception that the overwhelming majority of Americans shared his aversion to another communist regime in the Caribbean and would support the intervention – and he was right. The Organization of American States, which Johnson contemptuously dismissed as being so inept that it couldn't "pour piss out of a boot if the instructions were written on the heel," also tepidly endorsed the action.

Occurring after the beginning of the major US build-up in Vietnam, the Dominican intervention represented a transitional event in the 1960s from the World War II/Cold War consensus to the new skepticism about American international behavior. Opinion-makers, as demonstrated in the editorials of three leading American newspapers, warmly endorsed Johnson's decision to intervene. The *New York Times* stated that "there was a solid reason for the United States to put a marine landing force into Santo Domingo. The reason was to protect Americans and to evacuate those who desire to leave." Later, the *Times* noted that Johnson's determination not "to see another communist state established in this hemisphere will command national support." The *Washington Post* agreed: "the United States does not want to see the Dominican Republic become another communist Cuba." As might have been expected, the *Chicago Tribune* did not hesitate to interpret the Dominican rebellion as "animated by communist elements" against whom President Johnson had to act. Through most of the period of the military intervention itself, few opponents came forward in either political party or in any particular area of American life, although one notable exception was Senator Wayne Morse of Oregon who, foreshadowing the later opposition on Vietnam, charged that the United States had become "military power drunk." At least until the final phase of the American operation, when negotiations were conducted to establish a new Dominican government and some criticism surfaced – some of which came from the Chairman of the Senate Foreign Relations Committee, J. William Fulbright – Johnson enjoyed nearly the same level of support that Kennedy had received during the Cuban Missile Crisis. A part of the reason for this is that Johnson helped to mold opinion by vigorously promoting his policy in speaking engagements to a wide array of professional organizations around the country.[15]

That Johnson, who succeeded to the presidency on 22 November 1963 following the assassination of President Kennedy, shared the world view of almost every other policymaker of his generation seems abundantly clear: that appeasement did not pay; that America's primary interest lay in containing the expansionist aspirations of the Soviet Union and the People's Republic of China, and in successfully competing for influence in the developing world. Less interested in "nation-building" than in stopping communism, his approach to international problems tended to be more overtly military than Kennedy's had been, although he was guided by many of Kennedy's advisers and assumed he was continuing his predecessor's programs. Among "the best and the brightest" who stayed on with Johnson were Robert McNamara, who remained as Secretary of Defense until differences over Vietnam led to his resignation in 1968; McGeorge Bundy, who served as National Security Adviser until 1966; Walt Rostow, who moved from the State Department to take over Bundy's post; and Dean Rusk, who, as Secretary of State, gained influence in policy formation under Johnson. In addition to these influential advisers were many second-echelon players who helped to define Johnson's Vietnam policy.

Johnson inherited a problem in Vietnam that went back far beyond the administration of his immediate predecessor. A French colony in the nineteenth and early twentieth centuries, occupied by the Japanese during World War II, and the site of bitter fighting between indigenous nationalists and French imperialists between 1945 and 1954, Vietnam became a direct object of cold-war contention during the Eisenhower administration, when the United States supported a non-communist regime south of the 17th parallel, thereby obstructing unification of the country under the communist government of the north. The region received greater American attention in the late 1950s and early 1960s because the government in Hanoi, frustrated over its failure to achieve domination of the whole country through peaceful means, began an uprising against the troubled, increasingly unpopular, American-sponsored government of President Ngo Dinh Diem in the south. By the time of Kennedy's death in 1963 the conflict had reached a critical stage, wherein the United States had two basic options: to allow events to take their course, which would probably mean communist control of all of Vietnam, or to increase assistance to the south.

On 2 October 1963, the date of the return from a week-long visit to Vietnam by two of his most trusted advisers, General Maxwell Taylor and Robert McNamara, both of whom came back convinced of the need to save South Vietnam, President Kennedy issued a statement asserting that "the security of South Vietnam is a major interest of the United States."[16] In 1961 the United States had 948 troops in Vietnam, along with a handful of CIA personnel who were performing a variety of cloak-and-dagger activities to help the Diem government cope with the National Liberation Front – or "Vietcong" as it was labeled by President Diem to denote its communist affiliation. Kennedy also continued to provide technical and financial assistance to the South Vietnamese in accordance with his assessment of American interests.

In addition to giving the South Vietnamese lessons in political science and urging democratic reform, the Kennedy administration markedly increased the number of American military forces in Vietnam during 1962–3: by the middle of 1962 the number was up to 5,000; by the end of the year it was 11,000; by the time Johnson succeeded to the presidency there were over 16,000, all of them functioning as "advisers." Diem, whose overthrow on 1 November 1963 had been encouraged by the United States in the hope of producing a stronger government, was followed by a series of leaders, which weakened rather than strengthened the chances of resisting communist pressures.

Informing the Vietnam policies of both the Kennedy and Johnson administrations in the early and mid-1960s were assessments of the People's Republic of China as a peculiarly virulent and aggressive regime, and an interpretation of the Asian theater of World War II that portrayed Southeast Asia as having been of critical importance to the Allied nations. If a vital interest of the United States in the 1940s had been that no hostile power should dominate a large part of Asia and the Pacific, and if it had been necessary to wage a war partly to prevent the Japanese from establishing control of Southeast Asia, American officials reasoned that it was no less important in the 1960s to guarantee access to that region by the United States and its allies. An expansionist China, using one means or another to dominate that area, represented a threat at least as critical to American interests as the one posed earlier by Japan. Containing China thus became the central focus of American policy in Vietnam during the early phases of the increased US involvement in Southeast Asia.[17]

China had become the *bête noire* of American policymakers for a variety of reasons. As a former battlefield enemy in Korea, ally of the Soviet Union and bitter opponent of US policies in East Asia, China seemed determined to expand its influence by creating a series of client states in the region. American officials interpreted, in the darkest terms, such Chinese moves as the annexation of Tibet and the attack on India, not to mention the bombarding of the offshore islands in 1954–5 and 1958. President Kennedy came to the conclusion that the sobering effect of the Cuban Missile Crisis had created a favorable climate for a Soviet–American understanding to avoid mutual destruction. He saw little hope for such an understanding with China; indeed, he saw China as the more dangerous of the two cold-war enemies facing the United States. With their development of the atomic bomb in 1964, the Chinese leadership seemed capable of making good on their belligerent pronouncements about fostering wars of national liberation in Southeast Asia. Using the bomb for blackmail, they could, moreover, frighten the political leaders of Southeast Asia into closer association with China. The fact that all southeast Asian nations possessed very large Chinese populations made this close association seem all the more likely. In the case of Vietnam itself, much of which had been part of China until the tenth century, and with which it now shared a frontier, it seemed logical that China would seek domination or control. If all of Vietnam became communist, the communization of the rest of Southeast Asia, under Chinese direction, would become easier to achieve. Chinese involvement in the uprising against the government of Indonesia in the fall of 1965, though badly timed and a colossal failure, tended to confirm American assessments of Chinese intentions.

A part of the conventional wisdom influencing American policy was the "domino" theory, or some variation thereof, which was first enunciated by

President Eisenhower. If Vietnam fell to communism, other states in Southeast Asia would surely fall in turn, like dominoes, until all of the region, including the Philippines, Malaysia, Indonesia, and possibly New Zealand and Australia, had been lost. That such a development would prove inimical to American interests seemed axiomatic to US officials, not only because Americans would be denied access to an area rich in natural resources, but the major trade routes and sea lanes in that part of the world would also become inaccessible. All this region, it was assumed, would become closely associated with the People's Republic of China.

Two other concerns suffused American policy in the Kennedy–Johnson years: that Vietnam had considerable intrinsic importance and that the United States must show its resolve and its capacity to combat "wars of national liberation." Vietnam possessed sufficient quantities of manganese, tungsten, chromium, phosphate, tin, coal, zinc, rubber, rice and various exotic woods to make it a valuable prize in the Cold War. For nearly a century the French had reaped enormous profits from this rich but unfortunate country. If the United States and its allies did not require these materials for their own needs, it was nonetheless important to deny them to their enemies. Wars of national liberation, in which communist insurgents carried on guerrilla activity to disrupt the normal processes of life and issued propaganda to win over poverty-ridden peasants, presented a challenge that American officials believed they could not ignore. Developing countries could slide into the communist orbit, adding to the overall strength of China and the Soviet Union, just as decisively through "wars of national liberation" as through conventional wars of conquest. It was necessary that the United States demonstrate the futility of such a war in Vietnam, otherwise countless other wars of this type would occur.

If policymakers saw Vietnam as representing a valuable interest of the United States they were no less influenced by the other part of the prevailing consensus in their interpretation of events in that country. The Vietcong regularly displayed insufficient sensitivity to human values in their brutal murders and kidnapping of civilians in the south; and the regime in the north, while holding no brief for American democratic ideals, aggressively attempted to impose its dictatorial system on the people of the south. "Just like FDR and Hitler, just like Wilson and the Kaiser," Lyndon Johnson said, it was necessary "to quarantine aggressors over there."[18]

Because the communists made huge gains in 1964, President Johnson had either to increase American assistance or suffer the acute embarrassment associated with having "lost" another Asian country. The Republican candidate for the presidency, Senator Barry Goldwater of Arizona, advocated taking the war to North Vietnam and criticized administration policy as too soft and conciliatory. Although Johnson ridiculed Goldwater as a warmonger, he began to pursue secretly a number of the very policies advocated by Goldwater – to the point that within a year he had appropriated and implemented nearly every program recommended by his Republican opponent.

He increased the number of US advisers to about 23,000 by the end of 1964, began US air strikes in Laos, had the CIA infiltrate sabotage units into North Vietnam and increased American economic aid to the south. Then, in early August 1964, he used the issue of North Vietnamese torpedo boat attacks on the US destroyer *Maddox* ten miles off the North Vietnamese coast to secure Congressional passage of the Tonkin Gulf Resolution – a measure passed 466–0 in the House and 88–2 in the Senate – that authorized the president to "take all necessary measures to repel armed attack against the forces of the United States and to prevent further aggression."[19]

Accepting this as a sort of declaration of war, over the next three and one-half years Johnson took very extensive measures indeed. In response to a Vietcong attack on the US air base at Pleiku in early February 1965 and the killing of several American airmen, Johnson initiated air attacks on North Vietnam, attacks that soon became a campaign under the code name "Operation Rolling Thunder." Within a few months Johnson had sent 80,000 men to South Vietnam; by early 1969 the United States had 542,000 troops there engaged in the longest, most expensive and one of the bloodiest and most brutal wars in American history – a war that dragged on inconclusively, a war in which the United States seemed to lose sight of the proper connection between means and ends, a war inconsistent with American ideals, and a war that became increasingly unpopular with the American people.

A quick survey of the two types of opinion, mass and elite, indicates how minds changed during the course of the war. In 1964 and 1965, fully two-thirds of the American people stated that they paid no attention to the Vietnam question, and a high percentage could not locate the country on a map. During the initial build-up of 1965 and early 1966 a large majority of the American people supported administration policy and, while criticism and disaffection began to grow into 1967, most Americans preferred escalation to de-escalation or withdrawal. In other words, more people voiced dissatisfaction with the war because the United States was not taking strong enough steps to win it than objected to the intervention itself. Between 1968 and 1970 objections increased geometrically: by September 1970 over 55 per cent of mass opinion favored withdrawal from the war.[20]

Elite sentiment either paralleled or moved ahead of mass sentiment. At the end of 1965, J. William Fulbright of Arkansas, ardent anti-communist, supporter of the prevailing foreign policy consensus and backer of the Tonkin Gulf Resolution, came out against the war. Other key political figures in both political parties followed suit: on the Democratic side were, among others, Senators Frank Church of Idaho, Eugene McCarthy of Minnesota, Joseph Clark of Pennsylvania, George McGovern of South Dakota, Robert Kennedy of New York and Edward Kennedy of Massachusetts; among Republicans speaking out against the conflict by 1968 were Senators John Sherman Cooper of Kentucky, Thruston Morton of Kentucky, Mark Hatfield of Oregon, Charles Goodell of New York, Jacob Javits of New York and Paul "Pete" McClosky of California. Richard Nixon, the Republican candidate for the presidency in 1968, also began to question the wisdom of the debilitating US involvement in Southeast Asia. Other elites in a variety of professions, especially journalists and academics, came to the forefront of the antiwar movement.

Feelings about Vietnam were becoming so intense that when, on 23 January 1968, the North Koreans seized the US electronic intelligence vessel, the USS *Pueblo*, operating in international waters off the North Korean coast, the response in Congress and among the public was remarkably quiescent. The Vietnam involvement had created such general skepticism about American policy that a great many Americans assumed that the *Pueblo* had violated Korean waters. Even such hawks as Senator John Stennis of Mississippi warned against "rash overreaction," while Senator Fulbright spoke contemptuously of the *Pueblo* mission as "imprudent" and "stupid." A Harris poll showed that nearly 60 per cent of the American people favored a peaceful resolution of the crisis and negotiation rather than military action toward securing the return of the crew. Both the *New York Times* and *Wall Street Journal* cautioned that the United States should avoid another war at nearly whatever cost.[21]

Reaction to the *Pueblo* seizure was but one indication of the change in the national mood. On 30 January, as US officials contemplated what to do about the *Pueblo* incident, the North Vietnamese launched the so-called Tet Offensive, which had a devastating psychological impact on the nation. A massive military undertaking that included attacks on thirty-six South Vietnamese cities and led to fighting *within* the US embassy compound in Saigon, the North Vietnamese action, though extremely costly for them militarily, profoundly undermined the administration's promises of a successful conclusion to the war and further eroded public confidence. Indeed, the questioning of the war after Tet led to a breakdown in public civility, which further exacerbated the bitter divisions that already existed within the United States – and this began to take its toll on US policymakers in early 1968 and eventually contributed to a major policy reversal.

Two other developments stand out as notable in the policy reversal: a request by General William C. Westmoreland, Commander of US forces in Vietnam, in the wake of Tet, for 206,000 additional American troops; and a task force study organized by the new Secretary of Defense, Clark Clifford, which led him to oppose the conflict. Clifford's task force discussions – in which a number of his subordinates, most notably Assistant Secretary of Defense Paul Warnke, counselled against further escalation – convinced him that Westmoreland's request should not be fulfilled. Clifford now urged the president to negotiate an end to American involvement. As an old friend and longtime supporter of the war, Clifford could influence Johnson as few others could do; Johnson was profoundly shaken by this defection, which contributed significantly to his announcement on 31 March that he would not seek re-election to the presidency and that he would pursue a negotiated peace.

When Richard Nixon succeeded Lyndon Johnson after defeating the Democratic candidate, Vice President Hubert Humphrey, in the troubled presidential election of 1968, he did so with a definite set of predispositions about the place of Vietnam in the larger context of American foreign policy. As an old hard-line anti-communist, but as a greater proponent of *realpolitik* than he was of upholding principles, Nixon planned to implement a set of policies predicated less on ideology than on practical considerations of American interest. He and his National Security Adviser, Henry Kissinger, a Harvard professor and author of books on the nineteenth-century European balance of power as well as on the impact of nuclear weapons on American foreign policy, believed that the United States had to terminate its involvement in Vietnam. Nixon and Kissinger believed that the war was too costly, in terms of American lives and money, that it limited the nation's ability to act in other areas that were of greater importance, and that it was tearing at the fabric of American life in a way that undermined domestic support of US foreign policy as a whole.

A key to understanding the Nixon–Kissinger approach to Vietnam is that, while they wished to extricate the United States from that seemingly interminable war, they were determined to avoid the appearance of losing it. They hoped to engineer the withdrawal of US forces while a non-communist government remained in power in the south – at least for a decent interval. It is important to note that by 1968 a prime objective of the United States was, as Johnson's Assistant Secretary of Defense John McNaughton put it, "to avoid the harmful appearances" that would result if the United States failed to demonstrate its resolve.[22] What this meant in practice was that the credibility factor had begun to dominate American policy by the time Nixon came to office; and, unfortunately, it continued to dominate policy throughout his first term.

That an intangible like "credibility" became the primary concern of the US government is hardly surprising in view of developments affecting China in the late 1960s. The Chinese convulsion known as the Cultural Revolution, which was perpetrated by Chairman Mao Tse-tung, his wife, and a coterie of officials around them, had so enfeebled that nation, so isolated it internationally, that it could not endanger Southeast Asia – if indeed it had ever intended to do so. Nixon, long a vigorous defender of the Nationalists on Taiwan, began a series of steps that he expected to have a positive effect on the Chinese leadership: withdrawal of the Seventh Fleet from the Taiwan strait, use of the term "People's Republic of China" instead of "Mainland China," lifting of trade restrictions, and the initiation of a variety of cultural exchanges. Because the Chinese needed the United States as a counterweight to the Soviet Union, they were responsive. In April 1971 they invited an American table tennis team to visit China for a series of matches; in July they asked Kissinger to come to Peking (Beijing) to begin the normalization of relations; and in February 1972 the world witnessed something it had not expected to see, given the previous twenty-three years of Sino-American hostility: the president of the United States drinking mao-tai toasts with his Chinese hosts in Peking while a Chinese band played "America the Beautiful." This trip facilitated a new beginning, in everything but name, of diplomatic relations between the two countries.

To complement his opening to China, Nixon began a policy of détente with the Soviet Union: in May 1972, not long after his visit with the Chinese, he travelled to Moscow. The purpose of all this diplomatic to-ing and fro-ing was to create doubt in the minds of the leaders in each communist state about the other's agreements with the United States: to use improved relations with the Chinese to make the Soviets more manageable and to use better relations with the Soviets to make the Chinese more conciliatory. Nixon's strategy of détente involved extending credits to the Soviets, attempting to make them more dependent on the American technology that they so desperately needed to improve their economy, and improving trade and cultural ties. The strategy led, in the area of trade, to large sales of American wheat in 1972 – approximately 25 per cent of that year's crop – and to increased exports of a number of other American products to the Soviet Union. Détente also meant seeking areas of congruent Soviet–American interests and attempts to scale back the arms race. Significantly, out of Nixon's innovative initiative came such successes as the first strategic arms limitation agreement, SALT, and Soviet agreement on Western access to the city of Berlin.

During one of Henry Kissinger's discussions with Premier Chou En-lai after the opening to China, Chou, who recognized the central role the containment of China played in US Vietnam policy, asked why, given the fact that the United States and his country were working out their differences, the United States still had all those troops in Vietnam. Obviously, what the grand design had failed to achieve, as Chou's remark revealed, was positive Soviet and Chinese assistance in satisfactorily ending the Vietnam War.

Apart from attempting to secure Soviet–Chinese pressure on Hanoi, Nixon's strategy had several dimensions specific to Vietnam. One dimension was diplomatic, involving secret negotiations begun in 1969 between Kissinger and North Vietnamese representatives. Another was "Vietnamization." To defuse the debate in the United States and solidify the domestic foundations of his foreign policy, as well as to gain some leverage in the negotiations, Nixon attempted to connect the withdrawal of the hundreds of thousands of American troops to the willingness of North Vietnam to strike a face-saving deal for the United States: greater conciliation by Hanoi would bring a more rapid American withdrawal. Withdrawal – US forces were reduced by 400,000 within two years – meant turning over responsibility for the fighting to the South Vietnamese, to whom Nixon was providing huge amounts of arms and equipment. He combined this approach with removal of many of the restraints on the US military which, translated into action, meant more bombing of the north.

Ultimately, because Nixon and Kissinger would not accept the North Vietnamese prescription for ending the war – which consisted of unilateral removal of all US troops, repudiation of the South Vietnamese government of President Nguyen Van Thieu, and total, decisive victory for North Vietnam – it took them four years to conclude a war that they came into office determined to end quickly. During this four-year period they approved the secret bombing of Cambodia, the invasion of Cambodia in the spring of 1970, which triggered violent protests in the United States and the killing by National Guardsmen of unarmed Kent State University students, the US-supported South Vietnamese invasion of Laos in May 1971, and the bombing of North Vietnam in December 1972 – all of which was accompanied by the loss of 20,000 American men and approximately 600,000 Vietnamese. During the Christmas bombing of 1972, carried out to induce North Vietnamese concessions at the bargaining table and impress President Thieu with American resolve, Nixon, to quote Senator William Saxbe, seemed to "take leave of his senses." Henry Kissinger himself referred to his policy as "calculated barbarism." The saturation bombing conducted by the United States dealt devastating blows to targets in the Hanoi–Haiphong area, which had previously been off-limits, as well as causing the loss of at least fifteen B-52 bombers; but the strategy probably brought no better peace terms than might have been achieved the previous October.

An inversion of the norm in historical writing about American wars, the historiography of the conflict in Vietnam follows a contemporary–critical, revisionist–supportive pattern – and the synthesis that is now emerging is closer to the contemporary than to the revisionist interpretations. The literature is so vast that it is possible to address only a couple of the most important themes: the morality or immorality of American involvement and the question of whether or not the United States could have won.

Either directly or by implication a great many scholars have questioned the morality of American intervention in Vietnam. To some, like George Herring, who has written the best and most widely read short history of the war, the mere fact of the mistaken application of containment in that unhappy land not only undermined American interests but compromised long-standing moral ideals.[23] To others, like Gabriel Kolko, a new Left historian writing in the 1960s, the extension of American hegemony in the furtherance of the structural needs of the capitalist system predicates the moral indictment.[24] Frances Fitzgerald's popular work condemns the cultural intrusion of the United States on a peasant people whose customs and traditions American officials never understood.[25] Telford Taylor attacks the prosecution of the war, arguing that the bombing of innocent civilians, napalm attacks and such practices as the widespread use of chemical defoliants made American behavior particularly repugnant.[26]

The "revisionist" point of view – which in the context of the Vietnam War refers to the conservative defense of US policy – regards the war as highly moral in both its prosecution and its objectives. Norman Podhoretz, in *Why We Were in Vietnam*, states the revisionist case most forcefully, arguing that in attempting to contain communism, an evil, repressive system, the United

States acted *ipso facto* in pursuit of a moral objective. To Podhoretz, moreover, any comparison of American military action in Vietnam to atrocities of World War II are specious: the Allied bombing of Dresden, for instance, took 35,000 lives while the Christmas bombing of North Vietnam took only approximately 1,500. One of the earliest and most sophisticated of revisionist works, Guenter Lewy's *America in Vietnam*, makes the argument that not only did the United States fight in a morally defensible manner, but charges of genocide are outrageously exaggerated: the populations of South and North Vietnam, he points out, *increased* by 4 million and 3 million respectively over the 1965–73 period.

The revisionists, aided and abetted by the conservative political ideology in vogue in the 1980s, also contend that the United States could have won the war. Some, like Lewy, argue that greater emphasis on pacification would have done the trick. Harry Summers and Bruce Palmer Jr, writing as military strategists, say that a US declaration of war on North Vietnam and a greater conventional military effort would have resulted in victory – or that a mixed strategy of a naval blockade of North Vietnam combined with an American forcing of fixed battles would have won out. Frederick Nolting, who was US ambassador to South Vietnam between 1961 and 1963, joined the revisionist school in 1988 by arguing that a more faithful adherence to Kennedy's early strategy of support for President Ngo Dinh Diem would have changed the outcome.[27]

The revisionist arguments have found little support in the work of the postrevisionist scholars, who are convinced that the United States could not have won the war – at least not by any definition of winning that would have served American interests or conformed to the original objectives.[28]

Therein lay a central problem of the American experience in Vietnam: the balancing of means and ends. As President Nixon showed in the Christmas bombing in 1972, the United States might have gone on to devastate North Vietnam, might have gone further and "made the rubble bounce," might have undertaken a lengthy and costly occupation of the entire country, making the United States the full-fledged successor to the French. But such an effort at "winning" would surely have substantiated historian George Santayana's aphorism that "fanaticism consists in redoubling your effort when you have forgotten your aim."[29]

Neither the American public nor American policymakers would be quick to forget the tragedy of Vietnam, and a "Vietnam syndrome" influenced foreign policy in a variety of ways for many years to come. Every potential third-world intervention, whether in a peripheral area like Angola or in a vital one like central America, would stimulate debate in terms of the moral and material costs of Vietnam; every invocation of America's global mission would provoke intense questioning; every implication of America's benevolence or the superiority of its international behavior would thenceforth bring scornful reproach. On foreign policy, consensus gave way to skepticism and uncertainty. That is the larger meaning of the Vietnam years.

142   *Russell D. Buhite*

NOTES

1 Alexis de Tocqueville in Phillips Bradley (ed.), *Democracy in America* vol. I, New York, 1991, p. 267.
2 See Melvin Small, "Public Opinion," in Michael Hogan and Thomas G. Paterson (eds), *Explaining the History of American Foreign Relations*, New York, 1991, pp. 165–71; James N. Rosenau, *Public Opinion and Foreign Policy*, New York, 1961, pp. 35–41. The literature on public opinion and foreign policy is vast, done by a mix of historians and political scientists. Important studies include Melvin Small, *Johnson, Nixon and the Doves*, New Brunswick, N.J., 1988; Gabriel A. Almond, *The American People and Foreign Policy*, 2nd ed., New York, 1960; Ralph B. Levering, *The Public and American Foreign Policy, 1918–1978*, New York, 1978; Montague Kern, Patricia W. Levering, and Ralph B. Levering, *The Kennedy Crisis: The Press, The Presidency, and Foreign Policy*, Chapel Hill, N.C., 1983; Leonard A. Kusnitz, *Public Opinion and Foreign Policy: America's China Policy, 1949–1979*, Westport, Conn., 1984; Doris Graber, *Processing the News: How People Tame the Information Tide*, New York, 1984; Terry L. Deibel, *Presidents, Public Opinion, and Power: The Nixon, Carter and Reagan Years*, New York, 1987.
3 Ralph B. Levering, "Public Opinion, Foreign Policy, and American Politics since the 1960s," *Diplomatic History*, vol. 13, 1989, p. 385.
4 Levering, "Public Opinion," p. 386. Ole R. Holsti and James N. Rosenau, *American Leadership in World Affairs: Vietnam and the Breakdown of Consensus*, Boston, 1984, chaps 1 and 2.
5 Studies critical of the Alliance for Progress include Jerome Levinson and Juan de Onis, *The Alliance That Lost Its Way: A Critical Report on the Alliance for Progress*, Chicago, 1970; Joseph S. Tulchin, "The United States and Latin America in the 1960s," *Journal of Inter-American Studies and World Affairs*, vol. 30, 1988, pp. 1–36; and Stephen Rabe, "Controlling Revolutions: Latin America, the Alliance for Progress, and Cold War Anti-Communism," in Thomas G. Paterson (ed.), *Kennedy's Quest for Victory: American Foreign Policy, 1961–63*, New York, 1989, pp. 105–22. Rabe argues that the alliance was long on promises and short on delivery owing to a complex of factors including flawed planning and obstructions in Latin America. A recent essay evaluating the alliance in its Central American context provides a revisionist interpretation. See Craig Ferguson, "The Alliance for Progress and the Social Transformation of Central America," unpublished M.A. Thesis, University of Oklahoma, July 1990.
6 James G. Hershberg, "Before the Missiles of October: Did Kennedy Plan a Military Strike against Cuba," *Diplomatic History*, vol. 14, 1990, pp. 173–9, 168n. Arthur M. Schlesinger, Jr, *Robert Kennedy and His Times*, Boston, 1978, p. 482. Kennedy's obsession with Cuba is discussed in a number of other studies as well. Among the best are Thomas G. Paterson, "Fixation with Cuba: The Bay of Pigs, Missile Crisis, and Covert War against Fidel Castro," in Paterson (ed.), *Kennedy's Quest for Victory*, pp. 123–55; Barton J. Bernstein, "Pig in a Poke, Why did Kennedy Buy the Bay of Pigs Invasion?" *Foreign Service Journal*, vol. 62, 1985, pp. 28–33; Thomas G. Paterson and William J. Brophy, "October Missiles and November Elections: The Cuban Missile Crisis and American Politics, 1962," *Journal of American History*, vol. 73, 1986, pp. 87–119. See also Trumbull Higgins, *The Perfect Failure: Kennedy, Eisenhower, and the CIA at the Bay of Pigs*, New York, 1987, pp. 79–176, and Warren Hinckle and William W. Turner, *The Fish is Red: The Story of the Secret War against Castro*, New York, 1981.
7 Raymond L. Garthoff, "Cuban Missile Crisis: The Soviet Story," *Foreign Policy*, vol. 72, 1988, p. 73. See also Raymond Garthoff, "The Havana Conference on the

Cuban Missile Crisis," *Cold War International History Project Bulletin*, vol. 1, 1992, pp. 2–3.

8 Arthur M. Schlesinger Jr, *A Thousand Days: John F. Kennedy in the White House*, Boston, 1965; Elie Abel, *The Missile Crisis*, Philadelphia, Pa, 1966; Theodore Sorensen, *Kennedy*, New York, 1965; David A. Welch and James G. Blight, "An Introduction to the Ex Comm Transcripts," *International Security*, vol. 12, 1987/8, p. 8. Bundy quoted in Richard Ned Lebow, "Domestic Politics and the Cuban Missile Crisis: The Traditional and Revisionist Interpretation Reevaluated," *Diplomatic History*, vol. 14, 1990, p. 473. In addition to Schlesinger and Sorensen as cited above, many former Kennedy officials have written accounts of the crisis, all in one way or another praising Kennedy's calm and judicious handling of it. Most of them see this as JFK's finest hour, his actions unsullied by concerns other than national interest. Among the most prominent of these works are Robert F. Kennedy, *Thirteen Days: A Memoir of the Cuban Missile Crisis*, New York, 1969; McGeorge Bundy, *Danger and Survival: Choices about the Bomb in the First Fifty Years*, New York, 1988; George W. Ball, *The Past Has Another Pattern: Memoirs*, New York, 1982; Theodore C. Sorenson, *The Kennedy Legacy*, New York, 1969; Abram Chayes, *The Cuban Missile Crisis: International Crises and the Role of Law*, New York, 1974; Pierre Salinger, *With Kennedy*, Garden City, N.Y., 1966; Maxwell Taylor, *Swords and Plowshares*, New York, 1972; and Raymond L. Garthoff, *Reflections on the Cuban Missile Crisis*, Washington, 1987.

9 I. F. Stone, "The Brink," *New York Review of Books*, vol. 6, 14 April 1966, pp. 12–16; Ronald Steel, "End Game," *New York Review of Books*, vol. 12, 13 March 1969, pp. 15–18; Barton Bernstein, "The Week We Almost Went to War," *Bulletin of the Atomic Scientists*, vol. 32, 1976, pp. 12–21; Bernstein, "The Cuban Missile Crisis: Trading the Jupiters in Turkey?," *Political Science Quarterly*, vol. 95, 1980, pp. 97–125; Lebow, "Domestic Politics and the Cuban Missile Crisis," pp. 471–4.

10 Quoted in Lebow, "Domestic Politics and the Cuban Missile Crisis," p. 475.

11 Lebow, "Domestic Politics and the Cuban Missile Crisis."

12 Galbraith quoted in Lebow, "Domestic Politics and the Cuban Missile Crisis."

13 McNamara quoted in Lebow, "Domestic Politics and the Cuban Missile Crisis," pp. 476–7.

14 Merle Miller, *Lyndon: An Oral Biography*, New York, 1980, p. 518.

15 Quotations from Brigette Lebens Nacos, *The Press, Presidents, and Crises*, New York, 1990, pp. 59–61, 67. Johnson's intervention in the Dominican Republic is addressed in several studies that are decidedly critical of his actions and motives. Among the critical works are Piero Gleijeses, *The Dominican Crisis: The 1965 Constitutionalist Revolt and American Intervention*, Baltimore, Md, 1978; Jerome Slater, *Intervention and Negotiation: The United States and the Dominican Revolution*, New York, 1970; Abraham F. Lowenthal, *The Dominican Intervention*, Cambridge, 1972. Defense of Johnson's policy is provided in Bruce Palmer Jr, *Intervention in the Caribbean: The Dominican Crisis of 1965*, Lexington, Ky, 1989. Palmer sees the intervention as necessitated by a real danger of communist expansion in the western hemisphere.

16 Quoted in David W. Levy, *The Debate over Vietnam*, Baltimore, Md, 1991, p. 34.

17 Russell D. Buhite, *Soviet–American Relations in Asia, 1945–1954*, Norman, Okla., 1981, pp. 214–15.

18 Quoted in Doris Kearns, *Lyndon Johnson and the American Dream*, New York, 1976, p. 329.

19 *Congressional Record*, 88th Congress, 2nd sess., 7 August 1964, p. 18471.

20 William L. Lunch and Peter W. Sperlich, "American Public Opinion and the War in Vietnam," *Western Political Quarterly*, vol. 32, 1979, pp. 21–32.

21 *Congressional Record*, 90th Congress, 1st sess., 29 January 1968, p. 882;

Fulbright to Huey Cochran, 30 January 1968, Fulbright Papers, University of Arkansas Library, Fayetteville, Arkansas; William A. Armbruster, "The *Pueblo* Crisis and Public Opinion," *The Naval War College Review*, vol. 23, 1971, pp. 87–9.

22 Jonathan Schell, "Reflections, The Nixon Years – VI," *New Yorker*, vol. 51, 7 July 1975, pp. 46–7. There are a number of recent scholarly works on Kissinger and Nixon that not only assess the grand design but achieve a high degree of balance. Among the best of these are Robert D. Schulzinger, *Henry Kissinger: Doctor of Diplomacy*, New York, 1989; Stephen Ambrose, *Nixon: The Triumph of a Politician*, New York, 1989; Richard Thornton, *The Nixon–Kissinger Years: The Reshaping of American Foreign Policy*, New York, 1989; Herbert Parmet, *Richard Nixon and His America*, Boston, 1990; and Joan Hoff-Wilson, "Nixingerism, NATO, and Détente," *Diplomatic History*, vol. 13, 1989, pp. 501–26.

23 George C. Herring, *America's Longest War: The United States and Vietnam 1950–1975*, New York, 1979.

24 Gabriel Kolko, *The Roots of American Foreign Policy: An Analysis of Power and Purpose*, Boston, 1969.

25 Frances Fitzgerald, *Fire in the Lake: The Vietnamese and the Americans in Vietnam*, Boston, 1972.

26 Telford Taylor, *Nuremberg and Vietnam: An American Tragedy*, Chicago, 1970.

27 Harry G. Summers Jr, "Lessons: A Soldier's View," in Peter Braestrup (ed.), *Vietnam as History: Ten Years after the Paris Peace Accords*, Washington, D.C., 1984, pp. 109–14; Harry G. Summers Jr., *On Strategy: A Critical Analysis of the Vietnam War*, Novato, Calif., 1982; Bruce Palmer Jr, *The 25 Year War: America's Military Role in Vietnam*, Lexington, Ky, 1984. See also Robert A. Divine, "Vietnam Reconsidered," *Diplomatic History*, vol. 12, 1988, pp. 79–93; Frederick Nolting, *From Trust to Tragedy: The Political Memoirs of Frederick Nolting, Kennedy's Ambassador to Diem's Vietnam*, New York, 1988.

28 See, for example, George McT. Kahin, *Intervention: How America Became Involved in Vietnam*, New York, 1986. A good critique of the "win" perspective and summary of the literature may be found in Thomas G. Paterson, "Historical Memory and Illusive Victories: Vietnam and Central America," *Diplomatic History*, vol. 12, 1988, pp. 1–18. See esp. the note on p. 6.

29 Quoted in Ball, *The Past Has Another Pattern*, p. 387.

9   From détente to the Gulf
Walter LaFeber

Recent United States foreign policy has been a search to find solutions for
a series of problems that erupted between 1971 and 1974. These problems,
of course, did not suddenly appear during those years; they had deep
historical roots running back into the 1960s and beyond. By 1974, however,
they were so obvious and dangerous that they shaped the political agenda
for the next generation. The foreign policies of presidents Richard Nixon,
Gerald Ford, Jimmy Carter, Ronald Reagan, and George Bush can be
interpreted as varied responses to these dangers. The dangers, however,
were ultimately removed neither by these policies nor even by the collapse
of the communist bloc in 1989–91.

   By the mid-1980s, a decade of perspective enabled historians and policymakers to begin to understand the depth of the problems. In his history of the
Cold War, *America's Half-Century*, Thomas J. McCormick believed US
power in world affairs reached "high tide" in the 1960s, but "in the near-
decade" between 1968 and the American Bicentennial in 1976, the United
States began to bear a striking resemblance to Great Britain a century earlier:
while remaining the world's greatest power, "the United States nevertheless
showed clear evidence of decline in its capacity to perform its functions as
center" for the world's capitalist system. Power, especially of the economic
variety, flowed away from Americans who found themselves unable to enjoy
the living standards they had assumed to be their birthright before the 1970s.[1]
Paul Kennedy's *The Rise and Fall of the Great Powers* also argued that the
United States might be following Britain's example as a declining nation.
Placing his argument in five hundred years of history, and demonstrating that
a number of empires began their decline when they over-invested in military
power instead of economic productivity, Kennedy argued that the Soviets
faced a far greater danger of decline than did Americans, but that the United
States faced a sad future if it could not halt the economic downturn that
accelerated in the 1970s and 1980s.[2]

   A number of similar books that appeared in the 1980s triggered a wide-
ranging debate over how various foreign policies might solve these problems.
Many analysts, however, refused to accept the thesis that America was in
decline. Samuel P. Huntington argued that the most profound problems dated

only from the early 1980s, that they were results "not of the American economy, but of Reagan economics," and that they could therefore be easily solved by changing President Reagan's misguided policies. Huntington added that while other powers, such as Japan and West Germany, had grown economically powerful, the United States continued to hold about the same percentage of world economic activity in the 1980s as it enjoyed in the late 1960s; little actual decline was evident. He especially, however, disputed Kennedy's thesis that US military spending had undermined the nation's well-being. Americans' determination to over-consume and under-save had actually weakened their system: "If the United States falters economically, it will not be because U.S. soldiers . . . stand guard" in Germany, but "because U.S. men, women, and children overindulge themselves in the comfort of the good life. Consumerism, not militarism, is the threat to American strength."[3]

These accounts marked the boundaries of the debate that evolved after the early 1970s. Most histories of the 1970s and 1980s, it should be noted, sharply differed from those analyzing the pre-1972, actually pre-1969, years because of the types of documentation available. In studying foreign policy before Nixon, scholars have exploited the rich materials opening at the various presidential libraries; the millions of pages of formerly top-secret documents at the Lyndon B. Johnson Library in Austin, Texas, for example, have made possible dozens of excellent books on Vietnam, and the sources have been supplemented by the release, in however censored and unfortunate a form, of US Department of State papers in *Foreign Relations of the United States*, a series that has reached the early 1960s. For post-1969 materials, however, the Nixon, Ford, Carter, and Reagan presidential libraries are only slowly starting to release important foreign policy documents. Carter's personal diary, for example, remains largely closed. Many State, Defense, and Central Intelligence Agency documents can be found in the valuable *Declassified Documents Quarterly (DDQ)*, a service accessible to many university libraries that makes the important documents that have been declassified each week at the presidential libraries and government agencies available on microfiche. But the *DDQ* materials are not systematic, edited, or, often, complete, and must be used with care.

The student studying the post-1973 years therefore must provide proper context for the *DDQ* material with at least three other types of sources. First is memoir material by former officials. In certain instances, for example, the books by Carter administration officials that are noted in detail below are valuable and various points of view emerge clearly. Other memoirs, such as Henry Kissinger's two volumes, are detailed and important, but have not been sufficiently balanced by authoritative books of other officials who had different points of view. Some memoirs, such as those of Presidents Ford and Reagan, offer little new that is important to students.

A second type of available materials comprises accounts by journalists who have sources inside various governments and the means to obtain key documents. Seymour Hersh's scathing critique of Kissinger's diplomacy, and

Jane Mayer's and Doyle McManus's detailed analysis of Reagan's stumbling policies after 1984, are examples. *At the Highest Levels*, by Michael Beschloss and Strobe Talbott, was written from privileged access inside both the United States and former Soviet governments to provide the most detailed analysis of the historic 1989–91 years, including the destruction of the Soviet Union and the communist bloc, that we shall probably have for a generation. The danger with such accounts is that they usually rely on privileged interviews with former officials who might not, or might not want to, remember accurately what they did and said when in power. Moreover, the necessary documents to check such interviews remain closed. In the case of Beschloss and Talbott, this meant that they primarily based their book on information provided by those they talked to, or who would talk at length with them; this meant, in turn, that the authors missed the highly important Defense Department point of view that regarded Soviet policy from a different perspective than that of the White House and the State Department. Without documentation that is systematic and as complete as possible, even good journalism can have problems as history.[4]

The third type of material can be found in certain newspapers, including *The New York Times*, *Washington Post*, *Boston Globe*, *Chicago Tribune*, *Los Angeles Times*, and *Philadelphia Inquirer* that think of themselves as newspapers of record and have skilled reporters stationed worldwide. Ideologically, these journals cover a narrow political spectrum, with the *Boston Globe* perhaps the most liberal and the *Chicago Tribune* the most conservative. *Newsweek*, *Time*, *Foreign Affairs*, *Foreign Policy*, *New Republic*, *The Atlantic*, *New York Review of Books*, and *Harper's* are among respected periodicals that publish foreign affairs articles, but the student using them understands that, unlike the better newspapers, they often do not pretend to present a detailed record of events and usually advance sharp points of view that, while offering important perspectives, must be used with care.

And yet, even without the necessary documents, it is necessary to come to terms with the post-1972 years because they so clearly mark a fundamental turn in twentieth-century history. Before the early 1970s, the United States had enjoyed overwhelming superiority in nuclear weapons and was easily able to pay its own expenses. It dominated the international economy and feared few challengers. By 1971, however, President Nixon declared in a speech in Kansas City, Missouri that a new era was emerging. Instead of one or two superpowers, world affairs were being shaped by "five great economic superpowers" – the United States, the Soviet Union, Japan, Western Europe, and China – four of whom challenge Americans "on every front." If they did not want to suffer the fateful decline of ancient Greece and Rome, Nixon warned, Americans had to understand that "economic power will be the key to other kinds of power" in the future, and that their power would depend on how well they disciplined themselves to win that economic race. Nixon's view of history was a partial preview of McCormick's and Kennedy's arguments.

Nixon spoke from bitter experience. Burdened by the tremendous costs of the Vietnam War and resulting inflation, in 1971, for the first time since 1894, the nation suffered an unfavorable balance of merchandise trade. Americans were becoming less competitive in the vital international marketplace. Eyeing re-election in 1972, the president took four major steps to try to correct the growing problems. First, he understood that the United States was no longer strong enough economically to back the dollar, the only real international currency, with gold, as it had since 1945, because its gold supply was running out as the metal was used to pay debts overseas. Nixon instead announced that the dollar would "float" – that is, would be left to the whims of the marketplace where private business and other governments could directly influence its worth.

Next, he began to pull troops out of Vietnam and by 1973 accepted a peace that was advantageous to the communists in North Vietnam. Third, as he withdrew US troops, Nixon pushed others to pick up the burden – in the Pacific he asked more from Japan, in the Middle East he designated the willing Shah of Iran. Finally, in historic trips to Beijing and Moscow, Nixon set in place a détente policy that aimed at arms control and friendlier economic relations. By playing Chinese off against Russians, and vice versa, the president believed he had found a cheaper means of containing the two communist giants.

But "King Richard" had a brief reign. In 1973, Congress discovered that the president had committed a criminal act by trying to cover up a crime: the burglarizing of the Democratic Party headquarters in Washington's Watergate Hotel by White House agents in June 1972. In August 1974, Nixon avoided possible impeachment by becoming the first person to resign the presidency. Until 1973 the presidency was, without doubt, the world's most powerful office – in part because it controlled the globe's greatest military power, in part because Americans trusted the president. But that trust had been betrayed, and had been betrayed, moreover, just after the previous five presidents led the nation into the disastrous Vietnam conflict. Congress responded by passing the War Powers Act. For the first time since the founding of the Republic, the legislative branch tried in a systematic way to restrict the president's ability to commit troops to a possible or actual conflict.[5] The War Powers Act never became as effective as its supporters hoped, but the presidency had nevertheless been weakened.

Arthur Schlesinger Jr's *Imperial Presidency* appeared in 1973 to chronicle the historical rise of the strong Chief Executive and the beginnings of its fall. The book helped trigger a major debate among historians. Critics observed that Schlesinger's book was less coherent than it should have been because as a liberal Democrat he wanted a strong presidency to reform American society at home, but he also wanted a weaker executive that could not secretly or singlehandedly take the nation into war overseas. This distinction between domestic and foreign affairs, however, was becoming quite blurred. A strong domestic president who could control Congress and special public-interest groups so as to make reforms at home could too easily roll over Congress and public opposition in order to conduct a militant policy abroad. The United

States domestic economy, moreover, was becoming so integrated into a world economy – for example, the dependence of American automobile owners on Middle East oil – that Schlesinger's distinction between the two was becoming meaningless. The real question, as Johnson's former National Security Council adviser, McGeorge Bundy, pointed out, was how an over-militarized and over-extended foreign policy was returning home to bring down the imperial presidency. A key part of the answer, as Theodore Draper noted in his *Present History*, was how Nixon and his chief foreign-policy adviser, Henry Kissinger, tried to cover their activities at home and overseas in an attempt to save the policies and, indeed, the Nixon administration itself.[6]

Even if, therefore, the 1973 War Powers Act never worked as its authors hoped, the political arena in which the "imperial president" had grown so dominant was transformed. The president remained the world's most powerful figure, but he was increasingly being held accountable by a more aggressive Congress and new public groups who discovered how to lobby Congress effectively. Theodore Lowi, in his book *The Personal President*, saw dangers in this new situation. When tied up by Congress or the special interest groups, Lowi warned, the President could try to break loose with a spectacular overseas exploit, even a war, because historically the American people had almost always supported their Chief Executive in overseas adventures – even when such adventures failed. Congress was not able to stop such sudden presidential acts, Lowi noted, and therefore it would be dangerously tempting for presidents to get a political fix, as Lowi called it, for their political fortunes by striking out militarily abroad. This interpretation helped explain a number of US foreign adventures after 1972 that are noted below, including Reagan's invasion of Grenada in 1983 and Bush's decision to send 27,000 troops into Panama in late 1989. Lowi's book provided insight into how and why the post-1972 presidency was becoming more, not less, active.[7]

Certainly Nixon's and Kissinger's foreign policies were highly active in the Middle East in late 1973 after Egypt attacked Israel. When Washington aided Israel and pushed its allies to do the same, Arab oil producers retaliated by placing an embargo on vital oil shipments to the United States and some of its allies. As gasoline prices tripled, runaway inflation threatened western economies. Kissinger, whom Nixon had named secretary of state just before the war erupted, began to loosen the oil producers' grip by negotiating a truce in the war, and then working secretly with the Shah of Iran and other non-Arab producers to obtain large amounts of oil. Americans discovered that grave dangers now came not from just the communist military giants but from regions the French termed "the Third World," or the less industrialized but mineral-rich nations. Areas such as the Middle East, Latin America, Africa, and South Asia were becoming vital markets and sources of raw materials for the United States. But these regions were themselves undergoing tremendous change and instability as they tried to develop.[8]

Historians have concluded that Kissinger and Nixon left a mixed legacy in foreign affairs. By 1974–5 their policy of détente with the Soviets was collapsing. The policy was in part the victim of Congress's refusal to approve the economic deals that Nixon had made in Moscow that underpinned the political and arms-control agreement. The policy was also set back by the intervention of the United States and the Soviet Union on opposite sides of a growing, brutal, civil war in the east African nation of Angola that was freeing itself of Portuguese colonialism. Stephen Ambrose, in his standard biography of Nixon, appreciates the president's skilled breakthrough to China in 1971–2 and to the Soviet Union in 1972, but emphasizes the difficulty Nixon had in measuring and adjusting to the domestic restraints on his power. That difficulty led him first to secret diplomacy, then to criminal acts, and finally to resignation.[9]

Before coming to power, Kissinger had fully realized, as he had written beforehand, that obtaining sufficient domestic support was the "acid test" for a statesman in a democracy. As Robert Beisner noted, however, "Kissinger failed the 'acid test' . . . because he stepped outside the constraints imposed by the American political tradition without [being able to reshape] that tradition itself." Roger Morris, once a close aide of Kissinger, resigned after his boss and Nixon invaded Cambodia in 1970 to expand the war in Southeast Asia. Morris then became an important historian of the Nixon–Kissinger policies. He argued that Kissinger was brilliant in devising global strategies to deal with the new, post-1972 world that was emerging, but painfully deficient in understanding the domestic restraints on US officials, and he was to be criticized for his willingness to deceive Congress and the public, and sometimes even his own staff, as Kissinger attempted to break out of these restraints.[10]

In his two volumes of memoirs, Kissinger provided the most passionate and detailed response to such criticisms. He claimed that fundamental problems for the rational conduct of foreign affairs are built into the US political system, especially in terms of the public's tendency to swing back and forth between wanting to follow a tough interventionist policy and then, as in Vietnam or Africa, wanting to pull out rapidly and concentrate on issues at home. Kissinger also argued that Americans, without the long historical experiences of Europeans, did not appreciate the necessity to follow complex balance-of-power policies that required subtlety, patience, and, often, direct confrontation with those, such as the Soviets and their communist satellites, who tried to upset the global balance of power – a balance that was, after all, in favor of the United States. The inability of Americans to understand their world, Kissinger concluded, often forced leaders like himself to work secretly with other nations to maintain the proper balance. He argued that at times these associates could even include the Russians and Chinese because they shared with Americans the fear of instability, especially disorder that could lead to nuclear confrontation; moreover the communist giants had strong governments that, unlike even democratic regimes in such areas as Europe or Latin America, could deliver on their promises. Critics, led by Walter Isaacson and Seymour Hersh, countered by pointing out that Kissinger's secretive and devious approach undermined the public's long-term confidence in his and other officials' policies. The one topic on which these criticisms were muted was Kissinger's shuttle diplomacy in 1973–4 when he succeeded in stopping the Middle East war and starting a peace process. But as critics, led by Raymond Garthoff, pointed out, even this success came at a high price: by working successfully to shut Soviet influence out of these peace talks in the Middle East, and in other areas such as southern Africa and especially Angola, Kissinger angered Moscow and helped undermine the détente that he and Nixon had so painfully put into place.[11]

These criticisms have been brought into one detailed volume, Isaacson's *Kissinger*. Basing his book on 150 interviews as well as declassified documents (although too few from Nixon's and Kissinger's papers, which remain under their own control and largely closed), Isaacson has written the standard biography of the man and a highly influential analysis of the 1969–76 policies.

Kissinger remained as secretary of state under Nixon's appointed successor, Gerald R. Ford, who served as president from August 1974 until January 1977. The new president and Kissinger negotiated arms-control deals with the Soviets in 1975, but Congress refused to ratify them. As Steven Rearden has explained, a longtime government official, Paul Nitze, led conservative arms experts who blasted the 1975 deal for allowing the Soviets to enjoy an advantage in the largest rockets. Détente was rapidly giving way to a renewal of the Cold War, a war fought especially in the Third World. Kissinger lamented that the United States had to fight this war with new disadvantages, including a weaker presidency and an assertive, but disorganized, Congress. The father of the US containment policy against the Soviets, however, disagreed; George Kennan believed that although Congress and the public could certainly act irresponsibly, US officials themselves had refused to meet the Soviets half-way, especially in restraining the development of the most dangerous strategic nuclear weapons, during both 1956–61 and the post-1972 years.[12]

Over this intense discussion of how to come to terms with the new, post-1972 world perched the ghost of the US defeat in Vietnam. Kissinger constantly tried to exorcise this ghost by arguing that the tragedy in Southeast Asia must not prevent Americans from using military force to defend their interests elsewhere in the world. A few scholars tried to help Kissinger by arguing that the Vietnam struggle had indeed been misunderstood. Guenter Lewy, for example, believed the conflict was no more shameful than America's other twentieth-century wars, and he blamed US political and military officials for failing to devise a winning strategy. Others believed the United States had actually been winning the war until the media, especially television, turned Americans against the effort after early 1968. Historian Robert Divine, however, spoke for many by arguing that the conflict was indeed different, and dangerous, because there had been no clear-cut declaration of war and no convincing case made by the government for the terrible commitment.[13] Of special importance, a detailed, authoritative US Army history concluded that, overall, the media had actually supported the war throughout most of the 1960s, and that Vietnam had been lost because of problems of political and military strategy coming out of Washington, not because of misleading television news coming out of New York.[14] The ghost of Vietnam continued to haunt Americans, but at least the specter was more clearly defined: it was a tragedy caused not by some imagined media conspiracy or antiwar groups but by top officials who did not understand either the revolutionary situation they were entering in Vietnam or the very limited patience of the American people to support a long-term, costly, distant war. This new definition of Vietnam, arising out of the historio-graphical debate after the war, directly shaped US foreign policies after 1974, especially the realization on the part of officials, and notably the American military, that if they again used force abroad, it had to be short, decisive, and with clear-cut and obtainable objectives.

After narrowly defeating Ford in the 1976 election, President Jimmy Carter tried to expel the ghost of Vietnam quite differently than had Kissinger. Understanding how Americans had come to mistrust their national govern-mental institutions, Carter successfully portrayed himself as an outsider – a former Georgia governor with no Washington experience. Carter further concluded that he could both restore the confidence of Americans in their government and give himself a useful diplomatic tool by taking a high moral position – that is, by advocating "human rights" of political prisoners and the oppressed around the world. Supporting human rights could also place Americans on the side of democratic practices in the Third World and within the communist bloc. Patricia Derian received the task of directing human-rights policy in Carter's State Department.[15]

Her efforts, historians have argued, were soon undercut by contradictions within the president's foreign policies. Gaddis Smith pointed out that Carter wanted to achieve other foreign policy objectives more than he did those that concerned human rights. As Smith saw it, the president was pulled in different directions by the principles of morality, that is, pushing human rights, coming to diplomatic settlements with the Soviets and other opponents, and simply building up military strength to overpower those opponents. Carter, for example, welcomed Soviet dissidents and former political prison-ers to the White House until, as Stephen Cohen noted, an angry Moscow government cooled relations with the United States and began cracking down harder on internal dissenters. In the Middle East, as James Bill has argued, the Shah of Iran was one of the world's worst offenders against human rights, but Carter ignored the Shah's transgressions because he needed Iran's oil and military cooperation. In Central America, as historians Tommie Sue Mont-gomery and Lars Schoultz have observed, the president imposed sanctions against El Salvador's bloodthirsty regime, especially after Salvadoran soldiers raped and murdered four American women, including three nuns, in 1980. When, however, revolutionaries opened an offensive to topple the Salvadoran regime, Carter sent aid to prevent the Leftists from gaining power. US officials could never discover a workable human-rights policy.[16]

Carter also tried to put his foreign policy on a new course, while simultaneously dealing with the ghost of Vietnam, by downplaying the threat of communism. "Being confident of our own future," he declared at Notre Dame University, "we are now free of that inordinate fear of communism which once led us to embrace any dictator who joined us in that fear." Vietnam, he added, was "the best example" of such "intellectual and moral poverty."[17]

Those words reflected the views of his secretary of state, Cyrus Vance, who believed that the United States had to give priority to working with the more democratic factions in Africa, Asia, and Latin America, regardless of whether these factions were in power or helped by communists. Vance believed that Carter had to take political risks to settle US problems with third-world nations. This approach drove Carter and Vance to sign the historic Panama Canal treaties in 1977, which promised to turn over the canal to Panama in the year 2000, while protecting US interests in the region. Congress, after intense debate, passed the treaties by the bare two-thirds vote needed. As Burton Kaufman argues, Carter justifiably took credit for succeeding over bitter opposition from Americans who did not want to give back a foot of the strategic waterway that Theodore Roosevelt seized three-quarters of a century earlier. Carter and his supporters noted that the canal was too small for large oil-tankers and aircraft carriers, and it was not worth the blood that Panamanian nationalists seemed willing to shed to gain the canal region.[18] The real debate in the United States pivoted on the question of whether the Americans should retain the right to defend the canal through military intervention, if necessary, both before and after Panama was to take over the waterway. On this key point, as historian Michael Hogan noted, Carter's critics believe that it was congressional leaders, not the White House, that seized the initiative at a critical moment to hammer out the wording that gave the United States that right of intervention, but did not totally alienate the Panamanian government. The critics saw this episode as an example of how, even when Carter had the correct policy, he lacked the political skills to achieve it without rancor and political cost.[19]

By mid-1978, that is, just after Congress ratified the Panama Canal treaties, Vance's views were losing out to the quite different policies of Zbigniew Brzezinski, the National Security Council Adviser, who believed the Soviets posed the great danger. Brzezinski viewed third-world problems in the traditional anti-communist context of post-1945 US policy, and he disagreed with Vance's emphasis on the less industrialized world. The candid memoirs published by Vance, Brzezinski, and Carter provide striking insights into the Vance–Brzezinski contest for the capture of Carter's foreign policies. They also provide the most detailed histories available on the Carter administration's foreign policies. Brzezinski is outspoken in believing he was correct in pushing Carter to extend formal diplomatic relations to China in 1979 as a counterpoise to the Soviets, and also in arguing for a showdown with the Soviets when they attempted to work closely with Ethiopia's revolutionary government on the strategically important east coast of Africa. Vance, for his part, opposed closer relations with China because he believed they needlessly worsened ties with the Soviets, who feared being surrounded by a possible US–Chinese alliance. The secretary of state also argued that Africans could best settle African affairs, and that the east coast of the continent, especially the strategic "Horn of Africa" containing Ethiopia and Somalia, was not worth a superpower conflict. Of special importance, he wanted to treat the arms-control talks with the Soviets as separate from all other issues, in the belief that nothing was as important as preventing possible nuclear annihilation. Brzezinski, however, insisted on "linkage" – which meant, in effect, that the Soviets should not receive a SALT II deal until they promised to behave in such third-world areas as Africa.[20]

Most historians have concluded that Carter's foreign-policy problems were caused mainly by his inability to chart a consistent policy between the Vance and Brzezinski positions. When the president confronted a worsened US economy, and foreign-policy crises erupted, he moved closer to his NSC adviser's hard-line views. For example, in 1977, the United States and the Soviet Union signed a joint statement on Middle East policy, but in mid-1978 Carter brokered a peace treaty between Israel and Egypt without consulting the increasingly angry Russians. The turn in the Carter years, however, occurred most vividly in January–February 1979 when the Shah was driven from power in Iran, oil prices leaped upward, and the American economy declined. As gasoline prices rose 55 per cent in six months, the annual inflation rate, out of control since the early 1970s, reached 13 per cent in mid-1979, the highest rate since 1946. The crisis worsened in November 1979 when Iranian mobs, angry that Carter had allowed the Shah into the United States for medical treatment, stormed the US embassy and seized seventy-six hostages. Fifty-three were held throughout 1980 as Americans grew more frustrated and Carter prepared to run for re-election. Without any help from the Soviets, events in a third-world nation threatened the American system's economic and political foundations.

The published memoirs of the officials involved once again show how the Carter administration was nearly paralyzed by divisions. In Iran the most notable split occurred between US Ambassador William Sullivan, who thought the Shah was a lost cause and wanted to open relations with Ayatollah Khomeini, who ultimately overthrew the Shah, and Brzezinski's NSC, especially Gary Sick who was the specialist on Iran. Sick wanted the Shah to fight to the end against the Ayatollah and, in his own account of the crisis, accused Sullivan of not following instructions and of misleading the Carter administration by means of the dispatches he sent from Iran. Carter's biographer, Burton Kaufman, believes that "Sick was basically correct in his accusations." Above all, however, Kaufman argues that "the manner in which President Carter responded to the crisis pointed to one of the fundamental problems of his entire administration." Instead of either pushing the Shah toward full-fledged resistance or, on the other hand, cutting a deal with the increasingly powerful Ayatollah Khomeini, "Carter chose instead to waffle."[21]

As Iran turned bitterly anti-American, the president's problems were compounded when the Soviets invaded neighboring Afghanistan in December 1979 to save a pro-Moscow regime. The president issued a "Carter doctrine" warning that he would use force, if necessary, to keep the Soviets away from the strategically valuable, oil-rich Persian Gulf. The CIA secretly began sending aid to the Afghanistan resistance forces. Carter imposed economic sanctions against the Soviets and tried to convince his west European and Japanese allies to follow suit. They refused to do so; indeed, West Germany completed a new twenty-five-year trade agreement with Moscow. Carter's attempts to shore up the European alliance system seemed also to be crumbling because of failures to agree on arms-control procedures and the proper policies toward Iran and the Soviet Union. More fundamentally, as Stephen Gill observes, between 1973 and 1977 Brzezinski and New York banker David Rockefeller had realized the long-term structural damage that was weakening the western alliance. They tried to buttress US foreign policy by creating the Trilateral Commission. The Commission included representatives from Japan and Western Europe. It aimed to bridge the foreign policy differences among the three most powerful industrial hubs in the world, and to work out coordinated economic policies before trade wars erupted. The Trilateral approach, however, never worked effectively – as the Afghanistan crisis demonstrated. Growing economic and political strains, exemplified in West Germany's unwillingness to impose sanctions, gravely weakened the attempts to coordinate the policies of the three industrial regions.[22]

In April 1980, Vance resigned as secretary of state because he believed that a plan developed by Carter and Brzezinski to use military forces to free the hostages in Iran would fail and possibly lead to war with the Ayatollah's government. The rescue effort ended tragically in the Iranian desert before US troops could reach the hostages, whom the Iranians finally freed in January 1981. In his memoirs, Vance accused Brzezinski's policy, aimed at isolating and encircling the Soviet Union, of being a major reason why Moscow decided to invade Afghanistan: the Soviets had little "more to lose" in their relations with Washington.[23] Brzezinski was now free to push his anti-Soviet policies, and the frustrated, angry Carter listened. The president had promised in 1976 to cut up to $7 billion from the military budget, but now proposed a $20 billion increase. He had once promised to reduce arms sales to other nations, but now approved sales at a near-record pace of $15 billion. He authorized the building of two of the most destructive nuclear weapons ever devised, the multi-headed MX missile and the Trident II submarine.

Carter had begun his presidency by emphasizing human rights and promising to cut back the arms race. What had caused this stark reversal, this "tragedy" of the Carter administration, as Haynes Johnson characterized the president's failures? Some analysts argue that Carter failed to master Washington's politics – that is, he lost control of policy because he did not know how to form coalitions, manage the media, or define a vision that inspired others to follow.[24] Other scholars, however, believe Carter's problems went far beyond his political or operational style. Having no overall idea of how he wanted to accomplish his foreign policy objectives, he first tried an emphasis on human rights, then tried to work out arms deals with increasingly suspicious Russians, then excluded the Soviets from the Middle East talks, then took a hard-line military position in 1979–80. Unable to reconcile contradictions within his own early policies, such as human rights, and unable to choose between or reconcile the quite different perspectives of Vance and Brzezinski, Carter became confused, some historians argue, until he finally cut through his problems by reverting to a militarized, cold-war set of policies in 1979–80.[25]

In analyzing American mood swings and how they shaped US foreign policy in the 1970s and 1980s, Terry Deibel notes that during the 1980 presidential campaign Americans feared a "loss of control"; an unprecedented 84 per cent agreed that the nation was in "deep and serious trouble."[26] The nation badly wanted some good news. Ronald Reagan gave it to them. His most important speech writer, Peggy Noonan, afterwards wrote in an important memoir of the Reagan administration that the new president "was probably the sweetest, most innocent man ever to serve in the Oval Office." Born and educated in Illinois, Reagan was able to talk so effectively with Americans, and dominate their politics during the 1980s, because he embodied so much of the American dream. He began his career broadcasting baseball, where he learned the fundamentals of becoming a "great communicator," as he was to be known in the White House, then headed west where he found fame and wealth in that most American of pursuits, along with baseball, the movies.[27]

Historians largely agree that Reagan, especially during his first term, successfully sold most of his foreign policies because he knew how to talk to the American people and, as well, because he emphasized military strength and anti-communism in which Americans had devoutly believed since at least 1945. As Noonan emphasized in her book, Reagan's strength was not intellectual; he had, after all, once criticized California universities for "subsidizing intellectual curiosity."[28] In domestic affairs his call-to-action amounted to an appeal to the marketplace and individual initiative that justified two massive tax cuts for individuals and corporations between 1981 and 1986. More secure in their pocketbooks, Americans listened to Reagan's traditional appeal in foreign policy: the Soviet Union, he emphasized, was an "evil empire" that alone disturbed a world that would otherwise be at peace. Reagan, unlike Carter in his early presidential years, made the world a simple confrontation between good and bad, somewhat like the plots in many western films. Historian Robert Dallek noted how Reagan's domestic and foreign messages came seamlessly together: "Those upwardly mobile, middle class Americans who make anticommunism an extension of their fight for greater personal freedom at home also derive a sense of status from their militancy against the Soviets abroad." Reagan's "emotional patriotism," moreover, aimed "to compel a revival of respect for America overseas."[29]

Other analyses of the Reagan presidency quickly noted how foreign leaders came to fear the president's nationalistic and militant approach. Two distinguished experts on Western European affairs, Gordon Craig and Alexander George, quoted Chancellor Helmut Schmidt of West Germany: "We can afford no gestures of strength and no doughty demonstrations of steadfastness. We've had a noseful of that sort of thing!"[30] Reagan countered that Americans had to overcome the hesitations of such Old-World leaders as Schmidt and confront the Soviets directly. This could be done only after the US military was built to new levels. Between 1981 and 1986 the military budget nearly trebled to almost $300 billion each year, and Reagan used it with little concern for his allies in Western Europe and Japan. After rejecting Leonid Brezhnev's proposal for talks in 1981, the president reiterated his dislike of the SALT II arms agreement of 1979, made between Carter and Brezhnev, because he believed it was not sufficiently tough on the Soviets. Strobe Talbott's analysis of Reagan's policies toward the Soviets demonstrated the president's lack of knowledge: he was unaware, for example, of how dependent Soviet nuclear strategy was on the largest missiles, and consequently was puzzled when he urged that these missiles be sharply limited, only to have Moscow flatly reject his proposal. Talbott also emphasized how Reagan viewed arms control not as a give-and-take negotiation but as a policy "to dictate to the USSR an entirely new sort of arsenal" that destroyed those largest Soviet weapons without comparable US reductions.[31]

The high point of Reagan's anti-Moscow offensive occurred in March 1983 when, despite limited consultation with his advisers, he announced that his administration was committed to building a space-based defense system – a system which, when fully developed after years of research and many billions of dollars in expenditures, would supposedly shoot down incoming nuclear-tipped missiles before they could hit the United States. The intense, extended debate during the next decade over this Strategic Defense System (SDI) – or "Star Wars," as it was soon termed – actually moved little beyond the early positions for and against. Supporters of SDI believed that it could make nuclear war between the superpowers impossible; they believed this to the extent that Reagan said he would even share the technology with the Soviets, and that it would at the least protect the United States against nuclear threats from smaller, more primitive powers who had only a few bombs. Opponents argued that the Soviets would only build more missiles to overwhelm an SDI system and thus condemn the world to an all-out arms race. Scientists, led by Nobel Laureate Hans Bethe and Congress's Office of Technology Assessment, argued that the technology breakthroughs necessary for such a system – for example, a perfectly functioning computer that could accurately identify enemy missiles from decoys and instantly, and without glitches, shoot them down – was impossible to devise. Others argued that smaller powers would simply sneak nuclear weapons into the United States in ships or other kinds of subterfuge.[32]

Nevertheless, between 1983 and 1992, Congress agreed to invest between $2 billion and $4 billion annually into SDI before presidents George Bush and Bill Clinton severely cut back the project in 1992–3. During Reagan's term, "Star Wars" seemed to be an answer to the problems that had become prominent during the 1971–4 years: it promised to provide Americans with absolute security, and it had further appeal because, as historian Garry Wills noted, this new-found security would derive from "a unilateral American effort that does not depend on the goodwill or the nervous doubts of allies."[33]

This determination to act independently characterized Reagan's policy. In 1982, for example, he unilaterally sent 1400 marines into Beirut, Lebanon, ostensibly to separate the invading forces of Israel, armed by the United States, and Syria, armed by the Soviet Union. On 23 October 1982, a terrorist blew up 239 American soldiers in their barracks. Reagan vowed not to retreat, but he soon began to pull out the troops. He covered the humiliation in Lebanon by immediately using force on the small Caribbean island of Grenada, where he had refused to negotiate with a pro-Cuban government. The Grenada invasion was badly conducted. US troops had to refer to tourist maps to find targets; its costs included twenty American, twenty-four Cuban, and forty-five Grenadan lives; and it was criticized even by Reagan's close friend Margaret Thatcher, the Conservative prime minister of Great Britain. But the consensus among historians is that although the invasion was badly conducted, Americans gloried in the episode as a sign that they were overcoming their Vietnam-inspired fear of using military force.[34]

A forceful critique of Reagan's foreign policies, placed within historical context, was offered by former Undersecretary of State George Ball. He observed that the mid-1980s movie hero was, quite appropriately, "Rambo," who exemplified "a fervent commitment to physical violence as an instrument for the easy solution of complex problems," and who had "a compulsion to operate alone without regard for international constraints," much like "the lone cowboy who disdainfully conducts his own shootout." This was a traditional form of American isolationism, deeply rooted in history, because, in US foreign policy, isolationism has never meant simply staying at home – the American economy, for example, would never allow that kind of isolationism. It has meant instead freedom-of-action and a determination, if necessary, to go it alone and not be restrained by allies, such as West Europeans who disliked such use of military or economic power. As Ball pointed out, since 1970 this kind of go-it-alone-if-necessary approach had forced the United States to become increasingly isolated in the United Nations. Before 1970, US officials did not have to cast a veto in the UN Security Council to stop measures they disliked; but after 1970 fifty-two US vetoes had been cast, and thirty, or 57 per cent, occurred between 1981 and 1988. Other nations had not joined the United States on any of those thirty vetoes.[35]

In 1984–5 came the turn. After spending nearly $1 trillion on weapons in just four years, Americans found themselves trapped in a growing governmental debt that was increasing to more than $100 billion annually. More debt was added to US accounts during the Reagan years than during the first two hundred years of American history. As resources poured into weapons, competitiveness in civilian goods, automobiles, electronics declined, and US trade deficits grew. In 1985, for the first time since 1914, Americans were indebted to the rest of the world. By 1987, they surpassed Brazil and Mexico to be the globe's greatest debtor. Congress began to reduce the president's arms requests. By 1985, George Kennan, who had devised the "containment" theory, now argued, "What most needs to be contained . . . is not so much the Soviet Union as the weapons race itself."[36]

In the spring of 1985 Mikhail Gorbachev became head of the Soviet Union. He represented a new generation that, unlike the old, was trained in the professions, had some experience in the West, and understood that the communist system was not keeping up with the technological revolution. Gorbachev undertook to restructure the system (perestroika) while opening and invigorating it (glasnost); but he intended to make these changes while maintaining the Communist Party's control of the state. Beginning in November 1985, Gorbachev and Reagan held a series of summit conferences that slashed the number of nuclear weapons on both sides and helped to bring about Soviet troop withdrawal from Eastern Europe and Afghanistan; for the first time since 1972 a thaw in the Cold War occurred. As Gail Lapidus and Alexander Dallin observed, in words that most analysts accepted, not only the Russians had changed, but Reagan, facing severe economic and political constraints, had to forget his views about the "evil empire" and strike deals with the new communist leader.[37]

Even as Americans began to make settlements with the Soviets, however, problems in the Third World continued to perplex officials. Reagan was determined not only to contain but to roll back communist influence in the less industrialized world: "Our mission is to nourish and defend freedom and democracy" on "every continent, from Afghanistan to Nicaragua," he announced in 1985. Columnist Charles Krauthammer named this pledge to drive back Soviet-supported regimes in Angola, Afghanistan, Nicaragua, and Cambodia the "Reagan doctrine." Supporters, including Krauthammer, noted how the doctrine dealt with the post-1972 problems, for it aimed to drive back communist influence through relatively cheap, low-level counterinsurgency conflicts that – unlike Vietnam – would not disturb Americans by costing them many dollars or US lives. Critics, such as Robert Tucker and Michael Klare, warned that the Vietnam involvement had begun exactly this way, and that the American ability to "democratize" other peoples was limited.[38]

The Reagan doctrine worked in Afghanistan, however, where covert aid to the Afghan resistance helped force Soviet troops to begin returning home in 1988. It was less effective in Angola and Cambodia, and failed in Nicaragua to drive the Sandinista government from power before Reagan left office. Indeed, in Central America the doctrine nearly brought down the Reagan administration.

That story had its origins in late 1981 when the president secretly ordered the CIA to begin a massive covert campaign to overthrow the revolutionary Sandinista government. In 1979 the Sandinistas had destroyed the Anastasio Somoza dictatorship, which had long been supported by Washington. Reagan's effort was part of a larger plan to block the revolutions that were also sweeping through the neighboring nations of El Salvador and Guatemala. By 1985, however, the CIA's attempts to create an effective force of Nicaraguan "Contras" had failed. Congress, appalled by the Contras' human-rights atrocities and military disasters, cut off funding. Lt-Col. Oliver North of the National Security Council worked with CIA and State Department officials to circumvent Congress by raising funds for the Contras from private sources. As part of this effort, North and other officials broke US laws by selling arms to Iran, which since 1979 had sought to destroy American power in the Middle East, then sending the profits from the arms sales to the Contras. When discovered, North and other officials broke more laws by lying to Congress and destroying documents. Investigations concluded that Reagan had probably not violated laws, but his anti-communist zeal, combined with his lazy, inefficient oversight of the administration, had created a constitutional crisis that 57 per cent of Americans believed was as threatening as the Watergate scandal of 1972–4 that drove Nixon from office.[39]

Reagan left the presidency in early 1989 after working with Gorbachev to reduce the danger of nuclear holocaust and to improve Soviet–American relations to their best condition since World War II. Few US politicians, some historians argued, could have accomplished this as effectively – especially given his continued personal popularity, despite Iran–Contra scandals, and his immunity to attacks from right-wing, anti-Soviet Americans.[40] Critics, however, note how his administration failed to come to terms with other post-1971 legacies. The economy staggered under huge debt, was mired in low growth, suffered from energy inefficiency, especially when compared with the Japanese and German economies, and depended on as much imported oil as in 1973. The Reagan doctrine triumphed in Afghanistan, but failed in Central America, Africa, and Southeast Asia.[41]

George Bush brought a new energy to the presidency in 1989, as well as deep experience and wide knowledge in foreign policy. He had served as ambassador to the United Nations, US representative in China, and head of the CIA before becoming vice president in 1981. The new Chief Executive, who had grown up politically in the Cold War, saw the US–Soviet relationship as central, and was willing to use force to create a pro-American order in the Third World.

Between 1989 and 1991, however, the world that Bush had known largely disappeared. In 1989–90, Gorbachev allowed communist regimes in Eastern Europe to be replaced by democratic governments, and – to the shock of many both outside and inside the Soviet Union – tore down the hated wall that divided West and East Berlin. He then allowed the two Germanies to reunite in mid-1990. Eighteen months later Gorbachev himself was removed from power by democratic Russian factions headed by Boris Yeltsin. The Soviet

Union disintegrated. The ability of presidents such as Truman, Reagan, and Bush to gain public support for their foreign policy on the basis of opposing communism now disappeared, along with communism itself in most parts of the world. Without anti-communism as a rallying cry, without a Soviet danger on which to focus, Bush had to find other means to rally Americans around his policies. He could not find those means, nor could he discover the policies that would resolve the problems propelling the United States into one of its worst post-1945 economic recessions.

Historians have begun to judge Bush's role in the historic events of 1989–91. The judgments overall have been quite critical. The most detailed, authoritative account is Beschloss and Talbott, *At the Highest Levels*. Based on interviews with top officials in the American and former Soviet governments, the authors demonstrate that Bush committed two major errors. First, he was too slow in supporting Gorbachev because the president could not overcome his cold-war mentality and work with Gorbachev at a time when the Soviet leader might have moved his country more successfully toward economic and political reform. Second, when Bush finally realized that Gorbachev had to have strong support if he were to begin meaningful democratic reforms, the president swung over to his side – but it was too late. By that time a more democratic movement, led by Boris Yeltsin, was on the rise; Gorbachev's days in power were numbered. Gorbachev tried to save himself in early 1991 by bringing back to power some of the disreputable communists who had led the country into stagnation in the early 1980s. Bush nevertheless continued to side with Gorbachev. The White House let it be known that US officials considered Yeltsin too "boorish" and unpredictable. In August 1991, Soviet military and Communist Party leaders tried to overthrow Gorbachev and destroy Yeltsin. But Yeltsin and his supporters stopped the coup, gained power, and removed Gorbachev as head of the government. The Soviet Union disappeared and its former empire fractured into eleven republics that formed a Commonwealth of Independent States. Beschloss and Talbott, along with other observers, believe that Bush made these errors in part because he could not break free from his belief that the Cold War would continue in some form, and in part because he allowed his diplomacy to be determined by personal friendships, especially with Gorbachev after 1989, rather than by any rethinking of long-term US interests and Soviet realities.[42]

The Soviet collapse did allow Bush to utilize military force more easily in several areas of the Third World. In December 1989 the president invaded Panama with 27,000 troops to destroy the regime of Manuel Antonio Noriega. In the 1970s and early 1980s, Bush had worked closely with Noriega, but by 1989 the Panamanian's refusal to cooperate on Central American policy, his corruption and drug-running, his proximity to the Panama Canal, and – perhaps especially – his personal taunting of Bush, led the president to capture Noriega and, in a historic and controversial move, bring him to the United States for trial.[43] Noriega was sentenced to a long prison term.

A more dangerous crisis erupted in August 1990 when Saddam Hussein's Iraqi troops conquered the oil-producing kingdom of Kuwait. The two nations had fought for decades over borders and oil wells. Bush hesitated, then decided to block any Iraqi move toward Saudi Arabia, the most important and oil-rich friend of the United States among Arab nations, to liberate Kuwait, and to destroy Saddam Hussein's capacity to produce nuclear and chemical weapons. Dispatching 550,000 US troops, and masterfully creating and maintaining UN support, Bush destroyed much of the Iraqi army and liberated Kuwait in a 100-hour war in February 1991. His popularity leaped to all-time highs for twentieth-century presidents. But the honeymoon was short-lived. Investigations discovered that Bush's own misjudgments about Saddam Hussein had led the United States during the late 1980s to help build the Iraqi war machine as a counterforce to Iran. The president, moreover, had stopped the war before US and UN forces destroyed Saddam Hussein's nuclear capacity or the dictator himself.[44]

"By God," Bush announced after the victory, "we've kicked the Vietnam syndrome once and for all."[45] But not quite. The Vietnam experience haunted US officials who had feared a long, costly war, and who thus used over-whelming firepower to kill thousands of Iraqi civilians and 100,000 Iraqi soldiers in order that Americans back home would not condemn the war for lasting too long. Memories of Vietnam influenced US officials, especially those in the military who vividly recalled the embarrassments of the early 1970s in Southeast Asia and from antiwar protests at home. Nor did Americans think they any longer had the money to finance the war adequately. Their post-1971 economic problems now forced Bush to ask for money from allies, including $11 billion from an unwilling Germany and $13 billion from a reluctant Japan. Having become highly energy-efficient, the Germans and Japanese had less interest than Americans in fighting for Middle East oil.

President Bush repeatedly declared that the defeat of communism and the Iraqi army would bring about "a new world order." The world that confronted US foreign policy by 1992, however, uncomfortably resembled the world of 1971–3, despite the end of the Cold War. The dissolution of the Soviet empire spawned economic disasters and bloody ethnic–religious fighting in the former communist lands. The problems of the US economy meanwhile worsened, dependence on foreign energy resources grew, and American confidence in the institutions of government sank to lows approaching those of 1973–4. The "new world order" remained to be achieved. Americans could realize their part of this "order" by beginning to resolve the foreign and domestic policy problems whose historical roots, as Thomas McCormick and Paul Kennedy, among others, had pointed out, reached back at least to the early 1970s.

NOTES

1 Thomas J. McCormick, *America's Half-Century: United States Foreign Policy in the Cold War*, Baltimore, Md, 1989, especially pp. 153–5.
2 Paul Kennedy, *The Rise and Fall of the Great Powers*, New York, 1987, pp. 373–437. Another impressive argument along the same line is David P. Calleo, *Beyond American Hegemony*, New York, 1987.
3 Samuel P. Huntington, "The US – Decline or Renewal?," *Foreign Affairs*, vol. 67, 1988/89, pp. 84–8.
4 Seymour Hersh, *The Price of Power*, New York, 1983; Jane Mayer and Doyle McManus, *Landslide: The Unmaking of the President, 1984–1988*, New York, 1988; Michael Beschloss and Strobe Talbott, *At the Highest Levels*, New York, 1993.
5 Nixon's views can be found in US Government Printing Office, *Public Papers of the Presidents of the United States*. The 1971 volume (Washington, 1972), has the Kansas City speech, and the 1973 volume (Washington, 1974) contains Nixon's attempt to veto the War Powers Act. Advocates of the Act explain their position in Jacob K. Javits, *Who Makes War: The President Versus Congress*, New York, 1973; and Thomas F. Eagleton, *War and Presidential Power: A Chronicle of Congressional Surrender*, New York, 1974. Eagleton finally opposed the Act because it did not further restrict presidential powers.
6 Arthur Schlesinger Jr, *The Imperial Presidency*, Boston, 1973; McGeorge Bundy, "Vietnam, Watergate, and Presidential Powers," *Foreign Affairs*, vol. 68, 1979/80, pp. 397–404; Theodore Draper, *Present History*, New York, 1983. A thorough discussion of these economic changes, and their political meaning, can be found in Lester Thurow, *Head to Head: The Coming Economic Battle Among Japan, Europe, and America*, New York, 1992, especially pp. 30 and 53, for the post-1973 context. A different interpretation that stresses the seamlessness of the US domestic and international economies is Robert B. Reich, *The Work of Nations: Preparing Ourselves for 21st Century Capitalism*, New York, 1991.
7 Theodore Lowi, *The Personal President*, Ithaca, N.Y., 1985.
8 Eric Hobsbawm, "The Crisis of Today's Ideologies," *New Left Review*, vol. 192, 1992, pp. 56 and 59.
9 Stephen Ambrose, *Nixon*, 3 vols, New York, 1987–91.
10 Robert Beisner, "History and Henry Kissinger," *Diplomatic History*, vol. 14, 1990, p. 226; Roger Morris, *Uncertain Greatness*, New York, 1977.
11 Henry Kissinger, *White House Years*, Boston, 1979; Henry Kissinger, *Years of Upheaval*, Boston, 1982; Hersh, *Price of Power*; Raymond Garthoff, *Detente and Confrontation: American–Soviet Relations from Nixon to Reagan*, Washington, 1985; Walter Isaacson, *Kissinger: A Biography*, New York, 1992.
12 Steven Rearden, *Evolution of American Strategic Doctrine: Paul H. Nitze and the Soviet Challenge*, Boulder, Colo., 1984, p. 68. George Kennan, "The United States and the Soviet Union, 1917–1976," *Foreign Affairs*, vol. 54, 1976, especially p. 688.
13 Geunter Lewy, *America in Vietnam*, New York, 1978. Robert Divine, "Revisionism in Reverse," *Reviews in American History*, vol. 7, 1979, pp. 437–8, which has further references.
14 William Hammond, *Public Affairs: The Military and the Media, 1962–1968*, Washington, 1988, pp. 385–9. An alternative view, especially of the US response to the Tet offensive, is Peter Braestrup, *Big Story*, 2 vols, Boulder, Colo., 1977.
15 The administration's view is in Patricia M. Derian's statement in the US Department of State, *Current Policy*, no. 68, May 1979, and throughout Carter's memoirs, *Keeping Faith*, New York, 1982.
16 Gaddis Smith, *Morality, Reason and Power: American Diplomacy in the Carter

Years, New York, 1986; Stephen F. Cohen, "Soviet Domestic Politics and Foreign Policy," in Fred Warner Neal (ed.), *Detente or Debacle*, New York, 1979, p. 24; James A. Bill, *The Eagle and the Lion: The Tragedy of American–Iran Relations*, New Haven, Conn., 1988; Lars Schoultz, *Human Rights and the United States Policy Towards Latin America*, Princeton, N.J., 1981; Tommie Sue Montgomery, *Revolution in El Salvador*, Boulder, Colo., 1982; Walter LaFeber, *Inevitable Revolutions*, New York, 1993. The best explanation from the Carter administration's perspective is Robert Pastor, *Condemned to Repetition*, Princeton, N.J., 1987.

17 Quoted, with a helpful analysis, in Terry Deibel, *Presidents, Public Opinion and Power: the Nixon, Carter and Reagan Years*, New York, 1987, p. 40.

18 Burton I. Kaufman, *The Presidency of James Earl Carter Jr.*, Lawrence, Kan., 1993, pp. 89–90; Carter, *Keeping Faith*; Michael Conniff, *Panama and The United States*, Athens, Ga, 1992.

19 Michael J. Hogan, *The Panama Canal in American Politics*, Carbondale, Ill., 1986, pp. 6–7, 174–95; Walter LaFeber, *The Panama Canal: The Crisis in Historical Perspective*, New York, 1989, pp. 174–82.

20 Zbigniew K. Brzezinski, *Power and Principle: Memoirs of the National Security Adviser, 1977–1981*, New York, 1983, p. 185. Cyrus Vance, *Hard Choices: Critical Years in America's Foreign Policy*, New York, 1983, especially pp. 87–8, 99–103, 110–19. Carter, *Keeping Faith*, especially pp. 53–4, 193–200, 217–19.

21 Gary Sick, *All Fall Down: America's Tragic Encounter with Iran*, New York, 1985; William Sullivan, *Mission to Iran*, New York, 1981; Kaufman, *Presidency of Carter*, especially pp. 126–7.

22 Stephen Gill, *American Hegemony and the Trilateral Commission*, New York, 1990; while an important and representative statement is The Trilateral Commission, *The Crisis of International Cooperation*, New York, 1974.

23 Vance, *Hard Choices*, pp. 388–9.

24 Haynes Johnson, *In the Absence of Power*, New York, 1980; Martin Schram, *Running for President, 1976: The Carter Campaign*, New York, 1977; Richard E. Neustadt, *Presidential Power and the Modern Presidents: The Politics of Leadership from Roosevelt to Reagan*, New York, 1990; and for the problems with the press, Mark J. Rozell, *The Press and the Carter Presidency*, Boulder, Colo., 1989.

25 James Fallows, "Zbig Without Cy," *New Republic*, 10 May 1980, p. 19; Kaufman, *Presidency of Carter*, pp. 151–97; Walter LaFeber, "From Confusion to Cold War: The Memoirs of the Carter Administration," *Diplomatic History*, vol. 8, 1984, pp. 1–12.

26 Deibel, *Presidents, Public Opinion and Power*, pp. 14–15.

27 Peggy Noonan, *What I Saw at the Revolution: A Political Life in the Reagan Years*, New York, 1991, p. 149; Sidney Blumenthal, *The Rise of the Counter-Establishment: From Conservative Ideology to Political Power*, New York, 1986, p. 242. The best biography, and one that emphasizes these points, is Lou Cannon, *President Reagan, The Role of a Lifetime*, New York, 1991, pp. 38–45, 130, 150–1, 218–19; also see Garry Wills, *Reagan's America*, New York, 1987, for a similar interpretation.

28 Curtis Wilkie, "The President as Comic-Kaze," *Playboy*, vol. 30, June 1983, p. 62.

29 Robert Dallek, *Ronald Reagan, The Politics of Symbolism*, Cambridge, Mass., 1984, p. 133.

30 Gordon A. Craig and Alexander George, *Force and Statecraft: Diplomatic Problems of Our Time*, New York, 1983, p. 148; also Richard Barnet's thorough *The Alliance*, New York, 1983, especially pp. 385–90.

31 Strobe Talbott, *The Russians and Reagan*, New York, 1984, pp. 52–3; a good

discussion is Garthoff, *Detente and Confrontation*, pp. 1022–38.

32 The views of Reagan and his critics can be found in Paul Boyer (ed.), *Reagan as President, Contemporary Views of the Man, His Politics, and His Policies*, Chicago, 1990, pp. 206–19. Also in James Chace and Caleb Carr, *America Invulnerable*, New York, 1988, pp. 313–19; *Wall Street Journal*, 2 January 1985, "Letters to the Editor" section.

33 Wills, *Reagan's America*, p. 360.

34 The administration's view is in Department of State, *GIST*, January 1984, p. 1; Cannon, *President Reagan*, pp. 441–51.

35 George Ball, "A Report Card on Secretary Shultz," *New York Times*, 3 July 1988, p. E 15; George Ball lecture at American Academy of Arts and Science, 16 April 1986; manuscript in author's possession. The classical historical analysis of this US isolationism is Albert K. Weinberg, *Manifest Destiny*, Baltimore, Md, 1935.

36 Walter L. Hixson, *George F. Kennan: Cold War Iconoclast*, New York, 1989, chap. 14; *New York Times*, 14 May 1985, p. A 20; *Washington Post*, 17 April 1987, p. A 18.

37 Gail W. Lapidus and Alexander Dallin, "The Pacification of Ronald Reagan," in Boyer (ed.), *Reagan as President*, p. 257.

38 Department of State, "US Prosperity and the Developing Countries," *GIST*, January 1985, p. 1; Robert W. Tucker, "The New Reagan Doctrine," *New York Times*, 9 April 1986, p. A 27; Michael Klare and Peter Kornbluh, "Beware the Fatal Attraction of Small Wars," *Los Angeles Times*, 28 March 1988, p. 19. Charles Krauthammer's analysis can be found in *Washington Post*, 19 July 1985, p. A 25.

39 Arguments for and against the Reagan policies in Central America and the Iran–Contra scandal can be found in Boyer (ed.), *Reagan as President*, pp. 221–33, 234–45; the best account of Iran–Contra and its effects is Theodore Draper, *A Very Thin Line*, New York, 1991.

40 John Lewis Gaddis, *The United States and the End of the Cold War*, New York, 1992, applauds Reagan's role in ending the Cold War.

41 Boyer (ed.), *Reagan as President* is a good survey of these criticisms.

42 Beschloss and Talbott, *At the Highest Levels*, especially pp. 7–10, 19–42, 102–6. Some of these same points are made from another perspective in Don Oberdorfer, *The Turn*, New York, 1991.

43 Conniff, *Panama and the United States*, p. 167.

44 The most important accounts and critiques of the war are Jean Edward Smith, *George Bush's War*, New York, 1992; Stephen Graubard, *Mr. Bush's War: Adventures in the Politics of Illusion*, New York, 1992; Robert W. Tucker and David C. Hendrickson, *The Imperial Temptation*, New York, 1992. Stanley Hoffmann, "Bush Abroad," *The New York Review of Books*, 5 November 1992, pp. 54–9, gives a succinct overview of the president's foreign policies, and summarizes the general criticism of Bush's conduct of the Iraqi war by stating: "But the main trouble with celebrating either the morality or the success of the war is that – like just war theory itself – it neglects both what happened before and what happened after the period of crisis" (p. 56).

45 Tucker and Hendrickson, *Imperial Temptation*, pp. 69, 152.

10 The United States and the rise of the Third World

Dennis Merrill

It was not unusual during the Cold War era for Americans to tune in their evening television news only to catch the image of US soldiers slogging across the jungles, the beaches, or the city streets of some distant, third-world nation. From Truman through Reagan, officials portrayed US intervention as reactive and defensive. Violent revolutions and civil wars, they charged, had stemmed from Soviet subversion. While Washington harbored no expansionist designs, America had a duty to save the newly emerged nations from the grip of communism, and to place them on the path to democratic development.

The frequency of intervention was striking. In Korea, 1950, Lebanon, 1958, the Dominican Republic, 1965, and Vietnam, 1965–73, the United States resorted to direct military action. A partial listing of covert Central Intelligence Agency (CIA) efforts to overthrow foreign governments includes Iran, 1953, Guatemala, 1954, Cuba, 1961, and Chile, 1973. More than any other single event, America's disastrous engagement in Vietnam sparked historians, beginning in the 1960s, to challenge the official story. Surveying the vast destruction of the Vietnamese countryside, the staggering casualty rate, and the many points of government deception, these "revisionist" scholars searched for a fuller explanation of their country's behavior. The persistence of military interventions into the era following the Cold War – in Panama in 1990, the Persian Gulf in 1991 and Somalia in 1992 – only reinforces the need for new perspectives.

Recent scholarship explains third-world turmoil in historical rather than cold-war terms. Between 1945 and 1960 thirty-seven nations emerged from the ashes of dying colonial empires. Largely non-industrialized, non-white, and located in the southern half of the globe, the new nations reeled from the birthpangs of freedom. Proudly nationalistic, many proved reluctant to align with either the Soviet or the American camp. Thus, analysts referred to them as the "Third World" – a term that lent itself to oversimplification. In actuality, the new states, along with the developing nations of Latin America, varied widely in geography, culture, and aspirations.

The rise of the Third World coincided with another major development of twentieth-century history: the rise of the United States to world leadership.

While American power had been building for decades, widespread destruction in Europe and Asia left the United States after 1945 as the world's premier economic, military, and political power. With its own anti-colonial history, the United States often sympathized with the aspirations of the developing world. Yet as a global power with far-flung interests, it sought to manage a revolutionary world.

It was not an easy task. More than anything else, recent writings on United States/Third World relations show that the days when western powers could easily impose their will on others had passed. Still, Washington flexed its muscle. Sometimes policy succeeded and American interests remained secure. But US officials often failed to grasp the root causes of discontent and frequently stumbled when newly independent states resisted.

INTERPRETIVE OVERVIEW

Was American policy imperialistic? Part of the answer lies in how one defines the term. Some historians take a narrow view and insist that imperialism happens only when a stronger nation establishes *formal* political and military control over a weaker nation. By these standards, US policy after World War II was not imperialistic. The historic rise of the Third World determined that America's influence would differ from that of previous western powers.

Yet the quest for control, and the interventionism, betrayed a certain kind of expansionism. Historians most often use the term "hegemonic" to describe America's policies in the Cold War. A developed, industrial nation, they note, can deploy a vast economic arsenal – trade, investments, and foreign aid – to manipulate weaker states and to establish *informal* control. Diplomatic recognition and non-recognition, the limited use of force, and action taken before international forums also carry weight. The term "hegemony" does not imply that the developed nation always obtains its goals, it simply denotes power and ambition.

Historians have emphasized several factors in explaining why America acted hegemonically. The first generation of revisionist scholars during the 1960s turned to economic theories. In his pathbreaking *The Tragedy of American Diplomacy*, William Appleman Williams argued that US foreign policy since the turn of the century had centered on the pursuit of a world economic order characterized by the "open door."[1] Primarily interested in markets for a fast-growing economy, America had usually tried to avoid the costs of direct colonial rule. Instead, they preached that developing areas, especially in Asia, should be kept open to all external powers for purposes of trade and investment. The open door seemed perfectly suited to US needs since it promised to provide access to markets for the nation's competitive industrial economy without violating anti-colonial traditions. Of course, the United States often violated the spirit of the doctrine with its own interventionist policies in the Philippines, Guam, Puerto Rico, and much of the Caribbean region. Still, the open door served as the central organizing principle behind America's ever-growing economic empire in the early twentieth century.

Updating the open door thesis thirty years later, Gabriel Kolko argued in *Confronting the Third World* that US diplomacy during the Cold War revolved around a relentless effort to gain access to investment opportunities and markets.[2] Whereas direct US private investment had a book value of $7.5 billion in 1929 and only $11.8 billion in 1950, by 1966 those investments had reached $54.6 billion.[3] Although Western Europe and Canada remained the most active investment markets, America's growing dependence on imported minerals made investments in the Third World especially important. By 1960, the United States imported 32 per cent of its iron ore, 46 per cent of its copper, 60 per cent of its zinc, and 98 per cent of its bauxite, mainly from developing areas.[3] To acquire these materials and assert its "mastery" over the Third World, Washington worked to establish a stable, capitalist world order through trade agreements and the creation of multilateral institutions such as the International Monetary Fund and the World Bank. When political instability threatened to disrupt the economic environment, the United States utilized the CIA or resorted to military intervention.

Another group of revisionists, inspired by Marxist thought, emphasized the impact of US policy on third-world living standards. They challenged the conventional wisdom that investment and trade brought economic progress to developing areas. Instead, the producers of raw materials and other primary products suffered a disadvantaged position in the marketplace. Capitalist development, from this point of view, came to be seen as retarding industrial growth and serving mainly to enrich foreign investors and a small domestic elite, which then resulted in the creation of a world economy which was divided between have and have-not nations, in which the have-nots descended into a condition of "dependency" on richer, more powerful states. As the world's economic giant in the postcolonial era, the United States became the system's main beneficiary.[4]

Another economic interpretation has recently explored the impact of empire on the United States itself. Thomas J. McCormick's *America's Half-Century* uses "world systems" theory to explain how America after 1945 became the latest of a series of great powers which, since the fifteenth century, had worked to incorporate "peripheral" areas into the world capitalist system. At the outset, the process had enriched the United States. Indeed, most of the organized elements of America's "corporatist" society – business, labor, and government – supported the effort. Towards the end of the century, however, the country showed signs of decline. In the Third World, communist North Vietnam and Cuba defied US military power. Capitalist states such as South Korea and Taiwan defied dependency theory and assembled dynamic industrial economies. On the home front, America reeled from excessive defense spending and a deteriorating economic infrastructure. America's empire, McCormick concluded, seemed destined to follow the path laid down by its Spanish, Dutch, and British forebears.

While economics is obviously an important factor in foreign affairs, most historians agree that it cannot explain the totality of United States/Third World relations. While US investment in and trade with the Third World has been sizable, it has constituted only a small portion of total world commerce. And, if hegemony has contributed to overcommitment and budgetary woes, surely economics alone is not a sufficient explanation of them. Recognizing this complexity has led scholars to consider other factors to explain America's relations with the Third World.

One group of historians, led by John Lewis Gaddis and Gier Lundestad, point to geopolitical interests as the source of America's international behavior.[6] They describe how the term "national security" was redefined during and after World War II, when challenges to national well-being increasingly arose beyond the borders of the United States. A new concept of security emerged, which encompassed access to the strategic materials, such as oil, titanium, and chromium that undergirded modern, mechanized warfare. In an age of airpower and atomic weaponry, it also included access to forward bases overseas. These developments, considered in the light of Soviet expansionism, provided the basis for America's cold-war foreign policy.

National security analysts, also frequently referred to as foreign policy realists, do not necessarily condone the American record in the Third World. The game of power politics involves rules, and realists argue that the cardinal principle of diplomacy is to recognize *vital* interests and identify threats posed to those interests. Interests are deemed to be vital if they deliver a large "security dividend"; if the dividend is not substantial, then an alliance or a military intervention may not be worthwhile.

Melvyn P. Leffler has provided the most complete account of the origins of America's cold-war security policies in *A Preponderance of Power*.[7] While he generally praises the "Wisemen" of the Truman era for their prudent policies in Europe, where both American interests and the Soviet threat to them were substantial, he chastises them for their "foolish" decisions in the Third World. By making anti-communism a global policy, they failed to distinguish between vital and secondary interests. Assuming that third-world revolutionaries such as Vietnam's Ho Chi Minh owed their power to the Kremlin, they exaggerated the Soviet threat. Most important, according to Leffler, Washington consistently overestimated the strategic value of "peripheral" areas. In terms of war-making capacity, most developing areas outside of the petroleum-producing Middle East possessed only modest strategic value.

The national security thesis echoes economic theory in that it describes a hegemonic US foreign policy, but it differs from it in that it paints a policy that sprang more from imperial blunder than imperial design. At times, security decisions fell victim to domestic politics or bureaucratic infighting, but more often policymakers simply misread the international setting. Yet the security thesis also leaves a number of questions unanswered. If diplomats operated according to a careful calculation of their nation's strategic interests, why did they so frequently misunderstand the Third World, or misread Soviet intentions? What made them define American interests in the way they did? How do we account for their blurred vision?

To fill in the gaps, a third group of scholars have probed cultural and ideological factors. One of the most striking characteristics of the Third World for these historians is its cultural diversity: from predominantly Hindu India, to Confucian East Asia, to the Islamic Arab world. America's encounter with the non-western world, they stress, involved a collision of cultures, as well as a clash of economic and security interests. The methodological challenges to studying cultural relations are numerous: many US historians lack the language skills and anthropological tools to analyze cultural differences, while even definitions of "American" values and beliefs are not easily agreed upon. Still, interpretations of political and economic behavior that leave out the role of ideas run the risk of underestimating human complexity.

In *Ideology and U.S. Foreign Policy*, Michael Hunt explored the attitudes and assumptions that have guided and justified hegemony.[8] Convinced of America's national greatness, and informed by doctrines of Anglo-Saxon racial superiority, US officials have felt compelled to intervene in developing areas. During the Cold War, according to Hunt, the catalyst for intervention usually arose from Washington's distaste for revolutionary change. America's own historical experience, which had featured a limited, political revolution in the eighteenth century, did not prepare US leaders for the tumultuous social upheavals of modern times. From the communist Chinese revolution of 1949 through Nicaragua's Sandinista revolution in 1979, Washington viewed radical change as a threat to its interests, and as contrary to acceptable international conduct.

Hunt argues that American diplomats tried to accommodate the thirst for change by offering their own prescription for political and economic development.[9] Economic aid served as the mechanism; "modernization" provided the ideological foundation. Development would begin, American officials advised, when the Third World opened its doors to private capital and built the modern banking and commercial institutions needed to make capital work. Investment and technology, not class conflict and revolution, provided the key to the future. In some cases, historians of development have noted, the formula did promote growth. But it often underestimated the depth of third-world poverty, and failed to relieve the causes of unrest. Value laden and paternalistic, US development programs certainly reflected the deep cultural divide that separated developing states and the West.

The recent work of historians has demonstrated that US intervention in the Third World occurred for a variety of economic, strategic, and ideological reasons. What the interpretive schools have in common is that they link US policy to larger developments in world history. To comprehend US relations with any developing nation, historians must consider not only bilateral ties but also the position of the former colonial power, the views of neighboring states, the ambitions of other great powers, and the influence of multilateral institutions. In searching out the richness of these relations, scholars have not only illuminated the history of United States/Third World relations, they have also begun to redefine what it means to study American diplomacy.

A CHRONOLOGICAL OVERVIEW

The same internationalism evident in the various interpretations referred to above has been reflected in the growing number of case studies that deal with United States/Third World relations. Most of these studies, unlike many of the broader theoretical works, are based on archival research in US government records; but a significant number of them utilize British and French materials, as well as third-world sources – although such materials are usually less accessible. These studies offer a fuller account of how economic, security, and ideological factors have interacted in particular settings, while providing a sense of chronological development. This essay breaks the history of United States/Third World relations into three periods, although these overlap in time: 1941 through 1953, when rapid decolonization brought the United States into contact with many developing areas for the first time; 1953 through 1969, when European decline and the Cold War heightened America's presence in developing areas; 1969 to the present, when US influence became increasingly tenuous.

US relations with the Third World technically began at the turn of the century when America first reached beyond the shores of the continent in search of empire. The establishment of colonial rule in the Philippines, Puerto Rico, Guam, and Hawaii, along with "dollar diplomacy" and frequent military intervention in Latin America, foreshadowed Washington's future collision with third-world nationalism.[10] Yet in a more precise historical sense, this period in American diplomacy predated the rise of the Third World as an independent political force.

World War II marked the rise of the modern Third World, and initiated American involvement with it. The conflict badly weakened the empires of Europe and energized movements for national independence. In spite of America's own history of imperialism, US leaders often voiced sympathy with the aspirations of the emerging nations. In 1941, President Franklin Roosevelt joined with the British prime minister, Winston Churchill, in issuing the Atlantic Charter, an eloquent statement of the principle of self-determination. But when the allies sat down to implement the charter, controversy ensued. Pressed by Roosevelt to implement home rule in India, Churchill insisted that the charter applied only to those territories occupied by the Nazis.

In what would become a regular occurrence in United States/Third World relations, America backed away from its anti-colonial ideology. Both William Roger Louis in *Imperialism at Bay* and Christopher Thorne in *Allies of a Kind* concluded that the retreat flowed from American ambivalence on a number of issues.[11] First, the United States generally shared with its European allies the prevailing cultural and racial attitudes of the day, and doubted the capability of darker-skinned peoples to practice self-government. Indeed, few US officials envisioned immediate decolonization. Most subscribed to President Roosevelt's hopes for a gradual transition to trusteeship under the United Nations, followed by a period of carefully managed economic and political development.

Second, and perhaps more decisively, military exigencies – or what in a later day would be termed matters of national security – did not permit a breach in the Grand Alliance. As the war dragged on, and strategic realities increasingly impinged upon their decisions, US diplomats abandoned plans for a broad application of trusteeship. Demonstrating the power of strategic thinking, even the American military had, by the time the war ended, successfully vetoed the plans of the State Department to place Japanese-held islands in the Pacific under international trusteeship. Their usefulness as military bases proved too great to sacrifice.[12]

Decolonization went forward nonetheless. Weakened by the war, Britain, France, the Netherlands, and other colonial powers increasingly lost their hold on their empires. Nationalist movements, some of which were led by advocates of radical social change, swept across Asia, North Africa, and the Middle East. Washington might have welcomed these developments as harbingers of a more open, capitalistic world system. But by the late 1940s, the Cold War had reached fever pitch. President Harry S. Truman, in March 1947, addressed Congress in order to request economic and military aid for Greece and Turkey, both of which, he implied, faced communist aggression. In enunciating his famous "Truman doctrine," the president indicated that the containment of communism was about to become a global effort.

Cold-war anti-communism drew the United States deeper into third-world affairs while simultaneously restricting the options available to it in responding to nationalism. Recent research has revealed that the Truman administration, 1945–53, did not always oppose anti-colonial movements. When decolonization occurred peacefully, or when Soviet influence seemed to be absent, the administration accommodated it. Gary R. Hess has demonstrated that Washington looked favorably upon Britain's peaceful transfer of power to moderate nationalists in India and Pakistan in 1947.[13] Robert J. McMahon has argued that the United States gave its support to Indonesian freedom from Dutch colonial rule because the independence movement there was led by decidedly non-communist nationalists.[14] Finally, the Truman administration believed that its own policy of an early transition to self-rule in the Philippines could serve as a model for other colonial empires.[15]

Yet American support for anti-colonialism remained limited. For a variety of security and economic reasons associated with the Cold War, US officials often hoped that former colonial powers could maintain enough influence to assure regional stability. According to Scott A. Bills in *Empire and Cold War*, Washington sanctioned French rule in Algeria, Morocco, and Tunisia in order to strengthen France's support for the Cold War in Europe. In the former Italian colony of Cyrenaica, part of present-day Libya, it gave tacit support to Britain's occupying forces. In the Middle East, it hoped that London's policy of gradual devolution in Egypt would keep the strategically-valuable Suez Canal safely in western hands. It also counted on Britain to maintain stability in oil-rich Iraq and Iran.[16]

Washington opposed anti-colonial revolution most forcefully in French Indochina. The independence movement there had been controlled from its inception by Ho Chi Minh's communist Vietminh. Numerous scholars have examined the US perspective.[17] A pro-Soviet Indochina, policymakers reasoned, would demoralize France and weaken Western Europe. It would deny a source of raw materials and markets to Japan. Underlying all of this, officials assumed that the fall of Indochina would set into motion the "domino"-like collapse of the entire region. With these considerations in mind, the Truman administration in 1950 initiated America's long involvement in Vietnam when, for the first time, it extended US economic and military aid to French forces.

The Chinese communist revolution of 1949 and the Korean War in 1950 had a profound impact on relations between the United States and the Third World. In each case the Truman administration downplayed the indigenous sources of conflict and emphasized the Kremlin's role.[18] To demonstrate the credibility of the containment doctrine, America not only went to war in Korea but dramatically increased its commitment to non-communist regimes in nearby French Indochina, Formosa, and the Philippines.[19] By the end of 1950, most of East Asia had become a battleground in the Cold War.

Studies of US policy in Asia tend to emphasize America's limited economic presence there, and focus instead on the impact of geopolitics. But economics did play an important role in other regions of the Third World. Certainly in Latin America, where US investment had reached $6 billion and bilateral trade nearly $3 billion, the United States had more at stake than political credibility.[20] Walter LaFeber has used the term "neo-dependency" to describe the history of US relations with Central America.[21] In pursuit of investment opportunities and markets, and to safeguard the strategic Panama Canal, the United States had come to dominate much of Latin America long before the Cold War, which intensified, but did not substantially alter, that hegemonic system. Convinced that private enterprise best met the region's needs, Washington did not allocate substantial economic aid to Latin America; but military aid, especially after the outbreak of the Korean War, was provided to bolster friendly, authoritarian, client states.[22]

The administration moved more cautiously in the Middle East. Few historians deny that economic interests, particularly a concern for oil, dominated American policy in this region of the world. But any discussion of the topic requires a precise explanation of how Washington defined those interests. Aaron David Miller's *Search for Security* and David S. Painter's *Oil and the American Century* are particularly useful in this regard.[23] Although the United States during and after World War II imported only a small percentage of its petroleum needs, the oil of the Middle East played an increasingly important role in Europe's economic recovery, in the maintenance of international economic stability, and in strategic planning for protracted war. In short, the quest for oil related to a complex web of international economic and security interests. Thus, American-based multinational oil companies and cold-war diplomats worked together to assure the flow of petroleum products from states such as Saudi Arabia and Kuwait.

Although access to oil required friendly relations with Arab states, the United States pursued inconsistent policies. Stephen L. Spiegel has demonstrated in *The Other Arab–Israeli Conflict* how bureaucratic divisions within an administration can sidetrack policy.[24] He recounts the struggle between Truman's foreign policy and domestic advisers over the thorny issue of the creation of an independent Israeli state. Torn between a State Department that urged a delay in reaching a decision and a re-election campaign that seemed to require support for the emerging state, President Truman waffled. Finally, in 1948, owing to the dictates of domestic politics and personal philosophy, he gave strong support to the creation of Israel. The decision marked the beginning of what would become a ritualistic practice in US policy concerning the Middle East: the balancing of pro-Israeli with pro-Arab sentiments.

Most historians pinpoint the period from 1953 through 1969 as the era in which the United States fully entered the maelstrom of third-world affairs. By that time cold-war lines had hardened in Europe, but geopolitical lines had become more blurred in the Third World. French troops succumbed in 1954 to the Vietminh at the battle of Dienbienphu. Egypt's leader, Gamel Abdel Nasser, stood up to the British in 1956 at the Suez Canal. And by 1960 the continent of Africa, the last bastion of widespread colonial rule, had given birth to eighteen new nations. With its growing security and economic interests at stake, Washington increasingly intervened in third-world revolutions and civil wars, beseeched emerging nations to join in cold-war military alliances, and participated in third-world economic development.

The administration of Dwight D. Eisenhower, 1953–61, has won praise from historians in recent years for its handling of Soviet–American relations. Armed with recently released documents from the Eisenhower Library in Abilene, Kansas, scholars have been impressed by "Ike's" efforts to hold down defense spending, and his quest for nuclear arms talks.[25] But most historians of relations between the United States and the Third World have been far more critical. Confronted by the rise of radical nationalism and unrest, Eisenhower and his strongly anti-communist Secretary of State, John Foster Dulles, often mistakenly assumed that Soviet intrigue lay behind the tumult. Critics charge that the administration's policies often rolled back progressive social change and intensified regional conflicts.[26]

Eisenhower's initiatives in Asia illustrate these themes. Although the administration in 1953 broke the logjam in the Korean peace talks at

Panmunjom, it did not take advantage of that success to reorient American policy. The administration demonstrated restraint in 1954 when it decided not to come to France's aid at Dienbienphu.[27] Yet George Herring's classic study, *America's Longest War*, laments Eisenhower's decision to use economic and military aid to bolster the unpopular regime of Ngo Dinh Diem in the newly created, non-communist, Republic of South Vietnam. Herring also questions the necessity for the Southeast Asian Treaty Organization, SEATO, a military pact that included Britain, France, Australia, New Zealand, Thailand, the Philippines, and Pakistan.[28] Guided by cold-war logic, Eisenhower failed to grasp the indigenous origins of Vietnamese communism, and underestimated the difficulty of building and defending a new nation.

Studies of US policy in the Middle East are even more critical. Newly available documents, along with Iran's 1979 Shiite revolution, have inspired several new works on US–Iranian relations. James A. Bill's *The Eagle and the Lion* and Mark Hamilton Lytle's *The Origins of the Iranian–American Alliance* rank among the best.[29] Lytle focuses on the period from 1941 to 1953, when a combination of US concerns – access to oil, World War II planning, and the Cold War – initiated the American–Iranian marriage. Bill examines the history of that marriage up through its messy divorce in the 1980s. Both highlight the Eisenhower administration's role in the August 1953 CIA plan to overthrow the nationalistic government of Muhammad Musaddiq. Tired of the stalled negotiations over oil revenues between Iran and the British-owned Anglo-Iranian Oil Company, exaggerating Musaddiq's ties to the communist Tudeh Party, and ignorant of Iranian culture, the administration threw its weight behind Muhammad Reza Shah Pahlevi. In the process, it laid the groundwork for the explosive revolution that rocked US–Iranian relations a quarter of a century later.

The Eisenhower administration's push for military allies proved to be one of the most serious impediments to good relations with the Third World. In the Middle East, the creation in 1955 of the American-sponsored Baghdad Pact, which included Iraq, Pakistan, Turkey, and Great Britain, generated a major international crisis. Egypt's fiery nationalist, Gamel Abdel Nasser, viewed the pact as an unwelcome interference in the affairs of the Middle East. Even as Washington waved the promise of financial support for the High Aswan Dam, Nasser refused to join the alliance, made threatening gestures toward Israel, and accepted military aid from the Soviet bloc. When the United States condemned Cairo's ties to Moscow and withdrew funding for the dam, Nasser bristled with indignation.

To protest Washington's withdrawal of funds and create new sources of revenue, Nasser nationalized the British-run Suez Canal. Soon, British, French, and Israeli troops stormed across Sinai. Concerned that the Soviets might intervene to help Nasser and that the conflict might disrupt access to Arab oil, Eisenhower in this case opposed the reassertion of colonial control and deployed economic pressure to stop the aggression – actions that made him a hero in the Third World, at least for the moment. But historians such as Peter

Hahn, Diane Kunz, and Donald Neff agree that Suez ended up as a hollow victory. After the crisis, Eisenhower reverted to his old ways. When a military coup in Iraq brought to power a pro-Nasser regime in 1958, Eisenhower responded by sending US marines to nearby Lebanon and proclaiming the Eisenhower Doctrine, which promised American assistance against communism. The initiative deeply alienated the Egyptians and once again showed how the administration confused nationalism with communism.[30]

In response to the Baghdad Pact and the SEATO alliance in Asia, a number of states in the Third World, led by India's Jawaharlal Nehru and Indonesia's Achmed Sukarno, organized the first conference of nonaligned nations in April 1955 at Bandung, Indonesia. Anxious to assert their recently acquired freedom from colonialism, these nations denounced military alliances for violating national sovereignty and for producing regional conflicts. India was especially alarmed by the inclusion of Pakistan in both the Baghdad Pact and SEATO.[31] Antagonism between the two nations went back to Britain's partition of the subcontinent in 1947 between a predominantly Hindu India and a Muslim Pakistan. Although the nonaligned movement incorporated a kaleidoscope of political views, it became a rallying point for nationalism in the Third World. Public statements by US officials, however, at times implied that the nonaligned states sympathized with the Soviet cause. Secretary of State Dulles infuriated many of them when he declared in 1956 that neutralism in the Cold War was "an immoral and shortsighted conception."

H. W. Brands's *The Specter of Neutralism* and Dennis Merrill's *Bread and the Ballot* examine how the administration tried, in the late 1950s, to regain India's confidence and to demonstrate a greater appreciation for the non-aligned perspective.[32] Following a series of Soviet aid initiatives to India and other neutrals, Eisenhower softened some of his rhetoric and increased US economic assistance to the Third World. India, with its representative form of government, was acclaimed as a model for democratic development. Brands argues that the wooing of India reassured Nehru and re-established balance in US policy. But Merrill concludes that the continued military commitment to Pakistan undercut the diplomatic offensive, and contributed to growing tensions in South Asia. US policy drifted until the mid-1960s when war broke out between India and Pakistan and President Lyndon B. Johnson turned off the aid spigot to both nations.

While historians debate the finer points of US policy toward India, most argue that the Eisenhower administration's response to nationalism in Latin America amounted to little more than a reassertion of US hegemony. A defining moment in inter-American relations arrived with the election of President Jacobo Arbenz in Guatemala. A devout nationalist with widespread popular backing, Arbenz implemented sweeping land reforms, which included the confiscation of lands belonging to the Boston-based United Fruit Company. Charging that Guatemala had been infiltrated by communist agents, Washington in May 1954 orchestrated a CIA coup that overthrew Arbenz and canceled the social revolution. In seeking to explain US actions, some scholars have pointed to the elaborate lobbying efforts of the United Fruit Company, whose board of directors included CIA chief Alan Dulles.[33] Others have argued that opposition to communism determined policy.[34] The most recent treatment of the subject, Piero Gleijeses's *Shattered Hope*, concludes convincingly that no single villain can be blamed but that policy sprang from both economic and security concerns.[35]

Elsewhere in Latin America the administration followed a policy of calculated neglect. With the exception of a few cases where communism reared its head, the Eisenhower White House showed little interest in the region's economic underdevelopment, unequal distribution of land, and poverty. Eisenhower experimented with innovative diplomacy only after an angry mob assaulted Vice President Richard M. Nixon's motorcade during a trip in 1958 to Caracas, Venezuela, and even more so following Fidel Castro's triumphant march in 1959 into Havana. The creation of the Inter-American Development Bank in 1958, expanded funding for the World Bank in 1959, and the establishment of the Social Progress Trust Fund in 1960 ushered in a new era of US-backed development. But the effort involved only limited funds and remained tied to narrow cold-war aims.[36] John F. Kennedy's "New Frontier," 1961–3, tried to reorient United States/Third World relations somewhat by addressing more forcefully the underlying sources of discontent. During the Kennedy years, US influence in the Third World reached its highest level. He declared the 1960s to be the "development decade" and raised the level of economic aid, sent idealistic Peace Corps volunteers to distant rural villages, and promised a more tolerant attitude to nonaligned nations such as India and Egypt.[37] Yet Kennedy, no less than his predecessor, adhered to the prevailing cold-war dogma of his era. His legacy in the Third World remains ambiguous. The interpretive difficulties are compounded by his relatively brief tenure in office.

Most historians agree that Kennedy achieved his most impressive successes in Africa. Africa had long been considered by Washington to be a geopolitical backwater, but the Kennedy team looked upon the mineral-rich continent as a testing ground for third-world diplomacy. The New Frontier skillfully steered Portugal, its NATO ally, toward disengagement from its colony in Angola, and negotiated a UN settlement of the civil war in the Belgian Congo.[38] In one of the most thoroughly researched monographs on US policy in Africa, *Cold War and Black Liberation*, Thomas J. Noer discusses Kennedy's efforts to bring international pressure on the white government in South Africa to implement modest reforms of its racist apartheid system.[39] Interestingly, scholars agree that Kennedy proved supportive of nationalists in Africa mainly because that region had not yet become a major point of superpower competition.

In the Middle East, Kennedy initially took an even-handed approach and adopted a friendly attitude toward both Egypt and Israel. But Nasser's military intervention in the civil war in nearby Yemen in 1962 alienated even his fellow Arabs and forced Kennedy to distance himself from the

Egyptian ruler. Most specialists blame Kennedy's successor, Lyndon Johnson, for reversing policy during the Six Day War between Israel and the Arab states in 1967, and for assisting Tel Aviv with increased arms sales.[40] Stephen Spiegel draws attention to Johnson's inconsistencies. Support for Israel was contradicted by overtures to moderate Arab states. The administration endorsed UN Resolution 242 – which called for Israel to withdraw from the occupied West Bank, the Gaza Strip, the Golan Heights, and the Sinai – but never developed a plan for implementation. Torn between the pro-Arab sentiments of the State Department, and the pro-Israeli lobby in Congress, Johnson increased US involvement in the Middle East without charting a clear course for the future.[41]

Kennedy's darkest hour came in Cuba. While CIA plans to overthrow the Castro regime originated with the Eisenhower administration, it was Kennedy who ultimately oversaw the disastrous Bay of Pigs invasion. The New Frontier's accommodation of third-world nationalism apparently did not apply to states in the western hemisphere that befriended Moscow. Following the failure of the invasion, Kennedy ordered covert operations to weaken, overthrow, and even assassinate the Cuban dictator. In the end, the policy backfired. Rather than bend to US hegemony, Castro moved to the left, aligning Cuba more closely with the Soviet Union, and paving the way for the Cuban Missile Crisis.[42] Scholars have advanced a number of explanations for the US–Cuban confrontation. Thomas Paterson points to the impact of large historical forces that made western management of empires more fragile. America's relative economic decline in the late 1950s and early 1960s, he argues, helps to account for Castro's willingness to challenge US domination.[43] Writing from a Marxist perspective, Morris Morley, in *Imperial State and Revolution*, argued that American policies derived from Castro's radical economic policies, which resulted in the nationalization of many American-owned businesses and threatened the institutions of capitalism.[44]

No other initiative better illustrates Kennedy's ambiguous record than his embrace of "development diplomacy." Economic aid by no means began with the New Frontier, but no other administration pursued it with as much energy and conviction. In some ways the use of economic tactics represented a refreshing departure. President Kennedy decried Washington's traditional emphasis on military aid and alliances, and argued that America should help the Third World overcome its massive economic problems. But, at the same time, he viewed economic aid as a weapon in the Cold War, to be used to win new allies, to secure access to strategic raw materials, and to give third-world peoples greater faith in non-communist change. Most scholars agree that the much-heralded Alliance for Progress in Latin America came about primarily to prevent the advent of additional Castros.[45] Although Kennedy promised to use aid to back democratic governments in the Americas, cold-war politics often required support for authoritarian clients. When Brazil elected a leftist government that challenged US hegemony, the Johnson administration resorted to covert operations to help bring to power a more pliant military regime, which the United States then bolstered with aid.[46] And when civil war broke out in the Dominican Republic in 1965, Johnson abandoned development diplomacy altogether and sent in the marines.[47]

Although aid programs often revolved around cold-war politics, development studies offer a new focus of research for historians of US diplomacy. Beyond geopolitics, American developmentalism also reflected ideological and cultural assumptions. Their impact reached down and altered the social structure of each of those states that received assistance, usually with mixed results. In India, US agricultural programs introduced new hybrid seeds that dramatically increased productivity and helped make that country self-sufficient in food grains. But the absence of substantial land reform meant that widespread poverty continued.[48] In Iran, the Shah's American-backed, capitalistic "revolution from the top," which embodied only moderate land and legal reforms, helped modernize that country but failed to satisfy the aspirations of the middle class and deeply alienated conservative Shi'i religious leaders.[49] In a suggestive article, Emily Rosenberg has observed that development programs often had a negative effect on women in those societies where their subordinate role made them especially vulnerable to rapid social transformation.[50] In short, the blending of political, economic, and cultural factors involved in development encouraged both accommodation and discord in the relations of the United States with the Third World and demonstrate the growing complexity of modern international relations.

In spite of the emphasis on development, historians agree that the escalation of US military involvement in Vietnam ranks as the watershed event of the Kennedy–Johnson years. In many ways America's approach to Vietnam embodied all of the shortcomings inherent in its third-world policies as a whole. Underestimating the force of nationalism, the US found itself engaged in a multi-layered civil war. Once developmental policies had failed to ameliorate revolutionary conditions, the United States adopted a harsher counterinsurgency strategy. Soon America was bogged down in jungle warfare, faced a barrage of domestic and international criticism, and an economy weakened by runaway inflation and balance of payments difficulties.[51]

Because of the continued classification of government records, the monographic literature on United States/Third World relations in the post-Vietnam era is slim. We must rely mainly on general surveys of the period, regional studies, biographies of key leaders, and memoirs. Raymond Garthoff's sweeping *Detente and Confrontation* gives the best political overview. The strongest economic analysis is to be found in Thomas J. McCormick's *America's Half-Century.*[52] Robert D. Schulzinger's *Henry Kissinger: Doctor of Diplomacy* provides a scholarly introduction to Richard Nixon's years in the White House, 1969–74.[53] Gaddis Smith's *Morality, Reason, and Power* serves as the standard work on the administration of Jimmy Carter, 1977–81.[54] For Presidents Ronald Reagan, 1981–9 and George Bush, 1991–2 we must rely mainly on journalistic accounts.[55]

When historians sit down to write the history of recent United States/Third

World relations, they will be challenged by the sheer magnitude of the subject. Covert CIA operations across the globe, clandestine wars in Central America, deepening involvement in the diplomacy of the Middle East, growing dependence on oil, terrorism, famine, and third-world debt constitute only a partial listing of the important topics. Scholars will have to bear in mind, moreover, broader changes in the international setting that affected US policy toward developing areas. Détente with the Soviet Union, the rise of a more competitive, multi-polar international setting, and the decline and collapse of the Soviet Union have all profoundly influenced United States/ Third World relations.

Certain themes are nonetheless apparent. By the 1970s and 1980s the Third World itself had undergone several transformations. Although many developing states continued to depend on the export of primary products for their livelihood, many others – such as Mexico, Brazil, India, and South Korea – had emerged as newly industrialized countries (NICs), and as regional leaders. Others, such as Saudi Arabia and Kuwait, had demonstrated the power of oil by holding back supplies to make developed economies scream. Business leaders in the NICs no longer kowtowed to western firms, but instead pressured their governments to enact restrictions on foreign investors. In those nations that still struggled as producers of primary products – such as Nicaragua, El Salvador, and Angola – revolutionary slogans still held sway. In short, "North/South" relations became ever more contentious. The Third World had become more than ever what Richard E. Feinberg termed "the intemperate zone."[56]

American policymakers tried to adjust to the new realities by scaling back their commitments. Direct military intervention became the exception rather than the rule. Instead, the Nixon, Carter, Reagan, and Bush administrations came to rely on friends and allies in the Third World, proxies and clients from a more cynical perspective, to serve US goals. Nixon and Kissinger initiated the trend by throwing their support to Ferdinand Marcos of the Philippines, where air and naval bases assumed greater significance in the post-Vietnam setting. In the Middle East, they accelerated arms sales to the Shah of Iran. And after the Yom Kippur War of October 1973, they lent unwavering support and arms shipments to Israel. To undo the Sandinista revolution in Nicaragua, the Reagan administration armed supporters of the former US-backed dictator Anastacio Somoza. And in war-torn El Salvador both the Carter and Reagan administrations fought off a leftist insurgency by providing military and economic aid to that country's right-wing government.

Historians who have examined these policies concede that at times they served Washington's short-term needs. But over the long run they often generated foreign policy fiascos. James A. Bill emphasizes how support for the Shah, whose repressive SAVAK intelligence organization terrorized the political opposition, fueled the Iranian revolution of 1979.[57] Stanley Karnow's study of the Philippines, *In Our Image*, describes how support for Marcos over three administrations produced a backlash in the mid-1980s. Only astute diplomatic maneuvering by the Reagan administration in 1986 averted a disaster.[58] And numerous studies have shown how US policy toward Nicaragua and Central America contributed to the orgy of violence that consumed that region in the 1970s and 1980s.[59]

At times, US policymakers did seek creative alternatives in dealing with the Third World. Richard Nixon won widespread approval in 1972 when he reached out to the People's Republic of China. The rapprochement allowed Washington to exploit Sino-Soviet discord and opened new economic opportunities for American businesses.[60] Jimmy Carter in several cases demonstrated sensitivity to third-world nationalism. Walter LaFeber's *The Panama Canal*, chronicles the history of the Central American waterway and the Carter-sponsored treaty that will relinquish control of the inter-oceanic waterway by the year 2000.[61] William Quandt's *Peace Process* (1993) provides a rich account, from the perspective of a former official, of the delicate negotiations that led to the opening of relations between arch-enemies Israel and Egypt.[62]

Yet the swirl of events could easily overwhelm the best-intentioned administration. Iran posed an insurmountable challenge. When the Shah's regime teetered, Carter failed to initiate discussions with the new Islamic rulers. When the president allowed the Shah to enter the United States for medical treatment, Iranian students needed no further proof of where Washington stood. Urged on by their government, they stormed the American embassy in Tehran and initiated the tortuous Iranian hostage crisis.[63]

The Reagan administration initially decried Carter's weakness and tried to reassert American power. The Reagan White House launched in 1983 a military invasion to overthrow a leftist regime on the tiny Caribbean island of Grenada. In addition to the covert war against Nicaragua, it used the CIA to destabilize a communist regime in Angola, and to assist rebels in Soviet-occupied Afghanistan. In Lebanon, President Reagan sent in US marines to curb fighting between Christians and Muslims. And to punish the Libyan dictator Moammar Qadahfi for supporting terrorists he ordered US planes to bomb Tripoli.

Critics such as former State Department officials George Ball and Robert Pastor pointed to the meager results.[64] Grenada succumbed to US military power, but bloody civil wars plagued Nicaragua, El Salvador, Angola, and Afghanistan for the rest of the decade. In early 1984 243 US Marines fell victim to violence in the Middle East when their barracks came under terrorist attack. And following their withdrawal, the rate of hostage-taking and terrorism increased. In a desperate attempt to pry loose American hostages in Beirut, the administration made secret arms sales to Iran, one of the states in the Middle East most supportive of Lebanese terrorists. The controversy that followed badly scarred the Reagan presidency.

The period that immediately followed the end of the Cold War did not bring any respite for American policymakers. One legacy of the cold-war era that persisted into the new age was America's commitments to unsavory proxies.

Under President George Bush's leadership the United States carried out its first military intervention of the new era in Panama. John Dinges's *Our Man in Panama* explains how President Manuel Noriega had been a long-time informant for the CIA, and in the early 1980s an ally in the covert war against Nicaragua. But by 1990 the strongman's corruption and his links to Latin American drug lords made him a liability.[65] Cooperation with another third-world dictator during the 1980s also haunted Bush. Iraq's Saddam Hussein surprised the world in August 1990 with his conquest of Kuwait. For the previous five years, Washington had favored Hussein in his war against Iran. Now the United States feared that Iraqi militarism threatened oil supplies and regional stability. Bush assembled an effective international coalition, and in January 1991 launched Operation Desert Storm. The stunning ninety-day victory revived confidence in American power. Yet Hussein's ability to cling to authority in the immediate aftermath of the war suggested that the Third World still defied easy management by outsiders.[66]

CONCLUSION

From the Atlantic Charter to the Persian Gulf War, United States/Third World relations have evolved in unpredictable fashion. In recent years, historians have struggled to discern the larger trends behind the events. What have emerged are images of hegemonic purpose, yet evidence as well of inconsistency and ineffectiveness. We have begun to develop an appreciation for the large historical forces – decolonization, world war, cold war, and global economics – which have provided the context for relations. We have also explored the interaction between economic, national security, and ideological interests that define each relationship. Finally, we also have peeked inside government bureaucracies and glimpsed the idiosyncrasies that can affect diplomacy.

Yet in many ways our analysis is still primitive. In coming years, as archives continue to open, we will gain new dimensions of understanding. And as cold-war tensions fade, we will abandon more of yesterday's myths and view political and economic issues under more direct light. We will explore a host of new issues. Control over news gathering and information systems, environmentalism, and race relations are just a few of the subjects that merit further investigation. Increased availability of documents in developing nations in particular will provide new perspectives. A new generation of Western diplomatic historians, more fully trained in foreign languages and the study of foreign cultures, should prove eager to exploit new sources and to engage their Third World colleagues in dialogue.

While the future is impossible to predict, it is clear that United States/Third World relations will continue to be of central importance in tomorrow's world order. Political, economic, and technological trends in the twentieth century have made the world a smaller place. While the United States no longer dominates the globe as it did fifty years ago, it will still interact with all of the world's peoples. History has taught us that Washington's relations with the Third World can involve any combination of confrontation, accommodation, collaboration, and discord. Hopefully, historians can point the way toward policies that reinforce our more cooperative instincts.

NOTES

1 William Appleman Williams, *The Tragedy of American Diplomacy*, Cleveland, Ohio, 1959.
2 Gabriel Kolko, *Confronting the Third World: United States Foreign Policy, 1945–1980*, New York, 1988.
3 Statistics are drawn from Kolko's previous work *The Roots of American Foreign Policy*, Boston, 1969.
4 For a good introduction to dependency theory see Louis A. Pérez Jr, "Dependency," in Michael J. Hogan and Thomas G. Paterson (eds), *Explaining the History of American Foreign Relations*, New York, 1991.
5 Thomas J. McCormick, *America's Half-Century: United States Foreign Policy in the Cold War*, Baltimore, Md, 1989.
6 John Lewis Gaddis, *Strategies of Containment: A Critical Appraisal of Postwar American National Security Policy*, New York, 1982; Geir Lundestad, *The American "Empire" and Other Studies of US Foreign Policy in a Comparative Perspective*, New York, 1990.
7 Melvyn Leffler, *A Preponderance of Power: National Security, the Truman Administration, and the Cold War*, Stanford, Calif., 1992.
8 Michael Hunt, *Ideology and U.S. Foreign Policy*, New Haven, Conn., 1987.
9 Hunt, *Ideology and U.S. Foreign Policy*. Also see D. Michael Shafer, *Deadly Paradigms: The Failure of U.S. Counterinsurgency Policy*, Princeton, N.J., 1988. Also see: Richard Barnet, *Intervention and Revolution*, New York, 1968; Robert A. Packenham, *Liberal America and the Third World: Political Development Ideas in Foreign Aid and Social Science*, Princeton, N.J., 1973.
10 For concise overviews of American imperialism at the turn of the century see: Robert L. Beisner, *From the Old Diplomacy to the New, 1865–1900*, Arlington Heights, Il., 1986; Thomas G. Paterson and Stephen G. Rabe (eds), *Imperial Surge: The United States Abroad, the 1890s–early 1900s*, Lexington, Mass., 1992.
11 William Roger Louis, *Imperialism at Bay: The United States and the Decolonization of the British Empire, 1941–1945*, Oxford, 1977; Christopher Thorne, *Allies of a Kind: The United States, Britain, and the War Against Japan, 1941–1945*, New York, 1978.
12 Thorne, *Allies of a Kind*.
13 Gary R. Hess, *America Encounters India, 1941–1947*, Baltimore, Md, 1971.
14 Robert J. McMahon, *Colonialism and Cold War: The United States and the Struggle for Indonesian Independence, 1945–1949*, Ithaca, N.Y., 1981.
15 H. W. Brands, *Bound to Empire: The United States and the Philippines*, New York, 1992, pp. 227–9; Stanley Karnow, *In Our Image: America's Empire in the Philippines*, New York, 1989, pp. 323–55; Stephen Rosskamm Shalom, *The United States and the Philippines: A Study in Neocolonialism*, Philadelphia, Pa, 1981.
16 Scott L. Bills, *Empire and Cold War: The Roots of US–Third World Antagonism, 1945–1947*, New York, 1990.
17 Lloyd Gardner, *Approaching Vietnam: From World War II Through Dienbienphu, 1941–1954*, New York, 1988; George C. Herring, *America's Longest War: The*

United States and Vietnam, 1950–1975, New York, 1979, pp. 3–42; Gary R. Hess, *The United States' Emergence as a Southeast Asian Power, 1940–1950*, New York, 1987, pp. 311–22; Andrew J. Rotter, *The Path to Vietnam: Origins of the American Commitment to Southeast Asia*, Ithaca, N.Y., 1987.

18 The standard work on America's response to the Chinese revolution is Nancy B. Tucker, *Patterns in the Dust: Chinese–American Relations and the Recognition Controversy, 1949–1950*, New York, 1983. On Korea see Bruce Cumings, *The Origins of the Korean War*, 2 vols, Princeton, N.J., 1981 & 1992; Rosemary J. Foot, *The Wrong War: American Policy and Dimensions of the Korean Conflict*, Ithaca, N.Y., 1985; Burton I. Kaufman, *The Korean War: Challenges in Crisis, Credibility, and Command*, Philadelphia, Pa, 1986; James I. Matray, *The Reluctant Crusade: American Foreign Policy in Korea, 1941–1950*, Honolulu, Hawaii, 1985.

19 Gordon H. Chang, *Friends and Enemies: The United States, China, and the Soviet Union, 1948–1972*, Stanford, Calif., 1990, pp. 42–80; Hess, *The United States' Emergence*, pp. 331–71; Michael Schaller, *The American Occupation of Japan: The Origins of the Cold War in Asia*, New York, 1985, pp. 273–89.

20 Richard I. Immerman, *The CIA in Guatemala: The Foreign Policy of Intervention*, Austin, Tex., 1982, p. 8.

21 Walter LaFeber, *Inevitable Revolutions: The United States in Central America*, New York, 1984, pp. 5–18, 85–110.

22 David Green, "The Cold War Comes to Latin America," in Barton Bernstein (ed.), *Politics and Policies of the Truman Administration*, Chicago, 1970; Samuel Baily, *The United States and the Development of South America, 1945–1975*, New York, 1976; Chester J. Pach, *Arming the Free World: The Origins of the United States Military Assistance Program, 1945–1950*, Chapel Hill, N.C., 1991; Bryce Wood, *The Dismantling of the Good Neighbor Policy*, Austin, Tex., 1985.

23 Aaron David Miller, *Search for Security: Saudi Arabian Oil and American Foreign Policy, 1939–1949*, Chapel Hill, N.C., 1980; David S. Painter, *Oil and the American Century: The Political Economy of US Foreign Oil Policy, 1941–1954*, Baltimore, Md, 1986. Also see Bruce R. Kuniholm, *The Origins of the Cold War in the Near East: Great Power Conflict and Diplomacy in Iran, Turkey, and Greece*, Princeton, N.J., 1980.

24 Stephen L. Spiegel, *The Other Arab–Israeli Conflict: Making America's Middle East Policy from Truman to Reagan*, Chicago, 1985.

25 For overviews of the Eisenhower presidency see: Stephen Ambrose, *Eisenhower: The President*, New York, 1984; Robert A. Divine, *Eisenhower and the Cold War*, New York, 1981; Fred I. Greenstein, *The Hidden Hand Presidency: Eisenhower as Leader*, New York, 1982; Peter Lyon, *Eisenhower: Portrait of a Hero*, Boston, 1974.

26 For an excellent critique of Eisenhower's third-world policies see: Robert J. McMahon, "Eisenhower and Third World Nationalism: A Critique of the Revisionists," *Political Science Quarterly*, vol. 101, 1986, pp. 453–73.

27 On Dienbienphu see: John Prados, *"The Sky Would Fall": Operation Vulture, The U.S. Bombing Mission, Indochina, 1954*, New York, 1983; George C. Herring and Richard I. Immerman, "Eisenhower, Dulles, and Dienbienphu: 'The Day We Didn't Go To War' Revisited," *Journal of American History*, vol. 71, 1984, pp. 343–63.

28 Herring, *America's Longest War*, pp. 43–72. For the most recent work on Eisenhower and Vietnam see David L. Anderson, *Trapped by Success: The Eisenhower Administration and Vietnam, 1953–1961*, New York, 1991.

29 James A. Bill, *The Eagle and the Lion: The Tragedy of American–Iranian Relations*, New Haven, Conn., 1988; Mark Hamilton Lytle, *The Origins of the Iranian–American Alliance, 1941–1953*, New York, 1987.

30 Peter L. Hahn, *The United States, Great Britain, and Egypt*, Chapel Hill, N.C., 1991; Diane B. Kunz, *The Economic Diplomacy of the Suez Crisis*, Chapel Hill, N.C., 1991; Donald Neff, *Warriors at Suez: Eisenhower Takes America Into the Middle East*, New York, 1981.
31 Robert J. McMahon, "United States Cold War Strategy in South Asia: Making a Military Commitment to Pakistan, 1947–1954," *Journal of American History*, vol. 75, 1988, pp. 812–40.
32 H. W. Brands, *The Specter of Neutralism: The United States and the Emergence of the Third World, 1947–1960*, New York, 1988; Dennis Merrill, *Bread and the Ballot: The United States and India's Economic Development, 1947–1963*, Chapel Hill, N.C., 1990.
33 Steven C. Schlesinger and Stephen Kinzer, *Bitter Fruit: The Untold Story of the American Coup in Guatemala*, Garden City, N.Y., 2nd ed., 1983.
34 Immerman, *The CIA in Guatemala*.
35 Piero Gleijeses, *Shattered Hope: The Guatemalan Revolution and the United States, 1944–1954*, Princeton, N.J., 1991.
36 Stephen G. Rabe, *Eisenhower and Latin America: The Foreign Policy of Anti-communism*, Chapel Hill, N.C., 1988.
37 Standard works on the Kennedy presidency include Arthur M. Schlesinger Jr, *A Thousand Days: John F. Kennedy in the White House*, Boston, 1965; Richard J. Walton, *Cold War and Counter Revolution: The Foreign Policy of John F. Kennedy*, New York, 1972; Herbert Parmet, *J.F.K.: The Presidency of J.F.K.*, New York, 1983; Thomas G. Paterson (ed.), *Kennedy's Quest for Victory: American Foreign Policy, 1961–1963*, New York, 1989.
38 The standard work on Kennedy and Angola is Richard D. Mahoney, *JFK: Ordeal in Africa*, New York, 1983. On the Congo see Madeline Kalb, *Congo Cables: The Cold War in Africa From Eisenhower to Kennedy*, New York, 1982. For an overview of JFK's Africa policy see: Peter Duignan and L. H. Gann, *The United States and Africa: A History*, New York, 1984.
39 Thomas J. Noer, *Cold War and Black Liberation: The United States and White Rule in Africa, 1948–1968*, Columbia, Mo., 1985, pp. 61–95.
40 Douglas Little, "From Even Handed to Empty Handed: Seeking Order in the Middle East," in Paterson (ed.), *Kennedy's Quest for Victory*, pp. 156–77.
41 Spiegel, *The Other Arab–Israeli Conflict*, pp. 118–65.
42 Thomas G. Paterson, "Fixation With Cuba: The Bay of Pigs, Missile Crisis, and Covert War against Fidel Castro," in Paterson (ed.), *Kennedy's Quest for Victory*, pp. 123–55. Also see Morris H. Morley, *Imperial State and Revolution: The United States and Cuba, 1952–1986*, New York, 1987; Trumbell Higgins, *The Perfect Failure: Kennedy, Eisenhower, and the CIA at the Bay of Pigs*, New York, 1987; Jules R. Benjamin, *The United States and the Origins of the Cuban Revolution: An Empire of Liberty in an Age of National Liberation*, Princeton, N.J., 1990.
43 Paterson, *Kennedy's Quest for Victory*.
44 Morley, *Imperial State and Revolution*.
45 On the Alliance for Progress see Stephen G. Rabe, "Controlling Revolutions: Latin America, the Alliance for Progress, and Cold War Anti-Comnmunism," in Paterson (ed.), *Kennedy's Quest for Victory*, pp. 105–22; Baily, *The United States and the Development of South America*, pp. 82–117; Jerome Levinson and Juan de Onis, *The Alliance That Lost Its Way*, Chicago, 1970.
46 Gerald K. Haines, *The Americanization of Brazil: A Study of U.S. Cold War Diplomacy in the Third World, 1945–1954*, Wilmington, Del., 1989; Ruth Leacock, *Requiem for Revolution: The United States and Brazil, 1961–1969*, Kent State, Ohio, 1990; Phyllis R. Parker, *Brazil and the Quiet Intervention, 1964*, Austin, Tex., 1979.

47   Piero Gleijeses, *The Dominican Crisis: The 1965 Constitutionalist Revolt and American Intervention*, Baltimore, Md, 1978.
48   Merrill, *Bread and the Ballot*, pp. 169–211.
49   Bill, *The Eagle and the Lion*, pp. 131–53.
50   Emily Rosenberg, "Walking the Borders," in Hogan and Paterson (eds), *Explaining American Foreign Relations*, pp. 24–35.
51   Herring, *America's Longest War*, pp. 73–281; Larry Berman, *Planning a Tragedy: The Americanization of the War in Vietnam*, New York, 1982.
52   Raymond Garthoff, *Detente and Confrontation: American–Soviet Relations From Nixon to Reagan*, Washington, 1985; McCormick, *America's Half-Century*, pp. 155–243.
53   Robert D. Schulzinger, *Henry Kissinger: Doctor of Diplomacy*, New York, 1989. Also see Tad Szulc, *The Illusion of Peace: Foreign Policy in the Nixon Years*, New York, 1979; Seymour Hersh, *The Price of Power: Kissinger in the Nixon White House*, New York, 1983; Richard Nixon, *RN: The Memoirs of Richard Nixon*, New York, 1978; Henry Kissinger, *White House Years*, Boston, 1979; *Years of Upheaval*, Boston, 1982.
54   Gaddis Smith, *Morality, Reason, and Power: American Diplomacy in the Carter Years*, New York, 1986. Also see memoirs such as Jimmy Carter, *Keeping Faith*, New York, 1982; Zbigniew Brzezinski, *Power and Principle*, New York, 1985; Cyrus Vance, *Hard Choices*, New York, 1983.
55   Robert Dallek, *Ronald Reagan, The Politics of Symbolism*, Cambridge, Mass., 1984; Reagan era memoirs include Alexander Haig, *Caveat: Realism, Reagan, and Foreign Policy*, New York, 1984; Constantine Menges, *Inside the National Security Council: The True Story of the Making and the Unmaking of Reagan's Foreign Policy*, New York, 1988.
56   Richard E. Feinberg, *The Intemperate Zone: The Third World Challenge to U.S. Foreign Policy*, New York, 1983.
57   Bill, *The Eagle and the Lion*, pp. 154–292.
58   Karnow, *In Our Image*, pp. 356–434. Also see Raymond Bonner, *Waltzing With a Dictator: The Marcoses and the Making of American Policy*, New York, 1988; Brands, *Bound to Empire*, pp. 298–308.
59   Robert A. Pastor, *Condemned to Repetition: The United States and Nicaragua*, Princeton, N.J., 1987; LaFeber, *Inevitable Revolutions*, pp. 201–317.
60   Chang, *Friends and Enemies*, pp. 275–94.
61   Walter LaFeber, *The Panama Canal: The Crisis in Historical Perspective*, New York, 1978.
62   William Quandt, *Peace Process: American Diplomacy and the Arab–Israeli Conflict since 1967*, Washington and Berkeley, Calif., 1993, pp. 255–334.
63   Bill, *The Eagle and the Lion*, pp. 261–304.
64   George W. Ball, *Error and Betrayal in Lebanon: An Analysis of Israel's Invasion of Lebanon and the Implications for U.S.–Israeli Relations*, Washington, 1984; Pastor, *Condemned to Repetition*, pp. 230–336. On the Middle East also see Gary Sick, *All Fall Down: America's Tragic Encounter With Iran*, New York, 1985; Spiegel, *The Other Arab–Israeli Conflict*, pp. 395–429; Bill, *The Eagle and the Lion*, pp. 304–15, 409–24. On Central America also see Thomas W. Walker, *Revolution and Counterrevolution in Nicaragua, 1977–1989*, Boulder, Col., 1990; LaFeber, *Inevitable Revolutions*; Cynthia J. Arnson, *Crossroads: Congress, The Reagan Administration, and Central America*, New York, 1989.
65   John Dinges, *Our Man in Panama*, New York, 1990.
66   For a provocative first draft of history see Jean Edward Smith, *George Bush's War*, New York, 1992.

11 Reconsidering the nuclear arms race: the past as prelude?

James G. Hershberg

A professor of mine once told his class that the most important alliance during the Cold War was between the United States and the Soviet Union – he paused here – not to have a nuclear war. It was, to be sure, a tacit and well-disguised alliance, especially in the first two decades after World War II, when crises between the communist and capitalist worlds erupted at widely scattered flashpoints (Korea, Indochina, Suez, Berlin, Cuba) that had little in common save their symbolic significance on the superpower chessboard. After going to the brink over Cuba in 1962, Washington and Moscow did a better job for the next few decades of avoiding direct confrontations, but continued to augment and modernize their stockpiles. In November 1985, when he first met Soviet leader Mikhail Gorbachev, Ronald Reagan, who had condemned the Soviet Union as an "evil empire," remarked that if the Earth were attacked by extraterrestrials, surely the two adversaries (and former World War II allies) would cooperate militarily to defend the planet. But in a real sense, the ETs had already landed: nuclear weapons constituted as radical a departure from previous experience and as grave and palpable a threat to civilization as would any Martian invasion – and even implacable enemies were forced to limit their difficulties accordingly.

Now the Cold War is gone, but the nuclear arms race has outlived it. Clearly, the anti-communist convulsions of 1989–91 ended the post-World-War-II nuclear competition between the Western alliance and the erstwhile Soviet bloc. Having amassed a combined arsenal of well over fifty thousand nuclear warheads, Washington and Moscow had already begun to reverse the nuclear arms race with the conclusion in 1987 of a treaty to cut the levels of short and medium range nuclear missiles in Europe. In July 1991, George Bush and Mikhail Gorbachev signed a START (Strategic Arms Reduction Treaty) capping their strategic arsenals, and later that year, after the failure of a hardline coup in Moscow the following month, Bush and Gorbachev traded announcements of additional sweeping reductions in the strategic arsenals. In January 1993 Bush and Russian president Boris Yeltsin signed a START II pact mandating further large cuts, including a ban on land-based multiple-warhead missiles, although Russian ratification remained a question mark.

Yet this rush of staggering accomplishments, once unimaginable, was largely overshadowed by the disintegration of the USSR itself.[1]

These events terminated the second and, so far, most dangerous phase of the nuclear age – counting as the first leg the covert contest between the Anglo-American alliance and Nazi Germany during World War II.[2] The danger of an all-out East/West nuclear war, whether by premeditation or inadvertence, has been drastically reduced.[3] But, whereas the end of the division of Germany and Europe and the breakup of the Soviet Union irrevocably ended the Cold War, these same developments *increased* the risks of nuclear proliferation, at the very time that long-dormant volcanoes of nationalistic hatred are erupting across the landscape of the former Soviet realm. Never before has the world seen the disintegration of a nuclear superpower or empire – and the economic and political chaos in the former Soviet Union offers incentives for uncontrolled trafficking in nuclear weapons, delivery systems, plants, fuels, and trained personnel. Moreover, the removal of constraints upon the international environment imposed by the Cold War's bipolar alliance system has already encouraged regional powers and middling or smaller states with large ambitions to seek hegemony or security via the acquisition of weapons of mass destruction. Even if the immediate challenge of containing current proliferation dangers is met, the impossibility of disinventing nuclear weapons or technology assures that the nuclear peril will remain a significant aspect of industrialized civilization.[4]

These circumstances assure that the nuclear issue will continue to preoccupy US policymakers, who will long be guided by their understanding of the significance of nuclear weapons during the Cold War. Have nuclear weapons made the postwar world safer or more dangerous? Did their existence contribute to stability, deterring World War III, or to tensions between the superpowers that made an apocalyptic conflict more likely? Was the nuclear arms race avoidable or inevitable? What role did nuclear weapons and policies play in such events as the Cuban and Berlin crises? What lessons should be inferred from the Cold War nuclear arms race for the post-cold-war world? Did this competition artificially prolong the post-World-War-II order, freezing the superpower status quo, or hasten its conclusion? Are past ideas, agreements, and intellectual frameworks for controlling nuclear weapons still relevant?

There is no consensus on the answers to these questions and the process of re-evaluating the role of nuclear weapons during the Cold War is only beginning. This essay will not attempt a comprehensive recounting of this story – students may now turn to a number of excellent studies that have appeared in the United States since the nuclear weapons issue awoke from political slumber in the early 1980s.[5] Rather, my goal is to venture some observations on the (second) nuclear arms race, and to stimulate thought about how its legacy may influence future thinking about the nuclear issue.[6]

ENDING AT THE BEGINNING

To understand the end of the postwar nuclear arms race, it is a good idea to go back to its beginning. A look at the origins of the US–Soviet atomic rivalry offers insight into why Gorbachev and Reagan made such rapid progress when they started to break the nuclear stalemate.[7] As early as 1944, physicist Niels Bohr had secretly implored the leaders of the Anglo-American atomic collaboration that an "open world," in which the Allies shared their knowledge of atomic energy, was essential after the defeat of Nazi Germany in order to build mutual confidence and to avoid a secret Soviet atomic effort. Bohr based his idealistic proposal on a realistic recognition that the nuclear physics which made atomic bombs possible was known to scientists around the world, and that trying to retain exclusive national possession of the weapons would be futile and only exacerbate distrust and hostile competition. To improve the chances for what he jokingly referred to as "another experimental arrangement" of the international system, Bohr counselled Winston Churchill and Franklin Roosevelt to make an early, serious approach to Josef Stalin to invite his future cooperation prior to the first use of the bomb against Japan. The Allied leaders rebuffed this suggestion, but even FDR's pragmatic science advisers Vannevar Bush and James Conant independently arrived at Bohr's essential ideas, if not his tactical advice for a direct overture to Stalin, when they agreed that the United States should after the war create an international agency to exchange scientific and technical information related to atomic energy as a means of preventing the Soviet Union from secretly pursuing nuclear weaponry.[8]

But the rub of these proposals was that they required the Soviet Union (as well as the United States) to open territories, laboratories, and mines to international inspection: "We recognize that there will be great resistance to this measure, but believe the hazards to the future of the world are sufficiently great to warrant this attempt," wrote Bush and Conant to War Secretary Henry L. Stimson in September 1944.[9] Stimson became a convert, but even he was so taken aback by evidence of the Soviet police state mentality at the July 1945 Potsdam summit conference that he despaired at trying to achieve an arms agreement with Moscow, and even wondered whether the bomb itself could be used to bring about democratic change inside the USSR. Stimson later reverted to his earlier advocacy of nuclear arms control – but when Washington proposed in the United Nations the establishment of international control of atomic energy, the plan was doomed by the Soviets' rejection of the proposed international agency's authority to conduct intrusive on-site inspections and operate facilities on Soviet soil. It was, the Kremlin charged, nothing less than a US espionage scheme to undermine Soviet sovereignty and perpetuate America's atomic lead; to Washington, Moscow's intransigence on inspection proved that it eschewed serious negotiations and was more interested in building its own atomic bombs.[10]

This pattern held for the next four decades – from Eisenhower's "Open

Skies" proposal (1955) to negotiations for a comprehensive test ban treaty (1958–63) to endless haggling over the "verification" provisions of SALT (Strategic Arms Limitation Talks) treaties in the 1960s and 1970s, a sticking point remained the Soviet resistance to foreign inspections on its own territory. Limited agreements proved possible only because of monitoring capabilities provided by spy planes, satellites, and tracking stations, known in diplomatic parlance as "national technical means." This ingrained Soviet secrecy bred Western suspicion and skepticism and, at times, offered a pretext for US policymakers opposed to nuclear arms control to evade serious consideration of proposals to halt or reverse the arms race. Nuclear arms control, it was frequently said, was impossible so long as Moscow relied on dictatorial methods and censorship at home and kept its military activities shrouded from outside scrutiny.

That viewpoint began to lose its potency soon after Mikhail Gorbachev rose to the head of the Communist Party of the Soviet Union in March 1985. Shortly before their summit in November, Reagan aides suggested opening both sides' research laboratories for inspection to keep track of experimentation related to space-based defenses; they had counted on receiving the customary Soviet *nyet*, but to their surprise Gorbachev expressed sympathetic interest in the idea and unexpected candor in discussing military issues.[11] After a relapse during the Chernobyl nuclear plant disaster in April 1986, when Moscow tried to cover the accident up, Gorbachev showed an unprecedented willingness to open his country's politics and history to domestic debate and journalistic investigation and, over the opposition of key members of the armed forces, its military facilities to foreign inspection. A harbinger of this changed attitude came in Stockholm in September 1986 when an East–West agreement on measures to reduce the risks of military conflict was reached at the Conference on Confidence- and Security-Building Measures and Disarmament in Europe. Those talks had dragged on for years until the Soviets suddenly agreed to long-standing Western proposals to enforce a strict regime of mutual monitoring and advance notification of NATO and Warsaw Pact maneuvers and force movements throughout Europe, extending inside the Soviet Union as far as the Urals. Strikingly, the Soviets agreed to permit observers at Warsaw Pact exercises and surprise air or ground inspections, or both, with no right of refusal.[12] Though negotiations over a strategic arms reduction treaty remained stymied over Reagan's Strategic Defense Initiative, a breakthrough came in negotiations for a ban on medium- and intermediate-range missiles in Europe when the Soviets also called the US bluff on verification – and the Americans, after decades of carping that Moscow would not allow inspection, suddenly were worried about opening up their own secret facilities. "The Soviets backed us into a corner," said one US negotiator. "We had talked about intrusiveness – continually – and they took us up on it, saying, in effect, 'Absolutely. Right on. Any time. Any place.' We backpedalled. When it dawned on us that 'any place' included some highly sensitive installations, we drew back."[13] The

Intermediate Nuclear Forces (INF) agreement, complete with stringent on-site inspection provisions, was signed in Washington in December 1987, and soon Americans and Soviets were travelling to each other's military bases to observe the destruction of missiles and setting up monitoring equipment at manufacturing plants.

The *volte-face* on inspection and verification had reversed the dynamic of the nuclear arms race, undercutting the psychological barrier blocking genuine trust between the superpowers even during a period of relative cooperation. At least as important, the new Soviet openness undermined the entrenched domestic political opposition to nuclear arms control within the United States, prompting Reagan to embrace radical arms reductions ideas more quickly than some skeptical advisers. Nuclear arms reduction, not merely control, gained momentum. After four dangerous decades, the essential insight of Bohr and Conant in 1944 – that transparency was the precondition for stopping or preventing a nuclear arms race – was being validated.

INTERNATIONAL CONTROL – BACK ON THE AGENDA?

Another, closely related idea discarded at the dawn of the nuclear arms race was that of the international control of atomic energy. Briefly, at the end of World War II, the notion of a supranational authority to control the world-wide development of atomic energy for civilian and military purposes became official American policy. The US government adopted it, not out of idealism, generosity, or altruism, but because of a sober recognition that any deter-mined industrial power could rapidly acquire atomic weapons. As early as May 1944 – convinced that humanity faced either a "race between nations and in the next war destruction of civilization, or a scheme to remove atomic energy from the field of conflict" – Conant had concluded that "the only hope for humanity" was "an international commission on atomic energy with free access to all information and right of inspection."[14]

Truman formally, albeit ambivalently, endorsed the goal of international control in the fall of 1945, although some advisers believed that Washington was better off clinging to its atomic edge as long as possible. And Stalin was more interested in accelerating his country's covert atomic program than in trusting an unclear international scheme proposed by the United States. Rather than conduct direct negotiations with Moscow, Truman opted to bring the international control issue before the newly created United Nations. A State Department committee chaired by Dean Acheson, advised by a board of consultants led by Tennessee Valley Authority head David Lilienthal and including physicist J. Robert Oppenheimer, recommended the creation of an international atomic development authority that would not only police nuclear activities but take on the job of developing nuclear power for peaceful purposes, becoming a sort of global atomic TVA.

But when Truman's cautious negotiator, Bernard Baruch, formally intro-duced the US position to the United Nations Atomic Energy Commission in

June 1946, he toughened the Acheson–Lilienthal plan by rejecting the use of a veto and by adding provisions for "condign punishment" of offenders and for a staged implementation – the United States would hand over atomic data and facilities only after the control mechanisms went into operation. Not surprisingly, the Soviets proposed an opposite sequence: inspections and controls would go into effect only after all countries with atomic bombs (i.e. the United States) destroyed them and handed over all facilities to the international agency. The gap proved unbridgeable, and the talks soon degenerated into a desultory propaganda battle. In late December, the Baruch Plan passed, 10–0, with the USSR abstaining, but the Soviet refusal to participate consigned it to irrelevance. For the next forty years, the notion of international control of atomic energy, like the dream of an effective United Nations, was put into deep freeze.

But the superpower thaw in the late 1980s allowed the tentative re-emergence of the thinking that originally animated plans for postwar international collective action. This throwback first manifested itself in US–Soviet cooperation to calm regional disputes in third-world trouble spots such as Cambodia, Angola, Afghanistan, and Central America, and then appeared most strikingly in the Security Council's endorsement of force by a US-led military coalition against Iraq. The willingness of the Soviet Union and United States to act against an international aggressor even elicited suggestions to reactivate the United Nations' Military Staff Committee, moribund since 1945. Washington's insistence on retaining control of the war against Saddam Hussein precluded that, but the Security Council's subsequent approval of US-led humanitarian interventions in Cambodia, Somalia and Bosnia underlined the growing use of the international umbrella. Even Ronald Reagan, no fan of the United Nations, called in a speech at Oxford University in late 1992 for the creation of "a standing UN military force, an army of conscience," empowered to intervene in trouble spots around the world.

There are reasons to believe that this bolstering of international authority could be extended to the world weapons bazaar. During the Cold War, international atomic cooperation was limited to organizations composed of like-minded countries, like NATO and Euratom, or else constrained by financial, functional, and political parameters, like the International Atomic Energy Agency (IAEA), created by the United Nations in 1957. In the mid-1980s, charges that Reagan's "Star Wars" proposal would stimulate a destabilizing and costly US–Soviet race in defensive weapons accidentally evoked a variant of international control thinking when Reagan suggested that the United States would share the fruits of its own research and development. Gorbachev scoffed at the idea. Yet, if both sides were determined to go ahead with strategic defenses, a more sensible way to adapt the ideas behind Acheson–Lilienthal and Baruch would have been for Washington and Moscow to work collaboratively on defensive systems. Indeed, in 1992, Boris Yeltsin announced that Russia stood "ready jointly to work out and subsequently to create and jointly operate a global system of defense in place of SDI."[15]

That idea, met by silence from the Americans, pointed the way for other efforts that reprised past initiatives. In early 1992, thirty-seven years after it was first proposed, Eisenhower's "Open Skies" proposal, providing for mutual "observation overflights" of military facilities, was agreed to by the United States, its European allies, and the former Soviet republics and satellites. Echoing Acheson–Lilienthal's emphasis on power development, following the Soviet collapse the US government hired physicists in its former enemy's weapons plants and labs to work on nuclear fusion research rather than circulate their résumés to the highest bidder. Taking on some of the extensive reach that the UNAEC was originally supposed to possess, the IAEA assumed new powers to monitor the destruction of Iraq's nuclear capabilities after the 1991 Persian Gulf War, although it needs far more resources, authority, and aggressiveness to act effectively in detecting hidden nuclear programs.[16] Calls also arose for the creation of a new watchdog agency to limit the spread of ballistic missile technology.

Clearly, internationalization did not constitute a panacea to solve the world's nuclear or security problems at the end of World War II and does not now. The postwar record of international cooperation, moreover, hardly inspires confidence or lessens traditional US wariness toward the surrender of sovereignty.[17] It also remains evident that international organizations can only be effective given essential agreement on major issues among key powers. Still, with the Cold War's passing, internationalization of nuclear and military forces and development deserves another, searching appraisal, and a reexamination of past precedents.[18]

HIROSHIMA AND THE ARMS RACE

One seminal event of the nuclear age that never entirely faded from view and which continues to stir both emotions and historical controversy is the decision to drop the atomic bomb on Japan in 1945. The bombings of Hiroshima and Nagasaki contributed to the origins of the Cold War by enhancing distrust within the alliance against Hitler. Stalin is said to have made a single demand upon being told of the bombings: "Provide us with atomic weapons in the shortest possible time. You know that Hiroshima has shaken the whole world. The balance has been destroyed. Provide the bomb – it will remove a great danger from us."[19] Two principal arguments have emerged in the debate over Hiroshima: whether the atomic bomb was necessary to end the war against Japan without resorting to a full-scale American invasion of the home islands; and whether American policymakers were motivated primarily by military considerations vis-à-vis Japan or were, by the summer of 1945, more concerned with intimidating the Soviet Union in anticipation of contentious postwar diplomatic bargaining.[20]

One distinctive feature of the debate over Hiroshima is that it has never been completely divorced from contemporary political concerns. Initially, few Americans questioned the use of the bomb on Hiroshima (described in a

White House press release as a "Japanese Army base"): its usage seemed to be both a military necessity and a justifiable response to Japanese aggression and atrocities.[21] Although some of the scientists involved in the Manhattan Project warned that dropping the bomb on a city would provoke an arms race after the war,[22] others argued that it was not only justifiable but would alert the United States to the gravity of the challenge posed by nuclear weapons. "We have been very fortunate indeed in timing," Vannevar Bush, Roosevelt's chief science adviser, wrote to a friend less than a week after Hiroshima.

> If the scientific knowledge which rendered the development of the bomb possible had come into the world, say, five years earlier we might indeed have succumbed to the Nazis. On the other hand, if it had come five years later, there would have been great danger that this country, in its peacetime easy-going ways, would not have gone into the subject in the extraordinarily expensive manner which was necessary to put it over. Yet this whole thing would most certainly have come on civilization in one way or another during our lifetime. It is fortunate that it comes now, and in the hands of a democratic, peace-loving country, but it is also essential that that country realize fully just what it is and where it stands on the matter. No amount of demonstration would ever have produced this realization in the American public. It was necessary that events happen just as they have happened in the past week, and it was very fortunate that they thus occurred.[23]

Only a year later did doubts begin to surface. In the summer of 1946, a US government inquiry into the effectiveness of the country's wartime strategic bombing effort concluded that "certainly prior to December 31, 1945, and in all probability prior to November 1, 1945, Japan would have surrendered even if the atomic bombs had not been dropped, even if Russia had not entered the war, and even if no invasion had been planned or contemplated."[24] And the publication in the *New Yorker* magazine of John Hersey's description of the devastation of Hiroshima prompted a wave of horror and regret over the bomb's destructive powers.[25] A few critics even charged that the bombings had actually been intended to cow the Soviet Union.[26]

This sort of second-guessing alarmed several of those involved in the decision to drop the bomb, including James Conant, the president of Harvard, who feared that public repudiation of the decision would destroy the diplomatic usefulness of the weapon and prompt America to relapse into isolationism. He hoped that Washington's temporary monopoly would convince the Soviet Union to agree to an American-sponsored international control plan in the United Nations. Even though only a "small minority of the population" questioned the decision to use the bomb, this "sentimentalism" was bound to influence the next generation, he wrote former Stimson aide Harvey Bundy:

> The type of person who goes into teaching, particularly school teaching, will be influenced a great deal by this type of argument. We are in danger of repeating the fallacy which occurred after World War I. You will recall

that it became accepted doctrine among a group of so-called intellectuals who taught in our schools and colleges that the United States had made a great error in entering World War I, and that the error was brought about largely by the interests of the powerful groups . . . a small minority, if it represents the type of person who is both sentimental and verbally minded and in contact with our youth, may result in a distortion of history.[27]

Conant's alarms initiated a counterattack by the atomic establishment in the national press. Articles defending the use of the bomb soon appeared in *The Atlantic* by Karl T. Compton, and, more significantly, in *Harper's* by Stimson.[28] Stimson's somber and seemingly authoritative rejoinder helped to quiet the debate over Hiroshima and established what would become the orthodox explanation of the decision: that it was necessary as a military measure to defeat Japan and end the war at the earliest possible moment. Even before the article appeared, Conant enthusiastically congratulated Stimson, predicting that it would "play an important part in accomplishing" his goal of abolishing war because:

> if the propaganda against the use of the atomic bomb had been allowed to grow unchecked, the strength of our military position by virtue of having the bomb would have been correspondingly weakened, and with this weakening would have come a decrease in the probabilities of an inter-national agreement for the control of atomic energy. I am firmly convinced that the Russians will eventually agree to the American proposals for the establishment of an atomic energy authority of world-wide scope, *provided* they are convinced that we would have the bomb in quantity and would be prepared to use it without hesitation in another war. Therefore, I have been fearful lest those who have been motivated by humanitarian considerations in their arguments against the bomb were as a matter of fact tending to accomplish exactly the reverse of their avowed purpose.[29]

Stimson's justification for using the bomb, repeated in his memoir, *On Active Service in Peace and War*, was echoed by Truman and Churchill in their memoirs, and by numerous historians, the most important of whom was Herbert Feis.[30]

For almost two decades this orthodox perspective dominated the debate, and not until the opening of Stimson's private diary and other sources disclosed incontestable evidence that postwar considerations vis-à-vis Russia had influenced the thinking of Truman, Stimson, and James F. Byrnes about the bomb prior to Hiroshima could a documented revisionist interpretation emerge – as it did when Gar Alperovitz published *Atomic Diplomacy* in 1965, at a moment when revisionist historians were questioning the conduct of the US in other areas of the Cold War.[31] Several historians criticized Alperovitz, some bitterly, for asserting with more certainty than his evidence justified that the bomb had been used for political reasons.[32]

Atomic Diplomacy nevertheless transformed the historiographical debate.

Subsequent accounts challenged Truman's assertion that the bomb was the only way to avoid a large-scale American invasion of Japan, suggesting that other possibilities such as modifying the insistence on unconditional surrender, a demonstration explosion, or relying on Russia's entry into the war could have received more serious consideration; moreover, they place greater emphasis on anti-Soviet political and diplomatic purposes – such as ending the war in the Far East in time to exclude the Kremlin from the peacemaking process there. However, even liberal "postrevisionist" authors such as Martin Sherwin, Barton Bernstein, and Robert L. Messer have differed from Alperovitz: while endorsing and elaborating the thesis that Truman and his advisers hoped the use of the bomb would intimidate or impress Moscow, they see this as "secondary," "confirming," or a "bonus" to the motive of ending the war as quickly as possible at minimum cost in American lives.[33] As Bernstein has explained it, the argument on this point has been reduced to whether "anti-Soviet purposes constituted the primary reason for using the bomb (as Alperovitz's book also argued), or a secondary but necessary reason (as some others think), or a confirming but not essential reason (as I contend)."[34]

One point on which most historians seemed to agree in the 1980s was that Truman, Stimson, and Churchill had substantially exaggerated claims that military authorities had expected half a million, or a million, American casualties in an invasion of Japan. Debunking the "myth" that the bomb had saved 500,000 American lives, they cited military staff documents, which were presented to Truman in June 1945, predicting that a maximum of 40,000 US soldiers would die and 150,000 would be wounded in a full-fledged invasion;[35] they also showed that Truman, in preparing his memoirs, changed his figures to avoid contradicting Stimson.[36]

Such revelations might suggest that Conant had been justified in worrying that "sentimental" or "verbal-minded" historians would warp the minds of the next generation. But his hope that the bomb could serve the diplomatic function of bringing about international control proved unwarranted, as did his fear of recrudescent isolationism. Nearly half a century later, there is little evidence that the arguments of historians and other critics have altered the public approval of Truman's decision. US policymakers, moreover, still find it useful to remind the world that they have not backed away from the use of the bomb. During the war against Iraq, the Bush administration made one such excursion into history to send a warning to Saddam Hussein: as US warplanes pounded Iraqi targets, fears ran high in Washington that Baghdad might use chemical weapons to repel American ground forces poised to charge into Kuwait; in a nationally televised interview, Defense Secretary Dick Cheney pointedly agreed with columnist George Will that Harry Truman had acted morally, saved lives, and "made the right decision when he used the bomb on Hiroshima." Although Cheney disclaimed any intention to use atomic weapons – "at this point" – his historical allusion sent a clear message: the United States stood ready, able, and willing to match any escalation to weapons of mass destruction.[37]

NEW EVIDENCE FROM "THE OTHER SIDE"

Did the United States and the Soviet Union botch, ignore, sabotage, or otherwise miss opportunities to end or limit the nuclear arms race far earlier and at lower levels of danger than in fact occurred? Could agreement have been reached in 1944–7 for the international control of atomic weapons, or in 1949–52 to forestall the mutual development of the hydrogen bomb? What prevented Moscow and Washington from agreeing on a comprehensive ban on nuclear testing in 1958–63? Could the rise of multiple-warhead missile systems have been forestalled in the 1970s? The "missed" or "lost" opportunities question has been a staple of historiographical debates on the arms race. Yet the paucity of Soviet sources has led to a stunted, speculative debate that often yielded arguments over whether the United States tried hard enough or sincerely enough to explore the possibilities for an arms control breakthrough, rather than whether or not such a breakthrough was really likely or possible given Moscow's attitudes.

Now, however, these debates and other lingering mysteries of the arms race may become more susceptible to informed exploration as the Soviet nuclear program's archives become accessible and its officials and scientists tell their stories, and as the Cold War's end allows the US government to relax its traditionally tight-lipped policies about releasing nuclear-related documents, policies that have prompted historians to complain repeatedly about the slowness of the Department of Energy in releasing finding aids and documents of the now-defunct US Atomic Energy Commission. Keeping nuclear weapons technology secret is a plausible enough aim, but nuclear secrecy has also been employed for political reasons: National Security Council 30, a top secret directive approved in September 1948, noted that public debate or decisions on important nuclear policy questions, such as whether to use atomic weapons in warfare, could not be risked because it "might have the effect of placing before the American people a moral question of vital security significance at a time when the full security impact of the question had not become apparent."[38]

Yet these restrictions are negligible in comparison with the barriers that blocked access to Soviet archives during the Cold War, when it was impossible for independent historians to explore records dealing with the post-World-War-II era. Until the final years of the Soviet Union, analysts in the West had to read between the lines of official newspapers and announcements, interview émigrés and defectors, and utilize the occasional leaked document. Like the shadows in Plato's cave, the exterior manifestations of Soviet actions and policy pronouncements only hinted at the far more complicated processes that had led to them. One could never be certain, for example, whether the US atomic threat had successfully "deterred" the USSR from invading Western Europe in the late 1940s or early 1950s, from tightening the noose around West Berlin in the crisis of 1958–62, or from any other policy that it wished to pursue. The debate over Soviet nuclear strategy was, at best, only partly informed by reliable information: to what extent, for instance, did Soviet leaders genuinely believe that their country could "fight and win a nuclear war," as some right-wing American commentators (such as Harvard's Richard Pipes) claimed in the late 1970s?[39] This ignorance about the inner workings about the communist world also made it impossible to render an informed assessment of American national security policies.

The collapse of the Soviet state and the partial liberalization of access regulations by the new Russian government suddenly meant that documentation from "the other side" would enable historians to reexamine the nuclear arms race.[40] Some initial revelations have already appeared. Regarding the early arms race, for example, accounts and documents indicate that Soviet espionage penetration of the Manhattan Project was far more widespread than previously believed, and included information from a thus-far unidentified scientist in addition to the German-born British physicist Klaus Fuchs, whose activities were revealed in 1950.[41] (The best account of early Soviet nuclear decisions, synthesizing new archival and oral history sources, should be David Holloway's forthcoming *Stalin and the Bomb*).[42]

Information concerning several US–Soviet crises involving nuclear weapons is also appearing and, although the inquiry into the Soviet files is still preliminary, some intriguing patterns are beginning to emerge. In both the Berlin and the Cuban missile crises, it seems, Soviet documents and oral history interviews suggest that erroneous perceptions of the other side's intentions and behavior almost led to disaster. In the case of West Berlin, where Washington was committed to its defense even if nuclear weapons were necessary, Raymond Garthoff reported alarming new details of the tense US–Soviet tank confrontation at Checkpoint Charlie on the border between East and West Berlin in October 1961. Moscow, according to interviews with Soviet officials, had received a faulty intelligence report that US forces were planning to knock down the recently-erected Berlin Wall, and viewed the incident as a pretext; Washington, by contrast, was convinced that Moscow had provoked the incident to intimidate western officials in the city. Delicate back-channel contacts defused a crisis that neither side correctly understood.[43] From their research in East German and Soviet records, Hope Harrison and Vladislav Zubok made another discovery: at the same time that Washington viewed East German actions as precisely reflecting Moscow's wishes, Soviet officials were not always informed of East Germany's harassment of Western officials in Berlin, and were concerned that such actions could escalate tensions. Coming against a backdrop of Nikita Khrushchev's repeated threats to kick the West out of the city, aggressive East German initiatives could have been misinterpreted as being Soviet-inspired.[44]

A far more sensational revelation regarding Soviet actions during the Cuban Missile Crisis emerged from a conference of Russian, American, and Cuban scholars and former officials, which was held in Havana in 1992. At the meeting, the last in a five-year series of academic conferences on the crisis,[45] the Soviet military commander who planned the deployment of forces to Cuba in 1962, Gen. Anatoly Gribkov, claimed that Soviet ground troops there had possessed tactical nuclear weapons and the authority to use them against an American invasion force,[46] although he later backed off from the latter assertion. Kennedy and his advisers were aware of the presence of medium-range nuclear missiles, which they expected to disable in an air strike accompanying any invasion, but had no idea that they might face nuclear-equipped short-range missiles as well. According to Robert S. McNamara, Kennedy's Secretary of Defense, any Soviet use of tactical nuclear weapons would likely have killed many thousands of US troops, making an American nuclear response virtually inevitable.[47] Since a US invasion was being prepared throughout the crisis, and particularly during the climactic weekend of 27–8 October 1962, the consequences may have been even graver than previously believed had Kennedy followed the advice of some of his more bellicose advisers, and had Khrushchev not precipitously agreed to withdraw the missiles.

Similarly, the addition of a Cuban perspective has convinced many analysts of the crisis that the relationship between Havana and Moscow was far more complicated and tense than US policymakers believed at the time.[48] Washington would undoubtedly have blamed the Kremlin for any aggressive action that might have been taken; but it now appears that Castro urged the Soviets to launch a preemptive nuclear strike on the United States if it invaded Cuba.[49] Similarly, it now seems certain that the shooting-down of a U-2 plane at the height of the crisis on 27 October, which almost triggered a US air attack on a Soviet-manned SAM base, was done independently by a Soviet commander on the island, rather than on Moscow's instructions, as some US officials presumed.[50]

NUCLEAR WEAPONS – A FORCE FOR "STABILITY"?

Perhaps the most controversial question concerning nuclear weapons is whether their existence has, generally speaking, made the world safer by making war unthinkable or made it more dangerous by bringing global destruction within human capabilities. Not all specialists in the field regret the missing of the alleged "missed opportunities" to end or limit the arms race. "It is often simply assumed that the world would have been a safer place if these opportunities had been seized," wrote Marc Trachtenberg in 1990, but such claims "cannot be accepted uncritically." Citing the likelihood that any international control system would break down in the event of a war between nuclear powers, Trachtenberg concludes that "probably the safest thing was to allow the nuclear revolution to run its course the way it did."[51]

Trachtenberg's skepticism is symptomatic of the ambivalent reaction to the near-agreement to eliminate the weapons that occurred at the Reagan–Gorbachev summit meeting in Reykjavik, Iceland, in October 1986. In their hastily arranged, utterly unscripted sessions, they stunned the world by flirting with an agreement to eliminate all nuclear weapons in their arsenals by the year 2000. A mutual commitment to do so fell through at the last minute because Reagan refused to agree to a clause that would ban the testing of his beloved Strategic Defense Initiative.[52]

But even had the two leaders agreed to eliminate the weapons, they might have been repudiated, probably by the US government, NATO, and perhaps by the Soviet military establishment. Why? Partly because the military, the bureaucracy, and industrial organizations on both sides had vested interests in continuing the nuclear arms race, but also because many politicians, strategists, and others on both sides of the Cold War had taken to heart the subtitle of Stanley Kubrick's classic farce of the nuclear age: *Dr Strangelove – Or How I Learned to Stop Worrying and to Love the Bomb.* Only in a fraction of cases did this romance bloom from the passion for conquest (of physical nature or enemy states) that observers sometimes discerned in the character of men such as Edward Teller, Herman Kahn, or Curtis LeMay; rather, nuclear weapons inspired a kind of intellectual affection for the role they played in keeping the peace between the superpowers.

By the 1980s, an increasing number of specialists claimed that the principal impact of nuclear weapons had been to increase "stability" in US–Soviet relations, thereby reducing the chance of war. Moreover, this salutary development was alleged to have been growing more pronounced since the 1962 Cuban Missile Crisis, as countries possessing weapons of mass destruction inexorably underwent a process known as "nuclear learning," becoming more cautious, prudent, and judicious in their international behavior, less prone to reckless nuclear threats and better able to avoid rather than "manage" nuclear crises.

The most prominent exponent of this view was John Lewis Gaddis, director of the Contemporary Historical Institute at Ohio University. In an influential essay published in 1986, Gaddis argued that the Cold War, with its disparaging connotations, should instead be known as "The Long Peace" in order to represent the unusually long period of relative peace and prosperity in Western Europe, and between the superpowers, in comparison with previous, shorter intervals between major European wars. And the bomb was credited for this success. "It seems inescapable that what has really made the difference in inducing this unaccustomed caution has been the workings of the nuclear deterrent," Gaddis concluded, suggesting that "the development of nuclear weapons has had, on balance, a stabilizing effect on the postwar international system."[53]

John Mueller, a political scientist at the University of Rochester, dissented from this view when he argued in 1988 that nuclear weapons had been "irrelevant" to the postwar world's "general stability," since the horrors wrought by the conventional weapons of World War II were sufficient to deter a repetition. He agreed, however, that what influence nuclear weapons did exert was largely beneficial, helping to dissuade leaders from escalating tensions or risking war and, since 1962, had contributed to "crisis stability." Given this stability, Mueller concluded, "it may well be that the concerns about arms and the arms race are substantially overdone. That is, the often-exquisite numerology of the nuclear arms race has probably had little to do with the important dynamics of the Cold War era."[54] Gaddis responded by disputing Mueller's claim that nuclear weapons were "irrelevant" to the course of the Cold War, arguing that they served as a sort of insurance policy for peace (or non-war) between the superpowers, reinforcing their aversion to direct military clashes that might precipitate World War III and prolonging the bipolar postwar order; thus, the weapons may have been redundant, but in a vital, helpful, reassuring, and "relevant" manner.[55]

McGeorge Bundy, another believer in "nuclear learning," exuded optimism about humanity's ability to "cap the volcano" of nuclear weapons in his *Danger and Survival: Choices about the Bomb in the First Fifty Years.* Surveying the key crises of the nuclear era, Bundy concluded that the weapons had instilled caution in statesmen and become less dangerous as a "tradition of non-use" took root. "Nuclear weapons have been with the world since 1945," Bundy wrote, "and each ten-year period in that time has turned out to be less dangerous than the one before it."[56]

The importance of such historical views, of course, is that assumptions about the past impact of nuclear weapons will influence what is done with them in the future. If nuclear weapons are perceived as having imbued politicians with caution and responsibility, plans for the retention or even spread of nuclear weapons will multiply – witness John J. Mearsheimer's cover story in *The Atlantic* of August 1990, "Why We Will Soon Miss the Cold War."[57] Mearsheimer was positively effusive about the bomb. "Nuclear weapons seem to be in almost everybody's bad book," he wrote, "but the fact is that they are a powerful force for peace." By raising the potential horrors of war, he argued, nuclear weapons "favor" and "bolster" peace. With that thought in mind, Mearsheimer suggested that "nuclear proliferation in Europe" in the post-cold-war epoch "is the best hope for maintaining stability on the Continent." The centerpiece of this bomb-in-every-garage scenario is a nuclear-armed, unified Germany, which would otherwise feel "insecure" without a nuclear arsenal. While Mearsheimer preferred that a "well-managed proliferation" stop with Germany, he allowed that states in Eastern Europe should also be permitted to join the nuclear club if they so insist. Why stop there? Why not distribute nuclear weapons to other "insecure" states? If Mearsheimer's pro-proliferation idea wins adherents, perhaps proposals to create other "balances of terror" throughout a multi-polar international system will follow.

If, on the other hand, the historical record suggests that nuclear crises have occurred with enough frequency and seriousness to justify alarm rather than reassurance, and that nuclear weapons can exacerbate as well as ease tensions, then a greater sense of urgency about getting rid of them is a logical consequence. This will continue to be disputed, and the answer to whether we are better off with nuclear weapons or without them comes down as much to one's confidence or pessimism about human nature and fallibility as it does to rational calculations of "risk assessment" or "crisis stability."

Historians who have drawn comforting lessons from the outcome of nuclear crises over the past half-century have overlooked or downplayed some ominous trends. For a variety of reasons – technical malfunctions, the problems of controlling a vast military apparatus, the difficulty of "signaling" a nuclear adversary, misperceptions, etc. – the risks of accidental nuclear war, or of unintended escalation that might have led to nuclear war, appear to have been higher in several crises than was recognized at the time. In an important study of US nuclear strategy, Scott Sagan credited Washington with successfully avoiding nuclear war and deterring Moscow, but concluded that senior US officials have not always been in full control of their nuclear machinery.[58] Senior civilian and military leaders have added many safety features to the US nuclear arsenal to prevent accidental war or inadvertent escalation, but numerous close calls have nonetheless occurred. Nuclear peace has been maintained for forty years, but it is not assured for the future. The argument that the Cuban Missile Crisis was not followed by other, comparable, nuclear confrontations does not mean that "crisis management" had become easier.[59] Increasing technological sophistication over the course of the Cold War proved to be no guarantee against occasional, catastrophic malfunction, as demonstrated by Chernobyl, Three Mile Island, Challenger, and other disasters. Also, the growing complexity and size of the two powers' military apparatus appears to have made them more difficult to control, whatever their political leaders may have desired, and this would have been particularly so if both the US and the USSR simultaneously had raised their alert status during a moment of tension, thereby increasing the incentive for a preemptive strike.[60]

Moreover, the assertion that the superpowers gradually "learned" over time to behave more judiciously, cautiously, and safely with nuclear weapons may itself require reconsideration, if further research substantiates the recent claim that a secret US–Soviet crisis in the fall of 1983 brought the world "closer to apocalypse than any time since the Cuban missile crisis of 1962." The purported crisis was disclosed in 1990 by Oleg Gordievsky, a senior KGB officer who defected to the West in 1985 and subsequently co-authored a history of Soviet intelligence and co-edited two collections of smuggled KGB documents.[61] According to Gordievsky, the Moscow controllers of the KGB, then headed by Yuri Andropov, became convinced during the first term of the Reagan administration that the United States was "actively preparing for nuclear war." They took this fear so seriously, Gordievsky reports, that the KGB and Soviet military intelligence launched an espionage effort, Operation RYAN, to see if the United States and NATO were preparing a surprise nuclear first strike. Illustrating Soviet ignorance of Western society, the KGB instructed its London station that preparations for a nuclear attack on the Soviet Union might be indicated by "increased purchases of blood and the price paid for it" and the "mass slaughter of cattle and putting meat into long cold storage"; advance warning of a nuclear first strike might be obtained from leading Western bankers and church officials, including those of the Vatican.[62]

Matters reached a dangerous climax in late 1983, Gordievsky reports. Reaganesque rhetoric, "Star Wars," and the US military build-up had already convinced Andropov (who had succeeded Leonid Brezhnev) that America was slipping into an "outrageous military psychosis." Relations continued to deteriorate when the Soviets shot down the KAL 007 Korean airliner and the Americans invaded Grenada. But the Soviets were most alarmed when the Americans began, in October, to deploy in West Germany Pershing and cruise missiles, which were capable of hitting Soviet political and military command bunkers in a short flight time that was unprecedented. (Gordievsky said KGB headquarters inaccurately estimated they could reach key targets in only four to six minutes.) In response, the Soviets walked out of arms control talks in Geneva. Then, in early November, NATO forces conducted "Able Archer 83" – a training exercise "designed to practice nuclear-release procedures" – exacerbating Soviet fears. The Soviet intelligence apparatus, according to Gordievsky, was convinced that a nuclear strike was imminent: "the KGB concluded that American forces had really been placed on alert – and might even have begun the countdown to nuclear war."

Soviet fears ebbed after the NATO exercise concluded without a surprise attack and after the West took measures to calm the situation. But Gordievsky's account, if accurate, suggests that such a crisis, which could have led to nuclear war, happened largely because of misunderstandings and fears generated by the weapons themselves, and in particular by the quick-action Pershing and cruise missiles being deployed by the United States (in response to Soviet medium-range missiles aimed at Western Europe), and the nuclear-delivery systems associated with the NATO training exercise.

Gordievsky's story requires further investigation to determine how serious the danger really was. US intelligence, it appears, initially considered the matter a case of Soviet disinformation. But a classified reexamination of the episode undertaken by the president's Foreign Intelligence Advisory Board reported in February 1990 that previous US intelligence estimates had been "remiss in dismissing the possibility that the Soviet leadership actually believed the United States was planning a first strike," and that Soviet leaders, convinced that Washington was seeking, and winning, military superiority, "may have taken seriously the possibility of a US nuclear strike against the Soviet Union."[63]

What emerges is a recipe for disaster: the Soviets, ill-informed and paranoid, taking literally the extremist statements of Reagan and his advisers concerning the use of nuclear weapons and extrapolating the most sinister interpretation of them;[64] the Reagan administration being blithely unconcerned that reckless talk might lead to unintended and dangerous consequences. Gordievsky's chilling tale does not necessarily invalidate the reassuring conclusions reached by Gaddis, Mueller, Bundy, and others. It may indeed be, as Gaddis contends, that, "on balance," nuclear weapons have had a stabilizing effect on the postwar world. But any theory of "nuclear

learning" will have to explain why these supposedly well educated superpowers came so close to failing the test.

In any event, the chaos of the post-cold-war world may be inducing
some second thoughts. In a work published in 1992, Gaddis denounced
Mearsheimer's argument in favor of nuclear proliferation as "profoundly
wrong" and asked: "At what point does the risk of irrational action —
which presumably increases as the number of nuclear-capable states increases — outweigh the benefits of the 'sobering effect' nuclear capability
apparently brings?"[65]

With nuclear technology easier to obtain than ever, with a long list of
nations hurrying to develop nuclear weapons, with extreme ideologies and
unstable regimes continuing to cause international chaos, and with military
conflicts still erupting despite the "New World Order," we may already have
crossed the line where nuclear learning will cease to be effective. Half-hearted
inspection regimes, such as the IAEA and the Nuclear Non-Proliferation
Treaty, and unilateral anti-proliferation actions (such as Israel's 1981 bombing
of an Iraqi nuclear reactor), offer no more than band-aids or pain-killers for a
disease that has become chronic and that might prove to be terminal. Despite
mankind's success in surviving the first half-century of the nuclear age, the
long-term dangers are no less than they were when the Manhattan Project's
scientists and administrators saw international control as the only hope for
escaping atomic destruction. There is no time like the present to study the
history of the nuclear weapons race to determine whether current ideas,
institutions, and policies will be adequate to meet the new challenges.

NOTES

1 Two early accounts of the reversal in US–Soviet relations, making good use of
   interviews and leaked documents, are Don Oberdorfer, *The Turn: From the Cold
   War to a New Era: The United States and the Soviet Union 1983–1990*, New York,
   1991, and Michael Beschloss and Strobe Talbott, *At the Highest Levels: The Inside
   Story of the End of the Cold War*, Boston, 1993.
2 Nazi Germany's failure to develop atomic weapons during World War II is a
   subject of contentious debate between those who argue that the principal reason
   was practical difficulties (inadequate material resources and government support,
   poor organization, scientific errors, war-caused hardships) and others who argue
   that key German physicists working on nuclear fission, in particular Werner
   Heisenberg, were unenthusiastic about building an atomic bomb for Hitler and
   effectively sabotaged the effort. For an important new work that comes closer to
   the latter view, see Thomas Powers, *Heisenberg's War: The Secret History of the
   German Bomb*, New York, 1993. See also Samuel Gouldsmit, *Alsos*, New York,
   1947; Mark Walker, *German National Socialism and the Quest for Nuclear Power,
   1939–1949*, New York, 1989; and Jeremy Bernstein, "The Farm Hall Transcripts:
   The German Scientists and the Bomb," *New York Review of Books*, vol. 39, 13
   August 1992, pp. 47–53.
3 If not entirely eradicated, as Russian Foreign Minister Andrei V. Kozyrev
   reminded the world in startling fashion in December 1992 when he delivered a
   hardline speech to a meeting of the Conference on Security and Cooperation in

Europe, only to return a half hour later to tell the stunned gathering that he had only been dramatizing what might be heard should hardliners topple Yeltsin. Craig R. Whitney, "Russian Carries On Like the Bad Old Days, Then Says It Was All a Ruse," *New York Times*, 15 December 1992. Kozyrev's desperate stunt was reminiscent of one scenario contained in a secret Pentagon study of potential post-cold-war dangers, that a "single nation or a coalition of nations" might arise in the former Soviet Union "to adopt an adversarial security strategy and develop a military capability to threaten U.S. interests through global military competition." See Patrick E. Tyler, "7 Hypothetical Conflicts Foreseen by the Pentagon," *New York Times*, 17 February 1992.

4 For surveys of the international proliferation situation, see the annual reports of Leonard S. Spector of the Carnegie Endowment for International Peace; on the proliferation implications of the Soviet Union's demise, see Kurt M. Campbell, Ashton B. Carter, Steven E. Miller, and Charles Zraket, *Soviet Nuclear Fission: Control of the Nuclear Arsenal in a Disintegrating Soviet Union* [CSIA Studies in International Security No. 1], Cambridge, Mass., 1991, and Steven E. Miller, "Nuclear Proliferation Risks and the Former Soviet Union," paper prepared for the conference on "Nuclear Proliferation in the 1990s: Challenges and Opportunities," Woodrow Wilson International Center for Scholars, Washington, D.C., 1–2 December 1992.

5 The following list is a sampling of works offering overviews of the nuclear arms race from World War II onwards: Michael E. Mandelbaum, *The Nuclear Question: The United States and Nuclear Weapons, 1946–1976*, New York, 1979; Ronald W. Clark, *The Greatest Power on Earth*, New York, 1980; Gerard H. Clarfield and William M. Wiecek, *Nuclear America: Military and Civilian Nuclear Power in the United States, 1940–1980*, New York, 1984; Ronald E. Powaski, *March to Armageddon: The United States and the Nuclear Arms Race, 1939 to the Present*, New York, 1987; McGeorge Bundy, *Danger and Survival: Choices about the Bomb in the First Fifty Years*, New York, 1988; Charles R. Morris, *Iron Destinies, Lost Opportunities: The Post-War Arms Race*, New York, 1988; John Newhouse, *War and Peace in the Nuclear Age*, New York, 1989; Carl B. Feldbaum and Ronald J. Bee, *Looking the Tiger in the Eye: Confronting the Nuclear Threat*, New York, 1990; Jennifer E. Sims, *Icarus Restrained: An Intellectual History of Nuclear Arms Control, 1945–1960*, Boulder, Col., 1990. The essays of David Alan Rosenberg are essential for their use of declassified documents on the evolution of US nuclear policies: see Rosenberg, "The Origins of Overkill: Nuclear Weapons and American Strategy, 1945–60," *International Security*, vol. 7, 1983, pp. 3–71, and "Reality and Responsibility: Power and Process in the Making of United States Nuclear Strategy, 1945–1968," *Journal of Strategic Studies*, vol. 9, 1986, pp. 35–52. Several studies of nuclear strategy also provide an historical perspective: Lawrence Freedman, *The Evolution of Nuclear Strategy*, New York, 1981; Fred Kaplan, *Wizards of Armageddon*, New York, 1983; Gregg Herken, *Counsels of War*, New York, 1987, expanded edition; Janne E. Nolan, *Guardians of the Arsenal: The Politics of Nuclear Strategy*, New York, 1989. Three excellent anthologies of articles and documents are Donna Gregory, *The Nuclear Predicament: A Sourcebook*, New York, 1986; Philip L. Cantelon, Richard G. Hewlett, and Robert C. Williams, *The American Atom: A Documentary History of Nuclear Policies from the Discovery of Fission to the Present*, Philadelphia, Pa, 1991; and Jeffrey Porro (ed.), *The Nuclear Age Reader*, New York, 1989. A massive classified history commissioned by the US Department of Defense, released in 1990 in a sanitized version, is Ernest R. May, John D. Steinbrunner, and Thomas W. Wolfe, *History of the Strategic Arms Competition, 1945–1972*. Recommended for its analysis of the role of scientists in the arms race is Gregg Herken, *Cardinal Choices: Presidential Science Advising from the Atomic Bomb to SDI*, New York, 1992.

6 This historical approach admittedly neglects important thematic issues that deserve a serious reassessment, including the changes in the United States wrought by the nuclear arms race in the relationship among science, academia, industry, the federal government, and the military; the economics of the nuclear arms race; the environmental legacy of the nuclear weapons and energy industries; the cultural, literary, philosophical, and psychological impact of the nuclear age; the relationship between the civilian nuclear power industry and the weapons business; and the influence of nuclear weapons in the rise of government secrecy and the imperial presidency.

7 My analysis does not adopt the thesis, advanced by presidents Reagan and Bush and some of their admirers, that the Cold War and the nuclear arms race ended in the late 1980s because the Soviets were stretched to the breaking point trying to match the military budget increases and technological innovations such as the Strategic Defense Initiative introduced by the Republican administrations. These acts certainly exacerbated Moscow's woes, but there is considerable evidence to suggest that the Soviet systemic collapse resulted from a largely internal dynamic, the cumulative burdens of decades of mismanagement and internal political, economic, and spiritual decay, rather than any sudden external pressure.

8 Studies of the Manhattan Project and its relationship to the origins of the postwar arms race are Richard G. Hewlett and Oscar E. Anderson, Jr, *The New World, 1939/ 1946*, vol. 1, *A History of the United States Atomic Energy Commission*, University Park, Pa, 1962; Martin J. Sherwin, *A World Destroyed: The Atomic Bomb and the Grand Alliance*, New York, 1975; citations from the revised edition, *A World Destroyed: Hiroshima and the Origins of the Arms Race*, Vintage Books, 1987; Richard Rhodes, *The Making of the Atomic Bomb*, New York, 1986.

9 Conant and Bush to Stimson, 30 September 1944, in Sherwin, *A World Destroyed*, pp. 286–8.

10 On the international control negotiations see Bundy, *Danger and Survival*, chap. 4; on the evolving US mindset toward atomic weapons in the early postwar years, see Gregg Herken, *The Winning Weapon: The Atomic Bomb in the Cold War, 1945–1950*, New York, 1980.

11 Oberdorfer, *The Turn*, pp. 232–3.

12 See US Arms Control and Disarmament Agency, *Arms Control and Disarmament Agreements: Texts and Histories of the Negotiations*, Washington, 1990, pp. 319–35.

13 Newhouse, *War and Peace in the Nuclear Age*, pp. 400–1.

14 Conant, handwritten comments on Bush to Conant, "Shurcliff's memo on Post-War Policies," 17 April 1944, Atomic Energy Commission Historical Document 180, and Conant, "Some Thoughts on the International Control of Atomic Energy," 4 May 1944, S-1 files, Bush–Conant correspondence, folder 97, Office of Scientific Research and Development papers, Record Group 227, National Archives, Washington, D.C. The present author examines Conant's ideas in *Harvard to Hiroshima: James B. Conant and the Making of the Nuclear Age*, New York, Knopf, 1993.

15 Yeltsin speech of 29 January 1992, in FBIS-SOV-92-019.

16 See David Kay, "The IAEA – How Can It Be Strengthened?," paper delivered at the Woodrow Wilson Center conference on "Nuclear Proliferation in the 1990s: Challenges and Opportunities," 1–2 December 1992, and Gary Milhollin, "The Iraqi Bomb," *The New Yorker*, vol. 67, 1 February 1993, pp. 47–56.

17 For a skeptical view of the efficacy of collective security in the post-cold-war world see Josef Joffe, "Collective Security and the Future of Europe: Failed Dreams and Dead Ends," *Survival*, vol. 24, spring 1992, pp. 37–50.

18 See Gar Alperovitz and Kai Bird, "Dream of Total Disarmament Could Become Reality," *Los Angeles Times* Opinion section, 12 January 1992.

19 Quoted by A. Lavrent'yeva in "Stroiteli novogo mira," *V mire knig*, no. 9, 1970, p. 4, cited in David Holloway, *The Soviet Union and the Arms Race*, New Haven, Conn., 1983, 1984, p. 20.

20 Surveys of the historiographical debate over Hiroshima include Barton J. Bernstein, "The Atomic Bomb and American Foreign Policy, 1941–1945: An Historical Controversy," *Peace and Change*, vol. 2, Spring 1974, pp. 1–16; Bernstein, *The Atomic Bomb: The Critical Issues*, Boston, 1976, pp. vii–xix and 163–9; and J. Samuel Walker, "The Decision to Use the Bomb: A Historiographical Update," *Diplomatic History*, vol. 14, 1990, pp. 97–114.

21 On the depths of US hostility toward Japan, which had a racial dimension missing from the war with Germany, see John Dower, *War Without Mercy: Race and Power in the Pacific War*, New York, 1986. On the US public's reaction to Hiroshima see Michael J. Yavenditti, "The American People and the Use of Atomic Bombs on Japan: The 1940s," *The Historian*, vol. 36, 1974, pp. 221–47, and Paul Boyer, *By the Bomb's Early Light: American Thought and Culture at the Dawn of the Atomic Age*, New York, 1985, esp. chaps 1 & 16.

22 Most accounts of the Manhattan Project describe the scientists' objections, especially *A World Destroyed* and *The Making of the Atomic Bomb*, but also see Alice K. Smith, *A Peril and a Hope: The Scientists' Movement in America, 1945–1947*, Chicago, 1965.

23 Vannevar Bush to John T. Tate, 13 August 1945, Atomic Energy files, Carnegie Institution of Washington archives, Washington, D.C.

24 *US Strategic Bombing Survey, The Summary Report on the Pacific War*, Washington, D.C., 1946, p. 26.

25 John Hersey, "Reporter at Large: Hiroshima," *New Yorker*, 31 August 1946; Hersey, *Hiroshima*, New York, 1946. For analyses of the reactions to Hersey's article see Michael J. Yavenditti, "John Hersey and the American Conscience: The Reception of 'Hiroshima,'" *Pacific Historical Review*, vol. 43, 1974, pp. 24–49; and Boyer, *By the Bomb's Early Light*, pp. 205–10.

26 See, for example, Norman Cousins, "The Literacy of Survival," *The Saturday Review of Literature*, vol. 29, 14 September 1946, p. 14.

27 James B. Conant to Harvey H. Bundy, 23 September 1946, "Bu–By" correspondence folder, 1946–7, box 296, Conant Presidential Papers, Pusey Library, Harvard University, Cambridge, Mass.

28 Karl T. Compton, "If the Atomic Bomb Had Not Been Used," *Atlantic Monthly*, vol. 178, December 1946, pp. 54–6; Henry L. Stimson, "The Decision to Use the Atomic Bomb," *Harper's Magazine*, vol. 194, February 1947, pp. 97–107. The Stimson article was drafted by Harvey Bundy's son, McGeorge (who was helping Stimson with his memoirs), with aid from Conant and others involved in the decision. See James G. Hershberg, "James B. Conant, Nuclear Weapons, and the Cold War, 1945–1950," Ph.D. dissertation, Tufts University, 1989, chap. 3; this account was amplified in Barton J. Bernstein, "Seizing the Contested Terrain of Early Nuclear History: Stimson, Conant, and Their Allies Explain the Decision to Use the Atomic Bomb," *Diplomatic History*, vol. 17, 1993, pp. 35–72.

29 James B. Conant to Henry L. Stimson, 22 January 1947, box 154, folder 18, Stimson papers, Yale University. Underlining (italics) in original.

30 See the accounts in Henry L. Stimson and McGeorge Bundy, *On Active Service in War and Peace*, New York, 1947, 1948, chaps 23–4; Harry S. Truman, *Memoirs*, vol. 1: *Year of Decisions, 1945*, Garden City, N.Y., 1955, pp. 415–26; Winston S. Churchill, *Triumph and Tragedy*, Boston, 1953, pp. 628–9, 637–45; and Herbert Feis, *Japan Subdued: The Atomic Bomb and the End of World War Two in the Pacific*, Princeton, N.J., 1961.

31 Gar Alperovitz, *Atomic Diplomacy: Hiroshima and Potsdam*, New York, 1965; revised ed., 1985. Alperovitz's work prompted Feis gingerly to acknowledge the

influence of postwar considerations in the atomic deliberations in *The Atomic Bomb and the End of World War II*, Princeton, N.J., 1966. Alperovitz is currently working on another study of Hiroshima slated for publication in 1995.

32 See for example, Robert J. Maddox, "Atomic Diplomacy: A Study in Creative Writing," *Journal of American History*, vol. 59, 1973, pp. 925–34, and Bundy, *Danger and Survival*, pp. 88–9, 650–1 n. 78 & 79. In an unusually angry comment in his otherwise temperate and reflective *Danger and Survival*, Bundy, whose anger may have been a product of his abiding affection and respect for Stimson, heaps scorn on Blackett, Alperovitz, and others who believe that "a desire to impress the Russians with the power of the bomb was a major factor in the decision to use it. This assertion is false, and the evidence to support it rests on inferences so stretched as to be a discredit both to the judgment of those who have accepted such arguments." Bundy acknowledges that "later and more careful critics" have made cogent points about the absence of a thorough and thoughtful consideration of alternatives to using the bomb, and also agrees that Truman and his aides were "full of hope that the bomb would put new strength into the American power position" vis-à-vis the Russians.

33 See Sherwin, *A World Destroyed*; Barton J. Bernstein, "The Quest for Security: American Foreign Policy and International Control of Atomic Energy, 1942–1946," *Journal of American History*, vol. 40, 1974, pp. 1003–44; Bernstein, "Roosevelt, Truman, and the Atomic Bomb, 1941–1945: A Reinterpretation," *Political Science Quarterly*, vol. 90, 1975, pp. 23–69; and Robert L. Messer, *The End of an Alliance: James F. Byrnes, Roosevelt, Truman and the Origins of the Cold War*, Chapel Hill, N.C., 1982, esp. pp. 114–17. In recent years, Sherwin has become more critical of Truman's decision (see the introduction to the 1987 Vintage edition of *A World Destroyed*), Bernstein less so. The most important study of Japan's surrender assigns an important role to the bomb, but also argues that an earlier modification of the Allied demand for unconditional surrender might well have prompted Tokyo to capitulate without using atomic weapons. See Robert J. C. Butow, *Japan's Decision to Surrender*, Stanford, Calif., 1954, pp. 149–50, 158, 180–1, 231.

34 See Barton J. Bernstein, "Eclipsed by Hiroshima and Nagasaki," *International Security*, vol. 15, Spring 1991, pp. 149–73, esp. pp. 168–70, and the subsequent exchange between Bernstein, on the one hand, and Alperovitz and Messer, on the other, in *International Security*, vol. 16, Winter 1991/2, pp. 204–21 (the quotation in the text is on p. 219).

35 Rufus E. Miles, Jr, "Hiroshima: The Strange Myth of a Half a Million American Lives Saved," *International Security*, vol. 10, Fall 1985, pp. 121–40; Barton J. Bernstein, "A Postwar Myth: 500,000 U.S. Lives Saved," *Bulletin of the Atomic Scientists*, vol. 42, June/July 1986, pp. 38–40; Sherwin, *A World Destroyed*, intro. to 1987 ed.; Walker, "The Decision to Use the Bomb," pp. 105–6.

36 See Barton J. Bernstein, "Writing, Righting, or Wronging the Historical Record," *Diplomatic History*, vol. 16, 1992, pp. 163–73; and Hershberg, *James B. Conant*, chap. 16.

37 Transcript of "This Week with David Brinkley," ABC News, 3 February 1991.

38 NSC-30, "United States Policy on Atomic Weapons," 10 September 1948, in US State Department, *Foreign Relations of the United States, 1948*, vol. I, part 2, pp. 624–8.

39 See Richard Pipes, "Why the Soviet Union Thinks It Could Fight and Win a Nuclear War," *Commentary*, vol. 64, July 1977, pp. 21–34.

40 The most informed reports on the fast-changing Soviet/Russian archives scene have been written by Patricia Kennedy Grimsted and distributed by the International Research and Exchanges Board (IREX); good places to keep track of continuing developments include the journal *American Archivist*; the newsletter of

the American Association for the Advancement of Slavic Studies; and the *Bulletin* of the *Cold War International History Project*, Woodrow Wilson International Center for Scholars, Washington, D.C.

41 See Michael Dobbs, "How Soviets Stole US Atom Secrets," *Washington Post*, 4 October 1992; Serge Schmemann, "1st Soviet A-Bomb Built from U.S. Data, Russian Says," *New York Times*, 14 January 1993; and various articles in the May 1993 *Bulletin of the Atomic Scientists*.

42 Holloway's new book will undoubtedly supplant the standard English-language works on the origins and early history of the Soviet nuclear program: Arnold Kramish's *Nuclear Energy in the Soviet Union*, Stanford, Calif., 1959, and Holloway's *The Soviet Union and the Arms Race*, New Haven, Conn., 1983.

43 See Raymond L. Garthoff, "Berlin 1961: The Record Corrected," *Foreign Policy*, vol. 84, 1991, pp. 142–56.

44 See papers by Hope Harrison and Vladislav Zubok prepared for the Cold War International History Project's conference on Cold War history, Moscow, 12–15 January 1993, and published as working papers by the project.

45 The meetings were organized by James G. Blight and associates, at first at Harvard University's Center for Science and International Affairs and then at Brown University's Center for Foreign Policy Development; see James G. Blight and David A. Welch, *On the Brink: Americans and Soviets Reexamine the Cuban Missile Crisis*, New York, 1989; rev. ed., 1990; Blight, Bruce J. Allyn, and David A. Welch (eds), *Back to the Brink: Proceedings of the Moscow Conference on the Cuban Missile Crisis, January 27–28, 1989*, Lanham, Md, 1992; and James G. Blight, Bruce J. Allyn, and David A. Welch, with David Lewis, *Cuba on the Brink: Fidel Castro, the Missile Crisis, and the Collapse of Communism*, New York, 1993. Other new information and interpretations regarding the crisis are presented in Laurence Chang and Peter Kornbluh (eds), *The Cuban Missile Crisis: A National Security Archive Documents Reader*, New York, 1992, and James A. Nathan (ed.), *The Cuban Missile Crisis Revisited*, New York, 1992.

46 See Raymond L. Garthoff, "The Havana Conference on the Cuban Missile Crisis," *Cold War International History Project Bulletin*, no. 1, spring 1992, pp. 2–4; and Anatoly Gribkov, "An der Schwelle zum Atomkrieg" ["On the Threshold of Nuclear War"] and "Operation Anadyr," *Der Spiegel*, 13 & 20 April 1992. Documentation to substantiate Gribkov's assertion, which occasioned some skepticism among US analysts, was later located in Soviet Defense ministry archives; see the 26 October letter of James G. Blight and Bruce J. Allyn printed in *The New York Times*, 2 November 1992, p. A 18. However, subsequent accounts have cast doubt on Gribkov's assertion of predelegated authority to use nuclear weapons; see Mark Kramer's article in the *Cold War International History Project Bulletin*, no. 3, Fall 1993, pp. 40, 42–6.

47 Comments at press conference, 21 January 1992, National Press Club, Washington, D.C.

48 See Philip Brenner, "Cuba and the Missile Crisis," *Journal of Latin American Studies*, vol. 22, 1990, pp. 115–42, and Brenner, "Thirteen Months: Cuba's Perspective on the Missile Crisis," in Nathan (ed.), *The Cuban Missile Crisis Revisited*, pp. 187–217.

49 Castro to Khrushchev, 26 October 1962.

50 See Brenner, "Thirteen Months," pp. 198–9, 214, n. 85.

51 Marc Trachtenberg, "The Past and Future of Arms Control," *Daedelus*, vol. 120, winter 1991, pp. 203–16, quotation on p. 205.

52 See Oberdorfer, *The Turn*, pp. 189–205, 445–7.

53 John Lewis Gaddis, *The Long Peace: Inquiries into the History of the Cold War*, New York, 1987, pp. 215–45.

54 John Mueller, "The Essential Irrelevance of Nuclear Weapons: Stability in the

Postwar World," *International Security*, vol. 13, Fall 1988, pp. 55–79.

55 John Lewis Gaddis, "The Essential Relevance of Nuclear Weapons," in *The United States and the End of the Cold War: Implications, Reconsiderations, Provocations*, New York, 1992, pp. 105–18.

56 Bundy, *Danger and Survival*, p. 616.

57 John J. Mearsheimer, "Why We Will Soon Miss the Cold War," *The Atlantic*, vol. 266, August 1990, pp. 35–50; for a lengthier and more scholarly version of the argument see Mearsheimer, "Back to the Future: Instability in Europe After the Cold War," *International Security*, vol. 15, summer 1990, pp. 5–58, reprinted in Sean M. Lynn-Jones (ed.), *The Cold War and After: Prospects for Peace*, Cambridge, Mass., 1991, pp. 141–92.

58 Scott D. Sagan, *Moving Targets: Nuclear Strategy and National Security*, Princeton, N.J., 1989, pp. 5–6; see also Sagars *The limits of Safety: Organizations, Accidents and Nuclear Weapons*, Princeton, 1993.

59 For an extensive review of historical case studies and generic difficulties involved in controlling crises, particularly those involving nuclear weapons, see Alexander L. George (ed.), *Avoiding War: Problems of Crisis Management*, Boulder, Colo., 1991.

60 On the complexity of controlling nuclear forces see Paul Bracken, *The Command and Control of Nuclear Forces*, New Haven, Conn., 1983. A key ingredient in limiting escalation of the Cuban Missile Crisis was the failure of the Soviets to match the American high-level nuclear alert. See Marc Trachtenberg, "The Influence of Nuclear Weapons in the Cuban Missile Crisis," *International Security*, vol. 10, Summer 1985, reprinted in Trachtenberg, *History and Strategy*, Princeton, 1991, pp. 235–60, esp. pp. 253–5; and Scott D. Sagan, "Nuclear Alerts and Crisis Management," *International Security*, vol. 9, Spring 1985, pp. 99–139.

61 Christopher Andrew and Oleg Gordievsky, *KGB: The Inside Story*, New York, 1990; Andrew and Gordievsky (eds), *Instructions from the Centre: Top Secret Files on KGB Foreign Operations, 1975–1985*, London, 1991; and Andrew and Gordievsky (eds), "More 'Instructions from the Centre': Top Secret Files on KGB Global Operations, 1975–1985," *Intelligence and National Security*, vol. 7, 1992, pp. 1–128.

62 On "Operation Ryan" and the 1983 crisis see Andrew and Gordievsky, *KGB: The Inside Story*, pp. 581–605, and the directives and commentary in Andrew and Gordievsky (eds), *Instructions from the Centre*, pp. 67–90.

63 See Oberdorfer, *The Turn*, pp. 62–8, especially the footnote on p. 67.

64 For a compilation of the kind of statements that might have contributed to Soviet paranoia, see Robert Scheer, *With Enough Shovels: Reagan, Bush & Nuclear War*, New York, 1982.

65 Gaddis, "The Essential Relevance of Nuclear Weapons," pp. 117, 217 n. 38.

12 American diplomacy: retrospect and prospect

Joan Hoff

Shortly after the 1991 war in the Persian Gulf, a political cartoon depicted the United States "giving a [war] party" to which "the enemy [Iraq] had refused to come." Yet "Victory Celebrations" in Washington, D.C., New York, and other major cities in June 1991, accompanied by an uncharacteristically massive display of high tech armament, gave the distinct impression that the United States had won a "fun," essentially bloodless war – more like a Nintendo game played on a real world stage. Some newspaper columnists referred to the conflict in the Middle East as the best "splendid little war" the United States had fought since the Spanish–American War of 1898; others said it was equivalent to sending an elephant to stomp on a mouse.

Each of these images, conveyed by political cartoons, patriotic parades, and pundits is partly accurate. Saddam Hussein's forces did conduct a basically static defensive and often his troops refused to fight during this unbelievably short, 43-day and intensely technological "hyperwar." Certain stated military objectives, however, were achieved: the Iraqis left Kuwait; Saddam's army was destroyed, and Iraq's nuclear, chemical, biological, and Scud warfare capabilities were severely damaged – although not completely eliminated as initially reported. Most Allied political objectives were not achieved: Saddam remained in power, the "free" Kuwait remained undemocratic with its oil wells on fire and incapacitated until well into 1992, and the Middle East was left no more stable than before the war.

The achievement of this partial *status quo ante* resulted in the deaths of some 120,000 Iraqi soldiers and an estimated 200,000 civilians, largely due to disease and malnutrition. At the same time, 268 Americans were killed in combat-related action, and the war itself initially cost about $1 billion a day for the first three months, not including the ongoing expense of keeping an encampment of 300,000 Allied troops in Saudi Arabia, Iraq, and Kuwait. As of 18 May 1992, the cost to the United States alone was $7.3 billion, with the remainder to be paid by the Allied powers.[1] The United States, for the first time in the twentieth century, could not afford to finance its own participation in a war effort.

What then did the nation celebrate or honor with these parades in June? The end of the Cold War or the beginning of a New World Order? Secure access to half of the world's oil resources? Victory? Patriotism? Militarism? Successful testing of high tech weapons? Dead American veterans and their families? The end of the defeatist Vietnam syndrome? And what will American foreign policy become in the wake of the war? These questions have led to speculation about the need to reassess US diplomacy in the 1990s, and about whether the history of previous changes in American foreign policy can help envision what the country should or could do as the "pre-eminent" power in the world at the end of the twentieth century.

Since America's inception three very general and intertwined phenomena have influenced the way in which policymakers have formulated US foreign policy and the way in which diplomatic scholars have interpreted it. They are: first, a maddeningly unselfconscious ideology, which by the beginning of the twentieth century had conflated national greatness with the promotion of liberty abroad, usually meaning the American model of democracy and capitalism, and a racist and suspicious view of leftist revolutions in the rest of the world, waiting to be exacerbated by the Cold War; second, sea-changes that occurred in the economy of the United States, gradually up to 1890s and then dramatically after World War I and II and again at the end of the Cold War; and third, traumatic generational events, usually wars that have temporarily shaped both popular and elite thinking about how the nation should conduct itself on the international scene.[2]

The role of the United States in the world has obviously changed in the last two hundred years. Although most diplomatic historians now concentrate on the history of US foreign relations since the nation became a great power, a small minority maintain that the ideological, political, and cultural ways in which the United States consolidated itself into an "empire of liberty" in the course of the nineteenth century have determined its rapid and unprecedented global primacy in the twentieth century – as much, if not more than, its economic and military dominance – and, hence, are worthy of more scholarly consideration than they are now being accorded. After all, the American Union will survive at least into the twenty-first century, while the Soviet Union has not. Neither unwieldy empire was given much chance of surviving this long by many Europeans who commented on their tortuous formations through revolution and civil war.

There is much truth to the claim that the United States outlasted the "evil empire" because in the nineteenth century it triumphed over its own secessionist crisis with a federal system and "ideology and social structure that harnessed rather than suppressed the creative individuality of its citizenry, especially whites and males." In doing so, however, its concept of national greatness by 1900 included the messianic notion that by example, or force, as it turned out the United States should undertake an "experiment in self-duplication" for the rest of the world.[3] This experiment in global cloning was based on the assumption that its democratic and capitalistic brand of liberty was universally transferable and would benefit people abroad, as it had domestically, if they would only become clones of the "American way of life." In the course of the twentieth century this cloning process succeeded least when most forced and best when most inadvertent, as in the pervasive spread of American pop culture and desire for consumer products behind the Iron Curtain and into remote areas of the Third World.

Yet at the height of this cloning process in the wake of the Cold War, there is every indication that Americans have lost faith in their own system. During the 1992 presidential election, for example, evidence abounded that the land of equality, liberty, and opportunity was internally fragmenting in part because of a new wave of immigrants since 1965 that rivals the highest levels reached at the end of the nineteenth century. Unlike their predominantly European predecessors, however, these largely Hispanic and Asian new-comers are not as motivated to assimilate in order to be a part of the "American dream." Instead of being content with individual rights, they, along with a number of ethnic Americans, are advocating group rights and pressuring the establishment to recognize the existence of real, rather than rhetorical, diversity in the United States at the end of the twentieth century. Fragmentation also existed by 1992 among old stock, Protestant Americans, who during the decades of the Cold War subscribed to the "melting pot" theory of American society which largely blinded them to class differences and discrimination based on race, gender, and ethnicity. In the last decade of the twentieth century these WASPs found themselves being challenged not only from the bottom but from the top by a new elite group claiming to be a "merit class" based on their computer skills rather than traditional wealth. Not surprisingly, establishment Americans began talking more openly about the socio-economic fissures in the fabric of American society only *after* the fall of godless, classless communism. Instead of a "melting pot," the United States had become a "salad," whose demographic ingredients mixed, but did not merge. As evidence of their newly found class consciousness, the most affluent eighth of the US population by 1992 had begun to live in guarded suburban enclaves with security guards.[4]

The Los Angeles uprising in the spring of 1991 confirmed the separate world which poor African-Americans, whites, Hispanics, and Asians all inhabit in the inner cities of the nation's crime-infested, drug-ridden ghettos and from which fewer and fewer escape. Enraged volatility on the part of the "have-nots" and the privately financed security systems of the "haves" seem to be replacing the concept of civic responsibility and shared values in the country with the longest history of democratic government the world has ever known. Such domestic unrest combined with economic instability after over a decade of "Reagan[Bush]omics" cannot help but have an impact on US foreign policy, just as socio-economic turmoil did a century ago in the 1890s – except that then the American economy was on the rise and not in decline. Moreover, the Spanish–American War at the end of the nineteenth century, unlike the Gulf War, affirmed the basic tenets of US nationhood and launched what publisher Henry R. Luce belatedly in 1941 called the "American Century." Clearly the Gulf War did not – as George Bush learned the hard way. It remains to be seen whether the Clinton administration will be able to deal with this loss of confidence and fragmentation at home without turning away from pressing foreign policy issues.

Of all the new issues on the diplomatic horizon raised by the demise of the Soviet Union and complicated by depressed national economies all over the world, there is no doubt that pragmatic economic regionalism, rather than ideological or idealistic internationalism, will become a key force for understanding geopolitics in the twenty-first century. Since the 1970s such regionalism was represented in a configuration of economic power represented by the United States, Japan, and what was first known as the European Economic Community (EEC), which had emerged from the Rome Treaty of 1958. Japan's attempts to establish regional hegemony through agreements with the ASEAN nations (Thailand, Malaysia, Singapore, the Philippines, and Indonesia) simply emulated early attempts by the EEC to establish preferential access to the ACP nations of Africa, the Caribbean, and the Pacific through the 1975 Lomé Agreement. Both actions clearly presaged further developments in economic regionalism as did the initiation of plans for a European Monetary System in 1978, actions by OPEC beginning in 1973, and by less developed nations calling for a new economic order that takes into consideration North/South geographical configurations – other than in terms of exploitation of third-world resources – rather than simply East/West ones. When the North American Free Trade Agreement (NAFTA) becomes operational in 1994, it is anticipated that ASEAN exports to the United States will fall by $2 billion a year, promoting the Southeast Asian countries to consider establishing an ASEAN Free Trade Area of their own.[5]

Moreover, the European Economic Community will finally become a reality in the 1990s despite the painfully slow process involved in obtaining approval of the Maastricht Treaty by member nations of the Economic Community (EC), and by the lingering worldwide recession. In fact, the defeat of the treaty in Denmark, the close vote on the treaty by the French in September 1992 and opposition to it in Britain have temporarily retarded economic unity for Europe, including the establishment of a single currency through the Exchange Rate Mechanism (ERM) of the European Monetary System (EMS). Currency exchange instability at the fall of 1992 and beginning of 1993, however, further retarded this European economic unity and led to calls for the restoration of another Bretton Woods to calls for the re-establishing of a new version of the Bretton Woods System because monetary relations and trade relations are integrally connected. Floating exchange rates and freer trade do not go hand in hand. In fact instability of the former almost always produces complaints about unfair trading practices and pressures for protectionism. Much depends on whether the Clinton administration understands this and avoids calls in the United States for more protectionism.[6]

What creates integration of individual national economies may not promote it abroad. A global economy may temporarily be deemed not in the national interest, not only in the United States but also in Germany and France.

Competition in the form of economic regionalism may flourish for the rest of the 1990s because with the collapse of the Bretton Woods system in 1973 three rival trading blocs emerged. Each established a separate regional monetary order based on the yen, mark, and dollar – a situation that has contributed to exchange rate instability and currency speculation for the last twenty years.[7] The increased tension among these three major regional trading blocs will continue until the current global recession is over. Yet if this regional competition intensifies – even with a successful end to the seven-year-old Uruguay round of GATT talks – worldwide economic conditions could worsen in the 1990s.

Historically, economic crises are not usually resolved by experts who long labor over such agreements and plans but by politicians trying to hang on to or gain political power in relatively parochial national settings.[8] The negative popular mood in Europe about the Maastricht Treaty at the end of 1992 did not bode well for obtaining widespread understanding of the advantages of global, rather than national, economic solutions to the recession gripping most of Europe and the United States. One in eight citizens of EC countries knew little or nothing about it, but more significantly less than half thought their country would benefit from it while 34 per cent disagreed and the rest had no opinion.[9]

An aspect of economic regionalism often overlooked is that it is no less exploitative of third-world nations than previous multinational competition to control world resources. For example, the first post-cold-war National Security Strategy Report issued by the United States in March 1990 talked about "threats to our interests" that required the country to strengthen its "defense industrial base" by investing "in new facilities and equipment as well as in research and development," including high tech counterinsurgency and low-intensity conflict resolution weapons and tactics. The 1992 GATT talks are another negative example of western nations manipulating the infrastructures of the new regional and global economic systems for their own advantage. For example, they have established monopolies on patents and software programs and control over development and investment funds going to less developed areas. Highly publicized disputes between the United States and the EC over soybean subsidies and other agricultural disputes have concealed their basic agreement on protecting their own domestic and foreign economic interests at the expense of the rest of the world.[10] In a word, economic regionalism is not apt to be any more beneficial for nations outside developed areas than old-fashioned nationalistic economic rivalries were in the nineteenth century and for most of the twentieth. If anything, the EC nations and the United States seem only too willing to impose a nineteenth-century brand of "primitive" capitalism on third-world countries as they establish factories and plants outside their own national boundaries in search of cheap labor and few democratic or humane or environmental restrictions on their activities.

The current concern with economic regionalism, whether positive and negative, has increased the credence of those progressive and revisionist

studies that claimed economics was important for understanding the conduct
of American diplomacy. Looking back, it is possible to outline three different
stages in the economic development of the United States that have affected its
international relations. Beginning as a small, indebted, commercial and
agricultural nation following the American Revolution, the country became
a major industrial nation by the late nineteenth century with the aid of
considerable foreign investment, and finally a major international creditor
nation following World War I. In the last two centuries the United States
continuously adapted its foreign policy goals and doctrines to the evolution of
its economic, political, and military power. The Cold War marked the last
major adaptation of American diplomacy when, in the late 1940s, the Soviet
Union and the United States squared off in a bipolar conflict. This occurred
when America was at the height of its economic power in the world because
World War II had devastated the economies of Britain, Europe, Japan, and the
USSR. The United States is now in the process of adapting its foreign policy
for a fourth time in the twentieth century to meet the demands of a drastically
altered post-cold-war world in which it finds itself a greatly weakened giant.

With the dramatic and largely unexpected collapse of communism in
Central and Eastern Europe beginning in 1989, the Cold War technically
ended and, according to President George Bush, represented the "triumph
[and] . . . vindication of our ideals."[11] The world had not experienced such
political and demographic changes in Europe since the Napoleonic wars
almost two hundred years ago. Unlike the end of World War II, however,
when the United States found itself a victorious creditor nation with little
foreign economic or military competition, at the end of the Cold War in 1989
Americans faced serious debt problems at home and abroad in part because of
the burden garnered from forty years of almost single-handedly protecting the
"free" world from communism, and also because of revitalized regional
trade and technological competition from Asia and the European Community.
Ironically, the end of the Cold War was marked by a short, "hot" military
conflict instead of with a "cold" peaceful transition to a New World Order.
To one degree or another the United States has been pursuing a New World
Order since its inception.

From 1776 until 1900 American foreign policy adhered to several principles based entirely on the condition of the United States as a relatively
powerless, developing nation in a world dominated by England and France.
Accordingly, successive American presidents supported the following diplomatic principles to varying degrees: the right of people in the name of self-
determination to decide their own national boundaries, neutrality, freedom of
the seas, international cooperation in the form of arbitration over boundary
and fishing disputes, and continental expansion better known as Manifest
Destiny. Certain foreign policy events or developments accompanied these
diplomatic principles. For example, in 1793 George Washington's famous
Proclamation of Neutrality announced that America would "pursue a conduct
friendly and impartial toward the belligerent Powers" of Europe. Then three

years later, the nation's first president described America's political, but not *economic*, isolationism in his 1796 Farewell Address, which warned the nation against *permanent* alliances and involvement in the diplomatic affairs of other nations, but *not* against "temporary alliances for extraordinary emergencies" or commercial relations. For most of the nineteenth century the United States was a developing nation whose economic state did not allow it to play an important role in international affairs.

Although from the late eighteenth century until World War I, the United States defined neutrality and freedom of the seas in absolute terms, it did not yet have sufficient economic or military power to enforce its diplomatic principles. The same was true of such famous presidential declarations as the Monroe doctrine. Proclaimed by President Monroe in 1823, the doctrine was intended to prevent intervention by European powers in Latin America in particular, and the western hemisphere in general. However, the Monroe doctrine went virtually unnoticed abroad for most of the nineteenth century and was randomly violated. Likewise, until the twentieth century American political isolationism was dictated as much by its inferior trading position as by its geographical separation from Europe and Asia.

As a rapidly developing nation in the nineteenth century, the United States had the power and volition to pursue consistently only two diplomatic principles: continental expansionism and international arbitration of minor disputes. Thus, the country added contiguous territory – except for Alaska, the Philippines, Puerto Rico, Guam, and Hawaii – through treaties or wars with Native American Indians and foreign countries starting with the Louisiana Purchase in 1803, reaching new heights at the end of the Spanish–American War in 1898, and dwindling to such isolated acquisition as the Panama Canal Zone in 1904, several small islands after each world war. Related to this propensity for territorial expansionism in the nineteenth century was American commitment to economic expansionism.

No official name was given to this diplomatic principle until Secretary of State John Hay proclaimed the open door policy during the presidential administrations of William McKinley and Theodore Roosevelt. While this policy tried, unsuccessfully, to limit the economic and territorial expansion of foreign powers in China, the open door, the idea of equal economic opportunity where the United States faced seriously economic competition abroad, became the slogan under which the United States pursued economic expansionism for most of the twentieth century, except in the Caribbean where it simply established economic protectorates, lasting until the 1930s. At the time of its proclamation, however, America could not enforce the open door policy in a region where it had little economic and no military power. The other side of the open door policy is the closed door policy that the United States has followed whenever it had dominant economic influence, especially in Central and South America.[12]

Neither the Monroe doctrine nor the open door policy was intended by the administrations in which it originated to become a permanent feature of

American foreign policy, yet both did. The possibility that diplomatic principles designed for another era will live on after they have outlived their original purpose simply because growth in national power makes them enforceable, presages the danger represented by such proclamations. This "life after obsolescence" is especially true of presidential doctrines that become official doctrines without Congressional approval, a practice going back to Washington's Proclamation of Neutrality, but one that became more common with the onset of the Cold War.

In the first two decades of the twentieth century, as the United States became a world power, its economic and political interests became increasingly couched in idealistic terms about promoting democracy abroad. Since the seventeenth century, the United States had been content to be a city set on a hill with the "eies of all people uppon us," in Puritan John Winthrop's words – a moral model.[13] Although the country had been launched by a revolution based on the principle of self-determination, and despite all the talk about the superior morality and democratic way of American life in the nineteenth century, the United States did not seek to impose these principles abroad. This self-restraint diminished as the United States began to occupy militarily and/or establish protectorates in Caribbean countries in the early twentieth century. Diplomatic assertiveness in the name of democracy and morality dramatically increased under President Woodrow Wilson, who sent American troops into Mexico in order to "teach the South American republics to elect good men," and who coined the famous description of World War I as making the world "safe for democracy."[14]

While the promotion of liberty had been linked ideologically with the country's foreign policy since the turn of the century, until it acquired an overseas empire in the aftermath of the Spanish American War, the United States had not imposed its brand of liberty on foreign peoples outside its continental borders. The moral imperative of the United States to clone itself by exporting its economic and political system by force waned in the 1920s and 1930s only to return with new vigor once the Cold War began in the late 1940s, and continued until the end of the Cold War seemed to make it unnecessary as newly liberated nations began frantically to emulate what they thought was American capitalism and democracy. In other words, as the United States became more powerful and able to assert its national interests abroad, its foreign policy rhetoric became more, rather than less, ideological, despite disclaimers by American leaders and many diplomatic scholars to the contrary. The Cold War only highlighted the need to rationalize America's overwhelming economic and military power in other than pragmatic terms – it did not invent the process.

Following the emergence of the United States as a major world power in the course of World War I the country also dramatically reversed some of its positions on neutrality, freedom of the seas, and even self-determination. Now, instead of supporting such concepts, as it had at the outbreak of war in Europe in 1914, American leaders no longer defended the rights of neutral nations or honored their claims to freedom of the seas as their predecessors had before the nation became a major naval and economic power in the world. It also seriously compromised its former commitment to self-determination by sanctioning the arbitrary boundaries created by its former allies in Yugoslavia and the Middle East, for example, following World War I.

The United States also modified its concept of isolationism in the 1920s. Because the country became a leading industrial and creditor nation for the first time in that decade, politicians and businessmen cooperated in further limiting the country's practice of isolationism as the country's political and economic interests expanded during that decade. Instead, the United States began to practice what has been called "independent internationalism," referring to the combination of unilateral and collective actions after World War I as the United States remained active in international affairs but retained a sense of independent action.[15] Thus, while the United States condemned war and trimmed back its national defense system and military interventionism in Central America during the 1920s, it took a strong interest in a variety of international problems such as disarmament, war debts, and reparations, and the quite different postwar anxieties of both Germany and France. Where it lacked power, as in the Far East, it continued to advocate an open door economic policy; where it dominated, as in Latin America, it practiced closed door diplomacy. Although the Great Depression and events leading to World War II prompted more talk about isolationism in the 1930s, the economic size and military power of the United States has prevented it from effectively practicing isolationism from that time to the present, despite the passage of the misguided Neutrality Acts, which were designed to keep the United States – rather belatedly – out of the *First* World War, and not the *Second*.

Even though the United States did not join the League of Nations or the World Court in the interwar years, it began to participate in a greater number of international conferences on disarmament, peace, and international economic matters than ever before and, of course, became a major force behind the creation of the United Nations in 1945. So its nineteenth-century commitment to international arbitration, which had been particularly noticeable in the late nineteenth and early twentieth centuries with its participation in the peace conferences at The Hague in 1899 and 1907, continued until the outbreak of the Cold War. In fighting what was portrayed as a battle to the death with communism, the United States adopted an interventionist foreign policy known as globalism or internationalism based "on the assumption that the security and prosperity of every place on earth is vital to America's own."[16] Postwar leaders hoped that US global internationalism would be approved by non-communist countries under the auspices of the United Nations. When that support did not materialize, successive American presidents moved to negotiate regional collective security alliances such as the North Atlantic Treaty Organization (NATO) in 1949, the military agreement with Australia and New Zealand (ANZUS) Pact in 1951, the Southeast Asia Treaty

220   *Joan Hoff*

(SEATO) in 1954, the Central Treaty Organization (CENTO) in 1959 whereby the United States, along with Britain, agreed to aid Pakistan and Iran, and bilateral treaties of mutual defense with the Philippines, Japan, South Korea, and Nationalist China, and to the proclamation of a number of unilateral presidential doctrines on foreign policy beginning with the Truman doctrine in 1947 through the Reagan doctrine in 1984.[17]

Consequently, when the United Nations did not provide reliable support for America's efforts to combat communism all over the world in the 1950s and 1960s, opposition to this international organization increased in government and popular circles in the United States. This lack of UN support stemmed from the fact that since the 1950s two-thirds of the votes in the UN General Assembly have been controlled by nonaligned, developing nations from the Third World who believed that US globalism made them mere pawns in a bipolar cold-war game, especially when "hot wars" broke out between the two superpowers or their surrogates as in Korea, Vietnam, and Angola. The UN has only recently begun to return to favor in the United States as a result of its support for allied action in the Gulf War, made possible by a significant break in the unity of nonaligned nations on the question of outside interference in the Middle East.

Finally, as one of the two most powerful nations of the Cold War period, the United States tried to enforce the Monroe doctrine and the closed door policy in Latin America and to exercise influence in other parts of the world unilaterally through foreign aid or military intervention whenever it decided that its economic or security interests were threatened. Increasingly it honored the territorial integrity of undemocratic nations if they were noncommunist and interfered with or disapproved of self-determination if it resulted, or threatened to result, in the establishment of communist governments. This included at least two documented cases of governmental attempts to assassinate foreign leaders.[18] In the process the power of the presidents of the United States to wage undeclared overt and covert wars increased significantly.

Thus, President Eisenhower did not support nationwide elections in Vietnam in 1956, allowed the CIA to help overthrow the nationalist government of Iran in 1953, sent marines into Lebanon in 1958, and approved the organizing of indigenous military units to invade both Guatemala and Cuba. President Kennedy approved the invasion of the latter in 1961 in the infamous Bay of Pigs operation by CIA-trained commandos and initiated the introduction of American forces in Vietnam that same year. Under President Johnson 25,000 US and Organization of American States (OAS) troops were sent into the Dominican Republic to establish order and a conservative regime, while US soldiers in Vietnam reached a peak level of 542,000 in 1969 without any Congressional declaration of war. In the early 1970s President Nixon used the CIA to contribute to the downfall of the democratically elected socialist government of Salvador Allende Gossens in Chile, and under President Ford in 1975 the United States unsuccessfully engaged the CIA in an attempt to defeat the Soviet-backed Popular Movement for the Liberation of Angola (MPLA). In the 1980s US troops went into Lebanon and bombed Libya, and Presidents Reagan and Bush successfully presided over the invasions of both Grenada and Panama in the late 1980s. And then there was the Gulf War. The absolute necessity for any of these actions in the name of national interest has been questioned because in each case the outcome has not contributed to stability in the respective areas of the world in which US intervened.[19]

With the Cold War over, it is possible to reflect on its distinctively integrative characteristics, especially in the area of suppressing ethnic strife and promoting economic unity among the major non-communist, western nations. Obviously, its demise did not mean the end of integrative versus disintegrative forces or patterns in the historical landscape of the future.[20] The end of the Cold War does not mean, therefore, the "end of history" as neoconservatives in the United States and post-structuralists around the world are so prone to assert.[21] Rather, the end of the Cold War should allow us to evaluate economic and military institutions to see that many of them such as the Marshall Plan, NATO, GATT, the International Monetary Fund, the World Bank, and Exchange Rate Mechanism of the European Monetary System which came into existence after the collapse of the Bretton Woods System – all served integrative functions in the direction of producing regional security, and regional markets, and some modicum of currency stability because of the threat of communism. These same cold-war institutions, however, may not be reliable or adequate ones for structuring collective security and a global market of the future in a world without communism. GATT, and, of course, NATO, were, after all, originally conceived in the late 1940s as temporary; that is, ad hoc solutions and institutions which have long since assumed a life of their own and which may or may not be relevant in the altered world situation created by abrupt disappearance of the Cold War.[22] All of these manifestations of the Cold War – whether they be economic, ideological, or based on selective memories about past wars – are now being reconsidered in light of the demise of at the least most prominent bipolar aspects of that conflict – the superpower rivalry of the US and former USSR.[23]

One aspect of that rivalry that will probably receive more attention by diplomatic historians than previously is the impact of the Cold War on the American presidency and democratic form of government in the United States. Modern American presidents have conducted military and non-military foreign policy during the Cold War under the rhetoric of bipartisanship, which originally in the 1950s meant that leaders of the Republican and Democratic parties agreed to unite behind the diplomacy of anti-communism. However, as the domestic consensus for such anti-communist internationalism began to break down in the 1960s as a result of the lengthy and undeclared war in Vietnam, it became more and more difficult to maintain even the facade of bipartisanship. The term "nonpartisan" has often been used by more recent presidents to gain support for their foreign policies, but more and more it appears to mean "non-discussion" of diplomacy. How could foreign policy *not be discussed* in a country as democratic as the United States and how will this development affect the brand of democracy and capitalism exported to liberated areas in the post-cold-war period of the 1990s?

If the United States is to advise nascent democracies in other parts of the world effectively, to say nothing of honestly, it must look at the reality rather than the rhetoric about democracy in America.[24] Since the onset of the Cold War almost fifty years ago, American presidents have assumed "semi-constitutional" power in the conduct of foreign policy in the name of national security. For example, the Cold War gave US presidents authority to issue executive orders in violation of civil rights and to conduct the foreign military and political interventions cited above without Congressional approval. The domestic results of such actions have almost always been the censorship of information, suppression of dissent, and retreat from internal reform.[25] Thus, the presumed necessity of marshalling first a bipartisan and then a "non-partisan" foreign policy in order to fight communism abroad has increasingly stifled domestic political discussion about American foreign policy goals. In recent years "nonpartisan" has threatened to become a substitute for "non-discussion." A highly emotional moralistic and patriotic rhetoric, in which sports, sex, and religious symbols abound, characterizes the singularly *undemocratic* way foreign policy issues are now commonly presented to the American people.[26] This same emotionally charged "non-discussion" of issues, and suppression of independent press coverage, was too evident in government presentations of events leading up to and continuing through the Gulf War in 1991. Americans may have been inundated with TV coverage censored by the Pentagon, but they were not well informed.

A re-evaluation of American democratic habits not only in terms of declining voter participation in national elections since 1960 but also in terms of the unilateral, extra-legal power that the Cold War bestowed upon American presidents is in order. From the Oval Office these men often relied on policies that not only violated both the federal constitution and congressional legislation but also were designed secretly by unelected advisers in avoidance of democratic discussion of these policies at home. Examples include the secret bombing of Cambodia in the first Nixon administration, the secret National Security Council actions in violation of congressional legislation during the Iran–Contra affair under Reagan, and Irangate under Bush. Thus, in the course of the Cold War, a growing gap developed between the nation's needs at home and its expansive foreign policy goals. Any reconsideration of budgetary priorities and appropriations to resolve mounting domestic problems will not be undertaken in the 1990s if a lingering "Cold Warrior" mentality with all of its interventionist connotations continues to hamper the free exchange of ideas about controversial domestic and foreign issues.

Do traditional "Cold Warrior" attitudes continue to linger despite President George Bush's call for the New World Order? And in using this slogan, was his administration stressing the word "new" or the word "order?" Was the Gulf War representative of a "new" or the "old" US foreign policy? Is the American-dominated type of military coalition, such as prevailed during that conflict, the kind of international cooperation needed now that communism has been defeated? Since the Gulf War could not have taken place had the Soviet Union remained a major force in the Middle East, it could be interpreted as the United States assuming the role of armed policeman of the world in those instances when its national self-interest or security are involved – in this case, oil – but not in other parts of the world. To fight for freedom and stability in an area of the world that has yet to experience either, while continuing to ignore torture, murder, and military takeovers of governments in other areas, is not setting a new world standard for ethics either in the United States or internationally – whether it is done under the auspices of the UN or not. The Gulf War was simply a continuation of cold-war practices.

To date, there are only two things "new" about the New World Order and both are ethically problematic: the excessive use of high tech weapons on a third rate military power in the Middle East; and the fact that for the first time in its history the United States, in part because of its current debtor status among world nations, did not think that it could or should pay for the war by itself. Hence, the United States put together a coalition to fight the Gulf War to protect its own oil needs in the name of freedom for Kuwait. Will American economic self-interest ever be openly acknowledged as its economic weaknesses have been admitted? Will recognizing American economic vulnerability deter US military actions in the post-cold-war era, or will the day simply come when American soldiers are "hired out" as mercenaries in future wars paid for by other nations? In 1991 the exact impact that the debt-ridden economy of the United States will have on its foreign policy is not clear as it moves much less robustly than it did in the 1890s into a new century. Historically, however, it is clear that economic change has altered the course of America's position in the world and its diplomacy. By the end of the 1990s it will have done so again. But first the country has to fill the void left by the fact that for too long it leaned too hard on the Berlin Wall as a rationale for its foreign policy. With the wall and the Soviet Union gone, the United States can no longer "cry communist wolf" in the name of domestic or national security at home or abroad.

Judging from previous developments in the foreign policy of the United States, it is evident that diplomatic precedents based on a combination of a messianic, nationalist ideology, the nation's international economic position, and generational perceptions about the outcome of the "last" war will not be quickly discarded even in the face of dramatic events like the unexpected victory over communism in Eastern and Central Europe and the predictable victory over Iraq. Under these unexpectedly favorable international circumstances, it is quite conceivable that the United States should resist acting like an arrogant world bully now that the Soviet Union is on its knees and Iraq reduced to subsistence. Instead, America might logically begin to think more modestly and more realistically abroad, rather than expansively, in order to address serious domestic problems and become once again the moral and democratic "city set on a hill" for other nations to emulate or not – as they choose. Now that the United States has been freed from an immediate security challenge, it is time to place less emphasis on ordering the world and more on setting America's domestic house in order, including taking a hard look at the damage done by the Cold War to American values and its democratic political processes.

To date, however, the ideological connection between capitalism and democracy has become even more evident in the post-cold-war world. Because such a connection is unhistorical, it can almost be viewed as a Marxian joke. Except in this instance it is not Karl Marx I am referring to, but the Marx Brothers. Here I am in agreement with John Ralston Saul who has said that "neither history nor philosophy link free markets and free men. They have nothing more to do with each than the accidents of time and place." In fact, it can be historically documented that capitalism has worked best when there was less, not more, democracy in most western countries. One need only look at both England and the United States before universal male suffrage, child labor laws, and health regulations were enacted, although these occurred at different times in the nineteenth century in each country. Likewise, capitalism thrived in the undemocratic times of Louis Philippe, again under Emperor Napoleon III, under Kaiser Wilhelm II, and Nicholas II. Most recently in the United States, capitalism, in the form of maximization of profits based on the service sector and financial speculation, has functioned best when those voting in the United States had declined the most; namely, in the 1970s and 1980s.[27]

If, as appears to be the case, voting is no longer considered a premier prerequisite for democratic citizenship in the United States, why do Americans continue to stress it in their foreign policy for recently liberated countries? The decline in those voting in presidential elections has been steady for almost thirty years and even the 55 per cent of eligible voters who went to the polls in 1992, representing the highest percentage since 1972, did not bring the level up to anywhere near those of the 1950s and 1960s. There is no clear evidence that 1992 signified an upward swing in voter participation because it represented more anti-Bush sentiment than a positive endorsement of Clinton or Perot, just as 1972 was as much anti-McGovern as it was pro-Nixon. I stress this point because of the overexpectations currently being created by the United States and by other western nations in Eastern Europe and the former republics of the Soviet Union on the implicitly ideological assumption that capitalism guarantees democracy and vice versa. To say, as Richard D. Kauzlarich, Deputy Assistant Secretary for European and Canadian Affairs of the US State Department, did at an international conference on "The US and Europe" at the Irish Royal Academy in Dublin on 19 November 1992, that "economic reform without democratic government cannot succeed" is simply misleading as well as unhistorical.

Moreover, in Central and Eastern Europe and in republics within the former Soviet Union we have not questioned the results of suspicious "free" elections even when we know that some of the leaders being put forward, e.g. in Romania, parts of Yugoslavia, the Soviet Republic of Georgia, and most recently Lithuania, have no commitment to democracy. In the face of the collapse of communism Americans must be more discriminating in offering support to any and all new governments simply because they purport to be democratic and in weighing the merits of self-determination versus that of territorial integrity. After all, Hitler is not the only example in recent history of an individual exploiting free elections while simultaneously building a political system dedicated to destroying democratic government. We also have the examples of Indira Gandhi in India, Sukarno in Indonesia, Lee Kwan Yew in Singapore, and Ferdinand Marcos in the Philippines.[28]

Understanding the unhistorical and ideological aspects of connecting democracy and capitalism need not mean a retreat to some mythical iso-lationism, even if the United States does cut back its military and political involvement abroad. The immediate lesson of the end of the Cold War and the results of the 1992 presidential election need not become the self-fulfilling prophecy presaged by *Le Monde*: "Il est grand temps de nous occuper de nous."[29] The United States could and should take an active role in supporting genuine free trade rather than its traditional open/closed door strategy, although GATT negotiations with EC nations at the end of 1992 did not bode well for this approach. It could do much more than it has to destroy its own nuclear weapons, to prevent their spread, and to discontinue arming its "friends" all over the world – but especially in the Middle East. Likewise, it could take advantage of the Gulf War coalition to pursue genuine, rather than opportunistic or erratic, collective security through the United Nations that should include an expanded number of permanent members of the Security Council representing more than the four ex-colonial powers coming out of World War II.

The United States should also promote human rights through the United Nations, especially those of women, whose rights are being trampled in newly liberated nations, or in other parts of the world where they never had been given such rights. It could begin to do this *at home* by belatedly ratifying the major human rights treaties and conventions, some of which apply specific-ally to women. As the only leading democratic nation that has refused to sign these United Nations documents, the time seems right to do so if this is to be a new international world order based on a new commitment by the United States to all international laws and norms – not just some of them. It should also take seriously the concern of Biljana Kasic, a Zagreb feminist and political scientist, who in December 1992 demanded a revision of the Geneva Convention to designate rape as a war crime at long last. For too long the United States has turned a blind eye to the treatment of women in time of war by its own soldiers and those of other nations. For the first time in the history of modern warfare, the tragedy represented by the systematic rape and abuse of as many as twenty thousand women in Bosnia, mainly Muslims and Croatians but some Serbian women as well, could be used to internationalize the issue of rape and other gendered violence directed toward women. Up to now such atrocities have been either ignored as exaggerated wartime stories, or simply viewed as a "normal" part of warfare and, hence, seldom given credence in postwar legal documents and trials. This was most clearly shown when the mass rape of Bangladesh women by Pakistani soldiers in 1971 was quickly forgotten by the international community.[30]

An even more disturbing, but less emotionally visible global problem facing women is the fact that they are disappearing all over the world in such great numbers that they no longer constitute a majority of the planet's population. This could not happen except by design: through the abortion, almost exclusively, of female fetuses in India and China, or by the systematic neglect of the nutritional, medical, and health needs of women in Africa and Latin America. Technology will make gender manipulation possible in most advanced industrialized countries, once the separation of female and male chromosomes, which is now possible in cattle breeding, is perfected for the human race. In 1990 it was estimated that as many as 150 million females were "missing" in Asia, Africa, and Latin America. Perhaps these disappearances could be euphemistically labeled the "gender cleansing" of the world. Whatever it is called, it represents socio-economic crimes against women resulting in their deaths of global proportions that simply cannot be attributed to East/West or North/South cultural and economic differences. For reasons that are no longer a scientific mystery, we know that the normal sex/ratio balance of the world's population favors women.[31] Simply put, when females are given the same care by society as men, they tend to have better survival rates, and hence they should usually represent a majority of the world's population; despite this they are disappearing in increasing numbers without appropriate diplomatic response from the United States or world community.

Problems in the Middle East remained far from resolved at the end of 1992 despite the Gulf War and renewed Arab–Israeli peace talks. In fact, these talks broke down at the beginning of 1993 after Israel deported 415 Palestinian men into a no man's land in southern Lebanon and the incoming Clinton administration appeared willing to block any censure of Israel by the United Nations, much to the consternation of some of the Arab nations who had allied with the United States during the Gulf War because they see this as a contradiction of US condemnation of Serbian atrocities against Muslims in Bosnia–Herzegovina. This area of the world – where the Cold War can be said to have begun and ended – has perhaps changed the least because the American goal in the Middle East remains what it has been since World War II: strategic and economic domination because of its location and oil, and sometimes heavy-handedly pro-Israel.[32] Now that US domination cannot be disguised in anti-Soviet rhetoric, it is time to question whether US hegemony in the Middle East will make it any more peaceful in the future than it has been in the past, especially now that the Israelis amd Palestinians have reached an uneasy peace accord wihtout US help.

Yet in a truly global, interdependent, and collective world of the next century, the internal sense of socio-economic chaos and fragmentation in the United States may prove too much for its stagnating, debt-ridden economy, single issue politics, and rampant individualism to contain.[33] If the center does not hold at home, how can the United States successfully deal with the fragmentation abroad in the wake of the Cold War? It is even possible that policies of reintegration at home will be at odds with obtaining integration abroad. If so, America's decline on the world scene may be as precipitous as its rise to the pinnacle of power in the twentieth century. According to world systems theory this is already a foregone conclusion because all hegemonic powers ultimately destroy their economic power base by "overinvest[ing] in multinational ventures abroad and in military production at home" as they carry out their self-imposed dual roles of "global banker and global policeman."[34] Another way to view this dilemma facing the United States is that its post-World-War-II diplomacy was too successful in reconstructing the economies of Japan and Western Europe – so successful that it created its own major economic rivals. Thus, it may no longer be a question of whether the United States is on the decline, but how gracefully it can preside over the impermanence of its preeminence.

The answer may well lie in whether the Democrats under President Clinton can revive the economy of the United States and whether the Vietnam War generation, which his administration represents, continues to think that restraint rather than interventionism is the best course to follow in the post-cold-war world or whether the new administration will revert to the Reagan–Bush use of force that proved so popular in Grenada, Panama, and, at least temporarily, in the Gulf War. All these interventions appeared to have been based on the Pentagon's post-Vietnam doctrine of "invincible force," meaning that instead of employing a minimum amount of military power, the United States amassed overwhelming might and used it without reservation against much weaker opponents. This rationalization for the use of power is no less grounded in the Cold War than the gradual escalation of power in Vietnam was, and it should not be viewed as the product of a new post-cold-war way of thinking. This type of unrestricted, short-term use of military force has little meaning in areas of the world where mass starvation requires minimal but probably prolonged armed intervention for humanitarian purposes, as in Somalia, or where anti-genocidal practices require carefully planned surgical use of military intervention, as in the former Yugoslavia, because of the Serbian practice of "ethnic cleansing," or in Cambodia where Khmer Rouge savagery has reemerged, or in the Kurdistan portion of Iraq. Starvation, whether arising from civil war or natural disaster, and genocidal situations require intervention in the name of humanity and against genocidal tyranny. If there is to be a New World Order it must be based on an internationally shared principle of justice, not the whims of rogue leaders and armed gangs of terrorists. Without the adhesive provided by the Cold War, "rogue regimes," once symbolized primarily by Colonel Muammar Qadahfi of Libya, may become the "greatest threat to international stability in the post-Cold War era," along with the distinct possibility of disintegration within some of the newly formed countries in the Balkans and Baltic regions and in portions of the former Soviet Union, with their attendant ethnic and religious antagonisms.[35]

Another newly emerging cause of ethnic strife, civil war, and rogue insurgency facing US foreign policymakers is the dislocation associated with scarcities of renewable resources. Unlike competition over non-renewable resources, such as fossil fuels, iron ore, and rare minerals, the 1993 report of the Environmental Change and Acute Conflict project indicated that renewable resources are linked to highly complex systems that can lead to unforeseen and simultaneous environmental crises which, in turn, promote violence that will not follow the traditional pattern of wars over non-renewable resources. Instead, scattered outbursts within nations, especially in the Third World, are more likely to develop in the next fifty years. This means that highly developed nations like the United States should not be promoting "primitive" capitalism abroad, but environmentally sound industrialization that does not displace people to unmanageable cities or ecologically fragile areas like steep terrain. To date, the United States, as well as banks and international lending agencies, have not shown any great interest in systematically pursuing a foreign policy to offset the potential for scarcities of renewable resources to produce widespread, erratic conflict all over the world.[36]

It is also likely that many of the post-cold-war experiments in establishing nation states of questionable economic viability on the basis of nationalist and ethnic or religious fervor will fail to make the transition to either capitalism or democracy. The possibility that the New World Order will be characterized by numerous failed nation states was not anticipated by western nations when they first celebrated the death of communism. If this proves to be the case then it will necessitate giving more serious consideration to what former Secretary of State George Shultz has called "the new sovereignty" on the part of the United States rather than more mindless use of "invincible force" to gain political favor at home. According to Shultz, in the post-cold-war world "responsible powers" will have to make multinational decisions about when to violate previously impenetrable sovereignty on the part of "irresponsible powers" that violate human rights within their borders. "Ethnic cleansing" need not always take the genocidal form pursued by the Serbs in Bosnia; its more "civilized" form consists of restricting citizenship rights as Estonia did in 1992 to prevent non-native peoples, primarily Russians, from voting. Making multinational decisions through NATO, the United Nations, or international economic agencies about when and when not to violate sovereignty rights in the name of human rights will be much more complex than when the two major superpowers attempted to control the internal as well as external destinies of their client states. It may well be that collective economic instruments such as boycotts and sanctions will become more common tools of US presidents in the post-cold-war world than political summitry or unilateral military actions.[37] However, the increased and arbitrary nature of the power of American presidents because of the Cold War does not lend itself to the tedious and technical types of negotiations required at economic summit conferences to make economic sanctions more than symbolic gestures – as the Gulf War so aptly demonstrated.

Once again US foreign relations rests at a crossroads; its direction to be determined by a volatile mixture of an as yet undefined post-cold-war ideology of nationhood, economics, and generational conflict based on memories of World War II, Vietnam, and, most recently, the Gulf War. For the first time in its history, however, all three of the mainstays of US diplomacy – ideology, economics, and generational response to traumatic events – are in a state of disarray at the same time. At the very moment when America finally found itself in a position to realize its most laudable ideological pursuits – the exportation of liberty, i.e., capitalism and democracy without opposition from communism – there was debilitating disagreement at home about what the future held for Americans, let alone for the rest of the world. In the 1992 presidential election a depressed economy and depressing national debt of over $4 trillion, growing domestic socio-economic intolerance and political volatility, generational conflict over those whose mindsets came from World War II and those whose foreign policy imprinting occurred during the Vietnam War, and confusion over national values crowded out serious consideration of a re-evaluation of the future role of the United States in international affairs. The end of the Cold War by itself probably would have been enough to trigger an identity crisis in the United States. Combined with the weakest economy since the Great Depression, American foreign policy for the remainder of the 1990s is likely to reflect more drift than mastery – just as it did for most of the 1930s under the influence of that economic crisis.

America has survived such domestic disarray before. After a decade of turmoil a century ago in the 1890s a consensus emerged that rationalized a place of preeminence for the United States in world affairs. No doubt by the end of the 1990s another consensus will have emerged to rationalize the role that America will play in the twenty-first century. If it is based on the beliefs of the twentieth century that made the country great and whose origins came from the nineteenth century, then the United States will be relegated to a secondary role in the next century. If it took a particular type of nationalistic foreign policy to mold cultural, regional, ethnic, racial, and religious diversity of enormous proportions into a great nation at the end of the nineteenth century, it will take quite a different type of ideology and foreign policy to mend the cracks that have developed in the current brand of American domestic pluralism. The time has come to discard the unconsciousness of US ideology and redefine liberty in other than traditional capitalist and democratic terms. Market economies may still be the name of the game, but they are no longer nationally based. This may represent a difference of kind in global economic thinking, and not simply of degree, indicating that US presidents and their administrations in the 1990s can no longer ignore developments abroad as they struggle with the economy at home.

Increased racial intolerance at home may reinforce rather than diminish the racism and xenophobia that traditionally have been associated with US foreign relations in the twentieth century, while the United States struggles to put its own house in order. Stereotypical American opposition to leftist revolutions abroad may be automatically transferred to rightist takeovers in ethnic conflicts in Eastern Europe and the former republics of the Soviet Union. Or it may substitute antifundamentalist crusades for the now defunct anticommunist ones. Neither course will improve understanding on the part of the average American about how dramatically the position of the United States in the world has declined on the eve of the millennium, but either, if implemented, would mask addressing domestic problems with foreign policy adventurism. Most unfortunately, it would not lead to an understanding on the part of the American public that democracy at home or abroad is no guarantee of economic prosperity or guarantee of peace. Likewise, the free flow of commodities around the world, particularly when they disproportionately consist of arms and munitions, is also no guarantee of peace. If the Cold War was, indeed, the equivalent to a World War III, in the sense that it has had the impact on the world that such another global conflict would have had without the massive bloodshed and destruction,[38] then a major reassessment of US foreign policy is in order. The world has not seen such territorial and demographic changes since the Napoleonic era. Before a New World Order can come into existence the Cold War mentality, as evidenced in both the World War II and the Vietnam generation of leaders represented by George Bush, Ross Perot, and Bill Clinton in the 1992 presidential campaign must become a thing of the past. None of the presidential candidates addressed these important questions and foreign policy is not the new president's forte. It is the area where he is most likely to make safe, traditional appointments drawing on people from the Carter administration whose foreign policy was mediocre at best, with the exception of the Camp David Accords. While some new foreign policy faces are emerging around Clinton, none are without previous cold-war government experience.[39]

The same re-evaluation is required with respect to domestic problems and they are far from simply economic in nature – another fact ignored in the 1992 presidential election. These "ignored" domestic problems include the increasingly dysfunctional American political system and increased intolerance for diversity. If democracy cannot be revitalized domestically in the United States, communism may not be the only economic and ideological system to fail at the end of the twentieth century. Such a failure would give policymakers their first authentic post-cold-war generational trauma (because the Gulf War did not) on which to base future interpretations of US foreign policy, but America and Americans deserve better from their political leaders at this crucial watershed in their international and domestic history.

NOTES

1 *Newsweek*, 18 May 1992, p. 21.
2 Michael H. Hunt, *Ideology and U.S. Foreign Policy*, New Haven, Conn., 1987, pp. 17, 171, *passim*; Jerald A. Combs, *American Diplomatic History: Two Centuries of Changing Interpretations*, Berkeley, Calif., 1983, p. x, *passim*; and Jeffrey Kimball, "The Influence of Ideology on Interpretive Disagreement: A Report on a Survey of Diplomatic, Military and Peace Historians on the Causes of 20th Century U.S. Wars," *The History Teacher*, 17 May 1984, pp. 355–81.
3 David Reynolds, "Beyond Bipolarity in Space and Time," *Diplomatic History*, vol. 16, 1992, pp. 231, 233, first quotation; and John M. Carroll and George C. Herring (eds), *Modern American Diplomacy*, Wilmington, Del., 1986, p. 8, second quotation, p. 221.
4 *The Economist*, 5 September 1992, p. 23. The difference between a "melting pot" and a "salad" assumes postmodern overtones when it is remembered that "E pluribus unum" dates back to a recipe in an early poem by Virgil in which he said that the "ingredients do not merge; the union is simply the sum of its parts."
5 *International Herald Tribune*, 24 November 1992, p. 17.
6 *International Herald Tribune*, 19 November 1992, p. 2; *The Irish Times*, 23 November 1992, p. 11, and 1 December 1992, pp. 1, 12, 17–18; and David Wightman, "The U.S. and Europe," paper delivered at the Royal Irish Academy, 20 November 1992.
7 John Ralston Saul, *Voltaire's Bastards: The Dictatorship of Reason in the West*, London, 1992, pp. 271–2. For details see papers delivered at the Fourteenth Annual Conference of the National Committee for the Study of International Affairs at the Royal Irish Academy in Dublin, 19–20 November 1992: by Reinhardt Rummel, "German–American Relations in the Setting of a New Atlanticism," and by David Wightman, "Europe and Dollar." These will be published in the RIA's *Irish Studies in International Affairs*, vol. 4, 1993.
8 *International Herald Tribune*, 18 November, 1992, pp. 1, 11, and 14–15 November, 1992, p. 2.
9 *International Herald Tribune*, 14–15 November 1992, p. 2.
10 White House issued policy paper, "National Security Strategy of the United States," March 1990; Noam Chomsky, "A View from Below," *Diplomatic History*, vol. 16, 1992, pp. 85–103; and *International Herald Tribune*, November 1992; *The Irish Times*, 6 November 1992, p. 12.
11 Bush quoted from speech to the National Guard Convention, Salt Lake City, 15 September 1992.
12 Joan Hoff Wilson, *American Business and Foreign Policy, 1920–1933*, Lexington, Ky, 1971, pp. 9–10, 157–218.
13 Winthrop quoted in Edmund S. Morgan, *The Puritan Dilemma, The Story of John Winthrop*, Boston, 1958, p. 70.
14 Wilson quoted in Arthur S. Link, *Woodrow Wilson and the Progressive Era, 1910–1917*, New York, 1954, pp. 119, 281.
15 Wilson, *American Business and Foreign Policy*, pp. xiv–xvii, 26, 241.
16 Alan Tonelson, "What Is the National Interest?," *The Atlantic Monthly*, July 1991, p. 35.
17 The *Truman doctrine*, 1947, proclaimed initially in reference to Greece and Turkey, but later applied to other parts of the world, stated that "it must be the policy of the United States to support free peoples who are resisting subjugation

by armed minorities or by outside pressures." The *Eisenhower doctrine*, 1957, gave unilateral notice that the United States would intervene in the Middle East if any government threatened by a communist takeover requested aid. The *Johnson doctrine*, 1965, stated that the president could use military force whenever he thought communism threatened the western hemisphere and was first issued when LBJ sent troops into the Dominican Republic. The *Nixon doctrine*, 1969, originally aimed at "southern tier" third-world countries in East Asia, came to represent the formal institutionalization of the policy of Vietnamization; that is, it noted that while the United States continued to support regional security and national self-sufficiency for nations in the Far East, it would no longer commit American troops to this effort. The *Carter doctrine*, 1980, maintained that any attempt by the Soviet Union "to gain control of the Persian Gulf will be regarded as an assault on the vital interests of the United States." The *Reagan doctrine* announced that American foreign policy would actively promote democracy throughout the world by giving humanitarian and military aid to "democratic revolutions" wherever they occurred.

18 Glenn P. Hastedt, *American Foreign Policy: Past, Present, Future*, 2nd ed., Englewood Cliffs, N.J., 1991, pp. 217–37. Of the six cases of alleged US attempts to assassinate foreign leaders – Fidel Castro, Cuba; Patrice Lumumba, Congo (Zaire); Rafael Trujillo, Dominican Republic; General Rene Schneider, Chile and Salvador Allende, Chile; and Ngo Dinh Diem, Vietnam – only two were found to be substantiated by evidence: Castro and Lumumba.

19 Hastedt, *American Foreign Policy*, pp. 1–8.

20 John Gaddis, "The Cold War, The Long Peace, and the Future," *Diplomatic History*, vol. 16, 1992, pp. 242–4.

21 Francis Fukuyama, "The End of History?," *The National Interest*, vol. 16, summer 1989, pp. 4, 8, 9, 14; Fukuyama, *The End of History and the Last Man*, New York, 1992; and Joan Hoff and Christie Farnham, "Theories about the End of Everything," *Journal of Women's History*, vol. 1, 1990, pp. 6–12.

22 For details see papers delivered at the Fourteenth Annual Conference of the National Committee for the Study of International Affairs at the Royal Irish Academy in Dublin, 19–20 November 1992, by Reinhardt Rummel and by David Wightman.

23 For a review of these early reassessments see the two symposia in *Diplomatic History*, vol. 16, 1992, pp. 45–114 and vol. 16, 1992, pp. 223–318; and articles in *Foreign Affairs*, 1991.

24 Ideally, American democracy consists of four basic principles. First, there is the supposition that no other country in the world has trusted its past and future to so many free elections and the peaceful transition of power. The corollary to this is that, second, democratic government in the United States was and is owned and operated by voting citizens. Third, it is usually assumed that the unique American system of checks and balances, along with the two-party system, makes Americans impervious to the plutocratic, oligarchic, or autocratic pitfalls that have plagued other democracies because these ensure the enactment of just laws and policies that have been vigorously debated by an involved citizenry. Finally, judicial interpretations of the written Constitution have produced for Americans the greatest amount of civil liberties and freedom of expression ever granted by any government to its people. Few would quarrel with this description of American democracy – in theory. In practice, however, democratic citizenship in the United States falls far short of this idealization.

25 For a review of censorship patterns in the United States with emphasis on the twentieth century, see Joan Hoff-Wilson, "The Pluralist Society," in New York Public Library, *Censorship, 500 Years of Conflict*, New York, 1984, pp. 103–15.

26 For a discussion of ways in which the growth of state power has "de-democratized"

politics in the United States while at the same time promoting a superficial type of democracy abroad, see Sheldon S. Wolin, *The Presence of the Past, Essays on the State and the Constitution*, Baltimore, Md, 1989, pp. 180–207.

27 Saul, *Voltaire's Bastards*, pp. 359–61; and Joan Hoff, "The City on the Hill, America's Role in the World," in *The Humanities and the Art of Public Discussion*, Washington, 1991, pp. 16–26.

28 For more details see Hoff, "The City on the Hill."

29 *Le Monde*, Edition internationale, no. 2295 du jeudi 22 au mercredi 28 octobre, p. 9.

30 Elizabeth F. Defeis, "International Trends," *Journal of Women's History*, 1991; *International Herald Tribune*, 8 December 1992, p. 4; *Newsweek*, international edition, 4 January 1993, pp. 32–7; and "List of Rape/Death Camps in Bosnia–Herzegovina," and "General Report" on the need to protect women and children as victims and refugees, both dated 28 September 1992 and issued by the Croatian women's group "Tresnjevika."

31 Amartya Sen, "More than 100 Million Women Are Missing," *New York Review of Books*, 20 December 1990, pp. 61–6. Although more male babies are born than female ones, "considerable research has shown that if men and women received similar nutritional and general health care, women tend to live noticeably longer than men. Women seem to be, on the whole more resistant to disease and in general hardier than men . . . especially during the months immediately following birth" (p. 61).

32 Robert Jervis, "A Usable Past for the Future," and Nikki R. Keddie, "The End of the Cold War and the Middle East," *Diplomatic History*, vol. 16, winter 1992, pp. 82–3, 95, 103. *International Herald Tribune*, 2 November 1992, p. 4; 7–8 November 1992, p. 4; 9 November 1992, pp. 1, 7; 3 February 1993, p. 5. *Irish Times*, 29 January 1993, pp. 1, 6, 10; 4 February 1993, p. 6; 11 February 1993, pp. 1, 10.

33 *The Economist*, 5 September 1992, pp. 21–3, 52.

34 McCormick, "World System," in op. cit., pp. 94–5.

35 *International Herald Tribune*, 3 December 1992, p. 4; 8 December 1992, p. 4. *The Irish Times*, 7 December 1992, p. 8; 8 December 1992, p. 9. In explaining why President Bush ordered US troops into Somalia and not into Bosnia, Cambodia, or to aid the Marsh Arabs or Kurds in Iraq, a December 8 op/ed piece by William Pfaff stated that there was no political constituency in the United States other than for aid to Somalia that "the U.S. army's doctrine, under General Colin Powell, is to resist any assignment where it cannot deploy totally overwhelming force with unlimited weaponry." The term "rogue regime," and quotation comes from a forthcoming book by G. Henry M. Schuler, *Untamed Rogue: Our Failed and Farcical War Against Qadhafi*, New York, forthcoming.

36 *International Herald Tribune*, 4 February 1993, p. 6. The project on Environmental Change and Acute Conflict is co-directed by Jeffrey Boutwell and George Rathjens and is sponsored by the American Academy of Arts and Sciences. An article on the project's findings was published in the February 1993 issue of *Scientific American*.

37 Hastedt, *American Foreign Policy*, pp. 239–54; and *International Herald Tribune*, 1 December 1992, p. 5; and *The Irish Times*, 7 December 1992, p. 8; *Time*, 7 December 1992, p. 65.

38 John Mueller, "Quiet Cataclysm, Some After Thoughts about World War II," *Diplomatic History*, vol. 16, 1992, pp. 66–75.

39 *International Herald Tribune*, 6 November 1992, pp. 1–2; 7–8 November 1992, pp. 1, 3; 17 November 1992, pp. 1, 6; 18 November 1992, p. 1; and *New York Times*, 23 December 1992, pp. 1, 10.

Bibliography

I BOOKS

Abel, Elie, *The Missile Crisis*, Philadelphia, Pa, Lippincott, 1966.

Adler, Selig, *The Isolationist Impulse: Its Twentieth-Century Reaction*, New York, Abelard-Schuman, 1957.

Almond, Gabriel A., *The American People and Foreign Policy*, 2nd ed., New York, Praeger, 1960.

Allison, Graham T., *Essence of Decision: Explaining the Cuban Missile Crisis*, Boston, Little, Brown, 1971.

Alperovitz, Gar, *Atomic Diplomacy: Hiroshima and Potsdam*, New York, Simon & Schuster, 1965; revised ed., Penguin, 1985.

Ambrose, Stephen E., *Eisenhower: The President*, New York, Simon & Schuster, 1984.

——, *Nixon*, 3 vols, New York, Simon & Schuster, 1987–91.

Ambrosius, Lloyd E., *Woodrow Wilson and the American Diplomatic Tradition: The Treaty Fight in Perspective*, New York, Cambridge University Press, 1987.

——, *Wilsonian Statecraft: Theory and Practice of Liberal Internationalism during World War I*, Wilmington, Del., Scholarly Resources, 1991.

Anderson, David L., *Imperialism and Idealism: American Diplomats in China, 1861–1898*, Bloomington, Ind., Indiana University Press, 1985.

——, *Trapped by Success: The Eisenhower Administration and Vietnam, 1953–1961*, New York, Columbia University Press, 1991.

Anderson, Irvine H., *Aramco, The United States, and Saudi Arabia: A Study of the Dynamics of Foreign Oil Policy, 1933–50*, Princeton, N.J., Princeton University Press, 1981.

Andrew, Christopher, and Oleg Gordievsky, *KGB: The Inside Story*, New York, HarperCollins, 1990.

Arnold, David (ed.), *Imperial Medicine and Indigenous Societies*, Manchester, Manchester University Press, 1988.

Arnson, Cynthia J., *Crossroads: Congress, The Reagan Administration, and Central America*, New York, Pantheon Books, 1989.

Bailey, Thomas A., *Woodrow Wilson and the Great Betrayal*, Chicago, University of Chicago Press, 1951, 1984.

Baily, Samuel, *The United States and the Development of South America, 1945–1975*, New York, New Viewpoints, 1976.

Ball, George W., *Error and Betrayal in Lebanon: An Analysis of Israel's Invasion of Lebanon and the Implications for U.S.–Israeli Relations*, Washington, Foundation for Middle East Peace, 1984.

Barnet, Richard, *Intervention and Revolution*, New York, World Publishing Co., 1968.

——, *The Alliance: America, Europe, Japan: Makers of the Postwar World*, New York, Simon & Schuster, 1983.

Barnhart, Michael (ed.), *Congress and United States Foreign Policy*, Albany, N.Y., State University of New York Press, 1987.

Bass, Herbert J. (ed.), *America's Entry into World War I: Submarines, Sentiment, or Security*, New York, Holt, Rinehart & Winston, 1964.

Beard, Charles A., *The Open Door at Home: A Trial Philosophy of National Interest*, New York, Macmillan, 1934.

——, *The Idea of National Interest: An Analytical Study in American Foreign Policy*, New York, 1934; reprint, Chicago, Quadrangle Books, 1966.

——, *American Foreign Policy in the Making, 1932–40*, New Haven, Conn., Yale University Press, 1946.

——, *President Roosevelt and the Coming of the War, 1941: A Study in Appearances and Realities*, New Haven, Conn., Yale University Press, 1948.

Becker, William H., *The Dynamics of Business–Government Relations: Industry and Exports, 1893–1921*, Chicago, University of Chicago Press, 1982.

——, and Samuel F. Wells Jr (eds), *Economics and World Power: An Assessment of American Diplomacy Since 1789*, New York, Columbia University Press, 1984.

Beers, Burton F., *Vain Endeavor*, Durham, N.C., Duke University Press, 1962.

Beisner, Robert, *Twelve Against Empire: The Anti-Imperialists, 1898–1900*, New York, McGraw-Hill, 1968.

——, *From the Old Diplomacy to the New, 1865–1900*, New York, AHM, 1975; rev. ed., Arlington Heights, Ill., Harlan Davidson, 1986.

Bemis, Samuel Flagg, *The Latin American Policy of the United States: A Historical Interpretation*, New York, Harcourt, Brace & Co., 1943.

——, *A Diplomatic History of the United States*, New York, Holt, 1936, 1950, 1955, 1965.

Benjamin, Jules R. *The United States and the Origins of the Cuban Revolution: An Empire of Liberty in an Age of National Liberation*, Princeton, N.J., Princeton University Press, 1990.

Bennett, Edward M., *Franklin D. Roosevelt and the Search for Victory*, Wilmington, Del., Scholarly Resources, 1990.

Berkhofer Jr, Robert K., *The White Man's Indian: Images of the American Indian from Columbus to the Present*, New York, Knopf, 1978.

Berman, Larry, *Planning a Tragedy: The Americanization of the War in Vietnam*, New York, W. W. Norton, 1982.

Bernstein, Barton (ed.), *Politics and Policies of the Truman Administration*, Chicago, Quadrangle Books, 1970.

——, *The Atomic Bomb: The Critical Issues*, Boston, Little, Brown, 1976.

Beschloss, Michael R., *Kennedy and Roosevelt: The Uneasy Alliance*, New York, Norton, 1980.

——, *Mayday: The U-2 Affair*, New York, Harper & Row, 1986.

——, *The Crisis Years: Kennedy and Khrushchev, 1960–63*, New York, Edward Burlingame Books, 1991.

——, and Strobe Talbott, *At the Highest Levels: The Inside Story of the End of the Cold War*, Boston, Little, Brown & Co., 1993.

Bill, James A., *The Eagle and the Lion: The Tragedy of American–Iranian Relations*, New Haven, Conn., Yale University Press, 1988.

Billings-Yun, Melanie, *Decision Against War: Eisenhower and Dien Bien Phu, 1954*, New York, Columbia University Press, 1988.

Bills, Scott L., *Empire and Cold War: The Roots of US–Third World Antagonism, 1945–1947*, New York, St Martin's Press, 1990.

Bird, Kai, *The Chairman: John J. McCloy, The Making of the American Establishment*, New York, Simon & Schuster, 1992.

Blight, James G., and David A. Welch, *On the Brink: Americans and Soviets Reexamine the Cuban Missile Crisis*, New York, Hill & Wang, 1989; rev. ed., 1990.

——, Bruce J. Allyn, and David A. Welch (eds), *Back to the Brink: Proceedings of the Moscow Conference on the Cuban Missile Crisis, January 27–28, 1989*, Lanham, Md, University Press of America, 1992.

——, Bruce J. Allyn, and David A. Welch, with David Lewis, *Cuba on the Brink: Fidel Castro, the Missile Crisis, and the Collapse of Communism*, New York, Pantheon, 1993.

Block, Fred, *Postindustrial Possibilities: A Critique of Economic Discourse*, Berkeley, Calif., University of California Press, 1990.

Blumenthal, Sidney, *The Rise of the Counter-Establishment: From Conservative Ideology to Political Power*, New York, Times Books, 1986.

Bonner, Raymond, *Waltzing With a Dictator: The Marcoses and the Making of American Policy*, New York, Times Books, 1988.

Borden, William S., *The Pacific Alliance: United States Foreign Economic Policy and Japanese Trade Recovery, 1947–1955*, Madison, Wis., University of Wisconsin Press, 1984.

Borg, Dorothy, and Waldo Heinrichs (eds), *The Uncertain Years: Chinese–American Relations, 1947–1950*, New York, Columbia University Press, 1980.

Bourne, Kenneth, *Britain and the Balance of Power in North America, 1815–1908*, Berkeley, Calif., University of California Press, 1967.

Boyer, Paul, *By the Bomb's Early Light: American Thought and Culture at the Dawn of the Atomic Age*, New York, Pantheon, 1985.

—— (ed.), *Reagan as President, Contemporary Views of the Man, His Politics, and His Policies*, Chicago, Ivan R. Dee, 1990.

Bracken, Paul, *The Command and Control of Nuclear Forces*, New Haven, Conn., Yale University Press, 1983.

Braestrup, Peter, *Big Story: How the American Press and Television Reported and Interpreted the Crisis of Tet 1968 in Vietnam and Washington*, 2 vols, Boulder, Colo., Westview Press, 1977.

—— (ed.), *Vietnam as History: Ten Years after the Paris Peace Accords*, Washington, D.C., University Press of America, 1984.

Brands, H. W., *The Specter of Neutralism: The United States and the Emergence of the Third World, 1947–1960*, New York, Columbia University Press, 1988.

——, *Bound to Empire: The United States and the Philippines*, New York, Oxford University Press, 1992.

Buhite, Russell D., *Soviet–American Relations in Asia, 1945–1954*, Norman, Okla., University of Oklahoma Press, 1981.

Bundy, McGeorge, *Danger and Survival: Choices about the Bomb in the First Fifty Years*, New York, Random House, 1988.

Burns, James MacGregor, *Roosevelt: The Lion and the Fox*, New York, Harcourt Brace, 1956.

Burns, Richard D. (ed.), *Guide to American Foreign Relations Since 1700*, Santa Barbara, Calif., ABC-Clio, 1983.

Butow, Robert J. C., *Japan's Decision to Surrender*, Stanford, Calif., Stanford University Press, 1954.

Calhoun, Frederick S., *Power and Principle: Armed Intervention in Wilsonian Foreign Policy*, Kent, Ohio, Kent State University Press, 1986.

Calleo, David P., *Beyond American Hegemony*, New York, Basic Books, 1987.

Calvert, Peter, *The Mexican Revolution, 1910–1914: The Diplomacy of Anglo-American Conflict*, London, Cambridge University Press, 1968.

Campbell Jr, Charles S., *The Transformation of American Foreign Relations, 1865–1900*, New York, Harper & Row, 1976.

Campbell, Kurt M., Ashton B. Carter, Steven E. Miller, and Charles Zraket, *Soviet*

Nuclear Fission: Control of the Nuclear Arsenal in a Disintegrating Soviet Union, Cambridge, Mass., Center for Science and International Affairs, Harvard University, 1991.

Cannon, Lou, *President Reagan, The Role of a Lifetime*, New York, Simon & Schuster, 1991.

Cantelon, Philip L., Richard G. Hewlett, and Robert C. Williams, *The American Atom: A Documentary History of Nuclear Policies from the Discovery of Fission to the Present*, Philadelphia, University of Pennsylvania Press, 1991.

Chace, James, and Caleb Carr, *America Invulnerable: The Quest for Absolute Security from 1812 to Star Wars*, New York, Summit Books, 1988.

Challener, Richard D., *Admirals, Generals, and American Foreign Policy, 1898–1914*, Princeton, N.J., Princeton University Press, 1973.

Chang, Gordon H., *Friends and Enemies: The United States, China, and the Soviet Union, 1948–1972*, Stanford, Calif., Stanford University Press, 1990.

Chang, Laurence, and Peter Kornbluh (eds), *The Cuban Missile Crisis: A National Security Archive Documents Reader*, New York, The New Press, 1992.

Chayes, Abram, *The Cuban Missile Crisis: International Crises and the Role of Law*, New York, Oxford University Press, 1974.

Clarfield, Gerard H., and William M. Wiecek, *Nuclear America: Military and Civilian Nuclear Power in the United States, 1940–1980*, New York, Harper & Row, 1984.

Clark, Ronald W., *The Greatest Power on Earth*, New York, Harper & Row, 1980.

Clements, Kendrick, *William Jennings Bryan*, Knoxville, Tenn., University of Tennessee Press, 1982.

——, *Woodrow Wilson: World Statesman*, Boston, Twayne, 1987.

——, *The Presidency of Woodrow Wilson*, Lawrence, Kan., University Press of Kansas, 1992.

Clifford, J. Garry, *The Citizen Soldiers: The Plattsburg Training Camp Movement, 1913–1920*, Lexington, Ky, University Press of Kentucky, 1972.

——, and Samuel R. Spencer Jr, *The First Peacetime Draft*, Lawrence, Kan., University Press of Kansas, 1986.

Clymer, Kenton J., *Protestant Missionaries in the Philippines, 1898–1916: An Inquiry into the American Colonial Mentality*, Urbana, Ill., University of Illinois Press, 1986.

Coffman, Edward M., *The War to End All Wars: The American Military Experience in World War I*, New York, Oxford University Press, 1968.

Cohen, Warren I., *Dean Rusk*, Totowa, N.J., Cooper Square Publishers, 1980.

——, *Empire without Tears: America's Foreign Relations, 1921–1933*, Philadelphia, Pa, Temple University Press, 1987.

Cole, Wayne S., *Senator Gerald P. Nye and American Foreign Relations*, Minneapolis, Minn., University of Minnesota Press, 1962.

——, *Roosevelt and the Isolationists, 1932–1945*, Lincoln, Neb., University of Nebraska Press, 1983.

Collin, Richard H., *Theodore Roosevelt, Culture, Diplomacy and Expansion: A New View of American Imperialism*, Baton Rouge, La, Louisiana State University Press, 1985.

Combs, Jerald A., *The Jay Treaty: Political Battleground of the Founding Fathers*, Berkeley, Calif., University of California Press, 1970.

——, *American Diplomatic History: Two Centuries of Changing Interpretations*, Berkeley, Calif., University of California Press, 1983.

Coniff, Michael L., *Panama and the United States: The Forced Alliance*, Athens, Ga, University of Georgia Press, 1992.

Coogan, John W., *The End of Neutrality: The United States, Britain, and Maritime Rights, 1899–1915*, Ithaca, N.Y., Cornell University Press, 1981.

Cook, Blanche Wiesen, *The Declassified Eisenhower: A Startling Reappraisal of the Eisenhower Presidency*, New York, Doubleday, 1980.

Cooke, Jacob E., *Alexander Hamilton*, New York, Scribner's, 1982.

Cooper Jr, John Milton, *Walter Hines Page: The Southerner as American, 1855–1918*, Chapel Hill, N.C., University of North Carolina Press.

Corwin, Edwin S., *The President: Office and Powers 1787–1957*, New York, New York University Press, 1957.

Costigliola, Frank, *Awkward Dominion: American Political, Economic, and Cultural Relations with Europe, 1919–1933*, Ithaca, N.Y., Cornell University Press, 1984.

Crabb Jr, Cecil V., and Pat M. Holt, *Invitation to Struggle: Congress, the President and Foreign Policy*, Washington, Congressional Quarterly Press, 1980.

Craig, Gordon A., and Alexander George, *Force and Statecraft: Diplomatic Problems of Our Time*, New York, Oxford University Press, 1983.

Crook, David, *The North, the South, and the Powers, 1861–1865*, New York, Wiley, 1974.

Cumings, Bruce, *The Origins of the Korean War*, vol. 1, *Liberation and the Emergence of Separate Regimes, 1945–47*, 1981; vol. 2, *The Roaring of the Cataract*, Princeton, N.J., Princeton University Press, 1992.

Curry, Roy Watson, *Woodrow Wilson and Far Eastern Policy, 1913–1921*, New York, 1957; reprint, Octagon Books, 1968

Dahl, Robert A., *Congress and Foreign Policy*, New York, Harcourt Brace, 1950.

Dallek, Robert, *Franklin D. Roosevelt and American Foreign Policy, 1932–1945*, New York, Oxford University Press, 1979.

——, *The American Style of Foreign Policy: Cultural Politics and Foreign Affairs*, New York, Knopf, 1983.

——, *Ronald Reagan, The Politics of Symbolism*, Cambridge, Mass., Harvard University Press, 1984.

Dangerfield, Royden J., *In Defense of the Senate: A Study in Treaty Making*, Norman, Okla., 1933; reprint, Port Washington, N.Y., Kennikat Press, 1966.

DeConde, Alexander, *This Affair of Louisiana*, New York, Scribner, 1976.

Deibel, Terry L., *Presidents, Public Opinion, and Power: The Nixon, Carter and Reagan Years*, New York, Foreign Policy Association, 1987.

De Santis, Hugh, *The Diplomacy of Silence: The American Foreign Service, the Soviet Union, and the Cold War, 1933–1947*, Chicago, University of Chicago Press, 1980.

Destler, I. M., *Presidents, Bureaucrats, and Foreign Policy: The Politics of Organizational Reform*, Princeton, N.J., Princeton University Press, 1972.

Dinges, John, *Our Man in Panama*, New York, Random House, 1990.

Divine, Robert A., *The Illusion of Neutrality*, Chicago, University of Chicago Press, 1962.

——, *Roosevelt and World War II*, Baltimore, Md, Johns Hopkins University Press, 1969.

——, *Eisenhower and the Cold War*, New York, Oxford University Press, 1981.

Dobyns, Henry F., *Their Number Become Thinned: Native American Population Dynamics in Eastern North America*, Knoxville, Tenn., University of Tennessee Press, 1983.

Doenecke, Justus D., *Anti-Intervention: A Bibliographical Introduction to Isolationism and Pacifism from World War I to the Early Cold War*, New York, Garland, 1987.

——, and John E. Wilz, *From Isolation to War, 1931–1941*, 2nd ed., Arlington Heights, Ill., Harlan Davidson, 1991.

Dowd, Gregory E., *A Spirited Resistance: The North American Indian Struggle for Unity, 1745–1815*, Baltimore, Md, Johns Hopkins University Press, 1991.

Dower, John, *War Without Mercy: Race and Power in the Pacific War*, New York, Pantheon Books, 1986.

Draper, Theodore, *Present History*, New York, Random House, 1983.

——, *A Very Thin Line: The Iran–Contra Affairs*, New York, Hill & Wang, 1991.

Duignan, Peter, and L. H. Gann, *The United States and Africa: A History*, New York, Cambridge University Press, 1984.

Eagleton, Thomas F., *War and Presidential Power: A Chronicle of Congressional Surrender*, New York, Liveright, 1974.

Eccles, M. S., *Beckoning Frontiers*, New York, Knopf, 1951.

Fairbank, John K. (ed.), *The Missionary Enterprise in China*, Cambridge, Mass., Harvard University Press, 1974.

Feinberg, Richard E., *The Intemperate Zone: The Third World Challenge to U.S. Foreign Policy*, New York, Norton, 1983.

Feinman, Ronald L., *Twilight of Progressivism: The Western Republican Senators and the New Deal*, Baltimore, Md, Johns Hopkins University Press, 1981.

Feis, Herbert, *Japan Subdued: The Atomic Bomb and the End of World War Two in the Pacific*, Princeton, N.J., Princeton University Press, 1961.

——, *The Atomic Bomb and the End of World War II*, Princeton, N.J., Princeton University Press, 1966.

——, *From Trust to Terror: The Onset of the Cold War, 1945–1950*, New York, Norton, 1970.

Feldbaum, Carl B., and Ronald J. Bee, *Looking the Tiger in the Eye: Confronting the Nuclear Threat*, New York, Vintage, 1990.

Ferrell, Robert H., *American Diplomacy in the Great Depression*, New Haven, Conn., Yale University Press, 1952.

——, *Woodrow Wilson and World War I, 1917–1921*, New York, Harper & Row, 1985.

Fitzgerald, Frances, *Fire in the Lake: The Vietnamese and the Americans in Vietnam*, Boston, Little, Brown, 1972.

Fleming, Denna Frank, *The Treaty Veto of the American Senate*, New York, G. P. Putnam's Sons, 1930.

Floto, Inga, *Colonel House in Paris*, Princeton, N.J., Princeton University Press, 1980.

Foner, Philip S., *The Spanish–Cuban–American War and the Birth of American Imperialism, 1895–1902*, New York, Monthly Review Press, 1972.

Foot, Rosemary J., *The Wrong War: American Policy and Dimensions of the Korean Conflict*, Ithaca, N.Y., Cornell University Press, 1985.

Frank, Thomas N., and Edward Weisband, *Foreign Policy by Congress*, New York, Oxford University Press, 1979.

Freedman, Lawrence, *The Evolution of Nuclear Strategy*, New York, St Martin's Press, 1981.

Freedman, Max (ed.), *Roosevelt and Frankfurter: Their Correspondence, 1928–1945*, Boston, Little, Brown, 1967.

Gaddis, John Lewis, *The United States and the Origins of the Cold War, 1941–1947*, New York, Columbia University Press, 1972.

——, *Strategies of Containment: A Critical Appraisal of Postwar American National Security Policy*, New York, Oxford University Press, 1982.

——, *The Long Peace: Inquiries into the History of the Cold War*, New York, Oxford University Press, 1987.

——, *The United States and the End of the Cold War: Implications, Reconsiderations, Provocations*, New York, Oxford University Press, 1992.

Gardner, Lloyd, *Economic Aspects of New Deal Diplomacy*, Madison, Wis., University of Wisconsin Press, 1964.

——, *Architects of Illusion: Men and Ideas in American Foreign Policy, 1941–1949*, Chicago, Quadrangle Books, 1970.

——, *Safe for Democracy: The Anglo-American Response to Revolution, 1913–1923*, New York, Oxford University Press, 1984.

——, (ed.), *Redefining the Past: Essays in Diplomatic History in Honor of William Appleman Williams*, Corvallis, Ore., Oregon State University Press, 1986.

——, *Approaching Vietnam: From World War II Through Dienbienphu, 1941–1954*, New York, Norton, 1988.

Garthoff, Raymond, *Detente and Confrontation: American–Soviet Relations From Nixon to Reagan*, Washington, Brookings Institution, 1985.

——, *Reflections on the Cuban Missile Crisis*, Washington, Brookings Institution, 1987.

Gelb, Leslie, and Richard Betts, *The Irony of Vietnam: The System Worked*, Washington, Brookings Institution, 1979.

George, Alexander L. (ed.), *Avoiding War: Problems of Crisis Management*, Boulder, Colo., Westview Press, 1991.

Gibson, Martha L., *Weapons of Influence: The Legislative Veto, American Foreign Policy, and the Irony of Reform*, Boulder, Colo., Westview, 1992.

Gilbert, Felix, *To the Farewell Address: Ideas of Early American Foreign Policy*, Princeton, N.J., Princeton University Press, 1961.

Gilderhus, Mark T., *Diplomacy and Revolution: U.S.–Mexican Relations under Wilson and Carranza*, Tucson, Ariz., University of Arizona Press, 1977.

——, and David Healy, *Pan American Visions: Woodrow Wilson in the Western Hemisphere, 1913–1921*, Tucson, Ariz., University of Arizona Press, 1986.

Gill, Stephen, *American Hegemony and the Trilateral Commission*, New York, Cambridge University Press, 1990.

Gimbel, John, *The Origins of the Marshall Plan*, Stanford, Calif., Stanford University Press, 1976.

Gleijeses, Piero, *The Dominican Crisis: The 1965 Constitutionalist Revolt and American Intervention*, Baltimore, Md, Johns Hopkins University Press, 1978.

——, *Shattered Hope: The Guatemalan Revolution and the United States, 1944–1954*, Princeton, N.J., Princeton University Press, 1991.

Godfried, Nathan, *Bridging the Gap between Rich and Poor: American Economic Development Policy toward the Arab East, 1942–1949*, New York, Greenwood Press, 1987.

Gould, Lewis L., *The Spanish–American War and President McKinley*, Lawrence, Kan., University of Kansas Press, 1982.

Gouldsmit, Samuel, *Alsos*, New York, Schuman, 1947.

Graber, Doris, *Processing the News: How People Tame the Information Tide*, New York, Longman, 1984.

Graebner, Norman A., *Empire on the Pacific: A Study in American Continental Expansion*, New York, Ronald Press, 1955.

——, *Ideas and Diplomacy: Readings in the Intellectual Tradition of American Foreign Policy*, New York, Oxford University Press, 1964.

——, *Cold War Diplomacy: American Foreign Policy, 1945–1975*, New York, Oxford University Press, 1964.

Graham Jr, Otis, and Meghan R. Wander (eds), *Franklin D. Roosevelt: His Life and Times: An Encyclopedic View*, Boston, G. K. Hall, 1985.

Grassmuck, George, *Sectional Biases on Foreign Policy*, Baltimore, Md, Johns Hopkins University Press, 1951.

Graubard, Stephen, *Mr. Bush's War: Adventures in the Politics of Illusion*, New York, Hill & Wang, 1992.

Greenstein, Fred I., *The Hidden Hand Presidency: Eisenhower as Leader*, New York, Basic Books, 1982.

Gregory, Donna, *The Nuclear Predicament: A Sourcebook*, New York, St Martin's Press, 1986.

Gregory, Ross, *Walter Hines Page, Ambassador to the Court of St. James's*, Lexington, Ky, University Press of Kentucky, 1970.

Grenville, J. A. S., and George Berkeley Young, *Politics, Strategy, and American Diplomacy: Studies in Foreign Policy, 1873–1917*, New Haven, Conn., Yale University Press, 1966.

Guinsburg, Thomas N., *The Pursuit of Isolationism in the United States Senate from Versailles to Pearl Harbor*, New York, Garland, 1982.

Hagan, Kenneth J., *This People's Navy: The Making of American Sea Power*, New York, Free Press, 1991.

Hahn, Peter L., *The United States, Great Britain, and Egypt, 1945–1956: Strategy and Diplomacy in the Early Cold War*, Chapel Hill, N.C., University of North Carolina Press, 1991.

Haines, Gerald K., *The Americanization of Brazil: A Study of U.S. Cold War Diplomacy in the Third World, 1945–1954*, Wilmington, Del., Scholarly Resources, 1989.

Haley, P. Edward, *Congress and the Fall of South Vietnam and Cambodia*, Rutherford, N.J., Fairleigh Dickinson University Press, 1982.

Hammond, William, *Public Affairs: The Military and the Media, 1962–1968*, Washington, Center of Military History, US Army, 1988.

Harbutt, Fraser, *The Iron Curtain: Churchill, America and the Origins of the Cold War*, New York, Oxford University Press, 1986.

Headrick, Daniel R., *The Tentacles of Progress: Technological Transfer in the Age of Imperialism, 1850–1940*, New York, Oxford University Press, 1988.

Healy, David, *US Expansionism: The Imperialist Urge in the 1890s*, Madison, Wis., University of Wisconsin Press, 1970.

——, *Drive to Hegemony: The United States in the Caribbean, 1898–1917*, Madison, Wis., University of Wisconsin Press, 1988.

Heinrichs, Waldo H., *Threshold of War: Franklin D. Roosevelt and American Entry into World War II*, New York, Oxford University Press, 1988.

Henkin, Louis, *Constitutionalism, Democracy and Foreign Affairs*, New York, Columbia University Press, 1990.

Herken, Greg, *The Winning Weapon: The Atomic Bomb in the Cold War, 1945–1950*, New York, Knopf, 1980.

——, *Counsels of War*, New York, Oxford University Press, 1987.

——, *Cardinal Choices: Presidential Science Advising from the Atomic Bomb to SDI*, New York, Oxford University Press, 1992.

Herring, George C., *America's Longest War: The United States and Vietnam 1950–1975*, New York, Wiley, 1979.

Hersh, Seymour, *The Price of Power: Kissinger in the Nixon White House*, New York, Summit Books, 1983.

Hershberg, James, *James B. Conant: Harvard to Hiroshima and the Making of the Nuclear Age*, New York, Knopf, 1993.

Herwig, Holger H., *Politics of Frustration: The United States in German Naval Planning, 1889–1941*, Boston, Little, Brown, 1976.

Hess, Gary R., *America Encounters India, 1941–1947*, Baltimore, Md, Johns Hopkins University Press, 1971.

——, *The United States' Emergence as a Southeast Asian Power, 1940–1950*, New York, Columbia University Press, 1987.

Hewlett, Richard G, and Oscar E. Anderson Jr, *The New World, 1939–1946*, vol. 1, *A History of the United States Atomic Energy Commission*, University Park, Pa, Pennsylvania State University Press, 1962.

——, and Francis Duncan, *Atomic Shield, 1947/1952*, vol. 2, *A History of the United States Atomic Energy Commission*, University Park, Pa, Pennsylvania State University Press, 1969.

Hietala, Thomas R., *Manifest Design: Anxious Aggrandizement in Late Jacksonian America*, Ithaca, N.Y., Cornell University Press, 1985.

Higgins, Trumbull, *The Perfect Failure: Kennedy, Eisenhower, and the CIA at the Bay of Pigs*, New York, Norton, 1987.

Hilderbrand, Robert C., *Power and the People: Executive Management of Public Opinion in Foreign Affairs, 1897–1921*, Chapel Hill, N.C., University of North Carolina Press, 1981.

Hill, Larry D., *Emissaries to a Revolution*, Baton Rouge, La, Louisiana State University Press, 1973.

Hilsman, Roger, *The Politics of Policy Making in Defense and Foreign Affairs*, New York, Harper & Row, 1971.

Hinckle, Warren, and William W. Turner, *The Fish is Red: The Story of the Secret War against Castro*, New York, Harper & Row, 1981.

Hixson, Walter L., *George F. Kennan: Cold War Iconoclast*, New York, Columbia University Press, 1989.

Hofstadter, Richard, *The Progressive Historians: Turner, Beard, Parrington*, New York, Random House, 1968.

Hogan, Michael J., *Informal Entente: The Private Structure of Cooperation in Anglo-American Economic Diplomacy, 1918–1928*, Columbia, Mo., University of Missouri Press, 1977.

——, *The Panama Canal in American Politics: Domestic Advocacy and the Evolution of Policy*, Carbondale, Ill., Southern Illinois University Press, 1986.

——, *The Marshall Plan: America, Britain, and the Reconstruction of Western Europe, 1947–1952*, New York, Cambridge University Press, 1987.

——, and Thomas G. Paterson (eds), *Explaining the History of American Foreign Relations*, New York, Cambridge University Press, 1991.

Holloway, David, *The Soviet Union and the Arms Race*, New Haven, Conn., Yale University Press, 1984.

Holsti, Ole R., and James N. Rosenau, *American Leadership in World Affairs: Vietnam and the Breakdown of Consensus*, Boston, Allen & Unwin, 1984.

Holt, W. Stull, *Treaties Defeated by the Senate: A Study of the Struggle Between President and Senate Over the Conduct of Foreign Relations*, Baltimore, Md, 1933; reprint, Gloucester, Mass., Peter Smith, 1964.

Horsman, Reginald, *Expansion and American Indian Policy, 1783–1812*, East Lansing, Mich., Michigan State University Press, 1967.

——, *Race and Manifest Destiny: The Origins of American Racial Anglo-Saxonism*, Cambridge, Mass., Harvard University Press, 1981.

——, *The Diplomacy of the New Republic, 1776–1815*, Arlington Heights, Ill., Harlan Davidson, 1985.

Hunt, Michael H., *The Making of a Special Relationship: The United States and China to 1914*, New York, Columbia University Press, 1983.

——, *Ideology and U.S. Foreign Policy*, New Haven, Conn., Yale University Press, 1987.

Hunter, Jane, *The Gospel of Gentility: American Women Missionaries in Turn-of-the-Century China*, New Haven, Conn., Yale University Press, 1984.

Immerman, Richard H., *The CIA in Guatemala: The Foreign Policy of Intervention*, Austin, Tex., University of Texas Press, 1982.

—— (ed.), *John Foster Dulles and the Diplomacy of the Cold War: A Reappraisal*, Princeton, N.J., Princeton University Press, 1989.

Ireland, Timothy P., *Creating the Entangling Alliance: The Origins of the North Atlantic Treaty Organization*, Westport, Conn., Greenwood Press, 1981.

Iriye, Akira, *Across the Pacific: An Inner History of American–East Asian Relations*, New York, Harcourt, Brace & World, 1967.

Isaacson, Walter, *Kissinger: A Biography*, New York, Simon & Schuster, 1992.

——, and Evan Thomas, *The Wise Men: Six Friends and the World They Made*, New York, Simon & Schuster, 1986.

Israel, Jerry, *Progressivism and the Open Door: America and China, 1905–1921*, Pittsburgh, Pa, University of Pittsburgh Press, 1971.

Jablon, Howard, *The State Department and Foreign Policy, 1933–1937*, Lexington, Ky, University Press of Kentucky, 1983.

Javits, Jacob K., *Who Makes War: The President Versus Congress*, New York, William Morrow, 1973.

Jenks, Leland H., *Our Cuban Colony: A Study in Sugar*, New York, 1928; reprint, New York, Arno Press, 1970.

Jennings, Francis, *The Invasion of America: Indians, Colonialism, and the Cant of Conquest*, Chapel Hill, N.C., University of North Carolina Press, 1975.

Johnson, Haynes, *In the Absence of Power: Governing America*, New York, Viking Press, 1980.

Johnson, John J., *A Hemisphere Apart: The Foundations of United States Policy toward Latin America*, Baltimore, Md, Johns Hopkins University Press, 1990.

Johnson, Loch K., *A Season of Inquiry: The Senate Intelligence Investigation*, Lexington, Ky, University Press of Kentucky, 1985.

Jonas, Manfred, *Isolationism in America, 1935–1941*, Ithaca, N.Y., Cornell University Press, 1966.

Jones, Dorothy V., *License for Empire: Colonialism by Treaty in Early America*, Chicago, University of Chicago Press, 1982.

Jones, Howard (ed.), *Safeguarding the Republic: Essays and Documents in American Foreign Relations, 1890–1991*, New York, McGraw-Hill, 1992.

Joseph, Gilbert M., *Revolution from Without: Yucatan, Mexico, and the United States, 1880–1924*, New York, Cambridge University Press, 1982.

Kahin, George McT., *Intervention: How America Became Involved in Vietnam*, New York, Knopf, 1986.

Kalb, Madeline, *Congo Cables: The Cold War in Africa From Eisenhower to Kennedy*, New York, Macmillan, 1982.

Kaplan, Fred, *The Wizards of Armageddon*, New York, Simon & Schuster, 1983.

Karnow, Stanley, *In Our Image: America's Empire in the Philippines*, New York, Foreign Policy Association, 1989.

Kaufman, Burton I., *The Oil Cartel Case: A Documentary Study of Antitrust Activity in the Cold War Era*, Westport, Conn., Greenwood Press, 1978.

——, *Trade & Aid: Eisenhower's Foreign Economic Policy, 1953–1961*, Baltimore, Md, Johns Hopkins University Press, 1982.

——, *The Korean War: Challenges in Crisis, Credibility, and Command*, Philadelphia, Pa, Temple University Press, 1986.

——, *The Presidency of James Earl Carter Jr.*, Lawrence, Kan., University Press of Kansas, 1993.

Kay, Christobal, *Latin American Theories of Development and Underdevelopment*, New York, Routledge, 1989.

Kearns, Doris, *Lyndon Johnson and the American Dream*, New York, Harper & Row, 1976.

Kennan, George F., *Soviet–American Relations, 1917–1920*, Princeton, N.J., Princeton University Press, 1956.

Kennedy, Paul, *The Rise and Fall of the Great Powers: Economic Change and Military Conflict from 1500 to 2000*, New York, Random House, 1987.

Kepner Jr, Charles D., and Jay H. Soothill, *The Banana Empire: A Case Study of Economic Imperialism*, New York, 1935; reprint, New York, Russell & Russell, 1967.

Kern, Montague, Patricia W. Levering, and Ralph B. Levering, *The Kennedy Crisis: The Press, The Presidency, and Foreign Policy*, Chapel Hill, N.C., University of North Carolina Press, 1983.

Knight, Melvin H., *The Americans in Santo Domingo*, New York, Vanguard Press, 1928.

Kolko, Gabriel, *The Roots of American Foreign Policy: An Analysis of Power and Purpose*, Boston, Beacon Press, 1969.

Kolke, Gabriel, *Confronting the Third World: United States Foreign Policy, 1945–1980*, New York, Pantheon Books, 1988.

Kolko, Joyce and Gabriel, *The Limits of Power: The World and United States Foreign Policy, 1945–54*, New York, Harper & Row, 1972.

Komer, Robert W., *Bureaucracy at War: U.S. Performance in the Vietnam Conflict*, Boulder, Colo., Westview Press, 1986.

Kramish, Arnold, *Nuclear Energy in the Soviet Union*, Stanford, Calif., Stanford University Press, 1959.

Kroes, Rob (ed.), *The American Identity: Fusion and Fragmentation*, Amsterdam, Amerika Instituut, Universiteit van Amsterdam, 1980.

Kuklick, Bruce, *American Policy and the Division of Germany: The Clash with Russia over Reparations*, Ithaca, N.Y., Cornell University Press, 1972.

Kuniholm, Bruce R., *The Origins of the Cold War in the Near East: Great Power Conflict and Diplomacy in Iran, Turkey, and Greece*, Princeton, N.J., Princeton University Press, 1980.

Kunz, Diane B., *The Economic Diplomacy of the Suez Crisis*, Chapel Hill, N.C., University of North Carolina Press, 1991.

Kusnitz, Leonard A., *Public Opinion and Foreign Policy: America's China Policy, 1949–1979*, Westport, Conn., Greenwood Press, 1984.

LaFeber, Walter, *The New Empire: An Interpretation of American Expansion, 1860–1898*, Ithaca, N.Y., Cornell University Press, 1963.

——, *The Panama Canal: The Crisis in Historical Perspective*, New York, Oxford University Press, 1978; updated ed., 1989.

——, *Inevitable Revolutions: The United States in Central America*, New York, W. W. Norton, 1983, 1984, 2nd ed., 1993.

Langer, William, and S. Everett Gleason, *The Challenge to Isolation*, New York, Harper, 1952.

——, *The Undeclared War*, New York, Harper, 1953.

Langley, Lester D., *The Banana Wars: An Inner History of American Empire, 1900–1934*, Lexington, Ky, University Press of Kentucky, 1983.

Leacock, Ruth, *Requiem for Revolution: The United States and Brazil, 1961–1969*, Kent State, Ohio, Kent State University Press, 1990.

Leffler, Melvyn, *Elusive Quest: America's Pursuit of European Stability and French Security, 1919–1933*, Chapel Hill, N.C., University of North Carolina Press, 1979.

——, *A Preponderance of Power: National Security, the Truman Administration and the Cold War*, Stanford, Calif., Stanford University Press, 1992.

Lehman, John, *The Executive, Congress and Foreign Policy: Studies of the Nixon Administration*, New York, Praeger, 1974.

Lens, Sidney, *The Forging of the American Empire*, New York, Crowell, 1971.

Leopold, Richard W., *The Growth of American Foreign Policy*, New York, Alfred A. Knopf, 1962.

Leutze, James R., *Bargaining for Supremacy: Anglo-American Naval Collaboration, 1937–1941*, Chapel Hill, N.C., University of North Carolina Press, 1977.

Levering, Ralph B., *The Public and American Foreign Policy, 1918–1978*, New York, Morrow, 1978.

Levin, N. Gordon, *Woodrow Wilson and World Politics: America's Response to War and Revolution*, New York, Oxford University Press, 1968.

Levinson, Jerome, and Juan de Onis, *The Alliance That Lost Its Way: A Critical Report on the Alliance for Progress*, Chicago, Quadrangle Books, 1970.

Levy, David W., *The Debate over Vietnam*, Baltimore, Md, Johns Hopkins University Press, 1991.

Lewy, Guenter, *America in Vietnam: Illusion, Myth, and Reality*, New York, Oxford University Press, 1978.

Link, Arthur S., *Wilson the Diplomatist: A Look at His Major Foreign Policies*, Baltimore, Md, Johns Hopkins University Press, 1957.

——, *Woodrow Wilson: War, Revolution, and Peace*, Arlington Heights, Ill., AHM Publishing, 1979.

Livermore, Seward W., *Politics is Adjourned: Woodrow Wilson and the War Congress, 1916–1918*, Middletown, Conn., Wesleyan University Press, 1966.

Louis, William Roger, *Imperialism at Bay: The United States and the Decolonization of the British Empire, 1941–1945*, Oxford, Clarendon Press, 1977.

Lowi, Theodore, *The Personal President: Power Invested, Promise Unfulfilled*, Ithaca, N.Y., Cornell University Press, 1985.

Lundestad, Geir, *The American Non-Policy Towards Eastern Europe, 1943–1947*, New York, Humanities Press, 1975.

——, *America, Scandinavia, and the Cold War, 1945–1949*, New York, Columbia University Press, 1980.

——, *The American "Empire" and Other Studies of US Foreign Policy in a Comparative Perspective*, New York, Oxford University Press, 1990.

Lynn-Jones, Sean M. (ed.), *The Cold War and After: Prospects for Peace*, Cambridge, Mass., MIT Press, 1991.

Lyon, Peter, *Eisenhower: Portrait of a Hero*, Boston, Little, Brown, 1974.

Lytle, Mark Hamilton, *The Origins of the Iranian–American Alliance, 1941–1953*, New York, Holmes & Meier, 1987.

McCormick, Thomas J., *China Market: America's Quest for Informal Empire, 1893–1901*, Chicago, Quadrangle Books, 1967.

——, *America's Half-Century: United States Foreign Policy in the Cold War*, Johns Hopkins University Press, Baltimore, Md, 1989.

McCoy, Drew R., *The Elusive Republic: Political Economy in Jeffersonian America*, Chapel Hill, N.C., University of North Carolina Press, 1980.

McMahon, Robert J., *Colonialism and Cold War: The United States and the Struggle for Indonesian Independence, 1945–1949*, Ithaca, N.Y., Cornell University Press, 1981.

——, *The Cold War on the Periphery: The United States, India, and Pakistan, 1947–1965*, New York, forthcoming, 1994.

Maddux, Thomas R., *Years of Estrangement: American Relations with the Soviet Union, 1933–1941*, Tallahassee, Fl., University Presses of Florida, 1980.

Magdoff, Harry, *The Age of Imperialism: The Economics of US Foreign Policy*, New York, Monthly Review, 1969.

Mahoney, Richard D., *JFK: Ordeal in Africa*, New York, Oxford University Press, 1983.

Mandelbaum, Michael E., *The Nuclear Question: The United States and Nuclear Weapons, 1946–1976*, New York, Cambridge University Press, 1979.

Marks III, Frederick W., *Wind Over Sand: The Diplomacy of Franklin D. Roosevelt*, Athens, Ga, University of Georgia Press, 1988.

Marsh, Margaret A., *The Bankers in Bolivia: A Study in American Foreign Investment*, New York, Vanguard Press, 1928.

Matray, James I., *The Reluctant Crusade: American Foreign Policy in Korea, 1941–1950*, Honolulu, Hawaii, University of Hawaii Press, 1985.

May, Ernest R., *Imperial Democracy: The Emergence of America as a Great Power*, New York, Harcourt, Brace & World, 1961.

——, *American Imperialism: A Speculative Essay*, New York, Athenaeum, 1968.

——, *The "Lessons" of the Past: The Use and Misuse of History in American Foreign Policy*, New York, Oxford University Press, 1973.

——, *The Truman Administration and China, 1945–1949*, Philadelphia, Pa, Lippincott, 1975.

May, Glenn A., *Social Engineering in the Philippines: The Aims, Execution, and*

Impact of American Colonial Policy, 1900–1913, Westport, Conn., Greenwood Press, 1980.

May, Glenn A., *Battle for Batangas: A Philippine Province at War*, New Haven, Conn., Yale University Press, 1991.

May, Robert E., *The Southern Dream of a Caribbean Empire, 1854–1861*, Baton Rouge, La, Louisiana State University Press, 1973.

Mayer, Arno J., *Politics and Diplomacy of Peacemaking: Containment and Counterrevolution at Versailles*, New York, Knopf, 1967.

Mayer, Jane, and Doyle McManus, *Landslide: The Unmaking of the President, 1984–1988*, New York, Houghton Mifflin, 1988.

Mayers, David, *George Kennan and the Dilemmas of US Foreign Policy*, New York, Oxford University Press, 1988.

Melanson, Richard A., and David Mayers (eds), *Reevaluating Eisenhower: American Foreign Policy in the 1950's*, Urbana, Ill., University of Illinois Press, 1987.

Merrill, Dennis, *Bread and the Ballot: The United States and India's Economic Development, 1947–1963*, Chapel Hill, N.C., University of North Carolina Press, 1990.

Messer, Robert L., *The End of an Alliance: James F. Byrnes, Roosevelt, Truman and the Origins of the Cold War*, Chapel Hill, N.C., University of North Carolina Press, 1982.

Miller, Aaron David, *Search for Security: Saudi Arabian Oil and American Foreign Policy, 1939–1949*, Chapel Hill, N.C., University of North Carolina Press, 1980.

Miller, James E., *The United States and Italy: The Politics and Diplomacy of Stabilization*, Chapel Hill, N.C., University of North Carolina Press, 1986.

Miller, Merle, *Lyndon: An Oral Biography*, New York, Putnam, 1980.

Miller, Stuart C., *"Benevolent Assimilation": The American Conquest of the Philippines, 1899–1903*, New Haven, Conn., Yale University Press, 1982.

Minnen, Cornelis van, and John F. Sears (eds), *FDR and His Contemporaries: Foreign Perceptions of an American President*, New York, St Martin's Press, 1992.

Mommsen, Wolfgang J., *Theories of Imperialism*, New York, Random House, 1982.

——, and Jurgen Osterhammel (eds), *Imperialism and After: Continuities and Discontinuities*, Boston, Allen & Unwin, 1986.

Montgomery, Tommie Sue, *Revolution in El Salvador*, Boulder, Colo., Westview Press, 1982.

Morgan, H. Wayne, *America's Road to Empire: The War with Spain and Overseas Expansion*, New York, Wiley, 1965.

—— (ed.), *The Gilded Age: A Reappraisal*, Syracuse, N.Y., Syracuse University Press, 1970.

Morison, Elting E., *Turmoil and Tradition: A Study of the Life and Times of Henry L. Stimson*, Boston, Little, Brown & Co., 1960.

Morley, Morris H., *Imperial State and Revolution: The United States and Cuba, 1952–1986*, New York, Cambridge University Press, 1987.

Morris, Charles R., *Iron Destinies, Lost Opportunities: The Post-War Arms Race*, New York, Carroll & Graf, 1988.

Morris, Roger, *Uncertain Greatness: Henry Kissinger and American Foreign Policy*, New York, Harper & Row, 1977.

Moss, Norman, *Men Who Play God: The Story of the Hydrogen Bomb*, New York, Harper & Row, 1968.

Munro, Dana G., *Intervention and Dollar Diplomacy in the Caribbean, 1900–1921*, Princeton, N.J., Princeton University Press, 1964.

Nacos, Brigette Lebens, *The Press, Presidents, and Crises*, New York, Columbia University Press, 1990.

Nathan, James A. (ed.), *The Cuban Missile Crisis Revisited*, New York, St Martin's Press, 1992.

Neal, Fred Warner (ed.), *Detente or Debacle: Common Sense in U.S.–Soviet Relations*, New York, Norton, 1979.

Nearing, Scott, *The Making of a Radical: A Political Autobiography*, New York, Harper & Row, 1972.

——, and Joseph Freeman, *Dollar Diplomacy: A Study in American Imperialism*, New York, 1925; reprint, New York, Monthly Review Press, 1966.

Neff, Donald, *Warriors at Suez: Eisenhower Takes America Into the Middle East*, New York, Linden Press/Simon & Schuster, 1981.

Neustadt, Richard E., *Presidential Power and the Modern Presidents: The Politics of Leadership from Roosevelt to Reagan*, New York, Free Press, 1990.

Newhouse, John, *War and Peace in the Nuclear Age*, New York, Knopf, 1989.

Noer, Thomas J., *Cold War and Black Liberation: The United States and White Rule in Africa, 1948–1968*, Columbia, Mo., University of Missouri Press, 1985.

Nolan, Janne E., *Guardians of the Arsenal: The Politics of Nuclear Strategy*, New York, Basic Books, 1989.

Nore, Ellen, *Charles A. Beard, An Intellectual Biography*, Carbondale, Ill., Southern Illinois University Press, 1983.

Novick, Peter, *That Noble Dream: The "Objectivity Question" and the American Historical Profession*, New York, Cambridge University Press, 1988.

Oberdorfer, Don, *The Turn: From the Cold War to a New Era. The United States and the Soviet Union, 1983–1990*, New York, Poseidon Press, 1991.

Offner, John L., *An Unwanted War: The Diplomacy of the United States and Spain over Cuba, 1895–1898*, Chapel Hill, N.C., University of North Carolina Press, 1992.

Osgood, Robert E., *Ideals and Self-Interest in America's Foreign Relations: The Great Transformation of the Twentieth Century*, Chicago, University of Chicago Press, 1953.

Pach, Chester J., *Arming the Free World: The Origins of the United States Military Assistance Program, 1945–1950*, Chapel Hill, N.C., University of North Carolina Press, 1991.

——, and Elmo R. Richardson, *The Presidency of Dwight D. Eisenhower*, Lawrence, Kan., University Press of Kansas, 1991.

Packenham, Robert A., *Liberal America and the Third World: Political Development Ideas in Foreign Aid and Social Science*, Princeton, N.J., Princeton University Press, 1973.

Painter, David S., *Oil and the American Century: The Political Economy of US Foreign Oil Policy, 1941–1954*, Baltimore, Md, Johns Hopkins University Press, 1986.

Palmer Jr, Bruce, *The 25 Year War: America's Military Role in Vietnam*, Lexington, Ky, University Press of Kentucky, 1984.

Parker, Phyllis R., *Brazil and the Quiet Intervention, 1964*, Austin, Tex., University of Texas Press, 1979.

Parmet, Herbert, *J.F.K.: The Presidency of J.F.K.*, New York, Dial Press, 1983.

——, *Richard Nixon and His America*, Boston, Little, Brown, 1990.

Parrini, Carl P., *Heir to Empire: United States Economic Diplomacy, 1916–1923*, Pittsburgh, Pa, University of Pittsburgh Press, 1969.

Pastor, Robert A., *Condemned to Repetition: The United States and Nicaragua*, Princeton, N.J., Princeton University Press, 1987.

Paterson, Thomas G., *Soviet–American Confrontation: Postwar Reconstruction and the Origins of the Cold War*, Baltimore, Md, Johns Hopkins University Press, 1973.

——, *On Every Front: The Making and Unmaking of the Cold War*, New York, Norton, 1979; rev. ed., 1992.

—— (ed.), *Kennedy's Quest for Victory: American Foreign Policy, 1961–1963*, New York, Oxford University Press, 1989.

Paterson, Thomas G., and Stephen G. Rabe (eds), *Imperial Surge: The United States Abroad, the 1890s–early 1900s*, Lexington, Mass., D. C. Heath, 1992.

Patterson, James T., *Congressional Conservatism and the New Deal*, Lexington, Ky, University of Kentucky Press, 1967.

Pérez Jr, Louis A., *Cuba between Empires, 1878–1902*, Pittsburgh, Pa, University of Pittsburgh Press, 1983.

——, *Cuba and the United States: Ties of Singular Intimacy*, Athens, Ga, University of Georgia Press, 1990.

Perkins, Bradford, *The First Rapprochement: England and the United States, 1795–1805*, Philadelphia, Pa, University of Pennsylvania Press, 1955.

——, *Prologue to War: England and the United States, 1805–1812*, Berkeley, Calif., University of California Press, 1961.

——, *The Great Rapprochement: England and the United States, 1895–1914*, New York, Athenaeum, 1968.

Perkins, Dexter, *A History of the Monroe Doctrine*, Boston, Little, Brown, 1941.

——, *The American Approach to Foreign Policy*, Cambridge, Mass., Harvard University Press, 1955; rev. ed., 1962.

Perkins, Whitney T., *Denial of Empire: The United States and Its Dependencies*, Leyden, A. W. Sythoff, 1962.

Pletcher, David M., *The Diplomacy of Annexation: Texas, Oregon, and the Mexican War*, Colombia, Mo., University of Missouri Press, 1973.

Plummer, Brenda Gayle, *Haiti and the Great Powers, 1902–1915*, Baton Rouge, La, Louisiana State University Press, 1988.

Porro, Jeffrey (ed.), *The Nuclear Age Reader*, New York, Knopf, 1989.

Porter, David L., *The Seventy-Sixth Congress and World War II, 1939–1940*, Columbia, Mo., University of Missouri Press, 1979.

Powaski, Ronald E., *March to Armageddon: The United States and the Nuclear Arms Race, 1939 to the Present*, New York, Oxford University Press, 1987.

Powers, Thomas, *Heisenberg's War: The Secret History of the German Bomb*, New York, Knopf, 1993.

Pratt, Julius W., *Expansionists of 1898: The Acquisition of Hawaii and the Spanish Islands*, Baltimore, Md, 1936; reprint, Gloucester, Mass., P. Smith, 1959.

——, *America's Colonial Experiment: How the United States Gained, Governed, and In Part Gave Away a Colonial Empire*, 1950; reprint, Gloucester, Mass., P. Smith, 1964.

Quandt, William, *Camp David: Peacemaking and Politics*, Washington, Brookings Institution, 1986.

——, *Peace Process: American Diplomacy and the Arab–Israeli Conflict since 1967*, Washington and Berkeley, Calif., 1993.

Quirk, Robert E., *An Affair of Honor: Woodrow Wilson and the Occupation of Vera Cruz*, Lexington, Ky, University Press of Kentucky, 1962.

Rabe, Stephen G., *The Road to OPEC: United States Relations with Venezuela, 1919–1976*, Austin, Tex., University of Texas Press, 1982.

——, *Eisenhower and Latin America: The Foreign Policy of Anticommunism*, Chapel Hill, N.C., University of North Carolina Press, 1988.

Randall, Stephen J., *United States Foreign Oil Policy, 1919–1948: For Profits and Security*, Montreal, McGill-Queen's University Press, 1985.

Rauch, Basil, *Roosevelt: From Munich to Pearl Harbor*, New York, Creative Age, 1950.

Rearden, Steven, *Evolution of American Strategic Doctrine: Paul H. Nitze and the Soviet Challenge*, Boulder, Colo., Westview Press, 1984.

Reed, James, *The Missionary Mind and American East Asia Policy, 1911–1915*, Cambridge, Mass., Council on East Asian Studies, Harvard University, 1983.

Reich, Robert B., *The Work of Nations: Preparing Ourselves for 21st Century Capitalism*, New York, A. A. Knopf, 1991.

Reynolds, David, *The Creation of the Anglo-American Alliance 1937–41*, Chapel Hill, N.C., 1982.

Rhodes, Richard, *The Making of the Atomic Bomb*, New York, Simon & Schuster, 1986.

Ricard, Serge (ed.), *An American Empire: Expansionist Cultures and Policies, 1881–1917*, Aix-en-Provence, Université de Provence, 1990.

Rippy, J. Fred, *The Capitalists and Colombia*, New York, 1931; reprint, New York, Arno Press, 1976.

Rosenau, James N., *Public Opinion and Foreign Policy*, New York, Random House, 1961.

Rosenberg, Emily S., *Spreading the American Dream: American Economic and Cultural Expansion, 1890–1945*, New York, Hill & Wang, 1982.

Rotter, Andrew J., *The Path to Vietnam: Origins of the American Commitment to Southeast Asia*, Ithaca, N.Y., Cornell University Press, 1987.

Rourke, John T., *Congress and the Presidency in U.S. Foreign Policymaking: A Study of Interaction and Influence, 1945–82*, Boulder, Colo., Westview Press, 1983.

——, *Presidential Wars and American Democracy: Rally 'Round the Chief*, New York, Paragon House, 1992.

Rozell, Mark J., *The Press and the Carter Presidency*, Boulder, Colo., Westview Press, 1989.

Sagan, Scott D., *Moving Targets: Nuclear Strategy and National Security*, Princeton, N.J., Princeton University Press, 1989.

——, *The Limits of Safety: Organizations, Accidents and Nuclear Weapons*, Princeton, N.J., Princeton University Press, 1993.

Schaller, Michael, *The American Occupation of Japan: The Origins of the Cold War in Asia*, New York, Oxford University Press, 1985.

Scheer, Robert, *With Enough Shovels: Reagan, Bush & Nuclear War*, New York, Random House, 1982.

Schlesinger Jr, Arthur M., *A Thousand Days: John F. Kennedy in the White House*, Boston, Houghton Mifflin, 1965.

——, *The Imperial Presidency*, Boston, Houghton Mifflin, 1973.

——, *Robert Kennedy and His Times*, Boston, Houghton Mifflin, 1978.

Schlesinger, Stephen C., and Stephen Kinzer, *Bitter Fruit: The Untold Story of the American Coup in Guatemala*, Garden City, N.Y., Doubleday, 1982, 2nd ed., 1983.

Schoenbaum, Thomas J., *Waging Peace and War: Dean Rusk in the Truman, Kennedy, and Johnson Years*, New York, Simon & Schuster, 1988.

Schoonover, Thomas D., *The United States in Central America, 1860–1911: Episodes of Social Imperialism and Imperial Rivalry in the World System*, Durham, N.C., Duke University Press, 1991.

Schoultz, Lars, *Human Rights and the United States Policy Towards Latin America*, Princeton, N.J., Princeton University Press, 1981.

Schram, Martin, *Running for President, 1976: The Carter Campaign*, New York, Stein & Day, 1977.

Schrecker, Ellen W., *No Ivory Tower: McCarthyism and the Universities*, New York, Oxford University Press, 1986.

Schulzinger, Robert D., *Henry Kissinger: Doctor of Diplomacy*, New York, Columbia University Press, 1989.

Schwabe, Klaus, *Woodrow Wilson, Revolutionary Germany, and Peacemaking, 1918–1919*, Chapel Hill, N.C., University of North Carolina Press, 1985.

Schwartz, Thomas A., *America's Germany: John J. McCloy and the Federal Republic of Germany*, Cambridge, Mass., Harvard University Press, 1991.

Shafer, D. Michael, *Deadly Paradigms: The Failure of U.S. Counterinsurgency Policy*, Princeton, N.J., Princeton University Press, 1988.

Shalom, Stephen Rosskamm, *The United States and the Philippines: A Study in Neocolonialism*, Philadelphia, Pa, Institute for the Study of Human Issues, 1981.

Sherwin, Martin J., *A World Destroyed: The Atomic Bomb and the Grand Alliance*, New York, 1975, 1977; rev. ed., New York, Vintage Books, 1987.

Sick, Gary, *All Fall Down: America's Tragic Encounter With Iran*, New York, Random House, 1985.

Sims, Jennifer E., *Icarus Restrained: An Intellectual History of Nuclear Arms Control, 1945–1960*, Boulder, Colo., Westview Press, 1990.

Small, Melvin, *Johnson, Nixon and the Doves*, New Brunswick, N.J., Rutgers University Press, 1988.

Smith, Alice K., *A Peril and a Hope: The Scientists' Movement in America, 1945–1947*, Chicago, University of Chicago Press, 1965.

Smith, C. Gerard, *Doubletalk: The Story of SALT I*, Garden City, N.Y., Doubleday, 1980.

Smith, Daniel, *Robert Lansing and American Neutrality, 1914–1917*, Berkeley, Calif., University of California Press, 1958.

Smith, Gaddis, *Morality, Reason and Power: American Diplomacy in the Carter Years*, New York, Hill & Wang, 1986.

Smith, Jean Edward, *George Bush's War*, New York, H. Holt, 1992.

Smith, Robert Freeman, *The United States and Revolutionary Nationalism in Mexico, 1916–32*, Chicago, University of Chicago Press, 1972.

Smith, Tony, *The Pattern of Imperialism: The United States, Great Britain and the Late-Industrializing World since 1815*, New York, Cambridge University Press, 1981.

Sofaer, Abraham D., *War, Foreign Affairs and Constitutional Power: The Origins*, Cambridge, Mass., Ballinger, 1976.

Sorensen, Theodore, *Kennedy*, New York, Harper & Row, 1965.

——, *The Kennedy Legacy*, New York, Macmillan, 1969.

Spanier, John, *American Foreign Policy Since World War II*, 7th ed., New York, 1977.

Spiegel, Stephen L., *The Other Arab–Israeli Conflict: Making America's Middle East Policy from Truman to Reagan*, Chicago, University of Chicago Press, 1985.

Stanley, Peter W., *A Nation in the Making: The Philippines and the United States, 1899–1921*, Cambridge, Mass., Harvard University Press, 1974.

—— (ed.), *Reappraising an Empire: New Perspectives on Philippine–American History*, Cambridge, Mass., Council on East Asian Studies, Harvard University, 1984.

Stoff, Michael B., *Oil, War, and American Security: The Search for a National Policy on Foreign Oil, 1941–1947*, New Haven, Conn., Yale University Press, 1980.

Stone, Ralph A. *The Irreconcilables: The Fight Against the League of Nations*, Lexington, Ky, University Press of Kentucky, 1970.

Stromberg, Roland N., *Collective Security and American Foreign Policy*, New York, Praeger, 1963.

Stuart, Reginald, *United States Expansionism and British North America, 1775–1871*, Chapel Hill, N.C., University of North Carolina Press, 1988.

Summers Jr, Harry G., *On Strategy: A Critical Analysis of the Vietnam War*, Novato, Calif., Presidio Press, 1982.

Szulc, Tad, *The Illusion of Peace: Foreign Policy in the Nixon Years*, New York, Viking Press, 1979.

Talbott, Strobe, *Endgame: The Inside Story of SALT II*, New York, Harper & Row, 1979.

——, *Deadly Gambits: The Reagan Administration and the Stalemate in Nuclear Arms Control*, New York, Knopf, 1984.

——, *The Russians and Reagan*, New York, Vintage Books, 1984.

Tansill, Charles C., *The United States and Santo Domingo, 1798–1873*, Baltimore, Md, 1938; reprint, Gloucester, Mass., P. Smith, 1967.

——, *Back Door to War: The Roosevelt Foreign Policy, 1933–1941*, Chicago, Regnery, 1952.

Taylor, Telford, *Nuremberg and Vietnam: An American Tragedy*, Chicago, Quadrangle Books, 1970.

Thies, Wallace J., *When Governments Collide: Coercion and Diplomacy in Vietnam, 1964–1968*, Berkeley, Calif., University of California Press, 1980.

Thomas, Hugh, *Armed Truce: The Beginnings of the Cold War, 1945–1946*, New York, Athenaeum, 1987.

Thomson Jr, James C., Peter W. Stanley, and John Curtis Perry, *Sentimental Imperialists: The American Experience in East Asia*, New York, Harper & Row, 1981.

Thorne, Christopher, *Allies of a Kind: The United States, Britain, and the War Against Japan, 1941–1945*, New York, Oxford University Press, 1978.

Thornton, Richard, *The Nixon–Kissinger Years: The Reshaping of American Foreign Policy*, New York, Paragon House, 1989.

Thurow, Lester, *Head to Head: The Coming Economic Battle Among Japan, Europe, and America*, New York, Morrow, 1992.

Trachtenberg, Marc, *History and Strategy*, Princeton, N.J., Princeton University Press, 1991.

Tucker, Nancy Bernkopf, *Patterns in the Dust: Chinese–American Relations and the Recognition Controversy, 1949–50*, New York, Columbia University Press, 1983.

Tucker, Robert W., *The Radical Left and American Foreign Policy*, Baltimore, Md, Johns Hopkins University Press, 1971.

——, and David C. Hendrickson, *Empire of Liberty: The Statecraft of Thomas Jefferson*, New York, Oxford University Press, 1990.

——, and David C. Hendrickson, *The Imperial Temptation: The New World Order and America's Purpose*, New York, Council on Foreign Relations Press, 1992.

Turner, Julius, *Party and Constituency: Pressures on Congress*, Baltimore, Md, Johns Hopkins University Press, 1951.

Ulam, Adam, *The Rivals: America and Russia Since World War II*, New York, Viking Press, 1971.

Varg, Paul A., *The Making of A Myth: The United States and China, 1897–1912*, East Lansing, Mich., Michigan State University Press, 1968.

Wall, Irwin, *The United States and the Making of Postwar France, 1945–1954*, New York, Cambridge University Press, 1991.

Wallerstein, Immanuel, *The Capitalist World-Economy: Essays*, New York, Cambridge University Press, 1979.

Walter, Mark, *German National Socialism and the Quest for Nuclear Power, 1939–1949*, New York, Cambridge University Press, 1989.

Walton, Richard J., *Cold War and Counter Revolution: The Foreign Policy of John F. Kennedy*, New York, Viking Press, 1972.

Walworth, Arthur, *America's Moment, 1918: American Diplomacy at the End of World War I*, New York, Norton, 1977.

——, *Wilson and His Peacemakers: American Diplomacy at the Paris Peace Conference*, New York, Norton, 1986.

Watts, Steven, *The Republic Reborn: War and the Making of Liberal America, 1790–1820*, Baltimore, Md, Johns Hopkins University Press, 1987.

Weinberg, Albert K., *Manifest Destiny: A Study of Nationalist Expansionism and American History*, Baltimore, Md, 1935; reprint, New York, AMS Press, 1979.

West, Rachel, *The Department of State on the Eve of the First World War*, Athens, Ga, University of Georgia Press, 1978.

White, Richard, *The Middle Ground: Indians, Empire, and Republics in the Great Lake Region, 1650–1815*, New York, Cambridge University Press, 1991.

Whitfield, Stephen J., *Scott Nearing: Apostle of American Radicalism*, New York, Columbia University Press, 1974.

Wilcox, Francis O., *Congress, The Executive, and Foreign Policy*, New York, Harper & Row, 1971.

Williams, William A., *American–Russian Relations, 1781–1947*, New York, Holt, Rhinehart and Winston, 1952; reprint, New York, Octagon Books, 1971.

——, *The Tragedy of American Diplomacy*, Cleveland, Ohio, 1959; rev. and enl. ed., New York, 1962, 1972; new ed., New York, Norton, 1988.

Williams, William A., *The Roots of the Modern American Empire: A Study of the Growth and Shaping of a Social Consciousness in a Marketplace Society*, New York, Random House, 1969.

——, *Empire as a Way of Life: An Essay on the Causes and Character of America's Present Predicament Along with a Few Thoughts about an Alternative*, New York, Oxford University Press, 1980.

Wills, Garry, *Reagan's America*, Garden City, N.Y., 1987; rev. ed., New York, Penguin Books, 1988.

Wilson, Joan Hoff, *American Business and Foreign Policy, 1920–1933*, Lexington, Ky, University Press of Kentucky, 1971.

——, *Herbert Hoover: Forgotten Progressive*, Boston, Little, Brown & Co., 1975.

Wilson, Theodore A., *The First Summit: Roosevelt & Churchill at Placentia Bay, 1941*, Boston, Houghton Mifflin, 1969; rev. ed., Lawrence, Kan., University Press of Kansas, 1991.

Wilz, John E., *In Search of Peace: The Senate Munitions Inquiry, 1934–1936*, Baton Rouge, La, Louisiana State University Press, 1963.

Wisan, Joseph E., *The Cuban Crisis as Reflected in the New York Press, 1895–1898*, New York, 1934; reprint, New York, Octagon Books, 1965.

Wohlstetter, Roberta, *Pearl Harbor: Warning and Decision*, Stanford, Calif., Stanford University Press, 1962.

Wood, Bryce, *The Dismantling of the Good Neighbor Policy*, Austin, Tex., University of Texas Press, 1985.

Woods, Randall B., and Howard Jones, *The Dawning of the Cold War*, Athens, Ga, University of Georgia Press, 1991.

Yergin, Daniel, *Shattered Peace: The Origins of the Cold War*, Boston, Houghton Mifflin, 1977.

——, *The Prize: The Epic Quest for Oil, Money, and Power*, New York, Simon & Schuster, 1991.

York, Herbert, *The Advisors: Oppenheimer, Teller and the Superbomb*, San Francisco, Calif., 1976; reissue with new preface and epilogue, Stanford Calif., Stanford University Press, 1989.

Young, Marilyn Blatt, *The Rhetoric of Empire: America's China Policy, 1895–1901*, Cambridge, Mass., Harvard University Press, 1968.

II ARTICLES AND ESSAYS

Abrams, Richard H., "United States Intervention Abroad, The First Quarter Century," *American Historical Review*, vol. 79, 1974, pp. 72–102.

Allison, Graham T., and Morton H. Halperin, "Bureaucratic Politics: A Paradigm and Some Policy Implications," *World Politics*, vol. 24, 1972, pp. 40–80.

Armbruster, William A. "The *Pueblo* Crisis and Public Opinion," *The Naval War College Review*, vol. 23, 1971, pp. 84–110.

Art, Robert J., "Bureaucratic Politics and American Foreign Policy: A Critique," *Policy Sciences*, vol. 4, 1973, pp. 467–90.

Becker, William, "American Manufacturers and Foreign Markets, 1870–1900," *Business History Review*, vol. 47, 1973, pp. 466–81.

Beisner, Robert, "History and Henry Kissinger," *Diplomatic History*, vol. 14, 1990, pp. 511–28.

Bernstein, Barton J., "The Atomic Bomb and American Foreign Policy, 1941–1945: An Historical Controversy," *Peace and Change*, vol. 2, Spring 1974, pp. 1–16.

——, "The Quest for Security: American Foreign Policy and International Control of Atomic Energy, 1942–1946," *Journal of American History*, vol. 40, 1974, pp. 1003–44.

——, "Roosevelt, Truman, and the Atomic Bomb, 1941–1945: A Reinterpretation," *Political Science Quarterly*, vol. 90, 1975, pp. 23–69.

——, "The Week We Almost Went to War," *Bulletin of the Atomic Scientists*, vol. 32, February 1976, pp. 12–21.

——, "The Cuban Missile Crisis: Trading the Jupiters in Turkey?," *Political Science Quarterly*, vol. 95, 1980, pp. 97–125.

——, "Truman and the H-Bomb," *Bulletin of the Atomic Scientists*, vol. 40, March 1984, pp. 12–18.

——, "Pig in a Poke, Why did Kennedy Buy the Bay of Pigs Invasion?," *Foreign Service Journal*, vol. 62, 1985, pp. 28–33.

——, "A Postwar Myth: 500,000 U.S. Lives Saved," *Bulletin of the Atomic Scientists*, vol. 42, June/July 1986, pp. 38–40.

——, "Eclipsed by Hiroshima and Nagasaki," *International Security*, vol. 15, Spring 1991, pp. 149–73.

——, "Writing, Righting, or Wronging the Historical Record," *Diplomatic History*, vol. 16, 1992, pp. 163–73.

Billington, Ray Allen, "The Origins of Middle Western Isolationism," *Political Science Quarterly*, vol. 60, 1945, pp. 44–64.

Braeman, John, "The New Left and American Foreign Policy during the Age of Normalcy: A Re-examination," *Business History Review*, vol. 57, 1983, pp. 73–104.

Brands, H. W., "The Age of Vulnerability: Eisenhower and the National Insecurity State," *American Historical Review*, vol. 94, 1989, pp. 963–89.

——, "Fractal History, or Clio and the Chaotics," *Diplomatic History*, vol. 16, 1992, pp. 495–510.

Brauer, Kinley J., "The Great American Desert Revisited: Recent Literature and Prospects for the Study of American Foreign Relations, 1815–61," *Diplomatic History*, vol. 13, 1989, pp. 395–417.

Brenner, Philip, "Cuba and the Missile Crisis," *Journal of Latin American Studies*, vol. 22, 1990, pp. 115–42.

——, "Thirteen Months: Cuba's Perspective on the Missile Crisis," in James A. Nathan (ed.), *The Cuban Missile Crisis Revisited*, New York, St Martin's Press, 1992, pp. 187–217.

Bundy, McGeorge, "Vietnam, Watergate, and Presidential Powers," *Foreign Affairs*, vol. 68, 1979/80, pp. 397–404.

Campbell, A. E., "The Paradox of Imperialism: The American Case," in Wolfgang J. Mommsen and Jurgen Osterhammel (eds), *Imperialism and After: Continuities and Discontinuities*, Boston, Allen & Unwin, 1986, pp. 34–40.

Carleton, William G., "Isolationism and the Middle West," *Mississippi Valley Historical Review*, vol. 33, 1946, pp. 377–90.

Clifford, J. Garry, "Both Ends of the Telescope: New Perspectives on FDR and American Entry into World War II," *Diplomatic History*, vol. 13, 1989, pp. 213–30.

Cohen, Warren I., "Acheson, His Advisors, and China, 1949–1950," in Dorothy Borg and Waldo Heinrichs (eds), *The Uncertain Years: Chinese–American Relations, 1947–1950*, New York, Columbia University Press, 1980, pp. 13–52.

Cole, Wayne S., "Isolationism," in Otis Graham, Jr, and Meghan R. Wander (eds), *Franklin D. Roosevelt: His Life and Times*, Boston, G. K. Hall, 1985, pp. 211–13.

Cooper, John Milton, "An Irony of Fate," *Diplomatic History*, vol. 3, 1979, pp. 425–37.

Crapol, Edward P., "Coming to Terms with Empire: The Historiography of Late-Nineteenth Century American Foreign Relations," *Diplomatic History*, vol. 16, 1992, pp. 573–97.

Daniels, John D., "The Indian Population of North America in 1492," *William and Mary Quarterly*, 3rd series, vol. 49, 1992, pp. 298–320.

Dingman, Roger, "The Diplomacy of Dependency: The Philippines and Peacemaking with Japan," *Journal of Southeast Asian Studies*, vol. 27, 1986, pp. 307–21.

——, "Atomic Diplomacy During the Korean War," *International Security*, vol. 13, 1988/9, pp. 50–91.

Divine, Robert A., "Franklin D. Roosevelt and Collective Security, 1933," *Mississippi Valley Historical Review*, vol. 48, 1961, pp. 42–59.

——, "Vietnam Reconsidered," *Diplomatic History*, vol. 12, 1988, pp. 79–93.

Field Jr, James A., "American Imperialism: The Worst Chapter in Almost Any Book," *American Historical Review*, vol. 83, 1978, pp. 644–83.

Fleming, Thomas, "The Big Leak," *American Heritage*, vol. 38, 1987, pp. 64–71.

Fry, Joseph A., "Theodore Roosevelt and the Rise of America to World Power," in Howard Jones (ed.), *Safeguarding the Republic: Essays and Documents in American Foreign Relations, 1890–1991*, New York, McGraw-Hill, 1992, pp. 19–43.

Fukuyama, Francis, "The End of History?" *The National Interest*, vol. 16, summer 1989, pp. 3–18.

Gaddis, John Lewis, "The Emerging Post-Revisionist Thesis on the Origins of the Cold War," *Diplomatic History*, vol. 7, 1983, pp. 171–90.

——, "The Essential Relevance of Nuclear Weapons," in *The United States and the End of the Cold War: Implications, Reconsiderations, Provocations*, New York, Oxford University Press, 1992, pp. 105–18.

Galison, Peter, and Barton Bernstein, "In any Light: Scientists and the Decision to Build the Superbomb, 1952–54," *Historical Studies in the Physical and Biological Sciences*, vol. 19, 1989, pp. 267–347.

Garthoff, Raymond L., "Cuban Missile Crisis: The Soviet Story," *Foreign Policy*, vol. 72, 1988, pp. 61–80.

——, "Berlin 1961: The Record Corrected," *Foreign Policy*, vol. 84, 1991, pp. 142–56.

——, "The Havana Conference on the Cuban Missile Crisis," *Cold War International History Project Bulletin*, no. 1, spring 1992, pp. 2–4.

Gillette Jr, Howard E., "The Military Occupation of Cuba, 1899–1902: Workshop for American Progressivism," *American Quarterly*, vol. 25, 1973, pp. 410–25.

Glennon, Michael J., "The Gulf War and the Constitution," *Foreign Affairs*, vol. 70, 1991, pp. 84–101.

Graebner, Norman A., "Cold War Origins and the Continuing Debate: A Review of Recent Literature," *Journal of Conflict Resolution*, vol. 13, 1969, pp. 123–32.

Green, David, "The Cold War Comes to Latin America," in Barton Bernstein (ed.), *Politics and Policies of the Truman Administration*, Chicago, Quadrangle Books, 1970, pp. 149–95.

Harris, Paul W., "Cultural Imperialism and American Protestant Missionaries: Collaboration and Dependency in Mid-Nineteenth Century China," *Pacific Historical Review*, vol. 60, 1991, pp. 309–38.

Hawley, Ellis W., "The Discovery and Study of a 'Corporate Liberalism,'" *Business History Review*, vol. 52, 1978, pp. 309–20.

Herring, George C., "The Executive, Congress, and the Vietnam War, 1965–1975," in Michael Barnhart (ed.), *Congress and United States Foreign Policy*, Albany, N.Y., State University of New York Press, 1987, pp. 176–86.

——, and Richard I. Immerman, "Eisenhower, Dulles, and Dienbienphu: 'The Day We Didn't Go To War' Revisited," *Journal of American History*, vol. 71, 1984, pp. 343–63.

Hershberg, James G. "Before the Missiles of October: Did Kennedy Plan a Military Strike against Cuba," *Diplomatic History*, vol. 14, 1990, pp. 163–98.

Hess, Gary, "Global Expansion and Regional Balances: The Emerging Scholarship on United States Relations with India and Pakistan," *Pacific Historical Review*, vol. 56, 1987, pp. 259–95.

Hoff-Wilson, Joan, "Responses to Charles S. Maier, 'Marking Time: The Historiography of International Relations,'" *Diplomatic History*, vol. 5, 1981, pp. 377–82.

——, "Nixingerism, NATO, and Détente," *Diplomatic History*, vol. 13, 1989, pp. 501–26.

Hofstadter, Richard, "Manifest Destiny and the Philippines," in Daniel Aaron (ed.), *America in Crisis*, New York, Alfred A. Knopf, 1952, pp. 173–200.

Hogan, Michael J., "Corporatism," in Michael J. Hogan and Thomas G. Paterson (eds), *Explaining the History of American Foreign Relations*, New York, Cambridge University Press, 1991, pp. 226–36.

Holbo, Paul S., "Economics, Emotion, and Expansion: An Emerging Foreign Policy," in H. Wayne Morgan (ed.), *The Gilded Age*, Syracuse, N.Y., Syracuse University Press, 1970, pp. 199–221.

Holloway, David, "Entering the Nuclear Arms Race: The Soviet Decision to Build the Atomic Bomb, 1939," *Social Studies of Science*, vol. 11, 1981, pp. 159–97.

Horlacher, Friedrich W., "The Language of Late Nineteenth-Century American Expansionism," in Serge Ricard (ed.), *An American Empire: Expansionist Cultures and Policies, 1881–1917*, Aix-en-Provence, Université de Provence, 1990, pp. 32–49.

Hunt, Michael, "Ideology" [in A Roundtable: Explaining the History of American Foreign Relations], *Journal of American History*, vol. 77, 1990, pp. 108–24.

Huntington, Samuel P., "The US – Decline or Renewal?" *Foreign Affairs*, vol. 67, 1988/9, pp. 84–8.

Kahn, Gilbert N., "Presidential Passivity on a Nonsalient Issue: President Franklin D. Roosevelt and the 1935 World Court Fight," *Diplomatic History*, vol. 4, 1980, pp. 137–61.

Kennan, George, "The United States and the Soviet Union, 1917–1976," *Foreign Affairs*, vol. 54, 1976, pp. 670–90.

Krasner, Stephen D., "Are Bureaucracies Important, (or Allison Wonderland)," *Foreign Policy*, vol. 7, 1972, pp. 159–79.

Kuehl, Warren F., "Midwestern Newspapers and Isolationist Sentiment," *Diplomatic History*, vol. 3, 1979, pp. 283–306.

LaFeber, Walter, "Roosevelt, Churchill, and Indochina, 1942–45," *American Historical Review*, vol. 80, 1975, pp. 1277–95.

——, "From Confusion to Cold War: The Memoirs of the Carter Administration," *Diplomatic History*, vol. 8, 1984, pp. 1–12.

Lapidus, Gail W., and Alexander Dallin, "The Pacification of Ronald Reagan," in Paul Boyer (ed.), *Reagan as President, Contemporary Views of the Man, His Politics, and His Policies*, Chicago, Ivan R. Dee, 1990, pp. 256–9.

Lauren, Paul Gordon, "Human Rights in History . . .," *Diplomatic History*, vol. 3, 1978, pp. 257–78.

Lebow, Richard Ned, "Domestic Politics and the Cuban Missile Crisis: The Traditional and Revisionist Interpretation Reevaluated," *Diplomatic History*, vol. 14, 1990, pp. 471–92.

Levering, Ralph B., "Public Opinion, Foreign Policy, and American Politics since the 1960s," *Diplomatic History*, vol. 13, 1989, pp. 383–94.

Little, Douglas, "From Even Handed to Empty Handed: Seeking Order in the Middle East," in Thomas G. Paterson (ed.), *Kennedy's Quest for Victory: American Foreign Policy, 1961–1963*, New York, Oxford University Press, 1989, pp. 156–77.

Louis, W. Roger, "Dulles, Suez, and the British," in Richard Immerman (ed.), *John Foster Dulles and the Diplomacy of the Cold War*, Princeton, N.J., Princeton University Press, 1990, pp. 133–58.

Lunch, William L., and Peter W. Sperlich, "American Public Opinion and the War in Vietnam," *Western Political Quarterly*, vol. 32, 1979, pp. 21–32.

Lundestad, Geir, "Empire by Invitation? The United States and Western Europe, 1945–1952," *Journal of Peace Research*, vol. 23, 1986, pp. 263–77.

McCormick, Thomas J., "Drift or Mastery? A Corporatist Synthesis for American Diplomatic History," *Reviews in American History*, vol. 10, 1982, pp. 318–30.

McMahon, Robert J., "Eisenhower and Third World Nationalism: A Critique of the Revisionists," *Political Science Quarterly*, vol. 101, 1986, pp. 453–73.

——, "United States Cold War Strategy in South Asia: Making a Military Commitment to Pakistan, 1947–1954," *Journal of American History*, vol. 75, 1988, pp. 812–40.

——, "Credibility and World Power," *Diplomatic History*, vol. 15, 1991, pp. 455–71.

Maddox, Robert J., "Atomic Diplomacy: A Study in Creative Writing," *Journal of American History*, vol. 59, 1973, pp. 925–34.

May, Ernest R. "The American Commitment to Germany, 1949–1955," *Diplomatic History*, vol. 13, 1989, pp. 431–60.

——, "The U.S. Government, a Legacy of the Cold War," *Diplomatic History*, vol. 16, 1992, pp. 269–77.

Miles Jr, Rufus E., "Hiroshima: The Strange Myth of a Half a Million American Lives Saved," *International Security*, vol. 10, Fall 1985, pp. 121–40.

Mueller, John, "The Essential Irrelevance of Nuclear Weapons: Stability in the Postwar World," *International Security*, vol. 13, Fall 1988, pp. 55–79.

Nichols, Jeannette P., "The Middle West and the Coming of World War II," *Ohio State Archaeological and Historical Quarterly*, vol. 62, 1953, pp. 122–45.

Paterson, Thomas G., and William J. Brophy, "October Missiles and November Elections: The Cuban Missile Crisis and American Politics, 1962," *Journal of American History*, vol. 73, 1986, pp. 87–119.

——, "Oversight or Afterview?: Congress, the CIA, and Covert Operations Since 1947," in Michael Barnhart (ed.), *Congress and United States Foreign Policy*, Albany, N.Y., State University of New York Press, 1987, pp. 154–75.

——, "Historical Memory and Illusive Victories: Vietnam and Central America," *Diplomatic History*, vol. 12, 1988, pp. 1–18.

——, "Fixation with Cuba: The Bay of Pigs, Missile Crisis, and Covert War against Fidel Castro," in Thomas G. Paterson (ed.), *Kennedy's Quest for Victory: American Foreign Policy, 1961–63*, New York, Oxford University Press, 1989, pp. 123–55.

Pérez Jr, Louis A., "Dependency," in Michael J. Hogan and Thomas G. Paterson (eds), *Explaining the History of American Foreign Relations*, New York, Cambridge University Press, 1991, pp. 99–110.

Perkins, Bradford, "'The Tragedy of American Diplomacy': Twenty-five Years After," *Reviews in American History*, vol. 12, 1984, pp. 1–18; reprinted in Lloyd C. Gardner (ed.), *Redefining the Past: Essays in Diplomatic History in Honor of William Appleman Williams*, Corvallis, Ore., Oregon State University Press, 1986.

Pletcher, David M., "Rhetoric and Results: A Pragmatic View of American Economic Expansionism, 1865–1898," *Diplomatic History*, vol. 5, 1981, pp. 93–105.

Rabe, Stephen, "Controlling Revolutions: Latin America, the Alliance for Progress, and Cold War Anti-Communism," in Thomas G. Paterson (ed.), *Kennedy's Quest for Victory: American Foreign Policy, 1961–63*, New York, 1989, pp. 105–22.

——, "Eisenhower Revisionism: A Decade of Scholarship," *Diplomatic History*, vol. 17, 1993, pp. 97–116.

Reynolds, David, "The Origins of the Cold War: The European Dimension, 1944–51," *Historical Journal*, vol. 28, 1985, pp. 497–515.

Rosecrance, Richard, "Must America Decline?," *Wilson Quarterly*, vol. 14, 1990, pp. 67–85.

Rosen, Elliot, "Intranationalism vs. Internationalism: The Interregnum Struggle For the Sanctity of the New Deal," *Political Science Quarterly*, vol. 81, 1966, pp. 274–92.

Rosenberg, David Alan, "American Atomic Strategy and the Hydrogen Bomb Decision," *Journal of American History*, vol. 66, 1979, pp. 62–87.

——, "The Origins of Overkill: Nuclear Weapons and American Strategy, 1945–1960," *International Security*, vol. 7, Spring 1983, pp. 3–71.

——, "Reality and Responsibility: Power and Process in the Making of United States Nuclear Strategy, 1945–1968," *Journal of Strategic Studies*, vol. 9, 1986, pp. 35–52.

Rosenberg, Emily, "Gender" [in A Roundtable: Explaining the History of American Foreign Relations], *Journal of American History*, vol. 77, 1990, pp. 116–24.

——, "Walking the Borders," in Michael J. Hogan and Thomas G. Paterson (eds), *Explaining the History of American Foreign Relations*, New York, Cambridge University Press, 1991, pp. 24–35.

Sagan, Scott D., "Nuclear Alerts and Crisis Management," *International Security*, vol. 9, Spring 1985, 99–139.

Schilling, Warner R., "The H-Bomb Decision: How to Decide without Actually Choosing," *Political Science Quarterly*, vol. 76, 1961, pp. 24–46.

Schlesinger Jr, Arthur M., "Origins of the Cold War," *Foreign Affairs*, vol. 46, 1967, pp. 22–52.

——, "The Missionary Enterprise and Theories of Imperialism," in John K. Fairbank (ed.), *The Missionary Enterprise in China*, Cambridge, Mass., Harvard University Press, 1974, pp. 336–73.

——, "Franklin D. Roosevelt's Internationalism," in Cornelis van Minnen and John F. Sears (eds), *FDR and His Contemporaries: Foreign Perceptions of an American President*, New York, St Martin's Press, 1992, pp. 3–16.

Small, Melvin, "The United States and the German 'Threat' to the Hemisphere, 1904–1914," *The Americas*, vol. 28, 1972, pp. 252–70.

——, "Public Opinion," in Michael J. Hogan and Thomas G. Paterson (eds), *Explaining the History of American Foreign Relations*, New York, Cambridge University Press, 1991, pp. 165–71.

Smuckler, Ralph H., "The Region of Isolationism," *American Political Science Review*, vol. 47, 1953, pp. 386–401.

Steele, Richard E., "The Great Debate: Roosevelt, the Media, and the Coming of War, 1940–1941," *Journal of American History*, vol. 71, 1984, pp. 69–92.

Steele, Richard W., "Franklin D. Roosevelt and His Foreign Policy Critics," *Political Science Quarterly*, vol. 94, 1979, pp. 15–32.

Summers Jr, Harry G., "Lessons: A Soldier's View," in Peter Braestrup (ed.), *Vietnam as History: Ten Years after the Paris Peace Accords*, Washington, D.C., University Press of America, 1984, pp. 109–14.

Trachtenberg, Marc, "The Influence of Nuclear Weapons in the Cuban Missile Crisis," *International Security*, vol. 10, Summer 1985; reprinted in Trachtenberg, *History and Strategy*, Princeton, N.J., Princeton University Press, 1991, pp. 235–60.

Tucker, Nancy Bernkopf, "A House Divided: The United States, the Department of State, and China," in Warren I. Cohen and Akira Iriye (eds), *Great Powers in East Asia*, pp. 35–62.

Tulchin, Joseph S., "The United States and Latin America in the 1960s," *Journal of Inter-American Studies and World Affairs*, vol. 30, 1988, pp. 1–36.

Vandenbroucke, Lucien S. "Anatomy of a Failure: The Decision to Land at the Bay of Pigs," *Political Science Quarterly*, vol. 99, 1984, pp. 471–91.

Vlahos, Michael, "Culture and Foreign Policy," *Foreign Policy*, no. 82, spring 1991, pp. 59–78.

Walker, J. Samuel, "The Decision to Use the Bomb: A Historiographical Update," *Diplomatic History*, vol. 14, 1990, pp. 97–114.

Weinberg, Albert K., "The Historical Meaning of the American Doctrine of Isolation," *American Political Science Review*, vol. 34, 1940, pp. 539–47.

Welch, David A., and James G. Blight, "An Introduction to the Ex Comm Transcripts," *International Security*, vol. 12, Winter 1987/8, pp. 5–29.

Wilkins, Robert P., "The Non-Ethnic Roots of North Dakota Isolationism," *Nebraska History*, vol. 44, 1963, pp. 205–11.

Winks, Robin W., "The American Struggle with 'Imperialism': How Words Frighten," in Rob Kroes (ed.), *The American Identity: Fusion and Fragmentation*, Amsterdam, Amerika Instituut, Universiteit van Amsterdam, 1980, pp. 143–77.

Yavenditti, Michael J., "The American People and the Use of Atomic Bombs on Japan: The 1940s," *The Historian*, vol. 36, 1974, pp. 221–47.

——, "John Hersey and the American Conscience: The Reception of 'Hiroshima,'" *Pacific Historical Review*, vol. 43, 1974, pp. 24–49.

Index

Asia 31; and end of the Cold War
29, 145, 160–2, 187, 206, 216,
230; and Gulf War 26, 29,
179–80, 182, 196, 227; and
Irangate 222; and Panama 149,
221, 227; and SDI 158; and trade
policy 37, 213
Bush, Vannevar 189, 194
Byrnes, 107, 109, 113, 195

Cabral, Donald Reid 131
Cambodia 227; and Reagan doctrine
159; and US aid 25–6, 192; and
Vietnam war 140, 150, 222
Campbell, A.E. 65
Canada 3, 168
Carter, Jimmy: foreign policy of
152–7; and Senate 25; sources on
145–6; and the Third World
179–81
Castro, Fidel 127–8, 131, 177–8, 199
Central Treaty Organization
(CENTRO) 220
Central Intelligence Agency (CIA)
25, 27–8, 146, 166, 168, 177,
180–2, 221–2; and Afghanistan
155; and Cuba, 127–8, 131, 166,
178, 220; and end of the Cold War
37; and Guatemala 47, 166, 176;
and Iran 166, 175, 220; and
Nicaragua 160, 168; and Vietnam
133, 136
Chang, Gordon 118
Cheney, Dick 196
Chicago Tribue 30, 132, 147
Chile 166, 220
China: and US Cold War policy
113, 117–18, 126, 132, 134–5,
147–8, 150, 153–4, 181, 173; and
US during cultural revolution
138–9; and US economic policy 4,
7, 55–6, 217; and US immigration
12; and US intervention 4; and US
missionary activity 64–5; and US
security policy 31, 109, 134–5,
220; Woodrow Wilson and 73–7,
85–6
Chou En-lai 139
Church, Frank 25, 136
Churchill, Winston S. 106, 112, 171,
189, 195–6
Clark, Joseph 136
Clemenceau, Georges 75, 83
Clifford, Clark 137

Clinton, Bill 37, 158, 214, 224,
226–7, 230
Cohen, Stephen 152
Cohen, Warren I. 117
Colby, Bainbridge 74
Cole, Wayne S. 92, 96, 99–100
collective security 10, 94, 101, 206,
219, 221, 225
Collin, Richard H. 60
Colombia 61
Compton, Karl T. 195
Conant, James 189, 191, 194–6
Congress: and Cuban missile crisis
128; and isolationism 93, 96–7,
99–100; and US foreign policy
22–7, 32–3, 218, 220, 222; and
Panama Canal treaty 153; and
Pueblo crisis 137; Richard Nixon
and 148–51; and SDI 157–60; and
US aid 172; and Israeli lobby 178;
and US trade policy 37, 40, 56;
Woodrow Wilson and 82
containment 10, 22, 43, 112, 115,
139–40, 151, 159, 172–3
Cook, Blanche Wiesen 118
Cooper, John Sherman 136
corporatist school 22, 45–6, 48, 91,
106, 114–16, 119, 168
Corwin, Edward S. 23
Craig, Gordon 157
Cuba: and Spanish-American War
13, 15, 58–9; and US protectorate
4, 52, 62, 64–5
Cuban Missile Crisis 28, 126,
128–31, 134, 187, 198–200, 202
Cumings, Bruce 116, 119–20
Czechoslovakia 109

Dallek, Robert 58, 95–6, 101, 156
Dallin, Alexander 159
DeConcini, Dennis 25
Deibel, Terry 156
dependecy theory 54, 63, 65, 168
Derian, Patricia M. 152
détente 139, 148–9, 151
Diem, Ngo Dinh 119, 133, 141, 175
Dinges, John 182
Dingman, Roger 113
Divine, Robert A. 24, 151
Dobrynin, Anatoly 129
Doenecke, Justus 102
Dominican Republic 40, and US
intervention 75, 131–2, 166, 179,
220, 232; and US protectorate 51